My Journey Landing Heaven on Earth

Volume I

My Journey Landing Heaven on Earth

Volume I

Scenes from Developing Exopolitics,
Mapping the Omniverse, and Discovering
the Positive Timeline Equation 1973-2015

Upper Theatre: Recovery

Alfred Lambremont Webre

Author of

Exopolitics: Politics, Government
and Law in the Universe
The Omniverse

For copyright licenses, please contact:
Universebooks *www.universebooks.com*
Email: *Exopolitics@exopolitics.com*

Typesetting and Cover Design by *www.wordzworth.com*
Cover image credit: TarikVision

Library and Archives Canada Cataloguing in Publication
Webre, Alfred Lambremont, 1942-
Library of Congress
Cataloguing

Journeys
Alfred Lambremont Webre

ISBN: 978-0-9737663-3-2

1. Cosmology 2. Political Science 3. Autobiography 4. Memoir
I. Title.

Books by Alfred Lambremont Webre

The Omniverse
(Rochester, Vermont: Inner Traditions/Bear & Co. Dec. 2015)

The Dimensional Ecology of the Omniverse
(Vancouver, Canada: Universebooks.com, 2014);

Exopolitics: Politics, Government and Law in the Universe
(Vancouver, Canada: Universebooks.com, 2005);
(Granada, Spain: VesicaPiscis.eu 2009)

The Levesque Cases
(Ontario: PSP Books, 1990)

The Age of Cataclysm
(New York: G.P. Putnam's Sons, 1974);
(New York: Berkeley Medallion, 1975); (Capricorn Books, 1975);
(Tokyo: Ugaku Sha, 1975)

This book is dedicated to Source & GAGA

CONTENTS

ACT II

ACT III

UPPER THEATRE: RECOVERY

Journey: Volume I

Journey – Volume I is a non-fiction, true life history of personal experiences occurring around the founding of Exopolitics, the science of relations among intelligent civilizations in the multiverse, the mapping of the Omniverse, and the development of the Positive Future Equation

Positive Future = Positive Timeline + Unity Consciousness

JOURNEY:
VOLUME I

ALFRED LAMBREMONT WEBRE
J.D. M.ED

INTRODUCTION

Greetings! I am a soul navigating our time space hologram on a holographic timeline inside my Avatar, Alfred Lambremont Webre, on planet Earth as I compose these word pictures for you.

I am like all Souls, an entity that has teleported and is an emanation from the Spiritual Dimensions of the Omniverse.

My purpose in creating *Journey – Volume I* is to share with you specific personal, emotional, historical, scientific, and spiritual episodes from my Life's journey in this present incarnation.

This is a book from some of my personal experiences, for the record.

These experiences are for you who have expressed an interest in episodes from my inner and outer Life.

You will find here subjective reports of episodes that I as Soul have encountered along the way on Earth, navigating our collective timeline.

Here are moments of Self-Realization, Spiritual Awakening, Self-Actualizing as a human being, child, parent, husband, seeker, Earthling, Incarnate, telepath, social activist, Exopolitician. Here are Archetypes that may apply to your Life as well.

Some Life episodes are not covered in this Volume and are water shed Life-changing events for me, like my 4th birthday party in May 1946 at the back patio of my maternal grandmother's house in Vedado, Havana, Cuba where I was crowned King for the Day, and are of no external consequence and remain as cherished memories in a Lifetime where I have sworn to accept no public offices or emoluments.

I have been reliably told by professional seers that, in another dimension, I am a Prophesied Being.

In my Soul career professional seers tell me that I have had very little bad karma early that I have overcome and balanced out with much good karma of doing good for others.

What influence I have is behind the scenes, for in the public eye I am not and will never be world famous in this Lifetime, I am told.

The planetary perpetrators have isolated me from the bulk of humanity and Starseeds as CIA time traveled my book back to 1971 and Illuminati began war-level cointelpro against me around then and even before, starting with the Jesuits in early childhood [my maternal uncle was Deputy Black Pope].

My memories have been blocked from knowing prior lives or Inter-lives for security reasons, as some of my prior lives are ultra- famous, I am reliably told.

In this Life I am a Soul who, because I have excelled at fast-lane soul development, has the privilege of a lifetime or more on Earth helping educate Earthlings on the dimensional ecology of the Omniverse within which we all exist.

As a Soul, this Life on Earth for me is a bit like being an Assistant in Instruction at the great Graduate School of Soul Development we call that collective of all Universes known as the Multiverse. If you want to know more about Timelines, Universes, Multiverse, and Omniverse, my strong suggestion is that you also read my book *The Omniverse* in parallel.

Here, in Earth's time-space hologram, my Avatar Alfred Lambremont Webre is a figure in sciences sequestered from the mainstream literature, a Futurist, Developer of Exopolitics the science of relations among intelligent civilizations in the multiverse. My Avatar is a Discoverer of the dimensional ecology of and early mapper of the Omniverse, the totality of all universes in the multiverse and the intelligent civilization of souls, spiritual beings and Source in the Spiritual Dimension.

In *Journey – Volume I* you will discover that the design of my Life is such that in order to better understand how humans have been kept imprisoned and to teach and educate my fellow Earthlings how to exit their personal Matrix, I have been put myself through deep and searing experiences from which I gained much pain, insight, wisdom, drive, and courage to move forward.

For example, in my adult years I actively work with others worldwide to deconstruct the pedophile, ritual child sacrifice, and child trafficking networks that are established to service the feeding needs of the Draco reptilians *et al.* and their treaty and mind control hold over the Western power Matrix. Pedophilia and child sacrifice perhaps also by Coneheads, Ancient Vampire Illuminati (I have multiple sources for their existence at the top of our controller pyramid), and others are propagated in networks in Monarchies, Parliaments, Governments, Churches, schools, police, military, intelligence, media, multigenerational families.

CHILDHOOD SEXUAL ABUSE

So as prelude and forewarning to this deep understanding and mission, in the early 1950s when I was 9 years old, a male sexual predator in his mid 20s repeatedly sexually abused and sodomized me in rural Chaparra, Cuba and that was my introduction to the birds and the bees.

So traumatized was I by this childhood sexual abuse and sodomy that I did not share these events deeply with anyone except my parents in confidence in Brownsville, Texas, when I was fifty and to my therapist in weekly sexual abuse therapy for five years at the British Columbia Society for Survivors of Male Sexual Abuse starting sometime after my fifth Spouse Soul Mate Geri and I immigrated to Vancouver BC in 1998 and I began then to unwind from my long captivity under the American servants to the Reptilians, Ancient Vampire Illuminati, and other manipulatory controllers.

Later I was to deduce that this childhood sexual predation upon me might well have been arranged by a former member of the Danish World War II Underground and fellow engineer working with my father at the sugar mill in Oriente Province Cuba owned by the same Illuminati-controlled Cabal that assassinated John F.

Kennedy. This Danish engineer also apparently attempted to seduce my mother and undermine our family in a serpentine secretive way. All of the childhood sexual abuses against me occurred in a shed on the Danish man's property.

So there is some probable cause evidence that the secret society [Jesuits] attempting to set up the course of my inner architecture to fit their template with a childhood sexual sodomy on a targeted male did so on me in Chaparra in the early 1950s.

My guess is that it was the Illuminati Jesuits who set up the Danish engineer to set up the sexual abuse because one of my maternal uncles became the deputy to Pedro Arrupe SJ, the most notorious of the Black Popes who reportedly was fired as Black Pope after he attempted to assassinate the White Pope John Paul II because J2P2 was trying to disband the Jesuits.

J2P2 was what we in the Press Corps at Puebla Mexico called Pope John Paul II in a 1978 Council held next to the Cholula Pyramid of Quetzalcoatl, one of the largest pyramids then known in the world. We now know that Karol Wojztyla as Pope John Paul II, like Popes before and after him, committed ritual child sacrifice in an underground chamber 40 meters from the Vatican.[1]

Was it the Jesuit Vampire Illuminati's intent in setting up the childhood sodomy of me so that I would focus dedicating adult years to helping the public clean house at the Draco Reptilians, Vampire Illuminati, Vatican, the Jesuits, the UK Crown, CIA, the Iranian and Talmudic perverts, U.S. government, Dutch and Belgian Crown, Parliaments, schools, police, multigenerational families? I doubt it. That is the free will choice of my Sovereign Soul to break free from child hood trauma and apply my talents to humanity's benefit.

Or was this childhood sexual abuse random karma, built into the design of my Life, which I knew about before embarking on this time-space holographic virtual reality ride as/with my Avatar Alfred Lambremont Webre?

Since Illuminati such as Jesuits like to play "God" and as I seem to have been set up in/chosen an incarnation with a deputy to the Black Pope (Jesuit Superior General) as an uncle who once boasted to my mother that child sacrificer and cannibal Elizabeth Windsor had sent the Royal Yacht Britannia to pick him up as he was her "Spiritual Adviser", I can most plausibly assume that Reptilian elites like the Windsors were attempting to bend my body and psyche to their side any which way they could.

But wait! Let's rewind the virtual reality tape and start from the beginning on this my timeline [which as you shall see shifts all on its own on or about December 21, 2012].

I was born on Sunday May 24, 1942 at the US Naval Air Station at Pensacola Fla.

Sunday six months earlier had been the Illuminati False Flag of Pearl Harbor, orchestrated by 33rd degree Mason Franklin Del-Ano [He of the Anus] Roosevelt, whose Administration reportedly signed the Treaty with the Dracos in Balboa Panama in 1933. This allegiance to the self-serving rapacious Draco race (as opposed to more civilized human upper-dimensional advanced extraterrestrial civilizations) is only natural as I was to learn to my chagrin that the United States of America was infiltrated at its founding to be a Reptilian and Luciferian Nation. From its very birth, the USA was secretly perverted as an Illuminati Project by the 2nd chapter of the Illuminati, Skull & Bones founded in 1776 (not 1832 as the Brotherhood of Death cover story) at my Alma Mater Yale University.

In the minds of the 1st Chapter of the Illuminati, the 13 founding colonies of the United States represent the 13 Zionist families, led by the Rothschilds. George Washington was chosen as First President because he was a look alike of the then current Rothschild. Rothschild and associated Illuminati started the U.S. civil war between North and South, and then took over world finances through the U.S. Federal Reserve and World Wars I and II. The irony is that the early American Founding Fathers wrote and spoke openly against the dangers of the Zionists, agents of the Ancient Vampires.

Around the time of my human birth in 1942, there are underwater ET bases off Pensacola, Florida that may belong to positive galactic fleet.

So my Sovereign Soul may have vectored off the ruins of Atlantis North of Cuba and the ET bases to quadrant in at the U.S. Naval Airbase, enmeshing itself in the fetus in the womb of Juanita Bautista Chisholm, wife of US Navy Lt. JG Alfred Lambremont Webre, Jr., Class of Yale 1938 ROTC.

Assuming a normal birth, three months after my soul enmeshing itself into the fetus of my future, Avatar, baby Alfred was born at a U.S. Naval hospital six months after the Japanese false attack on another U.S. Naval Base at Pearl Harbor in Honolulu, Hawaii.

And thus I entered our Earth's time-space dimension as a babe, ready for action from my first breath.

Feature this! A premiere world conspiracy theorist to be is born at a U.S. Naval Air base during World War II only six months after the mother of all False Flags until that moment - Pearl Harbor. Was I born False Flag sensitive or what? Even my Florida State Birth Certificate was signed on a September 11. Now that is an Inside Job, as the September 11 False Flag Operation did not occur until 2001! So is it clear to you that unraveling False Flags are central to the design of my Life's work? A fellow colleague David Wilcock claims that 9/11 was Jesus true birthday according to the Gnostics and that the 9/11 False Flag was intended as a reversal on the Christic energy by the false Matrix forces.

1973 & HOLY SPIRIT EXPERIENCE

One night in February 1973 while in my SOHO loft study in Manhattan I was enveloped in an enormous translucent being whose vibration was the Sacred. The Being and I conversed telepathically. I asked, "Who are You?" and received the reply "I am the Holy Spirit" that reverberated inside me with a profundity that shook me to the core. After more telepathic exchange I asked, "And who am I?" The Being replied, "Thou are Peter and upon this Rock I shall build my Church." After this I was taken into missing time until the morning, with the sense that I would have assistance to offer humanity when the well being of the Earth was threatened.

I did not share this Holy Spirit experience with anyone for many years and placed it online briefly in the year 2000. For me, this experience was a watershed and I date my public mission from February 1973. As you will learn, I am as yet uncertain of the nature of the entity with whom I was communicating. I spent much time examining all of the possibilities that are as of this writing still unfolding.

TARGETED BY ELECTROMAGNETIC EMF REMOTE NEURAL INFLUENCING WEAPONS

From the moment of my birth the Draco Jesuit Vampire Illuminati Rothschild-Rockefeller forces attempted to deviate me from any semblance of upper theatre mission. In October 1977 while I was meeting with an Assistant Secretary of Defense in the Inner Ring of the Pentagon on my investigation of space-based weapons platforms as part of my initiative as Director of the proposed 1977 Carter White House Extraterrestrial Communication Study, I was hit with electromagnetic EMF remote neural influencing weapons that stunned my etheric and physical bodies. These weapons were deployed by black ops forces within the US government directly at me to stop the Carter White House ET Study that had already been approved at the White House level. These forces did not want the study going forward because the secret Treaties with manipulatory Dracos and greys would have been discovered and that Treaty regime ended, with their Elites elected from power in disgrace for cowardice in having sold humanity to planetary slavery and for their assassination of John F. Kennedy, a fellow Starseed.

Back home in Palo Alto, CA and SRI International where I continued as a Futurist developing the proposed 1977 Jimmy

Carter White House Extraterrestrial Communication Study (My version of "Fools rush in where Angels fear to Tread"), the EMF remote targeting and stalking by Reptilian ground security forces continued on my person unabated. One day I was admitted to the hospital with symptoms diagnosed as bipolar disorder manic phase because that is the only diagnosis that the medical system has for civilian persons who have been attacked by remote energy weapons of their own government.

The EMF remote neural influencing targeting on me had induced symptoms that may have mimicked bipolar mania and were in fact induced responses from my neurological and neurotransmitter system coupled with post traumatic stress from the sustained targeting by intelligence black ops agents wanting to shut down the first civilian led extraterrestrial communication study by the U.S. Government in history because we would have discovered the secret treaties with the Orion greys and Draco Reptilians allowing for the abduction and experimentation on humans, as well as the sacrifice of and consumption of human babies and children, and perhaps the capture and trade of their souls.

As one more challenge to my Avatar Alfred Lambremont Webre in 1977 I now added a false mental health diagnosis "bipolar disorder" or "manic depressive", also induced by the Matrix. No worries, by 1997 only 20 years later, I was fully recovered, a proud graduate psychotherapist with a degree in Counselling from the University of Texas at Brownsville. I have included my sworn Affidavit to the Disclosure Project, May 9, 2001, National Press Club, Washington, DC regarding these events in *Journey-Volume I*.

UPPER THEATRE: RECOVERY

You will also find *Upper Theatre: Recovery*, which I originally wrote in 1999 opposite a red school house in Kitsilano, Vancouver, BC in recovery from fives decades of focused targeting by the false Matrix.

Upper Theatre: Recovery is a parallel version of my Life 1973-1999 from the Archetypal perspective of Upper Theatre, for we humans can live both in Archetype and in 3D Avatar.

JOURNEY ALONG A POSITIVE TIMELINE

One other development in *Journey - Volume I* that affects us all in our Life Journeys is that our major collective holographic timeline on which we are all traveling in this time-space hologram incarnated in our Avatars on Earth shifted from a more catastrophic to a positive timeline on December 21, 2012 or thereabouts. Please see Act III, Scene 11 *Creating a Positive Future: Time Science Shows Our Earth is on a Positive Timeline in our Time Space Hologram by Alfred Lambremont Webre.*

Our holographic virtual reality we know our life on Earth is now governed by the equation:

Positive Future = Positive Reality + Unity Consciousness

My identity as Avatar Alfred Lambremont Webre in this life is simply to be a Soul maintaining its own Sovereignty, to learn and expose the Truth as best I can to my fellow Souls.

As I am told I am a Prophesied Being in another dimension, the negative Matrix was able to spot and monitor my incarnating on Earth in my Avatar Alfred Lambremont Webre. Fortunately for me, the Matrix never controlled my inner Life, my Soul and I am consciously on our holographic positive timeline at this writing.

My book *The Omniverse* is being published [in multiple languages] through Inner Traditions/Bear & Co. in December 2015, so I will break the quarantine into higher skill set of Starseeds and cosmic understandings as humanity's discovery of the Omniverse begins to enter the Noosphere as my social invention Exopolitics did in 2000.

On this present timeline I hold no public office or emoluments and my writings and application of my social inventions over the coming centuries like Exopolitics, the mapping of the

Omniverse, and the Positive Timeline Equation deconstruct the Matrix and is how I fulfill my Incarnation mission.

[**EDITOR'S NOTE:** *"Journey – Volume I* was scheduled to have been published in the year 2025, after the substantial projected landing of Christ Consciousness on Earth. The available evidence of a global extinction level false flag planned for September 22-28, 2015 to October 11-12, 2016 around Pope Francis Bergoglio [*Whore of Babylon* Revelation Archetype]; Barack Obama [*One Head of Two Headed Beast* Revelation Archetype], and the United Nations [*Seven-headed Ten-horned Beast* Revelation Archetype] led to an acceleration of the publishing schedule of *Journey – Volume I* from the year 2025 to June 15, 2015 as part of the deconstruction of this false flag event. *"Journey – Volume I* is a scientific experiment and a new book – *Journey: Volume II* – is planned for after October 11-12, 2016 to evaluate the results of deconstructing the September 23, 2015 Jade Helm False Flag"]

My Avatar
Alfred Lambremont Webre

Chronology

May 24, 1942
Date of Birth
U.S. Naval Air Station Hospital
Pensacola, Florida USA

1942–1946
Travel and resident in Grandparents' homes in Havana, Cuba &
Merion, Pennsylvania & wartime military bases

1947–49
Radburn, New Jersey

1949–1955
Chaparra, Cuba

1955–57
Napoleonville, Louisiana

1957–60
Cespedes, Cuba
Georgetown Preparatory School
Washington, DC

1960–67
Yale University
Yale Law School
Assistant in Instruction, Economics Department

1968
Fulbright Scholar
Montevideo Uruguay

1969–1972
New York City
Wall Street Lawyer
New York City Environmental Protection Administration

1973–1977
SOHO Loft – New York City

1973
The Holy Spirit Experience
Exopolitical Author
Director, Assassination Information Bureau
The Age of Cataclysm (1974 G.P. Putnam's)

1977–78
Menlo Park California
Futurist, Stanford Research Institute
Director, Proposed 1977 Carter White House Extraterrestrial
Communication Study
House Select Committee on Assassinations

1979–91
Los Angeles, San Francisco, New York, Ontario
Producer, Journalist, Attorney, Author, Consultant
Radio Talk Show Host

1991–1998
Lower Rio Grande Valley
Deputy Director, Brownsville Community Health Center
Adjunct Professor, Bill of Rights
University of Texas
Awarded MEd (Counseling) University of Texas

1998–Present
Vancouver, BC
Futurist, Author, Journalist
Exopolitics: Politics, Government and Law In the Universe
(2005: Universebooks.com)

2014
Positive Future Equation:
Positive Future = Positive Timeline + Unity Consciousness

2015
Journey – Volume I
(2015: Universebooks.com)
The Omniverse
(2015: Inner Traditions/Bear & Co.)

Exopolitics.com
NewsInsideOut.com
PositiveFuture.info
Omniversity.info

ACT I

1973 – 1977
THE HOLY SPIRIT

"In Act I the conflict of the story is discovered. In this act, the exposition, the introduction of the protagonist, and other characters that the protagonist meets take place, as well as the dramatic premise and inciting incident (the incident that sets the events of the story in motion) occurs approximately halfway through the first act."

SCENE 1

THE HOLY SPIRIT

February 1973, 2 AM
Location: Alfred's loft in downtown SOHO/Manhattan
130 Greene Street, 2nd floor, New York 10012

"Aelf-raed [Alfred] is derived from the Old English 'aelf' (elf) and 'raed' (counsel). Elves were considered to be supernatural beings having special powers of seeing into the future.' Alfred encapsulates the essence of his spirit as an 'Elfen Wise Counselor."

At 2 AM Alfred Lambremont Webre (pronounced "Weber") was awake, working at the front of his loft on Greene Street, just then gentrifying from industrial to artist-gallery. Before Alfred and his architect wife Teresa had converted it into an ultra modern artist space that eventually was featured in New York Magazine, the loft had been a warehouse for religious artifacts. The renovation had tossed out literally barrel after barrel filled with gilt-edged holy cards of Jesus, Mary, and the saints.

Alfred's 17-month old son Freddie was asleep in his small back bedroom. Teresa had gone to Vermont to design a ski house. He and Freddie were alone in the loft. Alfred was busy painting the shelves of his office bookcase, bright yellow and red. Even now he remembers the glare of the white florescent

19

lights on the tall frosted front windows of the loft. The silence was peaceful, calm, like a pillow spread around the white space and onto the hard maple floor.

Alfred remembers he was sitting for a time, as in meditation. His consciousness became single-focused. His visual field became acutely clear. After a while, Alfred felt encased in a translucent energy field. His consciousness deepened, thoughts resonating with powerful insights.

Gradually Alfred became aware of a living presence permeating the energy field around him. Then the presence became one with the energy field, responding softly then more loudly to his thoughts.

Alfred and the presence spoke back and forth, each to each, just at the edges of his consciousness. With each reverberation of communication Alfred's consciousness expanded out into union with this source.

Alfred and the presence were dialoguing, but more than that, he was integrating with the entity, in a state of profound reverence and oneness.

He felt at peace, united with a deep truth of reality – a mystic state.

Alfred and the presence stayed in this mutuality for an indeterminate period, for what felt like a timeless embrace.

He felt in the presence of a being of the order of the gods, something far and beyond any reality he could conceive.

Alfred felt he was being given a revelation.

The dialogue was a communion, edging toward the center of his consciousness. Alfred began to hear the outlines of the thought communications that grew between the entity and himself.

He became aware of the content of these thought communications. Alfred could make out that their dialogue had to do with the agenda of Spirit in our reality.

Though Alfred could not fully hear the communications yet, their meanings seemed to confirm what he had been deducing in his waking hours.

20

Alfred's mind raced with questions about the identity of the entity. What are the interdimensional and extraterrestrial intelligences? What is their agenda? How did he fit into their agenda? Could he interpret their plans? What is their agenda? How would it evolve?"

The entity now came into the center of Alfred's consciousness, holding it in invisible embrace.

The telepathic communications between Alfred and the entity became louder and more defined.

Each syllable, each word of thought emitted telepathically by the presence reverberated down the core of his being, like long musical notes played up and down the edges of his energy field.

All of a sudden Alfred's thoughts spoke first, loudly in his mind.

"Who are you?" he asked the presence.

A long deep pause ensued. Alfred felt safe, but forward in asking, as though he had been given permission to approach.

Profound was the thought communication that came back from the presence.

"I am the Holy Spirit," the presence said in thought.

Silence enveloped the two, Alfred and the presence.

Communion embraced them.

Realization overcame Alfred's being.

Elevation caught him in its gentle hand, and he rose in frequency of thought and feeling.

Alfred wanted to stay in the moment forever, and he stayed as long as he could remember, living in the deep embrace. He could feel his molecules changing; altered, transforming his naïve, human state.

"The Holy Spirit, holy of holies, third person of deity!" thought Alfred's human mind in a flash of recognition.

At any other higher level of energy gradient, Alfred knew he would have been rendered unconscious, or at least transfixed by the presence. Alfred rested in meditation on the most recent response by the presence.

Alfred let go of his evaluative, judgmental brain processes; and just experienced being at one with this moment.

He felt enthralled. Symbols of the "Holy Spirit" pushed him into circuits of profound reverence. His physical brain knew it could not the third person of all Source that was talking to him. His spirit felt like deity embraced him.

Alfred's mind did not want to leave this reverie. The presence's words "Holy Spirit" reverberated and reverberated.

At some moment, Alfred's mind wanted to know more.

So he asked,

"And who am I?" asked Alfred.

The Holy Spirit responded with thought waves that continued to embrace Alfred.

"Thou art Peter and upon this rock I shall found my church," responded the presence in clear thought communication.

"Me? The rock on which the Holy Spirit will found its church?" Alfred was simultaneously awed and shocked.

This answering phrase of the "Holy Spirit" entity was to become the dominant shift of Alfred's life.

The literature on inter-dimensional and extraterrestrial contactees tells us that contactees are often given messianic messages, which set them off on life long missions as "appointed" messengers to humankind.

Alfred's own immediate reactions were probably not too different from other alien experiencers.

His first reaction was profound validation. "Hey! The Holy Spirit knows what it is doing!"

His second reaction was… "Hey, this entity is playing head games with my ex-Catholic case!"

His third reaction was… "Hey, this is happening to me now, and I really do not know what it all means."

Alfred sank back into thought silence with the entity, feeling at once baffled, embraced, responsible, awed, and confused.

Alfred was not sure how long he stayed in a state of quiet reverie. It could have been an hour; it could have been less. He remembers thinking that his visitation with the Holy Spirit was at an end.

Then came the second act.

A force turned Alfred toward the center of the loft space and walked him slowly toward a table saw he had placed there for woodworking needed to finish the loft space.

The force ushered Alfred up to the table saw, bent him over, and brought his head and face right up to its edge.

The saw's brand name – "Rockwell" - stared him in the face.

As Alfred looked at the brand name – "Rockwell" - its letters and syllables began to morph about before his eyes.

The first syllable, "ROCK", became acutely large and came up to his eyeballs, vibrating before him.

The second syllable - "well" - zoomed away from Alfred. Vibrating in the air, the "well" syllable rapidly shrunk in size and completed an optical dissolve.

The bizarreness of the scene baffled him for a moment. He almost laughed at the cheekiness of it all. Really, now! Why do these high beings have to communicate through wavy, buzzing letters on the edge of a table saw? Alfred realized this was a message in symbolic code. An extension of the message he had just received from the Holy Spirit entity. Alfred did not come to this conclusion on his own. The Holy Spirit entity's thought-voice was telling this to him in his mind.

The voice walked him through the symbols in the message, several times.

The bizarreness of the vibrating "ROCK" syllable and the disappearing "well" syllable kept dancing before his eyes. Alfred continued in his befuddled state. He was being coaxed to understand, like a child learning basic meanings in a language from a teaching adult.

The voice in Alfred's mind was firm but gentle as Alfred began to decipher the symbolic communication.

How do "well" and "ROCK" relate? The question kept revolving in his mind.

The answer came in an *"aha!"* moment.

The "well" syllable had morphed smaller and smaller, eventually disappearing in an optical dissolve.

Alfred understood the meanings of the symbols.

"'Well' means the 'wellness of the earth'," he thought.

The "well" doing an optical dissolve means that the "wellness of the earth" will diminish and disappear.

Alfred envisioned a meaning to the disappearing "well" symbol – "There will be a time when conditions on the earth may become catastrophic for human kind."

Alfred's mind turned to decipher the meaning of the "ROCK" syllable.

What was the meaning of the "ROCK" syllable's morphing, magnified up against his eyes?

The Holy Spirit's words – "Thou are Peter and upon this Rock I will found my Church" – swirled around him. Alfred did not want to allow that "Rock" was referring to him. Literally. That was too scary. On the other hand, there was an underlying thrill that the "Rock" might mean him. Sort of the ultimate life challenge.

Then, Alfred "grokked" that the "Rock" in fact did not refer to him.

The "Rock" meant a new reality based on the reality of the Holy Spirit entity.

The total meaning of the symbolic message came in a flash.

"As the wellness of the earth disappears, the Rock will come to the fore!"

The Holy Spirit was giving Alfred a prophecy, or vision of the future, in symbolic terms.

Alfred took the gist of the prophecy to be that there are catastrophic times coming for the planet. And as these times come, a spiritual reality will come to the fore on earth.

It was now late, maybe an hour before dawn. Alfred was sitting quietly. His mind was exhausted, meditating on what had just transpired.

He felt he had entered an elite rank – humans who had been visited by higher intelligence. Alfred felt he had been admitted to a special message for mankind. The symbolic message was not for his sake only, but for the benefit of the planet.

It seemed logical. Other prophecies in time had been given by higher intelligence to humans, couched in symbolic terms.

Like other experiencers of higher intelligence, he was given not only a message but also a mission. Did Alfred have a responsibility to tell the world of future potential troubled times?

There was also a linguistic ambiguity in the message. Undoubtedly, the Holy Spirit entity carefully designed its response to Alfred to exploit this ambiguity.

Alfred was told explicitly, "Thou are Peter, and upon this Rock I shall found my church." In many Latinate languages, Peter and Rock are synonyms.

That message is a phrase from 18:16 in the gospel of Matthew in the New Testament. Christian religions, specifically Roman Catholicism, have used this phrase as evidence to represent the historical Jesus, who in the Christian church is seen as the "Son of God", on the planet.

Why would the Holy Spirit entity intentionally designate Alfred as "Peter the Rock"?

Ah. Well, apparently that's the way higher intelligence is. Higher intelligent interdimensional or extraterrestrial beings know how to motivate.

They know how to enroll a human being for the rest of her or his life.

They know how to couch their message in symbols that will sear the soul of their human charge.

Dimensional intelligence knows how to implant the symbols of divinity in a way that charges the human with the sense of a unique mission on earth.

So it was with Alfred.

Alfred's 1973 experience with the Holy Spirit entity occurred a month into his career as a student of parapsychology and extraterrestrial relations, prophecy and the paranormal. The visitation came at a strategic moment, and propelled him forward into ever deepening alternate realities. He felt he was on a pre-destined track in his life.

He had started a life-long mission.

For over three decades, Alfred told no one about the Holy Spirit and kept his secret deep within his heart.

Alfred felt the interaction with the Holy Spirit entity had transformed him at the molecular level. From then onward, he sensed the frequencies of his being vibrating at higher rates than the mundane human reality around him. Alfred navigated, rather than walked through the scenes of his life.

Who was the Holy Spirit entity? Who was Alfred? During the "missing time" episode with the Holy Spirit, Alfred felt he was shown a documentary of his future life. Was he taken aboard a spaceship? Was Alfred taken to another dimension? Was Alfred taken another planet?

EXCERPT FROM RECOVERY [Please see UPPER THEATRE]: In the early 1970s, Alfred began to explore the evidence for multi-dimensional reality and realized that the positivist world of electoral politics and "progressive" government was not addressing the full range of multi-dimensional challenges our planet in crisis demanded. In January 1973 Alfred's one boss, New York Mayor John Vliet Lindsay, decided to run for U.S. President. Another boss, EPA Administrator Jerome Kretchmer, decided to run for Mayor. Alfred decided to leave government where he was General Counsel to the New York City Environmental Protection Administration.

"I am the Holy Spirit."

One night in February 1973 Alfred was working in my studio at the front of his designer loft in SOHO (lower Manhattan) that had recently been featured in New York Magazine. Teresa, a Peruvian architect, was Alfred's then first wife. She was away in Vermont designing a ski-lodge. Alfred's two-year-old son Freddie was asleep in his bedroom of the loft.

Alfred and Teresa had found the loft as a former warehouse filled with barrels of religious articles like holy cards of Jesus and the Holy Family, and renovated it with a futuristic design.

Lost in the midst of his work on extraterrestrial life and hermeneutics (decoding prophecy), Alfred unexpectedly felt enveloped inside an enormous inter-dimensional energy being that came down around him at his desk. The being communicated to him telepathically, and its words reverberated throughout his mind and body. Alfred felt he was in the core of all that is Holy.

Alfred asked the being point blank, "Who are you?" With a telepathic depth that enthralled him beyond any sacred moment he had ever experienced, the being responded, "I am the Holy Spirit."

Alfred sat in profound, reverential stillness at this telepathic message, which had been delivered with an anthropomorphic representation of the third person of Triune Deity communicating to him, a human, in his loft on Greene Street, much as other Godheads had communicated to other prophets on mountaintops.

Never mind that Exopolitics now shows these other "God-heads" communicating to other extraterrestrial contactees were most probably interdimensional extraterrestrials seeding human religions. Never mind that Alfred had left the Roman Catholic religion 13 years before on entering Yale as a freshman in 1960. For Alfred, speaking with the interdimensional being in that moment was like speaking with the actual Holy Spirit.

"Thou are Peter, and upon this Rock I shall build my Church"

Some impulse prompted Alfred to ask his next question and it rolled off his telepathic transmitter. I telepathically asked the interdimensional being, "And who am I?"

The being responded in reverberations, "Thou are Peter and upon this Rock I shall build my Church". Alfred sat in stunned silence as the meaning of these words poured over him, again and again. He took the words of the Holy Spirit source personally in that moment. The

Holy Spirit source was calling him, Alfred Lambremont Webre, "Peter" (Latin for Rock), and a foundation of its "Church".

At one level, Alfred understood these to be the words of the New Testament Gospel of Matthew Chapter 16, verse 18, normally interpreted to be the words of the Christ designating his apostle Peter either literally or metaphorically a custodian of Christ's continuing revelation on Earth.

A deeper part of Alfred in that moment took the "Holy Spirit" words as an anointment and a revelation of his future mission and destiny on Earth. Alfred was led into hours of "missing time" and shown a virtual "movie" of a future Earth in crisis, a time when the "Rock" (Alfred) would come to the fore and help provide the Earth with needed solutions.

In short, Alfred's February 1973 experience exhibited all the hallmarks of an interdimensional, extraterrestrial encounter, a form of psychological operation to imbue the "contactee" (Alfred) with a deep, life-long sense of mission.

For years Alfred's encounter with the "Holy Spirit" was a watershed episode in his life that he largely kept to himself. Alfred wondered: "Was this truly a communication from Divinity? Was the 'Holy Spirit' a masquerading interdimensional spiritual being, extraterrestrial, manipulative human intelligence agency? Was the 'Holy Spirit' a dissociated part of my subconscious?"

The "Holy Spirit" experience played a central role in Alfred's private life. The "Holy Spirit" experience became his private, interdimensional, prophetic moment. Alfred trusted it as genuine, whatever its source. One psychic even told Alfred that he "might be" a reincarnation of the apostle Peter. The message of the "Holy Spirit" and the information Alfred saw in the virtual movie of the Earth future became the hidden engine behind his public life mission and actions.

Finally, after decades of inner consideration, Alfred decided to "accept" the "Holy Spirit" experience as what it most reasonably appeared to be – his multidimensional contact experience. Alfred's "Holy Spirit" episode was, he concluded, an encounter with an interdimensional or ex-

traterrestrial being using the "masquerade" of the "Holy Spirit" and a New Testament messianic text for the purpose of enrolling Alfred in an indeterminate mission that appeared to be part of an over-all long term plan for landing a positive timeline on planet Earth. The over-all purpose of the "Holy Spirit" encounter was to motivate Alfred, using the psychological conditioners employed with most extraterrestrial contactees, designating the contactee a "special messenger" – in this case the Rock on which the Church of the Holy Spirit would be founded in the new era.

The simplest explanation remains that Alfred attracted the Holy Spirit experience into his reality after he attracted the Messiah experience into his reality on January 3, 1973 and empowered it.

SCENE 2

CIA/DARPA Time Travel

1971-72, Weekday morning
Location: Alfred's office as General Counsel of the NYC EPA
Municipal Building, 23rd floor, 1 Centre Street, New York 10007

SCENE 3

SAME DAY, AFTERNOON

*Location: Large hall with windows
and about fifty chairs in nondescript office building
somewhere in the Delaware Valley, or near Washington, DC*

It is a weekday morning at Alfred's General Counsel office in the Mayor John Lindsay's New York City government's Environmental Protection Administration. Alfred is about to leave his office where he would unwittingly participate in a meeting with a joint CIA/DARPA and Project Pegasus secret time travel program. At the time, though Alfred is conscious of the cognitive dissonance he feels during his talk, he will think he is giving a talk on environmental protection to approximately fifty men in suits and ties. In fact, Alfred was giving a speech to fifty or so employees of CIA, DARPA and Project Pegasus who had all been briefed on the book "Exopolitics" Alfred would publish in 2005 and which CIA, DARPA and Project Pegasus had time traveled back to 1971.

CIA and DARPA had taken his 2005 book *"Exopolitics: Politics, Government and Law in the Universe"* from at least 2005 back to 1971 by U.S. secret government time travel, and had subjected it to enough investigation to want to examine him in person in 1971.[2] Perhaps CIA and DARPA had also used chronovision or actual physical time travel to perform physical (unconstitutional) surveillance of him from the past (1971) in the future (2000 forward), when the book "Exopolitics" was first published online, and when Alfred re-emerged as an exopolitical activist worldwide.

Alfred was to spend 40 years trying to understand why the military-intelligence apparatus worldwide was targeting him. Four decades later in 2013, Alfred will know the truth about how he was targeted by CIA and DARPA through time travel surveillance because of a book he would write nearly thirty years in the future. In the interim, Alfred will cope with the rigors of time travel surveillance and constant state terror against him, trying to survive specific clandestine power factions who were privy to this time travel information and who wished to destroy him before he could reach his destiny.

These power factions used a multiplicity of deadly tools at their command including attempts to assassinate or abduct and "disappear" Alfred, interference by Cointelpro social disruption campaigns, deployment of MKULTRA and mind control frequency weapons, and financial and professional isolation so that Alfred could not find mainstream employment in his field.

At the beginning of the 1970s, Alfred found himself disturbed by the fact that the Wall Street law firm he worked for, Cleary, Gottlieb, Steen & Hamilton, represented Pan American Airways and that he was handling legal matters for Pan American Airways account at a time when Pan Am reportedly had the contract to repatriate body bags containing dead U.S. soldiers from the war in Vietnam. Through his research, Alfred knew that the body bags his client was ferrying back from Vietnam were stuffed with heroin from the "Golden Triangle", a deliberate "opium war" by the global drug cartel to undermine the social fabric of the United Stated by addicting its underclass and its youth. Consequently, Alfred decided to leave Wall Street law for "public service" and environmental protection in 1970.

Prof. Howard Gillette, PhD of Rutgers University, a fellow Yale classmate of Alfred's, wrote of Alfred in his proposed book "Class Divide: Social Change and Yale's Class of 1964."

"In 1974 [George W. Bush's Attorney General] John Ashcroft [also Yale '64] was serving as auditor general for the State of Missouri, and a number of classmates had been drawn to New York to join Mayor John Lindsay's effort to fashion the first progressive Republican administration in that city since that of Fiorello LaGuardia during the Depression and World War II. Among the Lindsay appointments was 64's Alfred Webre. The son and grandson of sugar magnates operating in Louisiana and Cuba, Webre grew up bi-culturally, acutely aware of the roots his Cuban mother provided as well as ties to the United States where he attended private schools in Pennsylvania and Maryland. A soccer player who joined the children of Cuban workers in the sport, he was sympathetic to the social justice issues embraced by the revolution, even as his family suffered expropriation and exile from the island. Put under house arrest the summer before he was to attend Yale, his appearance at the reception opening the 1960 academic year sparked the interest of administrators who told him they were worried he would be prevented from attending. Caught between expectations that he would follow his father into business and other academic interests, he majored in industrial administration but took as many courses as he could in the humanities. With close friends captured in the Bay of Pigs fiasco, he nonetheless retained some sympathy for Fidel Castro, who had been a student in a school administrated by his uncle and a frequent visitor to his grandmother in Havana. "I lived in two worlds," he recalled, "always trying to reconcile them."

"Webre's post-graduate career appeared normal enough—a degree from Yale Law School, followed by a Fulbright fellowship to study in Latin America, a job at Cleary, Gottlieb, Steen & Hamilton, a leader in the practice of international law, and appointment as director of the fledging environmental protection office in the Lindsay administration. What was not so apparent was the growing difficulty Webre experienced trying to balance his establishment credentials with his growing radicalism. The choice of Yale Law and the fellowship that followed were prompted by a determination to avoid the draft. At Yale, his opposition to the war was nothing out of the ordinary, but when Webre arrived in Uruguay, he threw himself into the cause, giving

35

talks against the conflict in several Latin American countries. All the time, he conveyed a rebellious posture as the Spanish-speaking, motorcycle-riding critic, who apparently looked enough like Che Guevara's fellow rebel and biographer, Regis Debray, to be confused with him. The decision to work for Cleary, Gottlieb represented an effort to settle down and perhaps work towards an international law practice. Instead, the discovery that one of his clients, Pan American Airways, was implicated in smuggling drugs from Vietnam in body bags heightened his earlier disillusionment and prompted his resignation. He chose to join the Lindsay Administration as a means of tamping down his own political rebellion, which had been further complicated by becoming a cooperating attorney in the ACLU's defense of 21 Black Panthers charged in New York with attempted murder and conspiracies to blow up various police and school buildings, a railroad yard, and the Bronx Botanical Gardens."

Alfred had been brought into Cleary Gottlieb Steen & Hamilton in 1969 by Fowler Hamilton, John F. Kennedy's first nominee for CIA (later Kennedy's head of US AID). Alfred wondered why Fowler Hamilton had brought him into Cleary Gottlieb. At the time, he attributed the fortunate job offering to the happy coincidence that the Washington, DC lawyer representing his father's consulting firm in Africa knew Fowler Hamilton personally.

Alfred's first office at Cleary Gottlieb had been the "Ball Room," the former office of George W. Ball, Kennedy's Under Secretary of State, well known for his opposition to the escalation of the war in Vietnam. Alfred shared the Ball Room with two other law associates at Cleary and worked under senior partner James G. "Jimmy" Johnson, Jr. on financial matters for international and corporate legal clients including the now defunct Lehman Brothers, Asian Development Bank (for whom CIA agent Stanley Ann Dunham, Barry Soetoro/Barack H. Obama's birthmother later worked), the Government of Brazil, and the heroin-ferrying Pan Am airways.

By mid 1970, Alfred found the contradictions between his personal political beliefs and the activities of his legal clients like Pan Am airways too great to bear. One day, Alfred and Fowler Hamilton were in the office elevator together at the firm's offices at 52 Wall Street and Alfred proudly told Fowler about his civil liberties brief challenging the decision of N.Y. Judge John M. Murtagh to find Alfred's client in summary contempt of Court at the Panther 21 trial. Fowler Hamilton, founder of the venerable firm turned to Alfred with a stare, "John's a good Judge, Alfred." In 1964, Judge Murtagh has also adjudged the comedy of Lenny Alfred Bruce to be "patently offensive to the average person in the community." Eventually, the jury acquitted the Panther 21 of all charges in 45 minutes. That elevator meeting with Fowler Hamilton was a tipping point. There was no inner values future for Alfred at Cleary, Gottlieb.

Soon afterward several young associates invited Alfred to a luncheon at which Jerome Kretchmer, the newly appointed head of the NYC Environmental Protection Administration was speaking. Kretchmer said he was setting up a new legal office under Neil Fabricant, a former New York Civil Liberties Union lawyer. The other associates looked around at Alfred. It seemed they knew Alfred wanted to leave Wall Street.

Alfred made contact with Neil Fabricant who in turn got strong recommendations of Alfred's capabilities as a lawyer from his contacts at the New York Civil Liberties Union (NYCLU). Alfred's NYCLU brief on behalf of a Student for Democratic Society (SDS) member who had been sentenced to summary contempt at the New York Panther 21 trial had reportedly been circulated nation-wide in civil liberties circles including at the Chicago 7 trial of Abbie Hoffman, Jerry Rubin, David Dellinger, Tom Hayden, Rennie Davis, John Froines, Lee Weiner, and Bobby Seale before Judge Julius Hoffman.[3]

Fabricant made Alfred an offer to join NYCEPA as an environmental lawyer, and in mid-1970, Alfred took up a new office on the 23rd floor of New York's Municipal building, across from City Hall. Within a year, Fabricant had left the EPA to "drop out" and run a bookstore in upstate New York, and Alfred was appointed General Counsel.

Alfred's time as General Counsel was characterized by his usual "think outside the box" style that invariably resulted in getting his peers in municipal, state and federal government and in industry ruffled and upset, much to the satisfaction of the media and the public.

Alfred was often in the New York city newspapers, especially the New York Post, whose environmental reporter Steve Lawrence, reported widely on his activities enforcing the New York City air pollution, water pollution, noise pollution and solid waste laws and regulations with the half-dozen activist environmental lawyers in his office. One invitation for Alfred to speak came from a group called the "Delaware Valley Industrial Engineering Association." Alfred spoke publicly on environmental issues and when he was invited to speak by this group, Alfred routinely accepted.[4]

On the particular weekday morning in 1971-72 that was the scheduled day of Alfred's talk, a representative of the "Delaware Valley Industrial Engineering Association" came Alfred's General Counsel office on the 23rd floor of the New York City Municipal Building. Alfred and the representative set off in the representative's car. The representative was a middle-aged "grey" bureaucrat. He was different from the students and housewives in community-based environmental groups Alfred generally addressed.

On the road trip to the venue of his talk, Alfred exchanged small talk and pleasantries with the representative. The representative was, however, reserved, guarded, and silent and unlike the environmental activist group representatives Alfred was used to dealing with.

The car trip grew much longer than Alfred expected. Alfred queried his host where they were going. The representative simply smiled and said something like "We will get there soon." Inwardly, Alfred began to suspect that something was up, out of the ordinary to be sure.

The "Delaware Valley" generally refers to an area in southern

New Jersey and southeastern Pennsylvania. Unknown to Alfred, in 1971-72 many of the East-coast U.S. functions of CIA/DARPA's Project Pegasus secret time travel and teleportation project were centered in the area of New Jersey known as the "Delaware Valley", just the time period when he was now on his way to speak to the "Delaware Valley Industrial Engineering Association."

Alfred and his host finally arrived several hours later at a nondescript office building that could be anywhere in the "Delaware Valley" or even south toward Baltimore and Washington, DC. They entered a hall on one of the upper floors of the office building. There was a lectern at the front of the hall, where Alfred would speak.

There were about fifty or so people in the audience of the hall, all expecting Alfred. Like his host, the audience was not at all like the community-based environmental activist audiences that Alfred usually spoke to in New York City at that time. The people in this audience were all male, dressed uniformly in suits or shirts with ties.

As Alfred approached the podium and was being introduced, he scanned the audience. Alfred was an accomplished public speaker. At a public speaking course at New York's New School, the faculty member had remarked that Alfred's public speaking voice and impact reminded him of Robert F. Kennedy. As he began to speak, Alfred made out noticeable smirks on the faces of a number of the audience members, a sort of "voyeur gotcha" smirk. This was unusual, Alfred noted, as his environmental audiences at the time did not smirk, were not dressed in bland governmental office garb, and were not uniformly male bureaucratic intelligence agency types.

Alfred adjusted his standard environmental stump speech, tweaking it slightly toward the right for political cover as he sensed he was in the presence of illicit national security state surveillance. As Alfred spoke, he felt that he was being observed and covertly measured for performance in a way that did not relate at all to the content of his talk, which was the urban environmental agenda of the early 1970s. Alfred also felt he was being sent a subliminal series of messages. What the full content of the messages was he did not know, except the gist was "You are being watched."

Alfred made sure to put full energy into the windup of his talk, seeking to motivate the men in the room to protect the environment for all our sakes and for the sake of future generations. At the end of the talk, he was asked a few perfunctory questions and then soundly applauded, which surprised him. He was given a mug with the words "Delaware Valley Industrial Engineering Association" on it. Alfred kept the mug in his 23rd floor General Counsel EPA office as a memento.

For almost 35 years, Alfred's principal emotional memory associated with this incident was "cognitive dissonance." The audience and the true purpose in inviting him to speak did not add up. What did this episode with the "Delaware Valley Industrial Engineering Association" have to do with his then role as a crusading environmental lawyer?

Alfred was not ever able to track down a "Delaware Valley Industrial Engineering Association." He doubted that such an organization existed except as a cover for a CIA/DARPA 1971-72 covert time travel surveillance event of Alfred Lambremont Webre, then General Counsel of the New York Environmental Protection Administration and future author of the book "*Exopolitics: Politics, Government and Law in the Universe*", or perhaps, a time travel surveillance event of Alfred contactee of the Holy Spirit entity, identified as "Thou art Peter and Upon this Rock I will found my Church"?

Andrew D. Basiago, a childhood participant in CIA/DARPA's secret time travel projects (Project Pegasus) in the "Delaware Valley", reports he was in the presence of Alfred's book "Exopolitics: Politics, Government and Law in the Universe" in 1971-72. In 2005, Andy revealed that the reason CIA/DARPA was able to identify Jimmy Carter, who in 1971 was Governor of Georgia, as a future U.S. President, is that CIA/DARPA time travel was in possession of a copy of "Exopolitics: Politics, Government and Law in the Universe" by Alfred Lambremont Webre, a book that

Alfred would not write until 1999, would not be published as a trade book until 2005, and which bears a quote on its front pages of a statement made by President Jimmy Carter.

Alfred's book *"Exopolitics: A Decade of Contact"*, originally published by Universe Books as an online free book in 2000, historically defined and founded the field of Exopolitics, "the science of relations among intelligent civilizations in the multiverse." The book provides an articulation of a paradigm shift by which humanity becomes part of a populated, organized multiverse. Alfred's book *"Exopolitics: Politics, Government and Law in the Universe"* was a time travel artifact and, among other written works, had been physically retrieved from the future by CIA/DARPA's Project Pegasus and brought back in time to 1971 or a prior time.

In 1971 Alfred was General Counsel of the New York City Environmental Protection Administration. In 2005, with the publication of his book *"Exopolitics: Politics, Government and Law in the Universe"*, Alfred would learn directly from eyewitness Andrew D. Basiago, who in 1971 with two other witnesses saw a physical copy of "Exopolitics: Politics, Government and Law in the Universe" that CIA/DARPA had retrieved from 2005 (or later). Only then would it be confirmed to Alfred that he had been placed under covert time travel surveillance by the U.S. government since at least 1971.

Only by 2005 would Alfred come to know that thirty-five years of time-travel-driven MKULTRA and Cointelpro dirty tricks against him by the U.S. government and other interests would trace back to intelligence gathered by a narrow group of CIA/DARPA employees and time scientists he met at the "Delaware Valley Industrial Engineering Association". The work results of those CIA/DARPA employees were coordinated by then Nixon cabinet member Donald H. Rumsfeld. Rumsfeld, in turn, reported back to Nixon National Security Advisor Henry Alfred Kissinger. As Alfred was to surmise from Bernard Mendez, one of Nixon's secret time travel aides, Rumsfeld and Kissinger reported back on issues to time travel to President Richard M. Nixon himself.

SCENE 4

PARAPSYCHOLOGY & EXOPOLITICS

June 1973
Location: Outside Columbia University Library, on the lawn
New York, NY 10027

Alfred is sitting on the lawn outside Columbia University Library in conversation with Phillip Liss. It has been almost six months since Alfred left his job at NYC EPA to pursue free form research in parapsychology and extraterrestrial studies. Alfred's savings are depleting. Alfred decides he must write a book in this new field, generate a new source of income, and broadcast his new insights.

By the end of 1972, Alfred's search for a reality view beyond the "Western-positivist" paradigm had led him to the doors of parapsychology, the science of non-local consciousness, psi, telepathy, psychokinesis, life after death. Alfred phoned his cousin Ann Webre, a psychotherapist at the Karen Horney Institute in Manhattan, to ask if she knew an expert in parapsychology. "Yes," Ann said. "The husband of one of my fellow therapists at work is a professor of experimental psychology and is also a researcher in parapsychology." More phone calls ensued, and Alfred and Teresa were invited to the home of Rutger's professor Phillip Herman Liss, PhD for an open house on January 7, 1973.

Phillip H. Liss' biography lists him as a Woodrow Wilson Fellow who graduated with a PhD in physiological psychology in 1965, followed by an NIH postdoctoral fellow at the Nencki Institute of Experimental Psychology in Warsaw Poland. Phillip's teaching career started as a lecturer at MIT psychology department, followed by a year at the Center for Cognitive Studies, Harvard University. Phillip was then an Assistant professor of psychology at CUNY, and an Associate professor of psychology at the Institute for Cognitive Studies, Rutgers University, Newark, NJ until 1974 when Phillip's academic career abruptly ends for reasons that relate directly to Phillip's mental health diagnosis.

Phillip Liss comes into Alfred's life on January 7, 1973 and is to act as Alfred's mentor in parapsychology, extraterrestrial studies, conspiracy theory, and hermeneutics (decoding of prophetic texts) until the summer of 1976. In 1976, Alfred breaks with Phillip over his bizarre public behavior during a book promotion trip to Vancouver, British Columbia at the invitation of legendary Canadian television host Peter Gzowski for Alfred and Phillip to be on his national CBC-TV program.

Rutgers Professor Howard Gillette, PhD writes in "*Class Divide: Social Change and Yale's Class of 1964.*"

"*In 1974 Webre teamed up with Rutgers University psychologist Philip Liss in the publication of 'The Age of Cataclysm'. Joining his many classmates who used their tenth reunion year to express their disillusionment with contemporary politics even as Richard Nixon faced almost certain impeachment, Webre's volume might well have cited the Watergate break-in to reach the conclusion that the existing political parties were not up to meeting the challenges of the era. No such references appeared in the book. What drove the authors' recommendations, not just for the formation of a new federalist party but also for a world federation, was the considered belief, suggested by psychic readings and confirmed by the emerging science of plate tectonics— the study of the earth's crust—that the world was about to experience a prolonged period of natural catastrophes. In a sober and highly critical fashion the authors detailed how poorly prepared the United States and the world were to deal with the effects of earthquakes, flooding, drought, and other natural disasters that the authors claimed were sure to plague the earth. Far from being pessimistic, however, the authors predicted that as the challenges became clear and nations acted rationally to remove obstacles to cooperation, there would follow a 'profound revolution in the human process and in the individual mind as a prelude to world peace' and 'the unleashing of creativity, cooperation, and happiness without precedent in human history.' Claiming that psychic discoveries predicting these disasters could well represent the fulfillment of Biblical prophecies, the volume reflected Webre's continuing sense of straddling an establishment role even as it joined a growing body of literature melding science and unconventional spiritual beliefs.*

"Webre's view was not incidental. As rewarding as he found his career path in the Lindsay administration, it left something still to be desired. Looking outside what he called the positivist and enlightenment paradigm that had characterized his formal education, he began to investigate more intuitive areas of knowledge, most particularly parapsychology, which involved the study of telepathy, precognition, clairvoyance, near-death experiences, and reincarnation. Webre's investigations received a boost from the 1970 book Psychic Discoveries Behind the Iron Curtain, which introduced him to scientifically based research in non-rational experience. Among the subjects Webre found of particular interest in this text was the view, inspired by Yuri Gagarin's 1961 flight into space, that telepathy would ultimately form common language when cosmonauts first hailed spaceships from other solar systems. Webre's partnership with Philip Liss, a specialist in parapsychology and extraterritorial life, gave an edge to their 1974 joint publication. Unstated but clearly evident in the blend of parapsychology with standard policy formation was a life-changing experience Webre had recently undergone."

SCENE 5

THE CATASTROPHIC TIMELINE

1974
Location: Offices of Bill Targ,
Editor in Chief of GP Putnam's Sons
Madison Avenue, New York, NY 10022

Alfred and Phillip's book *"The Age of Cataclysm"*[5], published in 1974 at the top of the list by GP Putnam's brought contact with leading researchers, as well as exposure on national TV and radio talk shows. The book was also one of the first to define the "catastrophic timeline", a future envisioning a global coastal event, the turning inside out of a global conspiracy that assassinated John F. Kennedy and was installing a militaristic police state worldwide, and a new social and spiritual era on the planet integrating with intelligent extraterrestrial life.

Alfred's friend Neil Fabricant, who reminded Alfred of the actor Dustin Hoffman, was now back in New York City from his dropping-out adventure. Fabricant connected Alfred with the public interest environmental law program at the Ford Foundation under Edward "Ned" Ames.

In 1974, Alfred became the Ford Foundation's consultant, periodically traveling to the offices of the Natural Resources Defense Council and the Environmental Law Fund in New

York, Denver, and Berkeley, California. One day at lunch with Ned Ames in the Ford Foundation cafeteria, Ned said, "Alfred turn around, over there is McGeorge Bundy, Ford Foundation President. He almost never comes to the cafeteria." Bundy looked straight at Alfred. "Oh, no!" thought Alfred reflecting back on his experience of being surveilled by the 'Delaware Valley Industrial Engineering Association'. "Another top level CIA surveillance. What did Bundy know?" Bundy had been US National Security Adviser under Presidents Kennedy and Johnson.

The Ford Foundation consultantship provided Alfred with an income stream to pay rent on his loft and keep contact and credentials in the matrix world that Alfred was now re-framing from multiple dimensions, keeping in his inner most sanctum the words of the 1973 Holy Spirit entity, and somewhere in his subconscious the anomalous 1971 experience with the "Delaware Valley Industrial Engineering Association," in reality DARPA/CIA masquerading as an environmental group.

Alfred began his research in conversation sessions with Phillip Liss on the catastrophic timeline in 1973, when researching the earth sciences plausibility of a "remote viewing" by the American psychic Edgar Cayce (March 18, 1877 – January 3, 1945) of a "global coastal event". Alfred found when writing "The Age of Cataclysm" that earth sciences trends in geology and seismology were congruent with a "global coastal event" that Edgar Cayce had remote-viewed while in psychic trance.

The global coastal event that Cayce remote viewed had the following characteristics:

1   Destructive earthquake activity along USA west coast;

2   Disappearance of southern portions of Carolina & Georgia;

3   Disappearance of the greater portion of Japan under the sea;

4   Rapid earth changes in the upper portion of Europe;

5   Emptying of Great Lakes into Gulf of Mexico;

6   Rising of new lands along the east coast of USA;

7   Dramatic changes along USA east coast, including destruction of NYC;

8   Upheavals of Earth in Arctic & Antarctic;

9   Volcanic eruptions in torrid zones;

10 A shift in the axis of the Earth, with corresponding climatic changes, starting in 2001.

Alfred completed the basic research and text for "The Age of Cataclysm" in 1973. As Alfred was to discover in 2008, "The Age of Cataclysm" had found congruent parallels with contemporary (1971) secret time travel discoveries made by DARPA/CIA on their chronovisor probes of the year 2013. Both DARPA/CIA time travel in 1971 and *"The Age of Cataclysm"* in 1973 found evidence of a catastrophic timeline containing a global coastal event for Earth in the early 21st century.

Remote sensing in the time-space continuum[6]

Mr. Basiago has revealed that between 1969 and 1972, as a child participant in Project Pegasus, he both viewed past and future events through a device known as a chronovisor and teleported back and forth across the country in vortal tunnels opened in time-space via Tesla-based teleporters located at the Curtiss-Wright Aeronautical Company facility in Wood Ridge, NJ and the Sandia National Laboratory in Sandia, NM.

DARPA had, he explains, five reasons for involving American school children in such new, dangerous, and experimental activities. First, the Department of Defense wanted to test the mental and physical effects of teleportation on children. Second, Project Pegasus needed to use children because the holograms created by the chronovisors would collapse when adults stood within them. Third, the children were tabula rasa and would tend to see things during the time probes that adults would tend to miss. Fourth, the children were trainees who upon growing up would serve in a covert time-space program under DARPA that would operate in tandem with the overt space program under NASA. Lastly, the program sponsors found that adult time travelers were often becoming insane after moving between time lines, It was hoped that by working with gifted and talented children from childhood, the US government might create an adult cadre of "chrononauts" capable of dealing with the psychological effects of time travel.

In one time probe to the future undertaken by Project Pegasus from a chronovisor device located at ITT Defense Communications in Nutley, NJ, Mr. Basiago viewed the US Supreme Court building in Washington, DC, as it would be in the year 2013. During this probe, he found that the Supreme Court building was under 100 feet of stagnant water and reported this to the Lieutenant Commander from the Office of Naval Intelligence who debriefed him after the probe to the future was completed. He hastens to add that because the chronovisors did not identify absolute, deterministic futures but rather alternate futures in the "multi-verse," this catastrophic vision of Washington, DC might be from an alternative time line that does not materialize on our time line.

In contrast to the chronovisor probes, in which a form of virtual time travel was achieved, the teleporters developed by Project Pegasus allowed for physical teleportation to distant locations, sometimes with an adjustment forward or backward in time of days, weeks, months, or years. According to Mr. Basiago, by 1972, the US government was using "quantum displacement" of this kind to both send people forward in time several years to store sensitive military secrets in the future and backward in time several years to provide the government current intelligence about future events.

Was it not a remarkable coincidence that DARPA/CIA's secret time travel project that had held its "time travel surveillance event" on Alfred in 1971 would discover a catastrophic timeline containing a "global coastal event" in 1971 and that Alfred would document the same "global coastal event" timeline in September 1973, using the earth sciences and parapsychology? Is this the sort of work that the "Holy Spirit" entity was referring to when it spoke to Alfred in his Greene Street loft in February 1973?

Alfred was to write of the 1971 DARPA/CIA time travel probe of the 2013 catastrophic timeline.[7]

> As to whether this probe is indicative of a positive or catastrophic timeline in our near term future, "Mr. Basiago hastens to add that because the chronovisors did not identify absolute, deterministic futures but rather alternate futures in the 'multi-verse,' this catastrophic vision of Washington, DC might be from an alternative time line that does not materialize on our time line."

> Over 170 deep underground military bases (DUMBs)

> According to Mr. Basiago's whistleblower testimony, "Donald H. Rumsfeld was the defense attaché to Project Pegasus during the early 1970's, when Mr. Rumsfeld was officially serving as a counselor to President Nixon, a member of the Nixon cabinet and member of his Board of Wage and Price Stabilization."

> In all likelihood, Mr. Rumsfeld, as the defense attaché to Project Pegasus, would have known about and possibly had control over the data about the chronovisor probe to the U.S. Supreme court building in 2013 and derived via "quantum access" and brought back to the early 1970's for analysis by the DARPA research and development program under his administrative authority.

> U.S. Executive authority under U.S. President Richard M. Nixon or his successors can then have plausibly relied upon the DARPA Project Pegasus chronovisor "2013 Washington DC catastrophic timeline" information in making an executive decision of the U.S. government to proceed with the development of a network of deep underground military bases (DUMBs) that now reportedly may number over 170 DUMBs.

> If, as Mr. Basiago points out, "this catastrophic vision of Washington,

DC might be from an alternative time line that does not materialize on our time line," then the entire network of DUMB underground bases and socially repressive anomaly infrastructure used by the U.S. government and elites to implement this predicted 2013 "catastrophic timeline" would backfire against the governments and elites.

Alternate timelines

In August 2012, Mr. Basiago stated that during Project Pegasus all time travel to the past by child participants had been halted in the early 1970s because "each time a child time traveled to the past, she/he found a different result". This, Mr. Basiago said, could be indicative of alternative and differing timelines.

If a second DARPA chronovisor probe had been performed to the US Supreme Court Building in the year 2013, it is just as likely that the probe could have found an alternate 2013 timeline with the Supreme Court safe and functioning and Justices routinely hearing a case before legal counsel.

"The Age of Cataclysm" also marked Alfred's first published venture into Exopolitics – the science of relations among intelligent civilizations in the multi-verse as well as into conspiracy research, in this case a solution of the assassination of John F. Kennedy, in 1973 still a pressing issue in U.S. public life.

Out of Alfred and Phillip's conversations emerged the "Context Communication Theory of Extraterrestrial Communications".[8]

Exopolitics: Extraterrestrial Interventions & the Context Communication Theory

The Context Communication Theory of Extraterrestrial Communications, which this author developed in 1974, holds that UFO Encounters and Extraterrestrial encounters are symbolic communications from a higher intelligent species – or a different intelligent species – to our human species. An analogy is that of a dream, which is a communica-

tion from one's unconscious mind to the conscious mind, often in symbolic and multi-dimensional format. One uses a dream dictionary, for example, to interpret dreams. Like dreams, genuine Extraterrestrial interventions or UFO encounters can be interpreted as symbolic, multi-dimensional communications to the human community from a higher intelligent source. The Swiss psychologist Carl Jung referred to this symbolic aspect of UFOs when in his pioneering work "Flying Saucers" he called them UFOs "Mandalas" or archetypal devices for raising human consciousness.

At the time of the paperback edition (1975) of *"The Age of Cataclysm"*, the concept that the apparitions of the Virgin Mary at Garabandal, Spain (1961-65) or at Fatima, Portugal (1917) were artifacts created by extraterrestrial or interdimensional entities was an advanced, pioneering exopolitical concept.

"The Age of Cataclysm" had a stirring Epilogue, "The Future World Society," that Alfred dictated word for word with Phillip typing as Alfred spoke, the two pausing to edit and discuss as they reviewed the text. The Future World Society began with a Theory of the Millennium; how a utopia promised in sacred texts, including the Old and New Testaments, could be fulfilled on Earth. The discussion transitioned to the turning inside out of the power structure through coming 2nd American Revolution triggered by public exposure of the forces behind the assassination of John F. Kennedy. The discussion proposed a new Federalist political party that offered election of candidates through direct popular vote on televised debates, and suggested various structural transformations to governmental constitutions.

At its best, *"The Age of Cataclysm"* created an international media platform initiating dialogue on a number of issues on which Alfred became increasingly visible: possible looming catastrophic timeline; the science of intelligent civilizations in the multiverse and the extraterrestrial/interdimensional agenda in Earth dimension; parapsychology, the human mind's psi capacity, life after death; the Kennedy assassination and false flag state assassinations in general; prophecy and the coming End Times and Millennium.

SCENE 6

GLOBAL HOPE

Spring 1974
Location: Riverside Park,
overlooking the Hudson River
New York 10025

Phillip Liss was the first of several intellectual collaborators whom Alfred came to consider life influences in his new multi-dimensional arena, each one bringing Alfred key knowledge, insights and lessons in specific areas that rounded out Alfred's own capacity to understand multi-dimensional reality. For Alfred, each of these life influences was to come possessed with a powerful "meme" or inner thought-form that Alfred did not fully share, and that skewed the collaborator's own thoughts and actions.

In the case of Phillip H. Liss, that skewing, controlling meme was: "*I, Phillip Liss am the Jewish Messiah*". At a personal level, Alfred was philosophical toward Phillip Liss and his controlling meme. Alfred took a "Live and Let Live" attitude and looked on his experience with a brilliant experimental psychologist and parapsychologist with a meme as a life-learning experience. Alfred also realized Phillip Liss, as a significant intellectual collaborator, came to him with a pre-life contract, entered into in a non-local dimension of the inter-life, to be fulfilled in this incarnation as "Alfred". Close life collaborators and Alfred's interaction with them formed part of his soul and experience education in this lifetime.

If there is one thing Alfred could say about the Phillip Liss, it's that he was of good heart and good will. Phillip was genuinely ethical and concerned about the fate of the universe and humanity. Philip was kind to strangers and generous with beggars; brilliant in his chosen field on experimental psychology; and a good father and husband before he lost his sanity.

With the distance of the years, Alfred bore a growing fondness for Phillip Liss as an influential teacher and colleague in the business of life. Phillip was transparent; his heart-sourced motives were pure by and large.

Phillip Liss' enrollment as universe savior started with his delving into parapsychology. Phillip had a scientist's sharp mind and approached the study of precognition, telepathy, psychokinesis, and reincarnation with the same vigor as he had attacked experimental and cognitive psychology. Perhaps it was the death knell of ego tolling, but Phillip told Alfred how no one in contemporary parapsychology had the methodological grasp that he did. Phillip's mission, as he saw it, was to integrate the paranormal sciences with mainstream science, and to lead humankind from the darkness to a new dimension of universe understanding. From this perspective, Phillip's vision was right in line with the unification of science and spirituality promised for this age, Alfred benefited from Phillip's brilliant, integrative insights into parapsychology and extraterrestrial reality.

Phillip Liss' journey before meeting Alfred took Phillip through the labyrinth of the paranormal. Phillip told Alfred that disembodied voices spoke to him as he returned from a visit to a parapsychological institute in Eastern Europe in 1971. During this episode, he experienced more than the voices. Phillip reported that his personal reality morphed as the voices were speaking to him, in a way to reinforce and demonstrate their message. Given Phillip's medical diagnosis just a few years later, it is difficult to say whether those "voices" he heard were the early manifestation of symptoms of the disease or genuine telepathic communications with dimensional intelligence.

It may be that the "voices" were along some line between chemical imbalance and interaction with dimensional beings. One psychologist suggests that these voices may be "archons", or mind parasites that can infest a human mind. Was it the "voices" that told Phillip he was destined to integrate all knowledge for the new era? Phillip told Alfred that during the "voices" episodes, morphing subconscious thoughts would manifest before him, like little cartoon characters. Wristwatch hands would bounce back and forth, signaling messages from unseen dominions. Phillip said he could not only read people thoughts, but also see these thoughts as people thought them.

Who am I, thought Alfred, to contradict Phillip's report that he had been visited by a dimensional intelligence that enrolled him in a "messianic-type mission"? After all, the "Holy Spirit" entity had done the same to Alfred. As time went on, Alfred realized he was on one side of sanity's razor and Phillip was square on the other side. Phillip was caught in the scourge of mental chemical imbalance. The "voices" Phillip heard in his mind may have been artifacts of brain chemistry or archonic infestation or a combination of both.

Alfred considered whether his telepathic communication with the "Holy Spirit" entity could have been either a dissociated part of his own personality or electronic voice-to-skull communications from a government intelligence agency like the CIA, which he had surmised had him under surveillance.

Upon analysis and reflection, Alfred concluded the "Holy Spirit" was an inter-dimensional or extraterrestrial entity that had created an interdimensional missing time contact episode for him around themes of Earth transformation in a new era.

For a time, while Phillip Liss still had mental balance, he was Alfred's mentor and friend. Phillip helped liberate Alfred from the intellectual binds of his Jesuit and Yale-educated mind, from the arid deserts of matrix thinking, into greener pastures of the multi-dimensional mind. Phillip, the experimental psychologist and parapsychologist, introduced Alfred, the future psychotherapist, to the secret worlds that live invisibly in the recesses of the human mind.

At first in 1973 Phillip and Alfred tape-recorded all their conversational research sessions. They would meet in Alfred's SOHO loft or Phillip's Upper West Side/West End Avenue apartment from mid-morning to early morning next day; tape and tape after tape changed into the largish black tape recorder, sentences left hanging while the tapes were changed. Day number forty-one, tapes number nine, and Phillip and Alfred are in conversation, recorded for the ages.

During a typical early research session, Phillip would hold forth on a topic in parapsychology or extraterrestrial affairs, peppered by the occasional phrase of prompt from Alfred. Another day's topic would be Swedenborg's description of life after death and its relationship to findings recent articles on the survival of human consciousness after bodily death on the afterlife in the American Journal of the American Society for Psychical Research.

Emanuel Swedenborg (29 January 1688 – 29 March 1772) was a Swedish scientist and psychic of the eighteenth century. Known as one of the greatest scientists of his day, Swedenborg spent many of his later working days in trance communication with higher beings in the inner dimensions.

Swedenborg developed an elaborate description of the afterlife, holding that the "dead" persons, actually "live" souls, continued to live detailed lives in a series of dimensional spheres surrounding the earth. Swedenborg would visit with them, gathering data in the manner of a visiting sociologist. Some of the "dead" did not know they had passed on from earthly life.

Phillip Liss latched onto Swedenborg as his role model, a world-class psychic scientist. By Phillip's view, Swedenborg had paved the way for Phillip Liss to be a stepping-stone for his mission of integrating science and liberating mankind.

Synchronicity was always a fun topic for Phillip and Alfred's taped conversations. The psychologist Carl Jung's theories on synchronicity, meaningful coincidence, could mean that objective dimension of meaning exists in reality. The classic example is synchronicity is of a scarab beetle walking into Jung's window, just as a patient was telling him a dream about a scarab beetle.

Alfred and Phillip found themselves afloat in a sea of synchronicity, infusing their activities and thoughts. One grand synchronicity occurred as Alfred and Phillip walked along the Hudson River in Riverside Park, envisioning roles in the coming millennium. A large ship came down the river, its stern emblazoned with the name, "GLOBAL HOPE."

Other working sessions centered on the dimension of "meaning" in the multiverse that manifested itself in patterns of numbers, codes, and synchronicities. Phillip told Alfred "voices" had given him the inner meaning of the numbers the "voices" would use in their communications to him through stopped watches, etc. The numeral 2 meant "good," for example. Soon Alfred was applying these "inner meanings" to numerals in his own microcosm - automobile license numbers, phone numbers, etc. that would appear in a meaningful context.

Experimenting with the number-meaning system, Alfred felt he could walk down the streets of New York, spy a license plate number of a passing car and decode its meaning in relation to the context, in the manner of a tarot. License plates, telephone numbers, patterns became a sort of tarot guide to a situational reality, whether the advice sought was what might happen at a meeting Alfred was going to or the answer to an inner question Alfred asked.

The meaning of Alfred's own phone number at his Greene Street loft (212-9-666-030) by this code, for example, signified that Alfred's work to contain The Beast "666", or the New World Order, and to protect the harvest of human souls for Source (G*D) would be successful. This "inner meaning" of his phone number was congruent with the "Holy Spirit" message for Alfred as he saw it. The "inner meaning number tarot" proved remarkably accurate. Alfred experienced accessing a new, objective dimension of meaning in a living, intentional multiverse.

Alfred extended the synchronicity lens into his family history and birth. His maternal grandmother's family was from a town in Cuba called Sancti Spiritus, meaning "Holy Spirit" in Latin, a synchronicity with the "Holy Spirit" entity. Alfred discovered an apparent pattern in which the numbers in his birthday or birth year seemed appear more frequently in the news, in media, in motion pictures, TV than other numbers. The numerals in Alfred's birth date are 5-24-42. He noticed "42", "24", "542" and "524" seemed to appear more frequently, as in the actual headline, as in "Forty-two miners today narrowly escaped injury when..." Alfred made detailed maps and connections between prophecy and politics, highlighting the synchronous names, sounds, dates, and patterns. The links between politics and spirituality were of deep interest to him.

Phillip's governing "meme" would show its head in these synchronicity experiments. Phillip began to decode the Old Testament, to show how "his" coming had been foretold. Phillip was serious when he interpreted one prophetic verse of the Old Testament (Isaiah 11:1 "There shall come forth a shoot from the stump of Jesse") to refer to an incident where Phillip's cousin Jesse masturbated and ejaculated in front of him when they were adolescents. Sure there was synchronicity – down to the identical name of his cousin ("Jesse') and the slang for male ejaculation. When Alfred saw that Phillip genuinely believed he was foretold in Isaiah 11:1, he knew that Phillip had ventured into delusion, not into objective perception of multi-dimensionality.

Phillip and Alfred first intersected in the time-space hologram in 1973 two years after Phillip said he had his own experiences with "voices" that had spoken to him extensively whose communications he attempted to incorporate into his experimental psychologist's framework. When Alfred and Phillip first met, Phillip H. Liss, PhD was an associate professor of psychology at a prestigious university (Rutgers), with degrees from Harvard, MIT and McGill Universities. Phillip and Alfred worked together for three years until 1976, when Alfred broke with Phillip because of his increasingly bizarre behavior due possibly to a diagnosed schizophrenia.

Phillip's wife Barbara Liss told Alfred in the late 1990s that Phillip had passed away in Florida of ill health. The last time Alfred saw Phillip was at the United Nations during the 2nd Special Session on Disarmament in June 1982, where Alfred was an NGO delegate and a correspondent for the San Francisco Observer. Phillip was there as an NGO participant, being filmed delivering a plan for universal peace. Phillip told Alfred how after they had parted, New York City police had abducted him in a squad car, taken Phillip to an abandoned lot, and beaten him repeatedly in the face, shouting, "The man has a plan! The man has a plan!"

SCENE 7

JFK & HOUSE
SELECT COMMITTEE ON
ASSASSINATIONS (HSCA)

1976
Location: U.S. Congressional Dining Room,
Luncheon with Alfred, Gail Beagle, and
Rep. Henry B. Gonzalez (D-TX),
Chairman, House Banking Committee
U.S. Capitol, Washington, DC 20004

Alfred felt a deep connection to John F. Kennedy and his political legacy. When Kennedy was first elected President, Alfred's mother Juanita would attend mass and sit several rows behind Jack Kennedy in the Catholic Church in Palm Beach, Florida that Kennedy also would attend. During one summer college break in the early 1960s, Kennedy himself, wearing a pair of red Bermuda shorts, was on the rear deck of the Honey Fitz, the Presidential yacht, laughing out loud as Alfred and Tim Killen, his sailing partner, tried hurriedly to get their small sailboat out of the way of the wake of the yacht as it went by in the Palm Beach inlet. In the late 1960s, while a Wall Street lawyer in New York, Alfred became friends with LeMoyne "Lem" Billings, Jack Kennedy's roommate at the Choate School and life-long friend who reportedly had his own room at the Kennedy White House. Lem was visibly upset when Alfred forsook international corporate law Cleary Gottlieb for the environmental law with the Lindsay administration.

Yet Alfred found circles around these personal friends of Jack Kennedy friends to be venomous. Around 1970, two young friends of Lem Billings, both society girls whose sister Anne Stroud seemed sweet on Alfred and whose family ran International Basic Economy Corporation (IBEC) in Latin America for David Rockefeller and had a Maine estate next to David Rockefeller, came to Alfred's office at the EPA and gang-stalked him. The message of the gang stalking by Rockefeller intimates seemed to be: "We are watching you, Alfred!", meaning the Rockefeller inner circle is watching you.

Alfred discovered that as early as 1970, elite families working for David Rockefeller practiced MKULTRA gang stalking. The Rockefeller gang-stalking episode made it ultra-clear to Alfred that he made all the right choices in leaving behind the parties on Malcolm Forbes yacht at North East Harbor, Maine, the women connected to families running David Rockefeller organizations and their MKULTRA gang-stalking ethos, and in moving away from Wall Street.

Later, in 2005, Alfred would learn that DARPA/CIA ran its secret time travel experiments in the late 1960s and early 1970s in facilities of a company (now called Exxon) controlled by David Rockefeller. It was little wonder that players from the David Rockefeller court would be gang-stalking him at that time. Did the Rockefeller organization (in whose buildings the secret DARPA/CIA time travel experiments were taking place) know about Alfred's future Exopolitics activities, as did the DARPA/CIA time travel group covered as the "Delaware Valley Industrial Engineering Association"? Very likely, it would seem by the evidence.

In the aftermath of his break with Phillip Liss in 1976 on their return from their CBC-TV engagement with Peter Gzowski in Vancouver, BC, Alfred decided on a strategic reformulation. His media appearances and messaging around *"The Age of Cataclysm"*, engineered to be as technocratic and evidence-oriented as possible, had focused on a possible coming catastrophic timeline and global coastal event early in the 21st century.

"The Age of Cataclysm", which was popular enough to be in airport book stores, also questioned the official version of the John F. Kennedy assassination at a time when it was still somewhat dangerous to challenge the official verdict, and placed responsibility for the assassination and the cover-up on the matrix leadership, including the David Rockefeller-led clique that had gang-stalked Alfred earlier at his New York City EPA office.

Alfred and Phillip's analysis predicted that a public exposure of the assassination of John F. Kennedy would turn inside out a covert matrix power structure controlling the permanent war economy of the United States and the world. This public exposure and legal conviction of the powers behind the coup d'état that was the Kennedy assassination would in turn lead to breakthrough for a new positive future for Earth.

Alfred followed through on the reasoning developed in *"The Age of Cataclysm"*. A renewed public interest in solving the assassination of John F. Kennedy had been sparked by a 1975 showing of the Zapruder film on U.S. television, and there was a movement for a Congressional investigation. Alfred's activist self took over, and he developed a proposal for a citizen's campaign to re-open the investigation of the Kennedy investigation and mailed it to a group of notables to gather their support.

One notable who gave him a receptive hearing was the fiction writer Isaac Bashevis Singer, whose writing Alfred followed in the New Yorker. Isaac told Alfred, "If your intentions are good, you will have good results." Another notable family gave Alfred $2000.00 toward the campaign that he used to found the Citizens Campaign for a Congressional Investigation into

Political Assassinations (CCCIPA). Alfred also visited with leading edge Kennedy assassination researchers and authors around the U.S. on his various trips, building a network that one JFK assassination researcher called "the Webre underground." The insights of these researchers and authors confirmed that Alfred had been essentially correct in his conclusions about the prime movers behind Kennedy Assassination.

One researcher Alfred met was A.J. Weberman, whose apartment was close to Alfred's Greene Street loft. Weberman, known as the originator of "garbology" or journalistic research through the study of a subject's garbage, was a member of the Yippies (founded by Abbie Hoffman, author of "Steal this Book") had written a Concordance to the songs, poetry, and assorted writings of poet singer Bob Dylan, whose birthday on May 24 Alfred shared. Weberman had also written a key 1975 book on the Kennedy assassination, "Coup D'Etat in America".[9]

Webre visited Weberman at his apartment, and Weberman gave Webre useful tips on how to handle obvious surveillance phone calls that Webre was experiencing after he began his work calling for a new investigation. "Yeah, they're just trying to see how you react," Weberman told Webre after Webre explained that he was receiving harassing phone calls where either the caller would be silent or an obvious FBI agent-like voice would say, "Look out Al, they're going to get you!"

One day in 1976 the phone rang in Alfred's studio in his loft and on the line was the office of Rep. Henry B. Gonzalez in Washington, DC asking if Alfred would come down to Washington and meet with Rep. Gonzalez about starting a Congressional investigation of the assassination of John F. Kennedy. Alfred was not quite sure how Rep. Henry B. Gonzalez had gotten his phone number or why he had called on Alfred. Realizing the opportunity Rep. Gonzalez invitation presented to a new investigation of the Kennedy assassination, Alfred quickly agreed to the meeting and took a train down to Washington to move a Congressional investigation into the Kennedy assassination forward.

Alfred arrived at Rep. Gonzalez office in Washington, DC for his meeting and was met by Gail Beagle, the same female assistant who had spoken to him earlier on the phone. Rep. Gonzalez invited Alfred and Gail Beagle to lunch in the Congressional dining room, and the two listened while Alfred updated them on his organizing campaign to start a new investigation into political assassinations, particularly the John F. Kennedy assassination. That Rep. Gonzalez was the sponsor of HR 204 to establish a select committee on assassinations was in the forefront of Alfred's mind, especially because of the "204" synchronicity with his birthday number "24".

Rep. Gonzalez then said something Alfred found remarkable and strange. He said, "You know we thought you were that other researcher AJ Weberman," and laughed. All three laughed at the coincidence and the inadvertent error that had gotten Alfred to that meeting with Rep. Henry B. Gonzalez. Alfred agreed to focus his campaign on the passage of HR 204, and Rep. Gonzalez agreed to mail out flyers that Alfred would send him for the Citizens Campaign for a Congressional Investigation into Political Assassinations (CCCIPA).

Back in New York, Alfred reached out to the Assassination Information Bureau (AIB), a Cambridge, Massachusetts-based organization that was touring college campuses raising awareness on the Kennedy assassination. Following a seminal 1973 AIB conference on the Kennedy assassination, the AIB had made over six hundred presentations around the United States in the three years leading up to 1976. AIB was founded by Carl Oglesby, former President of Students for a Democratic Society (SDS) and then author of the 1976 book "The Yankee and Cowboy War: Conspiracies from Dallas to Watergate".[10] Alfred had defended an SDS member at the Panther 21 trial in New York on charges of summary contempt. AIB's other directors included Bob Katz, Jeff Goldberg and a philosophy professor from the University of Pennsylvania. AIB prided itself on its egalitarian structure. All principals were directors, as well as first-born males. Alfred was a first-born male, the eldest of nine siblings, so he fit right in. The paranoid naiveté of Carl Oglesby amused Alfred, when Uncle Carl claimed that "Alfred Lambremont Webre" was a made-up CIA name, as it was Alfred's grandfather's and father's name, and had a heritage in Louisiana political history.

Meeting in Cambridge, MA with the directors of AIB, Alfred recounted Rep. Gonzalez determination to secure that passage of HR 204 and establish a Congressional select committee to investigate not only the John F. Kennedy assassination, but also that of Dr. Martin Luther King, Jr., Robert F. Kennedy, George Wallace and perhaps others. The AIB directors were moved by Alfred's presentation. AIB and Alfred agreed on a coordinated strategy to both support the passage of Rep. Henry B. Gonzalez HR 204 and secure an official assassination investigation by Congressional committee. Carl Oglesby and the other directors also envisioned establishing an AIB "safe house" in Washington, DC to lobby for the passage of HR 204 and to monitor and influence the Congressional investigation once it began.

Celebrating the developments at the U.S. Congress, the AIB came down to New York to network and hold events, using Alfred's Greene Street loft as a base. AIB quickly brought author Norman Mailer on board supporting this new enterprise to accelerate the passage of HR 204. AIB and Alfred made the pilgrimage to Brooklyn Heights to cement the new alliance, where Mailer discoursed on the significance of the Kennedy assassination high fashion. After Alfred informed Mailer that he had voted for Norman Mailer and Jimmy Breslin for the Mayor ticket of New York in 1968, Norman Mailer started a mock boxing match with Alfred.

On September 17, 1976 House Resolution 1540 creating the House Select Committee on Assassinations was passed by a vote of 280–65. The AIB and CCCIPA claimed some credit for the passage of HR 204.

Alfred was eventually was asked to join the AIB Board of Directors. A February 15, 1979 MEMO: AIB Document Research

Proposal on AIB stationery with AIB offices at 1322 18th St. NW, Washington, DC 20036 shows the AIB Board of Directors as Jeffrey M Goldberg, Robert Katz, James Kostman, Martin A. Lee, Carl Oglesby, Alfred L. Webre, David B. Williams, and Harvey Yazijian. The AIB Advisory Board was filled with notables, all actively seeking resolution of the Kennedy assassination: David Dellinger, Allen Ginsberg, Tom Hayden, Murray Kempton, Norman Mailer, Jack Newfield, Philip Nobile, Marcus Raskin, and Peter Dale Scott.

The CIA successfully infiltrated the HSCA with the aim of implanting the meme that the John Kennedy assassination was an operation of the government of Cuba under Fidel Castro. Ultimately the Committee failed to find that the U.S. government was involved in any conspiracy to assassinate John F. Kennedy, Robert F. Kennedy, Martin Luther King and Malcolm X, contrary to the forensic facts.

SCENE 8

LINKING UP WITH UFO CONTACTEE JIMMY CARTER

December 1976
Dinner at Townhouse on Capitol Hill
with Jimmy Carter Inner Circle
Washington, DC 20002

With the Congressional establishment of the House Select Committee on Assassinations (HSCA) in September 1976, Alfred commuted between his Greene Street loft in lower Manhattan, New York and Washington, DC where the AIB and a growing network of researchers were gathering to monitor the HSCA investigation in a process Alfred called "public interest counter-intelligence".

Shortly after the November 1976 U.S. Presidential election, which Jimmy Carter narrowly won against former Warren Commission member Gerald Ford, a lawyer from Atlanta, Georgia had called Alfred to a meeting at the Carlyle, a mid-town Manhattan hotel. At the meeting, the lawyer told Alfred he was a representative of the incoming President Jimmy Carter to the House Select Committee on Assassinations. Alfred had gone to Georgetown Preparatory School with a member of the

Spalding family of prominent Atlanta lawyers and had no reason to doubt the Atlanta lawyer. The Atlanta lawyer representing Jimmy Carter at the HSCA invited Alfred to meet some of the Carter inner circle in Washington, DC.

Alfred's meeting with people in the incoming President Jimmy Carter's inner circle took place at a handsome town house on Capitol Hill in December 1976 during the Transition period of the Carter Presidency. The "inner circle" people at the dinner, all male, were not the "Georgia Mafia" or the "12 Apostles" ("JC & the 12 Apostles" was a nickname for the Carter team). The "inner circle" that night was close to people in the "Georgia Mafia" who would come to be important to Alfred's work in the coming two years, 1977-78.

At the dinner, Alfred listened closely and familiarized himself with the Jimmy Carter players and their sub-culture. "Are you going to work for Peanut?" asked one. Peanut was a term of endearment for Jimmy Carter by those in the inner circle. Carter domestic policy advisor Stuart Eizenstat[11] and Carter's press secretary Jody Powell[12] were to play key roles in Alfred's immediate future during the Carter Administration.

Though Alfred was invited to dinner with Carter aides in his role as public interest watchdog on the House Select Committee on Assassinations, Alfred was also intrigued by another aspect of Jimmy Carter's *persona*. Carter had won the White House on an explicit platform to open the U.S. government UFO and extraterrestrial files, and this policy related directly to the twin platform that Alfred had been working on since 1973 – Public recognition of the extraterrestrial presence.

During the 1976 Presidential campaign, Jimmy Carter had talked about his 1969 UFO sighting in Leary Georgia, later memorialized in Carter's 1973 UFO report. Describing his 1969 UFO sighting to reporters at a Southern Governor's conference during his 1976 Presidential campaign, Carter told a reporter, "It was the darndest thing I've ever seen. It was big, it was very bright, it changed colors, and it was about the size of the moon. We watched it for ten minutes, but none of us could figure out what it was. One thing's for sure; I'll never make fun of people who say they've seen unidentified objects in the sky. If I become president, I'll make every piece of information this country has about UFO sightings available to the public and the scientists."[13]

"Jimmy Carter

"Interest in extraterrestrial life and UFOs.

"President Carter claims to have witnessed an unidentified flying object in 1969; he remains the only U.S. President to have formally reported a UFO. He filed a report with the International UFO Bureau in Oklahoma City after a request from that organization. During his presidential campaign, Carter promised to reveal the truth about any alleged UFO cover-up.

"Through Stanford Research Institute, Mr. Alfred Webre was Principal Investigator for a proposed civilian scientific study of extraterrestrial communication presented to and developed with interested Carter White House staff. This took place during the period from May 1977 until the fall of 1977.

"President Carter, official statement placed on the Voyager spacecraft for its trip outside our solar system, June 16, 1977: 'We cast this message into the cosmos... Of the 200 billion stars in the Milky Way galaxy, some - - perhaps many - - may have inhabited planets and space faring civilizations. If one such civilization intercepts Voyager and can understand these recorded contents, here is our message: We are trying to survive our time so we may live into yours. We hope some day; having solved the problems we face, to join a community of Galactic Civilizations. This record represents our hope and our determination and our goodwill in a vast and awesome universe."[14]

That December 1976 night during his dinner with members of Carter's inner circle on Capitol Hill the idea came to Alfred of a Carter White House Investigation into the Extraterrestrial

Presence as a step President Jimmy Carter could feasibly undertake that was equal to the historic occasion of his election. Certainly, the fact that Carter had defeated Gerald Ford was cosmic justice, Alfred thought. Following 1966 UFO sightings in Michigan, Ford, who represented the state secured a hastily-arranged Congressional hearing on April 5, 1966 where the principal witness, Defense Secretary Robert Strange McNamara, architect of the Edsel and the Vietnam War, administered another classic military-industrial complex cover-up calling the UFOs swamp gas and an "illusion" at the Congressional hearings.

Alfred reasoned that Jimmy Carter's 1973 UFO report and his public mention of his own UFO experience on the 1976 Presidential campaign trail increased the probability that Carter himself was not only a "UFO contactee" but an "Extraterrestrial contactee", even though Carter consciously denied it. Carter's 1969 contact experience would have far-reaching implications if he were found to be an extraterrestrial contactee or abductee.

Alfred later speculated on the possibility that Jimmy Carter was in fact an Extraterrestrial abductee.

"Is Jimmy Carter an Extraterrestrial Abductee?

"Jimmy Carter's Profile as a potential UFO/ET Abductee. One principal regularity in the profiles of UFO/ET abductees appears to be that abductees have Close Encounters of the First Kind (Flying Saucer and/or Night Light Sightings), as well as Close Encounters of the Fourth Kind (UFO/ET Abductions).

"Under a classification system first introduced by astronomer and UFO researcher J. Allen Hynek, and in his book The UFO Experience: A Scientific Inquiry, a close encounter is an event where an individual encounters a UFO or Extraterrestrial Vehicle:

'Three of the six categories of unidentified flying object in the classification scheme devised by J. Allen Hynek. A close encounter of the first kind (CEI) is any UFO reported to have been within about 500 feet of

the witness. A close encounter of the second kind. A close encounter of the second kind (CEII) is a UFO that leaves markings on the ground, causes burns or paralysis, frightens animals, or interferes with engines or TV or radio reception. A close encounter of the third kind (CEIII) includes a purported sighting of the occupants of a UFO. To these categories, ufologists have added two others. A close encounter of the fourth kind (alien abduction). A close encounter of the fifth kind (CEV) is one in which it is claimed that communication takes place between a human and an alien. (CEII) is a UFO that leaves markings on the ground, causes burns or paralysis, frightens animals, or interferes with engines or TV or radio reception. A (CEIV) is one in which a person reports having been abducted (see alien abduction). A close encounter of the fifth kind (CEV) is one in which it is claimed that communication takes place between a human and an alien.' Close Encounters, Internet Encylopedia of Science.

Close Encounter of the First Kind, by one definitional system, include: 'A sighting of one or more unidentified flying objects, (1) Flying saucers [or Extraterrestrial Vehicles]; (2) Odd lights or [Night Lights]; (3) Aerial objects that are not attributable to human technology. Some would also include that the sighting(s) is/are at a distance of 600 feet (about 180 meters) or less, presumably to eliminate false identification of known object(s) or phenomenon.'

"Jimmy Carter by his own reported historical record had a Close Encounter of the First Kind.

"Did Jimmy Carter have a Close Encounter of the Fourth Kind? Threshold Test Met - By the available evidence, Jimmy Carter did have a Close Encounter of the First Kind. He passed the threshold test as a potential UFO/ET abductee. Jimmy Carter has had a Close Encounter of the First Kind. By the documentary evidence, Jimmy Carter fits a prime regularity on the profiles of UFO/ET abductees.

"Emotional and Psychic Bonding Threshold Raised - Moreover, Carter's own recorded verbal statements and recollections from close family members, such as his mother Lillian, a matriarchal figure in the Carter family, and in public statements such as to the Atlanta

Constitution, Carter clearly conveys a deep sense psychic and emotional bonding with the experience of the Close Encounter of the First Kind. Human emotional bonding experiences are a regularity of Close Encounters of the Fourth Kind. There is a threshold research question raised that the intense emotional bonding by Jimmy Carter in his repeated recollections of the Close Encounter of the First Kind may be a triggered response to a cloaked memory of a Close Encounter of the Fourth Kind." [15]

Jimmy Carter, incoming President of the United States might well be not only an Extraterrestrial contactee judging from his 1969 UFO contact experience, but an Extraterrestrial abductee as well, with Carter being taken aboard an Extraterrestrial craft and debriefed by members of an advanced intelligent civilization.

In any case, by the time Alfred was a guest at the dinner on Capitol Hill with members of Carter's inner circle, he felt a certain inner kinship with Jimmy Carter, given Alfred's February 1973 interdimensional experience with the "Holy Spirit" entity, relatively close in time with Carter's reported January 6, 1969 UFO contact experience and September 18, 1973.

Alfred left the December 1976 Carter inner circle dinner on Capitol Hill with the beginnings of a new strategy in mind. In parallel with his role as a public watchdog in the Congressional investigation of the Kennedy and other political assassinations at the House Select Committee on Assassinations in the new Congress in 1977, he would seek to launch the Carter White House Extraterrestrial Communication Study, the first ever civilian scientific public study of the extraterrestrial presence on Earth. In Alfred's mind, he was laying the seeds for social foundations upon which a new era could be built as the "Holy Spirit" entity had foretold.

SCENE 9

FUTURIST, STANFORD RESEARCH INSTITUTE

January 1977
Center for the Study of Social Policy
Stanford Research Institute (SRI)
Menlo Park, CA 94025

Back in New York after the Carter White House inner circle dinner Alfred visited psychic Ingo Swann at his Bowery loft in lower Manhattan with a mutual friend, Mary Schoonmaker. Mary suggested that Alfred visit her friends at Stanford Research Institute (SRI), Russell Targ and Dr. Hal Puthoff who were working with Ingo at SRI in their remote viewing experiments for the CIA. During a Christmas 1976 family trip to the San Francisco Bay Area, Alfred called Hal Puthoff and Russ Targ (whose father Bill Targ had been his editor at GP Putnam's Sons) and went to see them.

Puthoff and Targ advised Alfred that the most appropriate home for his proposed Jimmy Carter White House extraterrestrial study was at SRI's futurist unit, the Center for the Study of Social Policy. That same afternoon, Alfred met with SRI futurist Peter Schwartz (later futurist to Shell Oil Company and founder of the Global Business Network). Peter Schwartz readily understood the importance of the proposed Carter white House extraterrestrial study, and set up a group interview with the eminent futurists at the Center who ranged from Willis Harmon (then directing a Fifty Year Alternative Futures Study for CIA) and Duane Elgin, author of the book "Voluntary Simplicity" on the appropriate technology movement.[16]

SRI's futurists thought Alfred's presentation of the Carter White House extraterrestrial communication study, along with his analysis of the impact of the HSCA Congressional investigation of the Kennedy assassination was strong and recommended Alfred for a position at the Center. After about a month of security checks, Alfred was offered a position as a futurist at SRI. Wikipedia notes in its list of Notable People at SRI "Alfred Webre Was a futurist at SRI in the Center for the Study of Social Policy around 1977. He worked on studies in alternative futures, innovation diffusion, and social policy applications for clients including the Carter White House Extraterrestrial Communications Study."[17]

Alfred returned to New York to pack up his Greene Street loft and move with his wife Teresa and his six-year old son Freddie to Palo Alto, CA. His last public act in New York was as keynote speaker at the celebration of the 100th anniversary of healer and psychic Edgar Cayce's birth held at St. John the Divine Cathedral in New York in March 1977. Alfred was given this honor because of his authorship of the book *The Age of Cataclysm*, which included an analysis of the Cayce Earth changes predictions.

SCENE 10

U.S. Senate Advisory Committee

Late Spring 1977
U.S. Senate Committee Room
Washington, DC 20004

Arriving at Stanford Research Institute in the spring of 1977, Alfred went directly to Washington, DC to take Peter Schwartz's position as a member of a U.S. Senate Advisory Committee on U.S. National Security Needs through the year 2000. Alfred found himself in a U.S. Senate committee room in Washington, DC seated next to Senator Sam Nunn, Democrat of Georgia. Nunn, then acknowledged Dean of U.S. National Security in the U.S. Senate, focused his tortoise shell glasses on Alfred, the multi-dimensional thirty-five year old Stanford Research Institute Futurist seated next to him around a large, oval U.S. Senate Committee table.

Flanking Nunn and Webre around the table were twenty or so high-ranking leaders of the military-intelligence establishment of the United States, Illuminati of the U.S. war machine. These included Paul Nitze (1907-2004), nuclear hawk and a leading U.S. Cold War strategist; the then legendary head of

79

U.S. Air Force Intelligence; the Director of the Defense Intelligence Agency (DIA) and twenty more leaders of the intelligence "community". Across from Alfred was a colleague from the public-interest community, Rear Admiral Gene R. LaRoque, founder of the Center for Defense Information. Alfred was on this Panel by serendipity. His fellow SRI Futurist, Peter Schwartz said he could not attend and had asked Alfred to sit in his place. Was Alfred once again being "set up" to be on this Committee?

In the company of these aging white men, Alfred Lambremont Webre looked even younger than his age. In New York a year earlier, Webre performed inside the Museum of Modern Art (MOMA) as a modern dancer in the Elaine Summers and Marilyn Wood companies. Alfred had never danced before the age of thirty-three and after a few months performed modern dance as an avocation in the same way others visit the health club after a day at work. He performed modern dance in the skyscraper windows of a closed-down Park Avenue as part of a massive cityscape, and at another venue modern danced around a gentle John Lennon and his companion and some say Black Widow Yoko Ono as they sat together quietly on the floor of the New York University gymnasium performance.

Alfred was the eldest of nine children in a Canadian-Cuban-American, Louisiana French family, born at the U.S. Naval Air Station at Pensacola, Florida. Three decades later, at the dawn of the Twenty First Century, Alfred's seventh brother Septime Webre (who also had started to dance in early adulthood) would become a well-known ballet choreographer and Artistic Director of the Washington, D.C. Ballet. Alfred's natural grace would prove a life-saving survival skill in the months ahead of him as he sat around U.S. Senate conference table in May 1977, a member of the Senate Panel on U.S. National Security Needs Through the Year 2000.

In the U.S. Senate conference room, Sam Nunn leaned over and stared blankly at Alfred, then stared at a dark penciled doodle Alfred was drawing on the official committee member

U.S. Senate memo pad lying on the table between them. The doodle showed the likeness of a wine bottle, with squiggly lines coming out of an open elongated neck. Nunn stared at the capital letters scrawled next to the bottle,

"LET THE GENIE OUT OF THE BOTTLE!"

Alfred turned and threw a knowing glance across the table to Gene LaRoque. Months before, Rear Admiral Gene R. LaRoque, founder of the Center for Defense Information, and Alfred had collaborated on a book project, "Armageddon: The Chilling Prospect of Global Nuclear War". The work of preparing the book project had turned Alfred's stomach as he (vicariously) reconstructed the horrors experienced by the *hibaku-sha*, Hiroshima A-Bomb survivors.

"There are no victors; there are no vanquished. Each ground zero is the Void," Alfred and LaRocque wrote about the utter devastation of nuclear war.

Alfred leaned into the looming U.S. Senate Conference table, and its discussion on nuclear weapons, the "community" (parlance for the military-intelligence insider network), the business of war, and the staple behind U.S. power since 1945. It was a solemn, serious moment. Serendipity in an appointment as a futurist at SRI had placed him at the very center of U.S. military strategic long range planning, unless that "serendipity" was an intentional attempt by an unknown controller to manipulate.

Alfred felt some core of deep civilized values, of mature responsibility, of adherence to Universally-recognized standards of law was absent from the words of the assembled military and intelligence leaders, gathered to chart a course for the United States through the beginning Twenty First Century, then 23 years away. To most of the assembled brass around the table, nuclear war was a business with a tolerable cost, and Mutually Assured Destruction (MAD) was thinkable and war-gamed. Indeed, a future film documentary by a University of British Columbia law professor, "The Corporation", would classify the behavior of organizations such as the U.S. military-intelligence organizations as "psychopathic" under the DSM IV, the diagnostic and Statistical manual used to classify psychiatric disease and disorders.[18]

As a futurist, Alfred knew that individuals, organizations, nations, and even an entire world civilization like *homo sapiens* consciously create or determine alternative futures for themselves. A time scientist or a New Physicist could define the "future" as a quantum process in a time-space hologram which itself has quantum properties. Theoretically, there are multiple futures actually occurring now, but only one will become the "now" that you will experience. "Alternative Futures" to a futurist in 1977 was more like applied public policy, a methodological tool for a nascent integrated social science discipline. That is, an organization or a "nation" like can create hypothetical "alternative futures" for itself by planning main lines of infrastructure and social policy forward, for example, for 50-100 years or more. The society may then choose a healthy – or a destructive – future, depending on the inherent wisdom of the society.

Today was Alfred's first day on the U.S. Senate committee. He was a freshly minted futurist at SRI. Should he speak out morally as a human being or, as a technocrat, remain silent? Alfred pondered the dualities manifesting before him that day in the U.S. Senate. Here in 1977 at this table, the inside top leadership of the military-intelligence apparatus of the U.S. military-intelligence – the Pentagon, the Department of Defense, the U.S. Air Force was focusing on a futuristic task of creating the Alternative Future of Armageddon, the chilling prospect of global nuclear war.

At the same time, another "Alternative Future" was also on Alfred's mind – this one "out of the box" of conventional, non-classified military-intelligence planning. That "Alternative Future" this futurist intended to explore and develop was a future that incorporated interactive communications with advanced extraterrestrial civilizations visiting Earth.

The specific reason Alfred had come to SRI as a futurist was to co-create a civilian scientific study of extraterrestrial communication with the administration of President Jimmy Carter. In that way, an "Alternative Future" to a future Armageddon – a positive future based on interaction and integration with what appeared to be an advanced extraterrestrial civilization with peaceful intentions towards humanity – would be developed. This was to be the Mother of All Futurist Studies, under the authority of President James Earl Carter.

Alfred knew from his research in extraterrestrial studies that many of these same military-intelligence officials sitting around the table with him – and their predecessors in office - were instrumental in continuing the hostile information warfare by the U.S. government against advanced ethical extraterrestrial civilizations, as surrogates for manipulatory ETs to which the United States was under secret Treaty obligation. The litany of official disinformation and anti-extraterrestrial propaganda by the U.S. Central Intelligence Agency, the Defense Intelligence Agency, the U.S. Department of Defense, the U.S. Air Force and Navy and other agencies is legendary and stretches back to the 1940s: The Roswell Incident in 1947; Project Blue Book (1952-70); The Robertson Panel (1953).

Canadian official Wilbur Smith had stated that U.S. security classification on the Extraterrestrial presence is the highest, higher than on nuclear secrets. One purpose of the information war against advanced extraterrestrial civilization by the U.S. military-intelligence establishment may well have been to be able to create and maintain vast and profitable nuclear arsenals and an environmentally toxic nuclear power industry. Judging by the discussion around the table, Alfred thought in 1977, one aim of the U.S. arsenal may ultimately have been to wage Armageddon, or all-out nuclear war (scorching Earth and adjacent dimensions) – against the Extraterrestrials themselves.

At the conference table, Alfred turned a myriad of considerations in his mind. In that instant, Alfred decided to resist the obvious temptation to open up discussion of the Extraterrestrial

Issue as a key to the future of U.S. (and world) security needs through the year 2000. In a perfect world, Alfred would have put the ET issue at play into the U.S. Senate committee. In the light of hindsight, maybe that is what he should have done, and "leaked out" the planned Carter White House civilian scientific study into the assembled group of military-intelligence leaders who were, as they spoke, carrying out a covert war against advanced extraterrestrial civilizations. In that moment, he found it wisest to obtain formal SRI and White House approval before advertising his intentions publicly to what he perceived as the declared enemies of ethical extraterrestrial civilization, the U.S. government and the Pentagon.

Leaning out into the conference table and taking aim with calm *chi*, Alfred spoke out his words to the Director of the Defense Intelligence Agency. He recited words from memory drawn from "Armageddon: The Chilling Prospect of Global Nuclear War", the book project he and Gene LaRocque had worked on just months before. Serendipity and synchronicity- the power of meaningful coincidence – had brought him into the inner lair of the planners and executioners of nuclear war.

As the gaunt, Anglo face of the DIA officer blanched white, Webre slowly enunciated well-crafted words detailing the inhuman devastation and futility of nuclear war, ending with the words: "There are no victors; there are no vanquished. Each ground zero is the Void," A poignant silence overtook the room as Alfred finished his address. The Genie had been let out of the bottle. As the panel ended, Gene LaRocque drew near to Alfred, nodding, "You did quite a good job there." Now on to to the Extraterrestrials, thought Alfred.

Making his way back to the Stanford Research Institute campus in Menlo Park, California, Alfred realized he had little time to spare. He had to design an extraterrestrial communications study in short order, vet it through SRI and get Carter White House approval. Alfred's just completed episode at the U.S. Senate committee with the top military-intelligence officials of the United States had given him the clarity for the hard work and authoritative project leadership that lay ahead of him. Alfred quickly developed the outline of a civilian scientific study of extraterrestrial communication, the first of its kind in history. He located personnel within the Carter White House who reportedly were open to carrying extraterrestrial study forward in furtherance of Jimmy Carter's campaign promise.

SCENE 11

1977 CARTER WHITE HOUSE EXTRATERRESTRIAL STUDY

Summer 1977
Executive Office Building, White House
Washington, DC 20006

Alfred is on an airplane from San Francisco to Washington, DC that also carrying other Stanford Research Institute researchers for their briefings with U.S. government officials. On the plane with Alfred are SRI scientists Dr. Hal Puthoff and Russell Targ, under contract to develop the field of remote viewing for U.S. military and intelligence agencies. Puthoff and Targ were the first SRI scientists Alfred met when he approached SRI for a position as a Futurist after meeting their remote viewing subject Ingo Swann at his Bowery loft in New York City.

Remote viewing, a form of non-local time travel and teleportation, was to become a key tool in the development of Exopolitics, the science of relations among intelligent civilizations in the multiverse that Alfred founded in a 2005 book that the CIA already had physical possession of in 1971 via secret quantum access time travel technology. Remote viewers would be able in the 1990s to interact with intelligent Extraterrestrial civilizations and representatives of Universe governance bodies, as well as to locate an apparent intelligent, advanced civilization living underground on Mars.

Alfred's recent trip for SRI was to serve on a U.S. Senate Committee. On this trip for SRI, Alfred would meet in the White House Executive Office Building with a woman staff member of the Domestic Policy Staff under Stuart Eizenstat. Originally from Colorado, the woman staff member was enthusiastic about Carter's promise to open government UFO and extraterrestrial files. During the meeting, Alfred secured White House staff approval to submit a Stanford Research Institute proposal for an Extraterrestrial Communication Study project to the White House.

Back again at SRI, Alfred prepared a final proposal for the Jimmy Carter White House. UFO researcher Jacques Vallee, a colleague of Alfred's at the nearby Institute for the Future, contributed a written recommendation for the proposed White House study both from himself and Prof. Peter Sturrock, an eminent physicist at Stanford University who in 1975 had surveyed over 1300 members of the American Astronomical Society on the subject of UFOs. Strangely, just two years later Vallee was to publish the 1979 edition of his book "Messengers of Deception: UFO Contacts and Cults" that Alfred Lambremont Webre and Phillip H. Liss, PhD had formed a "UFO cult", and had compared Alfred to Aleister Crowley (1875-1947), an English occultist also known as "The Great Beast 666".[19]

Alfred and Vallee would have lunch often at SRI to discuss matters such as the "Context Communication Theory of Extraterrestrial Communication" that Alfred and Phillip Liss had developed and Vallee seemed genuinely interested as the theory was congruent with Vallee's own views. Valle must have been writing the manuscript for *Messengers of Deception: UFO Contacts and Cults* right at the exact time when Alfred and he were meeting and Vallee made his written contribution to the SRI 1977 Carter White House Extraterrestrial Communication Study proposal. When Alfred met with Vallee at his California investment banker's office in 1978, Vallee made no mention of his intended poison pen. Alfred later was to discover that this poison penmanship was typical of Vallee, and noted that Vallee had deleted all reference to Alfred and Phillip Liss in the 2008 edition of his book.

On August 30, 2000, Alfred swore an affidavit for the Disclosure Project before Zachary David Dubins, Notary Public, in Sacramento, CA. about the proposed 1977 Carter White House Extraterrestrial Communication Study.

AFFIDAVIT OF ALFRED LAMBREMONT WEBRE
Sworn August 30, 2000

STATE OF CALIFORNIA _____

|
|
|
|
| Affidavit of
| Alfred Lambremont
| Webre
|
|
|

SWORN AFFIDAVIT _____

I, Alfred Lambremont Webre, do affirm and swear the following to be true and factual:

1 My name is Alfred Lambremont Webre. I was born May 24, 1942 at the US Naval Air Base, Pensacola, Florida. My present address is 1512 West 40 Avenue, Vancouver, BC V6M 1V8. I hold a Bachelor of Science degree from Yale University, 1964. I hold a Juris Doctor degree from Yale Law School, 1967. I hold a Master of Education in Counseling from the University of Texas at Brownsville, 1997. I am a member of the Bar of the District of Columbia.

2 1977 Carter White House Extraterrestrial Communication Study - As Senior Policy Analyst at the Center for the Study of Social Policy at Stanford Research Institute (now "SRI International", Menlo Park, California), I was Principal Investigator for a proposed civilian scientific study of Extraterrestrial communication. This Study presented to and approved by appropriate White House staff of President

Jimmy Carter, during the period May 1977 until its unlawful termination of contract research on or about September 1977.

3   At the time of such unlawful termination, the Proposal for the 1977 Carter White House Extraterrestrial Communication Study had been approved for implementation by the management of Stanford Research Institute, and by appropriate White House Domestic Policy staff. On information and belief, the 1977 Carter White House Extraterrestrial Communication Study was also pending review by James Fletcher, the Administrator of NASA in or about September 1977.

PERSONS WITH DIRECT AND PERSONAL KNOWLEDGE OF THE 1977 CARTER WHITE HOUSE EXTRATERRESTRIAL COMMUNICATION STUDY

4   On information and belief, the persons, together with their then positions, having direct personal knowledge of the 1977 Carter White House Extraterrestrial Communication Study include at least the following:

A   Jacques Vallee, Institute for the Future, Palo Alto, CA. Position in Study: Scientific Investigator

B   Peter Sturrock, Chairman, Dept. of Physics, Stanford University. Position in Study: Scientific Adviser.

C   Tom Thomas, Supervisor, Center for the Study of Social Policy, Stanford Research Institute. Position in Study: Line Supervisor

D   Peter Schwartz, Senior Policy Analyst, Center for the Study of Social Policy, Stanford Research Institute. Position in Study: Policy Adviser. Present position: Chairman, Global Business Network

E   Willis Harmon, Senior Policy Analyst, Center for the Study of Social Policy, Stanford Research Institute. Adviser. Deceased.

F   John Doe (African American), Senior administrative official, Stanford Research Institute. Position in Study: Internal administration of Study.

G   John Doe2, SRI-Pentagon Liaison Officer, Washington, DC. Position in Study: Terminates 1977 Carter White House Extraterrestrial Communication Study through unlawful interference with contract, in or about September 1977.

H   James Fletcher, Administrator, National Aeronautic and Space Administration (NASA). Position in Study: Contract review of Proposal. NASA Administrator has copy of proposal and orders staff review in or about September 1977.

I   Jane Doe, Staff member, White House Domestic Policy Staff, Washington, DC. Position in Study: White House Liaison contract officer for Study, who reviewed and approved 1977 Carter White House Extraterrestrial Communication Study during period May 1977 to September 1977.

DESCRIPTION OF UNLAWFUL TERMINATION OF 1977 CARTER WHITE HOUSE EXTRATERRESTRIAL COMMUNICATION STUDY.

5   During the period May, 1977 until the unlawful termination of the Study in September, 1977, I met at the Executive Office Building, White House approximately every 20 days with appropriate White House staff to review and secure contract research approval of the 1977 Carter White House Extraterrestrial Communication Study. On information and

belief, my signature is recorded with the security gate of the Executive office building for each such visit. The only other occasion on which I have accessed the Executive office building and signed in at the Security Gate was in 1988, when handling a legal matter on behalf of a client who had brought legal action for acts of President George HW Bush, Sr.

6   During the period May to September, 1977, I presented verbal briefings, a written outline, and a written proposal for the 1977 Carter White House Extraterrestrial Communication Study to the appropriate White House staff member Jane Doe. The purpose of such presentations and proposal was to secure sole-source contract research approval from the White House, as well as to facilitate contract relations with the Study's proposed contracting agencies, NASA and National Science Foundation. Such presentations included the proposed Study as a collaborative effort of the National Science Foundation, NASA (National Aeronautic and Space Administration), Stanford Research Institute and the White House Science Advisor's Office and Domestic Policy Staff.

7   An outline and overview of the proposal for the 1977 Carter White House Extraterrestrial Communication Study is set out in Appendix I hereof. During the May 1977 - September 1977 period, such proposal was, on information and belief, in the possession of White House staff members of the Domestic Policy Staff and of the White House Science Advisers Office, in addition to White House staff member Jane Doe. The 1977 Carter White House Extraterrestrial Communication Study was designed as a major, civilian, scientific, multi-disciplinary study of the phenomena, with a duration of at least three (3) years.

8   The proposal for the 1977 Carter White House Extraterrestrial Communication Study was prepared with the direct, personal assistance of Jacques Vallee and Peter Sturrock,

both then expert scientists in the field. Jacques Vallee personally handed a version of the preliminary proposal to me on the morning of my airplane flight from Palo Alto, Ca. to Washington, DC in or about September 1977 to meet with White House staff on contract research approval of the proposal.

9   At a meeting in or about September 1977, Jane Doe of the White House Domestic Policy Staff approved in principle the 1977 Carter White House Extraterrestrial Communication Study as a sole source contract research project. Jane Doe also approved my representing to officials of the Study's cooperating agencies - National Science Foundation and NASA - that the White House had approved the Study for application for sole source funding. On information and belief, Jane Doe had authority to make such determination, and communicated such determination to appropriate personnel within the White House Domestic Policy staff and White House Science Adviser's office.

10   On information and belief, copies of the 1977 Carter White House Extraterrestrial Communication Study proposal are on file in the office archives of the NASA Administrator, and/or personal archives of the former Administrator. On information and belief, copies of 1977 Carter White House Extraterrestrial Communication Study proposal may be on file in archives of the White House Science Adviser, White House Domestic Policy Council, at the Carter Presidential Library or elsewhere. On information and belief, copies of the 1977 Carter White House Extraterrestrial Communication Study proposal may be in the files of SRI International or former SRI personnel, Study investigator Jacques Vallee, and Study adviser Peter Sturrock.

11   Following the September, 1977 meeting at which White House Domestic Policy staff approved the 1977 Carter White House Extraterrestrial Communication Study, I returned to SRI Headquarters in Palo Alto, Ca., and was directed to attend

a meeting with John Doe, an African American senior administrative officer of SRI. Also present at the meeting was Peter Schwartz, SRI policy adviser to the 1977 Carter White House Extraterrestrial Communication Study. John Doe stated to me that in a few minutes John Doe2, SRI-Pentagon liaison would be joining the meeting. John Doe indicated that John Doe2 had stated that SRI's research contracts with the Pentagon would be jeopardized if SRI went forward with the 1977 Carter White House Extraterrestrial Communication Study. John Doe stated that the Study was hereby being terminated and advised me, in his words, to "dissimulate" any negative reaction I might have.

12 John Doe2 entered the meeting, and stated to me that he had been personally informed by Pentagon officials that SRI's research contracts would be terminated by the Department of Defense if SRI proceeded with the 1977 Carter White House Extraterrestrial Communication Study. John Doe then stated that the 1977 Carter White House Extraterrestrial Communication Study was being terminated "because there are no UFOs."

13 I vociferously confronted John Doe2, and verbally presented evidence for the extraterrestrial presence and the UFO phenomena. At the end of the meeting, John Doe and John Doe2 verbally decided that the 1977 Carter White House Extraterrestrial Communication Study was immediately terminated. Both these persons were fully aware of the prior approval by the White House staff of the Study. On information and belief, SRI does not in practice terminate contract research with US government agencies after prior approval by the White House.

14 The evening of this meeting with John Doe and John Doe2, SRI staff member Peter Schwartz, who was present at the meeting, telephoned me at home and acknowledged my confrontation with John Doe2 earlier that day.

15 Starting in or about September, 1977, following termination of the 1977 Carter White House Extraterrestrial Communication Study, I was personally subjected to electronic and chemical intrusions on my person which bear the same symptomology and electronic signature as those ascribed to non-lethal "mind control" electronic and chemical weapons of the MKULTRA ("Mind Kontrol ULTRA") program.

16 During this time period, I was the target of three separate intrusions of such non-lethal weapons, two of which occurred with coordinated ground weapon's personnel.

17 Such three intrusions occurred at the Pentagon, in New Orleans, Louisiana prior to a meeting with Judge Jim Garrison at the New Orleans Athletic Club, and at the grounds of Stanford Research Institute at Palo Alto, Ca. As a result of such advanced non-lethal weapons intrusions, I was hospitalized for health reasons, forced to take a health-related leave of absence, and to resign from my position at SRI on health grounds.

18 On information and belief, I suffered adverse health effects from such non-lethal weapons attacks as were described in testimony before a US Senate Committee and other Congressional committees regarding the MKULTRA non-lethal weapons program of the US Central Intelligence Agency and other intelligence entities.

19 On information and belief, such non-lethal weapons intrusions against me were carried out as part of MKULTRA or related programs, at the direction of personnel of the US intelligence agencies, or surrogates thereof, for the purpose of deterring me from pursuing the 1977 Carter White House Extraterrestrial Communication Study. On information and belief, such attacks were carried out for the purpose of disabling me as a research professional, and destroying me as an economic entity.

20 On information and belief, such attacks have directly caused and contributed to serious personal health symptoms and syndromes I have suffered in the years 1977 to present, for which I am entitled to and seek lawful compensation.

21 On information and belief, such termination of the 1977 Carter White House Extraterrestrial Study as herein described constitutes unlawful and malicious interference with contract research, as well as a civil tort and criminal assault on my person.

22 On information and belief, the underlying public need for the research and public recommendations envisioned by the 1977 Carter White House Extraterrestrial Communication Study remain as necessary at present as at the time of the original proposal for the research.

SWORN TO AND SUBSCRIBED IN SACRAMENTO, CALIFORNIA THIS 30th DAY OF AUGUST, 2000.

Alfred Webre

Alfred Lambremont Webre

Zachary D Dubins
Notary Public Comm. #1231678, Comm. Exp. Aug. 8, 2003

Appendix I
To the Affidavit of
Alfred Lambremont Webre

1977 CARTER WHITE HOUSE EXTRATERRESTRIAL COMMUNICATION STUDY

The over-all purpose of the 1977 Carter White House Extraterrestrial Communication Study was to create, design and carry out an independent, civilian-led research compilation and evaluation of phenomena suggesting an

Extraterrestrial and Interdimensional intelligent presence on Earth. The outcome of the Study was to have been a public report by the White House, detailing the compiled evidence and evaluation, together with possible scientific models for the implications of the research. The White House report was to have contained public policy recommendations emerging from the evaluations and conclusions of the Study. These, if warranted, included transformation of secrecy regulations of US military-intelligence agencies. It is clear from the evidence that the phenomena to be studied are worldwide and in the public domain.

The scientific and public policy goal of the 1977 Carter White House Extraterrestrial Communication Study was to fill a substantial gap in civilian scientific knowledge of the UFO (Unidentified Flying Object), Extraterrestrial Biological Entities (EBEs), and related phenomena. This knowledge gap was created and maintained by excessive secrecy practices and regulations of US Department of Defence agencies in the various generations of its UFO-programs since the late 1940s, including but not limited to Project Grudge and Project Blue

Book, as well as other alleged secret programs.

Historically, the agencies proposed for the Study were:

- White House - Principal sponsorship and policy coordination of Study

- NASA - Consultative line agency regarding UFO and Near Space phenomena, including terrestrial-UFO or EBE interaction

- National Science Foundation - Advice and consultation by the National Science Board

- SRI International - Principal Investigators of Study

- Scientific experts on UFO, EBE and related phenomena - Scientific Advisers

It should be noted that the structure and contributors to the 1977 Carter White House Extraterrestrial Communication Study are similar and parallel to the COMETA Report, issued by a high-level private Committee in France after a three-year study. That Committee included the former head of the French equivalent of NASA. The COMETA Report endorses the Extraterrestrial hypothesis as the most plausible interpretation of the data. The 1977 Carter White House Extraterrestrial Communication Study antedated the COMETA Report by approximately twenty (20) years.

The 1977 Carter White House Extraterrestrial Communication Study was designed and structured around several research phases and tasks:

- Compilation of UFO, EBE. and related phenomena database - The Study team would compile a complete, objective, scientific data base of all UFO, EBE and related incidents from all available sources: US private and non-profit UFO and EBE data bases; International governmental, non-profit, and private UFO and EBE data bases (e.g. the Government of France, China, Russia, Brazil, Mexico); UFO and EBE data bases held by US military personnel and agencies, under a White House-mandated pardon from relevant security regulations affecting disclosure.

- Evaluation of UFO, EBE and related phenomena database - The Project team, employing its expertise in the areas of UFO, EBE, and related phenomena, would evaluate the compiled data base, and develop alternative interpretive models of data, including but not limited to the Extraterrestrial hypothesis. The Study contemplated contracting with relevant research scholars and experts in this field, as necessary.

- Report and Recommendations - The Study would produce a public report, including the full UFO, EBE, and related phenomena database, as well as the full results of the evaluation and model-building phases of the research. The Report would also include public policy recommendations as justified by its evidentiary and analytical conclusions. The Study proposal envisioned that recommendations might include:

- Global and regional UFO and EBE data banks, under independent scientific and community-based control.

- Public, international funding in the UFO, EBE and Extraterrestrial communication fields.

- Rescission of military-intelligence secrecy regulations that inhibit the flow of UFO and EBE reporting in the field.

- Design and implementation of a public Extraterrestrial Communication Program for intentional terrestrial non-hostile communication with such Extraterrestrial intelligence as might be posited by the Study.

- Design and implementation for an international public order system to facilitate integration of Earth into a Universe governmental order.

END OF AFFIDAVIT

The proposed 1977 Carter White House Extraterrestrial Communication Study

The proposed 1977 Carter White House Extraterrestrial Communication Study was designed as the first civilian led scientific study of the Extraterrestrial presence on Earth at the White House level, the first in history. In the 1976 U.S. presidential campaign, Jimmy Carter who in 1969 had encountered a UFO "about as bright the moon" in the company of members of Leary, Georgia Lions Club, promised if elected he would open U.S. secret UFO and extraterrestrial files

Starting in October 1977, the U.S. Department of Defense, probably acting on instructions from the CIA that CIA had obtained from secret 1970s time travel surveillance of Alfred's activities and writings after 2005, sabotaged the proposed 1977 Carter White House Extraterrestrial Communication Study even though the Study had White House staff approval. As part of their attack, the U.S Department of Defense attacked Alfred using directed energy weapons and trained anti-civilian Cointelpro ground agents.

This counter-offensive against the Carter White House ET Study started when, in October 1977, the Department of Defense liaison to Stanford Research Institute (SRI) established a meeting with an African American SRI executive to which Peter Schwartz, Alfred's fellow futurist and Alfred were called. The Defense liaison officer stated that if Alfred's Carter White House Extraterrestrial Communication Study went forward, the Department of Defense would "cancel all of its studies contracts with SRI". Moreover, he stated, the Carter White House study was invalid because "there were no UFOs".

"Dissimulate," the SRI African American executive signaled to Alfred. Alfred did not know what "dissimulate" meant. Always the public interest advocate, Alfred came down hard on the Defense liaison with the irrefutable facts of the Extraterrestrial presence. Peter Schwartz called Alfred after the meeting to reassure him. It was too late. Alfred's proposed 1977 Carter White House Extraterrestrial Communication Study, the first U.S. public civilian scientific study of the extraterres-

trial presence in history was summarily cancelled with no appeal.

Alfred's proposed 1977 Carter White House Extraterrestrial Communication Study, had it gone ahead, would have revealed the existence of secret human-extraterrestrial liaison programs, most especially with a human civilization under the surface of Mars. U.S. intelligence agencies were desperate to stop this.

More importantly, Alfred was to learn in 2005, the CIA and U.S. Department of Defense was using secret advanced time travel technology to learn of Alfred's future publications and activities. CIA and DARPA were well aware in 1977 of Alfred's 2005 future and were acting (ultimately unsuccessfully) to prevent it from coming about.

U.S. government Cointelpro 1977-78

Starting in October 1977, Alfred became subject to what are called "Cointelpro", psychological warfare attacks on him by trained U.S. military personnel and electromagnetic frequency weapons. Cointelpro attacks against Alfred happened in the inner ring of the Pentagon while he was meeting with an assistant secretary of defense. Cointelpro was carried out against him by men-in-black type intelligence agents at airports and public places; in constant surveillance by SRI security personnel, like the veteran; and, through Cointelpro alert networks, by uniformed personnel in the United States of America, local, state, and federal.

Alfred was on an international secret military, intelligence and police surveillance dragnet, all because of his interest in extraterrestrial life and Alfred's future activities in bringing Exopolitics into being circa the year 2000 and beyond.

At the time, of course, Alfred thought this Cointelpro was directed to terminate the 1977 Carter White House Extraterrestrial Communication Study. Much later, Cointelpro would be directed to suppress Alfred's actual future activities in the 21st century. DARPA and CIA used time travel technology in the 20th century to engage in illegal surveillance of Alfred's activities in the 21st Century.

ACT II

1978 – 1998
REFUGE & RECOVERY

"At this point, the main character encounters an obstacle that prevents the character from achieving his or her dramatic need. This is known as the complication. The main character reaches his or her lowest point and seems farthest from fulfilling the dramatic need or objective and it seems like there is no longer any way that the protagonist can succeed."

SCENE 1

SANGRE DE CRISTO
MOUNTAINS
ARIZONA

Christmas Eve, 1978
Alfred's VW Westphalia Campmobile
Location: Patagonia State Park
Sangre de Cristo Mountains, AZ 85624

Alfred spent his first Christmas Eve since leaving Stanford Research Institute (SRI) at Patagonia State Park in the Sangre de Cristo Mountains by the Mexican border near Nogales, AZ. Taking refuge in his mobile studio, a 1978 VW Westphalia Campmobile he nicknamed the "LordMobile", Alfred made busy writing a book on his experiences.

Behind lay the remains of Alfred's roles as director of proposed 1977 Carter White House Extraterrestrial Study and as a public watchdog over the House Select Committee on Assassinations, as well as the remains of Alfred's marriage with Teresa, his Peruvian-Chinese wife. Teresa found she could not handle her career as a woman architect, her role as a mother to their son Freddie, then eight years old, and also be wife to a man in the trenches of public interest counter-intelligence and extraterrestrial activism.

In 1977, while at SRI Alfred had been attacked with electromagnetic frequency weapons at the inner ring of the Pentagon; again at Washington, DC National airport; at Moissant International Airport (New Orleans, LA); and at the campus of Stanford Research Institute (SRI). The frequency weapons attacks were functionally intended to destroy Alfred as a social and economic entity, through severe injury to his neurological system and through the trauma that accompanied that injury.

Alfred pondered why he had been targeted with electromagnetic frequency weapons. Were the attacks intended to neutralize his role as director of the proposed White House extraterrestrial study? Or neutralize his role as a watchdog on the Congressional HCSA political assassination investigation? Were the attacks intentionally undertaken to destroy the possibility of his reaching a future as a positive planetary actor? Alfred concluded it was for all of these purposes.

Alfred did not know during this soul-trying period starting in 1978 what he would learn later, after publication of his book *"Exopolitics: Politics, Government and Law in the Universe"* in 2005 that he was under CIA time travel surveillance since at least 1971. Alfred was a high priority target for a CIA campaign of social disruption against his person that would apparently reach into the White House of every administration and into what Alfred came to know as an international war crimes racketeering organization that controlled key world processes and actors on the basis of information derived from secret time travel technology.

Elaborate teams of apparent plainclothes U.S. government operatives accompanied the 1977 frequency weapons attacks on Alfred. The agents gang-stalked Alfred in the aftermath of the attacks and sought to abduct or disable Alfred. With his agility as a modern dancer, Alfred managed to keep his center and foil their attempts.

These attacks were Alfred's first exposure as a target to the hidden MKULTRA/Cointelpro program against progressive activists. On one trip to Washington, DC, Alfred returned to Stanford Research Institute in California via New Orleans, LA to see his brother John Webre, then studying architecture at Tulane University, and so they could tour the traveling King Tut exhibit together, then visiting New Orleans. On the first day of Alfred's visit in New Orleans, he made an appointment to meet former District Attorney Jim Garrison,[20] the prominent Kennedy assassination prosecutor, at the New Orleans Athletic Club the next day. Alfred would never meet get to his appointment with Garrison. As he entered the King Tut exhibit, frequency or biochemical weapons so disoriented Alfred that he had to leave the exhibit and cancel his meeting with Jim Garrison.

Under increasing frequency weapons attacks and intelligence surveillance back at SRI, Alfred took a medical leave of absence from SRI in early 1978. Alfred's diagnosis fell somewhere between the "labels" of post-traumatic stress disorder (PTSD) and bi-polar disorder, intentionally caused by advanced electromagnetic frequency weapons whose attacks were designed to mimic the frequencies of diseases in the human body and trigger these diseases in target humans.

Alfred was to learn that the controllers who were targeting him within the U.S. government had developed electromagnetic frequency weapons that would induce a spectrum of medical conditions in the body of the targeted victim to disable or assassinate them, ranging from fast-acting cancer through heart disease and in Alfred's case post-traumatic stress disorder (PTSD)/bipolar disorder. The truth was that his neurological system had been severely traumatized by unrelenting covert frequency weapons attacks by the U.S. government.

Alfred took refuge from Stanford Research Institute and the frequency weapons attacks of the U.S. government in West Africa. He traveled to the city of Korhogo on the northern Ivory Coast. Alfred's father was helping build a sugar mill at Korhogo on a World Bank project. Alfred's mother Juanita and a number of his eight siblings were also then at Korhogo.

Alfred found initial spiritual refuge with the animist Senofu Tribe, whose tribal territory covers parts of northern Ivory Coast, Burkina Faso (then Upper Volta), and Mali. Korhogo was a seat of the Senofu Tribe, whose King with many wives had just died. Alfred made friends with the Prince of the Senofu, who was dating a blonde Peace Corps volunteer then stationed in Korhogo.

Soon Alfred left for a 3-month shoulder bag trek through Burkina Faso and Mali via bush taxi, leaving U.S. intelligence's Cointelpro against him behind. Alfred's favorite course at Yale Law School had been African Tribal Law. As he traveled in rural Mali, Burkina Faso, and Ivory Coast, Alfred read Alex Haley's book "Roots" and delved into deep personal impressions of his possible prior incarnations as an African Earthling human.

Alfred stayed in rural villages, speaking the *lingua franca* (French) and engaging in long conversations villagers and fellow travelers. Alfred's favorite haunts were the West African magic markets, where the *griots* (shamans) shopped. He collected tribal masks, intrigued by *Le masque qui parle* ("The mask that talks"), a tribal mask through which dimensional intelligences would speak, giving guidance to assembled village gatherings. Subjectively, Alfred felt his soul might have been connecting with influential prior African incarnations.

Returning back to Stanford Research Institute in mid-1978 after his West African sojourn in full health, Alfred soon discovered he was again under unrelenting surveillance and MKULTRA/Cointelpro-type attacks on the SRI campus. It was clear that the U.S. national security state considered Alfred a hostile civilian because of his research and interest in extraterrestrial life, coupled with his pursuit of Congressional investigations of the false flag operations of the John F. Kennedy and other political assassinations. How deep a level was the secret U.S. government's hostility Alfred would not discover until after 2005, when he began to discover that CIA and other alphabet agencies had begun "Person of Interest" surveillance of him as early as 1971, using secret time travel technology to spy on his writings and activities in 2005 and later.

Strategically, Alfred's soul sought a multi-dimensional worldwide platform on which to relate to Extraterrestrial civilizations' initiative for Earth, free of the destructive matrix of the Pentagon and U.S. Presidency he had just experienced at the hands of the U.S. Department of Defense. In mid-1978, Alfred resigned from Stanford Research Institute for good.

Alfred decided on a strategic retreat and resigned, to transform himself into a journalist. Paradoxically, the frequency weapons attacks had the effect of expanding Alfred's consciousness, even though causing him intolerable pain. Alfred came out of this ordeal "enlightened." For the balance of 1978, he traveled the United States. He went back to Yale, re-visited some of his law professors and experienced them as being in a "consciousness matrix" he had left behind.

Alfred went to Brooklyn to visit the Lubavitcher Rebbe; to Dealey Plaza (site of the Kennedy assassination); attended the Opera in New York and New Orleans and the result was the same. Alfred felt he was able to perceive the restrictive consciousness "matrix" within which humanity was acting out specific, limited roles.

Alfred returned to his family's home, a heritage house reigned over by his mother Juanita, a lively place with his father and his eight siblings at the Mexican border in Brownsville, Texas. Juanita was a "yellow dog" Democrat by her own description. The 1980 Ted Kennedy for President campaign was to bivouac one young Kennedy there.

Alfred was born at the U.S. Naval hospital on the U.S. Naval Air Station at Pensacola, Florida, U.S.A. at the height of World War II. His father, then Lieutenant (JG) Alfred Lambremont Webre, Jr. U.S. Navy, born in New Orleans on December 23, 1915 Jr., was of a Louisiana family founded by a German immigrant Johan Weber in the early 1700s. Lt. (JG) Webre freshly graduated from Yale class of '38 with graduate work at

MIT was NROTC. Ali was assigned to naval air cadet training at the Pensacola air base sometime before Pearl Harbor (Dec. 7, 1941).

Alfred's day of birth was a Sunday, the Feast day of "Our Lady Help of Christians" as his Catholic Cuban-American mother Juanita Bautista Chisholm Fernandez y Webre would tell Alfred as he grew to adulthood. A fellow Gemini like Alfred, Juanita had been born in Havana, Cuba on June 7, 1921, the seventh of nine children of a Scottish-Canadian-Massachusetts-Cuban family.

For Christmas 2012, Alfred's brother Septime Webre gifted him the National Geographic's GENO 2.0 DNA test.[21] The results showed Alfred's DNA was typical European DNA, except for Native American DNA on Alfred's mother's side that had crossed the land bridge over from Russia into the Americas starting about 23,000 years ago. For years at public events people asked Alfred if he was Native American because of his physical appearance. Alfred would answer, "I do not know," because this issue had never been discussed in his family.

Speculation in Alfred's family was that the Native American DNA could either be North American, from the Louisiana or New England branches of his mother's family, or Caribbean from the Cuban-based branches. Alfred's brother Louis Webre, the family genealogist wrote, "Through Everett Chisholm's maternal family, we are related to the Griswolds, the Verys, and other old New England families who immigrated during the Colonial era. The Native American DNA could possibly have come through them. [Alfred's father's side], the Greene family tree begins in the New World with John and Priscilla Alden, who came over in 1620 on the Mayflower. She uttered the famous line, 'Why don't you speak for yourself, John,' in 'The Courtship of Miles Standish'. Being that that branch has such deep roots in America, I believe that they are the source of the Native American DNA." The problem is that Alfred's father's side showed no Native American DNA. More likely, the Native American DNA was Caribbean, from the Taino[22] peoples of Cuba, intermingled with Carib, Arawak, and Ciboney DNA.

Alfred wrote to his siblings, "Taino, Arawak, Carib, and Ciboney are some possibilities for tribal origins of our Native American DNA. Here is my working hypothesis: The Cuban *guajiro* of pre-revolutionary Cuba is actually a bloodline remnant of the Taino/Arawak/Ciboney/Carib in Cuba." *Guajiro* is a modern Cuban term for a country peasant community with Indigenous features. Alfred continued, "Following up on the hypothesis that the *guajiros* are the bloodline descendants of the Taino/Caribe/Arawak/Ciboney indigenous genetic pool in Cuba, the attached photo is of a reconstruction of a Taino village in Cuba. The buildings are of the same basic form as a *bohio*, the palm-thatched roof house of a *guajiro* family. The *guajiro bohio* was derived from the Taino village dwelling, in my opinion. Cuban words like *guajiro, bohio, batey* are Taino, not Spanish in origin. *Batey* was a Taino ball game. In pre-revolutionary Cuba, *batey* was the Cuban word for the living quarters of sugar mill employees and workers, as those of us who grew up living in a *batey* well know." Historically, the *mestizo* descendants of Spanish settlers and Cuban indigenous were called *guajiros*.[23] The Taino culture was a festive, partying culture, just like Alfred.

Alfred's mother Juanita told him that his two grandfathers drank a toast to his mother's birth at the American Club in Havana, Cuba. In the toast, Alfred's Webre and Chisholm grandfathers envisioned Alfred's father and mother becoming engaged and getting married as adults. Their grandfatherly vision materialized when in December 1940, Alfred's Webre grandfather had a serious heart attack while staying at the home of Alfred's Chisholm grandfather. Grampo as he called his Webre grandfather usually stayed about six months out of the year in Cuba, consulting and designing sugar mills. He stayed at the Chisholm home, a large beige two-story house in the Vedado section of Havana whose second story was occupied by a Spanish *marques*.

Alfred's father, Alfred Jr. ("Ali" was his family nickname), Yale class of 1938, chose to take leave from a Master's degree at MIT (in chemical engineering) to travel down to Havana and take care of Grampo.

Ali met Juanita at the Chisholm house in Vedado, Havana on Christmas Eve 1940 and, true to the Webre-Chisholm grandfathers' vision, seven days later the Ali and Juanita were engaged that New Years Eve 1940.

Both the Webre's and the Chisholms were Roman Catholic families. So Ali and Juanita were married on April 27, 1941 in the Chapel of Colegio Belen, the Jesuit grade preparatory school whose Director later was to be Juanita's older brother Richard Chisholm, S.J., and among whose students was Albert Chisholm, Juanita's younger brother. Albert Chisholm played basketball with another Colegio Belen student, a young Fidel Castro (later to become *Lider Maximo* of the Cuban Revolution). As Director of Colegio Belen, Richard Chisholm, SJ had disciplinary problems with the young Fidel Castro and reportedly took a revolver away from him in class one day. Family lore has it that young Fidel came to Sunday dinner at the Chisholm house on occasion. This is appears to be part of the "Jesuit grooming" that Castro himself had as well.

Alfred's Webre Roman Catholic grandfather was born in St. James Parish, Louisiana (the "Webre seat") on Nov 7, 1881, *nee* Alfred Lambremont Webre. Grampo Webre was an inventor and mechanical engineer who taught at Tulane University and was a consultant to the world sugar industry. Grampo Webre died in November 1963 shortly before the John F. Kennedy assassination. Alfred, then a sophomore at Yale, was on his way to Grampo's funeral when he heard the news Kennedy had been shot. Alfred's greatest memories of Grampo Webre's funeral are of the immediate aftermath of the Kennedy assassination.

Alfred's Chisholm grandfather, Everett Chadbourne Chisholm, was an Episcopalian who allowed his Cuban wife Juana Fernandez Carbonell to raise their nine children Roman Catholic. Grandfather Chisholm was a graduate of the Massachusetts Institute of Technology and established an engineering company during the 1920s "sugar bubble" in Cuba. At the height of the sugar bubble, grandfather Chisholm was a wealthy man who sported the first Cadillac in Cuba, kept a house on

Riverside Drive in New York, and took his family by steamship to elite spas in the United States.

Alfred had not yet fathomed why he chose to be born into a family with "sugar karma". One researcher who would interview later Alfred on his own social invention, "Exopolitics", the science of relations among intelligent civilizations in the multiverse, wrote, "Sugar is a drug that has no nutritional value and is an addictive chemical [with harmful health effects]." Webre family lore has it that one of the first sugar mills in North America was built on the Webre plantation in the lower Mississippi River delta in the early 1700s, using equipment designed by a Haitian of African descent

In 1926, Alfred's Webre grandfather published a classic book, "Evaporation".[24] The "Webre Evaporator", an invention of Alfred's Webre grandfather, helped make the modern manufacture of sugar at the industrial scale more efficient. Webre and Chisholm were partners in the design and building of sugar mills, Cuba's leading industry. Family lore says that the Webre and Chisholm engineering partnership together designed and built a substantial number of the sugar mills in Cuba, which in the era of the 1920s sugar bubble were about half the sugar mills in the world.

The Balance of Light

Alfred entered this dimension Earth at the height of World War II on May 24, 1942. No important dates in history are listed in standard references as having happened on May 24, 1942. As a proper Aelfin-like proclamation to make about his birthdate, Alfred claimed his birth as an "important event in history" that occurred on May 24, 1942, the day that Alfred Lambremont Webre, who established Exopolitics, the science of relations among intelligence civilizations in the multiverse, was born.

Alfred's birthday is officially Queen Victoria's Birthday holiday in Canada, his 3rd homeland after Cuba and the United States. Alfred's life mission since birth has been to tilt the balance of Light on the planet as a

Lightworker, an incarnated "Early Indigo" soul dedicated to keeping the planet in the Light and out of the column of the forces of the Dark.

Alfred perceived that he was born into a planetary breakdown-breakthrough process in 1942 which is still transitioning from a condition of enforced dystopian war, disease, crime and poverty towards utopian expanding planetary breakthroughs of sustainability, abundance, enlightenment and cooperation.

Alfred understood that the exploitative, ecocidal, genocidal, exploitative forms of hereditary governance on planet Earth – The Pharaohs, Emperors, Kings, Queens, Presidents (Elected or Appointed) - were all artifacts of the Anunnaki extraterrestrial occupation of Earth, starting about 280,000 years ago at Adam's Calendar, South Africa.[25] The Anunnaki extraterrestrials intervened in an experiment by a consortium of upper dimensional, ethical extraterrestrial civilizations including the Pleiadians, the Alpha Centaurians, the Sirians and others to create the homo sapiens as a 12-strand DNA Light being in the 3rd dimension.[26]

Alfred perceived his incarnation plan into 3rd dimensional Earth to be structured around deep infiltrations into the three City States of the Satanic Illuminati – [VatLonUSA – Vatican-London-USA] The Vatican (The Pope), The British Crown (The Queen/King & the City of London) and the Illuminati-founded United States of America (Washington, DC), as well as a side infiltration into the Illuminati social invention of Communism (Cuba).

One mission of Alfred's life in this incarnation was to help in the deconstruction of Anunnaki/Illuminati exploitative hierarchy and its forms of governance, as well as of the masonic Illuminati City State "Triangle of Power" of the Vatican, City of London, Washington, DC one of whose portals dated back to at least the Roman Empire.

Alfred understood that, at one level of Exopolitical dimensional reality, World War II was a rollout of an attempted takeover of Earth, Mars and its Moons by a predatory faction of Draco Reptilian extraterrestrials aided by Orion Grey extraterrestrials.[27] The presumed "Vanquished" in World War II – the Third Reich – had actually migrated to

116

the United States after the end of the war under Operation Paper Clip. After World War II, and most especially after the assassination of John F. Kennedy on Nov. 22, 1963 by the Illuminati, the U.S. government, and all major governmental institutions worldwide, were actually at risk of infiltration and total takeover by a covert Illuminati controlled Fascist/Communist alliance operating under the moniker of the "New World Order (NWO)", seen as a worldwide police state.[28]

Alfred came to understand that the attempted rollout of the New World Order on Earth during his adult years was a manifestation of multiple dynamics in the dimensional ecology around Earth. At the cosmological level, the New World Order may represent the manifestation of archonic forces inherent in the Universe that Earth is a part of in the larger multiverse.

Alfred's colleague Laura Magdalene Eisenhower, great granddaughter of former U.S. President Dwight D. Eisenhower aided his understanding of the role of Archons, that are "hidden negative controllers of humankind, inorganic interdimensional entities that must now be exposed and exorcised from the individual human mind, from our human species, and from the planet as a whole as part of our collective evolution to a new state of consciousness and being."[29]

Archonic forces may have been present at the creation of our Universe and caused defects or faults in the very design of intelligent life in our Universe, such that "evil", "separation from Source", separation from God" exist in our Universe. Alternatively, Archons may have been brought into our Universe by space-faring travelers from our Universe who violated an injunction against venturing through a wormhole/stargate to a dark Universe populated by Archons.[30]

At a spiritual level, the rollout of the New World Order on Earth may represent the manifestation of Luciferic and Satanic diabolical dimensional forces. The Illuminati power structure of bloodline Monarchies (especially the UK and Dutch Crowns) and City of London bloodline banking families are Satanic and derive their power from diabolical dimensional entities they attract through ritual child sacrifice, mind control, and generational abuse.[31]

117

At the level of dimensional exopolitics, The New World Order rollout was the continued manifestation of the attempted takeover of 3rd dimensional Earth by the 4th dimensional Draco Reptilian/Orion Grey extraterrestrial alliance. The deconstruction of the New World Order would mean that is some real way the Draco Reptilian/Orion Grey extraterrestrial takeover had been deconstructed as well.

The deconstruction of the New World Order on Earth in Alfred's lifetime would involve cosmological intervention at the level of the Source or creator of our Universe to counteract the effects of archonic duality in our Universe. The broadcasts of unity consciousness through the interdimensional portal that intensified after October 28, 2011 and December 21, 2012 (or thereabouts) make duality consciousness ("I win-you lose") in our Universe more difficult to manifest, and counteract the effect of archons in our Universe.[32]

At the level of spiritual dimensions, the effects of historical negative ("diabolical") interdimensional entities such as Lucifer, Satan and others on the dimensional ecology of Earth as powerful positive spiritual entities are deployed in the dimensional ecology.

At the exopolitical level, the planned occupation of Earth, Mars and its moons by the Draco Reptilians and Orion Greys, originally reportedly timelined for 2000 – 2050, has now reportedly been stalled and even defeated by a consortium of ethical human civilizations from the Milky Way and Andromeda Galaxies that have destroyed major underground and undersea bases from which the Draco-Grey alliance controlled the Satanic/Illuminati power matrix on Earth.[33]

Alfred's birth month, May 1942, was the month when the genocide of the Warsaw ghetto Jews began at the hands of a Nazi movement. The Nazi leader Adolf Hitler was financed through the Skull & Bones Bush family at Alfred's alma mater Yale University. Alfred would come to understand that the City of London Illuminati bloodline bankers including the Rothschild family financed Hitler and the Nazis.[34]

Alfred will later successfully convict one representative of this blood-line, George W. Bush, for war crimes as a Judge on the Kuala Lumpur War Crimes Tribunal.[35]

The phrase echoing in Alfred's birthplace where he incarnates, a U.S. Naval Air Base, was "Praise the Lord and pass the ammunition!" Alfred, an Aelfin being of Light, chooses to descend into a lifetime on dimension Earth of simultaneously deconstructing war and developing the scientific bridges through his work in Exopolitics and the Dimensional Ecology of intelligent civilizations in the multiverse to higher dimensions for an evolving human race.

Alfred's physical incarnation and birth

As far as Alfred knows, the early, pre-birth stages of his present incarnation were normal and routine. If his incarnation was normal and routine, Alfred's soul teleported through an interdimensional portal from the inter-life in the Spiritual dimensions of the multiverse we all inhabit to the Earthly time-space hologram coordinates where his pregnant mother Juanita was located.[36]

Alfred's soul may have nestled next to his body-as-fetus in Juanita's womb for about three months prior to Alfred's physical birth on Sunday, May 24, 1942 War Time at the U.S. Naval Hospital, U.S. Naval Air Station, Pensacola, Florida, USA. Using a database of over 7000 replicable cases obtained by hypnotic regression of soul memories of the inter-life (afterlife), Dr. Michael Newton has found that the human soul typically will assume a non-local position next to the fetus they will inhabit about three months prior to birth.[37]

Juanita had become pregnant with Alfred in September 1941. His mother Juanita and Alfred's father Ali had been married on April 27, 1941 in the Chapel of the Belen (Bethlehem) Jesuit School in Havana, Cuba where Alfred's mother's family lived. Juanita's Jesuit older brother Richard Chisholm, SJ, was headmaster of Belen and later would become the Jesuit's liaison to Pope Paul VI during Vatican II in 1963-65 as well as assistant to Pedro Arrupe, SJ, the Director General of the

Jesuits, the "Black Pope". Such was the paradoxical incarnational design of Alfred's window into the Satanic Illuminati.[38]

Cointelpro circles later sought to propagandize about Alfred's Jesuit Uncle by charging that Alfred was a "Jesuit Coadjutor and Papal Knight", thereby seeking to deflect from the valid exposes that Alfred was in fact making. Alfred was to discover that every time he would make a major move to publicly expose the false flag operation of 9/11, Cointelpro would inevitably attack him.

[cia-drugs] To CIA-Drugs from Alfred Webre re: Eric Jon Phelps
Alfred Lambremont Webre JD MEd
Mon, 01 Sep 2008 22:18:12 -0700
Date: Sept; 1, 2008
To CIA-Drugs from Alfred Webre
re: Eric John Phelps

Hi All! - My friend and colleague independent scientist Leuren Moret today pointed out to me the below post of an article by Eric John Phelps, which I had not seen and I wanted to set the record straight on Phelps statements, which rise - in the opinion of my attorney – to libel and slander. That is they are reckless misstatements of fact done maliciously to impugn my good standing in the community.

For the record, just prior to 2008 Conspiracy Con conference at which Eric Jon Phelps was a Keynote Speaker, on the advice of legal counsel, I approached the organizer and brought to his attention a similar libelous article which Phelps had published on CTRL. As a result, the organizer of Conspiracy Con offered me a free pass to the conference to monitor Phelps, as he understood that Phelps article was libelous. In addition he called Phelps and cautioned against any further libel. The Conspiracy Con organizer indicated tome that Phelps agreed he would cease this libel. I agreed I would not pursue any further legal action at that point against Phelps. In addition, I was verbally invited to speak at the 2009 Conspiracy Con.

It is a preposterous fabrication that I am "A Jesuit Co-Adjutor" whatever that term might be. I have not formal or informal connection to the Jesuits or the Catholic church or any of its agencies. I went to Georgetown Preparatory, a Jesuit High School because my parents sent me there. I have not been a practicing Catholic since 1960, the year I graduated from Georgetown Prep and entered Yale. My family was very Catholic. My uncle Richard Chisholm, SJ, worked for Arrupe the Father General of the Jesuits during Vatican II. The last time I saw my uncle, who is now dead, was on a summer vacation in Rome in 1969, when I saw him briefly for two hours as a tourist. We were estranged because I rejected Catholicism.

At Yale I was not in Skull & Bones or any of the above ground Secret Societies. I was in Torch & Talon, a now defunct underground Secret Society. We rented a beach house in Branford CT and held a psychological encounter group twice a week, supporting ourselves through our problems at that life stage.

[EDITOR'S NOTE: In fact on the night Alfred was designated to tell his "life story" at Torch & Talon a Skull & Bones, oil industry shill-member infiltrated the meeting and interrupted Alfred with irrelevant interjections so that Alfred could not really communicate his story that night].

As my affidavit at the Disclosure Project shows, I was a whistleblower at Stanford Research Institute and led an Extraterrestrial Communication Project, for which I was attacked with electromagnetic weapons by US military intelligence agents.

I have been a broadcaster and activist all of my public life, and am extremely proud of my record.

Alfred Lambremont Webre, JD, MEd
Vancouver, BC
Sept.1, 2008 - Labor Day

9/11 War Crimes Tribunal
http://peaceinspace.blogs.com/911/

Re: *PAPAL KNIGHT,ALFRED WEBRE… ROMEs' JESUIT
GATEKEEPER for the 9/11"TRUTH" MOVEMENT*
by Eric Jon Phelps
<snip>

*A young Fidel Castro was a student in Havana, Cuba at Belen under
Richard Chisholm SJ's tutelage. Fidel played basketball with Alfred's
mother Juanita's youngest brother Albert and occasionally, Alfred was
told, showed up for Sunday dinner at Alfred's grandmother Abuelita's
house in Vedado, Havana, Cuba.*

*Juanita's elder brother Edward was in the movie business in Cuba and
after the 1959 revolution befriended Juanita Castro, Fidel's sister who
worked for the Cuban Institute of Cinematographic Art and Industry.
In August 1960, because of this Cuban movie business connection,
Alfred's mother Juanita was able to communicate with Juanita Castro.
Fidel Castro's sister in turn used her clout to successfully intervene
and release Alfred from a rural jail in the Oriente Province sugar mill
"Central Manati" (now "Central Argelia Libre)[39] that Alfred's father
managed for the Czarnikow-Rionda Sugar Company then a Braga
Brothers family firm at 120 Wall Street.[40] In 1969, Alfred met the one
of the Braga Brother owners of Czarnikow-Rionda at an elite gathering in River House in New York. The owner's daughter stated bitterly
to Alfred that John F. Kennedy was "guttersnipe" and that she was
glad he had been eliminated.*

*At the time that Central Manati/Argelia Libre was expropriated by
the Cuban Revolution, Alfred was the goalie on the Manati soccer
team and was scheduled to go to Jamaica to play with the team. What
upset Alfred deeply about the expropriation was that he could not go
and play in Jamaica for Cuba.*

*Juanita Castro threatened the Cuban Army Lieutenant holding Al-
fred just before he was to have been transferred to a Cuban Army
prison where his life would have been tragically derailed for the mundane crime of driving without a license. The Cuban revolution was*

targeting Alfred for being the eldest son of the manager of a Wall Street-owned latifundium, a Roman era term the revolution used for Cuban sugar estates owned by foreign interests.

In her 2009 autobiography "Fidel y Raúl, Mis Hermanos: La Historia Secreta", Juanita Castro revealed she had begun collaborating with the CIA in Cuba in 1961 in order to secure the release or political prisoners. If her dates are correct, then Alfred was released by virtue of Juanita Castro, head of the Cuban Institute of Cinematographic Art and Industry and not by virtue of Juanita Castro, covert CIA agent.[41]

In a historical irony, Alfred's brother Philip a few years later worked for the Cuban revolution as a member of the Venceremos Brigade, "a coalition of young people formed as a means of showing solidarity with the Cuban Revolution by working side by side with Cuban workers and challenging U.S. policies towards Cuba."[42] Another brother Septime, artistic director of the Washington, DC ballet took his ballet to Cuba during the second Bill Clinton Administration (1997-2001) at the invitation of the Ballet Nacional de Cuba to unqualified success. The New York Times reported, ""The enterprising Mr. Webre arrived in Havana with an entourage of 130 dancers, students, choreographers and theater directors and presenters from around the United States to meet their Cuban counterparts. One thing the group found was a rigorous program of training, one that has turned out world-class dancers like Jose Manuel Carreno of American Ballet Theater and Carlos Acosta, now with the Royal Ballet. The state-run program, headed by Ms. Alonso, has a highly organized curriculum and is tuition free."[43]

Along with the Cuban Ambassador to Canada, Alfred spoke at the Canada-Cuba Friendship Society in Vancouver, BC in 2001 where he urged Cuba to sign the Space Preservation Treaty banning space-based weapons.[44]

From Alfred's point of view, his family experiences with the Jesuits, Fidel Castro, and the Cuban Revolution were coordinated in the interlife prior to his birth so that Alfred could experience first hand the forces of the Vatican, the Jesuits, the British Crown, City of London/Wall Street capitalist networks, and New World Order phenomena like Communism in the context of a political revolution as an incarnating Starseed and Lightworker. That way Alfred would organically self-realize that he was on a parallel positive timeline outside these forces of catastrophic, entropic breakdown reality.

Alfred's father Ali had been U.S. Naval ROTC while he was at Yale University (class of 1938), and after Pearl Harbor (December 7, 1941) became a Lieutenant (JG) in the U.S. Navy, assigned to the Pensacola Naval Air Station, known as "the cradle of naval aviation," training 1100 air cadets per month. Alfred's birth certificate shows that Ali and Juanita lived at 1222 Poppy Street, Aero Vista, Warrington, adjacent to the Air Station.

His mother Juanita told Alfred that her pregnancy and his physical birth were normal. Juanita said she and Ali were at the Pensacola Air Base Officer's Club on Sunday May 24, 1942 when she felt labor pangs. She went to the hospital and Alfred was born that night without complications. Alfred's birth certificate simply states he was born "live" and is signed by a physician in the U.S. Naval Hospital at Pensacola who later lived in Escondido, California.

The hyper-vigilance and state of permanent alert at wartime Pensacola Air Station may have imprinted itself on Alfred's aura and etheric body as he emerged into that Sunday night of May 24, 1942. Alfred's interlife planning could have considered a wartime U.S. Naval Air Station a fitting place for the aura of a spiritual warrior to be born, given Alfred's method of life-development as transformation of self through immersion into opposites.

Alfred worked to dissolve any body and emotional trauma associated with his physical birth at Pensacola Naval Air Station by "re-birthing" with Alfred's rebirther healer-housemate Linda Thistle in the early 1980s in Los Angeles, California. Rebirthing is a technique for accessing and dissolving any trauma surrounding birth.[45]

Alfred "rebirthed" frequently during his interlude (1980-82) at Mi Casa, a historic building in Los Angeles on Havenhurst Avenue off

Sunset Boulevard. Alfred's bedroom balcony in what was reportedly at one time Cary Grant's old duplex faced the balcony of film icon Bette Davis' apartment. Bette Davis and Alfred occasionally saw each other across the property, which made Alfred feel like he was actually in "Hollywood" while developing motion pictures.

One film Alfred developed was called "Chappie", telling the story of the first African American 4-star General and the Tuskegee Airmen, the African American fighter squadron based at Pensacola, Florida. Two motion picture versions of the film that Alfred was developing in the early 1980s eventually were made. One was "The Tuskegee Airmen" (1995) a TV movie starring Laurence Fishburne. The other film was a Lucasfilm production "Red Tails" (2012).[46] Alfred was working out some deeper thread about his May 1942 birth at Pensacola's Naval Air Station.

"May 24 the Feast Day of "Our Lady Help of Christians"

Even late in life, the family story his mother Juanita repeated about Alfred's birth was her happiness that he was born on Sunday May 24, the Feast of "Our Lady Help of Christians". During childhood, every time Juanita would remind Alfred about the significance of his birthdate, it made him feel special and appreciated by her.

Alfred's habit as an adult was to listen to Juanita's Roman Catholic references with attentive "clinicism" (clinical cynicism). He had not been a practicing Roman Catholic during his adult life. Alfred did not oppose Christianity. Quite the contrary, he found the version of the life of Jesus in the Urantia Book, for example, compelling. It was the perversion of Christianity that the Papacy and the Vatican had introduced, morphing the Roman Emperor into the Pope for geopolitical and spiritual materialism purposes that Alfred abhorred.[47]

Alfred assumed "Our Lady Help of Christians" referred to a vague intervention by the Virgin Mary in support of Catholic virtue. Alfred did not understand what May 24, the Feast of "Our Lady Help of Christians" was meant to commemorate, or why Juanita would find it

125

so compelling that Alfred was born on that day. Perhaps Juanita herself did not know what "May 24 the Feast Day of "Our Lady Help of Christians" was meant to commemorate, except that the words had a comforting Roman Catholic, "Marian" ring to them.

When designing his present life and before incarnating as Alfred Lambremont Webre, Alfred would have reviewed the significance of his birthday of "May 24 the Feast Day of Our Lady Help of Christians" with his soul groups and guides in the interlife. In the interlife, his mother Juanita and Alfred would also have reviewed prior to incarnation the fact that Juanita frequently reminded Alfred of the significance of Alfred's birthdate on May 24.

In Juanita's mind as a believing Roman Catholic, Alfred's being born on "May 24 the Feast Day of Our Lady Help of Christians" had a different significance than it had in Alfred's mind. Alfred was a midlife contactee of an extraterrestrial or interdimensional entity masquerading as the "Holy Spirit" that may well have been engaging in a manipulative psyop when it told Alfred in February 1973 "Thou art Peter and on this Rock I will build my Church." There is the possibility – not likely in Alfred's mind - that the "Holy Spirit" experience was an electromagnetic experience, manufactured by human frequency weapons.

Alfred did not get the opportunity to share his "Holy Spirit" encounter with his mother Juanita while she was still alive. He never quite found the context or opportunity to do so in a way that would have been an "I-Thou" communication in which Juanita was fully listening. Alfred's 1973 "Holy Spirit" experience was too charged with cognitive dissonance for a believing Catholic to absorb, especially with Alfred's exopolitical framing of the "Holy Spirit" as manipulatory extraterrestrials or interdimensional entities.

After Alfred's "Holy Spirit" contact in February 1973, whenever his mother Juanita would remind him that he was born on "May 24 the Feast Day of Our Lady Help of Christians", the "Holy Spirit" encounter would come silently to his mind. Alfred's mind had been conditioned to link the significance of his birthdate May 24 "Feast Day of

Our Lady Help of Christians" and the "Holy Spirit's" special "Messianic" message to Alfred.

From 1971 forward, Satanic/Illuminati power matrix forces like the Ancient Vampire Illuminati, Coneheads, the Jesuits, British Crown, City of London Rothschild bloodline bankers, Skull & Bones CIA Rockefeller interests and their New World Order Israel-Mossad contractors sought to eliminate Alfred and prevent him from manifesting his future to bring Exopolitics, the science of relations among intelligence civilizations in the multiverse, to the light of day.

For his mother Juanita, that Alfred's May 24 birthday fell on the Feast Day of Our Lady Help of Christians cemented in her mind that Alfred had a higher, otherworldly mission to fulfill in his life. Her deep conviction this was true was vital in keeping Alfred alive when his mother Juanita was his only line of defense against these attacks.

Napoleon, Pope Pius VII, and "May 24 the Feast Day of Our Lady Help of Christians"

On researching the Catholic Encyclopedia, Alfred learned "May 24 the Feast Day of Our Lady Help of Christians" celebrates the return of Pope Pius VII to Rome on May 24, 1814, following Napoleon's arresting Pope Pius VII at Savona on July 15, 1808. Pope Pius VII fled Rome again when Napoleon left Elba and returned to Paris, and finally settled back in Rome on September 15, 1815 after the defeat of Napoleon at Waterloo.[48]

Ironically, May 24 the Feast Day of Our Lady Help of Christians, Alfred's birthday, seems to have been about realpolitik and power politics between Napoleon and the Papacy, both of which were power matrix forces of their day. Some authors claim that the French Revolution and Napoleon, like the later Bolshevik Revolutions and the Nazi movement, were financed by and instruments for the advancement of a world agenda led by Illuminati City of London bloodline bankers. If this analysis is true, Alfred's birthdate on May 24, the Feast Day of Our Lady Help of Christians, sets out a priority agenda in his life once again.

Alfred's birthday May 24 as the Feast Day of Our Lady Help of Christians may be a portal foretelling dominant missions that Alfred must perform without enmeshing himself in the duality of Napoleon vs. Papacy that was all about geopolitical power. Alfred's missions include the exposure of the covert, destructive roles of the Satanic/Illuminati, whose networks include the Pope and the Vatican, British Crown and City of London bloodline bankers on our planet, with cameo roles for the Skull & Bones, CIA and the Rockefeller networks.

The Satanic/Illuminati are nasty planetary remnant artifacts of the Anunnaki extraterrestrial intervention on our planet 280,000 years ago. Their 20th & 21st century social inventions include the promotion of Vladimir Lenin, the Bolsheviks, and the genocidal propagation of the meme "Communism" in Russia; World War I and its genocidal atrocities; the propagation of genocidal Communism in China under Mao Zedong, a Yale Skull & Bones, Illuminati asset; the promotion of Adolph Hitler & the Nazis; genocidal World War II; the global drug trade ("DOPE INC") and its false flag events such as the Vietnam War and the takedown of Mexico; subversion of world democracy; covert takedown of the United States through false flag operations of the assassinations of John F. Kennedy, Rev. Martin Luther King, Jr., Robert F. Kennedy, Malcolm X, and September 11, 2001; destruction of the DNA of humans and all living things through ionizing radiation from atmospheric nuclear weapons testing; depleted uranium (DU) weapons, and nuclear power plants; and, as of this writing, attempts to start World War III, and impose a New World Order (NWO) police state worldwide.[49]

Alfred's birth certificate

Like his birthdate on May 24 the Feast Day of Our Lady Help of Christians, Alfred's birth certificate reveals synchronicities about his life mission and future tasks. With synchronistic foreshadowing, the Acting Director of the Bureau of Vital Statistics signed the Certified Copy of Alfred's Birth Certificate on September 11, 1947. Public deconstructing of the false flag operation of September 11, 2001

("9/11") whose intent was to trigger World War III and impose a global police state will be a focus of Alfred's incarnation mission.

That focus will extend in his present incarnation to Alfred's participation in public deconstruction, and in some cases prosecution and judgment (including as a War Crimes Judge) of key principals behind many 20th and 21st Century false flag operations, including, as of this writing, the assassination of John F. Kennedy (November 22, 1963); 9/11 (September 11, 2001); Hurricane Katrina (August 28, 2005); the BP Gulf Oil spill (April 20, 2010); and the Fukushima HAARP Radiation false flag operation (March 11, 2011).[50]

One of the deeper synchronistic events of Alfred's life was to participate as a Judge on the Kuala Lumpur War Crimes Tribunal in its Judgment against former U.S. President George W. Bush and former U.K. Prime Minister Tony Blair for crimes against peace in their illegal March 19, 2003 invasion of Iraq. The Tribunal's Judgment was delivered on November 22, 2011, the 48th anniversary of the assassination of U.S. President John F. Kennedy in Dealey Plaza, Dallas, Texas. George H.W. Bush, then a covert CIA operative, served as a field coordinator for the assassination and was photographed in Dealey Plaza standing by the Texas School Book Depository.[51] On the 48th anniversary, the Tribunal delivered a Judgment (partially written by Alfred) condemning George W. Bush, Bush Sr.'s son was a Nuremberg-level war criminal for launching an illegal genocidal war using fraud and deceit.[52]

Little wonder it is that, with a birth venue of the Pensacola Naval Air Base (Cradle of naval air power) and a birth date of May 24 (Our Lady Help of Christians), Alfred would have an adult mission so focused on de-constructing the permanent war economy on Earth.

Alfred's birth on a U.S. Naval Air Station in the midst of World War II prepared his aura well for a life subjected to secret U.S. government time-travel surveillance[53] while assisting in the liberation of planet Earth and humanity from the grip of a 280,000 years old exploitative, self-perpetuating, multi-dimensional, hierarchy of negative spiritual entities, predatory extraterrestrials, and corrupt, service-to-self human power elites.

Alfred as an early Indigo soul

At a multi-dimensional level, World War II (1939-1945), like World War I (1914-1918), was the Earthly roll-out of an inter-dimensional and extraterrestrial agenda for the attempted takeover of Earth, Mars, our moons and our contiguous planets by predatory spiritual entities and extraterrestrial civilizations. Negative dimensional forces and a corrupt elite seek the imposition on Earth of a dysfunctional new world order of a global police state, and a techno-servant class in an elite theme park.

Together with a cadre of dedicated souls, Alfred incarnated in to help prevent this global police state, and with the assistance of ethical extraterrestrial and interdimensional Spiritual forces, return Earth to its rightful place in the Source-oriented legions of human life-bearing planets.

On May 24, 1942, Alfred's soul and body began the birth process in his mother Juanita's womb. With physical birth, Alfred's soul entered life on Earth as an early Indigo soul, part of a multiverse army of extraterrestrial Walk-ins, other early Indigos, Indigos, Crystal children, extraterrestrials left on Earth as infants, and Extraterrestrial hybrids that form the new humanity helping birthing Earth into its non-catastrophic, positive timeline – the Fifth World of Native American prophecy. And in May 2013 Alfred would discover from the National Geographic GENO 2.0 project that he in fact had Native American DNA that crossed land bridge from Siberia into North and South America 23,000 years ago.[54]

Exopolitics, Extraterrestrials and the Positive Timeline

Alfred's lifespan as of this writing is longer than that of the U.S. Military-Industrial Empire, created in 1945 by the same multi-generational Satanic Illuminati royal and banking bloodline families that earlier created Bolshevism/Communism and its dialectical opposite Fascism as a mechanism for profit taking in the matrix of an artificial war economy.[55]

Alfred chose to begin his life in this human incarnation on a U.S. Naval Air Station in the midst of World War II next to the undersea bases of an advanced extraterrestrial civilization in the Gulf of Mexico, off of Pensacola, Florida for a multiplicity of strategic life reasons, all closely evaluated in the inter-life period Alfred enjoyed between lives in the Spiritual dimensions.

For those wanting to confirm the scientific probability of re-incarnation of human consciousness or souls in successive human bodily life, the books of Canadian Dr. Ian Stevenson, MD (1918-2007), formerly Professor at the University of Virginia Medical School are a good start, especially his Cases of the Reincarnation Type series.[56]

The drama of the World War II Naval Air Station time-space setting of Alfred's birth is a fitting entry portal for his specific human soul whose priority life purposes will come to include reinforcing humanity's experience of a positive timeline in the time space hologram we collectively inhabit.

Among Alfred's contributions in his present lifetime will be the founding and propagation of "Exopolitics", the science of relations among intelligent civilizations in the multiverse. Exopolitics in turn can accelerate individual, cultural, institutional, and collective interface between Earthling humans and other intelligent civilizations in the multiverse. Exopolitics can provide a stable platform for understanding and interfacing from our time-space dimension to contiguous dimensions of the multiverse we inhabit.

Likewise, among Alfred's contributions as of this writing are the first scientific mapping of the Omniverse, or the sum totality of all of the universes of the Multiverse plus the intelligent civilization of souls, spiritual beings and Source (God) in the Spiritual Dimensions.

May 24, the "Holy Spirit" and the Dimensional Ecology

Among the indicators of Alfred's life priorities as a revelator of the dimensional ecology to his fellows in the time-space dimension are: (1)

131

his birthdate on May 24 the Feast Day of Our Lady Help of Christians, and (2) his 1973 Holy Spirit - "Thou art Peter and upon this Rock I will found my Church" experiences, even if that 1973 experience was a manipulatory extraterrestrial telepathic masquerade.

Alfred's priority life mission is to reveal more of the dimensional ecology of the multiverse. The dimensional ecology hypothesis states: "We earthlings live in a dimensional ecology of intelligent life that encompasses extraterrestrials in parallel dimensions and universes, souls in the after-life dimensions, spiritual beings in the spiritual dimensions and Source within a multiverse, or all that is."[57]

In some real way, the message of the "Holy Spirit", however genuine or manipulative, empowers Alfred to act as though his being and his works can be a figurative foundation for the emergence of dimensional consciousness that permanently takes Earth into a new and positive era. In being a foundation, then Alfred can act as one who helps those in Unity consciousness ("We are all One") – "Christ consciousness" - rather than duality consciousness ("I win you lose").

Primogeniture in the Webre family and Havana Chisholm clan

Within his genetic family, Alfred's birth at Pensacola Naval Air Station automatically gave him primogeniture ("first-born") status in his immediate Webre family that would eventually grew to nine siblings, as well as in the Havana Chisholm clan.

Alfred was Ali and Juanita's first of nine children, eight sons and a daughter (the youngest child). In Alfred's immediate Webre family, after him would be born Richard Chadbourne Webre (1945-81); Philip Chisholm Webre (1948); John Chisholm Webre (1952); Louis LeBourgeois Webre (1957); Joseph LeBourgeois Webre (1960-94); J. Septime Webre (1961); Charles Everett Webre (1963) and Jane Marie Noemie Webre (1964), all with names resounding in the Webre-Chisholm family tree.

Alfred's birth also made him first born in the Havana Chisholm clan, Juanita's family based in Havana, Cuba. Juanita was the seventh of

nine Chisholms and was the first to have a child (Alfred) among Al-
fred's Chisholm aunts and uncles. Primogeniture was to serve Alfred
well during World War II. Ali shipped out from Pensacola Air Base to
various theaters of war soon after Alfred's birth. Juanita and Alfred
traveled back to the Chisholm home in Vedado, Havana, Cuba, filled
with maiden aunts delighting to watch over him.

In mid-1978 Alfred was forging a new career as a journalist. Eager to move on from his family home at Brownsville, Texas, with the help of his mother Juanita, Alfred acquired a VW Westphalia Campmobile as a traveling studio and home, complete with kitchen.

Leaving Brownsville after Thanksgiving 1978, Alfred headed west toward the Sangre de Cristo Mountains in Arizona, intent on completing his new book. Within a few days journey Alfred came upon a Patagonia, Arizona state park deep within the mountains, there to celebrate an authentic Christmas, amidst the lowing Winnebagoes.

That Christmas Eve 1978, Alfred could take stock of his former plans to help trigger a transformation out of the "matrix" through the coupled modalities of proposed 1977 Carter White House Extraterrestrial Communication study of the extraterrestrial presence and the public revelation of the forces behind the John F. Kennedy assassination through the House Select Committee on Assassinations. The controllers ordering the MKULTRA/Cointelpro-style frequency weapons attacks on Alfred had destroyed any chance he would have a role in either the Carter White House Extraterrestrial Study, which would have been the first public scientific affirmation of the extraterrestrial presence, or in the Congressional HSCA investigation of the John F. Kennedy Assassination.

Historically, it turned out that no official public study or disclosure of the extraterrestrial presence took place under the direction of the Jimmy Carter White House and the House Select Committee on Assassinations was infiltrated and derailed to a false conclusion that no agency of the U.S. government was involved in the John F. Kennedy assassination, when the opposite was the truth.[58] The controller force that attacked Alfred with frequency weapons also succeeded in preventing the intended outcomes in both the Carter White House and the U.S. Congress.

Alfred was to conclude that an international war crimes racketeering organization had been the prime movers behind the assassination of John F. Kennedy.[59] Richard E. Sprague, a deep ally of Rep. Henry B. Gonzalez and the first staff director of the HCSA committee, called his version of the perpetrators of the Kennedy assassination the "Power Control Group (PCG)". While he was still at Stanford Research Institute, Alfred would get panicked telephone calls from Gail Beagle, Rep. Henry B. Gonzalez, stating that the FBI was trying to intimidate Rep. Gonzalez and shut down the investigation. Gonzalez ally, Richard E. Sprague documented in detail how the U.S. Central Intelligence Agency (CIA), the agency coordinating the false flag operation of the Kennedy assassination, infiltrated and neutralized the House Select Committee on Assassinations.[60]

Alfred's VW Westphalia Campmobile was well equipped for a 1978 traveling journalist's studio (in the pre-digital era), with typewriter, tape recorder, cameras, portable television, stereo and earphones. Parked in the Sangre de Cristo Mountains that Christmas Eve 1978, Alfred started to document his experiences in humorous and pun-filled poetic text. The manuscript was called "EyE G*D on Urth", and Alfred felt joy at the literary scope of what was becoming epic lyric prose. Years later it would be reported to Alfred that one literary agent in England – more details later - had compared his unpublished manuscript to the works of James Joyce.

Each night after writing Alfred stood under the stars, listening to music on his headphones, marveling at the breadth of creation. Beneath starry Arizona skies, Alfred prayed and called out to angelic and ethical Extraterrestrial forces to help liberate

Earth from its occupation by a tyrannical global political order, led by a corrupt elite and U.S. military-intelligence in league with predatory extraterrestrials and a diabolical interdimensional force. That is how Alfred saw Earth's plight in that moment. One night with all his heart and understanding Alfred sent out a telepathic prayer, "Calling all Angels" in creation to come to Earth and save it.

"EyE G*D on Urth" was built around a self-realization Alfred had during the long months of Cointelpro attack by the U.S. military and intelligence agencies against him. He realized that his soul was a holographic fragment of the Creator Source of the multi-verse, or all that is. Alfred's realization, "I am a holographic fragment of G*d as are all humans with souls" kept him alive and well during a Cointelpro campaign against Alfred whose purpose was to destroy him. *"EyE G*D on Urth"* was a message to all readers that we humans, literally and scientifically, are "G*d" in the sense that each fragment of the G*d hologram contains the entire hologram – Creator Source G*d. Our soul power is sufficient to defeat an takeover of our planet by a diabolical interdimensional and extraterrestrial predatory alliance working through a corrupt, power elite.

Soon Alfred finished about a third of the manuscript, and he left the mountain lair. Pope John Paul II, he learned, was about to make his first trip to Mexico. Alfred secured journalist credentials on the basis of his published work and headed for a Papal enclave close on the twin volcanoes of Popocatépetl and Iztaccihuatl (Sleeping Woman") and the town of Cholula, built near one of the largest pyramids in the world. Cholula was the ancient seat of the Quetzalcoatl, the Plumed Serpent, the God-Man returned.

SCENE 2

QUETZALCOATL

February 1979
Alfred's VW Westphalia Campmobile
Location: A pumpkin field
Between Popocatépetl & Iztaccihuatl
and the Pyramid of Quetzalcoatl, Cholula, Mexico

Now a journalist, Alfred traveled on his mobile studio to Mexico City where Jody Powell, Carter's Press Secretary, personally granted him White House press credentials to cover Jimmy Carter's Mexican visit. Alfred would also cover the French President Valéry Giscard d'Estaing's Mexican visit, all the while attending, as a journalist, a closed six weeks spiritual enclave with Pope John Paul II at Puebla, Mexico. "J2P2", as the assembled press called the Pope after the Star Wars robot, was intent on stamping out Liberation theology and the identification of Catholic ministry with political and social transformation.

Alfred arrived at a pumpkin field close by Puebla and Cholula, Mexico in January 1979 after doing multi-dimensional battle with U.S. Government military and intelligence agencies as director of the proposed Jimmy Carter White House Extraterrestrial Communication Study.

Alfred's book "*EyE G*D on Urth*" was largely written in this pumpkin field in 1979 in Alfred's traveling studio, the "Lord-Mobile". On one side of the pumpkin field lay the Great Pyramid of Cholula, dedicated to Quetzalcoatl, the plumed serpent, God-Man. On the other side of the pumpkin field lay the twin volcano-spirits, "Popocatépetl" (the Smoking Mountain) and "Iztaccíhuatl" (Sleeping Woman).

By day, Alfred was a Vatican-credentialed journalist covering Pope John Paul II's January-February 1979 Latin American Bishop's conference to deconstruct Liberation Theology. Alfred sported 1978 shoulder-length hair, long beard and mustache and looked the stereotypical image of Jesus or Rasputin. Alfred had occasion to be in a small huddle with the new celebrity Pope, "J2P2". Up close and personal, "J2P2" was a regular guy, smiling, jocular, kidding around. [If the testimony of J2P2's engaging in ritual child sacrifice in an underground chamber 40 meters from the Vatican are correct, how easily is the media – including a 1978 Alfred - fooled by appearances.

On the other side of Puebla at a Counter-Conference held by proponents of Liberation Theology the stakes were high. Chunky like a boxer, Archbishop Oscar Romero of El Salvador led the Puebla Counter-Conference. In 1980, Romero would be assassinated allegedly by Contras, most probably by the CIA/Vatican because he championed the poor. Honest journalism covers the world of polarities to expose the truth, and Alfred alternated between the Vatican Conference and the Counter-Conference as a gateway into the deeper currents of the reality occurring at Puebla.

As White House-credentialed journalist, Alfred attended briefings in Mexico City by then White House press secretary Jody Powell, covering U.S. President Jimmy Carter's 1979 visit to Mexico's President Lopez Portillo (whose wife was deeply involved in extraterrestrial life and UFOs).

During the Carter visit, Alfred took part in Leonard Bernstein's stirring rendition of Beethoven's Fifth Symphony ("Fate") at Mexico City's Opera House. A member of the audience stood to shout: *"Viva Mexico, La Mujer Dormida Debe Dar a Luz!"* The phrase "Long Live Mexico! Sleeping Woman will give birth!" referred to "Iztaccíhuatl", the volcano bookend at Alfred's pumpkin field, giving birth to a New Era of universal consciousness. The phrase also referred to a current book entitled "La Mujer Dormida Debe Dar a Luz", alluding to Mexico's role in a coming era of consciousness transformation.[61]

As Popocatépetl and Iztaccíhuatl are singularities, interdimensional portals for the entry into Earth's time-space dimension or density of interdimensional UFO craft of dimensional civilizations, it is literally true that Sleeping Woman will give birth, to new consciousness arriving in the form of interdimensional intelligence from the dimensional ecology surrounding Earth and the concurrent awakening of interdimensional intelligence in humanity.

As a Mexican Presidential-credentialed journalist covering French President Valéry Marie René Georges Giscard d'Estaing's 1979 visit to meet Lopez Portillo, Alfred watched Mexican waiters pour water on Giscard d'Estaing during the final joint press conference to dampen his perceived French arrogance. Alfred took the press bus to the airport to catch Giscard d'Estaing departure ceremony back to France. At the end of the ceremony, Mexican secret service surrounded Alfred on the airport tarmac. Alfred reached inside his suit-jacket pocket and took out a folded piece of white paper. That was enough of an official move to make the Mexican secret service scatter.

As the media boarded the press bus back to the Mexican Presidential Palace, the Mexican press attaché said to Alfred: *"Misión completa!"* "Mission Accomplished!" In that singular moment Alfred "saw" that the Mexican secret service, like the U.S. military and intelligence agencies months earlier in 1978, had no earthly idea of the Divine source that was motivating Alfred's work.

Alfred thought the Mexican secret service perceived him to

be some sort of intelligence correspondent stringer covering their President's 1979 meetings with visiting NATO heads of State like France and the USA for some agency back in the USA. In later years, Alfred would consider that perhaps the Mexican secret service was tipped off by CIA time travel surveillance teams to carry out Cointelpro on Alfred as part of ongoing CIA time travel surveillance because of CIA 1971 time travel information about Alfred's Exopolitical activities in 2000 and subsequent years.

At the time, in 1978, Alfred was "covering" his own dynamic interaction with a living, communicating multi-verse every night in the pumpkin field between Quetzalcoatl's Pyramid and the Sleeping Woman volcano spirit as Alfred wrote "EyE G*D on Urth".

"The pen is mightier that the sword" was Alfred's working motto. He knew from long years of conspiracy research of the central role of the Vatican in sustaining the demonic rule and corrupt elite of Earth. It was on learning that Pope John Paul II was making his first visit to Mexico to a six weeks conference to attempt an evisceration of Liberation Theology that Alfred took the "LordMobile" across the border into Mexico just south of the Sangre de Cristo Mountains on his way to Puebla and J2P2's conference, to cover the conference as a journalist and to continue writing EyE G*D on Urth, the Holy Spirit's Peter spiritually confronting the Vatican's Peter, who ran covert pedophile networks, ritual sacrifices of children, illicit banks, and continued to brainwash mankind with false doctrines about the nature of the afterlife and Source.[62]

Insights poured out of Alfred into "EyE G*D on Urth" every night and every morning in the pumpkin field between "Popocatépetl" and "Iztaccíhuatl" and the Great Cholula Pyramid of Quetzalcoatl before the daily press briefings at the J2P2 Conference in nearby Puebla.

One morning as Alfred was writing "EyE G*D on Urth" in the pumpkin field, he was admitted to a telepathic conversation between an entity that identified itself as the "Earth" and another that identified itself as the "Moon". The "Earth" entity said, "Alfred we are going to show you how we make an Earthquake." At that moment, the ground under the LordMobile shook with a regional earthquake that was officially measured as occurring in the area of Cholula, Puebla, and the "Popocatépetl" and "Iztac-cíhuatl". "What was the intelligence that spoke to me telepathical-ly?" thought Alfred. "Was it the secret extraterrestrial mind control platform that resides in the Moon as artificial satellite? Was it Gaia, the living Earth who spoke to me? Was it an interdimen-sional source? Was it extraterrestrial? Was it the secret Saturn-Moon-as-artificial-satellite Matrix, communicating to him? Was it secret government artificial telepathy? Was it Alfred's own precog-nition? What source created the Earthquake, which as real? Was it an artificial earthquake, or was it an authentic secret demonstra-tion of living power by the Urth to Eye?"

Alfred the author of "EyE G*D on Urth" took this telepathic communication about the earthquake as a real demonstration of some benevolent, ethical, supra-natural power behind his enterprise and determined to complete his written work.

Of course, there are many other possibilities than ethical, supra-natural power interacting with Alfred by voice and simultaneous earthquake. At the human level, that telepathic communication could have been voice to skull technology, and an earthquake created through seismic warfare via HAARP or satellite or other directed energy weapon.

At the crypto-terrestrial and extraterrestrial level, the voice and simultaneous earthquake could have been sourced from a multiplicity of any one of a number of causes: Was it the false matrix of the Saturn-Moon complex of extraterrestrial bases of the giant extraterrestrials in concert with the crypto-terrestrial giants, Coneheads and even Ancient Vampire Illuminati on Earth as part of their game plan? Or was it the Angelic and Celestial planetary caretakers under a restored Planetary Prince after the termination of the Lucifer Rebellion? Alfred opted with the latter, as it had a sacred and not manipulatory and fearful note and tone.

One night in the pumpkin field Alfred felt an inner signal that it was time to return from Mexico to United States of America with his written memoirs and seek a publisher. That is what authors did in those days before the World Wide Web, the Internet and Self-Publishing. Alfred had every intention of returning to his newfound sacred site by the Great Pyramid Of Quetzalcoatl. Alfred had accepted a university teaching position as a Futurist at the nearby Universidad de La Americas in Puebla for the fall 1979 academic year. His plan was to return to the USA, secure the publication of *"EyE G*D on Urth"*, and return to Puebla in the fall. What a logical plan for Alfred to arrive at in his working hypotheses, goals, perceptions of global information and belief systems and the resources at hand, all packed into the compact space of a VW Westphalia and a lifestyle where about $250.00 was a God send.

Los Angeles and the 1979 Academy Awards

Alfred crossed the border at Tijuana/San Diego at about 6 AM on April 9, 1979. By that evening, ever the reporter with a tape recorder in hand, he was at the Dorothy Chandler Pavilion in Los Angeles covering the aftermath of the 51st Academy Awards, hosted by Johnny Carson. One thing led to another and Alfred was soon at Carpinteria, California writing a screenplay on the life of Edgar Cayce for two producers from Paramount Pictures. Alfred took the opportunity because of the synchronicity that he had been the keynote speaker at a 1977 celebration of Edgar Cayce's birth at St. John the Divine Cathedral in New York City, chosen because of his 1974 book *"The Age of Cataclysm"* integrating earth sciences and the Edgar Cayce Earth Changes prophecies.

Meanwhile, Alfred's lifetime friend from Yale undergraduate days and now Rashneesh Sanyasin Shudananda introduced Alfred to a man claiming to be the cousin of war criminal and "Alfred" media meme artist Henry Alfred Kissinger. This man in turn offered to take a copy of *"EyE G*D on Urth"* to a literary agent in the United Kingdom. The "literary agent" turned out to be a part of a secret society known as the Cambridge Apostles at the University of Cambridge and art adviser to Queen Elizabeth II. The literary agent, named Sir Anthony Blunt, was stripped of his honours after he was exposed as a former Soviet spy one of the "Cambridge Five" by Margaret Thatcher in the House of Commons on November 15, 1979.[63]

Anthony Blunt's opinion of "*EyE G*D on Urth*", Alfred was told, was "it reminded him the genius of James Joyce, and it needed a little editing." That is as far as "*EyE G*D on Urth*" got to see publication as a trade book. To this day Alfred does not know what Anthony Blunt did with his copy of "*EyE G*D on Urth*", the only extant copy of the manuscript. Alfred burned his last remaining copy of "*EyE G*D on Urth*" in 1984 in a moment in the back yard of his psychotherapist friend's Anna Allred's house in Little Rock, Arkansas, where Anna would bump into Bill Clinton jogging nearby her home and Alfred briefly taught journalism at the University of Arkansas. Alfred thought destroying the manuscript would leave behind him the pain of the CIA's social disruption, Cointelpro war against him. Perhaps one day the remaining manuscript will surface?

SCENE 3

HOLLYWOOD & PEACE MOVEMENT

August 1982
Palais des Nations
Avenue de la Paix 14 1211
Genève 10, Switzerland

Since leaving the pumpkin field at the pyramid of Quetzalcoatl and arriving at the 1979 Academy Awards banquet, Alfred was to arrive at The Point, Bancroft, Ontario, Canada in October 1982 by way of Australia, West Hollywood, San Francisco, New York, Vienna, Amsterdam, Geneva, and Washington, DC.

Alfred spent his May 24, 1980 birthday in a courtroom in Melbourne, Australia, helping Anna Swadling (whom he would soon wed as his second wife, in Auckland, New Zealand) rescue her kidnapped son. Synchronistically, Queen Elizabeth Windsor, Head of State of Australia, with full escort, drove in front of the courthouse while Alfred sat upstairs in the courtroom waiting room.[64]

Anna's father, it turned out, was high-ranking in Australia's government aviation administration with connections to ASIO, Australia's CIA. Anna's father's cryptic parting comments to

Alfred in Melbourne were, "666! That's about the size of it." Clearly, ASIO/CIA was trying to project "666" onto Alfred while Alfred was exposing the UK Monarchy as in the service of "666", the Antichrist.

Anna's estranged husband had kidnapped her child while Anna and Alfred were on a first date in Los Angeles in the Hollywood Hills. Anna had been deported from the United States by US Immigration authorities that camped outside her hillside home on Ivar Avenue until Alfred left for work one morning in late 1979 after Alfred had appeared on the Los Angeles PBS TV station as part of a panel on nuclear disarmament.

At Anna's Immigration hearing, Alfred denounced Anna's arrest as illegal, stated Anna was his fiancé, and indicated to surprised Immigration agents that he would travel to Australia with her to marry so Anna could re-enter the U.S. once she had re-covered her kidnapped son. Clearly Anna had been targeted because of Alfred's PBS TV appearance.

Anna had been a reader of the Urantia Book[65] in Melbourne, and during the six months wait for the custody proceeding in Melbourne, Alfred carefully, from back to front, read the Urantia Book, a 2097 page text interdimensionally reportedly "channeled" over the period 1925-42 and published in 1955. The text described what Alfred perceived as the basics of Exopolitics, describing a highly populated and organized multiverse and Omniverse, starting with dimensionally interactive parallel central and super universes, and local universes.

The Urantia Book text included a history of Earth ("Urth" – "Urantia") as a life-bearing planet, even stating the purported planetary registry number of Earth among the registry of life-bearing planets (which reportedly ends in "666"). Finally, the text included a detailed history of the life of Jesus of Nazareth. The text described Jesus as a Paradise Son of God who incarnated as part of a complex Universe governance plan to end a rebellion in this quadrant of the Universe by governance officials including "Lucifer". The Urantia Book had been presented to Alfred once before, during a 3 hour talk show on Princeton, NJ. This interlude in Melbourne allowed Alfred to evaluate the text as one element of a future conceptual foundation for the development of the field of Exopolitics, the science of relations among intelligent civilizations in the multiverse.[66]

Anna was unable to obtain custody of her son. Alfred and Anna were married in Auckland, New Zealand and headed back to Los Angeles, via Vancouver, BC where Anna would wait while an immigration visa was granted. Like Teresa, Anna found herself unable to handle the stress of losing custody of her son and handling the constant Cointelpro attacks that marriage with Alfred entailed. While they lived in Melbourne, for example, Anna found a telescopic rifle left on her desk at the legal office at which she worked. Soon after the couple returned to Los Angeles, they separated amicably. Alfred moved into Mi Casa on Havenhurst between Sunset and Fountain, taking what was reportedly Cary Grant's former duplex in the National Register of Historic Buildings complex with Linda Thistle, a rebirther therapist friend.

A reader of Alfred's book *"The Age of Cataclysm"* nominated him to California Governor Jerry Brown's Governor's Emergency Task Force on Earthquake Preparedness.[67] Alfred had the satisfaction of attending a Governor's committee meeting at the campus of Stanford Research Institute, where just two years earlier he had been targeted by SRI/CIA surveillance and functionally forced to resign.

Alfred decided to go "Hollywood" in his own way. He breakfasted at Schwab's drugstore just around the corner on Sunset, went to Hollywood parties. Alfred developed film properties, including "Chappie" a film about the Tuskegee African American World War II airmen, centered on "Chappie" James, the first black 4-star general, born in Pensacola, Florida. The day after the local U.S. Air Force office gave Alfred a formal letter promising full support with aircraft and logistics a helicopter flew 10 feet over his balcony at Mi Casa. For a while William Morris, the then super agency, agreed to represent Alfred's documentary on

Canadian Futurist television pioneer Marshal McLuhan for a PBS production and then one day inexplicably returned all of the materials, much to the dismay of the McLuhan family in Canada who somehow thought Alfred was not doing anything when in fact it was William Morris Agency who was sitting on the Marshal McLuhan file, probably because Alfred was the client.

More Cointelpro against Alfred, although once Alfred went into the William Morris office in New York on his way back from a business trip to the Vatican on a record deal on J2P2's live speeches, and the Illuminati handlers sat a very star-struck pop star obviously instructed to sit next to Alfred in the lobby as Alfred sat waiting for a meeting to discuss J2P2 records (nothing came of the meeting BTW).

It was through a twist of fate that Alfred came to represent J2P2, Pope John Paul II, in the recording industry. Through Anna, a Hollywood record company engaged Alfred as its diplomatic counsel in negotiating the rights to sell records of the Pope's speeches. Alfred flew to the Vatican, which opened its business office on the day of Saints Peter and Paul (an official holiday) to negotiate the contract. A bomb had gone off in the Vatican that morning before the business meeting. Alfred spent the rest of the day inside St. Peter's Basilica, in deep meditation. Alfred called on G*d/Source to cleanse this Vatican global network of child genocide, banking fraud, and mind control in whose headquarters he found himself. Like all duality deals around Alfred, this record deal fell apart.

Back in Hollywood the organizers of Peacequake, a peace concert planned for Sunday and Monday May 30 & 31, 1982 in San Francisco Civic Center Plaza in support of the UN 2nd Special Session of Disarmament in June 1982, invited Alfred to come to San Francisco and help organize the event. Feeling the pull of peace activism, Alfred decided to leave behind the slice of the military-religion-entertainment complex he was experiencing in Los Angeles. Alfred moved into the Haight-Ashbury, sleeping on a fellow organizer's couch, and jumped into the Bay Area counter-culture.

The Monday May 24, 1982 San Francisco Board of Supervisors meeting minutes show a resolution authorizing the closing of downtown streets for "Peacequake '82":

> *"Supervisor Nelder requested that a letter be sent to the General Manager of the Recreation and Park Department, requesting the following information: 1) Whether a large group was refused permission to use Kezar Stadium for a rally because of faulty electricity, inoperable restrooms and dangerous stands at that facility; 2) Whether high school teams play there and what is done to protect them and their fans; 3) Why the department refused to allow Peacequake '82 to use the Polo Field as an alternative to Kezar Stadium; 4) What, in the opinion of the department, would be necessary to permit large groups to use Kezar Stadium or the Polo Field for gatherings; and 5) What was the day of the week, the date and place in Golden Gate Park of the last large group rally or gathering, and the difference between that group and Peacequake '82?"*

> *"Monday, May 24, 1982 Absent: Supervisor Silver - i. [Street Closings] Resolution authorizing temporary closing of portions of various streets at various hours. File 42-82-31, Resolution No. 360-82 (Fulton Street, between Larkin and Hyde Streets from 6:00 a.m. to 6:00 p.m. May 29, 1982 and from 10:00 a.m. to 6:00 p.m., May 30-31, 1982; Polk Street between McAllister and Grove Streets; and Larkin Street between McAllister and Grove Streets, 10:00 a.m. to 6:00 p.m., May 30 and 31, 1982; with barricades to be removed at 6:00 p.m., for "Peacequake "82".[68]*

Author Gore Vidal spoke at Peacequake as San Francisco Police Department squad cars, their driver doors open, parked in tandem along the edge of San Francisco Civic Center Plaza, giving a extraordinary neo-Fascist tint to the scenario. The show had gone on because Alfred and key organizers had rushed at the last minute to Apple co-founder Steve Wozniak's home on the Peninsula to collect a $5000 check Steve had pledged to cover expenses, the other key contributors being Northern California marijuana farmers.

Even then President Ronald Reagan chimed in with his opinion on Peacequake and other demonstrations, saying he "understood" why people are protesting.

From Peacequake, Alfred traveled down to the Rose Bowl in Pasadena, where a peace demonstration was held, featuring another May 24 Gemini, Bob Dylan who came hesitantly onto the stage. In the stands, Alfred found himself surrounded by U.S. Marine guards. Why were they there? While in San Francisco, Alfred secured credentials from "The Guardian", a Bay Area underground newspaper, to be its UN correspondent at the 2nd Special Session on Disarmament. Soon after the Rose Bowl event, Alfred flew to New York, arriving the day of a massive demonstration in Central Park. As Alfred crossed Central Park, a group of at least 50 New York policemen swarmed around him. Why was he being swarmed and what agency was directing the swarming? Was this ongoing campaign of social disruption related to the 1971 CIA's time travel pre-identification of Alfred's book "Exopolitics" and his future activities?

While a Wall Street lawyer at Cleary Gottlieb, Alfred had been at the United Nations on international legal matters and knew his way around the organization. He obtained UN press credentials as a journalist for "The Guardian", as well as UN credentials as a Non-Governmental Organization representative for Peacequake at the 2nd Special Session on Disarmament. Alfred was again wearing shoulder-length hair and a beard (his peace warrior stance). As he flashed his credentials at the New York City policewomen at the entrance to the UN, one gave out an audible gasp as if she recognized him from briefing photos. Some party inside law enforcement intelligence was clearly circulating photos of Alfred with false and alarming information on them.

Once inside the UN, Alfred set about to learn the hidden Exopolitical terrain. He sat in on the Security Council, watched U.S ambassador Jeane Kirkpatrick and the Israeli delegation gang-stalk each other, under electronic MKULTRA mind control.[69]

When the credentialed press was invited to the U.S. delegation for a briefing, they were doused with electromagnetic frequency weapons. Alfred was able to detect the frequency weapons attack because of his exposure to attacks at the Pentagon during the Carter White House Extraterrestrial Study at Stanford Research Institute.

Alfred found that another journalist, Saskia, who wrote for De Waarheid (The Truth), the Dutch Communist Party newspaper.[70] Saskia explained that the Dutch Communist Party was independent. Saskia (who was among the few journalists fully aware of all dimensions) and Alfred soon became news buddies.

Alfred became friendly with Thomas Banyacya, prophet and translator for the delegation of Hopi Elders who came to the House of Mica (United Nations) to forestall the Gourd of Ashes (Nuclear weapons) from falling on humanity as their prophecy foretold.[71] Thomas and Alfred hung out, laying on the grass to the side of St. John the Divine Cathedral in New York between sessions at the United Nations. One day, Alfred helped Hopi Elders whom he encountered lost on an upper floor of the UN Secretariat building find their scheduled meeting. Alfred felt as thought he played a small synchronistic part in fulfilling their prophesized Hopi mission.

On December 18, 1978, three and one-half years before the 2nd Special Session on Disarmament and a year after the sabotage of the 1977 Carter White House Extraterrestrial Study, the United Nations General Assembly had voted to approve decision 33/426, inviting U.N. Member States: "to take appropriate steps to coordinate on a national level scientific research and investigation into extraterrestrial life, including unidentified flying objects, and to inform the Secretary-General of the observations, research and evaluation of such activities."

The full text of United Nations General Assembly Decision 33/426 (1978) read:

[Reproduced from Resolutions and Decisions Adopted by the General Assembly during its 33rd Session (1978-1979): A/33/45 (GAOR, 33rd Session, Suppl. No. 45)]

33/426. Establishment of an agency or a department of the United Nations for undertaking, coordinating and disseminating the results of research into unidentified flying objects and related phenomena.

At its 87th plenary meeting, on 18 December 1978, the General Assembly, on the recommendation of the Special Political Committee adopted the following text as representing the consensus of the members of the Assembly:

1   "The General Assembly has taken note of the statements made, and draft resolutions submitted, by Grenada at the thirty-second and thirty-third sessions of the General Assembly regarding unidentified flying objects and related phenomena."

2   "The General Assembly invites interested Member States to take appropriate steps to coordinate on a national level scientific research and investigation into extraterrestrial life, including unidentified flying objects, and to inform the Secretary-General of the observations, research and evaluation of such activities."

3   "The General Assembly requests the Secretary-general to transmit the statements of the delegation of Grenada and the relevant documentation to the Committee on the Peaceful Uses of Outer Space, so that it may consider them at its session in 1979."

4   "The Committee on the Peaceful Uses of Outer Space will permit Grenada, upon its request, to present its views to the Committee at its session in 1979. The committee's deliberation will be included in its report which will be considered by the General Assembly at its thirty-fourth session."[72]

In the United Nations Press Room, Alfred saw a notice for UNISPACE, the UN Outer Space Conference, to be held in Vienna that summer of 1982.[73] He decided to cover UNISPACE as a journalist for a U.S. press agency. A friend, whose mother was Austrian ambassador to India, lent Alfred her Vienna apartment, just a few blocks from Conference at Schonbrunn Palace. At UNISPACE itself, UN delegates and media were, like delegates and press at the 2nd Special Session on Disarmament, terrestrial in outlook. Alfred spent time with the Cuban and Russian astronauts, marveling that there was a Cuban astronaut. He met Kurt Waldheim, former ET enthusiast, alleged Nazi war criminal and UN Secretary General, who on July 14, 1978 had met with researchers at the United Nations in preparation for a presentation on the Extraterrestrial/UFO presence to the UN Political Committee.

As was the United Nations in New York, Alfred found UNISPACE in Vienna was a fundamental news and policy vacuum. He decided to move on UN European headquarters located in the Palais de Nations in Geneva. UN Geneva, like UN Vienna and UN New York, turned out to be a real-news vacuum. Importantly, Alfred met future friends in the "peace in space" movement some of whom were also extraterrestrial contactees. He befriended three activists with whom he would collaborate on projects – futurist Barbara Marx Hubbard with whom Alfred would collaborate for a short while on developing the Good News Network, as well as space activist Dr. Carol Rosin who became a lifelong friend and ally, and "2001: A Space Odyssey" author Arthur C. Clarke, with whom Alfred would collaborate on the Institute for Cooperation in Space (ICIS).

Berne, Switzerland yielded an fascinating interview with the Soviet embassy on nuclear disarmament issues that leading newspapers in the U.S. carried, though Alfred almost missed he interview because a U.S. attaché kept him hung up on purpose over lunch.

Alfred boarded a train across Germany to Amsterdam to meet up with Saskia and De Waarheid. As Alfred emerged onto the passageway from his compartment on the train, he caught sight of an African-American U.S. serviceman in uniform who quickly ducked back into his own cabin when he saw Alfred had spied him. Once again, some party in the U.S. military was ordering up close and personal surveillance of Alfred. Why was this surveillance of Alfred undertaken, and who was ultimately ordering it? What was its connection to the 1971 CIA time travel surveillance of Alfred, and to the Department of Defense's crushing of the 1977 Carter White House Extraterrestrial Communication Study?

Barbara Marx Hubbard invited Alfred to take up residence at Greystone in Washington, DC that fall of 1982. While still in the Netherlands, Alfred wanted to cover the Women's peace movement that was then successfully blocking NATO cruise missile encampments. He and Saskia jointly interviewed the Dutch Minster of Defense on the subject of cruise missiles.

With Saskia's help, Alfred arranged to visit to interview women activists at a women's peace camp, set up outside a NATO military base. The night before the scheduled interview, the women's peace camp was overrun by thugs, the camp demolished, and women beat up. Unknown parties, probably within CIA and the U.S. military-intelligence complex, were running the same destructive methodology: Keep constant surveillance on Alfred (by whatever means including exotic time travel); intercept any progressive activity by Alfred with Cointelpro and social disruption so as to neutralize the activity (in this case the Women's peace camps) and Alfred's personal progress.

Alfred's first act back in New York was to lose his beard and shoulder- length hair at a hair salon in favor of a more techno-cratic look on his way to Reagan's Washington, DC. Once in Washington, DC in the early autumn of 1982, he met a core of dynamic people. Col. Jim Channon, one of the founders of the men who stare at goats introduced his circle to Arpanet, the early Internet.[74]

De Waarheid, the Dutch communist party newspaper, wanted him to be their Washington correspondent, filing stories from the White House and the Congress. Alfred shied away from a dualistic terrestrial confrontation that being a White House and Congressional correspondent for a communist newspaper in the Reagan administration might bring, especially since the paradigm of De Waarheid was terrestrial and would not allow him to cover the Exopolitical news.

Regardless, Alfred's instincts were right about Ronald Reagan's Washington, and he took the earliest opportunity in 1983 to move onto Pierre Trudeau's Canada and the Institute of Applied Metaphysics (IAM) in Coe Hill and Bancroft, Ontario.

SCENE 4

THE POINT

Oct 1982 – Jan 1991
THE POINT
Bancroft, Ontario
Canada K0L 1C0

Alfred asked himself a question: "What is it about me that I have attracted a 'Messiah' [Phillip H. Liss, PhD] and a 'God' [Pierre R. Levesque] into my life?" He concluded these were mighty karmic contracts and obligations he had incurred from prior lives for soul growth in his present life.

Each in their own respective ways, both Phillip Liss and Pierre Levesque taught Alfred deeply about mind control victims and how the Satanic/Illuminati national security state integrates MKULTRA and MONARCH mind control programmed assets into its statecraft and political control through the creation of cults that can infiltrate the social and political fabric.[75]

Alfred met "G*d", known in the flesh as Pierre R. Levesque, in 1982 when he and futurist Barbara Marx Hubbard were together invited to visit The Point, a 1500 acre estate that was part of a rural commune of the Institute of Applied Metaphysics (IAM) in northern Ontario. Alfred later came to represent plaintiff Pierre R. Levesque as his attorney and legal agent in the courts of Canada and the United States in the approximately 25 complex litigation cases (1987-91), prosecuting invasions of privacy against defendants Time Inc., HBO, David Rockefeller, George HW Bush, *et al.*

Alfred's book on this legal saga, "The Levesque Cases"[76], became something of a legend among circles of "Targeted Individuals" (those harassed by U.S. government directed energy weapons attacks). Alfred was able to collect a default judgment of $750 million against the Government of Ontario for its unlawful harassment of Pierre R. Levesque. This default judgment was later improperly over-turned by a Masonically-controlled Ontario judge. The preface to "The Levesque Cases" read:

"PIERRE R. LEVESQUE commenced his litigation in October 1987, seeking monetary damages and an apology for the 1984 broadcast by Time Warner Inc. cable television of a film that was a deliberate character assassination. In two years of intense court battles, he exposed a centrally coordinated criminal network, extending from the highest governmental offices in the United States and Canada to media conglomerates such as Time Warner, Inc., intent on destroying personal economic enterprise and personal liberties...

> *"It may come as no real surprise that the U.S. Central Intelligence Agency and Time Warner Inc. appear to be core organizations coordinating the network in courts, governments and media of Canada and the United States."*

> *"More surprising may be the evidential conclusion that high government officials such as the President of the Unites States, the Prime Minister of Canada, and the Attorney General for Ontario serve as willing executives of this clandestine network. The evidence suggests, moreover, that this international criminal network may look to a single individual for worldwide direction."*[77]

The original members of IAM reported they had been taken on board an extraterrestrial craft *en masse* in the early 1970s and given a planetary mission to usher in a new era around Pierre R. Leveque who was the Earthly incarnation of Deity. Alfred was familiar with this syndrome, having encountered it before with Prof. Phillip H. Liss, PhD, "The Messiah". Coincidently, Pierre R. Levesque was also trained as a psychologist.

At one level, by October 1982 IAM had established a functioning community, with a base in Ontario and education outposts in key capitals of the world. Alfred was then based in Washington, DC as a guest in futurist Barbara Marx Hubbard's family estate "Greystone", and had recently returned from covering peace activities in Western Europe for U.S. newspapers, his articles appearing in the Chicago Tribune and the Baltimore Sun.

Alfred found the constant surveillance in Washington, DC during the then Reagan Administration stifling. Once, as he was returning to his place of residence at "Greystone", the former residence of chief justice Charles Evan Hughes in Rock Creek Park, from a meeting with television people in Baltimore, Alfred was swarmed a half dozen by Reagan White House U.S. Secret Service cars that surrounded his car. Later, noting Ronald Reagan's personal close encounters with UFOs and interdimensional extraterrestrial civilizations, often wondered what Reagan's personal attitude toward him was or would have been as they shared many interests – (1) Extraterrestrials; (2) Hollywood; (3) Conspiracy theories; (4) Attempted recruitment by the FBI as an informant, which happened to Alfred one Saturday in 1979 at poolside in an apartment complex where he was staying with his law school buddy Jonathan Adler in Los Angeles and which Alfred flatly ejected from his reality.

Alfred gladly accepted IAM's invitation to stay in their rural Ontario community and thus remove himself from the overt fascism he experienced in Ronald Reagan's Washington. For several years before it imploded, IAM was Alfred's safe refuge from persecution by the CIA and the U.S. government

Cointelpro, obsessing over him because of what they had discovered about Alfred and his book *"Exopolitics: Politics, Government and Law in the Universe"* through secret time travel to 2005 and beyond.

Once at IAM, Alfred discovered the "Kingdom of Heaven and Earth," a governmental structure of the commune, with Pierre, the King of Heaven and Earth, and his consort Winifred Barton the Queen (with whom Alfred developed a life-long friendship). The Kingdom had its own currency, Privy Council, and monarchical regalia. Alfred was asked to write "The Throne Speech" or the platform for the Kingdom. Alfred did so, and found the task to be fun, like being at a role-playing recreational retreat.

In 1984 Pierre ("G*d") and Winifred ("Mrs. G*d") had a falling out, the commune divided into two camps – Pierre vs. Win. IAM imploded as a functioning organization. Alfred left the Ontario base of IAM and ultimately settled in New York City, where through his friend Neil Fabricant he became a consultant to the New York State Legislative Institute and through his friend Mary Houston a radio talk show host on WBAI-FM, with four live programs a week at one point while the station was still in its old headquarters across from Penn Station.[78]

Pierre contacted Alfred in New York City in 1987 and asked him to represent him in his legal battle against Cointelpro activities. As his attorney, Alfred was able to obtain a $750 million default judgment against the Government of Ontario for Pierre R. Leveque on grounds of invasion of privacy and malicious interference with business. That judgment was overturned in an illegal proceeding by the same covert Cointelpro network operating in the courts of Canada that had harassed Alfred in the United States since the proposed 1977 Carter White House Extraterrestrial Communication Study.[79]

One day in 1998, after Alfred and his soul mate Geri had moved to Vancouver, BC, Canada, Alfred received a call from Lenore, Pierre's second wife, telling him that Pierre had been found dead in his Ontario home at The Point. The circumstances appeared to Alfred to be false Matrix Cointelpro, lethally attacking Pierre with directed energy weapons.

EXCERPT FROM RECOVERY: Now that Pierre R. Levesque passed over into the next dimensions, Alfred felt he could write his truth. They battled, Pierre and Alfred, in this dimension we call human life. For some unknown karmic reason, only one of them - Alfred - made it out alive from their cosmic sumo-wrestling match. In his own eyes, Pierre was God. To Alfred, Pierre became the polar opposite, a Devil. Each became the other's nemesis. At first, Alfred was willing to consider Pierre as some unique manifestation of cosmic truth. In the end, Pierre showed Alfred that Pierre was indeed acting out as a manifestation of cosmic falsehood.

Alfred's abiding memories of his early times in the Canadian base camps of the "Kingdom of Heaven" were of reading the Urantia Book in the solitude of his room, as a compass against the disorientation of cultist thought-control. There were many levels to the thought control, not all with bad results. Alfred used the insights of the Urantia Book sacred text to discern and evaluate what was sourcing the rarified energies of the "Kingdom of Heaven" in Ontario, now his mystery.

Alfred soon fell into a mental push-me-pull-you. No, the Kingdom was a cult, and he should leave. Yes, the Kingdom was a universe administration base, and he should volunteer his energies.

On some days Alfred perceived the "Kingdom" as a model base for a universe plan on earth. The Kingdom's layout could function as a model for a natural base for an extraterrestrial planetary ruler, which the Urantia Book tells us, was a defined past stage in the development of inhabited planets such as Earth. On these moments, Alfred felt he could see the unfolding of evolutionary planetary development right before his eyes.

Then Alfred's perceptual matrix would flip. Alfred would come up against some invisible ceiling of thought and spirit in the cult of the

161

"Kingdom of Heaven", which after all had been established following a 1973 mass UFO abduction. Alfred saw their initiation rituals in royal regalia vapid and garish imitations of what deity should be. The cult members, by and large, were good-willed, gentle, people who otherwise befriended Alfred, became as robots, blindly wearing their cult-cap symbols. Foreswearing their critical faculties, the cult members pledged their allegiance to a giant, obscured lie, in Alfred's view.

Alfred was in a double bind. Alfred could not fully enter into the "Kingdom of Heaven", and by the same token Alfred could not entirely leave because to the south, in the United States, lay the CIA Cointelpro networks he had experienced at Stanford Research Institute and in the aftermath of the sabotage of the 1977 Carter White House Extraterrestrial Communication Study.

There was moreover, Alfred would discover, a deeper drama holding him in the "Kingdom of Heaven". The drama was, perhaps, the residue of prior life dramas, unfolding around the history of the distant past. The Kingdom's cultist leader who called himself God and Alfred had met before in spiritual battle on earth. A powerful psychic had informed Alfred that in an earlier galactic cycle, perhaps during Atlantean times, Pierre had treacherously led Alfred to his death while Alfred was on a positive planetary mission. Once again, Pierre and Alfred had come face to face in this lifetime upon this planet to complete a final chapter in their struggle in a battle of the invisible titans. The struggle between Pierre and Alfred turned out to be a struggle to the death.

Alfred can see clearly now how his years with Phillip Liss were preparation for the battle with Pierre Levesque, and how these years saved his life. Phillip Liss was a brilliant psychologist and scholar, with a breath-taking intellectual scope and a human of gentle good will. His diagnosed mental illness (schizophrenia) flawed his perceptions, but he brought a solid foundation of science to his work.

Pierre Levesque, by contrast, was a college dropout in psychology, who could bedazzle his cult members with pseudo-insight and who drew blanks on even the most fundamental areas of psychology. Pierre Levesque was also a master manipulator and psychological predator.

It was a source of endless fascination to him that Phillip Liss and Pierre Levesque had the same initials in their name "P.L.". Alfred always took that to be a meaningful synchronicity, but with a changing interpretation. Were Alfred's years working with Phillip Liss a preparation to help Pierre Levesque as a social benefactor, or to stop Pierre Levesque as a harbinger of social ill?

With Phillip Liss, Alfred, a future psychotherapist himself, learned how to work with the world of a schizophrenic who thought himself The Christ. Both Phillip Liss and Pierre Levesque were hospitalized for psychotic episodes. In formal terms, Pierre Levesque could be diagnosed as a paranoid schizophrenic with borderline personality disorder. Yet Pierre Levesque was calculating where Phillip Liss was transparent. Pierre Levesque could plan quietly for months, and then turn on you with overwhelming force, deadly in its intent.

Alfred's putative diagnosis of Pierre R. Levesque as paranoid schizophrenic with borderline personality disorder does have congruence with the mission of the CIA MONARCH's mind control program. Pierre R. Levesque exhibited many of the characteristics of individuals programmed with MONARCH multiples personalities. Pierre Levesque's background from a Canadian military family, and his prior employment as a Canadian Customs and Immigration officer may have exposed him to mind control training. Experts Cisco Wheeler and Fritz Springmeier write in "The Illuminati Formula Used to Create an Undetectable Total Mind Controlled Slave", "For many years, they were able to shut-up and quietly discard their programmed multiples by labeling them Paranoid Schizophrenics. But therapists are now correctly identifying these people as programmed multiples and are not only diagnosing them better but giving them better treatment."[80]

If this is the case, the CIA was able to create a cult leader in Pierre Levesque through MONARCH and other mind control that they could manipulate through embedded triggers in music videos and other media that Pierre Levesque would use to give directives to the Kingdom of Heaven cult.

163

In the "Kingdom of Heaven", Pierre Levesque built a cult around the projections of his schizophrenia. Those who internalized these projections lived in some safe, delusional island of consciousness. There was some deeper level of Alfred's being that rejected these delusional projections. Alfred was always the outsider, even after he was Pierre's attorney and strategic confidante, and Pierre himself had set aside the outward trappings of the Kingdom of Heaven for a life of blue jeans and marijuana.

As a persona, Pierre Levesque was the antithesis of Phillip Liss. Pierre Levesque was tall, solidly built, fashion-conscious, a gourmet cook, elegant and dark. To those who fell within his sway, his power could seem overwhelming. He was a master of manipulation and thought-control. Pierre Levesque embodied the manipulative genius. He would draw you into his needs, and then ruthlessly remove the ground from beneath your feet.

Pierre Levesque's projection held that all reality, every jot and tittle within the universe revolved around his consciousness. His reality became the idiom for the cult. Sometimes his perceptions were ridiculous. "You know what it's like to be me?" he once asked me, "knowing that every time I take a shit, the world wants to take a shit as well?"

Pierre Levesque felt he governed earth and all reality, he thought, through the projection of his energy – his Vibe. One weapon Pierre used against his enemies was to tie up their body parts by manipulating circuits of the Vibe. At times, when he perceived that one human clique or another was obstructing his wishes, he would shut down sex. "No sex for six months for them," he bragged. "I've shut down sex." Or he would contract their anuses so that bowel movements became painful. "I've shut down their ass-holes," he would tell a dozen or so members of the cult gathered for Saturday night pool games.

This was the ridiculous side of Pierre Levesque's maneuvers. There were also moments of the sublime. There were those personal, quiet moments within in the womb of the cult, when one contemplated being in the conscious presence of the deity incarnated, a part of the mind of God. These flights of expansive spiritual insight were the ultimate power drug of Pierre Levesque's cult. Within the Kingdom of Heaven, the peace of being connected to Pierre Levesque was known as "honey," the peace beyond human understanding. Sublime was the joy to be in Pierre Levesque's aura, leading the ultimate meaningful life, a missionary in service of the Source of all creation.

Alfred still had vivid memories of that chilled Ontario winter day in 1984, trees laden down to the ground with ten-foot icicles. The troops of the Kingdom of Heaven were massing at their base, ready for orders to descend upon New York and Washington as ambassadors for the Lord, as the cult called Pierre Levesque. Quick excitement, electricity was in the air. The troops felt that rare state of embarking on a high mission as they loaded on the rag-tag fleet of Kingdom vehicles headed south.

That was the moment of thrill. Then, as the citizens of the Kingdom of Heaven hit the unsuspecting fabric of the United States, came a less sublime reality.

Blam! The citizens hit the wall of a schizophrenic's delusional projections. No one they met in the U.S. knew that Pierre Levesque had arrived, or whom Pierre Levesque was. No one knew Pierre Levesque had declared was a spiritual war for humanity's liberation. Alfred's own beloved mother Juanita, whom Alfred visited on a fund-raising trip to Texas, waved Pierre Levesque's proclamations in his face, saying, "This is a cult! It's a cult!"

In his humble, hallucinating way, Phillip Liss' concern for the future of humanity was genuine. When he was lucid, his messianic vision was classically utopian, progressive, generous and free of grasping power hunger.

Pierre Levesque's game, by contrast, was power in the absolute, not the human welfare. In Alfred's presence, Pierre threatened to motivate psychically the North Koreans and Russians to rain nuclear missiles down on the United States if he were bodily threatened by the US military.

"Thy Will Be Done" was more than a figurative motto within the Kingdom. Pierre lived inside the delusion that his projected thoughts

*and energy could trigger nuclear conflagration on earth, or stop it at
will. Whatever the cost, the highest good in all reality was his personal
well being.*

*Within the cult and in the world at large, Pierre Levesque carried his
psychopathology to institutional extremes. He was, by his view, the
"King of Kings." In his later years, Pierre called the diminishing group
of former Kingdom of Heaven citizens around him "the cult of no-
cult." Still, an informal fear-inducing protocol of acceptable behavior
was informally enforced.*

*At Saturday night gatherings, Pierre Levesque, fueled with alcohol
and marijuana, bombarded with stream-of-consciousness diatribes.
Any topic was fair game – personal attacks on members and their
marriages; intimate details of his own marriage; revelations of how
world nations were treating him. To escape the scorching attention of
a personal attack, members of the groups retreated into private paralysis with a peculiar behavior called "bob and nod". Easy, just nod at
everything Pierre Levesque says, bob up and down if he looks at you,
and the paranoid-schizophrenic will not lash out at you. Inducing fear
was Pierre's main weapon.*

*The King of King's obsession was ruling Earth. "I run this planet," he
told Alfred in the privacy of his kitchen one afternoon as our legal
battles were intensifying. "More energy runs through here on a single
day than through the New York stock exchange." All of nature supported Pierre Levesque in his reign, the birds, the weather, the animals, the oceans, and the stars.*

*In his mind, television was one of Pierre Levesque's primary tools to
dominate the Earth. His house was in the midst of a forest, by a lake
on his 1500-acre private estate. As one drove by the winding unpaved
road toward the lake, three large satellite dish antennas sprouted from
the roof. Inside, Pierre projected his thoughts and energy at a large-
screen television. The screen was Pierre's window to the world, and the
world's channel back to him. Pierre Levesque "broadcast" his will
through the screen, out the antenna, and back into the television sets
and minds of all humanity.*

Pierre Levesque took his television work seriously. He kept a regular broadcasting schedule, heavily weighted toward dead-of-the-night programming. Night was when the noise of the world fell, and he could best reach his human subjects. But night was not the only time Pierre broadcast to the world. It happened during the day, every day, especially on live television. Then Pierre would talk back and forth with the television personalities, with politicians and heads of state, and see that he got his will across.

Or so Pierre Levesque, and the chosen, thought and knew.

Pierre Levesque's favorites were his public affairs broadcasts, usually through the news or public affairs live TV channels. Through public affairs broadcasts, Pierre Levesque kept "fleet" alert and organized. "Fleet" consisted of those human souls who were more "irritable" or attuned to him, and most closely in the service of his mission to save the earth. Fleet members could be found in every walk of life – in military uniform, in politics, in the arts and music, and – importantly – in music videos.

Through public affairs broadcasts, Pierre Levesque communicated directly with the leaders of the world – live and in living color. Leaders and heads of state could make or break their careers by how they came across to Pierre Levesque. As the King of Kings, Pierre judged his human leaders not by the clear words they uttered, but by their masonry – conscious or unconscious. Their body language, gestures, words were judged by Pierre Levesque for their symbolic impact. Finger wagging was a no-no. It meant that the finger-wagger wanted to injure or destroy Pierre. Any politician who wagged his finger at the TV camera when Pierre was watching risked the destruction of his life and soul.

Politicians who angered Pierre Levesque did so at their risk. He used his maximal negative psychic power to bring them down. One day, as Alfred was visiting him, Pierre began an attack session against a politician then appearing on TV. "You'd better leave," Pierre told Alfred. "This could be harmful to your health." Alfred quickly left Pierre's house.

No one was immune from Pierre Levesque's wrath, not even the leader of the free world. The last time Alfred saw Pierre alive, at his annual January birthday dinner on January 8, 1998, Pierre turned to Alfred with a face full of rage, and spurt out the words, "I've decided to send him to hell." He was referring to the then U.S. President, William Jefferson Clinton. About a week later, a sex scandal surrounding the President of the United States and Monica Lewinsky broke in the public news for the first time.[81] Was there cause and effect between Pierre R. Levesque and Bill Clinton? Well, you can be sure that Pierre Levesque thought he triggered the U.S. President's public problems.

Pierre Levesque's public affairs strategy was based on nation-blocks, races, religions, and social streams that he felt supported him or blocked his plans. Some embodied Pierre Levesque more purely than others. He was NATO. He was Islam. He was the Asians. He was the Africans. Opposed to Pierre Levesque were networks of organized crime and the secret world elite, a hidden cabal that maintains itself throughout the centuries with cultural masonry and manipulation of property, government and law. In other words, the Satanic/Illuminati war crimes racketeering organization that Alfred was pursuing as well.

The United States was his obsession; he had a love-hate relationship with the U.S. government, as well as the U.S. public. The public was his special flock, and had prayed to him to rescue them from orga-nized crime. But the U.S. public was also "managed," easily manipu-lated by the masonry of the hidden elite – its media, politics, and culture. The anti- Pierre Levesque media would promote themes and images that were designed to covertly undercut his sway in the United States and by extension the world public.

One striking example of Pierre Levesque's symbolic judgments oc-curred during Pierre's legal battles to marry his second wife Lenore. In Pierre Levesque's eyes, virtually the entirety of world affairs was a reflection of his war against the Ontario government to release his adoptive charge Lenore and marry her. The Chinese government carried out its infamous public massacre of student dissidents in Tiananmen Square on June 3-4, 1989 at the height of Ontario

Children's Aid Society legal proceedings to take Lenore into protective custody, thus blocking the marriage.[82]

By Pierre Levesque's view, the Tiananmen Square massacre was a direct attack upon himself by gangs of organized crime who controlled the Chinese government. The Chinese had staged the massacre intentionally to prevent his marriage. The message sent to the world at large was that Lenore, his bride-to-be – symbolized by the Chinese students (Lenore, Pierre's bride was a high school student) – must "get down" or be crushed.

In the world of music video, Pierre Levesque reigned supreme. Music videos were all about Pierre Levesque, either for him or against him. Music videos were his most active broadcasting arena, amplifying the "good" videos and psychically shooting down the "bad."

Pierre Levesque perceived "good" music videos as updates of his journey on earth, broadcast to fleet around the world. Each music video, its music, words, artists, story line, production values told the story of Pierre Levesque on earth as it was unfolding. Tune into music videos and you would be tuned into the coming of the Lord.

An example? Well, do you remember Talking Heads in 1984? Did you know that "Burning Down the House"[83] was all about the disintegration of the Kingdom of Heaven cult, the Pierre vs. Win battle? If you didn't, then you weren't tuned in to God's Play as closely as those who were in the know.

There may have been MKULTRA or MONARCH mind control manipulation embedded in this video that triggered Pierre Levesque's paranoid projections and acting out as part of a Satanic/Illuminati feedback loop.[84]

Music videos were not all good, though. There was a war in music video land. The tuned in vee-jays knew this, and would talk to Pierre Levesque live on the air while he watched the TV screen, and brought them into the workings of his mind and will. The more enlightened the Vee-jay was, the more the mix of good and bad videos reflected the battle of the bands. It was hard to predict from video to video whether

Pierre Levesque would judge a particular musical artist as being for or against Pierre, and therefore good or evil. One band could be heroes because of a single music video, only to be shot down by Pierre a few months later for a video that went against him.

Pierre Levesque's public work in the music video war formed the legal basis for the more than twenty legal cases he brought in the courts of the United States and Canada at the end of the eighties. He sued Home Box Office, Time Inc., RCA, and others for broadcasting footage of his private life that denigrated him, the central focus of the music video industry.

Alfred won a default judgment for Pierre Levesque against the government of Ontario in the amount of $750 million. Despite the paper victory, Pierre Levesque did not collect a penny. He was too busy trying to destroy and kill his Rival – his attorney whose quick wits had secured the default judgment in the first place.

That was Pierre Levesque for you, the mind controlled ultimate paranoid schizophrenic. Snatching defeat from the jaws of victory, Pierre Levesque was ultimately a self-saboteur.

At the cosmic, reincarnation level, Alfred's battle with Pierre Levesque was the secret basis of their relationship. On the surface, Alfred served Pierre as attorney. Officially, Pierre entrusted Alfred with representation of the Crown, first as minister of External Affairs of the Kingdom of Heaven, and then as a lawyer in the courts. Pierre lavished Alfred with attentions, accommodations, and long evenings playing storyteller.

Deep down, when relating to Alfred, Pierre projected onto Alfred that Alfred was God's nemesis, the "Antichrist", just like Anna's father, the ASIO/CIA connected official had done in Australia earlier in 1980. "There you are hidden, under layers and layers of masonry," Pierre told Alfred through the thick smoke of marijuana, as Pierre's plan to kill Alfred was coming to a head. Alfred was torn with grief. How could a true manifestation of Deity God condemn a soul who has deeply supported him? At one point earlier Pierre had said to Alfred, "I was told the Antichrist had hairy ears, referring to Alfred's hairy ears."

Their rivalry was evident almost from the first time they came together in this life. Not that Alfred ever intended consciously to confront Pierre. It was Alfred's Light, his stance that directly challenged Pierre's self-declared God-hood. Alfred made Pierre's "Big Lie" manifest, not by doing anything. Just by being. If Pierre did not destroy Alfred, he would eventually implode himself.

Is Alfred now still so filled with emotion by Pierre's memory? Did Alfred still feel the pain and fear of his betrayal? Betrayal, that's the source of Alfred's reverberation, his drive to clear the air and set the record straight about Pierre, a bent, infirm man. Alfred was appalled at the utter baseness of one who would try to murder another who is risking his life for him.

Pierre Levesque harbored murderous thoughts about Alfred from the beginning of their alliance. The harder Alfred would try and serve his interests, the darker his suspicions became. He thought Alfred came to steal his powers, to make off with his messianic legacy. "I can look into the TV screen and have them talk back to me. Can you do that?" Pierre asked Alfred.

Alfred bobbed and nodded, and did not tell Pierre that this perception was an artifact of frequency weapons attacks and was illusory. Alfred too had that phenomenon happen to him in the aftermath of the CIA frequency weapons attacks upon him after the CIA sabotage of the Carter White House Extraterrestrial Study. Alfred was concerned that if he told Pierre, he would have flown into a rage and attacked him physically on the spot.

Alfred can still almost summon up the emotion that he felt when Pierre Levesque held him captive for over a week at his snow-bound base in Ontario, trying to engineer his physical assassination. When Pierre failed at first to mobilize group opinion to kill Alfred, he visited Alfred in the house where Alfred was held under guard. "I could kill you with my bare hands," he told Alfred while they were alone. "And I have fleet's permission to do it."

[EDITOR'S NOTE: This text was written in 1999. It is now May 2015 and Alfred feels he has forgiven Pierre, who in fact taught him much intentionally and indirectly.]

Alfred survived a quintessential cult experience – assassination at the hands of cult members, under the direction of a charismatic but psychotic cult leader who has branded one as a traitor.

And why was Alfred considered a traitor? Well, "fleet" told Pierre on television that Alfred was a traitor to the Kingdom of Heaven. According to Pierre Levesque, fleet spoke to Pierre on television, and told him Alfred was the Antichrist, masquerading as a Soviet spy, disguised as a lawyer representing Pierre Levesque. Alfred was Evil incarnated according to Pierre's version of what fleet told him on their telepathic communications on television. Now that's a notion for the ages. Or should one say, a psychological re-projection by Pierre, who was seeing his own shadow self and was repelled by it.

Alfred survived Pierre Levesque's assassination attempt only because Alfred escaped in the late hours of the night after his guards had gone to sleep. The snow had been cleared from Alfred's pickup truck. Alfred rushed about the house, packing his blazer and his briefcase. A miracle! The truck started in the sub-freezing cold. A few hours later Alfred had crossed the border into the United States, then in full mobilization for Operation Desert Storm on January 17, 1991.[85]

Alfred went from a war in Heaven to the war on earth, and saw that one war was just an extension of the other. Pierre in Heaven was a tool of the war powers on earth. Was Pierre Levesque, his former client, a tool of the forces of war on earth?

Pierre Levesque himself possessed formidable psychic powers, which he used in the most sophisticated ways in an attempt to impose his will on Earth. And psychic weapons are the leading edge of human warfare. Pierre Levesque and the temporal forces of war had one singularly specific element in common – misuse of psychic powers.

Alfred's judgment was that Pierre Levesque and the war forces on earth both sought power in that narrow but diabolical arena – the use of psychic powers as dualistic instruments of destruction. Alfred did not know if Pierre Levesque and the forces of war were actually able to coordinate in the psychic realm. Alfred did know that Pierre claimed that this was so. Pierre Levesque's view was that fleet, friendly intelligence agencies and armies, did his will. Those spy, police, and military agencies that did not, did so at their peril.

Alfred's term at Stanford Research Institute, a leading think tank in the United States, brought him into direct contact with the US military's experiments in "remote viewing," the application of psychic powers to military spying. "Psying equals spying." These experiments were with human psychic spies. Alfred knew Dr. Hal Puthoff and Russell Targ, the remote viewing experimenters, who were his initial contacts at SRI. Alfred knew Ingo Swann, one of their principal psychics, a colorful character from New York. Alfred knew of the surface design of their experiments – delving into military sites and file cabinets of military enemies of the United States, then most prominently the Soviet Union.

Understand his circumstances at SRI once again. Alfred was a triple undercover agent, on the surface a futurist in their elite unit of half a dozen futurists who developed policy for the organs of government in the United States. At the next layer of the onion, Alfred was an undercover agent, self-appointed EyE, psychic hero, vindicator sworn to bring down the forces of darkness, most especially those forces which perverted the divine powers within each of us in the cause of war. And, in his third undercover role, Alfred was the chosen vessel of the Holy Spirit entity gaming in dangerous waters in order to foster higher intelligent beings' world plan.

That was his spiritual hat, his holy man role.

In a word, Alfred was highly motivated at SRI to be a triple-spy himself, gleaning the motivation and outcomes of the Central Intelligence Agency and other spy agencies' funding of the psychic spy research. Alfred was sure the psychic spy project was cover, mere icing on the cake to cover other, more diabolical misuses of divinely given psychic powers to the service of war.

Alfred played double fake-out games with the US intelligence agencies throughout his stay at the think-tank. Being used to soft technocrats who rolled over on command, they had not idea what forces they were dealing with in EyE. Or so Alfred thought in the safety of his triple disguise, about to be obliterated by well-placed electromagnetic pulse rays directed by US intelligence agencies at his delicate aura.

Alfred learned first hand that not only was psychic spying – the use of our psychic energy in an act of war – operational in the US arsenal. So too were machines that used electromagnetic energy to try and destroy the human aura, and ultimately to attempt assassination upon the human soul.

Those machines were electromagnetic pulse generators, and extremely low frequency (ELF) weapons, secretly deployed against the civilian population of the United States by its own covert government. Their purposes are neutralization of perceived dissidents against the state, and mind-control of moods and thoughts of targeted mass regions of the US population.

Yes, the psychics at SRI were just cover, stuff for newspaper headlines, and a manipulative way to surface opinion about psychic warfare without compromising the utter secrecy of these neo-Atlantean weapons. Alfred knew the Central Intelligence Agency ran a super-secret remote-viewing project, using batteries of psychics to influence distant targets to kill others or themselves.

Pierre Levesque could do, in a limited way, what these batteries of psychics or frequency weapons could do. Pierre's favorite weapon was the Boomerang. Pierre did not have to do anything to destroy or hurt an enemy; he just had to "be". The Boomerang operated through the Vibe. The boomerang effect automatically self-sabotaged any person harboring a hostile thought or intention, or planning or undertaking a hostile act against Pierre. No problem; just trust the Vibe! The boomerang would turn the negative energy against Pierre's enemy.

Within the psychic bubble of the cult, the boomerang was omnipotent. The boomerang delivered a stunning, destructive load of negative psy-

chic energy that literally ripped apart the lives of us erring humans. He relished telling us how a former cult member who challenged him became violently ill all afternoon, a victim of the boomerang.

And, oh how painful it was when Alfred came under the boomerang's effect himself, for his deviant thoughts and errant motivations. One of Pierre's favorite boomerangs was a fatal disease, like cancer. "You know," Pierre told Alfred when Alfred's mother died of cancer, "I've found that when a person dies of cancer, it's usually because they were opposed to me." Pierre knew his mother forcefully opposed his cult.

Once as Alfred was visiting Pierre's house, Alfred saw the name of US Senator and presidential candidate Paul Tsongas written on Pierre's lists. Paul Tsongas had been Alfred's law school classmate and sometime roommate while both prepared to take the Washington, DC Bar exam in June 1967. Alfred's hypothesis was that Pierre meant to send this Senator support through the TV screen as the Senator was vocally opposed to the Central American wars. When Paul Tsongas died of lymphatic cancer, Alfred began to wonder. Was his friend Paul Tsongas a candidate for death by boomerang? Was he done in by covert viral frequency weapons warfare? Or was it just ordinary cancer that caused his death?

Life with Pierre Levesque was the hall of mirrors

The boomerang was not limited to members of the cult and their families. It also applied to the world at large; nations, police forces, armies, rock and roll bands, politicians, religious leaders, presidents and Queens all reaped the boomerang. In fact, the story of contemporary history was seen as a crazy quilt careening of the boomerang through the life and times of straying human beings.

At times, it was hard to tell if the disintegration brought down on a particular human public figure was by the boomerang, or by the personal intervention of Pierre Levesque himself. Where the gravity of the situation merited, Pierre would psychically swoop down on a target human, and literally blow their life away.

The Crown of England was one of Pierre's least favorite institutions. By right of the oath that a British monarch takes, the British Throne belonged to Pierre Levesque. For not recognizing this, Pierre Levesque sent the British Throne 1992, an annum horribilis, a meltdown of family, castles, and royal legitimacy.

A similar fate befell the Pope. By rights, the seat of Peter should have been Pierre Levesque's. Pierre sent the Pope a disintegrating Church, and public embarrassments. But whether it was the boomerang or Pierre's personal intervention was hard to tell. Pierre's destructive psychic whammies happened alike to his subjects on the planet, as well as to members of his cult.

Pierre Levesque also perceived he ruled the Earth by regularly surfing CSPAN, his favorite public affairs TV channel, zooming in on live hearings, speeches, and political debates. Pierre Levesque targeted his enemies and friends, and zapped them with the psychic power of the Absolute as the cult called him. Alfred knew Pierre Levesque studied his targets carefully. In Pierre Levesque's world, no political act of substance took place but that his energy – for or against – was not involved. So far was Pierre Levesque's political influence, that he many times regaled friends with the tale of the US Secretary of State turning to face the camera in a live hearing, and telling a Congressional panel, "Now that's Power!" Referring, of course, to Pierre Levesque who was watching through the TV screen.

Over the years, Alfred took his fair share of psychic whammies, both from batteries of psychics or frequency weapons. Alfred always had a hard time trying to trace the frequency weapons attacks he was undergoing. They were so hard to tell apart that, after a while, Alfred assumed they were intertwined.

If you have ever been at the receiving end of a frequency weapons attack, it can be devastating. The mind reels in disorientation; an electrical wall presses down all over you, activating your body at the molecular level. If you do not know you are the victim of a frequency weapons attack, you can end up incapacitated. If you're a seasoned target of frequency weapons government mind-control, you tend to grit your teeth and wonder, "When will this be over?" Or, as Alfred would think, "How can I locate these bastards, and out them into public view?"

Once, after a stint as a NGO representative at the United Nations, Alfred was traveling by train from New York to Toronto. The frequency weapons wave came on as Alfred was between cars. The frequency weapons ray was so intense that Alfred lost momentary touch with where he was. Alfred tried to move back into the railway car, but could not. Alfred knew exactly what was targeting him at that moment – a covert frequency weapons mind-control attack. So Alfred just waited it out.

At The Point - the single Point of Consciousness on earth, as Pierre Levesque's estate was known - frequency weapons attacks were timed for Saturday night, when the cult would gather for dinners and pool games. They usually peaked around midnight. The intent of the attacks seemed to be to induce inter-personal conflict, disorientation, and fear. These are verified effects in human groups of the frequency weapons technology. Whole cities can be targeted by frequency weapons; its residents put through mood changes and paralyzing fear.

In this case, the frequency weapons attacks seemed coordinated with the US and Canadian government's strategies to neutralize Pierre Levesque's lawsuits against them. The more intense the legal battle became the more intense and frequent the frequency weapons attacks. Pierre could not fully decipher how the frequency weapons field was generated or targeted. Was it deployed by satellite? Was it deployed by land-based equipment? But he became an expert at picking up the sub-auditory noise frequency weapons put out just before the wave was felt, and thus enjoyed some degree of Civil Defense warning.

The attacks reached their height during the week that Lenore, Pierre Levesque's bride, was in detention by the government of Ontario. After Lenore was released by order of the court, the frequency weapons attacks fell off and went back to their usual Saturday night specials.

Good counter measures to frequency weapons grew out of the collective experiences. First and foremost was a strong sense of humor –

laughing one's way through a frequency weapons attack rather than falling prey to the sense of panic and disorientation. A party atmosphere certainly helped – lots of loud music, good cheer, drinking and marijuana smoking were a good recipe for keeping one's sense of balance intact. So effective was marijuana in neutralizing the frequency weapons waves that it occurred to the group that this was one real reason why the Canadian and US governments were so fiercely anti-marijuana.

Marijuana gave an effective defense to frequency weapons! When a natural herb can so easily neutralize the multi-billion dollar Orwellian mind-control machine, one can see why dope would squarely collide with the government's drug enforcement policy. The drug enforcement policy may actually about preventing the populace from defending itself against anti-population frequency weapons.

During his latter days at The Point, Alfred was zapped with frequency weapons on his way to visit Pierre Levesque, and zapped in the days directly after his semi-annual visits. His most vivid frequency weapons memory was a trip Alfred made to The Point, via Texas and San Francisco. On the San Francisco leg of the trip, Alfred was bathed with frequency weapons during the entire week of a public health conference he was attending.

Then Alfred traveled for a weekend stay at The Point, where Pierre Levesque's first private expletive at him was, "You crooked lawyer!" for not agreeing to move back up to The Point, his murder attempt against him notwithstanding. Pierre apologized and kept up his negative aggression all weekend.

When Alfred arrived back in Texas, the psychic remote viewing or frequency weapons attacks became so intense that Alfred remembers seeing visible waves of energy inside the cab of his pickup truck, as he struggled to keep control of the vehicle. They say politics make strange bedfellows. If both Pierre and the secret frequency weapons machines were zapping him, were not Pierre and the hidden government in concert at some level?

There may be some chance the intelligence bowels of the secret state, in its very depths, had Pierre Levesque as some sort of secret psychic King, most actively during the seventies, eighties, and the beginning of the nineties. Pierre may have been a kind of psychic icon to the rulers of the secret state. Then again, maybe this was not the case. Maybe Pierre Levesque was a legend in his mind only. It's hard to tell what was truly what in these halls of psychic mirrors. Or perhaps EyE was a secret occult icon from the way the former defense officials and other luminaries scurried their chairs to sit next to him at lunch at the US Senate. If anyone was a secret King of the secret state that King was Pierre Levesque – or one of the other usual suspects of planetary demonology.

Alfred's career with Pierre Levesque had two phases. There was one phase before, and one phase after Pierre's assassination attempt against him. Both phases lasted seven years, as if in some biblical allusion. During his second 7-year phase with Pierre, Alfred undertook a super-human effort to regain his health from the stress of surviving the assassination attempt against him, and to place his Light in Pierre's face.

After his escape from Pierre in January 1991, Alfred languished in deep depression for two years at his family home in the lower Rio Grande valley, convinced that he had died and that his life was over. This was an intensely painful time for Alfred, who spent long mornings in bed for days on end.

After a year, Alfred ventured to the edge out of the family compound to retrieve the mail. Once or twice a friend took him out to the nature preserves and seashore close by. Alfred cried when he saw the sunset, and its majestic colors. Alfred spent his day in full-time monitoring of the 1992 US presidential campaign on the public affairs channels.

Juanita, Alfred's mother, contracted esophageal cancer, and his world began to unravel. Alfred knew his life support would end with her coming death, and he would have to rejoin the world. A family friend threw him a life preserver and brought him into the community health movement. Alfred now had an entire clinic looking after his health, this time a clinic full of public health doctors, whom Alfred administered. Alfred quickly emerged back into relatively normal mood range, and returned to working life.

Almost three years to the day from his nighttime flight from The Point to avoid certain death at the hands of the cult, Alfred decided to return. Whatever his fears, Alfred needed to stand in front of Pierre Levesque, and silently confront him with his attempted deeds. Alfred says silently, because Pierre had gone to elaborate lengths to cover up his murder attempt. He and Pierre were to play a pantomime for seven years. Pierre agreed to pretend to woo Alfred. Alfred agreed to pretend to want to support Pierre. Each of them was really waiting for the opportunity to plunge the knife in the back of the other.

On his first visit, Pierre praised his boots and his health. He preempted any moves Alfred would make to delve into the dark hours when he had tried to do him in. "Alfred probably doesn't remember anything of what was going on," Pierre announced to the cult. Of course, Alfred was double-bluffing him, dissembling as if Alfred was too confused to remember. Alfred watched Pierre like a hawk, taking in every centimeter of his nervous cover up. As the evening wore on, Pierre began to relax once he saw Alfred did not seem to be seeking revenge.

Soon we were back in our usual routine. It was the "Pierre and his trusted elder advisor" show. Another twist in the bob and nod shuffle on those weekends Alfred would visit the Point. Alfred visited the cult-mind with a twist. Alfred knew that Pierre was a paranoid murderer wannabe, and he could not shake that perception. Alfred kept his head low and tried to bring some measure of normal-think to other cult members. "Thanks! We really needed that around here," one member told him after Alfred spoke about the benefits of the Internet. Alfred decided money was his best way to anchor inside the cult. Pierre loved money. Alfred brought up fat checks during his semi-annual visits. They were both on their best behavior.

During one visit to The Point, Alfred became "leader of the US government." A federal public health officer called Alfred on the telephone, and Pierre psychically picked up the call while watching live TV at his home.

"One moment I was leader of the US government; suddenly you are," He told him that evening. Alfred did not tell Pierre about the call, wondering about Pierre's delusions. *"I want to move up here,"* Alfred retorted, wanting to wrench every advantage out of his new role as leader-in-hallucination. Pierre ran back into the kitchen. *"You hear that, dear,"* he told his wife Lenore. *"Alfred is moving up to The Point!"* The two shook hands on the deal. Their cat-and-mouse game had escalated, back in a Mexican standoff.

On that same specific August day in 1995, at that very moment, Alfred's own soul mate and fifth wife-to-be, Geri, was a half a continent away, unbeknownst to him. *"I felt this inner activation,"* Geri later told Alfred. *"I knew everything in his life was going to change profoundly."*

Spirit brought Geri and Alfred together on the Internet in April 1996. *"Gaga"* was the nickname his soul mate and Alfred now gave themselves, a combination of their first name initials. Gaga were married January 1, 1997 and set out to visit The Point on their honeymoon. In the past, Alfred had to face Pierre's murderous intent alone, and surrounded by a malleable group of cult members. Gaga's yin-yang power brought its own Light into Pierre's face. The results proved fatal for Pierre and liberating for Alfred.

Gaga decided on some psychic counter measures. In a Gaga psychic reading, Geri and Alfred learned that many incarnations ago – Atlantean times - Pierre had imprisoned Alfred as a tool for power, and banished Gaga. Gaga had come together in this lifetime to stop Pierre and his psychotic power. Soon after Gaga confronted his deteriorating sanity, Pierre died of a massive heart attack, brought on by drugs, drink, and the psychotic blasphemy of thinking one is "God". Yet – the truth is that Pierre Levesque may well have died of a massive frequency weapons attack.

Pierre Levesque was dead!

Alfred heard the news in a sobbing phone call from Lenore his widow. Later, as Alfred was crossing the Georgia Strait from Salt Spring Island, BC on a mega-ferry the full impact hit him. Alfred's aging fa-

ther, himself a Catholic deacon, told him, "You know, it's a horrible thing to say, but Pierre was better off dead than alive." Seven years before, his father had refused to believe that Pierre had tried to murder him. In the end, the truth would out.

Alfred put to rest his years with Pierre Levesque in a letter to Lenore, his widow, expressing his own post-mortem confrontation of what had possessed her husband.

I do not know if I have ever mentioned this to you directly, but I feel a sense of moral responsibility toward you arising from my representing you in adoption proceedings several years ago. As a being, I wish to clear myself of any karma that I may have in that regard. I wish to let you know reality as I perceive it.

Clinically: I do not believe your husband was God. Quite the contrary, I believe he probably could be diagnosed as paranoid-schizophrenic, with borderline personality disorder. His astrological chart shows heavy delusional tendencies, and susceptibility to alcohol and drug abuse.

I believe he fits the classic mold of an authoritarian cult leader, and myself and others around him functioned as enablers or facilitators of this mold.

I believe his passing is a blessing in the end to me, and to those who were involved with him.

During my seven years in Brownsville, I undertook deep psychological work and earned a Counseling degree in part to restore my self-esteem and sense of inner self I felt I lost during the Queen-King of Heaven years of my life.

I cannot lead you or anyone else involved to these insights and conclusions. Your own process is for you to find. I enclose two pages of observations from a book on recovery from cults and abusive relationships that I have found helpful personally.

Please know that if you would ever like to write or talk over some of these concepts, just know that you will always find an open door.

Alfred

There is one common bond in the two hidden histories of Pierre Levesque and Phillip Liss. Each paid a steep price by claiming to be deity.

Phillip Liss' claim of deity cost him his sanity, life-long. He lost his own claim to healthy perception. When Alfred last knew him, Phillip was a kind soul, dressed in the smelly rags of the street psychotic.

Pierre Levesque lost his very life, and gained banishment, possibly, to an afterlife unknown. Pierre Levesque went over the edge in life, and arrogantly tried to abrogate the divine prerogatives of creating and nurturing human souls. Pierre's threat to take away souls was constant. "I take away souls," he would say. "I am the bottom line. I give souls and I take them away. No one gets off this planet without going through me"

He bragged about destroying souls of human leaders, judges, lawyers, artists and the media people who opposed him. Pierre Levesque monitored their speeches, hearings, pronouncements, music videos, news and public affairs programs on the live TV. If these reached a threshold, Pierre Levesque said he took their souls away. Of course, the whole exercise was Pierre's delusional exercise. But what Pierre's hallucinations did was to corrode Pierre's own soul.

Pierre Levesque made murdering a soulless errant member easier for the cult. In his hubris, Pierre told the cult he had taken away his soul as preparation for his attempt to destroy him. The cult believed him. Alfred remembers a bewildered cult member staring at him as though he was some vampire they were about to kill. "He doesn't believe you have a soul," Alfred's cult wife Francoise told him, his then fourth spouse.

After Pierre Levesque's first attempt to rouse the cult to kill Alfred failed, Pierre raised the delusional ante. "I took away your soul, but left it in your body," he told Alfred during a face-off. "That way the soul goes to Hell, as well as the body." Pierre was really into soul torture, wishing the most horrible depravity to his imagined enemies.

In the safety of the rear view mirror, Alfred now saw his battle with Pierre as the first true mission Alfred undertook on behalf of the Holy

Spirit entity. His mission was to bring his Light into the face of Pierre's rogue soul, and watch that soul take a path of spiritual surrender or self-destruction. His test run, as it were; his pilot project; his shakedown cruise. Fifteen years of Alfred's surviving on rugged self-control, as Pierre's troubled body and soul finally imploded in self-destruction, the completion of a karmic drama stretching back millennia. If Alfred survived his spiritual test in the battle against Pierre Levesque, then Alfred might be ready for other, larger missions in the future.

When Alfred first seeped into the dimensions of the Kingdom of Heaven, Urantia was his private guide. Each night, Alfred would consult the book asking, "Why am I here?" Each night the book told him Alfred was steadfast on an intended path. "Hang tight," Urantia told him in divination. "You are developing a spiritual marriage with IAM the Institute of Applied Metaphysics." Why or how Alfred was to pursue this marriage was not yet clear. As the cult began to trust him, and Alfred rose in rank to be a minister, a most unlikely ally came to aid his mission. She was Winifred Barton, Pierre Levesque's first wife, the "Queen of Heaven and Earth," a mystic herself, well versed in esoteric traditions and profoundly sensitive to the workings of spiritual law.

"No wonder you have been able to stay on course all these years, Alfred, " she told him over the short-wave radio network the cult used to communicate between bases. "If it were not for Urantia, you would have lost yourself." Soon Alfred invited Winifred to the Lodge by the Lake to present Urantia to a seminar of the ministers of the Kingdom. Alfred arrived to find Pierre was not in present company. Alfred felt divided. Either Pierre had condoned our gathering because he understood what Urantia was, or he was indifferent. Little did Alfred know then - Urantia had evoked his profound enmity.

Alfred sat in the circle, keeping close eye contact, bringing the words of the purported fifth epochal revelation to this planet. The prior epochal revelation was, according to Urantia, a person (Jesus of Nazareth), the human incarnation of the God that creates our local universe. The *revelation for this epoch was not a person, but a book. Urantia is our planetary lesson plan for at least the next millennium.*

Then Alfred saw the moment had arrived. Alfred was to proclaim the fifth epochal revelation right there, inside the Kingdom of Heaven and Earth. Layering upon layering.

Alfred raised Urantia above his head, intoning:

"I now proclaim the fifth epochal revelation."

That will get their cultic psyches going, Alfred thought. This public act will land Urantia inside the Kingdom mind-space.

Well, it did, and two months later the Kingdom of Heaven was in civil war, disintegrating into camps of cult members caught in the destructive crossfire of a battle to the death between Pierre and his Queen.

Pierre's bitterness against Urantia grew after this event. He railed against it often at gatherings where Alfred was present, knowing Alfred had brought the seeds of his destruction into his very camp.

All this was irony, however. It was not the information of Urantia that was eating Pierre away from the inside. Pierre's own resistance was dragging him into the direction of early termination.

Just one fair reading of Urantia's rendering of the source and journey of the human soul would have blocked off Pierre's destructive hallucination that he controlled human souls.

Alfred had brought into Pierre's reality a spiritual text. He could have stopped his self-destruction in just one opening to the majesty of how true divine creation works; how inhabited planets are developed and grown; how our own irregular planet has suffered in rebellion; what our future history and destination are.

Alfred has one bright moment-memory of Pierre, standing by a raging fireplace after dinner, turning to Alfred, and calling to him.

"You are Melchizedek," Pierre said to Alfred, reaching the deeper realms of his higher self. According to Urantia, Melchizedek's original mission was an emergency measure of the universe administration, at

a time when consciousness of the one true God was in danger of disappearing.

Years earlier, in the Netherlands, on the way back from Geneva and The Hague, over another dinner, Alfred had listened closely to the man performing the Dutch translation of the Urantia book. The man's knowledge of Urantia was encyclopedic. As they finished eating, the man unraveled a mystery contained within the mysteries of Urantia.

"The Urantia book says that there may be a surprise in our generation on earth," he told Alfred. "The surprise could be many things. It could be the Second Coming of the God of our local universe."

Alfred did not know what this surprise might be. Alfred's mission took him on a headlong search for this surprise

Then, one Urantia friend wrote him, "As for the Dutch comment/prediction, I would say it possibly had to do with the return of Machiventa Melchizedek."

After years with Pierre R. Levesque, Alfred put away the playthings of symbol and self and stood naked, unencumbered by his former masks.

SCENE 5

GLOBAL BROADCASTING

1984-87
United Nations
New York, NY 10017

Late one afternoon in 1986, surrounded by over 20 blue-unformed UN security guards who were swarming him, Alfred sat in an otherwise empty United Nations cafeteria wondering if he ever would be able to shake off CIA Cointelpro. He often went to the United Nations for lunch because it was conveniently in midtown Manhattan and served excellent affordable food. Alfred could access the UN cafeteria as NGO representative for the Communications Coordination Committee of the United Nations (CCCUN), the oldest Non-Governmental Organization at the United Nations, founded in 1946. Through CCCUN, Alfred pursued global broadcasting at the United Nations.

Alfred worked hard at pioneering in global broadcasting the public interest, piggy-backing on the up to four radio talk shows a week he broadcast as a volunteer programmer at NPR's listener-sponsor radio station WBAI-FM. Alfred and his co-host Mary Houston produced the "Instant of Cooperation",[86] the first live broadcast in history between the United States and the then Soviet Union. Gosteleradio, the official Radio-TV organ in "perestroika" (restructuring) Russia, engaged a full sound stage and orchestra for the program and reportedly broadcast the program across all 11 Russian times zones. Alfred spent $25.00 to rent a transponder on the National Public Radio satellite and used his personal computer faxed NPR stations to download the program signal.

Though 21st Century audiences would find it commonplace when poet Allan Ginsburg spoke live from New York on "The Instant of Cooperation" with a leading Russian poet, it was a historic first. In a follow-up program "Moscow-New York Live," Alfred broke through the "Iron Curtain" by linking up a person on the streets of Moscow to speak live with a person on the streets of Jersey City who had called into the program and broke down crying when he realized he was speaking through the "Iron Curtain" still then in place. "The Instant of Cooperation" was nominated for an award on the floor of the UN General Assembly, and Alfred was invited to Russia to meet Gorbachev, then still President of the Soviet Union and running *glasnost* (transparency).

By conscious choice, Alfred produced and hosted a 'Harmonic Convergence' national radio show in the U.S. on August 17, 1987 that was anchored at one of the National Public Radio (NPR) member stations in Boulder, Colo., and carried via live via the NPR satellite by a respectable number of NPR stations in the U.S.[87]

Researcher Jose Arguelles, author of the "Mayan Factor," was one of Alfred's live guests on the NPR satellite radio program. After the August 17, 1987 NPR satellite program, a reporter from the Washington Post called Alfred at the local Boulder, CO. listener-supported radio for an extensive interview on the meaning of the Harmonic Convergence (one of the Washington, DC area NPR member stations had broadcast the Harmonic Convergence program). Alfred does not know if the Washington Post ever published that interview. He subjectively felt at the time that, as a communicator and broadcaster, he was involved in an important process of linking U.S. mainstream audiences into deeper universe energy wave processes.

SCENE 6

PUBLIC HEALTH

1995
Harvard School of Public Health
677 Huntington Avenue
Boston, MA 02115

Alfred listened attentively to a lecture by Michael Dukakis, the 1988 Democratic Presidential contender, at the Harvard School of Public Health on the public importance of community public health. Alfred was the only attorney in the lecture hall, and to that time the only attorney ever admitted to the Harvard's certificate program for physicians working at federal community health centers in the United States. Since leaving Canada and returning to his family home in the Rio Grande Valley of Texas, Alfred had accepted his friend Paula Gomez' offer and had become an administrator at the Brownsville Community Health Center (BCHC). Alfred was also completing a Masters degree in counseling at the University of Texas (Brownsville). "Lawyers take people apart. Now I want to put people back together," Alfred thought.

Alfred grew up mainly outside his family home, enrolled in Roman Catholic schools starting in the first grade in Havana, Cuba at the age of 7, staying with grandparents or in boarding schools. At one Roman Catholic boarding school (St. Leo's, St. Leo, Florida), [88] run by the Benedictines of Pope Joseph Ratzinger fame, the monks beat Alfred for writing home that he was homesick, and a number of monks were expelled for sexual abuse of children. Alfred completed 7th and 8th grade in one year, won all of the academic trophies for his grade level, had to ward off love letters from one monk, and managed not to get assaulted sexually by any of the monks.

By moving back to his family home at Brownsville, Texas, Alfred bonded with his parents Juanita and Ali in a way that he never had in childhood or adolescence. Alfred reintegrated with his six surviving siblings when they would visit on holidays or to tend to one or another of his parents. Alfred's siblings Richard, mentally challenged from birth, and Joseph, born with massive cerebral palsy, had already passed over. Alfred took up Aikido martial arts, walked along the beaches at nearby Padre Island. When his mother Juanita passed over from esophageal cancer plausibly contracted from asbestos at her work place at Texas Rural Legal Aid, Alfred and his father Ali ran the family home together.

Alfred threw himself into his work in community public health in the Rio Grande Valley and into his studies in psychotherapy. The "Valley" was predominantly Spanish speaking, and Alfred felt at home in the Hispanic side of his culture and DNA. He spent a fair amount of time in Matamoros, Brownsville's twin city on the Mexican side of the border, leading a psychotherapy group once a week in in Spanish for patients with "mood disorders" as part of his University of Texas practicum under the guidance of a Mexican psychiatrist. Alfred found the Mexican patients to be as bright and motivated as the Americans in the weekly psychotherapy group he led for his practicum on the US side of the border.

Alfred decided to become involved in mainstream elected politics, and was elected delegate to the 1996 Texas Democratic Convention [89] at Dallas, where then FLOTUS (First Lady) Hillary Clinton gave the keynote address. The Democrats were functionally the only significant political party in the Valley. Juanita had been active in Democratic politics, and Gov. Ann Richards had often visited the Webre family home.

Alfred was increasingly recognized as an up and coming leader in community public health circles in Texas. Then came a conference that would transform Alfred's life once again. On Tuesday April 9, 1996, Alfred was in San Antonio, Texas to speak at a conference on community health. Carmen Rocco, a physician and researcher into birth defects in Maquiladora factories along the U.S-Mexican border invited Alfred, and a number of fellow physicians to go to the piano bars along the San Antonio River. On returning to his hotel room, Alfred decided to go online search for persons with psychic capacity and expertise in parapsychology among the members of then new-fangled Aol.com.

The Aol.com member that Alfred chose out of this Internet haystack happened to be online and was Geri DeStefano PhD, his Soul mate and future wife, then living in the Bay Area, California. Alfred and Geri had a high-energy 45-day period of long phone calls (this way before Skype). Alfred flew to California to meet Geri, a psychotherapist and psychic. On January 1, 1998 Geri and Alfred were married in Brownsville, in Alfred's family home.

The birds in the old growth trees in Alfred's family home had told him he should return to Canada to "help save the world." Alfred had met Texas Gov. George W. Bush, a man he later would judge to be a war criminal, in Brownsville, Texas on the same day on which Bush had signed a bill that denied Hispanic children health care and executed a Mexican prisoner over the objections of Pope Paul II.

On April 4, 1998, Alfred and Geri arrived in Vancouver, Canada with all their possessions in a VW Westphalia Camp-mobile. They landed in Canada with a business visa to establish EcoSustainable Products and sell shade grown organic coffee and organic teas online.

Unbeknownst to his conscious mind, Alfred's formal life in Exopolitics was renewing itself.

ACT III

1999 – 2015
EXOPOLITICS, OMNIVERSE
& POSITIVE FUTURE

"The climax occurs as well as the dénouement,
a brief period of calm at the end of a film where a state of
equilibrium returns. In other words, it is simply the resolution."

SCENE 1

THE AIR WAR

Christmas 2014
"The Hobbit: The Battle of the Five Armies"
Motion Picture Theatre
Vancouver, BC

By Christmas 2014 in Vancouver BC with Geri his Soul Spouse Alfred had become accustomed to the "Air War" as one more feature of his Incarnation. By the "Air War" Alfred referred to the creation of mass negative memes [negative propaganda thought forms] directed specifically against "Alfred" and his Archetype that the powers behind the false Matrix broadcast through motion pictures, television, advertising, popular music, and Internet that had the effect of inoculating specific human populations against Alfred's emergence in any position of idea-credibility or leadership.

AIR WAR IN THE HOBBIT – "ALFRID" [ALFRED] THE INVENTED HOBBIT CHARACTER WHO NEVER WAS

Going out for a Christmas 2014 Hobbit movie outing with his family in Vancouver, BC turned into a typical Air War encounter and Illuminati hit for Alfred, as well as a strategic realization of the depth and threat perception with which the false Matrix controllers viewed Alfred. [Editor's Note: Come Oh Reader with an Open Mind, for these Insights are for those with Eyes to See and Ears to Hear and Souls to Embrace and Comprehend.]

In summary, *"The Hobbit: The Battle of the Five Armies* is a 2014 epic fantasy adventure film, directed by Peter Jackson and written by Jackson, Fran Walsh, Philippa Boyens, and Guillermo del Toro. It is the third and final installment in the three-part film adaptation based on the novel The Hobbit by J. R. R. Tolkien, following An Unexpected Journey (2012) and The Desolation of Smaug (2013), and together they act as a prequel to Jackson's The Lord of the Rings film trilogy... The film was a box office success, grossing over \$955 million worldwide, surpassing both The Fellowship of the Ring and The Two Towers nominally, making it the second highest-grossing film of 2014 and the 26th highest-grossing film of all time. At the 87th Academy Awards, the film received a nomination for Best Sound Editing."[90]

If one searches the Cast of the movie, you will find actor Ryan Gage played the character "Alfrid" [pronounced "Alfred" in the actual film]. Ryan Gage "is an English actor who has most recently appeared in The Hobbit: The Desolation of Smaug and The Hobbit: The Battle of the Five Armies as Alfrid and The Musketeers as King Louis XIII... This is a list of original characters found in Peter Jackson's film adaptations of J. R. R. Tolkien's The Hobbit."

ENTER ALFRID

Now let's look at the moral character and role model of ALFRID in the largest grossing THE HOBBIT movie EVER! The name ALFRID is stated over and over and over in this film. If you do not GET this, Oh gentle Reader, you will NEVER get this example of the Air War! ;-)

"Alfrid (portrayed by Ryan Gage) is a cowardly and greedy man who is a government official of the town of Esgaroth and the Master of

Lake-town's conniving servant. Ultimately, Alfrid is betrayed by the Master and forced to fend for himself during Smaug's attack on Laketown. After almost getting lynched by the angry survivors, Alfrid ends up working under Bard before fleeing from Dale with some looted gold during the Battle of the Five Armies."[91]

As I type these words now I am filled with Rage that my name and Persona would be so sullied before (b) millions of subconscious minds throughout our fair planet, indeed the Noosphere, the currency the Black Magicians of Hollywood deal in.

All because various layers of self-appointed networks and bloodlines (what a hard-like terminology) want to stay in some power, or create some loosh energy to feed some dimensional other energy beingness? That's crazy and loopy and self-destructive to the biosphere.

The Irony of course is that the original book *The Hobbit* by JRR Tolkien does not have a character in it named "Alfrid". You can search the book online. Just search "The Hobbit – Free Download or PDF online" and the Search "Alfrid". Or read the whole book online for free.

The character ALFRID was invented whole cloth for the purposes of the Air Water against Alfred in compliance with the CIA or Mossad or New World Order or FuckWad network in Peter Jackson's shop in NZ or [hey wait it's the standard contract clause in Hollywood – "do you have the Alfred hit clause in this Picture?"]. Oh it's not in the fine print, it's off contract – you know in the wink and the handshake.

Well Let's take a look at some television.

AIR WAR ON ALFRED & 9/11 BY JON STEWART & DAILY SHOW

Jon Stewart carries out Satanic Illuminati hit on Daily Show?: October 23, 2013

By Alfred Lambremont Webre

VANCOUVER, BC – This article is for those readers with eyes to see and ears to hear and a desire to understand the methods the Satanic Illuminati media networks used in conjunction with other New World Order operations to target specific Truth movement workers. The article connects dots, and the reader, as always, is free to perceive those dots as connected or not connected.

This is experimental territory because the technology of targeting employed in this hit is such that if the targeted person states that he or she is being targeted, then he or she is conventionally perceived as a paranoid schizophrenic. Thus, technology is designed such that the target is in a double bind. If he or she reveals the hit, he or she is discredited. At least that's how the Satanic Illuminati have set up their global psyops targeting system.

CASE STUDY OF A MAJOR MEDIA ILLUMINATI HIT

One purpose of Satanic Illuminati major media hits on targeted Truth movement workers lies in the realm of dark magic – to attempt to take the positive spiritual and social energy generated by the causes in which the worker is active and direct them to the negative. This can be done by creating an anonymous smear website against the target on the Internet and then enroll a cooperating Illuminati major media asset - like a Jon Stewart (born Jonathan Stuart Leibowitz, November 28, 1962) on The Daily Show - to load key cue words about the smear into the collective mind through a "Capstone incantation" on their major media program.

Major Illuminati assets like politicians can also be enrolled into loading cue words about a targeted individual into the collective mind, in which case the "Capstone incantation" may take place during say a U.S. President's State of the Nation address.

COMEDY CENTRAL AS AN ILLUMINATI PSYOPS CENTRAL

There is ample evidence that Comedy Central's flagship program The Colbert Report has been used to target Truth workers attempting disclosure around important new secret technologies now controlled by the Illuminati, such as time travel and teleportation.

The Colbert Report invited former U.S. chrononaut Andrew D. Basiago to do a straightforward, policy-oriented interview that was to be focused on how teleportation can provide a way for the United States to free itself from dependence on foreign sources of oil, filmed the interview in Portland, Oregon in June 2012, and then recently in post-production added a 1953 CIA Robertson Panel-like "hit" on the CIA's Mars jump room program of the early 1980's that included not only Andrew D. Basiago, U.S. President Barack H. Obama, and former DARPA director Regina E. Dugan, but Andy's fellow chrononauts who have stepped forward as whistle blowers, William B. Stillings and Bernard Mendez.[1]

JON STEWART'S "CAPSTONE INCANTATION": OCT. 23, 2013

In the opening segment of his Oct. 23, 2013 Daily Show, host Jon Stewart [at 0.27] suddenly states a *non-sequitur* reference to the upcoming 50th anniversary of the JFK assassination [Nov. 22, 2013] that, on analysis, is an Illuminati "Capstone incantation", stating emphatically:

Jon Stewart: *"But first, Fifty years ago in Dallas an assassination that changed the country…"*

WATCH ON VIDEO

http://www.ctv.ca/DailyShowwithJonStewart.aspx?vp=140174

While he is making the "Capstone Incantation", Jon Stewart looks away from the camera while a background image of "Wall

Street" behind him is a setup for the first legitimate segment of the program. Stewart mutters that what he just said was "a joke" based on off-stage conversations.

Yet, there is no joke and no context for the Incantation. That is because there was no Daily Show joke in those words and that "Capstone Incantation" was actually part of a larger Illuminati hit, carried out through covert Illuminati assets like Jon Stewart and anonymous Illuminati assets on the Internet and elsewhere.

THE JFK ASSASSINATION 50TH ANNIVERSARY REFERENCE

The hypothesis of this article is that the JFK assassination 50th anniversary reference by Jon Stewart is actually an Illuminati ritualistic incantation, targeted as part of an Illuminati network hit on a specific target.

Jon Stewart: *"But first, Fifty years ago in Dallas an assassination that changed the country..."*

This is an Illuminati "hit" incantation that is meant to be part of an anonymous hit that took place on the Internet earlier that same day Oct. 23, 2013. The anonymous website took a comment on an ExopoliticsTV interview I had done in honor of the 50th anniversary of the JFK assassination with expert Ole Dammegard and conflated the comment into my being a "shape-shifting reptilian".[2]

Shape-Shifting Reptilian Caught On Video?
October 23, 2013 - Alternative, New World Order, Sci-Tech, Uncategorized - Tagged: aliens, david icke, new world order, nwo, reptilian, shapeshifter, strange, weird
Bizarre clip from a recent Alfred Webre video on YouTube. The clip seems to show Alfred shape-shifting mid way through an interview with Ole Dammegard.
http://theviralpost.com/shape-shifting-reptillian-caught-on-video/

I had in fact already responded to a viewer's question about my life-long speech impediment a day earlier. Here is the dialogue from ExopoliticsTV comments on Oct. 22, 2013 [Synchronistically, "International Stuttering Awareness Day"]:

- BeHisLikeness 1 day ago: "What happened to Alfred at 42:12? Looks like he had a seizure of some kind."

- Alfred Lambremont Webre 1 day ago: "It's called a "stupor", and is a life-long stammering behavior. Alfred's brain sees an entire sentence and attempts to say it all at once rather than allowing his speech to flow naturally. Thank you for asking that question."

- BeHisLikeness 23 hours ago: "No, thank you for answering my question. It was rather disturbing in light of all the videos that are going around about Reptilians... (please don't be offended)... Not that I am really convinced of a Reptilian race... Again, thank you for answering this question for me."[3]

Under the hypothesis of this article, an Illuminati cooperating asset had scanned this comment and transformed it into a smear "hit" against its target on an anonymous website and on the same day (Oct 23, 2013), had enrolled an Illuminati major media asset (Jon Stewart) into performing a "Capstone Incantation" against its target on that night's Daily Show.

THIS SOUNDS CRAZY?

To a conventional point of view, this line of reasoning sounds crazy. A classic paranoid schizophrenic diagnosis (I have a graduate degree in psychological counseling) is that the diagnosed individual reports that he or she is hearing segments on television about their lives, or voices in their skull.

Well, that is how Satanic Illuminati mind control technology is intentionally hidden and kept secret by its controllers, behind mental health diagnosis so that if the targeted individual comes forward, he or she can be labeled a paranoid schizophrenic. Voice to skull mind control technology is now well documented.[4]

Similarly with the secret Satanic Illuminati major media "hit" networks like the ones at Comedy Central with Jon Stewart and Stephen Colbert. When targeted individual come forward to report on Illuminati major media "hits", the expectation of the controllers is that the targeted individual would be seen as "paranoid schizophrenic" or at least not credible.

WHAT MAKES THIS HYPOTHESIS CREDIBLE?

In the absence of tangible evidence connecting Jon Stewart's non-contextual utterance about the 50th anniversary of the JFK assassination on the Oct. 23, 2013 Daily Show to an anonymous Internet "hit" on a targeted individual on the same day, what are the grounds to believe there is a connection?

That is a question I asked myself late into the wee hours of Thursday Oct. 24, 2013. Was this bizarre statement by Jon Stewart, which I watched on my television at 11 PM Pacific Time in Vancouver, BC, Canada, connected to the anonymous Internet hit I had just experienced hours before around an interview I had completed with a world expert on the 50th anniversary of the JFK assassination?

Initially I was skeptical, and finally came to an affirmative conclusion after asking a neutral adviser the next day who looked at the evidence and concluded that there were objective signs that (1) Jon Stewart is a Satanic Illuminati operative, and (2) that he had knowingly delivered his utterance about the 50th anniversary of the JFK assassination on the Oct. 23, 2013 Daily Show as a "Capstone Incantation" hit.

This does not mean that Jon Stewart knows the details of the hit, only that he was provided the Capstone Incantation and agreed to deliver it. Remember, Jon Stewart earns $25-30 million a year and is commercial television's most highly paid host even as he is in basic cable, ahead of Letterman and others in the major television networks.[5]

WHY THE HIT ON ALFRED?

A key question is: Why the hit on Alfred Lambremont Webre? The conventional mind would ask: How can I conceivably say that the Satanic Illuminati would "waste their time" to mobilize one of the Illuminati battle-ships (Jon Stewart-Daily Show) on me? I am not a mainstream public figure. I do not hold public office. I live outside of the United States. I lead a simple lifestyle.

THIS HAS BEEN HAPPENING SINCE 1973

One clue to why Alfred is that these sorts of "hits" by the secret Satanic Illuminati major media networks have been happening to me for 40 years, since 1973. I intend to report on them extensively in an upcoming book.

CNN'S PIERS MORGAN DOES AN ILLUMINATI HIT ON ALFRED

On April 4, 2011, this reporter Alfred Lambremont Webre was defamed publicly as an "idiot" and a "crackpot" by CNN's "foppish" and "pompous" anchor Piers Stefan O'Meara (whose stage name is "Piers Morgan") on Piers Morgan Tonight during Mr. Morgan's interview of the former Minnesota Governor and professional wrestler James George Janos (whose stage name is "JesseVentura.") Piers Morgan is another Illuminati major media asset who participates in Capstone Incantations for Illuminati networks.

At issue was the fact that I had called U.S. President Barack H. Obama a lifelong CIA "asset" during my interview with "Jesse Ventura" on a segment about the Gulf oil spill on his TruTV show Conspiracy Theory. In the CNN interview, "Piers Morgan" first cuts to a scene on the Ninth Ward levee in New Orleans, where I am seen calling Mr. Obama a CIA asset as I stand with "Jesse Ventura" starting at about 30 minutes into this segment of this episode of Gov. Ventura's Conspiracy Theory:

http://www.youtube.com/watch?v=vWVQvVSeRdA

My statements about Mr. Obama's background as an asset of the CIA, appearing at approximately 32 minutes into Piers Morgan's interview with "Jesse Ventura," were played numerous times over the air by CNN and can be viewed here:

http://www.youtube.com/watch?v=peztNH3Ksww

In the remainder of the CNN segment, "Piers Morgan" then states the epithets of "idiot" and "crackpot" at me for having stated that Mr. Obama is a lifelong CIA "asset."

After filming the Conspiracy Theory segment in New Orleans, Michael Braverman, Gov. Ventura's producer, told an associate of mine "the Governor is very pleased with Alfred Webre's interview. We hardly had to edit Alfred at all."

TIME TRAVEL PRE-IDENTIFICATION

Another clue lies in secret time travel technology that U.S. government has had since 1971, the year it began its unlawful and unconstitutional time travel surveillance of Alfred Lambremont Webre.

In June 2014, my Yale University Class of 1964 will celebrate its 50th anniversary. As part of the 50th anniversary, each of us graduates was asked to prepare a 500-word statement of his life since graduation.

Here is my 500-word statement to Yale. It may give you some clues as to why the Satanic Illuminati are continuing their major media "Capstone Incantations" on me. And yes, you are welcome to support these activities at *exopolitics@exopolitics.com*. Thank you.

ALFRED LAMBREMONT WEBRE, 64, 67L

On the eve of our 50th reunion I find myself a Futurist. My 2005 book, *"Exopolitics: Politics, Government and Law in the Universe"*

(Universebooks.com 2005) and its earlier online versions are credited with founding Exopolitics, the science of relations among intelligent civilizations in the multiverse. A Cambridge educated participant in the secret U.S. government time travel and teleportation Project Pegasus, former U.S. chrononaut Andrew D. Basiago, reported publicly he physically saw my 2005 book "Exopolitics" in 1971 after the CIA used advanced time travel technology to time travel teleport my book from 2005 back in time to 1971.

In 1971 I was General Counsel of New York City's Environmental Protection Administration. I was invited then to give an environmental talk to fifty officials whom I would learn after 2005 were CIA and Department of Defense officials who had been briefed on my future book "Exopolitics" and knew I would become the future developer of the Exopolitics and Dimensional Ecology models of the multiverse. This intelligence mattered to the CIA because in 1977 while a Futurist at Stanford Research Institute, I became the director of the Jimmy Carter White House Extraterrestrial Communication Study.

As a legacy I am developing the 10+ Policies for a Positive Future. These are some of key policies for a future sustainable, free, and thriving multi-dimensional world. Will you support me in this effort and assist in my work toward these goals?

10+ POLICIES FOR A POSITIVE FUTURE:

1   Extraterrestrial disclosure - A full public disclosure of the presence of intelligent civilizations in Earth's environment and a global referendum as to whether and on what conditions humanity should enter into relations with organized Omniverse society, including a world-sponsored Mars Protection Treaty.

2   Criminalization of war and the war industry

3   Criminal prosecution and conviction of members of war crimes racketeering organizations and restorative justice for war crimes victims

4   Implementation of teleportation as a global, national, regional and local transportation system. Implementation of new non-polluting "free" energy systems for powering cities, homes, vehicles, and our civilization.

5   Recognition of the rights of animals to be protected from murder, slaughter, torture, and cruel and inhumane treatment

6   Worldwide debt forgiveness for countries and individuals

7   Reinvention of money as a human right and public utility like air, water or electricity available for creative investment at public money utilities

8   Social guarantees in the form of annual income, health care, and elementary, secondary, and post-secondary education for every person on the planet, for life

9   Virtual direct democracy – Direct citizen voting at the local, regional, national and international level.

10   Disestablishment of monarchies and religions worldwide – Separation of state, religion, and bloodline families.

11   More – Please feel free to suggest more key policies.

If you are interested, you can find a full version of these policies at *www.Exopolitics.com* and you can email me at *exopolitics@exopolitics.com*.

Thank you.

In Light and Cosmic Love, Alfred ;-)

492 words

[1] "The Colbert Report's Unethical And Opportunistic Post-Production Edit Of Their Interview Of Andrew D. Basiago" http://bit.ly/SWoibo

Andrew D. Basiago & Alfred Webre with Host Roxy Lopez, "The Colbert Report",

[2] Alfred Lambremont Webre, "Stupor", a stammering speech disability, is spun as 'reptilian' shape-shifting on increasingly venomous Internet", http://bit.ly/18QtUf2

[3] Comments, "CIA Operation 40 and JFK, RFK, John Lennon assassinations, Watergate, 9/11: Expert Ole Dammegard", http://bit.ly/1d3KnNX

[4] Eleanor White, "What is Voice to Skull?", http://bit.ly/1afo2KQ

[5] Variety, "Jon Stewart is TV's Highest-paid Host, http://bit.ly/Hi4zkC

[6] Alfred Lambremont Webre, "Hidden story behind Jesse Ventura & Piers Morgan's CNN clash over Obama CIA ties", http://bit.ly/1dp6mS5

Thursday, 24 October 2013

AIR WAR AGAINST GAGA

Then the Air War even goes after Geri and Alfred's relationship nickname (*GAGA* – *GeriAlfredGeriAlfred* = GAGA ;-)

Take this specially made film by Gwyneth Paltrow – Yes *Shakespeare in Love* Gwyneth Paltrow – That One!

ENTER SHALLOW HAL

SHALLOW HAL the motion picture was released in 2001, three years after Geri and I settled in our new home and marriage in Vancouver, BC. SHALLOW HAL is a form of mass psychological warfare in my opinion in that its basic character design and plot development was a reversal of Geri and my intimate relationship, centered around an onscreen privacy violation and black magicke projection complete with our private relationship nickname "GAGA" etched on the frosted glass panes of the swinging doors to a public bar in one central scene of SHALLOW HAL as the Illuminati "Hit" signature.

In SHALLOW HAL, "A shallow man [Hal] falls in love with a 300 pound woman because of her 'inner beauty'." The film features life coach Tony Robbins whose Fire Walk I did in Manhattan while I was a radio talk show host at WBAI-FM in the mid-1980s. In the film, ""By a twist of fate, Hal becomes trapped in an elevator with famous American life coach Tony Robbins. Getting to know Hal while awaiting the workmen's effort to get the elevator operational again, Tony Robbins sympathizes with Hal's work disappointment but tries to figure out his ideas about women, so he hypnotizes him into only seeing physical manifestations of a person's inner beauty. Hal agrees to Robbins' suggestion but does not catch on to the fact it is hypnosis, and later meets and is smitten by Rosemary Shanahan (Gwyneth Paltrow), the daughter of Steve Shanahan (Joe Viterelli), the president of the company where Hal is employed. Rosemary is morbidly obese, but Hal sees her as a slender and beautiful trophy blonde because of her kind and generous personality. Mr. Shanahan is not certain about Hal dating his daughter, thinking that Hal may be going to any lengths to get to the top of the corporate ladder. Used to being overlooked by men due to her appearance, Rosemary initially interprets Hal's interest in her as mocking, but begins to date Hal when she realizes his feelings for her are authentic."[92]

Through SHALLOW HAL and remote frequency weapons, the controllers of Hollywood and the entertainment industry, the false Matrix that promotes pedophile, ritual child sacrifice, and child trafficking, inserted a false public image of our private lives and marriage and inoculated us with a negative image in the subconscious collective mind of the world public – the Noosphere as it were.

Because Geri was a thyroid cancer survivor, she had issues with personal weight at the time that SHALLOW HAL released. After the worldwide screening of the movie Geri's weight escalated to 298 pounds, just two pounds short of the 300 pound weight of the morbidly obese character played by Gwyneth Paltrow in the film [Geri's weight is now 150 pounds after a gastric bypass procedure gifted to her].

In April 2015 I mentioned the SHALLOW HAL and Gwyneth Paltrow targeting of Geri and me and GAGA to Charles Seven, my colleague in London, who herself is targeted by an international criminal syndicate over the theft of her Intellectual Property and its sale in television markets in 120 countries. Seven replied that she had a dream a few days earlier in which Gwyneth Paltrow's hair turned white and then fell out. If this is a prophetic dream to mean that the controllers now intend to assassinate Gwyneth Paltrow with a fast acting cancer in the same way that they assassinated another Air War film star actor, Philip Seymour Hoffman, then I am officially blowing the whistle here so that Gwyneth Paltrow, who was divorced on April 20, 2015, not get so assassinated.

THE MASTER: TRASHING ALFRED AND PIERRE AT THE POINT

In the Air War film THE MASTER, a mass propaganda reversal of the relationship of Alfred and Pierre R. Leveque at The Point, the star actor Philip Seymour Hoffman was most probably assassinated by suicide in my opinion on orders from Matrix controllers because "dead men tell no tales".

In summary, "The Master is a 2012 American drama film written, directed, and co-produced by Paul Thomas Anderson and starring Joaquin Phoenix, Philip Seymour Hoffman, and

Amy Adams. It tells the story of Freddie Quell (Phoenix), a World War II veteran struggling to adjust to a post-war society, who meets Lancaster Dodd (Hoffman), a leader of a religious movement known as "The Cause". Dodd sees something in Quell and accepts him into the movement. Freddie takes a liking to "The Cause" and begins traveling with Dodd along the East Coast to spread the teachings... The film was partly inspired by Scientology founder L. Ron Hubbard, as well as early drafts of There Will Be Blood, stories Jason Robards had told Anderson about his drinking days in the Navy during the war, and the life story of John Steinbeck.

> "The film officially premiered on September 1, 2012, at the Venice Film Festival where it won the FIPRESCI Award for Best Film. The Master was released on September 14, 2012, in the United States to critical acclaim. The film received three Academy Award nominations: Best Actor for Phoenix, Best Supporting Actor for Hoffman, and Best Supporting Actress for Adams."

The Plot is that "Freddie Quell is a sex-obsessed alcoholic World War II veteran from Lynn, Massachusetts struggling to adjust to a post-war society. He becomes a portrait photographer at a department store but is soon fired for getting into a drunken fight with a customer. Freddie then finds work at a Salinas, California cabbage farm, but his moonshine poisons one of the elderly Filipino migrant workers and he is chased off.

> "One night, intoxicated, Freddie finds himself in San Francisco and stows away on the yacht of a follower of Lancaster Dodd, the leader of a philosophical movement known as 'The Cause.' When he is discovered, Dodd describes Freddie as 'aberrated' and invites him to stay and attend the marriage of Dodd's daughter, Elizabeth, as long as he will make more of his mysterious brew (made with paint thinner), which Dodd has developed a taste for. Dodd begins an exercise with Freddie called Processing, a flurry of disturbing psychological questions aimed at conquering Freddie's past

traumas… At film's end, He gives Freddie an ultimatum: stay with
"The Cause" and devote himself to it for the rest of his life or leave
and never return. Dodd then serenades Freddie with the song Slow
Boat to China. Freddie leaves and picks up a woman at a local pub,
then repeats questions from his first Processing session with Dodd as
he is having sex with her. Finally, he appears to curl up on a beach
next to the crude sand sculpture of a woman the sailors built during
the war."[93]

THE MASTER is another in a long line of Air War productions designed around the negative content of Alfred's family nickname FREDDIE, the nickname his Jesuit Deputy Black Pope uncle always called him. Certainly actor Philip Seymour Hoffman seemed to have paid with his life by assassination by the controllers, under the cover of a revenge killing by disgruntled Scientology. Alfred is a Horse in Chinese astrology. "Horse" was the Illuminati symbology used in this ritual sacrifice of actor Philip Seymour Hoffman. "Phillip Seymour Hoffman died on 2/2/14, the 33rd day of the year, Superbowl Sunday and Groundhog's Day. He died from a heroine overdose. Phillip is Greek for 'horse lover'. 2014 is the Year of the Horse. Phil Everly and James Avery (Uncle Phil) also died this year, so far. Horse is slang for heroine. Katy Perry performed 'Dark Horse' at The Grammy's." [94]

TWENTIETH CENTURY FOX FLIES TO VANCOUVER TO FILM ALFRED, ALLEGEDLY FOR THE DAY THE EARTH STOOD STILL

Then there was the day that 20th Century Fox flew a film crew to Vancouver, BC to film Alfred speaking about Exopolitics for a mini documentary that would be allegedly released on April 7, 2009 with the DVD of THE DAY THE EARTH STOOD STILL starring Keanu Reeves as Klaatu. The film crew arrived, complete with Producer, camera and lighting crew and Alfred duly spoke into the 20th Century Fox camera for posterity.

Here is a draft press release, for the record:

LOS ANGELES, CA – Twentieth Century Fox, which made history on December 12, 2008 by transmitting the first motion picture into deep space, causing THE DAY THE EARTH STOOD STILL to become the world's first galactic motion picture release, is about to make motion picture history again.

Twentieth Century Fox, the producers of the re-make of this classic science fiction film starring Keanu Reeves, is breaking a 60-year taboo imposed by the CIA's 1953 Robertson Panel report about extraterrestrial contact and the existence of intelligent life on other planets, including Mars. In 1953, the Robertson Panel decreed that for reasons of "national security," extraterrestrial life would be debunked in the mainstream media and those claiming contact with extraterrestrials would be publicly ridiculed.

Twentieth Century Fox hired New Wave Entertainment of Burbank, CA to produce a documentary film on the exopolitical implications of extraterrestrial visitation to Earth. According to the exopolitics model, the Universe is filled with intelligent, organized civilizations, some of which are visiting Earth at this time. The documentary film will be included as a feature on the DVD of THE DAY THE EARTH STOOD STILL, which will soon be released internationally.

The producers turned to futurist Alfred Lambremont Webre, international director of the Institute for Cooperation in Space (ICIS), chairman of the Mars Anomaly Research Society (MARS), the Seattle Exopolitics examiner at Examiner.com, and author of Exopolitics: Politics, Government and Law in the Universe, a book that helped found exopolitics, as the star of the film. Also appearing is Seth Shostak of the SETI Institute to espouse the SETI viewpoint. Other commentators may appear in the documentary as well.

THE DAY THE EARTH STOOD STILL documentary marks the first time that an exopolitical documentary has been released in conjunction with a major motion picture.

The Alfred's mini-documentary never made it onto the DVD, as most probably the whole exercise was a Matrix hit to get film footage of Alfred to use as a model in future Air War productions.

Of course, prior to the Press Release, when Alfrid went to Blockbuster and rented the DVD of THE DAY THE EARTH STOOD STILL, the Exopolitics mini-documentary was not in the DVD. As was stipulated in the contract-release that Alfrid signed with 20th Century Fox's contractor, the contractor was under no legal obligation to use the footage.[95]

Please understand that only an initiated few along the Matrix network may fully understand and are aware of the inner meaning of the "ALFRED" and "FREDDIE" code words that appear in media titles, scripts, advertising as masonry to sustain the Matrix, as referring to an actual human being Alfred Lambremont Webre, always in a negative context. Now you too Reader are in on the masonry as well. [EDITOR'S NOTE: Oh I cannot try to prove it to you. Only you can change your mind and fully innerstand the "ALFRED" and "FREDDIE" code words as referring to Alfred.].

Alfred has a book on the Air War, which is in the planning stages.

SCENE 2

EXOPOLITICS: A DECADE OF CONTACT

October 13, 2000
Presidential Politics of UFOs/Disclosure Town Hall Meeting
Santa Clara Convention Center at Great America
5001 Great America Parkway, Santa Clara, CA 95054

Exopolitics: A Decade of Contact

Summary: "The truest conception of our human circumstance is that we are on an isolated planet in the midst of a populated, evolving, highly organized inter-planetary, inter-galactic, [inter-dimensional], universal society. We are isolated because we are in intentional quarantine by a structured, rational universe administration. Are we as a planet on the verge of being re-integrated into universe society? That's very likely. The signs are all around us."- Alfred Lambremont Webre, 1999

Alfred and Geri initially settled in an apartment two blocks from Kitsilano Beach in Vancouver, British Columbia. Their balcony overlooked a red brick elementary school house with park-like grounds. The scene inspired Alfred to write, and, with Geri's encouragement, he wrote three books in real time. The first book was *"Recovery"*, a memoir of his years from 1973 onward. The second book was *"Earth Changes: A Spiritual Approach"*[96], an updating in 1999 of "The Age of Cataclysm" he had written in 1973.

The third book Alfred wrote in 1999 was *"Exopolitics: A Decade of Contact"*[97], the online version of the trade book *"Exopolitics: Politics, Government and Law in the Universe"*. DARPA and CIA time travel would, according to witness evidence and Alfred's own 1971 New York City EPA experiences, have had the trade book "Exopolitics" in their possession since at least 1971.

In 1999, as he sat down to write the "Exopolitics" manuscript, Alfred had no conscious knowledge that in fact the book he would eventually publish in fact at that moment in time probably lay somewhere in the classified storage facilities of U.S. time travel projects as well as time travel surveillance projects, with computer-accessed summaries of his case in what Alfred would come to imagine as the DARPA/CIA "time travel surveillance police".

In real time in 1999, Alfred would awaken every morning early with a general concept that he was writing a treatise, a 'Field Theory' of how intelligent civilizations interacted in the multiverse, or totality of universes and parallel dimensions. Alfred wrote *Exopolitics* using the "headlight" method of writing, where the author simply starts writing and drives the vehicle of the text by the headlights of discovery in writing as it occurs, rather than by a pre-determined outlined or summary. For the content of *Exopolitics*, Alfred drew upon the sum total of his accumulated 26 years of original research into Extraterrestrial civilizations, starting in 1973.

The opening passages of *Exopolitics: A Decade of Contact* read

Caveat lector: Our human civilization is at the very beginnings of its era of Universe consciousness. Any factual errors in descriptions of the structure of a Universe government and of the dynamics of Universe politics, while they may be intuitively well grounded, are the sole responsibility of the author.

PART ONE

LOOKING AT THE UNIVERSE UPSIDE DOWN

How most of the story modern man and woman know about Earth and its outer space environs is wrong. How it is logical and rational that we live in a highly populated and organized Universe society of life-bearing planets. How Universe politics have placed Earth in a planetary quarantine. How that quarantine may be lifting, and what we can do to hasten a universe reunion.

CHAPTER ONE

INTRODUCTION TO EXOPOLITICS

Is there intelligent life elsewhere in the Universe? The true story unfolding in the Universe may turn our concepts upside down.

In reality, Earth appears to be an isolated planet in the midst of a populated Universe. Universe society consists of highly organized and consciously evolving, advanced civilizations. Universe civilizations function within our own interstellar Universe, as well as within other dimensions in the Universe at large. Advanced Universe civilizations exist in other dimensions parallel to our own. They access our own planet, galaxy, and all of interstellar space.

Life-bearing planets such as Earth are part of a collective Universe whole, operating under Universal law. Think of Earth as part of a Universe commons. Life is implanted and cultivated here under the tutelage of more advanced societies, in accordance with the over-all principles of Universe ecology.

Where necessary, Universal law applies restrictive measures to a planet that endangers the collective whole. Universe government can remove a planet from open circulation within Universe society. This fate appears to have happened to Earth in our distant past. Earth has suffered for aeons as an exopolitical outcast among the community of Universe civilizations.

Earth is isolated because it is under intentional quarantine by a structured, rational Universe society. There are signs around us of a Universe initiative to reintegrate Earth into interplanetary society. It is possible that Earth may be permitted to rejoin Universe society, under certain conditions, or at a future time certain.

The above version of our Universe reality may sound vaguely familiar to you. It is the stock of most science fiction, after all. The notion of a populated Universe may have the ring of truth for you. It may raise a tingle along the back of your neck, a truth too close for comfort. Or you may react to the concept of a populated Universe as flaky and unscientific.

Your own beliefs about a populated Universe - whatever they might be - fall along a spectrum of public opinion that is frequently measured. A 1996 Gallup poll showed that 72 percent of the U.S. adult population believes there is some form of extraterrestrial life, and 45 percent believes the Earth has been visited by extraterrestrial life. There are indications that public opinion about extraterrestrial visitation is similar in other regions of the planet. The proportion of extraterrestrial-sensitive world youth may be even higher than the adult populations who believe in an extraterrestrial presence.

Nearly 100 million adult humans in the United States of America (45 percent of the adult population) believe that extraterrestrial civilization has visited Earth. Approximately 100 million U.S. citizens vote in a U.S. Presidential election (the U.S. Federal Election Commission reports that 96,277,634 people voted in the 1996 presidential general election)! About 100,000,000 persons voted in the disputed 2000 U.S. Presidential election.

It is safe to assume that the 100 million US adults who believe in extraterrestrial life could not all be delusional, pre-programmed, or brainwashed. These extraterrestrial-sensitive humans are responding to something they sense is true, deep in their intuition – that extraterrestrials have visited Earth. It is also safe to assume that human intuition is reality-oriented enough to filter out false propaganda from Universe reality. For example, some extraterrestrial "visitations" are actually psychological warfare operations conducted by human military-intelligence agencies.

Other public opinion polls confirm the role of intuition in belief about extraterrestrial life. An October 2000 ABC-NEWS poll found that 47% of US adults believe that intelligent life exists on other planets in the Universe. Demographically, the poll found that belief in extraterrestrial life is held by more men (51%) than women (43%); more college-educated (51%) than high school graduates (43%); more Democrats (53%) than Republicans (38%).

The ABC-NEWS poll found that sixty percent of those who think intelligent extraterrestrial life exists believe that extraterrestrials have visited earth. Overall, 27% of U.S. adults believe that extraterrestrials visit Earth. (The poll excluded "spiritual alien" and "telepathic alien" visits.).

As with the 1996 Gallup poll, personal intuition appears to be a key component of human opinion that extraterrestrial intelligent life exists and visits Earth. In the 2000 ABC-NEWS poll, fully two-thirds of those who think extraterrestrials visit Earth base their conclusions on "speculation." One third of respondents base an opinion on external evidence they have read or seen. Inner intuition may thus be a basis for the insights of at least two-thirds of extraterrestrial-sensitive persons.

Estimates of the U.S. population that thinks extraterrestrial civilizations visit Earth range from 45% in the 1996 Gallup poll, to 27% of the adult population in the 2000 ABC NEWS poll. Somewhere between 50 and 100 million adults in the United States alone believe extraterrestrial civilizations visit Earth. The United States is only five percent of the world's total population.

On November 11, 1999, a less statistically based poll (which included a number of leading astronomers and astrophysicists) was released in the United States on a documentary cable television program. Seventy percent of those surveyed said they believe there is intelligent life in the Universe, including in our own Milky Way galaxy. Eighty percent believe alien civilizations are more advanced than Earth's. Sixty-five percent of the participants think Earth would be conquered if aliens chose to "invade" us. Twenty-six percent think Earth would fight back and win.

These polls may in fact indicate a bottom-line reality about the Universe, which the poll participants intuitively sense: We humans are actually part of a highly advanced, organized interstellar civilization, from which we are in deliberate isolation. This Universe society of intelligent, planetary civilizations is a highly organized and civilized interstellar government that would not attack Earth. It is not violent, war-like, or destructive. Although we are currently in isolation from the rest of interplanetary society, we are part of a peaceful Universal government.

CHAPTER TWO

THE INFANCY OF EXOPOLITICS

Exopolitics, the study of political process and governance in interstellar society, is in its infancy. Yet exopolitics is a key channel to transforming our human future. Exopolitics' immediate goal is a decade of human education and community politics about the extraterrestrial initiative – a Decade of Contact.

Earth may be only one of countless populated planets in an organized Universe that is under the guidance of an advanced Universe society. A near majority of the human population intuitively knows the truth. Extraterrestrial civilizations visit Earth, and an interplanetary federation governs Earth itself. Humanity does not know of or see this Universe government, because Earth has been under deliberate quarantine, isolated from the rest of interstellar society.

We do not yet know the official reasons for this Universe quarantine. Earth may be quarantined for evolutionary reasons, as a planet not yet advanced enough for social interaction with the rest of Universe society. Perhaps a "minimal interference" rule may be at work, whereby more advanced civilizations are prohibited from interfering with a less evolved Universe civilization. Or Earth may be quarantined for essentially exopolitical reasons – reasons of Universe law or politics. For instance, Earth may have somehow violated interplanetary norms in our distant past, and now must prove itself worthy of participation in the body politic of the Universe.

Early in the new millennium in January 2000, Alfred launched "Exopolitics: A Decade of Contact" online as a free e-book to seed the new Exopolitics paradigm.

222

A NOTE TO OUR NEW READERS

Thank you for visiting UniverseBooks.com.

This is your complementary eBook for your personal use. Please book-mark this page

and/or save it to your hard drive for printing and reading. Please tell your friends about us. You may quote from this eBook, so long as attribution is made. If you have any questions, please email us. The Editors at UniverseBooks.com copyright 2000-2001 all rights reserved.

Alfred found an initial receptive audience on the Internet to the concepts in *"Exopolitics: A Decade of Contact"*. From New Zealand, Nicky Molloy was one of several to write reviews of "Exopolitics":

EXOPOLITICS (Part One)
By Alfred Lambremont Webre
UniverseBooks.com
Reviewed by Nicky Molloy

This is one of the most deeply thought provoking books I've read in some time.

Alfred appears right in his perception that almost a majority of US adults know intuitively that we are a part of a populated universe and have been kept in the dark about the implications of this. Can our intuition override deliberate disinformation about this distributed by officials? The rest of society who choose not to believe there is life out there have been deceived from birth. This could possibly constitute the need to evolve more and may even as Alfred suggests reveal the real reason why we have been quarantined from active participation in Universe society, by the rulers of the universe - exopolitical reasons, reasons of Universal politics.

Have the rest of the interplanetary federation deliberately shunned us and left us alone to transmute our violent, warlike and destructive tendencies?

Could there be unseen Universal guardians watching over the Earth - and I would also ask, maybe even an unseen planetary ruler acting as owner of this planet, answerable to Universal rulers?

Alfred suggests that how much we know about Earth and its environs is exactly backwards. He suggests we live in a highly populated and organized society of life bearing planets. Universal politics, which have kept Earth in this planetary quarantine are obviously lifting now. He suggests things we can do to hasten the imminent Universe reunion. For this he suggests a "Users Guide to Life" issued at birth, containing standard instructions for at least four elements of our life on earth.

This guide would reassess and contradict key tenets of our world view -

from evolution to creation beliefs, which contain an element of truth about the origin and structure of the cosmos. It would show how all we've believed cosmologically is exactly backwards. However some have broken free and have Universe consciousness already. He suggests religion, an expression of the collective human intuition, may be one of our more fruitful access points to working models for the study of intelligent civilization in inter-stellar space.

Alfred puts forth the idea that the "User's Guide" could incorporate the disciplines of human religious traditions -Christianity, Buddhism, Islam, Judaism and Hinduism because they contain ancient and potentially fruitful models of the first principles, under which the universe is organized. He writes that religion was the repository of the collective human intuitive reality sense and itself often originally claimed to be influenced or created by higher intelligence itself. His suggestion is, that we can trust this intuition and guide it with the principles of scientific method.

However this would imply in my opinion, that all religions have worth, which I don't agree with in principle as they vary far from the ideal in some cases. But certainly some good, provided all the bad is disposed with, could be selected to add to a common Universal 'belief reality' that possibly the Universal society have collectively decided is 'truth'. We don't know yet if they have a common collective belief system but plans are afoot here now to create a global religion through UN's United Religions Initiative. But could it end up a love and tolerate your fellow man, be fair to all set of rules which deny initiative original thought?

Alfred is more positive and suggests the Universe is the product and creation of advanced, intelligent civilizations. However I would ask do they also have radical individualists, rebels out there? Those who do not conform to a Universe society that is ordered and run intelligently - logic would answer yes. He suggests four reasons why we do not officially recognize the populated, organized universe.

1 THE GARDEN OF EDEN HYPOTHESIS.
   A quarantine imposed by Universal government for disobedience.

2 THE EVOLUTION HYPOTHESIS.
   We have only now evolved to the stage of acquiring science necessary to locating other intelligent civilizations.

3 OSTRICH HEAD IN SAND HYPOTHESIS.
   The Universe may appear devoid of intelligent life, because we are not able to perceive the ongoing signals and visitations of ETs.

4 THE CONSPIRACY HYPOTHESIS.
   Covert Intelligence agencies and human forces want to keep earth isolated for their own power reasons - flooding humanity with bogus "disinformational" UFO sightings and alien "abductions".

Alfred suggests each of these is true. Our "User's Guide" would tell us that the laws of physics, astrophysics and astronomy are our only mode of determining the true realities and dynamics of the Universe. Also that the ancient models of the world's religions and philosophies provide very suggestive models of exopolitics. He writes of a way to break free of illusions and become ready to reintegrate into an intelligent Universal society.

Here is his plan - The intuitive method of knowledge is what human culture since time immemorial has used to survive. If we already 'intuit' that Earth is part of an interplanetary society of advanced civilizations, then why not let go altogether of the illusion that earth is not being monitored now? Are you ready for a dramatic change in our collective planetary life? He says our intuition is as powerful, if not more powerful, than our intellect. We should use it to contemplate freely the vision of a populated, regulated Universe, with travel, commerce, interplanetary universities and communications media. He suggests visualizing planetary societies, varying intelligent species and an inter-stellar federation of planets.

Interplanetary government orders are under Universal law, whose full nature is beyond the conceptual understanding of human government on earth. This includes Universal courts, administrative tribunes and enforcement technology of interplanetary society. He continues that Universal government functions according to classical principles that we on Earth can understand.

So far this all seems reasonable to me that from the mature vision of Alfred conception of this, it could well operate smoothly and orderly in

Universal society. I would be wondering about those species/races that don't conform to Universal law - do they see earth as a hideout, due to our lack of strong leadership and lack of defence technology? (Excerpt).[98]

Alfred reached out to the media. On May 11, 2000, reporter Sally Suddock wrote:

Book says Carter ET investigation scuttled

May 11, 2000 08:15 CST

Add to the reports and legends of presidential experiences with UFO and ET issues a new book that describes President Jimmy Carter's encounter with government cover-up.

Written as a serialized electronic book by a former Stanford Research Institute (SRI) futurist, "Exopolitics" reports that a White House study of extraterrestrial communication was "secretly suppressed at the behest of Pentagon officials" in 1977-78.

Author Alfred Webre alleges that the effort to cut off the study was led by the Defense Department liaison at SRI. It was to have been undertaken jointly by the National Science Foundation and SRI's Center for the Study of Social Policy. Webre says he was to have been the principal investigator for the study.

Webre writes that the Carter White House incident is part of what he terms exopolitics-"the process of government and politics in the Universe." "Is there intelligent life in the Universe?" the author asks. "In fact, the truest conception of our human circumstance may be that we are on an isolated planet in the midst of a populated, evolving, highly organized inter-planetary, inter-galactic, universal society.

Earth is isolated because we are in intentional quarantine by a structured, rational universe society." Webre's context communication theory of extraterrestrial intervention was first introduced in his earlier book "The Age of Cataclysm", published by Putnam's in 1974.

He's frequently consulted by national and international media on commentary and near space issues. In the summer of 1999, Webre appeared on over 60 media programs in the U.S. and elsewhere on issues of near space catastrophe.

Another book is a work of futuristic political journalism, "The Levesque Cases," published in 1990 by PSP Books, Ontario. EXPOLITICS is published by Universe Books.

—Staff Writer Sally Suddock[99]

Professor Leo Sprinkle, PhD of the University of Wyoming invited Alfred to deliver a keynote address on Exopolitics at the June 2000 Rocky Mountain Conference on UFO Investigation,[100] held at the University in Laramie, Wyoming. When

227

Alfred flew in from Vancouver, BC, the obligatory Wyoming State police patrol car pointed in Cointelpro fashion at the car sent to greet Alfred as he approached the campus. "The more things change, the more they remain the same," thought Alfred. Alfred prepared a slide show presentation on Exopolitics, the new field of relations among intelligent civilizations in the multiverse. Later, Prof. Sprinkle, an *eminence gris* in the realm of extraterrestrial studies, wrote a review that welcomed Exopolitics into the social sciences.

Any review of a scholarly work should address three questions: What is the stated goal of the author? How well does the author meet that goal? How does the book contribute to the literature of that discipline or special field?

The reader of a review should be given not only an intellectual assessment of the book, but also some insights into the author's intents and achievements, as perceived by the reviewer. Thus, the reader of the review can determine the bias of the reviewer and then decide whether to buy and/or read the book.

The author of the book that you are about to read, Exopolitics, both educates and exhorts the reader to accept a bold and optimistic view of Earth and humanity. Well written, and well edited, the book explores the status of an isolated planet that is ready to join the cosmic community – "Universe society."

The author, Alfred Lambremont Webre, has advanced degrees in law and applied psychology. He offers his readers the results of many professional activities, including his work as a futurist at Stanford Research Institute. In 1977, he directed a project to develop an extraterrestrial (ET) communication proposal for the White House staff during President Jimmy Carter's Administration.

Exopolitics provides an outline, or a model, for evaluating the current status and possible future of humanity. The stated goal is to provide a bridge between the current concept of Earth as an isolated planet and the future concept of Earth as a member of cosmic cultures, in a multidimensional Universe society.

Webre prepares the reader not only for changes in political "realities," but also for changes in scientific "realities." He emphasizes the principle of a holographic Universe. Both spiritual and material dimensions are ONE. Thus, spiritual and ethical, as well as scientific and technical, development, are signs of a planetary society that is ready for universal "reunion" in politics, government, and law.

Webre addresses a variety of questions: Is the story of the Garden of Eden a reflection of human origins in a cosmic context? Is Earth isolated because of quarantine by ET societies? Is humanity's history of violence – and current plans for military weapons in space – a significant factor in any quarantine by ET societies? Was there a rebellion by Earth's "gods," or governors, against the administrators of a larger cosmic community? Is the UFO phenomenon an indication of the strategy of an ET program? Does the Disclosure Project represent the means by which humanity formally recognizes the ET presence?

The author offers the concepts of "reflectivity" and "dimensionality" as methods by which humans become aware of higher consciousness and higher truth. Thus, both external (empirical) and internal (intuitive) methods are emphasized for exploring and evaluating truth.

For example, Webre uses the results of various public opinion polls as evidence to support dual hypotheses: Most adults are aware of both the ET presence and the UFO cover-up. Approximately half of U.S. adults agree with the statement that ETs are visiting Earth, and more than half agree with the statement that governmental officials are withholding information about UFO reports.

Webre states: "A transformational Exobiology, Exoarcheology, and Exopolitics would construct a bridge of knowledge and relationship with advanced civilizations in the Universe." He calls for a Decade of Contact to prepare humanity for its alignment with Universe society.

In the reviewer's opinion, the author has done well in describing his goal, which is to present a model of Universe politics, and an approach by which humanity might align itself with the law and governance of a Universe society.

Has the author done well in meeting that goal? The reviewer recognizes that there can be a variety of evaluations, depending upon the attitudes of any reader.

The general reader might ask: How does the author know about Universe laws and government? Observation? Intuition? Information from ET societies?

Persons of "enlightened" views (from meditation, UFO and ET encounters, and advanced education) are likely to applaud as well as agree with Webre. Persons with "practical" concerns (e.g., job security, skepticism about intellectuals, and fear of "aliens") are not likely to read the book or react to the model. Persons with certain affiliations or "special interests" (e.g., scientism, religiosity, and covert operations) are likely to discount the model and reject the book.

Perhaps the current "game" will continue, in which the dominant culture maintains that "logical positivism" is the method and "physical evidence" is the measure of the method. If current conditions continue, then the UFO cover-up will continue, and the dominant culture will continue to deny the ET presence.

Webre argues that conditions, however, are changing. There are a variety of Earth conditions (e.g., pollution, global warming, and extinction of plants and animals) and a variety of human concerns (e.g., wars, cultural and religious conflicts, the gap between the rich and poor, and suppression of free energy technologies) that calls out for a new view of Earth and a new view of humanity.

Does the model of Exopolitics provide that perspective? How does the book Exopolitics contribute to the literature on Exopolitics?

The literature on Exopolitics can be grouped into four categories:

1 Statements from writers of channeled messages from extraterrestrial (ET) or extra-dimensional (ED) entities, which describe ET or multidimensional communities;

2 *Reports from persons who describe encounters with ET/ED beings, and the messages from the beings about their worlds;*

3 *Reports from persons who describe travels to other planets, or dimensions, and their observations of those communities;*

4 *Comments from writers who analyze statements (e.g., "science fiction," speculation, and UFO/ET experiences) about various topics of Exopolitics.*

This review cannot summarize the vast literature of ET contact (consider the Vedic traditions, the writings of Zecharia Sitchin, the Old and New Testament), but it can give a few examples of recent writings for comparison with Exopolitics.

Members of the current scientific community usually focus on the physical and biological conditions that are needed for life to emerge on other (distant) planets. They may be supportive of SETI (the Search for Extraterrestrial Intelligence), but they seldom view UFO reports as an indication of ET visitation.

That gap between many scientists and most UFO investigators may be narrowing. For example, a recent article that explores the ET hypothesis – "Inflation-Theory Implications for Extraterrestrial Visitation," Journal of the British Interplanetary Society, vol. 58, 2005, pp. 43-50) was written by James Deardorff, Bernard Haisch, Bruce Maccabee, and Hal E. Puthoff, who are mainstream scientists as well as UFO investigators.

Few psychologists and psychiatrists have participated in UFO research. The death of John Mack, M.D. in 2004, however, was the subject of several editorials, including Stephen Basset's "Exopolitics" column in the December-January 2005 edition of UFO magazine, pp. 16-18. Dr. Mack, a professor of psychiatry at Harvard University, had authored two books on UFO "abductees," and he had founded the Program for Extraordinary Experience Research (PEER).

Philip Krapf, a former news editor for the Los Angeles Times, has described his visits aboard ships of an ET civilization and their plans for contact with nations on Earth.

231

Courtney Brown, Ph.D., a professor of political science, has described his sessions of remote viewing, and his analysis of the political structure of an ET civilization.

C.B. "Scott" Jones, Ph.D. convened a group of international speakers in 1995, at a conference called When Cosmic Cultures Meet. The purpose of the conference, held in Washington, D.C., was to prepare both the public and government officials for possible disclosure of the ET presence.

The Disclosure Project, directed by Steven Greer, M.D., has videotaped testimony from hundreds of former military and government officials about their knowledge of the UFO cover-up.

Michael Salla, Ph.D., author of Exopolitics: Political Implications of the Extraterrestrial Presence, has reviewed international politics as influenced by the ET presence. He attempts to evaluate the levels of evidence for various aspects of the "politics of Exopolitics."

Paul von Ward, author of Gods, Genes, and Consciousness, analyzes evidence from various sources (archeological, cultural, genetic, historical, and technical knowledge) that ABs (Advanced Beings) have helped humans to establish Earth civilizations. His focus on "religious" traditions, and "scientific" traditions, provides an analysis of factors that sustain wars and other conflicts among cultures and nations. He offers an approach to ease the conflicts between different cultures with different "gods."

Ida M. Kannenberg has authored a fourth book, Reconciliation, with the assistance of high-level entities, THOTH and TRES. She analyzes the argument that humanity is spiritually ready to reassess its relationship with other levels of cosmic consciousness.

Lisette Larkins has authored three books on her communications with ETs, emphasizing that anyone can communicate, telepathically, with extraterrestrial beings.

These brief examples indicate that a wide array of literature is available for any reader who wishes to evaluate the contribution of Webre and his model of Exopolitics.

If the reader of the review has doubts about intuitive processes for apprehending "truth," then the book, Power Versus Force, by David R. Hawkins, M.D., Ph.D., can provide an empirical method for assessing levels of consciousness or calibrating levels of truth.

If you have doubts about the UFO cover-up, then UFOs and the National Security State, a history by Richard Dolan, can provide the historical information needed to accept the reality of the ET presence and the UFO cover-up.

In my opinion, the author of this volume, Alfred Lambremont Webre, has presented to readers a small package that contains a huge gift – a new vision of humanity's place in the Cosmos. Most books about Exopolitics are written from the perspective of humanity, or from the perspective of the individual writer.

Webre has provided a perspective of universal law and government that rises above the mundane politics of humanity and Earth, and views humans not as Planetary Persons but as Cosmic Citizens.

When the reader is ready, his Exopolitics provides an individual and collective blueprint for developing a social structure on Earth that assists humanity, in a Decade of Contact, to join and participate in Universe society.

– R. Leo Sprinkle, Ph.D., counseling psychologist, professor emeritus at the University of Wyoming, distinguished Ufologist and author[101]

Alfred reached out to leading activists and audiences in the extraterrestrial and UFO arena with the intent to enrich their fields with the newly derived concepts of Exopolitics.

On July 4, 2000, Alfred appeared on Coast to Coast, the premiere talk show for UFO and Extraterrestrial issues with 10-20 million listeners on average.[102] In August 2000, Alfred flew from Vancouver, BC to Sacramento, CA to have his witness testimony regarding the Carter White House study for the Disclosure Project video-taped, at the same time as a life-long US government employee whose job it was to accompany nuclear warheads as they were recycled at U.S. military bases around the planet. Alfred's fellow witness testified that UFO craft would shadow the aircraft carrying US nuclear warheads. On August 30, 2000, Alfred swore his affidavit about the 1977 Carter White House Extraterrestrial Communication Study and submitted it to the Disclosure Project.[103]

Alfred delivered a lecture on Exopolitics at the October 2000 UFO Presidential Town Hall in Santa Clara, CA., where all but one of the declared candidates in the 2000 US Presidential election were no-shows.[104] Alfred enjoyed the opportunity in frame Exopolitics in terms of U.S. Presidential politics.

TOWN HALL
Santa Clara Convention Center/San Jose, CA.
Friday October 13, 2000
Statement By Alfred Lambremont Webre, JD, MEd

We are here tonight to repudiate secret acts of nearly a quarter century ago. In 1977, a U.S. White House administration openly acknowledged its ignorance about a wider Universe reality in our midst. The highest democratically elected authority in this land sought the most creative of our sciences in understanding the open approaches of an Extraterrestrial intelligence. Then, an information war scuttled that Carter White House study of extraterrestrial communication, even as its work was beginning. A narrow plutocratic clique - hosted in the United States of America - has attempted to lead our entire planetary generation into believing a planetary lie: that we are alone in the Universe.

If there is an Extraterrestrial presence in Earth's dimension, why here and now? Perhaps that Extraterrestrial intelligence is impelled to assist us out of our petroleum-nuclear planetary coffin. Our petroleum-nuclear civilization has made toxic our oceans, atmosphere, and landmasses. The hole in the ozone layer has now expanded from Antarctica to hover over a city in southernmost Chile, expanding the threat of human skin cancer and the disappearance of food-chain vegetation. Global warming and greenhouse gases, caused by our petroleum-nuclear civilization (as well as by solar and galactic activity), threaten Earth's species, habitats, and basic ecology. Already, our polar ice cap is melting. Earth's ionosphere and magnetosphere are being dangerously affected by global electromagnetic weapons and mind control systems such as HAARP and other monstrosities. Electromagnetic weapons affect the human brain's limbic system, and can trigger earth changes by altering the magnetosphere and tectonic plate systems. Universe society may be here to give our planet life-saving assistance. It may be a matter of planetary ecology and the directives of an advanced Extraterrestrial civilization. Some of us call that civilization Universe society.

We may have a decade or so to turn the direction of the petroleum-nuclear civilization around. Public disclosure by all governments of possible extraterrestrial presence may be absolutely necessary to our survival. The Extraterrestrial presence may be a vital component of our saving the ecology of Earth. They may be here to assist us beyond petroleum-nuclear into cosmic free energy sources; beyond our planetary regime of war, disease, crime and poverty into a Universe-based future.

Consider that Earth's ecology may be the true goal of extraterrestrial disclosure. Saving the Earth may be why we are really here tonight. To rally in the full measure of our political understandings and say - Enough! No more lies!

Let us push for a special Decade of Contact in all countries, a transformation of our human self-image. The Decade of Contact is a proactive, education-based process of global integration with Universe society. Our entire terrestrial fabric - environmental, energy, governmental, educational, scientific, technological, and philosophical - calls out for a new Universe-based reality. Let us save our precious Earth. Healing Earth's ecology can be a new, explicit goal of the disclosure process.

Tonight we birth a new vision - a planetary campaign for a Universe-based ecology. Let's start right here and now by demanding open

235

hearings in the California Legislature at Sacramento, and in the United States Congress at Washington, DC, on the extraterrestrial presence, and on exo-solutions in solving our global environmental crisis. We shall also be seeking Open Hearings in other planetary venues, for example: Mexico and Brazil in this hemisphere; France, Sweden, and Russia in Europe; China and Japan in Asia.

Tonight we are entering a new domain of politics - Universe exopolitics. We shift tonight from a terrestrial-bound community to a Universe-directed body politic, which is our fundamental cosmic entitlement. The transformation starts within all of us. For we ourselves are the Universe transformation. We are the exo-government. We are the new Universal human. Thank you.[105]

In 2000 Alfred began publishing on the theory and practice (praxis) of Exopolitics, for example, in a leading magazine in UFO and extraterrestrial commentary, UFO Magazine, and with this promote the Exopolitics model more widely.

Towards a Decade of Contact: Preparing for re-integration into Universe society

—Alfred Lambremont Webre, JD, MEd

VANCOUVER, B.C. – In the late 1980s, I was asked to meet with a Gallup family heir who wished to explore a collaborative venture for a public opinion poll of "transformational" attitudes worldwide. Before our meeting, I half expected a dull, cautious businessman-bureaucrat. Instead, in sauntered in a brilliant imagination, a bright intellect, with the twinkle of cosmic change. This Gallup seemed more like a utopian resident of Sir Francis Bacon's New Atlantis (some interpret Bacon's unfinished work as an allegory about Earth's coming integration with a larger Universe society), rather than the stereotypical captain of corporate America. That meeting was my first expansive Gallup encounter.

A decade or so later, I once again encountered an expansive Gallup. This time my encounter was not with a scion, but with a Gallup pub-

lic opinion poll. The subject matter of the poll related to my research on Exopolitics, the study of politics, government, and law in the Universe. I found the Gallup organization had compiled a public opinion poll that illuminated key terrestrial dynamics of the study of governmental structures and political processes in the Universe.

Yes, you read that sentence correctly. It did say, "Key terrestrial dynamics of the study of governmental structures and political processes in the Universe." Our terrestrial law of Space now ends at the upper atmosphere, or at best at the Moon. Everything beyond those near-earth orbits is, legally speaking, the Void. No living entity or system of government or law is presumed to exist there. Human law assumes that no supra-human politics or regulation exists in outer or dimensional Space.

Enter Exopolitics

Exopolitics, as a discipline for understanding Universe society through its politics and government, may turn our dominant view of the Universe upside down and inside out. As exopolitics posits, the truest conception of our human circumstance may be that we are on an isolated planet in the midst of a populated, evolving, highly organized inter-planetary, inter-galactic, multi-dimensional Universe society.

From an exopolitical perspective, Earth only appears to be isolated because we are in intentional quarantine, imposed by the technology and justice of structured, rational Universe society. We may be isolated from the rest of Universe society as the result of a formal, Universe governmental and political process.

Are we as a planet on the verge of being re-integrated into Universe society? That's very likely. The signs are all around us. In fact, as the Gallup organization polls suggests, contemporary human attitudes about our populated Universe may themselves constitute one of the main signs of our pending reintegration into Universe society.

As with other historical transformations of human society, politics may be a key mechanism for navigating Earth's integration into Universe society. Politics is a process by which the interests of individuals, groups, and institutions will mediate, compromise, and create a collective future. Politics, however, does not end at Earth's edge. Politics is a process that is universal. Earth's integration into Universe society is occurring as part of a definable political process within Universe government. That process is part of the discipline we can term exopolitics.

The Exopolitical Majority

Does the exopolitical version of our Universe reality sound vaguely familiar to you? Does it raise a tingle along the back of your neck? Does it have the ring of truth? Or do you react to it as flaky and unscientific? Well, you can compare your own attitudes about exopolitical reality in the results of a very significant public opinion poll by, yes, the Gallup organization. This poll has profound exopolitical implications. This Gallup poll is almost like a "tracking poll" for extraterrestrial politics.

Each of our personal opinions about the reality of an extraterrestrial presence on Earth now falls along a spectrum of public opinion that has already been scientifically measured by the Gallup organization. A 1996 Gallup poll showed that 72 percent of the U.S. adult population believes there is some form of extraterrestrial life. Fully 45 percent of the adult population believes the Earth is visited by extraterrestrial life.

By extension, we may assume that public opinion about extraterrestrial visitation may be roughly the same in the other regions of the planet. The proportion of world youth that likewise believe extraterrestrials have visited Earth may be even higher than the adult population. These polls, I am sure, will be measured in the not too distant future, if they have not been measured already.

The Gallup poll now shows that nearly 100 million adult humans in the United States – 45 percent of its adult population – believe that Extraterrestrial civilization has visited or visits Earth.

Let's explore the political dimensions of this finding. One hundred million adults is approximately the number of U.S. adults who vote *in a U.S. Presidential election! The U.S. Federal Election Commission reports that 96,277,634 persons voted in the 1996 Presidential general election.*

We can assume that as a whole these 100 million adults aren't delusional, mind-controlled, or brainwashed. Our poll population can intuitively filter out those extraterrestrial "visitations" which are staged secret psychological warfare operations by human military-intelligence agencies. A more recent poll shows that 70 percent of U.S. adults believe the U.S. government is covering up an extraterrestrial presence.

By the very premises of public opinion polls, these 100 million extraterrestrial-sensitive humans are responding to something they believe is true. Down deep in their intuition they hold that extraterrestrials have visited Earth. Philosopher Immanuel Kant would call this perfectly valid intuitive knowledge. In short, human intuition is reality-oriented enough to filter out false propaganda from Universe reality.

What are the implications of the finding that more adult U.S. citizens believe extraterrestrials visit Earth than vote in a U.S. Presidential election? Public opinion polls are prime tools in terrestrial politics. Suppose a public opinion poll were to show that 100 million U.S. adults were favor of a particular type of health care or social security plan. You can safely bet that governments and politicians (especially at election time!) would be jumping to meet these poll-driven political demands.

By contrast, a valid public opinion poll showing that 100 million U.S. adults believe there is an extraterrestrial presence is not driving any political outcomes. No mainstream politicians have defined extraterrestrial presence as a live political or public policy issue. No sizable number of citizens of any terrestrial nation is moved to call upon their local politicians or the political process to connect with the extraterrestrial presence, or study it, or even acknowledge it officially. Why is this anomaly occurring in politics and government?

You could say that a major reason for the disconnection between terrestrial politics and the extraterrestrial issue is cultural and contextual. Our modern human culture has not yet placed these issues – the extra-

239

terrestrial presence, terrestrial politics, and Universe society – in the same context. Our "mainstream" collective human mind literally cannot now see how governments and politics might be connected to an extraterrestrial initiative.

But cultural context is not the whole cause. Public interest research shows that a determined covert terrestrial network may be attempting to "engineer" human attitudes toward the extraterrestrial initiative, and in turn, toward Universe society. Two principal tools of this attitude engineering are official secrecy about actual extraterrestrial contact, and a raging information war against the extraterrestrial presence.

These quasi-official, secret "black operations" networks appear to be hosted largely in the anglophile countries of United States, United Kingdom, Australia, New Zealand, and Canada. Coincidentally, these anti-extraterrestrial networks are in the countries that manage "Echelon," a secret Internet surveillance operation.

The recent unofficial three-year COMETA study formally suggested the hypothesis of an extraterrestrial presence as viable based on the evidence. The senior French scientists, along with former space and Air Force officials, who completed the COMETA study may be taking sides in the information war. Whether consciously or not, functionally they act as informal diplomatic allies of Universe society. The French government itself has sued the Echelon countries for industrial espionage in violation of the European Union. Thus there may be the makings of a diplomatic divide in the global anti-Extraterrestrial information war!

The anti-Extraterrestrial information war has been in place since the early 1950s. This war has no terrestrial political sanction, has not been approved by any constitutional body, and violates the norms of international law. The illegal information war is, on analysis, a principal exopolitical block to Earth's fuller integration with Universe society.

The Disclosure Movement

Not surprisingly, a public disclosure movement is emerging in North America and worldwide. Its focus is to force credible disclosure of offi-

cial contact, and to stop the information war against the extraterrestrial presence. Disclosure movements have longstanding political and constitutional roots in the U.S. and elsewhere. Public interest groups have often used the political and constitutional process to make public and stop secret unconstitutional wars and programs. Such was the case in the Watergate cover-up, the Iran-Contra drug-weapons scheme, and the war in Central America (which killed more than a million persons, with questionable constitutional authorization).

Public disclosure of extraterrestrial contact and of the information war is a nexus point where terrestrial politics and exopolitics meet. To mix many metaphors, disclosure is "where the rubber meets the road." Public disclosure is how exopolitics acquires "traction" in human awareness and terrestrial politics. Disclosure is the procedural antecedent to full, sustained, institutional contact with an extraterrestrial (and multidimensional) Universe society.

Televised public legislative hearings on extraterrestrial scientific and public policy issues are a key strategic option for triggering official disclosure. The political and mass-educational impacts of an open, uncensored legislative hearing before a bipartisan, gender-balanced panel of U.S. Congresspersons could be profound.

Televised legislative and educational panels in different regions of the Earth could follow. France, Brazil and Japan are fruitful of venues for public disclosure hearings that readily come to mind. Hearings in these countries may be even more open than hearings in the U.S., the prime venue of the information war. The U.S., with only five percent of the world's population, may be serving as unwitting host for the brunt of the anti-extraterrestrial information war.

Official legislative hearings can create a credible forum for high-impact disclosure testimony and evidence. The prime function of televised public disclosure is global public education about an extraterrestrial presence. There are many concurrent disclosure activities that could provide valuable testimony and evidence for official hearings. These include high-level French participants in the three-year COMETA study, as well as witnesses in Washington, D.C.-based CSETI's disclosure project (where I recently submitted testimony on a 1977 Carter White House extraterrestrial communication study).

Exopolitics: The "Alien" vs. Extraterrestrial Distinction

The information war is designed to sow confused, negative human attitudes about extraterrestrial reality. Many "alien abductions" may in reality be classic psychological warfare operations, and a phenomenon of the information war. Abduction experiences may be a mixture of: 1) growth-oriented dimensional experiences of an archetypal nature, as described by Harvard Professor John Mack; 2) psychological operations by various sides in the information war; 3) MILAB or terrestrial military-intelligence operations, mimicking "alien abductions" as part of the information war (thus, many abductions may be "psywar" phenomena of the anti-extraterrestrial information war).

From an exopolitical perspective, I use the term "extraterrestrial" to refer to organized Universe society as it exists in interstellar and multidimensional space. Extraterrestrial societies are the participants in the exopolitical process. Exopolitics is a fundamental organizing, mediating, social, and governmental process in our interplanetary and interdimensional space. Exopolitics is how a highly populated and regulated Universe governs itself.

Exopolitics is designed to elicit and illustrate basic principles and dynamics of politics, government, and law in the Universe.

Towards a Decade of Contact: A Vision

How can the human population get beyond the anti-extraterrestrial conceptual traps our institutions and terrestrial leaders keep constructing for us? One way is to build a new, participatory exopolitical process whose purpose is to foment and structure humankind's preparedness to enter interplanetary society.

This participatory process is the Decade of Contact. As a society, we can dedicate a ten-year period of human education and community action around integrating Earth into Universe society. The Decade of

Contact is both a process and a public attitude. Extraterrestrial contact is our doorway into re-integration with Universe society. Extraterrestrial contact is an interactive process, both with our fellow humans and with Universe society itself. Just how many decades it will take to re-establish working contact with the organized Universe seems to be partially in our own hands.

The Decade of Contact is simple and straightforward. Any individual, group, age group, institution, nation, or government can participate. Participants in the Decade of Contact commit to transform their lives, their institutional focus, and resources to re-establishing integration with organized interplanetary society. Rejoining Universe society is an exopolitical process, and will happen only as political momentum gathers at the personal, local, regional, and global levels. The process of Universe integration may take time in lift-off, like a space vehicle starting its long journey with slow lift-off from Earth.

Mobilizing the human species to integrate with Universe society will take place in many concurrent ways. A key task is the gathering of information, research, and scientific and educational resources about Universe society. Our dominant terrestrial model of reality is functionally a legacy from the Middle Ages. Our collective new knowledge base must be assembled from an exopolitical context.

There are also important cultural components to the Decade of Contact, as human awareness builds to a critical mass. These include political movements, public events, concerts, music, art, and media to celebrate Universe society. Our reunion with Universe society is a ground of our basic human rights. The contact process transforms our civilization from within, from a terrestrial culture to a Universal one.

Transformation of human society will occur when we reach a Universe-sensitive critical mass. With approximately 45 percent of Earth's population now extraterrestrial-conscious, can critical mass be far behind?[106]

Copyright © 2000 Alfred Lambremont Webre

By early 2001, Alfred became more involved in helping a core of Disclosure Project witnesses organize a press conference to be held at the National Press Club on May 9, 2001. A collective of activists and witnesses came together to organize the Press Conference, including Alfred's friend Dr. Carol Rosin whom he had met at the UNISPACE conference in Vienna. As it turned out, Alfred was in the midst of obtaining his Canadian permanent resident status and could not leave Canada to participate in person in Washington, DC as an organizer or witness. Alfred participated from Vancouver, BC via phone, Internet, and email, helping with Congressional liaison and international media contacts.

The May 9, 2001 Disclosure Project press conference was itself significant in many ways. For one, despite a documented attempt by a clandestine U.S. government agency at suppressing the online webcast, the webcast itself was reportedly one of the largest recorded to date. Handling media relations, Alfred found evidence, not surprisingly that key media were censoring coverage of the event. The newspaper Space.com even had one article online at its website with the command "DO NOT PUBLISH".

DO NOT PUBLISH: UFO Group Demands Congressional Hearing
By Leonard David
Senior Space Writer
posted: 12:08 pm ET
09 May 2001

WASHINGTON -- There is compelling evidence that Unidentified Flying Objects (UFOs) visit the friendly skies of Earth. These extraterrestrial visitations suggest the presence of advanced extraterrestrial life forms, making use of advanced energy and propulsion technology. Witnesses throughout the world and spanning every branch of the armed services are coming forward to attest to this fact and demand that the U.S. Congress take up the issue.

The Disclosure Project, a nonprofit research organization, today called upon the U.S. President and Congress to support open congressional hearings on the matter.

These testimonies establish once and for all that we are not alone. Technologies related to extraterrestrial phenomena are capable of providing solutions to the global energy crisis, and other environmental and security challenges.

- Steven Greer, head of the Disclosure Project

For dozens of tight-lipped officials, many who are sworn to secrecy, the group is asking for amnesty so these individuals can inform the public-at-large regarding decades of high-level secrecy about UFOs and extraterrestrials.

Best case yet

According to the Disclosure Project head, Steven Greer, witnesses from such groups as the Federal Aviation Administration, Air Force Intelligence, the Central Intelligence Agency (CIA) and the National Reconnaissance Office are ready to step forward and make the best case yet that there is an extraterrestrial presence.

"These testimonies establish once and for all that we are not alone," Greer said. "Technologies related to extraterrestrial phenomena are capable of providing solutions to the global energy crisis, and other environmental and security challenges," he said.

Greer said the Crozet, Virginia-based Disclosure Project has gleaned some 120 hours of digital video testimony from witnesses regarding a long-standing cover-up, as well as amassing around 1200 pages of testimony transcript.

While the data collected speaks for itself, Greer called upon the public to "demand that Congress and the President and the leaders of other countries hold hearings into this subject without delay."

Past hearings

Greer said the only previously held congressional hearings were conducted in 1968, by the House Science and Astronautics Committee in the 90th Congress.

The testimony of first-hand witnesses, thousands of government documents, hundreds of photographs, and evidence to show past landings have been amassed by the group. The materials collected will be made available for any serious scientific or congressional inquiry, Greer said.

According to Alfred Webre, the congressional coordinator for the group, there are several lawmakers who have seen the legislative platform of the Disclosure Project and are prepared to sponsor it within the halls of the U.S. Congress. He would not identify those individuals, telling SPACE.com that private meetings are now underway to gain broad support for the group's findings and recommendations.

"The issue is why are they here, and what institutional interface can we build with extraterrestrial civilizations," Webre said in a phone interview, from his Vancouver, Canada office.

"All indications are that we are a lower-order, intelligent species. So my focus has been on the institutional aspects to very rationally and proactively build an institutional base outward. Right now, we have an outmoded and antiquated 50-year policy of official denial that nobody now believes. At the same time, the necessary work to build the institutional infrastructure to deal with the presence of UFOs and extraterrestrials is not happening," Webre said.

ET craft recovered

"We are talking about a new space policy and paradigm if you assume that the universe may be populated and regulated," Webre said. He said the group is hopeful of motivating Congress to hold hearings on their findings perhaps as early as this year, or in 2002, he said.

Today, Greer said, that the evidence and testimony point to the fact that Earth is indeed being visited by advanced extraterrestrial civiliza-

tions and has been for some time. Moreover, this fact is the most classified-compartmented program within the U.S. and many other countries. Advanced spacecraft of extraterrestrial origin have been downed, retrieved and studied since at least the 1940s, and possibly as early as the 1930s.

Greer said that by studying an ET craft, new breakthroughs in energy generation and propulsion have been made. In fact, classified, above top-secret projects possess fully operational anti-gravity propulsion devices and new energy generation systems. If these energy sources are declassified, he said, civilization could be empowered and free of environmental damage.

Among a number of recommended steps to incorporate the science behind UFOs, the President of the United States should create a new scientific research organization. This group would be charted to integrate the knowledge and technologies behind UFOs with mainstream scientific and academic institutions.[107]

No Congressional hearings came out of the Disclosure Project witnesses calling for a Congressional investigation. Rep. Dennis Kucinich (Dem-Ohio), who later would be publicly outed by his friend actor and author Shirley MacLaine as having had a personal UFO experience, failed to take on this important task (Shirley later would favorably interview Alfred on Exopolitics).[108] The Disclosure Project press conference was to be the first of several Alfred-related initiatives over the years where Dennis Kucinich failed to deliver, including a treaty to ban space based weapons and the banning of chemtrails spraying.

The May 9, 2001 Disclosure Project press conference marked a watershed in the field of Extraterrestrial research and public awareness. One important change, Alfred noticed after the Disclosure Project, was that interactions among the Extraterrestrial and UFO community of researchers became markedly more dualistic, conflictive, combative and at times resembling internecine warfare.

The unity that had surrounded Alfred with the publication of his book *"Exopolitics: A Decade of Contact"* in January 2000 began to unravel in duality after Alfred became a Disclosure Project witness. For example, on July 1, 2000 (Canada Day), Alfred was the honored guest on the leading Extraterrestrial-UFO radio show in Canada, based in Toronto. Less than a year later, after it became publicly known that Alfred was a Disclosure Project witness, the host of the Toronto-based radio show, declared Alfred *persona non-grata* on the prominent email list he ran and attacked Alfred because of his being a Disclosure Project witness.

Alfred found the duality and conflict pattern repeating itself over and over during the years 2001–2013, by specific government-connected officials or officialist gatekeepers in the Ufology and Extraterrestrial studies.

A collateral victim was the science of Exopolitics – the study of relations among intelligent civilizations in the multi-verse - at its infancy, finding itself throttled by apparently negatively-intentioned "leader-gatekeepers" and groups. This duality would accelerate as soon as Alfred introduced the subjects of time travel, teleportation and life on Mars into Exopolitics and the study of relations among intelligent civilizations.

SCENE 3

WORLD AFFAIRS

2007
India International Centre
#40, Max Mueller Marg,
Lodhi Estate, New Delhi,
DL 110003, India

In 2007, Alfred traveled to India from Kuala Lumpur, Malaysia, where he had just been appointed Judge on the Kuala Lumpur War Crimes Tribunal.[109] In New Delhi, India, he spoke at the India International Centre[110] as a guest of World Affairs Journal.[111] Two years earlier in 2005, still not conscious of the role of time travel, teleportation, and secret U.S. – Mars extraterrestrial relations that was at the core of Earthling exopolitics, Alfred had published "Directions Towards an Exopolitics Initiative"[112] in World Affairs.

As Alfred would discover in his dealings with the United Nations and other international and national governments over the next several years, his proposed initiatives would require a grass-roots transformation world-wide, starting with the United Nations.

WORLD AFFAIRS
The Journal of International Issues

DIRECTIONS TOWARDS AN EXOPOLITICS INITIATIVE

By Alfred Lambremont Webre, JD, Med
International Director,
Institute for Cooperation in Space (ICIS)
Vancouver, B.C., CANADA
Copyright 2005, all rights reserved

Part I
Exopolitics: The Twenty-First Century World View

Humanity's efforts to establish a peaceful world order and comprehensive legal jurisdiction in outer space have been largely shaped by the Twentieth Century worldview of the organization of intelligent life in the Universe. Our permanent war economy on Earth will transform into a peaceful, cooperative, sustainable Space Age society as humanity and our institutions allow a new world view of Earth's role a populated, organized Universe society to predominate in our inner and outer reality, and in our public policies and governmental, legal and political life.

The dominant scientific, philosophical, political, social, religious, military and diplomatic paradigm of the Twentieth Century – its Universal world view - held that all intelligent life ends at the geo-stationery orbit, some 22,242 miles above the surface of the Earth. Likewise, the dominant academic canon of the last century held that intelligent civilizations exist only on our Earth.[1]

---

[1] Humanity's fundamental legal instruments for outer space, such as the 1967 United Nations Outer Space Treaty, while theoretically legally operative at the geo-stationery orbit of Earth, as well as on celestial bodies

throughout our Milky Way Galaxy and in galaxies far, far away from our own, are based on the operative world view of our last century, however flawed that world view might be in scientific fact.

The keystone 1967 Outer Space Treaty has acquired normative status under international law, and is widely recognized by Earth's international community. As of January 1, 2003, fully 125 (out of a possible 191) U.N. Member Nations had signed the Treaty, including 98 ratifications by national legislative bodies. The Outer Space Treaty, which "provides the basic framework on international space law, includes the following principles:

- the exploration and use of outer space shall be carried out for the benefit and in the interests of all countries and shall be the province of all mankind;
- outer space shall be free for exploration and use by all States;
- outer space is not subject to national appropriation by claim of sovereignty, by means of use or occupation, or by any other means;
- States shall not place nuclear weapons or other weapons of mass destruction in orbit or on celestial bodies or station them in outer space in any other manner;
- the Moon and other celestial bodies shall be used exclusively for peaceful purposes;
- astronauts shall be regarded as the envoys of mankind;
- States shall be responsible for national space activities whether carried out by governmental or non-governmental activities;
- States shall be liable for damage caused by their space objects; and
- States shall avoid harmful contamination of space and celestial bodies."

With the possible exception of one such principle, "astronauts shall be regarded as the envoys of mankind," the operating world view underlying each of these principles is that the Outer Space Treaty is drafted for a Universe which is a limitless void, and in which intelligent life appears only on Earth. For example, the principle, "the exploration and use of outer space shall be carried out for the benefit and in the interests of all countries and shall be the province of all mankind," applies by its terms only to "mankind" and not to other intelligent civilization in the Universe.

Yet even jurisprudence itself informs us that principles of natural law such as Justice are Universal and operate beyond the geostationary orbit. Justice, a natural law basis for all social law, is operative on Earth, and is likewise operative on our Moon (Luna), on our sister planet Mars, in our sister solar system the Pleiades, on every celestial body, and elsewhere in the Universes.

The United Nations Outer Space Office has published a useful summary of international legal standards for outer space:

- The Treaty on Principles Governing the Activities of States in the Exploration and Use of Outer Space, including the Moon and Other Celestial Bodies (the "Outer Space Treaty", adopted by the General Assembly in its resolution 2222 (XXI)), opened for signature on 27 January 1967, entered into force on 10 October 1967, 98 ratifications and 27 signatures (as of 1 January 2003);

- The Agreement on the Rescue of Astronauts, the Return of Astronauts and the Return of Objects Launched into Outer Space (the "Rescue Agreement", adopted by the General Assembly in its resolution 2345 (XXII)), opened for signature on 22 April 1968, entered into force on 3 December 1968, 88 ratifications, 25 signatures, and 1 acceptance of rights and obligations (as of 1 January 2003);

- The Convention on International Liability for Damage Caused by Space Objects (the "Liability Convention", adopted by the General Assembly in its resolution 2777 (XXVI)), opened for signature on 29 March 1972, entered into force on 1 September 1972, 82 ratifications, 25 signatures, and 2 acceptances of rights and obligations (as of 1 January 2003);

- The Convention on Registration of Objects Launched into Outer Space (the "Registration Convention", adopted by the General Assembly in its resolution 3235 (XXIX)), opened for signature on 14 January 1975, entered into force on 15 September 1976, 44 ratifications, 4 signatures, and 2 acceptances of rights and obligations (as of 1 January 2003);

"The Agreement Governing the Activities of States on the Moon and Other Celestial Bodies (the "Moon Agreement", adopted by the General Assembly in its resolution 34/68), opened for signature on 18 December 1979, entered into force on 11 July 1984, 10 ratifications and 5 signatures (as of 1 January 2003).

"The international legal principles in these five treaties provide for non-appropriation of outer space by any one country, arms control, the freedom of exploration, liability for damage caused by space objects, the safety and rescue of spacecraft and astronauts, the prevention of harmful interference with space activities and the environment, the notification and registration of space activities, scientific investigation and the exploitation of natural resources in outer space and the settlement of disputes. Each of the treaties lays great stress on the notion that the domain of outer space, the activities carried out therein and whatever benefits might accrue therefrom should be devoted to enhancing the well-being of all countries and humankind, and each includes elements elaborating the common idea of promoting international cooperation in outer space activities.

"The five sets of legal principles adopted by the United Nations General Assembly provide for the application of international law and promotion of international cooperation and understanding in space activities, the dissemination and exchange of information through transnational direct television broadcasting via satellites and remote satellite observations of Earth and general standards regulating the safe use of nuclear power sources necessary for the exploration and use of outer space.
"The five declarations and legal principles are:

- The Declaration of Legal Principles Governing the Activities of States in the Exploration and Uses of Outer Space (General Assembly resolution 1962 (XVIII) of 13 December 1963);

- The Principles Governing the Use by States of Artificial Earth Satellites for International Direct Television Broadcasting (resolution 37/92 of 10 December 1982);

- The Principles Relating to Remote Sensing of the Earth from Outer Space (resolution 41/65 of 3 December 1986);

- The Principles Relevant to the Use of Nuclear Power Sources in Outer Space (resolution 47/68 of 14 December 1992);

"The Declaration on International Cooperation in the Exploration and Use of Outer Space for the Benefit and in the Interest of All States, Taking into Particular Account the Needs of Developing Countries (resolution 51/122 of 13 December 1996).

Source: Office for Outer Space Affairs, United Nations Office at Vienna, Austria: http://www.oosa.unvienna.org/SpaceLaw/treaties.html

A world view for the Twenty-First Century – the Exopolitics model - informs us that, in reality, Earth appears to be an isolated planet in the midst of a populated, evolving, highly organized inter-planetary, inter-galactic, multi-dimensional Universe society, composed of intelligent civilizations subject to Universal law, operating under Universal governance, and mediated by Universe politics. The Exopolitics model sees our Earth as an entry-level inhabited planet, now in a transitional process of social assimilation and structural integration into in a larger, organized Universe society. [2]

The Exopolitics model operates on Twenty-First Century science, and is based on replicable data derived through the scientific method using Scientific Remote Viewing.[3] Scientific Remote Viewing is based upon the remote viewing methodologies developed at Stanford Research Institute (SRI) in the latter 1970s by my former SRI colleagues Dr. Hal Puthoff and Russell Targ under contract with defence and intelligence agencies of the government of the United States of America.[4]

The essential structure and dynamics of the Exopolitics model – that the Universe is populated by intelligent civilizations, organized under governing bodies and operating according to law – is preliminarily confirmed by replicable scientific remote viewing data. Data from scientific remote viewers suggest that a spiritually and technologically advanced galactic federa-

---

[2] The Exopolitics model is set out in detail in the treatise EXOPOLITICS: POLITICS, GOVERNMENT AND LAW IN THE UNIVERSE (Universebooks 2005) by Alfred Lambremont Webre, JD, Med

[3] A comprehensive treatment of the scientific principles underlying Scientific Remote Viewing is set out in REMOTE VIEWING: THE SCIENCE AND THEORY OF NONPHYSICAL PERCEPTION (Farsight Press 2005) by Courtney Brown, PhD.

[4] See, for example, PUTHOFF, Hal E., "CIA-initiated Remote Viewing at Stanford Research Institute," Austin, Institute for Advanced Studies, 1995; see also, LORA, Doris and TARG, Russell, "How I was a Psychic Spy for the CIA and found God," Institute for Noetic Sciences (IONS), November 2003.

tion of inhabited worlds exists. It can be described as a sort of loosely organized spiritual government of our Milky Way galaxy. Scientific Remote Viewing uses access to a sub-space in the time-space matrix to achieve replicable, interactive communication with the consciousness of entities belonging to Off-Planet Cultures, and with the individual consciousness of representatives of governance bodies of Universe society. The sub-space context in the time-space matrix which Scientific Remote Viewing achieves is more suited to communication with representative of Off-Planet Cultures which are, in one specific case, literally approximately one million years more advanced than our own, making face-to-face negotiations difficult for our entry-level human species.[5]

Part II
An Exopolitical Initiative

Early Exopolitical Initiatives: Canada – Since the mid-Twentieth Century, humanity had been episodically transitioning toward public policies overtly based on the Exopolitics model. Over 40 years ago, the then Minister of Defence of Canada undertook an early Exopolitical Initiative: a public act based on the principles of the Exopolitics model. In 1963, Hon. Paul Theodore Hellyer became Minister of National Defence of Canada in the cabinet of Canadian Prime Minister Lester B. Pearson, himself a Nobel Peace Prize Laureate. As Minister of Defence, Minister Hellyer oversaw the controversial integration and unification of the Canadian Army, the Royal Canadian Navy and the Royal Canadian Air Force into a single organization, the Canadian Forces. Throughout his life, the Hon. Paul Hellyer has been

---

[5]   For an introduction to replicable data derived by Scientific Remote Viewing of interactive communications in sub-space with Off-Planet Cultures, please see BROWN, Courtney, *Cosmic Explorers*, New York, NY, Dutton, 1999; and BROWN, Courtney, *Cosmic Voyage*, New York, NY, Dutton, 1996.

opposed to the weaponization of space. He supports the Space Preservation Treaty to ban space weapons.[6] The Institute for Cooperation in Space supports the initiative for a United Nations Space Preservation Treaty and Treaty –signing Conference to ban all space-based weapons and warfare in space.[7]

On June 3, 1967, while Minister of Defence, Paul Hellyer flew in by helicopter to officially inaugurate an Extraterrestrial landing pad in St. Paul, Alberta, Canada. The town had built the landing pad as its Canadian Centennial celebration project, and as a symbol of keeping space free from human warfare. The sign beside the pad reads: "The area under the World's First UFO Landing Pad was designated international by the Town of St. Paul as a symbol of our faith that mankind will maintain the outer universe free from national wars and strife. That future travel in space will be safe for all intergalactic beings, all visitors from earth or otherwise are welcome to this territory and to the Town of St. Paul."[8] Hellyer later went on to become Deputy

---

[6] See Space Preservation Treaty. Institute for Cooperation in Space (ICIS). http://www.peaceinspace.com

[7] See: "Canada's Foreign Minister Pierre Pettigrew hints at supporting a U.N. Space Preservation Treaty Conference" Excerpt: GENEVA - In a March 14, 2005 speech to the United Nations Conference on Disarmament, Pierre Pettigrew, Minister of Foreign Affairs of Canada alluded to the possibility that Canada and other nations might be willing to look outside of the United Nations Conference on Disarmament, deadlocked for eight years, for a multi-lateral agreement banning weapons and warfare in space."
Source: Campaign for Cooperation in Space: peaceinspace.org http://peaceinspace.blogs.com/peaceinspaceorg/2005/03/canadas_foreign.html

[8] Source: The Life of Paul T. Hellyer, The Wikipedia Encyclopedia. May 7, 2005. "To turn us in the direction of re-unification with the rest of creation the author [Alfred Lambremont Webre, JD, Med] is proposing a "Decade of Contact" – an "era of openness, public hearings, publicly funded research, and education about extraterrestrial reality." That could be just the antidote the world needs to end its greed-driven, power-centered madness." Honorable Paul T. Hellyer, *Minister of National*

Prime Minister of Canada under Prime Minister Pierre Eliot Trudeau.

Early Exopolitical Initiatives: United Nations - Over a quarter century ago, the international community approved in principle the foundations of a transitional organizational and legal infrastructure based on an Exopolitical world view that Earth may well be part of an organized, populated Universe society. The United Nations General Assembly first approved a Resolution based on principles underlying the Exopolitics model on December 18, 1978, when the UN General Assembly adopted *decision 33/426, 1978*, stating that: "The General Assembly invites interested Member States to take appropriate steps to coordinate on a national level scientific research and investigation into extraterrestrial life, including unidentified flying objects, and to inform the Secretary-General of the observations, research and evaluation of such activities."[9]

Defense under Canadian Prime Minister Lester B. Pearson and Deputy Prime Minister of Canada under Prime Minister Pierre Trudeau

[9] The full text of UN General Assembly decision 33/426, 1978 reads as follows:

Summary: At its 87th plenary meeting, on 18 December 1978, the UN General Assembly, on the recommendation of the Special Political Committee recommended the establishment of an agency or a department of the United Nations for undertaking, co-coordinating and disseminating the results of research into unidentified flying objects and related phenomena.

UN General Assembly decision 33/426, 1978

Establishment of an agency or a department of the United Nations for undertaking, coordinating and disseminating the results of research into unidentified flying objects and related phenomena

At its 87th plenary meeting, on 18 December 1978, the General Assembly, on the recommendation of the Special Political Committee adopted the following text as representing the consensus of the members of the Assembly:

A Modern Exopolitical Initiative –The Exopolitical Initiative is a 10-year internationally and nationally funded formal process designed to support a sea change in humanity's understanding of its position in a populated Universe, and to support our social, legal, governmental, and exopolitical integration into a larger Universe society. The Exopolitics Initiative is epochal and unprecedented in scale and scope of activity, and consists of at least two mutually-reinforcing programmes:

A Decade of Contact - A 10 year process of formal, funded process of public education, scientific research, educational curricula development and implementation, strategic planning, community activity, and public outreach concerning terrestrial society's full cultural, political, social, legal, and governmental integration into a larger Universe society.

Star Dreams Initiative (SDI) – Public interest diplomacy, using modalities such as Scientific Remote Viewing, with spiritually

---

"1. The General Assembly has taken note of the statements made, and draft resolutions submitted, by Grenada at the thirty-second and thirty-third sessions of the General Assembly regarding unidentified flying objects and related phenomena.

"2. The General Assembly invites interested Member States to take appropriate steps to coordinate on a national level scientific research and investigation into extraterrestrial life, including unidentified flying objects, and to inform the Secretary-General of the observations, research and evaluation of such activities.

"3. The General Assembly requests the Secretary-general to transmit the statements of the delegation of Grenada and the relevant documentation to the Committee on the Peaceful Uses of Outer Space, so that it may consider them at its session in 1979.

"4. The Committee on the Peaceful Uses of Outer Space will permit Grenada, upon its request, to present its views to the Committee at its session in 1979. The committee's deliberation will be included in its report which will be considered by the General Assembly at its thirty-fourth session."

advanced Off-Planet Cultures now visiting Earth, where contact between our planetary civilizations has been authorized and recommended by Universe governance authorities.

A modern Exopolitical Initiative must be undertaken forthwith, under the auspices of the United Nations, as authorized by UN General Assembly *decision 33/426, 1978,* which remains valid and in force. This Exopolitical Initiative should be undertaken by the United Nations, as our planet's most viable representative to Universe society. At least one of the spiritually-advanced Off-Planet Cultures now authorized to enter into formal integration with our human society has stated that it does not wish to initiate negotiations with any one individual Member Nation government, and will prefer to deal with the United Nations as a representative body of Earth.[10]

On March, 10, 2005, The Institute for Cooperation in Space (ICIS) tabled such a Proposal for A Canadian Exopolitics Initiative in a public hearing in Winnipeg, Manitoba, Canada before the Senate of Canada's Standing Committee on National Security and Defence, in order to help facilitate the process of marshaling the interest and support of United Nations Member Nations, as well as the human population, in undertaking an Exopolitical Initiative.[11]

---

[10] Please see interactive communications with Off-Planet Cultures in BROWN, Courtney, *Cosmic Explorers,* New York, NY, Dutton, 1999; and BROWN, Courtney, *Cosmic Voyage,* New York, NY, Dutton, 1996.

[11] See: STATEMENT AND PROPOSAL FOR A CANADIAN EXOPOLITICS INITIATIVE, SENATE OF CANADA, Standing Committee on National Security and Defence, March 10, 2005, Winnipeg, MB, To: Senators Colin Kenny; J. Michael Forrestall; Norman K. Atkins; Tommy Banks; Jane Cordy; Joseph A. Day; Michael A. Meighen; Jim Munson and Pierre Claude Nolin.

Part III
Star Dreams Initiative (SDI) - Integrating with Off-Planet
Cultures now visiting Earth[12]

Public Interest Diplomacy - Members of the Institute for
Cooperation in Space (ICIS) have engaged in public interest
diplomacy with Non-Governmental Organizations, media
organizations, and governmental organizations of the Soviet
Union during the *glasnost* period in the latter 1980s. In 1987,
for example, the author of this article developed, co-produced
and co-hosted the first live radio broadcast in human history
between the United States of America and the Soviet Union.
The historic 4-hour programme was carried live in the Soviet
Union by *Gosteleradio*, the official state broadcasting entity, and
in the United States of America by a station of the Pacifica
Network using a National Public Radio satellite transponder.
The programme featured live interaction between prominent
Soviet and United States poets, actors and other cultural figures.
In a subsequent such ("Moscow-New York Live"), bystanders on
the streets of Jersey City, New Jersey in the United States were
connected live on international radio with bystanders on the
street in Moscow. Some of the citizens interviewed wept openly
on the air at the emotion of an Iron Curtain of separation being
instantly deconstructed through a public interest diplomacy
radio programme. This programme was organized as a conscious
act of public interest diplomacy, paid for in the Pacifica Network broadcast by non-profit contributions, and later was
nominated for an award to be given in the United Nations
General Assembly.[13]

The Star Dreams Initiative (SDI) is a programme of public

---

[12] Please see EXOPOLITICS: POLITICS, GOVERNMENT AND LAW
IN THE UNIVERSE (Universebooks 2005), pp. 87 – 107 for a detailed
discussion of concepts introduced in Part III of this article, Star Dreams
Initiative (SDI) - Integrating with Off-Planet Cultures now visiting Earth.

[13] See Wikipedia Encyclopedia, Life of Alfred Lambremont Webre, May 8,
2005.

interest diplomacy with spiritually advanced Off-Planet Cultures now visiting Earth.

"'Public interest diplomacy' is a terrestrial concept developed by western non-governmental organizations (NGOs) that established unprecedented, transparent, quasi-diplomatic relations with sectors of the Soviet Union during the glasnost period of the 1990s. Public interest diplomacy in the form of a Star Dreams Initiative requires empathic cooperation between representatives of the mainstream terrestrial culture and a participating Off-Planet Culture. As with glasnost, this cooperation can only happen through nurturing relationships between the parties. Public interest diplomacy also has as one of its goals influencing government policies so that they can be in the best interests of the human collective. [14]

Agape-centered public interest diplomacy – Public interest diplomacy in a Star Dreams Initiative (SDI) takes place amongst Universe civilizations with vastly different stages of evolution and cultural frames of reference. *Agape* is the ingredient that functionally levels the playing field between the vastly different Universe civilizations involved. Public interest diplomacy with spiritually advanced Off-Planet Cultures must be *Agape*-centered. *Agape* is defined as Cosmic Love rather than emotional or inter-personal love. Agape, a deep sense of the Cosmic Love and interconnectedness of the Universe, rather than conflict, appears to be the central organizing principle of advanced civilizations in Universe society. One scientist summarizes his findings, based upon interactive observations and communications via Scientific Remote Viewing with specific spiritually advanced Off-Planet Cultures, as follows:

"Somehow love is the theme... the glue that keeps the Universe together. But only highly evolved beings realize the full extent of this

---

[14]   See EXOPOLITICS: POLITICS, GOVERNMENT AND LAW IN THE UNIVERSE (Universebooks 2005), page 99.

reality. I do not claim to know why love is a glue of the universe. We tend to think of love as a mushy emotion. My remote viewing of highly evolved beings suggests that the human concept of love is very primitive, but I really do not know of any other word to describe the flavor of what I sense. Whatever love is in these evolved beings, it is not mushy. It is matched with clear thinking and effective action. There is a smoothness in their lives that is enviable."[15]

A functional dialogue between humanity and spiritually advanced Off-Planet Cultures requires that the ethics and functional states of being of participants in a Star Dreams Initiative (SDI) be Agape-centered, rather than dominated by a zero-sum power-based consciousness. Humanity's collective and individual human rights can be protected in negotiations with spiritually advanced Off-Planet Cultures by our adherence and enforcement of existing international standards such as the Universal Declaration of Human Rights.[16]

Structure & Goals of a Star Dreams Initiative (SDI) – One key treatise on public interest diplomacy with Off-Planet Cultures states that:

---

[15]   BROWN, Courtney, *Cosmic Voyage, op. cit.*, p. 173.
[16]   United Nations. Universal Declaration of Human Rights, Adopted and proclaimed by General Assembly resolution 217 A (III) of 10 December 1948 *"On December 10, 1948 the General Assembly of the United Nations adopted and proclaimed the Universal Declaration of Human Rights the full text of which appears in the following pages. Following this historic act the Assembly called upon all Member countries to publicize the text of the Declaration and "to cause it to be disseminated, displayed, read and expounded principally in schools and other educational institutions, without distinction based on the political status of countries or territories."* National legal standards protecting fundamental human rights are also operative to protect humanity's fundamental rights in public interest diplomacy with spiritually advanced Off-Planet Cultures, and must be protected and enforced. See, for example, the Charter of Rights and Freedoms, Constitution of Canada; The Bill of Rights, Constitution of the United States of America.

"The goals of public interest diplomacy include a negotiated, consensual plan for mutual, transparent, open interaction and public diplomatic relations between recognized scientific, ethical-religious, and governmental bodies of the terrestrial and specific off-planet culture(s) engaging in a Star Dreams Initiative. This overall plan would include appropriate inter-species treaties under principles of international and universal law. Public interest diplomacy, where appropriate, may include representatives and advisory observers of galactic, interplanetary governing authorities.

"A Star Dreams Initiative should develop interactive protocols, setting out the parameters of the project and appropriate proposals for outreach, contact, and public interest diplomacy. These would include interplanetary treaties establishing formal relations and detailing essential functions, such as fundamental declarations of principles governing rights, government, ownership, and other key principles of space law, bans on space weapons and warfare in space, outer space exploration standards, security, technology transfer, and interplanetary immigration."[17]

The structure and goals of a Star Dreams Initiative would include, in addition to the initiating Non-Governmental Organizations, the key parties of humanity's governance organizations as well as representatives of spiritually advanced Off-Planet Cultures which have been specifically authorized by Universe governance authorities to enter into full planetary relations with humanity on Earth.

Star Dreams Initiative (SDI) Participants - For example, as authorized by UN General Assembly *decision 33/426, 1978* our Earth's representative participants in a Star Dreams Initiative would include:

- United Nations Secretary-General

---

[17] See EXOPOLITICS: POLITICS, GOVERNMENT AND LAW IN THE UNIVERSE (Universebooks 2005), Part IV.

- United Nations Office for Outer Space Affairs
- United Nations Security Council
- United Nations General Assembly
- Member nations of the UN Committee on the Peaceful Uses of Outer Space
- Interested Non-Governmental Organizations (NGOs), educational institutions, and educational and public media.

Off-planet culture representatives (via direct participation, scientific remote viewing, or other modality) would include:

- Spiritually-advanced Off-Planet Culture governmental representatives, as identified in scientific remote viewing sessions or other outreach modalities
- Universe governance authorities which have authorized specific initiative to integrate humanity and another planetary society, as identified in scientific remote viewing sessions or other outreach modalities
- Other interested Spiritually advanced Off-Planet Culture participants.

Central Goals of a Star Dreams Initiative (SDI) – The central goals of a public interest diplomacy Star Dreams Initiative (SDI) include:

- Transformation of the permanent warfare economy on Earth into a sustainable, cooperative, peaceful, Space Age, Universe-oriented society
- Establishing interactive, substantive communication and contact with off-planet cultures engaging our planet at this time through programmed stages of interaction
- Integration of Earth and human society into a larger, organized, advanced, spiritually developed Universe society

Part IV
Conclusion

As stated at the outset, humanity's permanent war economy on Earth will transform into a peaceful, cooperative, sustainable Space Age society as humanity and our institutions allow a new world view of Earth's role a populated, organized Universe society to predominate in our inner and outer reality, and in our public policies and governmental, legal and political life. A Star Dreams Initiative (SDI) for public interest diplomacy with spiritually advanced Off-Planet Cultures now visiting Earth and authorized by Universe governance authorities to engage in planetary integration with our terrestrial society offers a practical avenue for this historic, epochal transformation.

SCENE 4

EXOPOLITICS & TIME TRAVEL

13th-14th-15th May 2005
Nexus Conference 2005
Grand Krasnapolsky Hotel,
Dam, 9. 1012 JS
Amsterdam, The Netherlands

"Exopolitics: Politics, Government And Law In The Universe" by Alfred Lambremont Webre, JD, MEd is the first book in history whose author was informed that his book was teleported by time travel technology from the future to the past. Alfred was so informed by Andrew D. Basiago, a former time travel participant in a highly classified U.S. Government program for time travel teleportation of objects and information from the future to the past for study by U.S. intelligence officials. As such, the book Exopolitics is a Quantum Access Time-Travel artefact." Proposed time travel notice, 2005

One Spring day in 2005 while working with his editor, Alfred learned from an eyewitness that his book *"Exopolitics: Politics, Government and Law in the Universe"* had been time-traveled by the U.S. government (DARPA and CIA) using secret time travel technology, physically taking the book "Exopolitics" back from at least 2005 to a U.S. government time travel project at least 1971.

267

The eyewitness and his editor were the same person Andrew D. Basiago who was editing Alfred's 1999 manuscript *"Exopolitics: A Decade of Contact"* that Alfred had published on the Internet in 2000 as a free e-book to seed the Exopolitics paradigm. Alfred learned from Andy that DARPA, the Defense Advanced Research Projects Agency, had time travel teleported a physical copy of the published trade book "Exopolitics" and that Andy had witnessed as copy of "Exopolitics" in 1971 as part of his experiences as a childhood participant in Project Pegasus, DARPA's time travel project.[113]

Andy told Alfred that as a 9-year-old child time traveler for DARPA's Project Pegasus, Andy first saw the book "Exopolitics" and heard its author's name, "Alfred Lambremont Webre", in 1971. Andy's father, Raymond F. Basiago, was in Project Pegasus and has brought a copy of Alfred's 2005 book "Exopolitics" in a classified time travel security satchel and shown it to Andy and one other witness, Connie Chavez, Raymond's friend in 1971.

According to Andy, once Andy had been pre-identified via time travel as a future whistleblower, all of Andy's books were retrieved from the future via time travel. Alfred's book "Exopolitics", which Andy edited, was part of this time travel dragnet. At this point, Alfred also came under time travel investigation.

Alfred's first emotions when learning that his innovative work "Exopolitics" had been traveled back in time by the U.S. Central Intelligence Agency for surveillance using DARPA secret time travel technology were anger and a sense of having his deep soul-privacy invaded for illegal, unconstitutional purposes by a secret U.S. government agency. Alfred's process was similar to the stages of Kübler-Ross model for the five stages of grief – denial, anger, bargaining, depression, and acceptance, occurring in no specific sequence.[114]

Alfred re-framed his perceptions of key past experiences once he emotionally was able to accept Andy's revelation that his book "Exopolitics" had been time traveled by DARPA/CIA from at least 2005 to back to at least 1971. One significant incident jumped out directly in Alfred's memory. This was the 1971 environmental speech Alfred had given to the "Delaware Valley Industrial Engineering Association".[115] Alfred had experienced that event with profound cognitive dissonance, as though the event were something other than it was advertised to be, and was, in fact, a U.S. government covert intelligence agency psyop.

Alfred deduced that a 1971 time travel surveillance of Alfred by CIA and DARPA personnel then in possession of his 2005 book "*Exopolitics: Politics, Government, and Law in the Universe*", had been conducted in the guise of an "Environmental speech" by then General Counsel of the New York City Environmental Protection Administration, Alfred Lambremont Webre. DARPA and CIA had been briefed on information assembled about Alfred via time travel, were in possession of his book "Exopolitics", and created a pseudo-event – an environmental lecture by Alfred - in order to subject Alfred to intelligence surveillance methods, determine a course of action to neutralize the future Alfred, and subliminally threaten Alfred by smirking, grimacing and making various neurolinguistic gestures during Alfred's talk.

Alfred's 1971 searing personal experience of 50 or so DARPA/CIA employees conducting intelligence surveillance of him in a psyop event informed by secret time travel technology provided Alfred with his own eye-witness testimony collaborating the eye-witness evidence Andy had just provided of his book "Exopolitics: Politics, Government and Law in the Universe" having been time traveled back to 1971. As a war crimes Judge, Alfred knew that the legal rules of evidence entitled him to take official notice and credence of Andy's eyewitness claim that DARPA/CIA had time traveled Alfred's book "Exopolitics" from 2005 to 1971.

Alfred and his editor Andy did not incorporate a public notice in the first Edition of "Exopolitics: Politics, Government and Law in the Universe" to the effect that the book had been time traveled to the past by DARPA and CIA.

At the time, shortly before the 2005 publication of the book "Exopolitics", this time travel notice would have been technically possible to insert into the first edition of *"Exopolitics: Politics, Government and Law in the Universe"*.

Inserting this time travel notice would have produced a different artifact from the original "Exopolitics" book artifact that DARPA/CIA had time traveled to the past (at least 1971) from the future (at least 2005). Under the laws of time science, the time line in which Andy would have both witnessed in 1971 Alfred's book "Exopolitics" without a time travel notice would not exist.

Thus, Alfred's book *"Exopolitics: Politics, Government and Law in the Universe"* rolled out into the world in 2005 with no public notice that the book was a time travel artifact, or that it had been time traveled and digested by U.S. military and intelligence agencies including DARPA and CIA as early as 1971.

Initially, UFO and extraterrestrial affairs researchers welcomed the content of Alfred's book "Exopolitics: Politics, Government and Law in the Universe" in 2005. As Alfred subsequently rolled out the exopolitical reality behind the book *"Exopolitics: Politics, Government and Law in the Universe"*, distorted and vocal opposition from gatekeeping UFO and extraterrestrial research gatekeepers to Alfred's conclusions arose even though they had only recently endorsed his book.

Alfred enjoyed solid public support for the evidential conclusions that the CIA had time traveled the book from 2005 back to 1971; that the U.S.-Mars extraterrestrial relations were at the core of modern exopolitics and were driving the official machinery of government secrecy, ranging from the Obama White House, to NASA, to main stream media, to gatekeepers within the UFO and extraterrestrial affairs research community (often simultaneously and with coordinated talking points).

The deconstruction of the quantum time travel cover-up began with the publication of Alfred's book *"Exopolitics: Politics, Government and Law in the Universe"*[116]. The initial publication notice for Alfred's book "Exopolitics" purposely did not mention the book's identity as a time travel artifact, that it was in itself forensic evidence of the existence of secret U.S. time travel technology as early as 1971.

EXOPOLITICS: POLITICS, GOVERNMENT AND LAW IN THE UNIVERSE, by Alfred Lambremont Webre, JD, MEd (Universebooks.com 2005).

Exopolitics is the evolution of Alfred Lambremont Webre's ground-breaking work as a futurist at the Stanford Research Institute, where in 1977 he directed a proposed extraterrestrial communication study project for the Carter White House. This project was initiated because Carter had seen a UFO in 1969 and was interested in the subject, as are millions of others today.

It may turn the dominant view of our Universe upside down. It reveals that we live on an isolated planet in the midst of a populated, evolving, and highly organized inter-planetary, inter-galactic, and multi-dimensional Universe society. It explores why Earth seems to have been quarantined for eons from a more evolved Universe society. It suggests specific steps to end our isolation, by reaching out to the technologically and spiritually advanced civilizations that are engaging our world at this unique time in human history.

A growing number of mainstream scientists are concluding that civilization – as we know it – may be extinct by the end of this century because of probable ecological catastrophes caused by climate change. To survive, we must transform the permanent warfare economy into a sustainable, cooperative Space Age society, release our addiction to fossil fuels, and move toward new, clean, renewable energy sources. An exopolitical approach to these challenges may well provide us with ecologically sound, life-saving solutions – a legacy of hope for our children and all future human generations.

What people are saying about Exopolitics

Excerpts from Reviews of Exopolitics:

"TIME *magazine has an annual practice of selecting The Man (or Woman) of the Year. A more appropriate ritual for the new millennium might be to select The Mind of the Year, and if that were so, Alfred Lambremont Webre would rank high on my list of suggested nominees. Among modern philosophers, Webre finds himself one of a very select few at the center of the birth of a discipline of critical importance for the future – Exopolitics.*"

—Paul Davids, Executive Producer of the film Roswell, starring Martin Sheen

"*Alfred Webre can be regarded as the founding father of Exopolitics as a field of human inquiry. His involvement with the study of the UFO phenomenon includes work with the Carter Administration and with the prestigious Stanford Research Institute, which are impressive credentials in this most controversial of emerging sciences. His book,* Exopolitics, *gives an overview of the field and offers a blueprint for humanity as it moves toward taking its place on a wider stage. It is a roadmap to the stars.*"

—Nick Pope, *UFO Desk Officer for the United Kingdom's Ministry of Defence, 1991-1994*

"*The final reality is that the story must be told and will be told. Exopolitics is a logical, rational, and scholarly attempt to clarify and present to the world the structure of an existing reality that can become a valuable tool in educating and expanding human consciousness. To this effort, I commend Alfred Webre and other members of the Institute for Cooperation in Space (ICIS) for their courage and dedication. I give my full support and encouragement to this endeavor, and I pray that it succeeds. If we ever mature as a race, we must recognize our extended family and reach out to them with courage and fellowship. Exopolitics can show us the way.*"

—Robert O. Dean, *Command Sergeant-Major, USAF (Retired), who served as an intelligence analyst with Cosmic Top Secret clearance, Supreme Headquarters Allied Powers Europe (SHAPE)*

"Alfred Lambremont Webre defines "Exopolitics" as a new discipline for understanding "Universe society" through its politics and government. In such terms, it would '...posit that the truest conception of our earthly circumstance may be that we are on an isolated planet in the midst of a populated, evolving, highly organized inter-planetary, inter-galactic, multi-dimensional Universe society.'

"In this context, Webre's championship of the new discipline of "Exopolitics" is a very credible academic and scientific pursuit. His extraordinary qualifications as a former researcher and a futurist at SRI's Center for the Study of Social Policy, and as an advisor to government on this subject, contributes to this study's significance as a contribution to knowledge at the beginning of the 21st century."

—*Father John Rossner, Ph.D., D.Sc., D.Litt., President, International Institute for Integral Human Sciences, Adjunct Professor, Religion and Culture, Concordia University, Montreal, Quebec, Canada*

"As our globe gets smaller and smaller, our eyes start to focus more and more on the many worlds around us. It is not just that we need more physical space for ourselves, but also existentially. We are contemporaries of God and we are duty-bound to reveal more of His greatness. Consequently, we must ask ourselves, how shall we discover more and more of Him? Alfred Webre's book makes us realize that this may be possible in ways we did not imagine some years ago."

—*Rabbi Dr. Nathan Lopes Cardozo, noted author, scholar, and lecturer, Dean, the David Cardozo School, Machon Ohr Aharon*

"I urge everyone who has an open mind to read this exciting and fascinating book, which is so thought provoking that it breaks all barriers of logic and rationalism and makes ancient theories tangible and real."

—*Uri Geller, world-renowned psychic and best-selling author, www.urigeller.com*

273

"Alfred Webre's treatise, Exopolitics, bodes well for those of us interested in the next step we must take as a species to evolve as universal beings. Here again, much will be made about the cover-up of our universal heritage, but, in truth, we need to move beyond that controversy to an awareness of the global significance of our arising consciousness and our realization of a greater cosmic reality. This, so aptly communicated in Alfred's work, is the needed direction to take and the role that must be played by humanity at this time. Exopolitics is an inspiration, providing for me a greater understanding of my own evolving comprehension of the extraterrestrial presence and our place in the Universe."

—Robert L. Nichol, filmmaker and educator, producer of the award-winning documentary, Star Dreams: Exploring the Mystery of the Crop Circles

"Exopolitics – Politics, Government, and Law in the Universe. That is a bold book title, given that most of this planet's human population is taught that we are a unique life form alone in the Universe. But author Alfred Lambremont Webre speaks as a futurist with a background at the Center for the Study of Social Policy at Stanford Research Institute, and as the current International Director of the Institute for Cooperation in Space.

"Exopolitics emerges at a time when astronomers are finding many planets beyond Earth and quantum string astrophysicists even describe other universes parallel to this one. If the Universe is filled with life, and even has multiple dimensions, then numerous life forms and their various agendas would inevitably mean 'social food fights,' and, as Alfred Webre describes it, would also require government and law in the Universe.

—Linda Moulton Howe, reporter and editor, Earthfiles.com, science and environment news contributor, Clear Channel's Premiere Radio Networks

"Alfred Lambremont Webre's odyssey into the realm of life in the vast Universe surrounding planet Earth is indeed a fascinating journey if you read it with an open mind. He postulates a Universe that includes

*many planets sustaining life more advanced than our own – all sub-
ject to universal governance based on the rule of law."*

—*Honorable Paul T. Hellyer, Minister of National Defense under
Canadian Prime Minister Lester B. Pearson and Deputy Prime Minister of Canada under Prime Minister Pierre Trudeau*

*"His brilliant treatise, Exopolitics, forms a conceptual bridge between
the familiar, locked-in, consensually limited thinking of our terrestrial
society and the expanded options that humanity will enjoy in what
Webre calls "Universe Society." In light of my chosen areas of interest
and advocacy – especially, socio-economic, environmental, geopolitical, and spiritual awareness issues related to truly paradigm-shifting
energy inventions – I find that, for me, his insights ring true.*

*"Exopolitics states that we, the human race, are collectively the exo-
government, the planetary Universe society. This is also the position
taken by the emerging grassroots movement that is pursuing new energy research and development. That movement is in its infancy, but an
organization called the New Energy Movement is dedicated to nurturing and sustaining it.*

*"I highly recommend Alfred Lambremont Webre's new book, Exopoli-
tics. It inspires hope for a better future, one in which humanity pro-
gresses beyond its present addictions to petroleum and war, and
beyond its resistance to beneficial change, toward a higher level of
spiritual awareness. My own experiences validate his assertion that the
Universe is ultimately a spiritual domain."*

—*Jeane Manning, author, The Coming Energy Revolution: The
Search for Free Energy*

*"Exopolitics: Politics, Government and Law in the Universe is an
exciting new book by Alfred Webre, a former futurist at the Stanford
Research Institute, advisor to the Carter administration on the extraterrestrial question, and Fulbright scholar, who received his law degree
from Yale. At present, he is the International Director of the Interna-*

tional Institute for Cooperation in Space and founder of the No Weapons in Space Campaign. He is an activist working to prevent the weaponization of space and to transform our economy from one based on war to one based on peace and sustainability.

"Take the time to listen to the message of Exopolitics. We all have a lot of work to do so that humanity can re-enter the cosmic community. Remember – you are the transformation that is needed to make this possibility a reality."

—Michael Mannion, co-founder, The Mindshift Institute, author, Project Mindshift: The Re-Education of the American Public Concerning Extraterrestrial Life.

"Alfred Webre's new book Exopolitics: Politics, Government and Law in the Universe is truly a must read for everyone. It lays the groundwork and the understandings necessary to assist Earth humanity to fulfill its destiny, which is to join the greater family of man throughout the universe. It should be on the bedstand of every politician, minister, and all those in leadership positions inspiring humanity for a better tomorrow."

—James Gilliland www.eceti.org

"In my opinion, the author of this volume, Alfred Lambremont Webre, has presented to readers a small package that contains a huge gift – a new vision of humanity's place in the Cosmos. Most books about Exopolitics are written from the perspective of humanity, or from the perspective of the individual writer. Webre has provided a perspective of universal law and government that rises above the mundane politics of humanity and Earth, and views humans not as Planetary Persons but as Cosmic Citizens.

"When the reader is ready, his Exopolitics provides an individual and collective blueprint for developing a social structure on Earth that assists humanity, in a Decade of Contact, to join and participate in Universe society."

—R. Leo Sprinkle, Ph.D., counseling psychologist, professor emeritus at the University of Wyoming, distinguished Ufologist and author

"Right now, if we could only get our species to look up with wonder at the potential vastness of life and its inherent complexity, we would be on a much better track than our current embrace of denial offers us. Webre's book is a hopeful and inspiring outlook concerning our future as a species. This is an outlook worth exploring in its fullness."

—Courtney Brown, Ph.D. is the founder of the Farsight Institute, a non-profit research and educational organization dedicated to the study of the "remote viewing" phenomenon.[117]

SCENE 5

ALFRED'S STORY (CIRCA 2007)

Summer 2007
1607 North Beach Road
Salt Spring Island, BC V8K 1A8
Canada

This is the story of Alfred Lambremont Webre's multi-dimensional journey to bring about interplanetary diplomacy on Earth. Alfred discovers and assists U.S. government whistleblowers to expose a cosmic Watergate uncovering a quantum cover-up of the use of secret time-travel technology by the U.S. government to alter political and governmental history.

Alfred's story includes his intervention with dimensional intelligences; his inside story of the 1977 Carter White House Extraterrestrial Communication Project; [118] *and the time-travel teleportation by DARPA, the U.S. Defense Advanced Project Research Agency and CIA, of futurist Alfred's book "Exopolitics: Politics, Government And Law In The Universe", which founded the science of relations among intelligent civilizations in the multiverse.* [119]

Part One: Visitors

Los Marcianos Llegaron Ya/ The Martians have Arrived

Alfred reviews his interest in Extraterrestrial-related phenomena as a child in his maternal country, Cuba and in his paternal country, the United States. Alfred relates his family history of Catholicism and his agnosticism in early adulthood as a crusading environmental lawyer to the personal shift that happens when he re-discovers that humanity may not be the only intelligent species visiting Earth.

A Call From the Cosmos

Alfred's life purpose fundamentally changes when, in early 1973, he is visited by an Extraterrestrial, dimensional presence that identifies itself telepathically as "the Holy Spirit." In technical parlance, Alfred becomes a "Contactee." The Holy Spirit telepathically tells Alfred, "Thou Art Peter and Upon this Rock I will found my Church." With Alfred in profound spiritual awe, the Holy Spirit entity telepathically transmits a vision of the future for Earth. Alfred plunges into deep study, discovering a blueprint of the structure of organized civilization in the Universe.

Age of Cataclysm/ Age of Planetary Birth

Transformed by his encounter with higher intelligence, Alfred starts communicating publicly in 1973 about the urgency of preparing for ecological cataclysms and an outreach to Extraterrestrial civilizations. He uncovers a pattern of future Earth Changes suggested by converging prophecies, psychic predictions, astronomy, seismology and geology. Alfred's 1974 book "The Age of Cataclysm" is the first to correlate Earth Sciences with parapsychology and psychical research, precognition, psychic prediction and prophecy, leading to a first 1970s wave of popular Earth Changes awareness.

Alfred develops the context communication theory of Extraterrestrial communication, holding that Close Encounters with higher intelligence should be interpreted as symbolic communications to humanity

– as dreams are a symbolic communication from the subconscious to one's conscious mind. He can now accept and integrate his Holy Spirit experience in a science-based framework.

Part Two: The 1977 Carter White House Extraterrestrial Communication Project

Jimmy Carter's 1969 Close Encounter

Alfred describes Jimmy Carter's vivid, publicly reported 1969 Close Encounter in the company of ten members of the Leary, Georgia Lion's Club while he was running for Governor of Georgia. Alfred discusses the documentation and reliability of the sighting. By the evidence, though, Jimmy Carter has never publicly confirmed knowledge of the Extraterrestrial presence. Jimmy Carter (1969) and Alfred Lambremont Webre (1973) were profoundly touched within four years of each other by multi-dimensional life-transforming experiences sourced by a higher intelligence.

On January 6, 1969, in the company of ten or more members of the Leary, Georgia Lion's Club, James Earl Carter had a close encounter with nocturnal lights, which he publicly reported on July 18, 1973 while Governor of Georgia. "It seemed to move towards us from a distance, stop, move partially away, return, then depart. Bluish at first; then reddish - luminous - not solid," stated Carter. "At times," Carter reported, "it was as bright as the moon, and about as big as the moon - maybe a bit smaller. The object was luminous; not solid." Despite some controversy with professional UFO skeptics, it seems a scientific certainty that the object Carter and his fellow Lions Club members saw was not Venus, an airplane, or another identified celestial object. As recently as 1997, Carter stated publicly that he "knew of no extraterrestrials" and did "not think any [extraterrestrials] were on the UFO he saw."[120]

Alfred's context communication theory of Extraterrestrial communication holds that Jimmy Carter's close encounter is a multi-dimensional communication, embedded with profound symbolic and cueing infor-

mation from a higher intelligence behind the Close Encounter experience. In his seminal book "Flying Saucers: A Modern Myth of Things Seen in the Sky,"[121] Swiss psychologist Carl Jung analyzes a UFO Encounter as a "Mandala" or "Sacred God-Form", whose function is to help elevate the spiritual energy-frequency of humanity and the Earth.

At the University of Wyoming, Alfred delivers a key-note presentation taking Jimmy Carter's hand-written UFO Report and substituting the words ""Mandala" or a Sacred God-Form," gives us a first-hand glimpse into the subliminal information Carter's higher-intelligence experience may have brought him: "The God-Form seemed to move towards us from a distance, stop, move partially away, return, then depart. Bluish at first; then reddish - luminous - not solid," stated Carter. "At times," Carter reported, "The God-Form was as bright as the moon, and about as big as the moon - maybe a bit smaller. The God-Form object was luminous; not solid." Two years after this life-transforming Close Encounter, Carter was the 83rd Governor of Georgia (1971-75), and eight years later, Carter became 39th President of the United States (1977-81).

Alfred discusses the documented effects on the personality, consciousness and lives of persons who have had Close Encounters of the type Jimmy Carter underwent. Alfred discusses the forensic evidence that Jimmy Carter may be a UFO/ET abductee, taken aboard ET spacecraft for physical and mental examinations and debriefings. Hypothetically, Carter's experiences during the ET/UFO abductions may have included teleportation, time travel, and an intimate experience of these secret ET-human liaison programs as detailed in Jim Sparks accounts.

In other words, in the UFO/ET abductions, the ETs could have been preparing Jimmy Carter along a parallel consciousness track for a proposed Disclosure role as U.S. President, unbeknownst to Carter's terrestrial handlers at the Rockefeller Trilateral Commission level. Jim Sparks' account of the Short Greys is that they feel that the U.S. Administration has violated all of the environmental and human rights aspects of their secret agreements, and are not in accord with the

Rockefeller Trilateralists, and City of London Zionists that have privatized and attempted to impose the ET Truth embargo for 60 years.

As director of the 1977 proposed Carter White House Extraterrestrial Communication Study, Alfred can understand in retrospect a possible Abduction-facilitated mechanism by which one individual determined Stanford Research Institute futurist could design and assemble a world-class scientific proposed study at the level of the U.S. Presidency in the course of several months in the Spring and Summer of 1977 while a multi-track pattern of other Carter-related Extraterrestrial Disclosure studies, such as those initiated by Daniel Sheehan and Marcia S. Smith, could unfold.

Washington, E.T. & the 1976 Election of James Earl Carter

It is 1975, and Rep. Henry B. Gonzalez of Texas approaches Alfred, who has publicly advocated a re-investigation of the Kennedy assassination, to meet him at the U.S. House of Representatives. The two men agree on a public campaign for a congressional investigation of the assassination of John F Kennedy, later to include those of Martin Luther King, Robert F. Kennedy and Malcolm X.

The historic 1976 U.S. Presidential Campaign had started. The Republican candidate, U.S. President Gerald Ford had already undertaken two key acts of strategic deception. Ford was a former member of the 1964 Warren Commission. In a 2001 article in the respected journal of the British Forensic Society, Science and Justice, Dr. D.B. Thomas argues "that there is a 96 percent chance that there was a shot from the grassy knoll to the right of the President's [John F. Kennedy] limousine in addition to the three fired from the Texas Book Depository by Lee Harvey Oswald."

The Warren Report was official U.S. Government disinformation

A 1966 UFO Flap involving a constituent of his in Michigan prompted Republican House Minority Leader Ford to call for U.S. Congressional hearings. Eventually, the U.S. House of Representatives

Foreign Affairs Committee held hearings, calling military-intelligence-friendly witnesses, such as the architect of the Vietnam War, Defense Secretary Robert S. McNamara who "categorically denied" there was any truth to the UFO phenomena other than reports such as that by U.S. Air Force consultant Dr. J. Allen Hynek that the UFOs were produced by "Swamp Gas."

CIA MKULTRA and MONARCH mind control survivor and former Presidential sex slave Cathy O'Brien, whom Alfred met while both were speakers at the 2013 Free Your Mind Conference[122] in Philadelphia, writes that Gerald R. Ford "promised [Cathy O'Brien's] father immunity from prosecution if he would see [Cathy O'Brien] into MKULTRA mind control."[123] CIA MKULTRA and MONARCH mind control, Alfred would learn has been a major instrumentality of Satanic/Illuminati infiltration of the U.S. government and of the extraterrestrial disclosure agenda.

The Democratic candidate, Governor Jimmy Carter was on record as having stated at a Southern Governors Conference "I don't laugh at people anymore when they say they've seen UFOs. I've seen one myself. It was the darndest thing I have ever seen. It was big, it was bright, it changed colors, and it was about the size of the moon." On the campaign trail, Carter takes a crafted position, reminding audiences of his personal Close Encounter, promising to make available government UFO sightings, and refusing to commit to re-open a U.S. Government investigation.

When asked by National Enquirer correspondent Jim McCandish if he would open UFO files when elected President, Carter actually states: "Carter: Well, no. What I would do is make information we have about those sightings available to the public (three words unclear). I have never tried to identify what I saw. You know, it was a light in the western sky that was very unique. I had never seen it before. There were about 20 of us who saw it. None of us could figure out what it was. I don't think it was anything solid. It was just like a light. It was a curious aberration, so I don't make fun of people who say they've see unidentified objects in the sky." When asked if he will re-open the U.S. Government investigation of UFOs, Carter stated, "I don't know yet."

Jimmy Carter, the Close Encounter Candidate ran a successful campaign. He performed well in Campaign debates. He won both the Democratic Nomination and the General Election with 50.1% of the popular vote, "one of only two Democratic Party Presidential Candidates to win a majority of the popular vote since Franklin Delano Roosevelt in 1944."

The 1976 U.S. Presidential Campaign was the first openly waged on the extraterrestrial issue. For the Democrats, Jimmy Carter, a populist Georgia Governor-with-a-Close-Encounter, who promises to make public all secret U.S. government documents on UFOs if elected. For the Republicans, incumbent President Gerald R. Ford, former Warren Commission member, and protégé of Vice President Nelson Rockefeller.

Rockefeller, with his intellectual mentor Henry Kissinger, since the 1950s had secretly dictated U.S. government policy on extraterrestrial societies through such groups as Majestic 12, PI-40, and the Study Group. As a member of the U.S. House Armed Services Committee, Gerald Ford had been politically forced to convene public hearings after massive UFO flaps over his constituency in Michigan in 1966. Ford had presided over public Congressional hearings designed to keep the UFO issue secret.

Alfred describes Carter's first public commitment to open secret U.S. government files on UFOs and extraterrestrial issues if elected President, and his campaign stops and press conferences on the extraterrestrial issue. In the end, Close Encounter Carter defeats Pentagon asset Gerald Ford for the Presidency of the U.S. Carter is now left to fulfill his promise to make the extraterrestrial secret files public.

Extraterrestrials, Stanford Research Institute & Futurist Alfred Webre

Alfred opens with the Carter Presidential Transition of autumn 1976. Alfred is in the Capitol Hill home of a close Jimmy Carter associate discussing staffing of the U.S. House of Representatives Select Committee on Assassinations, then newly formed and chaired by Rep.

Henry Gonzalez of Texas. The campaign that Gonzalez and Alfred had agreed on for a congressional investigation of the assassination of John F Kennedy, Martin Luther King, Robert F. Kennedy and Malcolm X, had enrolled Mrs. Martin Luther King and the Congressional Black Caucus, leading to Congressional approval of the investigation.

A member of the Carter Transition Team comes by the house for supper, with inside tales of the Carter Transition White House. He mentions Presidential nicknames: "Peanut" for Carter and "JC and the Twelve Apostles" for the inner Carter circle. The messianic references trigger resonance to memories of the Holy Spirit experience. Alfred intuits a possible opening within the Carter White House for an objective, scientific Extraterrestrial communication study. This study would lend the considerable scientific resources of the U.S. government in support to open research and communication with ethical Extraterrestrial civilization.

By coincidence, Alfred meets Ingo Swann,[124] the subject for Dr. Hal Puthoff and Russell Targ's military-intelligence-financed remote viewing experiments at his Bowery loft in New York City. Later, in the 1980s and 1990s, remote viewing was to become a leading scientific modality for replicable interactive communication with Off-Planet cultures. Swann suggests that Alfred meet with Puthoff and Targ at their laboratory at Stanford Research Institute (SRI) in California. On a Christmas 1976 trip to the San Francisco Bay Area, Alfred calls on Hal Puthoff and Russell Targ, who in turn refer him to Peter Schwartz a futurist with the Center for the Study of Social Policy at SRI.[125]

Alfred briefs Peter Schwartz, and then the staff of the Center – some of the world's leading futurists. Alfred receives an appointment as an SRI futurist with a commitment to seek an Extraterrestrial communication study with the Carter White House, starting in the late Spring of 1977, four years after his Encounter with the Holy Spirit and eight years after Jimmy Carter's Close Encounter outside the Leary, Georgia Lion's Club.

Alfred joins SRI with the indication that he would be able to continue his research on extraterrestrial communication, furthering his Context

Communication Theory of Extraterrestrial Communication, which Alfred defined as:

"The Context Communication Theory of Extraterrestrial Communication, which this author developed in 1974, [22] holds that UFO Encounters and Extraterrestrial encounters may be validly interpreted as symbolic communications from a higher intelligent species – or a different intelligent species – to our human species. An analogy is that of a dream, which is a communication from one's unconscious mind to the conscious mind, often in symbolic and multi-dimensional format. One uses a dream dictionary, for example, to interpret dreams. Similarly, genuine Extraterrestrial interventions or encounters can be interpreted as symbolic, multi-dimensional communications to the human community from a higher intelligent source. The Swiss psychologist Carl Jung referred to this symbolic aspect of UFOs when in his pioneering work "Flying Saucers" he called them UFOs "Mandalas" or archetypal devices for raising human consciousness."[126]

The 1977 Carter White House Extraterrestrial Communication Project

Alfred provides the background of U.S. President Jimmy Carter's historical firsts: first President to report a UFO Close Encounter publicly (in 1969), and first to win the Presidency by promising to open U.S. official UFO files (in 1976). Alfred details his development and securing approval of the 1977 Carter White House ET Communication Study.

In the spring of 1977, Alfred Lambremont Webre was one of an elite group of Futurists at Stanford Research Institute (SRI), with a specialty in communication with Off-Planet Cultures. In January 1977, Jimmy Carter became the first elected U.S. President who had publicly reported a Close Encounter with a UFO. Carter had campaigned promising to make U.S. government files on UFOs and Extraterrestrials public when elected. Alfred quickly sought and obtained approval from SRI officials and from Carter White House Domestic policy staff for a White House Extraterrestrial Communication Project, the first civilian scientific study of a possible extraterrestrial presence in Earth's near environment.

An historical report[127] of the 1977 proposed Carter White House Extraterrestrial Communication Study states:

"Carter Extraterrestrial Communication Study"

"UFO Studies Done and Proposed by the Carter Administration

"Preliminary Study Proposals

"It is not a well know fact that the Carter administration actually proposed and hosted a number UFO studies. When Carter first entered the White House it was known from his public declaration of having been a UFO witness, that he was familiar with what the objects were. Further, his campaign promise to release everything held by the U.S. government on the subject, placed the new President into a position where studies would be required to get at the facts.

One study that was proposed and which almost got off the ground was one proposed by the Stanford Research Institute. It has been called the 'Carter Extraterrestrial Communication Study.'

"In May 1977, only months after the inauguration of Jimmy Carter, the preliminaries of a project to study extraterrestrial communications was set up at the Center for the Study of Social Policy at the Stanford Research Institute.

"The study was headed by Dr. Alfred Webre, a Yale trained lawyer and Senior Policy Analyst at the Center. Peter Schwartz, another senior Policy Analyst, was an advisor to the project. Tom Thomas, the Supervisor of the Center had approved and signed off on the proposal.

"During his interview, prior to being brought on to the Stanford staff, Webre has asked "to do an extraterrestrial project." This study would be based on a theory Webre had published in the early 1970s called the Context Communication Theory of Extraterrestrials, which held that extraterrestrial phenomena could be interpreted by certain laws.

"While campaigning Jimmy Carter for President had made his declaration of his sighting and intention to release all the UFO data. It

*provided Webre the ideal opportunity for his study. 'It was a godsend,'
stated Webre. 'We took Carter on his word.'*

"Webre immediately began to identify 'people inside the Carter White
House who were sympathetic to the UFO issue.'

"The study proposed containing no classified aspects. The initial
contact within the Carter white House for the proposal was Stuart
Eizenstat, director of Carter's Domestic Policy Staff. Webre pitched
the outline of the proposed study. The White House agreed, and the
work began.

"Webre flew from California to Washington to meet in the Executive
Office Building with White House Domestic Policy Staff every two or
three weeks. 'The proposal was known and approved within the Domestic Policy Staff of the White House,' said Webre, 'and it was in
circulation with the White House Science Advisors Office.' The meeting continued with the Carter White House from May 1977 till September 1977.

"'I was signed in and out [of the White House Executive Office Building]
and I would meet with her [the White House liaison] around the proposals. The structure of the proposal was that the White House would
remain the overall policy director on this research proposal, which was
envisioned to be about three years long. Once a final report was issued
under the proposal it would become a White House document, and
would come out under their agency and their policy recommendations.'

"The study to provide knowledge on the subject, and propose a future
course of action, had three phases:

"Creation of a data base of UFOs and extraterrestrials in private and
non-private collections. The proposal involved obtaining data worldwide as opposed to simply the United States

"Evaluation phase where searches would be made for 'alternate models using the best scientific minds available'.

"The final report and recommendations, and the creation of 'a permanent, open, global data-base under independent control for UFO and EBE (extraterrestrial biological entity) encounters'. The final report would have included 'recommendation for the [rescinding] of intelligence and military secrecy regulations, which interfere with the flow of UFO and EBE data in the open civilian, scientific, and public domain. Hopefully it could have developed an "extraterrestrial communication project to establish non-hostile, open communication from an authoritative human source to whatever intelligence the project might find.'

"The extraterrestrial communications project came to the proposal stage in September 1977. The White House signed off on it, and Webre and the others involved from SRI "were given the directive to begin the personnel approaches with NASA, and with the National Science Foundation who would be the actual funding agencies for the proposal under the overall direction of the White House. James Fletcher, the NASA administrator, was provided a copy of the proposal, and began reviewing it.

"Webre flew back to California to prepare for the next step at SRI. The move by the White House to green light the project, however, had set off alarm bells in the Pentagon among those whose job it was to protect the UFO secret.

"When Webre arrived back at SRI, he reported that he was called back into the office of the Senior SRI Official, [an African American], along with Peter Schwartz. Into the room walked [a man] who was the SRI liaison at the Pentagon. He announced that the project was to be terminated. The reason for the termination of the White House approved proposal was, 'There are no UFOs.' He stated that he had been informed by someone in the Pentagon that 'if the study went forward, SRI's contracts with the Pentagon would be terminated.'

"As most of the contracts at SRI were tied into the Pentagon, the writing was on the wall for 'extraterrestrial communication'. Webre was told by the SRI liaison 'to simulate,' and play along with it. In this

way the liaison stated he would keep his job.

The Senior SRI Officer sided with the Pentagon liaison, and the extra-terrestrial communication study for the Carter White House was dead."[128]

Unbeknownst to the 1977 Alfred (to be known in 2005 as the father of the discipline of Exopolitics), in 1971 his landmark book "Exopolitics: Politics, Government And Law In The Universe" ("Exopolitics"), which would be published in 2005, had been teleported back in time from the future (sometime after 2005) to the past (1971) by Project Pegasus, a classified U.S. Department of Defense program. Project Pegasus included the retrieval of objects from the future back to the present for examination by DARPA, the U.S. Defense Advanced Research Projects Agency.

The Defense attaché to Project Pegasus in 1971 was Nixon Administration official and later Bush Secretary of Defense Donald Rumsfeld. Alfred was to learn of his book's time travel in 2005 from Andrew "Andy" D. Basiago, a whistleblower former time-traveler participant on classified Project Pegasus who in 1971 had physically witnessed Alfred's time-traveled book.

Alfred's was not the only Extraterrestrial project undertaken by the 1977 Carter White House. Alfred's later colleague at the Institute for Cooperation in Space (ICIS), Daniel Sheehan had reportedly been requested by the Congressional research Service to investigate alleged extraterrestrial artifacts in the U.S. National Archives. Sheehan's ET investigations proceeded without any reported injuries upon his person. Sheehan had served as General Counsel for the Jesuits, and attorney for the Pentagon Papers, Karen Silkwood, and Harvard Prof. John Mack.[129]

As Alfred proceeded to implement the 1977 SRI and White House-approved Extraterrestrial Communication project, in the fall of 1977, he was brutally attacked with directed energy weapons and barely survived with his life. The attacks upon Alfred began as he was on official Stanford Research Institute business in the inner ring of the

Pentagon, where he was attacked with Mind Control weapons in the offices of an Assistant Secretary of Defense in the Carter Administration. On his return trip to SRI, Men in Black (MIBs) at the Washington, DC National Airport who doused him with directed energy weapons and attempted to abduct him, surrounded Alfred.

On his return from that Washington trip to SRI, Alfred was called into a high-level meeting with SRI officials and liaison between SRI and the Pentagon, who informed Alfred that his White House-approved project was being terminated "because there are no UFOs." Unless the Project was terminated, DOD had informed him that SRI would lose all of the DOD studies contracts, amounting to about $25 million of SRI's $100 million total budget. Following this meeting, coordinated teams of Men In Black, security forces and directed energy weapons attacked Alfred, forcing him to take permanent leave and eventually resign from SRI.

By the evidence, the U.S. Department of Defense overtly directly intervened to stop a Jimmy Carter White House-approved Extraterrestrial Communication project. Covertly, a clandestine security force employing directed energy weapons brutally attacked project director Alfred Lambremont Webre, who barely survived with his life.

Uncovering The Quantum Cover-Up

What might have motivated those Project Pegasus-privy leaders within the U.S. Department of Defense to target the Alfred-White House Extraterrestrial Project, when we know other Carter White House ET-investigation projects, like that led by attorney Daniel Sheehan, were not so targeted?

Alfred and Andy had met in the early 2000s. In 2004, Andy had become Alfred's literary lawyer and Editor of Alfred's forthcoming book Exopolitics. Alfred learns from Andy that through the process of editing "Exopolitics" for publication, Andy is able to identify "Exopolitics" as the time-traveled book he had physically witnessed as part of classified Project Pegasus in 1971, and Alfred Lambremont Webre as its author whose name he heard uttered in 1971 before his memories were erased by Project Pegasus personnel. Andy is a former Project Pegasus participant who, as 9 year-old child time-traveler tasked with retrieving time-scrolls from the future, physically saw Alfred's book "Exopolitics" in 1971 after it had been retrieved from the future for study by DARPA, Defense Advanced Projects Agency.

According to Andy, Project Pegasus was a classified United States government time travel project for the teleportation of persons and objects and persons backwards and forwards in time. Project Pegasus included the retrieval of objects from the future back to the present for study by DARPA, U.S. Defense Advanced Research Projects Agency. By eye-witness testimony, these time-teleported objects from the future included works like "Exopolitics", which set out a model for peaceful integration with advanced extraterrestrial societies, unlike the U.S. Department of Defense and Central Intelligence Agency, which since Projects Sign (1948), Grudge (1949) and Blue Book (1952), had been publicly pursuing a hostile information war against ethical extraterrestrial societies.

From the vantage point of time travel, we can identify at least three (3) levels of Cover-Up for stopping the proposed 1977 Carter White House Extraterrestrial Communication Study, and attempting to eliminate its author and director, Alfred Lambremont Webre.

Cover-up Level One – Stop the 1977 Carter White House Extraterrestrial Communication Study because it will lead to open, scientific study of extraterrestrial communication with human culture. The U.S. secret information war against ethical extraterrestrial societies demands a continued Cover-up of the existence of ethical extraterrestrial societies seeking to interact with humanity.

Cover-up Level Two – Stop the 1977 Carter White House Extraterrestrial Communication Study because its Director, Alfred Lambremont Webre, is the author of a time-travel targeted book, "Exopolitics", of Project Pegasus a highly classified time travel project for obtaining information about the future and studying it for defense and political control purposes through the DARPA, Defense Advanced Projects

Research Agency. This poses a security risk to Project Pegasus and to the U.S. Government's secret time travel technology as Alfred and the 1977 White House Project may use that project's authority to discover and make public relevant time-travel secrets and U.S. government secret relations with unethical extraterrestrial civilizations.

Cover-up Level Three – Intervene in the time stream in 1977, and eliminate the future "father" of the science of Exopolitics, by destroying Alfred Lambremont Webre, director of the 1977 Carter White House ET Study. This stops the publication of the book "Exopolitics" and cripples the development of the discipline of Exopolitics, as a bridge of humanity's integrating with a wider, intelligent Universe society, thereby winning a crucial coup in the on-going "war" against ethical extraterrestrial society.

Synchronicity, the power of meaningful coincidence as Swiss psychologist Carl Jung defined the term, led Project Pegasus participant Andrew D. Basiago to remember and reveal to author Alfred Lambremont Webre that his book was teleported from the future back to 1971 in a secret Pentagon program led by Donald Rumsfeld, a high ranking Republican official in the Nixon and Bush administrations.

Andy's eyewitness testimony in turn may have explained why the Department of Defense so brutally attacked the 1977 Carter White House Extraterrestrial Communication study and its director, Alfred Lambremont Webre. Alfred's coming forward with how the 1977 Carter study was repressed thus may constitute a public leak of a secret U.S. government time travel program used for illicit political control.

Assembling the Carter White House Study

At Stanford Research Institute in spring 1977, Alfred's first assignment is in the U.S. Senate, where he is a member of the U.S. Senate Panel of U.S. National Security Needs Through the Year 2000. Later, in May 2001, Alfred was to be a Disclosure Project witness[130], his testimony made public at National Press Club press conference in Wash-

ington, D.C. Alfred's fellow witnesses, high-level U.S. military-intelligence whistleblowers, would confirm that Extraterrestrial intelligence has demonstrated a public concern about the potential devastation of nuclear war and nuclear weapons. This included Extraterrestrial craft shutting down U.S. Air Force Silos for launching Intercontinental Ballistic Missiles (ICBMs) equipped with nuclear-warheads.

Sam Nunn,[131] Democrat of Georgia acknowledged Dean of U.S. National Security in the U.S. Senate, focuses his tortoise shell glasses on the multi-dimensional thirty-five year old Stanford Research Institute Futurist seated next to him around a large, oval U.S. Senate Committee table. Flanking Nunn and Alfred around the table are twenty or so leaders of the military-intelligence establishment of the United States, Illuminati of the U.S. war machine. Across from Alfred was a colleague from the public-interest community, Rear Admiral Gene R. LaRocque,[132] founder of the Center for Defense Information.

Alfred turns a multiplicity of considerations in his mind. In that instant, Alfred decides to resist the obvious temptation to open up discussion of the Extraterrestrial Issue as a key to the future of U.S. (and world) security needs through the year 2000. In a perfect world, he would have put the ET issue at play into the U.S. Senate panel. In the light of hindsight, maybe that is what he should have done, and "leaked out" the planned Carter White House civilian scientific study into the assembled company of military-intelligence leaders who were, as they spoke, carrying out a clandestine war against advanced extraterrestrial civilizations. In that moment, he found it wisest to get formal SRI and White House approval before advertising his intentions publicly to the declared enemies of extraterrestrial civilization, the U.S. Pentagon.

Alfred brings to mind the well-documented Extraterrestrial civilization concern against human nuclear weapons and nuclear war. He leans out into the U.S. Senate table and taking aim with calm chi, speaks out his words to the Director of the Defense Intelligence Agency. He recites words from memory drawn from "Armageddon: The Chilling

Prospect of Global Nuclear War", the book proposal he and Gene LaRocque had worked on just months before.

Serendipity and synchronicity- the power of meaningful coincidence – have brought him into the inner lair of the planners and executioners of nuclear war. As the face of the DIA Chief paled, Alfred slowly enunciated well-crafted words detailing the inhuman devastation and futility of nuclear war, ending with the words: "There are no victors; there are no vanquished. Each ground zero is the Void," A poignant silence overtook the room as Alfred finished his address. The Genie had been let out of the bottle. As the panel ended, Gene LaRocque drew near to Alfred, nodding, "You did quite a good job there." Now onto to Extraterrestrial communication, thought Alfred.

SRI and Carter White House Approve the Study

Making his way back to the SRI campus in Menlo Park, California, Alfred realizes he has little time to spare. He tackles the challenges of designing a Study of Extraterrestrial communication, vetting it through SRI and getting Carter White House approval. The experience in the U.S. Senate with the leaders of the U.S. military-intelligence establishment has given him the clarity for the hard work and authoritative project leadership that lay ahead. SRI's business is to perform contract research for the U.S. government and other agencies.

Alfred designs a scientific Extraterrestrial Communication Study. The U.S. government and research agencies proposed for the 1977 Carter White House Study placed the White House itself in the role of Principal sponsor and policy coordinator of the proposed Study. The National Science Board, for whom Alfred is already doing contract research is to provide scientific advice and consultation, and outreach into the scientific community. The National Aeronautic and Space Administration (NASA) is designed as the consultative line agency regarding UFO and Near Space phenomena, including terrestrial, UFO or Extraterrestrial Biological Entity interaction.

The over-all purpose of the proposed 1977 Carter White House Extraterrestrial Communication Study was to create, design and implement an independent, civilian-led research compilation and evaluation of phenomena suggesting an extraterrestrial and/or Inter-dimensional intelligent presence in the near-Earth environment. Stanford Research Institute's Center for the Study of Social Policy are to be the Principal Investigators of Study, assisted by a Panel of leading Scientific Advisers on Unidentified Flying Objects (UFOs), Extraterrestrial issues, and related phenomena.

The designed outcome of the Study was to have been a public White House report, detailing the compiled evidence and evaluation, together with possible scientific models for the implications of the research. The White House report was to have contained public policy recommendations emerging from the evaluations and conclusions of the Study. These, if warranted, included transformation of secrecy regulations of U.S. military-intelligence agencies.

The scientific and public policy goal of the proposed 1977 Carter White House Extraterrestrial Communication Study was to fill a substantial gap in civilian scientific knowledge of the UFO (Unidentified Flying Object phenomenon), Extraterrestrial Biological Entities (EBEs), and related phenomena. This knowledge gap was created and maintained by excessive secrecy practices and regulations of U.S. Department of Defense and intelligence agencies in the various generations of its UFO-programs since the late 1940s, including but not limited to Project Grudge and Project Blue Book, as well as other alleged secret programs. [133]

Alfred describes a plane ride from San Francisco to Washington, DC, carrying him and other SRI personnel for their briefings with U.S. government officials. On the plane with Alfred are SRI scientists Dr. Hal Puthoff and Russell Targ, who are then developing the science of remote viewing for U.S. military and intelligence agencies. Puthoff and Targ were the first SRI scientists Alfred met when he approached SRI in late 1976 for a position as a Futurist after meeting their remote viewing subject Ingo Swann at his Bowery loft in New York City.

Alfred describes how remote viewing was to become a key tool in the development of Exopolitics, a new political science of relations with

Off-Planet cultures. Remote viewers would be able in the 1990s to interact with intelligent Off-Planet Cultures and representatives of Universe governance bodies, as well as locate an apparent intelligent, advanced civilization living underground on Mars.

Alfred describes his meetings in the spring of 1977 in the White House Executive Office Building, securing White House approval for the Extraterrestrial Communication Study. After his experiences with the U.S. Senate committee, Alfred networks his political connections and quickly locates Carter White House Domestic Policy staff that is known to be friendly to a scientific, White House-led investigation of the Extraterrestrial issue. In the Executive Office Building, Alfred briefs friendly White House staff of the proposed Extraterrestrial Communication Study, and receives agreement to present his Proposal to administrators within the Domestic Policy Staff.

Returning to SRI, Alfred briefs the administrator of the Futurist Center, as well as other Futurists, on his White House meeting, and receives approval to proceed with entering to contract research with the carter White House on the proposed Extraterrestrial Communication Study. White House Domestic Policy staff indicates that the Proposal has been approved at administrative levels and invited Alfred to submit formal contract research applications. For the 1977 Carter White House Extraterrestrial Communication Study. A historic milestone is at hand.

Life is good for Alfred as SRI officials approved the project, and expert researchers such as Jacques Vallee, then at the Institute for the Future in Palo Alto, contributed input to the study.

The Empire Strikes Back

Alfred reconstructs the total termination of the 1977 Carter White House Extraterrestrial Communication Study in the fall of 1977, and the directed energy weapons attacks and Men In Black (MIBs) deployments against him. These include motion picture like sequences at the Pentagon, across from the White House, at the King Tut Art Ex-

hibit in New Orleans, at the New Orleans Airport, and on the campus
of Stanford Research Institute.

The Case of the Congressional Research Service & Daniel Sheehan

Alfred opens with attorney Daniel Sheehan as he described his 1977
encounter in secret U.S. National Archives with photographs and
drawings of apparent artifacts from extraterrestrial spacecraft. Alfred
describes how, according to Sheehan, he makes drawings and notes of
these and smuggles them out of the National Archives. Alfred describes how Sheehan, who was then legal counsel to the Jesuit order,
was commissioned on this study via the Carter White House. Alfred
shows that no injury or attacks took place on the person of Sheehan,
who was later in 2001 to become an associate of Alfred's as General
Counsel to the Institute for Cooperation In Space (ICIS).

Ambush At The Inner Ring of the Pentagon

It is October 1977 and Alfred sits in a high level office in the Inner
Ring of the Pentagon, waiting to meet with an Assistant Secretary of
Defense of the United States. Peter Schwartz, a fellow SRI futurist,
informed Alfred that the Department of Defense was planning space-
based platforms for placing weapons in space. He offered to set up a
meeting with this Assistant Secretary, who is conducting a study to
determine the weapons' feasibility. As a space-based weapon could be
used against Extraterrestrial society, Alfred made an appointment
with the official to find out more.

As Alfred sat across from the official's female military Executive Assistant, she starts to engage in what mind control experts such as researcher David Lawson have identified "Electronically Assisted
Vigilante Gang Stalking."[134] The Executive Assistant suddenly raises
up an apparent newspaper that she has on her desk, and flashes its
front page at Alfred. The word "SEX" is written as a bold headline
dominating the top third of the newspaper. She flashes it back down.
Alfred feels a tingling at his legs, his neck, his arms, the symptoms of
EMF harassment with Electromagnetic directed energy weapons. He

299

realizes he has not walked into a meeting, but rather a Mind Control Ambush. Earlier that day, at Alfred's hotel just across from the White House, an intelligence operative in a dark suit and black glasses had menacingly stared at Alfred from the street, in an attempted textbook mind control routine, as Alfred had dinner in the Hotel dining room.

Maintaining equilibrium, Alfred establishes an inner aura against the vigilante harassment and waits about a half hour for the meeting in tense silence, he and the female Executive Assistant alone in the room.

Meeting with the official, Alfred cannot determine if the official is also party to the MKULTRA mind control electronically assisted vigilante harassment. Alfred acts as nothing out of the ordinary has taken place. The official acknowledges that his department is working on developing space-based platforms for weapons and asks Alfred whether he would like to work on a strategy study. Alfred effectively declines, saying, "I'll have to think about it.

Ambush in New Orleans: Judge Jim Garrison & King Tut's Tomb

Alfred was shocked by the paramilitary MKULTRA mind control attack at the Pentagon, yet survived it. He now leaves Washington for New Orleans and an appointment with Judge Jim Garrison who as New Orleans District Attorney had indicted co-conspirators for the assassination of President John F. Kennedy. Since 1976, Alfred had been acting as an informal adviser to U.S. Congressman Henry B. Gonzalez (D-Texas), and, as Co-Director of the Assassination Information Bureau, had helped Gonzalez successfully convene the House Select Committee on Assassinations, underway to investigate the assassinations of U.S. leaders John F. Kennedy, Martin Luther King, Robert F. Kennedy and Malcolm X.

Alfred calls Jim Garrison and sets up a meeting for the next day at the New Orleans Athletic Club. He wants to ask Garrison what he knows about the Kennedy assassination. The traveling Exhibit of King Tutankhamen, Pharaoh of the Eighteenth dynasty of Egypt (1341 BC – 1323 BC) was then in New Orleans. With a day off, Alfred decides to tour the Exhibit with his brother John, who was studying Architecture at Tulane University.

As Alfred enters the Exhibit, his mind suddenly reels, as though his coffee had been spiked with an overdose of some hallucinogenic drug. Research into the MKULTRA program demonstrated that LSD and related drugs were used by U.S. government military-intelligence agencies to as Mind Control drugs to incapacitate targeted individuals.

Stunned, Alfred is overcome and sits down on a bench by the entranceway, his mind trying to stay focused. He becomes internally agitated and confused. He is physically and emotionally ill, and must take a plane back to SRI the next evening. Alfred is not in a condition to meet with Jim Garrison. Even in his disoriented state, Alfred realizes that he has been attacked with military-intelligence Mind Control weapons in order to prevent his meeting with Garrison.

All the Pentagon's Men In Black

Alfred is at Moissant International Airport in New Orleans the next day, a Sunday. Alfred is at the airport gate, waiting for his flight to San Francisco, holding his tennis racket.

Alfred feels the now familiar disorienting sting of EMF directed energy weapons. He looks up and is surrounded by five military-intelligence operatives, dressed in black suits, with pork-pie hats and dark sunglasses. Each operative wears a tie clip in the form of a sharpshooter's rifle mounted with telescopic sight.

The operatives deploy with military precision around Alfred into different formations, performing mind control electronically assisted harassment. There are other people in the airline flight gate waiting area. The precision mind control technology is such that others seem not to notice the military maneuvers going on. Alfred realizes that the object of the mind control deployment is to induce him to panic and flight. Alfred understands that, in a state of panic and flight, he would be vulnerable to kidnapping either by the MIB operatives or under the cover of police "arrest."

301

His mother, Juanita is a Chisholm.[135] *He remembers a Chisholm clan motto in the family room – Feros Ferios. "I am Fierce with the Fierce." Calmly, Alfred sits in the waiting room on the territory he has staked out and throws his chi back at the Mind Control pack of MIBs, who eventually vanish.*

The Pentagon Tells SRI "There Are No UFOs"

Back at SRI, Alfred is called into an emergency meeting with fellow Futurist Peter Schwartz and a supportive African American SRI Vice President. The purpose of the meeting is to terminate the 1977 Carter White House Extraterrestrial Communication Study, although Alfred does not know this as he goes into the meeting.

The two men tell Alfred that the SRI Liaison to the Department of Defense is to join them. Alfred is asked to "dissimulate" or conceal any feelings at the outcome of the meeting. The Department of Defense has communicated to SRI that unless the 1977 Carter White House Extraterrestrial Study is terminated, the Department will terminate all of its missile studies contracts with SRI. At that time, SRI's annual budget was approximately $100 million, and the portion of that budget made up of Department of Defense-related projects was substantial.

The meeting with the SRI liaison is a donnybrook. The SRI Liaison states Department of Defense has asked the White House Study be terminated "because there are no UFOs." He is asking Alfred to participate in a cover-up, which he cannot do on principle. So Alfred challenges the DOD conclusion and recites the primary evidentiary cases for UFOs and for Extraterrestrial presence. The meeting ends in anger. That night Peter Schwartz calls Alfred at his home and expresses his concern. No other SRI contract research would be so terminated.

In the weeks following this meeting, Alfred is stalked by clandestine teams of security personnel and attacked repeatedly with directed energy weapons. A cordon of mind control electronically assisted harassment tightens around Alfred on the SRI Campus, led by the former security guard at the Center for the Study of Social Policy, a veteran

CIA *mind control operative who reportedly led early mind control LSD trips in the desert. These attacks result in Alfred's taking a temporary leave from SRI. Alfred eventually resigns in 1978.*

Targeted by the Mind Control Empire: 1978-2000

Stress forces Alfred to resign from SRI. He becomes a worldwide-targeted individual of U.S. covert mind control electronically assisted harassment. In the eyes of the U.S. national security state, one key fact qualified Alfred's status as a target for psychic, mind control, and electromagnetic pulse weapons. That key fact was Alfred's pre-identification via DARPA/CIA time travel about his contact with, and espousal of, interdimensional and extraterrestrial intelligent beings. Alfred is an Experiencer who has tried to make a difference, and that fact alone makes him an official non-entity and target. A citizen to be discredited under secret government mandates of the United States.

Not only is Alfred an Experiencer; he has been time travel pre-identified as an Extraterrestrial activist. He is proclaiming the truth of an Extraterrestrial society outreach in books, on radio and television. He is catalyzing a counter-policy against the ultra secrecy pronounced by the US government in the late 1940s and early 1950s. He is in the inner sanctum of a military-intelligence think tank, lobbying the Carter White House in a project to re-open the extraterrestrial policy.

Had Alfred been an environmental activist, or human rights activist, or even a JFK assassination researcher, he might have been targeted by covert mind control electronically assisted harassment. But most probably nowhere to the extent than being a time travel pre-identified Extraterrestrial activist brought out, on every continent where he traveled; in the most mundane settings; on virtually every telephone and e-mail station he used.

Alfred was not paranoid – just hyper-observant. Somewhere in the bowels of DOD/CIA, an order went out to neutralize Alfred. It had to be from the very control center of the time travel surveillance. Alfred cannot account for the almost complete surveillance and attack that has been with him now since 1977.

No matter where Alfred traveled – Canada, the United States, Africa, Europe or Mexico. Expertly coordinated police surveillance units shadowed Alfred closely, isolating him from his life, and hoping he would break. Even Alfred's parental visits with his son Freddie were shadowed by a burly Berkeley, CA policeman, standing within 10 feet of father and son as they played in a Berkeley, CA park. There is only one unit of the secret government that can muster that kind of international police authority, the international clandestine apparatus structured and deployed in furtherance of the time travel and extraterrestrial cover-up.

Though a target, Alfred continues on his public quest, as a United Nations Non-Governmental Organization representative; as a radio talk show host promoting Universe society, producing the first live radio program between the United States and the then Soviet Union in history. In 2000, after a quarter century of research, Alfred publishes the first edition of "Exopolitics" as a free Internet book, a first conceptual bridging discipline between terrestrial and extraterrestrial civilization.

Part Three: Quantum Cover-Up: Back To The Future

Alfred reconstructs his eyewitness account of being informed by Andy that his 2005 book "Exopolitics: Politics, Government and Law in the Universe" was time travel teleported back to 1971 by Project Pegasus, a classified project under Defense attaché Donald Rumsfeld, an official of the pre-Watergate Nixon Administration. Alfred will detail his concurrent life as General Counsel of New York City's Environmental Protection Administration in 1971, as a crusading environmental lawyer, and will detail his own first hand experiences of being surveilled in 1971 by about 50 DARPA and CIA employees who had knowledge of his 2005 book "Exopolitics".

Eyewitness Account: Time traveling "Exopolitics" to 1971

Alfred opens describing his eyewitness account of learning that his book "Exopolitics" was time traveled back to 1971 by a classified program of retrieving objects from the future to the past for analysis by DARPA. Alfred analyses his own account and discusses its credibility, based on Alfred's own independent memories of his 1971 surveillance meeting with about 50 DARPA and CIA personnel, internal consistency, evidentiary value according to the rules of evidence, circumstantial evidence, documentation to date, such as Alfred's written statements and affidavit. Alfred points out that his book "Exopolitics" was based on his experience around the 1977 Carter White House study, and led to the founding of the field of "Exopolitics", a crucial discipline in reconciling human and Off-Planet cultures.

Alfred shows his learning that DARPA/CIA had time traveled his book back to 1971 is a key to understanding the full significance of the 1977 Carter White House Extraterrestrial Communication Study because it reveals relevant events of the quantum cover-up that have remained secret to date. Alfred concludes that there is a quantum cover-up in the use of secret time-travel technology by the U.S. government to alter political and governmental history, with Alfred's learning that his book was time traveled to 1971, Alfred's 1971 time travel surveillance meeting with the same DARPA/CIA officials involved in time traveling "Exopolitics" and Alfred's inside account of the 1977 Carter White House Extraterrestrial Communication Project as a case study in point.

Eyewitness Account: Alfred, Andy, and "Exopolitics" in 2005

In the year 2000, fellow lawyer Andy contacts Alfred. In periodic phone conversations, Andy tells Alfred of his child hood experiences as a participant in a classified U.S. government program. He asks Alfred to become part of an informal advisory group helping Andy reconstruct his involvement in the classified project.

In late 2004, Andy became Alfred's literary lawyer and Editor of Alfred's forthcoming book "Exopolitics: Politics, Government And Law

In The Universe" (first published as a trade book by Universebooks in April 2005). In March 2005, in the process of editing "Exopolitics" for publication, Andy is able to identify Alfred's book "Exopolitics" as the book he had physically seen in 1971, in front of two other witnesses after the book had been teleported from the future to the past by classified time travel technology.

Personnel of the U.S. Defense Advanced Projects Agency (DARPA) carried out time travel teleportation under a classified Project Pegasus for retrieval of objects and information from the future for analysis. Alfred learns Andy retrieves a memory of having heard Alfred's name mentioned, "Who is Alfred Lambremont Webre," by another 1971 witness, and of an U.S. astronaut's name on the cover of the book he saw in 1971. Dr. Brian O'Leary, former U.S. Astronaut, is, in fact, on the cover of Alfred's 2005 book "Exopolitics". Alfred recounts the moments when he learns of Andy's retrieved memories. Alfred vividly portrays his sense of shock at hearing this, and feeling of his privacy violated by DARPA/CIA secret and unauthorized time travel of his Work in 1971.

Alfred's book "Exopolitics" is about to be first published in the very form in which Andy witnessed it in 1971 only several weeks later in April 2005, when Andy tells him of his discovery. If what Andy says is true, his 2005 book, was in the hands of the U.S. Department of Defense Advanced Research Projects Agency (DARPA) in 1971, a full six years before the 1977 Carter White House Extraterrestrial Communication Study got underway. Alfred has a profound realization that Andy's quantum revelation that "Exopolitics" is a time-traveled book is a Rosetta stone helping answer many puzzling aspects. That fact that high military-intelligence officials of the Pentagon had his book "Exopolitics" in hand in 1971 would account for the brutal termination of the 1977 White House Study, and Alfred's later life as a targeted individual of the world-wide permanent warfare state.

Uncovering the Quantum Coverup

Alfred's hearing Andy's account in 2005 of Andy's having witnessed in 1971 a time-teleported copy of Alfred's book "Exopolitics", a book based on the 1977 Carter White House ET Communication Study, provides a key in unlocking the mysteries of the quantum cover-up of time travel teleportation and the state of Extraterrestrial relations with the U.S. government. Alfred resolves to expose that DARPA/CIA has secretly surveilled him and his work using time travel technology, and to help Andy and other whistleblowers bring their knowledge about the quantum cover-up to public attention. Alfred will help uncover three levels of the quantum cover-up by discussing the motives of the U.S. Department of Defense toward the 1977 Carter White House Extraterrestrial Communication Study:

Cover-up Level One – Stopping open scientific study of extraterrestrial communication by terminating the 1977 Carter White House ET Study

Cover-up Level Two – Eliminating any security risk that secret U.S. time travel will be discovered by terminating a White House program led by a former target of Project Pegasus – Alfred Lambremont Webre and his book "Exopolitics".

Cover-up Level Three – Intervene in the time stream and cripple the future known development of "Exopolitics" by eliminating its founder, Alfred Webre.

The quantum cover-up has now been initially uncovered.

Time Travel: The Hidden Factor in the 1977 Carter White House Extraterrestrial Communication Study

Alfred identifies US government time travel technology as a hidden key factor, instrumental in the sudden and violent collapse of the 1977 Carter White House Extraterrestrial Communication study. Alfred analyzes the case of Daniel Sheehan, Alfred's future colleague, who likewise in 1977 undertook an extraterrestrial-related study on behalf of the Jimmy Carter White House. No personal harm befell Sheehan, and he actually used official authority to verify the existence of extraterrestrial artifacts at the U.S. Archives. Alfred shows that, by contrast, he was attacked just after he had begun the SRI study at a time when only a preliminary project plan existed – hardly an official threat. Whoever ordered the attacks upon Alfred and the 1977 White House Extraterrestrial Study Project was privy to more information that was available to Alfred himself. Alfred shows that in 1971 classified personnel of DARPA/CIA were in possession of Alfred's book "Exopolitics" in 1971 and that 50 DARPA/CIA personnel had engaged in a time travel surveillance Alfred in 1971, six years before the 1977 study. The Defense attaché of Project Pegasus in 1971 was Donald Rumsfeld, a political appointee of a right-wing Richard President Nixon, who was soon to resign to avoid impeachment for unconstitutional invasion of privacy.

From the vantage point of time travel, Alfred will identify at least three (3) levels of Cover-Up for stopping the proposed 1977 Carter White House Extraterrestrial Communication Study, and attempting to destroy its creator and director, Alfred Lambremont Webre.

Alfred asks: What might have motivated the U.S. Department of Defense to target the 1977 Carter White House Extraterrestrial Study? Other Extraterrestrial studies were reportedly commissioned in 1977 by the Carter White House. None of these was brutally terminated by the U.S. Department of Defense, as was the 1977 Carter White House study led by Alfred.

A key to this puzzle may lie in Andy's quantum time travel revelations about Alfred's book "Exopolitics", which sets out a blueprint for peaceful integration with advanced extraterrestrial societies. The U.S. Department of Defense since 1948, in Projects Sign, Grudge and Blue Book, has been clandestinely pursuing a hostile information war against ethical Extraterrestrial societies.

Cover-up Level One – Stop Scientific Knowledge of ET Communications

Alfred reconstructs one layer of motives of those who ordered the attacks upon him, and gave the order that the Pentagon would discontinue its contracts with SRI if the 1977 White House Extraterrestrial Communication Study went forward. Alfred shows that the nature of the attacks on him – with coordinated teams of Men In Black (MIBs) and directed energy weapons – strongly indicate the attacks came from a military-intelligence unit deployed to eliminate unacceptable risks to the Pentagon's information war against extraterrestrial society, then ongoing since at least the early 1950s. Alfred shows that the attacks on him – lethal in intent - were meant, at one level, to stop the 1977 Carter White House Extraterrestrial Communication study. The risk that a successful, open scientific White House extraterrestrial study would seriously impair the secret information war against ethical extraterrestrial societies by opening mainstream public and scientific opinion to the reality of extraterrestrial life visiting Earth.

Stop the 1977 Carter White House Extraterrestrial Communication Study because it will lead to open, scientific study of extraterrestrial communication with human culture. The U.S. secret information war against ethical extraterrestrial societies demands a continued cover-up of the existence of ethical extraterrestrial societies seeking to interact with humanity.

Cover-up Level Two – The Risk That Secret U.S. Government Time Travel Would Become Public

Alfred shows that the parties that ordered the attacks on him and the 1977 White House Extraterrestrial Communication Study had greater motivation than stopping a budding ET study by one researcher. Alfred shows that DARPA/CIA would have known Alfred Lambremont Webre's identity as the future author of "Exopolitics", a work crucial to future human-extraterrestrial relations, for at least six years in 1977. As the 1977 White House Study and Alfred would have had White House clearance as the study would have proceeded, there would have been a unusually real possibility that Alfred and his colleagues could have uncovered traces of secret U.S. time travel projects, particularly as these time travel programmes were entangled with other clandestine U.S. programmes with extraterrestrial races. As a high profile "time travel target," Alfred posed too much of a risk to the secret time travel projects to be allowed to go forward.

Stop the 1977 Carter White House Extraterrestrial Communication Study because its Director, Alfred Lambremont Webre, is the future au-

thor of "Exopolitics", a time-travel targeted book, in the possession since 1971 of DARPA, Defense Advanced Projects Research Agency. This circumstance poses a security risk to the U.S. department of Defense's secret time travel technology, as Alfred and the 1977 White House Extraterrestrial Communication Study may in the course of investigation, discover and make public relevant time-travel secrets and U.S. government secret relations with unethical extraterrestrial civilizations.

Cover-up Level Three – Sabotage Alfred, Change The Time Stream, and Cripple Exopolitics Forever

Alfred demonstrates the motivations of those ordering the attacks on him as being identical to those employing time-travel technology. The motivation of time travel technology is to acquire knowledge and/or power by intervening in the time stream through time teleportation of objects or information from the future to the past or the past to the future. Alfred shows that, in this case, it is most likely that those who sought to assassinate him did so by using intelligence gained through a secret time-travel program in order to how to intervene maximally in the time stream and achieve future power. These individuals knew through time travel technology that Alfred would author a vital book on Exopolitics, and would be a key player in extraterrestrial-human affairs. Eliminating Alfred stops the publication of the book "Exopolitics" and cripples the development of the discipline of Exopolitics as a bridge of humanity's integrating with a wider, intelligent Universe society, thereby winning a substantial coup in the on-going "war" against ethical extraterrestrial society. Only those with access to time travel technology would develop such strategies.

Synchronicity, the power of meaningful coincidence as Swiss psychologist Carl Jung defined the term, creates Andy's quantum revelation to Alfred that his book was teleported from the future back to 1971 in a secret Pentagon time-travel program. This quantum revelation explains why the Department of Defense came down so brutally on the 1977 Carter White House Extraterrestrial Communication Project and on Alfred Lambremont Webre, the future author of "Exopolitics".

The Quantum Cover-Up: A Secret Government Agency Can Access A Book Thirty Years Before It Is Written

Alfred discusses that the synchronicity or meaningful coincidence of Alfred meeting whistleblower Andy that led to Alfred's discovery of his case in the quantum Cover-Up. Alfred's case is one of the time travel of the key book "Exopolitics" back to 1971, along with the illegal use of intelligence that has been gained by time travel technology in order to terminate a White House study on extraterrestrial intelligence that had been promised by an elected U.S. President to his constituency. If this is true for one book in 2005 that was time-teleported back to 1971, with deep implications for 1977, then how far does the quantum Cover-Up extend in U.S. and world affairs?

A Quantum Cover-Up Has Been Uncovered. Let The Deconstruction of The Cosmic Watergate Begin!

Alfred shows how his story helps uncover the cover-up of the larger misuse of time travel technology, and the secreting from public science and public benefit of the time dimension as a quantum property of Nature. Alfred welcomes our looking at the time dimension as a newly found resource for humanity's benefit, and will seek that time travel technology and time science be dedicated to the public good. This includes the public release and application of associated non-polluting teleportation technologies as a replacement for polluting and land-use intensive petroleum and nuclear transportation technologies. All of these events have led to a positive outcome. Alfred's story makes public the eye-witness testimony of a participant in Project Pegasus who witnesses the time-travel teleported book "Exopolitics" in 1971, though it would not be written until 1999 nor published until 2005. Alfred's story helps uncover the cover-up of the misuse of time travel technology, and the secreting from public science and public benefit of the time dimension as a quantum property of nature. Exopolitics is a new political science, launched to help humankind integrate into a higher, organized Universe society.

SCENE 6

TIME TRAVEL, 9/11 &
POLITICAL CONTROL

Thanksgiving week,
November 20 - 23, 2006
Office of the incoming chairman
Rep. John Conyers (Dem.-Mich.)
2426 Rayburn H.O.B.
Washington, DC 20515

Like most people alive on 9/11, Alfred remembers where he was when he first learned of the events of September 11, 2001. Alfred had spoken at an Extraterrestrial disclosure conference at Simon Fraser University in Vancouver on September 9, 2001,[136] and was awaiting a meeting with the former Foreign Minister of Canada Lloyd Axworthy on September 12, 2001 to discuss Canada's sponsoring the Space Preservation Treaty banning space-based weapons.[137] Shortly after the first "plane" [actually a remote-controlled UFO cloaked to appear as a plane from below[138]] hit the North Tower WTC1 of the World Trade Center in New York, Alfred's colleague Carol called him and said, "Turn on CNN." Alfred did, and saw watched the molecular dissociation of the World Trace Center towers by multiple causes, including directed energy weapons, most plausibly the HAARP-chemtrails weapons system.

Around mid-morning, Alfred received from a trusted source a copy of an email from a U.S. sailor aboard a U.S. Navy ship reportedly off the East coast stating that the events unfolding on September 11, 2001 were a U.S. military operation. Alfred published the email online at then EcoNews and became one of the first official news sources to publish the reality of the 9/11 false flag inside job. Another sailor aboard the U.S. Navy ship later confirmed the U.S. sailor's email in a message to his mother.

Alfred began publishing the evidence confirming 9/11 was a false flag operation. He spoke at 9/11 conferences in Vancouver, BC (June 22-24, 2007),[139] Madison, WI (August 3-5, 2007),[140] and at Cooper Union in New York City (September 8-9, 2007),[141] and exposed an international war crimes racketeering organization that was coordinating 9/11 to create the New World Order through a global war on terror and domestic police state worldwide.[142]

Through an associate, Alfred brought the 9/11 Treason Independent Prosecutor Act[143] to Rep. John Conyers, the incoming Chairman of the U.S. House of Representatives Judiciary Committee. Rep. John Conyers' Executive Assistant personally assured Alfred's associate that Conyers personally reviewed the legislation over the Nov. 23, 2006 Thanksgiving weekend. Rep. John Conyers refused to act or even comment on the legislation even though the subject matter stood squarely within the mandate of the Judiciary Committee and a Memorandum summarized prima facie evidence demonstrating treason by the sitting President, Vice President and Secretary of Defense of the United States in that all three had knowingly participated in an "armed attack upon the United States", and thus met the constitutional test for treason.

The *SEPTEMBER 11 TREASON INDEPENDENT PROSECUTOR ACT*

QUESTION: What is The SEPTEMBER 11 TREASON INDEPENDENT PROSECUTOR ACT?

ANSWER: *The Act is a Public Act of the United States Congress, and a Joint Resolution of the U.S. Senate and U.S. House of Representatives in the U.S. Congress. It can be introduced by any U.S. Senator and any U.S. Representative at no cost simply by handing the Act to the Clerk according to official rules.*

QUESTION: What is the purpose of The SEPTEMBER 11 TREASON INDEPENDENT PROSECUTOR ACT?

ANSWER: *The Act would appoint an Independent Prosecutor under the authority of Article III (3) of the U.S. Constitution to prosecute Treason against these United States of America by U.S. President George W. Bush, U.S. Vice President Richard B. Cheney, U.S. Secretary of Defense Donald H. Rumsfeld and other John and Jane Does for planning and carrying out the acts of treason, as defined in Article III (3) of the U.S. Constitution, by conspiring to carry out, carrying out, and/or causing to be carried out an armed attack upon these United States on September 11, 2001, as part of a False Flag Operation. Article III of the U.S. Constitution provides that, "Sect. 3. Treason against the United States, shall consist only in levying war against them, or in adhering to their enemies, giving them aid and comfort..."*

On September 11, 1998, the U.S. House of Representatives Judiciary Committee released a report by Independent Prosecutor, Kenneth Starr, which eventually led to an Article of Impeachment against President William Jefferson Clinton under Article II of the U.S. Constitution.

QUESTION: *What are the main grounds for concluding that there is prima facie evidence that the named individuals - U.S. President George W. Bush, U.S. Vice President Richard B. Cheney, U.S. Secretary of Defense Donald H. Rumsfeld - abused the power of their office and committed Article III Treason on September 11, 2001?*

315

ANSWER: *This is what the Legislative Memorandum accompanying The SEPTEMBER 11, 2001 TREASON INDEPENDENT PROSECUTOR ACT states:*

VII. Summation: The 9/11 Attacks as Acts of Treason

The facts recited above constitute prima facie evidence that the named individuals---U.S. President George W. Bush, U.S. Vice President Richard B. Cheney, U.S. Secretary of Defense Donald H. Rumsfeld--- and other John and Jane Does are independently and jointly guilty of Treason against these United States under Article III (3) of the U.S. Constitution, because:

I. The attacks of 9/11, as portrayed in the official account, could not have succeeded if standard operating procedures between the FAA and NORAD had been followed. The Pentagon, under the leadership of Donald Rumsfeld, has provided three mutually inconsistent accounts of NORAD's response, which means that at least two of them are false. Moreover, the third account, articulated by the 9/11 Commission, is contradicted by a wide range of facts, including evidence that the FAA had notified NORAD in a timely fashion. There must have been stand-down orders, and these could have come only from the highest levels of the Pentagon and the White House.

II. Overwhelming evidence exists that the collapses of the Twin Towers and Building 7 were instances of controlled demolition. But al-Qaeda operatives could not have obtained the needed access to the buildings to plant the explosives and would not have ensured that the buildings come straight down. The controlled demolition, therefore, had to be the work of insiders. That President Bush was one of those insiders is suggested by the fact that his brother and cousin were principals in the company in charge of WTC security. Complicity at the highest levels of the federal government is also indicated by the removal of evidence (the collapsed steel), which is normally a federal offense. Finally, if the airplane strikes could have occurred only with the consent of the president and the secretary of defense (as suggested in the previous point), the coordination of these strikes with the demolition of the buildings implies their involvement in the latter as well.

III. *Overwhelming evidence also exists for the conclusion that the attack on the Pentagon was an inside job. That the official story could not be true is evident from many facts: Hani Hanjour's incompetence; the choice of the west wing as the target; the impossibility of a commercial airliner's coming back to Washington undetected and hitting the Pentagon unless permitted; and the lack of physical evidence consistent with an attack by a Boeing 757. That the strike was an inside job is implied by the falsity of the official story, the evidence that the strike was made by a military aircraft, the removal of evidence, and the government's refusal to release videos of the strike. This operation could hardly have been planned without the involvement of Secretary of Defense Rumsfeld.*

IV. *Complicity at the highest levels of the federal government is also indicated by President Bush's remaining at the school after it was evident---given the truth of the official account---that the United States was experiencing a surprise attack. This behavior makes sense only if Bush and his lead Secret Service agent knew that there would be no attack on the school.*

V. *The complicity of Vice President Cheney in the attack on the Pentagon and the downing of Flight 93 is implied by the testimony of Secretary Mineta in conjunction with the false claims of the 9/11 Commission, under the guidance of administration insider Philip Zelikow, as to when Cheney went to the PEOC and when he issued the shoot-down authorization.*

VI. *The conclusion from the evidence that members of the Bush administration orchestrated the attacks of 9/11 is reinforced by the fact that they had some huge projects---prosecuting wars in Afghanistan and Iraq and obtaining funding to accelerate the technological transformation of the military---that would likely be possible only in the event of "a new Pearl Harbor."*

On the basis of this and other evidence, the conclusion that the Bush-Cheney administration was complicit in the 9/11 attacks has been reached by many Americans, including intellectuals and former military officers. It is time for an independent official investigation into this evidence.

CAVEAT LECTOR: This memorandum is based upon the best public research resources presently available. It is presented not as a full treatment of the subject but as merely a brief summary pointing to the existence of sufficient prima facie evidence to warrant the appointment of an independent prosecutor.

The SEPTEMBER 11, 2001 TREASON INDEPENDENT PROSECUTOR ACT

Joint Res. _____ 1__ th CONGRESS _____ Session

Joint Res. _____

To appoint an Independent Prosecutor under the authority of Article III (3) of the U.S. Constitution to prosecute Treason against these United States of America by U.S. President George W. Bush, U.S. Vice President Richard B. Cheney, U.S. Secretary of Defense Donald H. Rumsfeld and other John and Jane Does for planning and carrying out the acts of treason, as defined in Article III (3) of the U.S. Constitution, by conspiring to carry out, carrying out and/or causing to be carried out an armed attack upon these United States on September 11, 2001, as part of a strategic deception operation.

JOINT RESOLUTION OF THE U.S. SENATE & HOUSE OF REPRESENTATIVES

Date: _____

Sen. _____ and Rep._____

introduced the following Joint Resolution of the Congress of the United States

A JOINT RESOLUTION OF THE U.S. SENATE & HOUSE OF REPRESENTATIVES

To appoint an Independent Prosecutor under the authority of Article III (3) of the U.S. Constitution to prosecute Treason against these United States of America by U.S. President George W. Bush, U.S. Vice President Richard B. Cheney, U.S. Secretary of Defense Donald H. Rumsfeld and other John and Jane Does for planning and carrying out the acts of treason, as defined in Article III (3) of the U.S. Constitution, by conspiring to carry out, carrying out and/or causing to be carried out an armed attack upon these United States on September 11, 2001, as part of a strategic deception operation.

Be it enacted by the Senate and House of Representatives of the United States of America in Congress assembled,

WHEREAS, U.S. President George W. Bush, U.S. Vice President Richard B. Cheney, U.S. Secretary of Defense Donald H. Rumsfeld and other John and Jane Does planned and carried out acts of treason, as defined in Article III (3) of the U.S. Constitution, by conspiring to carry out, carrying out and/or causing to be carried out an armed attack upon these United States on September 11, 2001, as part of a strategic deception operation; and

WHEREAS, the goals of the strategic deception operation of September 11, 2001 included providing a pretext for the unilateral abrogation of the ABM Treaty (announced by U.S. President George W. Bush on June 13, 2002) and for the weaponization of space; for the abrogation of fundamental rights guaranteed by the Bill of Rights in the U.S. Constitution; and for the launching of illegal wars of aggression in violation of international law and the Charter of the United Nations.

WHEREAS, There is a sufficient legal threshold of evidence to issue an indictment for the crime of Treason against these individuals under the US Constitution, which in Article III (3) provides: "Sect. 3. Treason against the United States, shall consist only in levying war against them, or in adhering to their enemies, giving them aid and comfort. No person shall be convicted of treason unless on the testimony of two witnesses to the same overt act, or on open confession in open court."

SECTION 1. SHORT TITLE.

This Act may be cited as the 'The SEPTEMBER 11, 2001 TREASON Independent Prosecutor Act'.

SEC. 2. REAFFIRMATION OF CONSTITUTIONAL PROHIBITION AGAINST TREASON AGAINST THESE

UNITED STATES.

Congress reaffirms the prohibition under the US Constitution, which in Article III (3) provides: "Sect. 3. Treason against the United States, shall consist only in levying war against them, or in adhering to their enemies, giving them aid and comfort. No person shall be convicted of treason unless on the testimony of two witnesses to the same overt act, or on open confession in open court."

SEC. 3. APPOINTMENT AND FUNDING OF A SEPTEMBER 11, 2001 INDEPENDENT PROSECUTOR. Congress hereby appoints and fully funds an Independent Prosecutor under the authority of Article III (3) of the U.S. Constitution to prosecute Treason against these United States of America by George Walker Bush, Richard B. Cheney, Donald H. Rumsfeld and other John and Jane Does for planning and carrying out the acts of treason, as defined in Article III (3) of the U.S. Constitution, by conspiring to carry out, carrying out and/or causing to be carried out an armed attack upon these United States on September 11, 2001, as part of a strategic deception operation.

SEC. 4. REPORTS. The SEPTEMBER 11, 2001 TREASON Independent Prosecutor shall submit public progress reports to the Congress every 90 days.

END[144]

Alfred published a series of exposes showing the link between time travel, other exotic black budget technologies such as HAARP, directed energy weapons, mini-nukes, remote-controlled UFOs holographically cloaked as airliners, and the false flag operation of 9/11. [145]

Alfred began by publicly revealing the role of time travel technology in the pre-identification of the 9/11 events.

Secret DARPA time travel program may hold key to understanding the deep politics of 9/11

By Alfred Lambremont Webre, JD, MEd

This is the first of a multi-part series on exotic and quantum access technologies, their application to the events of September 11, 2001, and the consequent implications for our society.

In a 2006 paper entitled, "False Flag Operations, 9/11, and the Exopolitical Perspective", Dr. Michael E. Salla identifies five exopolitical factors behind false flag operations, including the false flag operation of September 11, 2001. Although Dr. Salla identifies exotic scalar weapons as the "fourth exopolitical factor" in false flag operations, his 2006 article does not disclose how exopolitically-related factors specifically may have played out in the case of 9/11.

Since then, a key whistle blower, Andrew D. Basiago, has emerged with evidence that secret U.S. time travel technologies were used as early as 1971 to acquire first-hand documentary knowledge about September 11, 2001 – fully three decades before the horrific events of that fateful day.

Mr. Basiago, a child participant in DARPA's time travel program, Project Pegasus, has publicly stated how in 1971 he viewed moving images of the attack on the Twin Towers on September 11, 2001 that had been obtained from the future and brought back to the early 1970's.

DARPA is the chief research and development arm of the US military, the Defense Advanced Research Projects Agency. DARPA created the precursor to the Internet, "Arpanet," and has a penchant for trumpeting its advances, such as putting surveillance cameras on the backs of bumblebees and other exotic achievements in military science.

Mr. Basiago claims that DARPA's secret technical accomplishments go far beyond what it has publicly acknowledged and that by 1970 DARPA had achieved teleportation-based time travel as well as advanced electro-optical means of discerning past and future events via different technologies that provide quantum access.

Mr. Basiago has described how while serving in Project Pegasus, he viewed moving images of 9/11 at the secured U.S. defense-technical facility where they were processed after being retrieved from the future, the Aerojet Corporation facility that once stood at the corner of Bullock Avenue and Leroy Place in Socorro, New Mexico.

According to Mr. Basiago's whistleblower testimony, Donald H. Rumsfeld, the sitting U.S. Secretary of Defense on September 11, 2001, was the defense attaché to Project Pegasus during the early 1970's, when Mr. Rumsfeld was officially serving as a counselor to President Nixon and member of his Board of Wage and Price Stabilization.

In all likelihood, Mr. Rumsfeld, as the defense attaché to Project Pegasus, would have known about and possibly had control over the data about 9/11 derived via "quantum access" and brought back to the early 1970's for analysis by the DARPA research and development program under his administrative authority.

Mr. Basiago's eyewitness account that Secretary Rumsfeld and others knew about 9/11 decades in advance because data about it was gathered via DARPA's secret time travel program unlocks several of the more enigmatic facts in the 9/11 literature and may be the key to society's unraveling of the ultimate accountability for the false flag operation that took place on September 11, 2001.

This series will explore Mr. Basiago's whistleblower eyewitness evidence regarding how secret U.S. government time travel technologies relate to 9/11 in future installments of this series.

Corroborative evidence of Andrew D. Basiago's secret U.S. government time travel includes a Photo of Andrew D. Basiago on Nov. 19, 1863 at the site of Pres. Abraham Lincoln's Gettysburg Address.

This article introduces readers to quantum access evidence in the form of a time travel artifact that resulted from Andrew D. Basiago's childhood participation in DARPA's secret time travel program in the early 1970's. The ALTA reports and Web Bot technology have identified Mr. Basiago, an emerging figure in the disclosure movement, as a "planetary whistleblower" based on the global significance of his revelations. Exploring this time travel artifact will help establish a frame of reference for readers to better evaluate evidence gathered by quantum access technology and time travel participants like Mr. Basiago.

Corroborative documentary evidence of the veracity of Mr. Basiago's time travel expeditions on behalf of the U.S. government exists. This documentary evidence consists of a photograph of Mr. Basiago taken at the scene of U.S. President Abraham Lincoln's Gettysburg Address on November 19, 1863 after he was teleported to that location in the time-space continuum via DARPA time travel technology.

Andrew D. Basiago at Gettysburg, PA on November 19, 1863 (Gettysburg Address)

The photograph of Andrew D. Basiago [Figure 1] as a Project Pegasus time travel participant was taken at the site of U.S. President Abraham Lincoln's Gettysburg Address on November 19, 1863, to which Mr. Basiago had been teleported back in time by DARPA.

Mr. Basiago has publicly answered questions about this corroborating photographic evidence of his time travel experiences in the secret U.S. government program in which time travel was achieved.

Q: Is this [Figure 1] the photo of you on November 19, 1863? [Note: Please consult footnote at the end of this article to view a copy of this photograph. Thank you.]

Andrew D. Basiago: Yes. I am the boy standing in the foreground of the image at center-left, looking to his right. My shoes were lost in the transit through the quantum plenum that took me from the plasma confinement chamber at the time lab in East Hanover, NJ in 1972 to Gettysburg, PA on the day that Abraham Lincoln gave his famous address there in 1863. When I walked into downtown Gettysburg, where the shops were, after walking into town along the north-south arterial that led into Gettysburg, a cobbler by the name of John Lawrence Burns accosted me and took me inside a millinery shop and furnished me with a pair of men's street shoes and a Union winter parka that he took from a stack of military clothing in a storeroom at the back of the shop. In this image, one can see how over-sized the shoes were. I can confirm that this image was taken right after Presi-

dent Lincoln arrived on the dais, because when I walked over to this location and stood in this manner to detract attention from my shoes, I had been standing over by the dais, and Lincoln had not yet arrived, and I only stood in this position for several minutes before the quantum field effect produced by the plasma confinement chamber ended and I found myself back in the time lab in New Jersey.

Q: This is incredible, Andrew! I did not know there were pictures. Was this a picture (Figure 1) discovered that just happened to have you in it, or was this picture taken by those with you and you brought it back?

Andrew D. Basiago: To my knowledge, this was the only photograph that was taken in a past or future time when I was time traveling for DARPA's Project Pegasus. I think another breakthrough will come in the form of accounts from residents of Santa Fe [New Mexico] about children suddenly appearing at the state capitol complex there in the early 1970's. Our arrivals were sometimes witnessed. Several of my own arrivals were witnessed. I have spoken with area residents who knew that individuals were teleporting into Santa Fe in the early 1970's. Some of that knowledge resulted from the arrival of teleportees, including myself, being seen by others; other knowledge resulted from the fact that employees of LANL [Los Alamos National Laboratory, Los Alamos, NM] were bringing stories about the teleportation that was going on home from work and sharing them with their children around the dinner table in Los Alamos and White Rock.

Q: What were you looking at [in the photograph in Figure 1]?

Andrew D. Basiago: Nothing, intentionally. I was wearing a hodge-podge of clothes: the Union bugle boy uniform that I had been issued back in East Hanover, NJ in 1972; the Union winter parka that Burns had outfitted me in when I walked into town shivering in the brisk autumn air; the huge men's shoes that he gave me when I walked into town barefoot. When I walked over to the dais, several women were gossiping about me (presumably, because I was apparently a bugle boy separated from his regiment or a carpetbagger). I was questioned by two Union officers about where my regiment was bivouacked. I also had a strange encounter with my father, who was dressed as a Penn-

sylvania farmer and standing in front of the dais, in which he intentionally ignored me. He later said that encountering me there at Gettysburg was how he found out I was going to be in the program. But he was startled to see me and not expecting me to be there, [he] acted like he didn't know who I was. After I was questioned by the two Union officers, I was concerned that I should make myself inconspicuous. We had been trained to avoid being conspicuous, being questioned, being arrested, being detained, and so on, because these things might create complications that would prevent us from getting back to the present. So, self-conscious about the huge shoes that I was wearing and trying to avoid being further noticed, I walked about 100 paces from the dais and stood with my back to the dais looking in the opposite direction from where I knew Lincoln would be arriving. I hoped that by affecting an air of non-chalance in this manner, I would avoid further scrutiny by those present. It didn't work! I ended up becoming the first time traveler from the future to be photographed!

Andrew D. Basiago answers questions about Project Pegasus and 9/11

Q: Why would the US take part in 9/11?

Andrew D. Basiago: What I know is that in the early 1970's, Project Pegasus had moving images of one of the planes hitting one of the Twin Towers on 9/11; that 9/11 was known and spoken of by project principals; and that the defense attaché to Project Pegasus was Donald Rumsfeld, the individual who was serving as Defense Secretary during 9/11. The evidence from Project Pegasus shows that the US government knew about the 9/11 attacks many years in advance, not necessarily that it "took part" in those attacks.

Q: If Project Pegasus knew about 9/11 before it would happen, why wasn't 9/11 prevented from occurring?

Andrew D. Basiago: That's a good question. What I know is that it was the consensus of the US officials administering Project Pegasus that information about future events should be used to engage in contingency planning for future events but not to "play God" and change the future by preventing or altering future events. A paradox exists such that acting to change future events based on prior knowledge of them results in diminished accurate knowledge of future events. So, there is an institutional reluctance to change future events based upon prior knowledge of them because of the impact of doing so on the quality of the intelligence database concerning future events.

Q: How much information about the future has Project Pegasus learned about?

Andrew D. Basiago: My experiences in Project Pegasus indicate that by 1970, the US government was using chronovision to capture remotely and record on film a vast amount of footage of past and future events. When we visited the project location at Flemington, NJ -- where I was shown remote images of the signing of the US Constitution in 1787 and saw George Washington and Benjamin Franklin as they appeared in life -- we could see that the technicians there were filming reams and reams of scenes of past events on 16 mm film stock and storing it in film canisters. Presumably, this process is done digitally today.

Q: Is Project Pegasus still active?

Andrew D. Basiago: I do not know whether Project Pegasus is still active, but the intelligence infrastructure that evolved from it is in all likelihood very active at this time. Project Pegasus was a small, highly secret research and development program launched in the late 1960's. However, the technologies that it developed gave the US government the keys to past and future events. My guess is that the quantum access capabilities that Project Pegasus provided the US government are now headquartered at some form of national intelligence center that provides the President, the intelligence community and the military information about future events.

Q: Was just the military involved or was the government also involved?

Andrew D. Basiago: Project Pegasus combined individuals employed by the US military (Navy, DARPA), the US intelligence community

(CIA) and civilian defense contractors (e.g., Parsons). It was a research and development program of the US Department of Defense (DoD).

Q: How could a father actually put his son through all of these violent and possibly fatal transportation experiments?

Andrew D. Basiago: It is my position that my father and I were proud to serve our country during its hour of maximum danger and were also privileged to be involved in America's early activities in time-space exploration. My father did not involve me in Project Pegasus. Rather, we were approached by the US government and told we had to be involved for reasons that remain a mystery. In all likelihood, we were identified by project personnel from the future, who knew from the perspective of their time that we had been involved in the program, and hence we were brought into the program to create the future program that had knowledge of our past involvement.

Q: Why was not an adult the one transported so that the information brought back might be more precise?

Andrew D. Basiago: Children were involved for five main reasons. First, we were experimental test subjects into the physical and mental effects of teleportation on children. Second, we were necessary participants because the holograms produced by the chronovisors would collapse if adults were involved and so small, cooperative, intelligent human beings were needed as the time travelers in the chronovisor probes, and therefore a decision was made to involve gifted and talented American school children. Third, we were regarded as better participant-observers of the past and future events accessed in the program because children are tabula rasa -- blank slates whose perceptions are not skewed by the selection bias produced by their previous experiences. Fourth, we were trainees who were expected to become America's first generation of "chrononauts" in a fully-fledged time-space program when we grew up. Fifth and lastly, the Department of Defense found that when adults were involved in time travel, the psychologically destabilizing effects of moving between alternate time lines was causing some adult time travelers to become insane, so it was hoped that by training time travelers

327

from childhood a competent cadre of US time travelers could be formed.

Q: How could a child possibly be put through all of this and also re-member everything he saw or even understand what he saw or heard?

Andrew D. Basiago: I am a gifted individual with exceptional powers of observation and memory. These gifts were identified when I was being trained in Project Pegasus. In one test, I recited back random numbers provided to me verbally to 84 places. I was identified as the future whistle blower about Project Pegasus even while I was still serving on the project. I have spent over 10 years investigating my experiences and proving them to an historical certainty. I am an individual who did remember what I saw and heard, so it is not valid to say that I couldn't have done so because a child couldn't or shouldn't have been able to. That involves the fallacy of using the general to refute the specific. I not only remembered much of what I saw and heard, but I later wrote it down and went back and investigated it and proved my memories. Consequently, I am now able to provide an insider's ac-count of the US government's time-space program at the time of its emergence in the late 1960's and early 1970's.[146]

Although there was a wide public following Alfred's reporting on time travel revelations about 9/11, the 9/11 "Truth Movement" itself was resistant to this information. On September 11, 2012, Washington attorney and former childhood participant in DARPA's Project Pegasus (1968-73) Andrew D. Basiago filed a sworn affidavit with the 9/11 War Crimes Tribunal, Judges Constance Fogal and Alfred Lambremont Webre, JD, MEd, with regard to the application of DARPA secret time travel technology in accessing moving images of the events of September 11, 2001 as early as 1971.[147] As a Judge on the 9/11 War Crimes Tribunal, Alfred properly introduced into evidence the affidavit of Andrew D. Basiago swearing to his personal knowledge of Donald H. Rumsfeld and others foreknowledge in 1971 of the events of September 11, 2011 on the basis of secret time travel probes by DARPA.

Alfred's judicial ruling resulted in a walk out of all but four of the more than twenty witnesses before the 9/11 War Crimes Tribunal, orchestrated by University of Wisconsin Prof. Jim Fetzer who together with his associate Kevin Barrett began publishing a series of articles bashing Alfred and Andy Basiago on the grounds that the time travel revelations were disinformation meant to trivialize the 9/11 Tribunal.[148] Fetzer, Barrett, and the walkout witnesses could not fathom that Judge Alfred was in fact ruling properly on factual sworn evidence from a 9/11 eyewitness, Andrew D. Basiago.

In April 2013 as speakers at the Free Your Mind Conference, Fetzer who led the walk out, and Alfred made peace over a meal at the City Tavern on Old Philadelphia, agreeing that they had had a "misunderstanding."[149]

Alfred also published seminal, breakthrough insights on the role of time travel in governance and political control, appearing first in Veritas Magazine in Australia. A time travel surveillance guinea pig himself, Alfred stated that "The U.S. government has had Tesla-based quantum access time travel technology for over 40 years. Time travel technology has been weaponized with its principal impacts to date being for the sequestration in time loops of secret military installations, such as U.S. secret bases on Mars, political control of the human population, political surveillance, and attempted imposition of a catastrophic timeline on humanity by withholding or manipulating information about future events."[150]

Time Travel and Political Control

By Alfred Lambremont Webre, JD, MEd

NOTE: This article is part of a continuing series on quantum access and other exotic technologies that have been developed by black budget military and intelligence projects and applied to date principally for weapons uses, rather than for the benefit of humanity, who in the end have paid with public funds for their original development. This article originally appeared in Veritas Magazine, Australia.

The U.S. government has had Tesla-based quantum access time travel technology for over 40 years. Time travel technology has been weaponized with its principal impacts to date being for the sequestration in time loops of secret military installations, such as U.S. secret bases on Mars, political control of the human population, political surveillance, and attempted imposition of a catastrophic timeline on humanity by withholding or manipulating information about future events.

I Confirmation of U.S.' use of Tesla-based time travel technology

Two independent whistleblowers from the U.S. national security state have come forward with congruent, sophisticated, and extensive insider accounts of their experiences with Tesla-based time travel technology developed by the U.S. Department of Defense.

Mars colony eyewitness Michael Relfe is a whistleblower and a former member of the U.S. armed forces who, in 1976, was recruited as a permanent member of the secret Mars colony. In 1976 (Earth time), he teleported to the Mars colony and spent 20 years as a permanent member of its staff. In 1996 (Mars time), Mr. Relfe was time-travelled via teleportation and age-regressed 20 years, landing back at a U.S. military base in 1976 (Earth time). He then served six years in the U.S. military on Earth before being honorably discharged in 1982.

In a two-volume book, "The Mars Records"[151], authored by his wife, Stephanie Relfe, B.Sc., Mr. Relfe describes the two types of individuals at the secret Mars colony:

"To clarify: Remember there are two kinds of people that I remember.

"1. People visiting Mars temporarily (politicians, etc.) – They travel to and from Mars by jump gate. They visit for a few weeks and return. They are not time travelled back. They are VIP's. They are OFF LIMITS!!

"2. Permanent staff – They spend 20 years' duty cycle. At the end of their duty cycle, they are age reversed and time shot back to their space-time origin point. They are sent back with memories blocked.

They are sent back to complete their destiny on Earth." (Vol. 2, p. 204)

Four independent whistleblower witnesses, including Michael Relfe, have confirmed the existence of one or more U.S. secret bases on Mars, as forward strategic military bases for occupation or defence of the solar system. These whistleblower witnesses include, besides Michael Relfe, former U.S. Army Command Sgt. Major Robert Dean, former participant in DARPA's Project Pegasus Andrew D. Basiago and former U.S. Department of Defense scientist Arthur Neumann.

Andrew D. Basiago is a former participant in DARPA Project Pegasus (1968-72) that developed Tesla-based quantum teleportation and time travel in the time space hologram, initiating the U.S. program of time-space Chrononauts.

According to Mr. Basiago, the U.S. government already had a fully operational teleportation capability in 1967-68, and by 1969-70, was actively training a cadre of gifted and talented American schoolchildren, including himself, to become America's first generation of "chrononauts" or time-space explorers.

This training, he said, culminated in 1981, when, as a 19-year-old, he teleported to Mars, first by himself after being prepared for the trip by CIA officer Courtney M. Hunt, and then a second time in the company of Hunt. Both trips, Mr. Basiago said, were made via a "jump room" located at a CIA facility in El Segundo, CA. The apparent purpose of the trips to Mars was to familiarize him with Mars because the CIA knew of his destiny pertaining to publicly establishing the fact that Mars is an inhabited planet and deemed it important that he visit Mars and experience its conditions first-hand.

Mr. Basiago's involvement in advanced U.S. time-space research as a child, as well as Courtney M. Hunt's identity as a career CIA officer, have been confirmed by Dr. Jean Maria Arrigo, an ethicist who works closely with U.S. military and intelligence agencies, and by U.S. Army Captain Ernest Garcia, whose storied career in U.S. intelligence included both serving as a guard on the Dead Sea Scroll expeditions of

331

Israeli archaeologist Yigal Yadin and as the Army security attaché to Project Pegasus.

Remote sensing in the time-space continuum

Mr. Basiago has revealed that between 1969 and 1972, as a child partici-pant in Project Pegasus, he both viewed past and future events through a device known as a "chronovisor" and teleported back and forth across the country in vortal tunnels opened in time-space via Tesla-based teleporters located at the Curtiss-Wright Aeronautical Company facility in Wood Ridge, NJ and the Sandia National Laboratory in Sandia, NM.

A chronovisor is a device that uses a screen or holographic template to locate and display scenes from the past or future in the time-space hologram. The chronovisor was originally developed by two Vatican scientists in conjunction with Enrico Fermi and later refined by DARPA scientists.

DARPA had, he explains, five reasons for involving American school-children in such new, dangerous, and experimental activities:

1. First, the Department of Defense wanted to test the mental and physical effects of teleportation on children.

2. Second, Project Pegasus needed to use children because the holo-grams created by the chronovisors would collapse when adults stood within them.

3. Third, the children were tabula rasa (of the mind that has not yet gained impressions of experience) and would tend to see things during the time probes that adults would tend to miss.

4. Fourth, the children were trainees who upon growing up would serve in a covert time-space program under DARPA that would oper-ate in tandem with the overt space program under NASA.

5. Lastly, the program sponsors found that after moving between time lines, adult time travellers were often becoming insane, and it was hoped that by working with gifted and talented children from child-hood, the U.S. government might create an adult cadre of

"chrononauts" capable of dealing with the psychological effects of time travel.

In contrast to the chronovisor probes, in which a form of virtual time travel was achieved, the teleporters developed by Project Pegasus allowed for physical teleportation to distant locations, sometimes with an adjustment forward or backward in time of days, weeks, months, or years. According to Mr. Basiago, by 1972, the U.S. government was using "quantum displacement" of this kind to both send people forward several years in time to store sensitive military secrets in the future and backward several years in time to provide the government with intelligence about future events.

II The weaponization of time travel

DARPA's Project Pegasus (1968-73) under which the U.S. government program of quantum access Tesla-based teleportation and time travel was developed was historically under the control of then-U.S. President Richard M. Nixon's cabinet member Donald H. Rumsfeld. According to Mr. Basiago's whistleblower testimony, Donald H. Rumsfeld, the sitting U.S. Secretary of Defence on September 11, 2001, was the defence attaché to Project Pegasus during the early 1970's, when Mr. Rumsfeld was officially serving as a counselor to President Nixon and member of his Board of Wage and Price Stabilization.

Mr. Rumsfeld approached his Project Pegasus responsibilities with the intent to weaponize teleportation and time travel to the U.S. government's advantage. He has been quoted as stating in Project Pegasus meetings at the time that the chief mission of teleportation was to deliver troops to the appropriate place in the battlefield.

Sequestration of secret U.S. military bases

It is clear from Michael Relfe's two books on his 20 years at the secret U.S. base on Mars that U.S. time travel was principally used to the hide the presence of U.S. secret military installations on Mars from the public so that the installations remained accessible only to time scientists of the U.S. DoD.

Mr. Relfe was recruited into the U.S. armed forces and time travel/teleported to Mars in 1976. Only individuals with access to secret time science records or technology of the U.S. Department of Defense could prove the existence of the U.S. secret Mars base from Michael Relfe's conventional U.S. service records.

Time travel and political control of the human population

Time travel pre-identification and secret training of U.S. Presidents

On a November 11, 2009 Coast to Coast AM radio program, Mr. Basiago publicly stated that DARPA'S Project Pegasus program involving time travel was identifying future persons of interest, including those who would serve as U.S. president, and then informing such persons of their destinies. Mr. Basiago stated that in the early 1970s, in the company of his late father, Raymond F. Basiago, an engineer for The Ralph M. Parsons Company who worked on classified aerospace projects was present at a lunch in Albuquerque, New Mexico at which (then) future U.S. Presidents George H.W. Bush and George W. Bush were guests shortly after they were informed that both would one day serve as President.

He also stated that in the early 1970s, the DARPA program, Project Pegasus, had identified future Presidents Jimmy Carter and Bill Clinton utilizing time travel technology. Mr. Basiago met (then) future President Barack Obama in Los Angeles, CA in 1982 Mr. while attending UCLA. Mr. Obama, then a student at Columbia University, was visiting former classmates at Occidental College in Los Angeles. A statement was made by the ally of Mr. Obama in the anti-apartheid movement which revealed that Mr. Obama, then age 20, already knew that he would one day be the President.

Project Pegasus time travel was also used for political surveillance of future societal change agents.

Mr. Basiago revealed that the reason Project Pegasus was able to identify Mr. Carter, who was the then Governor of Georgia, in 1971, as a future U.S. President, is that the program was in possession of a copy of "Exopolitics: Politics, Government and Law in the Universe" by Alfred Lambremont Webre—a book that this reporter would not write until 1999 and would not be published as a library book until 2005, but which bears a quote on its front pages of a statement made by President Jimmy Carter.

According to him, Mr. Webre's book "Exopolitics" was, among other written works, physically retrieved from the future by Project Pegasus and brought back in time to 1971 or a prior time. At that time, 1971, Mr. Webre was General Counsel of the New York City Environmental Protection Administration and had been placed under time travel surveillance by the U.S. government.

Mr. Basiago has also stated that Project Pegasus identified Laura Magdalene Eisenhower, the great granddaughter of U.S. President Dwight D. Eisenhower, as a his future ally.

Thus, there is historical precedent for the covert political surveillance, via remote sensing in time, of a person of interest like Laura Magdalene Eisenhower, great-granddaughter of U.S. President Dwight D. Eisenhower.

Time travel and 9/11

Mr. Basiago has publicly stated how in 1971 he viewed moving images of the attack on the Twin Towers on September 11, 2001 that had been obtained from the future and brought back to the early 1970's.

He has described how while serving in Project Pegasus, he viewed moving images of 9/11 at the secured U.S. defence-technical facility where they were processed after being retrieved from the future (at the Aerojet Corporation facility that once stood at the corner of Bullock Avenue and Leroy Place in Socorro, New Mexico).

In all likelihood, Mr. Rumsfeld, as the defence attaché to Project Pegasus, would have known about and possibly had control over the data about 9/11 derived via "quantum access" and brought it back to the early 1970's for analysis by the DARPA research and development program under his administrative authority.

Mr. Basiago's eyewitness account that Secretary Rumsfeld and others knew about 9/11 decades in advance because data about it was gathered via DARPA's secret time travel program unlocks several of the more enigmatic facts in the 9/11 literature and may be the key to society's unraveling of the ultimate accountability for the false flag operation that took place on September 11, 2001.

Time travel and natural catastrophe

A chronovisor probe in the early 1970s by DARPA's Project Pegasus chose an archetypal target in Washington, DC. Project Pegasus chose to view the U.S. Supreme Court building in 2013 via chronovisor and Project Pegasus participant and Mr. Basiago "found that the Supreme Court building was under 100 feet of stagnant water".

A Farsight Institute remote viewing study of natural catastrophe targeted the archetypal target right across from the U.S. Supreme Court Building—the U.S. Capitol building—in 2013.

In all, 39% of the remote viewer reports viewed the U.S. Capitol in ruins alongside deep water.

Mr. Basiago has also stated that "that because the chronovisors did not identify absolute, deterministic futures but rather alternate futures in the "multi-verse," this catastrophic vision of Washington, DC might be from an alternative time line that does not materialize on our time line."

Results showed that 29% of Farsight remote viewers targeting the U.S. Capitol in 2013 did not see a Washington, DC devastated by natural catastrophe.

Here, then, we have the 2012-13 catastrophic and 2012-13 non-catastrophic futures side by side. DARPA's Project Pegasus chronovisor technology for probing future events in the time-space hologram was state-of-the-art in the early 1970s. Project Pegasus itself was under the policy oversight of Donald H. Rumsfeld as a Nixon cabinet member. It may have been that Presidential-level decisions were made in the early 1970s to commence underground shelter preparations, on the basis of Project Pegasus and other time-travel intelligence about the 2012-13 catastrophic timeline.

It is reasonable to speculate whether the U.S. and other governments and elites may have made a fundamental miscalculation and wrong conclusion in assuming that a 2012-13 cataclysmic timeline will be the actual future, when in fact it was an alternative future that would not materialize as the actual deterministic future in 2012-13.

It is also reasonable to speculate that the governments and political and financial elites have made a colossal moral error in creating safe underground bases for themselves, while making plans to leave an unwitting humanity on the surface to be 'depopulated' by a combination of giant solar flares, meteors from space, and a Mad Max scenario playing out — all of which is a future that does not materialize.

In a July 7, 2010 presentation, Dr. Courtney Brown of the Farsight Institute stated there are anomalies that suggest the U.S. government and elites are heavily invested in covertly preparing for the 2012-13 catastrophic timeline, while keeping the bulk of the human population in the dark.

These anomalies, such as rapid expansion of deep underground military bases to accommodate all U.S. government, military and police forces, and political and financial elites, suggest that they have accepted that the 2012-13 catastrophic future is the most probable future, and are feverishly completing underground facilities on Earth (as well as secret bases on Mars).

Societal impact of chronovision and teleportation

Basiago's Pegasus revelations establish that a secret, advanced U.S. time-space program emerged 40 years ago. For four decades, this program has used esoteric technologies involving chronovision and teleportation to perform "remote sensing in time" of past and future events. For the past three decades, teleportation has also been used to send individuals from Earth to strategic U.S. bases on Mars. He is adamant that these technologies be revealed so that their positive and negative aspects can be debated and their positive aspects used to the advantage of humanity.

Chronovision, he said, could be used to create an international network of virtual museums in which images from the past would be shown to enlighten and educate the public. Misapplied, such technology could also be used to create a Fascist society based on 24-hour surveillance of individuals by government, which may have been portended by the DARPA project called "Total Information Awareness" that President George W. Bush established and placed under Admiral John Poindexter.

Teleportation is a second quantum access technology developed with public funds that the public is being denied the full benefits of. Teleportation could be used, Basiago said, to move people and goods more quickly and efficiently around the globe, without the pollution caused by planes, trains, and automobiles or the negative land use effects from airports, railroad tracks, and highways. Yet, if it is not declassified, teleportation will remain what it has been for 40 years, that is, a weapon for use only by the U.S. military, to have the option to put troops precisely where they are needed on battlefields.

"I take my responsibilities as a planetary whistleblower very seriously," Basiago said.

"This is a truth campaign for positive human development on this planet. The people of this planet have a right to a true telling of the natural history of the solar system that we inhabit. This includes the truth that Mars is an inhabited planet and also that the United States' secret space program has already sent individuals from this planet to the Red Planet. If we are to achieve a sustainable human future on this planet, we must demand that the US government reveal the teleportation that has been used to reach Mars so that it can now be used to revolutionize human transport on Earth. The people of this planet have a right to inhabit a future global society in which all human beings enjoy the life-advantaging benefits of all of the *technologies that all of human ingenuity has ever produced. In both of these cases, whether a treaty protecting Mars or a global network of teleports results, the truth shall set us free."*[152]

THE AFFIDAVIT OF ANDREW D. BASIAGO ON 9/11, SWORN SEPTEMBER 11, 2012

In the interest of completeness for the public record, the affidavit of Andrew D. Basiago that Judge Alfred Lambremont Webre introduced as evidence before the 9/11 War Crimes Tribunal asserting that the U.S. government had secret time travel pre-identification of the events of 9/11 30 years in advance on 1971, and that caused all but four of the Tribunal witnesses to walk out can be accessed on the 9/11 War Crimes Tribunal website at 911warcrimestribunal.org.[153]

SCENE 7

HERE COME DA JUDGE

November 22, 2011
Kuala Lumpur War Crimes Tribunal
Kuala Lumpur, Malaysia

On January 30, 2007, Tun Dr. Mahathir bin Mohamad, former Prime Minister of Malaysia, appointed Alfred as a Judge on the Kuala Lumpur War Crimes Tribunal. According to its charter, "the Kuala Lumpur War Crime Tribunal aims to adjudicate prosecutions brought by the Kuala Lumpur War Crime Commission particularly those which involve:

1   Crimes against peace;

2   Crimes against humanity;

3   Crimes of genocide; and

4   War crimes

thereby holding perpetrators of war crimes to account for their actions especially when relevant international judicial organs fail to do so."[154]

A few days after the establishment of the Tribunal, the BBC tried exopolitical wedge politics in its initial reporting, singling out Alfred because of his interests in extraterrestrial issues.

BBC NEWS
Blair, Bush in 'war crimes trial'
By Jonathan Kent
Kuala Lumpur

A tribunal to try UK Prime Minister Tony Blair and US President George Bush for war crimes will be convened on Wednesday.

It is no surprise that neither man will be attending the proceedings - they may not even be aware that it is taking place.

But start it will, at a conference in Kuala Lumpur called as part of the former Malaysian Prime Minister Mahathir Mohamad's campaign to criminalize war.

Dry Mahathir is not expected to sit on the tribunal. He couldn't quite be characterized as impartial.

Dry Mahathir said: "What is Blair if not the co-murderer of 500,000 Iraqi children and the liar who told the British that Saddam had WMD (Weapons of Mass Destruction) which could be launched against Britain within 45 minutes?

"History should remember Blair and Bush as the 'killers of children'."

The former UN humanitarian coordinator in Iraq Hans Von Sponeck shares a platform with author Alfred Lambremont Webre.

Mr. Webre claims to have uncovered a vast conspiracy to profit from wars. He's also keenly interested in intelligent extra-terrestrial life.

Meanwhile a Downing Street spokesman responded simply: "We believe the invasion of Iraq was lawful, and we believe that the UN confirmed with resolution 1723 that the presence of the multi-national force remains legal."

And never the twain shall meet.[155]

On November 22, 2011, the Kuala Lumpur War Crimes Tribunal on which Alfred served as a Judge found former U.S. President George W. Bush and former U.K. Prime Minister Tony Blair guilty of crimes against peace - the Nuremberg level war crime - for the illegal invasion of and war in Iraq.[156]

KL tribunal convicts two former leaders with 'crimes against peace'

PETALING JAYA: The Kuala Lumpur War Crimes Tribunal unanimously found former United States president George W. Bush and former British Prime Minister Tony Blair guilty of "crimes against peace".

The tribunal found that the two had planned, prepared and invaded the state of Iraq on March 19, 2003, in violation of the United Nations Charter and international law.

"The charge is proven beyond reasonable doubt. The accused are found guilty," read an official media statement from Perdana Global Peace Foundation, organizers of the tribunal.

"War criminals have to be dealt with, convict Bush and Blair as charged. A guilty verdict will serve as a notice to the world that war criminals may run but can never ultimately hide from truth and justice," the statement read.

The tribunal noted that the UN Security Council Resolution 1441 did not authorize any use of force against Iraq but the US proceeded to invade Iraq under the pretext of the Sept 11 attacks and weapons of mass destruction.

"Weapons investigators had established that Iraq had no weapons of mass destruction. Iraq was also not posing any threat to any nation at the relevant time that was immediate that would have justified any form of pre-emptive strike."

With the findings, the tribunal has ordered that Bush and Blair's names be included in the war register of the Kuala Lumpur War Crimes Commission.

It also ordered the findings of the tribunal to be publicized to all nations who are signatories of the Rome Statute.

The tribunal, held for four days here, was initiated by former prime minister Tun Dry Mahathir Mohamad, who is also the Perdana Global Peace Foundation president.

The tribunal members were Datuk Abdul Kadir Sulaiman, Tunku Sofiah Jewa, Prof. Salleh Buang, Alfred Lambremont Webre and Prof Emeritus Datuk Dr. Shad Saleem Faruqi. Prof Niloufer Bhagwat and Datuk Zakaria Yatim were recused as tribunal members.

The Star, Kuala Lumpur, November 23, 2011[157]

Some synchronistic, karmic justice occurred to the "Bush" crime family through this judgment. The date of the judgment, November 22, 2011, was the 48th anniversary of the assassination of John F. Kennedy on November 22, 1963. George W. Bush's father, George H.W. Bush, was photographed in Dealey Plaza, Dallas, Texas on that date, standing by the Texas School Depository Building in his role as field coordinator of the JFK assassination, set in motion by an international war crimes racketeering organization led by the U.K. Monarchy and City of London bloodline bankers.[158]

During week following the Nov. 22, 2011 Tribunal judgment, while Alfred was in speaking in Johannesburg, South Africa and visiting the Anunnaki extraterrestrial landing site at Adam's Calendar, the Kuala Lumpur War Crimes Commission petitioned three neighboring African governments to arrest George W. Bush as he visited these nations on a coincidental "humanitarian" visit.

George W. Bush Must be Arrested in Africa

Amnesty International has urged African nations to arrest former US President George W. Bush during his visit to the continent this month.

--*"International law requires that there be no safe haven for those responsible for torture; Ethiopia, Tanzania and Zambia must seize this opportunity to fulfill their obligations and end the impunity George W. Bush has so far enjoyed," senior legal advisor for Amnesty International, Matt Pollard said.*

According to the international rights group, African nations have the obligation to bring Bush to justice for his role in war crimes, Reuters reported.

This is while Bush's stay in Africa is aimed at raising awareness of cervical and breast cancers, as well as HIV/AIDS.

Last month, the Kuala Lumpur War Crimes Tribunal found Bush and former British Prime Minister Tony Blair guilty of committing crimes against humanity during the Iraq war.

Earlier this year, Bush canceled a trip to Switzerland due to fears of being arrested over allegations of ordering the torture of prisoners held in overseas military bases.

President from 2001 to 2009, Bush authorized the use of waterboarding, as well as other interrogation techniques, considered to be torture by human rights groups.

Rohama, December 3, 2011[159]

Tony Blair, accustomed to travel freely internationally, also found himself subject to arrest under the judgment of the Kuala Lumpur War Crimes Tribunal when he attempted to visit Johannesburg, South Africa in 2012.

Call to arrest Tony Blair during SA visit gains momentum
By Rebecca Davis

Former British Prime Minister Tony Blair is in town this week to address a leadership summit in Johannesburg. He may want to watch his back, though: a group called the Society for the Protection of our Con-

stitution has launched an urgent application to the NPA to issue a warrant for Blair's arrest for the 2003 Iraq invasion.

In November 2011, a body called the Kuala Lumpur War Crimes Commission conducted a tribunal to try George W Bush and Tony Blair in absentia for crimes against peace, crimes against humanity and genocide. The tribunal was presided over by five judges and included representations on behalf of the defendants made by court-appointed defence counsel. The unanimous verdict found Bush and Blair guilty, but acknowledged the verdict was non-enforceable, though the findings were reported to the International Criminal Court in The Hague. The neutrality of proceedings were questionable, however, as the tribunal was the initiative of former Malaysian Prime Minister Mahathir Mohamad, who is staunchly anti-West and has accused the ICC of bias in terms of the figures it chooses to prosecute.

Daily Maverick, 27 Aug 2012 [160]*(South Africa)*

On May 10, 2012 the Kuala Lumpur War Crimes Tribunal, with Alfred as a Judge, found George W. Bush, Richard B. Cheney, Donald H. Rumsfeld, together with former Attorney General Alberto Gonzales, Cheney's General Counsel David Addington, Rumsfeld's General Counsel William Haynes, Assistant Attorney General Jay Bybee, and former Deputy Assistant Attorney General John Yoo, guilty of war crimes and torture in Iraq, Afghanistan, and Guantanamo and conspiracy to violate the Geneva Conventions.[161]

BREAKING: Tribunal finds Bush, seven others guilty of war crimes
By Global Research
Global Research, May 11, 2012
BERNAMA 11 May 2012

KUALA LUMPUR: The Kuala Lumpur War Crimes Tribunal yesterday found former US president George W Bush and seven of his associates guilty of the charge of 'Crime of Torture and War Crimes'.

The associates were former US vice-president Dick Cheney; former defence secretary Donald Rumsfeld; Bush's former counsel Alberto Gonzales; Cheney's then-general counsel David Addington; Rumsfeld's then-general counsel William Haynes; then-assistant attorney general Jay Bybee; and former deputy assistant attorney general John Yoo.

In a unanimous decision, former Court of Appeal president Tan Sri Lamin Mohd Yunus who headed the quorum of the tribunal, ruled the prosecution had proved its case beyond reasonable doubt.

"We, therefore, found that the accused are guilty of the charge," said Lamin.

The other four judges comprise Tunku Sofiah Jewa, Alfred Lambremont Webre, Professor Salleh Buang and Mohd Saari Yusuf. The panel arrived at the decision after hearing evidence from five prosecution witnesses and submissions from the prosecution and defence side.

In the days ahead Global Research will be providing details and analysis on the legal procedure. Global Research has been involved from the outset in the Kuala Lumpur Initiative to Criminalize War.

Michel Chossudovsky is member of the Kuala Lumpur War Crimes Commission (KLWCC), which organized the Tribunal Hearings.

Kuala Lumpur, May 12, 2012

The hearing took place over a four-day period, beginning May 7, whereby, three witnesses testified in the proceedings, while others gave their testimony, by way of statutory declarations.

Prof Gurdial Singh Nijar led the prosecution team while Jason Kay Kit Leon who was appointed 'amicus curiae' (friend of the court), represented the accused.

The eight accused were charged with the crime of torture, that they had willfully participated in the formulation of executive orders and directives to exclude the applicability of international conventions and laws, namely Convention against Torture 1984, Geneva Con-

vention 1949, Universal Declaration of Human Rights and the United Nations Charter, in relation to the war launched by the US and others in Afghanistan in 2001 and Iraq in March 2003.

Additionally, and/or on the basis and in furtherance thereof, the accused authorized, connived in, the commission of acts of torture and cruel, degrading and inhumane treatment against victims in violation of international law, treaties and aforesaid conventions.

Reading the 19-page verdict, Lamin said after considering the evidence adduced by the prosecution and submissions by both parties, the tribunal was satisfied the eight accused were guilty of the charge and convicted as criminals for torture and cruel, inhumane and degrading treatment of the complainant war crime victims. — Bernama Global Research, 11 May 2012[162]

And then as usual, the controllers of the false Matrix could not let Alfred be comfortable, even as a War Crimes Judge.

HOW AND WHY THE KUALA LUMPUR WAR CRIMES TRIBUNAL WAS DESTABILIZED

By Alfred Lambremont Webre, JD, MEd

VANCOUVER, BC - The objective of the attack on the Kuala Lumpur War Crimes Tribunal described in this article was to use "Meme warfare" to start an internecine war upon targeted Judges of the Kuala Lumpur War Crimes Tribunal, and thereby destabilize the Tribunal, a non-profit NGO citizen's tribunal of conscience sworn to carry out a vision architected by former Malaysian Prime Minister Dr. Tun Mahathir Bin Mohamad.[1]

That internecine war, induced by a standard covert operating Cointelpro procedures of U.S., U.K. and Israeli intelligence agencies known as "Meme warfare", had the specific objectives of (1) destabilizing the Tribunal by making it a "shooting gallery for shooting down or disqualifying Judges" so that multiple Judges could be disqualified as "Zionists" on specious grounds;

(2) discrediting the Tribunal as an objective adjudicatory body in the area of war crimes; (3) discrediting it as a functioning body to deliver credible justice in the area of Israel war crimes in Palestine 1948 – Present.[2]

The Tribunal to date had issued two important judgments against former Prime Minister Tony Blair, former U.S. President George W. Bush and his cabinet members Cheney, Rumsfeld, Gonzales and their lawyers for war crimes and torture in Iraq.[3] The Tribunal had scheduled the trial of Israel's war crimes in Palestine for August 20-24, 2013 and for November 20-25, 2013. I had participated in both trials of the Tribunal against Bush et al. and the first hearing on Israeli war crimes in Palestine. I was scheduled as a Judge on the Tribunal for the hearing on November 20-25, 2013.

MEME WARFARE: HOW TO OVERTHROW THE POWERS THAT BE ON A LOW BUDGET

According to author "Meme Warfare" author Stephen DeVoy,[4]

- Meme - "A meme is a mental construct that copies itself from mind to mind. It reproduces by inducing its carrier to engage in behavior that causes the meme to copy to other minds. It is a mental construct conjoined with a set of instructions which compel its host to engage in activities that increase the probability of the entire instruction set being copied from a host's mind into the minds of others."

- Memeplex - "A meme may have a higher chance of replication across a longer expanse of time if it aggregates with other memes. When aggregated, complementary memes enhance one another's probability of replication. Thus, just as DNA found advantage in aggregating into complex aggregations of genes, some memes find advantage in aggregating into complexes of memes. This more complex form is called the memeplex."

- Meme Warfare "Meme warfare is the subversion or destruction of a memeplex by means of memetic engineering. Meme warriors design memes targeting existing memeplexes. Such memes are intended to infect an existing memeplex, hinder an existing memeplex, or form a part of a competing memeplex. In the later case, the goal may be to create a new memeplex intended to replace the old memeplex."

MEME WARFARE AGAINST THE TRIBUNAL JUDGES & AGAINST TRIBUNAL

The memeplex "Zionist", falsely applied, was the weapon of choice in the Meme warfare designed to destabilize the Kuala Lumpur War Crimes Tribunal.

On analysis of the evidence below, it appears that there are four primary individuals who were overtly involved in the initiative to engage in "Meme warfare" and destabilize the Kuala Lumpur War Crimes Tribunal. These individuals appear to have consciously or unconsciously engaged in Meme warfare to a varying degree with the objective of destabilizing the Tribunal. It remains to be seen whether any of these individuals was covertly influenced to do so by outside intelligence agencies or groups, although some there is suggestive evidence of a cover-up and a conspiracy to destabilize the Tribunal. The individuals are present or past members of the Kuala Lumpur War Crimes Commission or present or past Prosecutors.[5]

The four individuals who, by the evidence, either consciously or unconsciously engaged in Meme warfare to destabilize the Kuala Lumpur War Crimes Tribunal are (in alphabetical order):

- Former Prosecutor Francis Boyle, academic and former Judge on the Kuala Lumpur War Crimes Tribunal and Prosecutor on the War Crimes Commission; Former Legal Counsel to the Palestinian Authority and Lt. Ehren Watada.

    Website: *http://www.law.illinois.edu/faculty/profile/francisboyle*

- Former Prosecutor Matthias Chang, former political adviser to Tun Dr. Mahathir bin Mohamad when Dr. Mahathir was Prime Minister and former Prosecutor of the Legal Team of the Kuala Lumpur War Crimes Commission. Self-professed high-ranking freemason inducted by a Grand Master freemason in the UK.

  Website: *http://futurefastforward.com/*

- Commissioner Michel Chossudovsky, Canadian academic and journalist, Member of Kuala Lumpur War Crimes Tribunal. Voted against having Tribunal trial of Israeli war crimes in Palestine.

  Website: *http://www.globalresearch.ca*

- Secretary-General Dr. Yaacob Merican, Secretary General of the Kuala Lumpur Foundation to Criminalize War

  Website: *http://www.criminalisewar.org*

SECRETARY-GENERAL YAACOB MERICAN & THE KUALA LUMPUR FOUNDATION TO CRIMINALIZE WAR

The timeline of the Meme war against the Judges of the Kuala Lumpur War Crimes Tribunal starts for me when the Foundation Secretary-General Dr. Yaacob Merican, began in May 2012, for some unknown reason, to lean on me for outreach to recruit Judges and Prosecutors for the Tribunal when that was really his job and function. Yaacob Merican invited me to a sumptuous luncheon at a spectacular Islamic art gallery and in front of a retinue of personnel from the Kuala Lumpur Foundation to Criminalize War, asked me to recruit "Caucasian" Judges for the Tribunal. Internally, I felt that his request was borderline political, but not unlawful. As I was a supporter of the non-profit peace efforts of Tun Mahathir, I complied with Secretary-General Yaacob Merican's requests in good faith as part of my contributions to this charitable peace effort. I saw my helping the Foundation recruit non-Malaysian Judges and Prosecutors as in no way providing grounds for my recusal as a "biased" Judge under the law.

In the law, judicial bias has to do with a tangible interest that the Judge has in the outcome of litigation. In the case of the Tribunal's trial of Israeli war crimes in Palestine 1948-present, I am neither Israeli nor Palestinian nor have any tangible interest in Palestine or Israel and therefore I am not biased according to the law. I am Director of Exopolitics Israel, Exopolitics Palestine, and Exopolitics Iran, and a war crimes correspondent for Press TV and have covered the Palestinian-Israeli conflict. These functions do not disqualify me as a Judge.

According to the law in most nations, "Laws or court rules provide for recusal of judges. Although the details vary, the following are nearly universal grounds for recusal.

- The judge is related to a party, attorney, or spouse of either party (usually) within three degrees of kinship.

- The judge is a party.

- The judge is a material witness unless pleading purporting to make the Judge a party is false (determined by presiding judge, but see Substitution (law)).

- The judge has previously acted in the case in question as an attorney for a party, or participated in some other capacity.

- The judge prepared any legal instrument (such as a contract or will) whose validity or construction is at issue.

- Appellate judge previously handled case as a trial judge.

- The judge has personal or financial interest in the outcome. This particular ground varies by jurisdiction. Some require recusal if there is any interest at all in the outcome, while others only require recusal if there is interest beyond a certain value.

- The judge determines he or she cannot act impartially."[6]

Timeline of a Meme War

1. Feb. 11, 2013: I forwarded to Secretary-General Yaacob Merican my report on new Judges for the Kuala Lumpur War Crimes Tribunal, and suggested that he "consult with Prof. Boyle both as to additional names for persons who can be KLWC Tribunal Judges as well as assisting the Amicus Curiae team." Former Prosecutor Boyle had formerly been a Judge of the Kuala Lumpur War Crimes Tribunal before switching over to the Prosecution. Secretary-General Yaacob's concern at that point seems to have been obtaining "Caucasian" Judges, who would presumably counter-balance the predominantly "Malaysian" Tribunal Judges. No mention was made of "Zionist", "Pro-Israel", or other similar Meme.

LETTER OF ALFRED L. WEBRE FEB. 11, 2013

---------- Forwarded message ----------

From: Alfred Lambremont Webre, JD MEd <webre@shaw.ca>

Date: Mon, Feb 11, 2013 at 12:34 PM

Subject: Re: KLFWC Tribunal on Palestine May 2013

To: Yaacob Merican <tokmama.yaacob@gmail.com>

Dear Dr. Yaacob - Hi! Thank you very much for the news about the forthcoming KLWC Tribunal on Palestine, tentatively scheduled for 5 to 10 May 2013. I have marked the dates on my calendar.

My apologies for not having written sooner. Here is my report.

I contacted the following persons qualified to be Judges on the KLWC Tribunal.

1. Judge Baltazar Garzon (Spain)

Bio:

http://en.wikipedia.org/wiki/Baltasar_Garz%C3%B3n

2. *Hon. Ramsay Clark (U.S.)*

Bio: http://en.wikipedia.org/wiki/Ramsey_Clark

3. *Gail Davidson (Canada)*

Bio: http://www.lrwc.org/gail-davidson-board-of-directors/

Gail Davidson was honored to be invited, and indicated she felt she was too busy to take on the responsibilities of being a Judge on the KLWC Tribunal.

Baltazar Garzon - I was unable to get a formal response from Judge Baltazar Garzon, who until recently was the subject of a political trial brought against him in Spain (See article).

http://www.bbc.co.uk/news/world-16965790

You may want to evaluate whether you want to ask him to be on the KLWC Tribunal. This is the best address I could get for him

Fundación Internacional Baltasar Garzón

C/ Antonio Diaz-caÑabate, 10Madrid, 28007

011-34- 911 729 69

Ramsay Clark represented Saddam Hussein, as you know. I have not yet been able to get a formal acceptance from him. I suggest that the Commission contact Ramsay Clark directly with the invitation to be a KLWC Tribunal Judge.

OFFICE:

Ramsey Clark & Lawrence W Schilling

36 E 12th St 6th Fl

New York, NY 10003-4604

Phone/Fax: (212) 475-3232

Professor Boyle - My suggestion is that you may want to consult with Prof. Boyle both as to additional names for persons who can

be KLWC Tribunal Judges as well as assisting the Amicus Curiae team.

Please let me know if you need any information, etc.

Best wishes, Alfred

On Sun, Feb 10, 2013 at 11:42 PM, Yaacob Merican
<tokmama.yaacob@gmail.com> wrote:

Dear Alfred,

It has been quite some time since we last heard from you. I hope that you are in the best of health and that you are free, if things go according to plan, that is, to sit on the KLWC Tribunal on Palestine tentatively scheduled to be held from 5 to 10 May 2013.

I recollect that before your departure from K.L. after your last visit to Malaysia, you gave assurance that you would forward to me some names of persons (at least two) with international law qualifications (together with their résumés) for consideration of the Trustees of the KLFCW **to empanel two more additional Caucasian judges on the KLWC Tribunal.**

Time is getting closer to the scheduled Palestine Tribunal Hearing and I would appreciate it very much if I could have your nominations as soon as possible.

Would you also be able to propose a name or two international lawyers of Professor Boyle's calibre, to assist the Amicus Curiae team in the aforementioned Tribunal Hearing, please?

Warmest regards

Yaacob

Sec-Gen, KLFCW

2. June 6, 2013: The next major milestone occurs when Secretary-General Yaacob asks me if I know of "a pro-Israeli international lawyer with a caliber at par with the Prosecution's Francis Boyle." [Former U.S. Representative] Cynthia McKinney is trying her level best to secure for the Amicus Curiae team the services of a pro-Israeli international lawyer with a caliber at par with the Prosecution's Francis Boyle. Time is if the essence. Would you know of anyone personally who would agree to act as such during the forthcoming hearing."?

INTENT OF THE REQUEST FOR A PRO-ISRAELI INTERNATIONAL LAWYER?

This request by Secretary-General Yaacob Merican is a key issue in Meme warfare. To understand if his request for "Pro-Israeli defense counsel" is part of Meme warfare, *one must know who issued the original request to obtain pro-Israel defense counsel and with what intent.*

- Did the request of pro-Israeli defense counsel originate with Secretary-General Yaacob or from another individual or organization that transmitted it to Secretary-General Yaacob?

- Who was that outside individual or organization? What was their intent?

- Why did "Caucasian" suddenly become "Pro-Israeli"?

- Why was "time of the essence"?

- What was the intent of this request?

- If the intent of the original request was to set up a Meme warfare situation around the meme "Zionist" to destabilize the Judges, then Secretary-General Yaacob's request constitutes Meme warfare.

Secretary-General Yaacob Merican's request - It is this request for *"the services of a pro-Israeli international lawyer with a caliber at par with the Prosecution's Francis Boyle"* that sets up the

Meme warfare against three Judges of the Tribunal. Judge Eric David and Judge Mike Hourigan, two of the Judges recommended by Former U.S. Rep. Cynthia McKinney were attacked as "Zionist", and I was to be attacked as "Zionist" because I acceded to Secretary-General Yaacob Merican's innocent-seeming request and searched (unsuccessfully) for pro-Israeli Judges.

---------- *Forwarded message* ----------

From: Yaacob Merican <tokmama.yaacob@gmail.com>

Date: Thu, Jun 6, 2013 at 7:02 PM

Subject: Re: KLFWC Tribunal on Palestine May 2013

To: "Alfred Lambremont Webre, JD MEd" <webre@shaw.ca>

Dear Alfred,

Many thanks for your e-mail.

The KLWC Tribunal Hearing on Palestine is confirmed to take place as scheduled from Wednesday 21 to Saturday 24 August 2013 in Kuala Lumpur.

Please schedule your flight arrangements so that you would arrive in Kuala Lumpur at the latest by the morning of Tuesday 20 August 2013.

Cynthia McKinney is trying her level best to secure for the Amicus Curiae team the services of a pro-Israeli international lawyer with a caliber at par with the Prosecution's Francis Boyle. Time is if the essence. Would you know of anyone personally who would agree to act as such during the forthcoming hearing.

Warmest regards.

Yaacob

On Fri, Jun 7, 2013 at 8:47 AM, Alfred Lambremont Webre, JD MEd <webre@shaw.ca> wrote:

Dear Dr. Yaacob - Hi! I was recently at the Kuala Lumpur Foundation to Criminalise War website and I happened to notice the following:

UPCOMING EVENTS

Kuala Lumpur War Crimes Tribunal–Hearing on Palestine

Date: 21 – 24 August, 2013 at 2nd Floor, No. 88, Jalan Perdana, Taman Tasik Perdana, Kuala Lumpur

Recently my attendance was requested at a public event scheduled for August 24, 2013. I told the host of that event I could tentatively not attend because there was a Kuala Lumpur Tribunal hearing scheduled for that date.

My schedule starts filling up about three months in advance.

Can you please advise me via return email if I should set aside the dates of 21-24 August 2013 to attend the above hearing as a Judge on the Tribunal?

Many thanks and best wishes, Alfred

To avoid a Pro-Palestinian "Kangaroo Court"?

I assumed, without asking Secretary-General Yaacob Merican, that the order for pro-Israeli defense counsel was a good faith requirement to avoid the trial seeming to be a "Kangaroo Court" in favor of the Palestinians, which had been a major criticism leveled at the Tribunal to date internationally.

Therefore, with the help of my co-director at Exopolitics Israel, I proceeded to contact Ambassador Alan Baker, former Israeli Ambassador to Canada who lives in Israel and is an international lawyer. His associate Prof. Robbie Sabel, Professor of International Law at Hebrew University in Jerusalem, declined to appear for Israel. I contacted my former classmate Prof. Bruce Ackerman of Yale Law School as well as my former teacher Prof. Guido Calabresi of Yale Law School. Both of these scholars recommended Prof. Alan Dershowitz of Harvard, who

Former Prosecutor Francis Boyle had told me was the "default go-to person on Israel" in the United States. Prof. Dershowitz reply, citing Former Prosecutor Francis Boyle's libel of him and Harvard Law School as his principal reason for not wanting to help recommend someone to represent Israel.

Alan Dershowitz dersh@law.harvard.edu via shaw.ca

Jun 7 to webre

"Thank you. I will think about it. Part of me doesn't want to add any legitimacy to Boyle who is an extreme supporter of terrorism and an extremist anti Israel agitator with no credibility. . . He has called me a war criminal and has accused harvard law school of complicity in war crimes. But I will respond to your inquiry."

"Who appointed him to prosecute the case?"

Sent from my iPhone

On Jun 7, 2013, at 4:42 PM, "webre@shaw.ca" <webre@shaw.ca> wrote:

> Dear Prof. Dershowitz - Hi! My classmate Prof. Bruce Ackerman of Yale Law School suggested that I contact you with a specific question.

> I am a Judge on the Kuala Lumpur War Crimes Tribunal. The Tribunal has a hearing scheduled for August 21-24, 2013 on alleged Israeli war crimes in its invasion of Gaza in January 2009.

> The Prosecutor is Prof. Francis Boyle of the Univ of Illinois who has tried cases before the International Criminal Court.

> I was asked to locate a pro-Israel lawyer of Prof. Boyle's stature who would like to serve as amicus curiae representing Israel.

> This is the website of the Tribunal.

> http://criminalisewar.org/the-foundation/judges-commissioners/

> I would very much appreciate your letting me know if can you kindly

suggest of any names of qualified lawyers who may be interested and contact info via return email.

> Best wishes,

> Alfred Webre

>

> Alfred Lambremont Webre, JD, MEd

> Vancouver, B.C. V6N3E5 CANADA

> Tel/Fax: 604-733-8134

> Skype: peaceinspace

> Email: webre@shaw.ca

>

MEME WARFARE DISTORTIONS AND FALSEHOODS

With that outreach my effort to recruit pro-Israeli defense counsel ended. Please notice that I did not ask Prof. Dershowitz to participate in the trial, merely to suggest the names of Pro-Israeli counsel who might be interested in representing Israel. I asked Prof. Dershowitz, "I would very much appreciate your letting me know if can you kindly suggest of any names of qualified lawyers who may be interested and contact info via return email."

In the heat of Meme warfare against me, both Former Prosecutor Francis Boyle and Former Prosecutor Matthias Chang would falsely state that I was a Zionist by falsely alleging that I had "asked Dershowitz to represent Israel." That is an exaggeration and distortion of the facts that is standard in Meme warfare, and demonstrative of how the minds and *persona* of Former Prosecutor Francis Boyle and Former Prosecutor Matthias Chang had become thoroughly infected with the "Zionist" Meme in this attack and how they sought by Meme warfare to attach the Meme to me in people's minds.

Through Judge Eric David, one of the two Judges that Cynthia McKinney had recommended to Secretary-General Yaacob Merican, I later learned that Cynthia McKinney had contacted Prof. Alan Dershowitz who had declined to participate. Clearly both former U.S. Rep Cynthia McKinney and I were both set up to search for "pro-Israel" defense counsel as part of Meme warfare against the Judges of the Tribunal.

3. August 20, 2013 – Orchid Room, Hotel Majestic, Kuala Lumpur, Malaysia. Conversation with Former Prosecutor Francis Boyle – I am seated next to Prosecutor Francis Boyle at a luncheon prior to the trial of Israeli war crimes in Palestine 1948- present, which was to start the next day. I casually mention to Former Prosecutor Francis Boyle that I am very proud that the Kuala Lumpur Foundation to Criminalize War had reached out to pro-Israeli Counsel to balance the trial and tell him that I had contacted counsel in Israel, Professors at Yale and Harvard Law School who had recommended Alan Dershowitz, but that Prof. Dershowitz had chosen not to recommend anyone. Former Prosecutor Francis Boyle launched into a lengthy, detailed dissertation on the feud between himself and specific professors at Yale Law School and Harvard Law School including Prof. Dershowitz. *At no time during the luncheon did Former Prosecutor Francis Boyle raise any objection to my having searched for pro-Israeli defense counsel on behalf of Israel or of having contacted Prof. Dershowitz.*

August 20, 2013 - Meme Warfare against Tribunal Judges – The evening before the trial, Commissioner Michel Chossudovsky, a controlling member of the Kuala Lumpur War Crimes Commission, and Former Prosecutor Boyle began to secretly conspiring to engage in Meme warfare and seek the recusal of three Judges on false Meme warfare grounds of "Zionism" or New World Order affiliations. We now know this because Cynthia McKinney leaked the emails in which Chossudovsky stated he wished to purge three of the Tribunal Judges (See emails below).

1 Judge Eric David, a Judge that Cynthia McKinney had nominated, on grounds that he was a Mossad agent, without providing any evidence thereof;

2 Judge Mike Hourigan because he had been at one time been associated with the UN Tribunal on Ruanda; and

3 Chief Judge of the Tribunal because he had been associated with the UN Tribunal on Yugoslavia.

CHOSSUDOVSKY AND BOYLE MEME WARFARE AGAINST TRIBUNAL JUDGES

Readers can download the full email exchange (PDF) leaked by former U.S. Rep. Cynthia McKinney showing clear Meme warfare against Judges Eric David and Michael Hourigan in the day before the trial on Israeli war crimes in Palestine at the following:

Download CHOSSUDOVSKYemail scan

CLICK TO DOWNLOAD PDF: *http://bit.ly/HLIwme*

4. August 21 – 22, 2013 - Meme warfare against Judges at hearing – Former Prosecutor Francis Boyle and Commissioner Michel Chossudovsky waged continual Meme warfare against Judge Eric David during the two-day hearing, demanding his recusal on the grounds of being a Mossad agent without offering any evidence thereof other than repetition of the Memeplex "Zionist". Vowing to shut the Tribunal down, Former Prosecutor Francis Boyle staged a sit-in of the Palestinian witnesses in the courtroom, playing on their minds with Meme warfare as well.

The irony is that on August 20, 2013, the Judges of the Kuala Lumpur War Crimes Tribunal had held an initial chambers discussion of the case, structured around a Defense motion to dismiss the charges against the State of Israel. On the basis of the discussion, Judge Eric David drafted a brilliant opinion in favor of the Palestinians, denying Israeli's motion for dismissal of the State of Israel as a defendant. Because of the Meme warfare of Chossudovsky and Boyle, the Judges never got to consider this motion publicly as a Tribunal.

Moreover, the internal discussion of the Judges on August 20, 2013 showed that (1) the Tribunal would have voted unanimously to find that Israel's war crimes in Palestine constituted crimes against humanity, and (2) the Tribunal would have voted 6-1 to find that Israel's war crimes in Palestine constituted genocide, the one dissenting vote being Judge Eric David, who believed the acts amounted to crimes against humanity, not genocide (consistent with his public positions).

Facts and actual judicial impartiality does not matter to Meme warfare, however. What matters is the destabilization of targeted Judges the Tribunal.

FINAL JUDGMENT OF THE TRIBUNAL

The Meme warfare of Former Prosecutor Francis Boyle is documented in the Final Judgment of the Tribunal, which readers can download and read (PDF).

Download KLWCT-Judgment-22-August-2013

DOWNLOAD PDF BY CLICKING HERE: *http://bit.ly/1fuDndL*

After the conclusion of the trial, Former Prosecutor Francis Boyle resigns as Prosecutor.

5. November 1, 2013 – The next event for me in the timeline of the destabilization of the Kuala Lumpur War Crimes Tribunal is my receipt on Nov. 1, 2013 of a letter from Former Prosecutor Matthias Chang demanding my recusal as a Judge, again using "Zionist" Meme warfare against me. The timing of Former Prosecutor Matthias Chang's letter is remarkable as it is sent 20 days prior to the next scheduled hearing of the Kuala Lumpur War Crimes Tribunal, as if a convenient legal maneuver to set up "Zionist" Meme warfare for my recusal on the Nov. 20-25, 2013 trial of Israel's war crimes in Palestine.

Former Prosecutor Matthias Chang's letter is also includes a telltale Meme warfare fundamental error – the same error that Former Prosecutor Francis Boyle stated - that I had attempted to recruit Alan Dershowitz to represent Israel. In fact, I only asked Prof. Dershowitz if he could suggest potential counsel for Israel.

The only person I had told that I approached Prof. Alan Dershowitz to suggest names of possible defense counsel for Israel was Former Prosecutor Francis Boyle, in the luncheon at the Hotel Majestic.

1   Therefore was it former Prosecutor Francis Boyle who contacted former prosecutor Matthias Chang with erroneous information about me to continuing Meme warfare against me as a Judge of the Tribunal?

2   Was this how former Prosecutor Matthias Chang who then took up the Meme warfare against me on this false premise?

3   Or did former Prosecutor Francis Boyle tell someone else in his network, such as Kuala Lumpur War Crimes Commissioner Michel Chossudovsky who then contacted Former Prosecutor Matthias Chang to continue Meme warfare?

Meme Warfare Mind Map

A Meme warfare mind map of the destabilization of the Kuala Lumpur War Crimes Tribunal will be most enlightening and illustrative for all tribunals of conscience worldwide to illustrate for informed citizenry how Meme warfare is used to destabilize tribunals of conscience and NGOs.

Former Prosecutor Matthias Chang states, *"It has come to my knowledge that you attempted to get the services of Dershowitz (sic) to represent Israel in the hearing which was postponed and now to be reconvened in November."*

After this initial falsehood, Former Prosecutor Matthias Chang's subsequent emails degenerate into a Meme warfare rant. Readers are welcome to access them by downloading the following PDF. What is clear is that Former Prosecutor Francis Boyle and Former Prosecutor Matthias Chang are conspiratorially engaged in Meme warfare to destabilize me as a Judge as well as the Tribunal.

Download MATTHIAS.CHANG.LETTERS

DOWNLOAD PDF BY CLICKING HERE: *http://bit.ly/18k3i2I*

6. November 4, 2013 – The next milestone in the timeline of "Zionist" Meme warfare to destabilize targeted Judges is a letter from the Chief Judge of the Tribunal stating that since I had now "openly taken the position of being an "Applicant/Complainant" before the Tribunal for a restraining order" against Commissioner Chossudovsky, Former Prosecutor Chang and others, "it has now become highly improper for you to be part of the panel of Judges at the Hearing."

The fact is that I had not served a formal motion on the court. I only emailed a notice of *intent to file.* Here the Tribunal Chief Judge, with no due process, was apparently guided by Secretary-General Yaacob Merican, who generally presents the Chief Judge with administrative matters, into joining in the reality distortions of "Zionist" Meme warfare against the targeted Judges.

Readers can view the Chief Judge's letter (PDF), which appears to be more continuation of "Zionist" Meme warfare against me as a Judge of the Tribunal below.

Download KLWCT

DOWNLOAD PDF BY CLICKING ON THE FOLLOWING: *http://bit.ly/HQrcvT*

TEXT OF NOTICE OF INTENT

"I hereby serve notice of intent to apply to the Tribunal for a restraining order against Michael Chossudovsky, Mathias

Chang, and all present and former members of the KLWCC and prosecution team, former KLWC Tribunal judges from directly or directly applying for or lobbying for the recusal of KLWC Tribunal Judges, based on a clear abuse of the recusal privilege in this case."

Very truly yours,

Alfred Lambremont Webre, JD, MEd
Member, District of Columbia Bar
JUDGE, KUALA LUMPUR WAR CRIMES TRIBUNAL
Nov. 1, 2013
VANCOUVER, BC, CANADA

FULL LETTER OF ALFRED LAMBREMONT WEBRE

Date: Fri, 1 Nov 2013 10:00:54 -0700

Subject: Denial of request for recusal and application for restraining order

From: webre@shaw.ca

To: tokmama.yaacob@gmail.com

CC: webre@shaw.ca; musaesquire@hotmail.com; tokma-ma@streamyx.com; mikehourigan@gmail.com; edavid@ulb.ac.be; sallehbuang@gmail.com; sallehbuang@hotmail.com; shad-saleem@yahoo.co.uk; tunkusofiahjw@gmail.com; changmatthi-as@hotmail.com; nijar46@hotmail.com; jasonkaykl@gmail.com

Dear Dr. Yaacob - Hi! I have received this mischievous email from Matthias Chang requesting my recusal because I carried out your request as Chairman of the KLWC Commission to make inquiries of defense counsel for the matter of Palestine, as I had done previously in my searches for additional Judges for the War Crimes Tribunal, in which I contacted Ramsey Clark and Baltazar Garzon.

When you contacted me to search for defense council for Israel, I did not see any conflict in my capacity as a Judge of a citizen's tribunal of conscience, and I as usual did my best to fulfill your request as Chairman of the KLWC Commission.

As you and defense counsel Jason Kay know, I contacted Ambassador Alan Baker, former Israeli Ambassador to Canada who lives in Israel and is an international lawyer. His associate Prof. Robbie Sabel, Professor of International Law at Hebrew University in Jerusalem, declined to appear for Israel. I contacted my former classmate Prof. Bruce Ackerman of Yale Law School as well as Prof. Guido Calabresi of Yale Law School. Both of these scholars recommended Prof. Alan Dershowitz of Harvard. My sister, Jane M.N. Webre, Esq. had defeated Prof. Dershowitz in an appeal case and had told me about his methods, so I contacted Prof. Dershowitz.

Prof. Dershowitz reply

Here is Prof. Dershowitz reply, citing Francis Boyle's libel of him and Harvard Law School as his principal reason for not appearing for Israel.

Alan Dershowitz dersh@law.harvard.edu via shaw.ca

Jun 7

to webre

Thank you. I will think about it. Part of me doesn't want to add any legitimacy to Boyle who is an extreme supporter of terrorism and an extremist anti Israel agitator with no credibility. . . He has called me a war criminal and has accused harvard law school of complicity in war crimes. But I will respond to your inquiry.

Who appointed him to prosecute the case?

Sent from my iPhone

On Jun 7, 2013, at 4:42 PM, "webre@shaw.ca" <webre@shaw.ca> wrote:

> Info: Dear Prof. Dershowitz - Hi! My classmate Prof. Bruce Ackerman of Yale Law School suggested that I contact you with a specific question.

> I am a Judge on the Kuala Lumpur War Crimes Tribunal. The Tribunal has a hearing scheduled for August 21-24, 2013 on alleged Israeli war crimes in its invasion of Gaza in January 2009.

> The Prosecutor is Prof. Francis Boyle of the Univ of Illinois who has tried cases before the International Criminal Court.

> I was asked to locate a pro-Israel lawyer of Prof. Boyle's stature who would like to serve as amicus curiae representing Israel.

> This is the website of the Tribunal.

> http://criminalisewar.org/the-foundation/judges-commissioners/

> I would very much appreciate your letting me know if can you kindly suggest of any names of qualified lawyers who may be interested and contact info via return email.

> Best wishes,

> Alfred Webre

> Alfred Lambremont Webre, JD, MEd

> Vancouver, B.C. V6N3E5 CANADA

> Tel/Fax: 604-733-8134

> Skype: peaceinspace

> Email: webre@shaw.ca

> IMPORTANT - DISCLAIMER: This message is intended for the use of the individual or entity to which it is addressed and may contain information that is privileged, confidential and exempt from disclosure under applicable law. If the reader of this message is not the intended recipient, or the employee or agent responsible for delivering this message to the intended recipient, you are hereby notified that any dissemination or copying of this communication is strictly prohibited. If you receive this communication in error, please notify us immediately by telephone at 604-733-8134 and/or email and delete the original message. Thank you.

>

> *Name: Judge Alfred Lambremont Webre*

>

> *email: webre@shaw.ca*

>

I do not consider my actions to be grounds for recusal, far from it. I consider Mr. Chang's letter to be that of a mischievous interloper, in continuation of the considerable mischief perpetrated on the Tribunal at our last sitting in this matter by the former prosecutor, Francis Boyle. Indeed, Mr. Boyle's reputation for libel and unfounded slander preceded him at Harvard at Prof. Dershowitz states above. I consider Mr. Chang's letter to be a continuation of lobbying outside the court room by parties in the KLWC Commission (such as Michel Chossudovsky, who lobbied extensively for the recusal of 3 Judges including the Chief Judge at our last sitting) or formerly part of the KLWC Commission (such as Mr. Chang) to attempt to deter this Tribunal in its difficult case in the matter of Palestine.

Legal Authority

As legal authority, I cite the Judgment of the Kuala Lumpur War Crimes Tribunal of 22 August 2013, Case No. 3- CHG-2013, Case No. 4- CHG - 2013, KLWCC vs. Amos Yaron and State of Israel, www.criminalisewar.org

I point to the statement of the Tribunal of "Deep concern and regret that there has been a serious breach of decorum and improper conduct on the part of Mr. Boyle, co-counsel for the Prosecution."

Application for restraining order against present and former members of the KLWCC, prosecution, and persons associated with the Perdana Peace Foundation and Criminalizewar

I hereby serve notice of intent to apply to the Tribunal for a restraining order against Michael Chossudovsky, Mathias Chang, and all present and former members of the KLWCC and prosecution team, former

KLWC Tribunal judges from directly or directly applying for or lobbying for the recusal of KLWC Tribunal Judges, based on a clear abuse of the recusal privilege in this case.

Very truly yours,

Alfred Lambremont Webre, JD, MEd

Member, District of Columbia Bar

JUDGE, KUALA LUMPUR WAR CRIMES TRIBUNAL

Nov. 1, 2013

VANCOUVER, BC, CANADA

LETTER FROM FORMER KLWCC PROSECUTOR CHANG

---------- Forwarded message ----------

From: matthias chang <changmatthias@hotmail.com>

Date: Fri, Nov 1, 2013 at 6:18 AM

Subject: Kuala Lumpur war Crimes Tribunal

To: Alfred Webre <icis.complex@gmail.com>, Alfred Webre <alfred.webre@gmail.com>, Alfred Webre <peace@peaceinspace.org>

Dear Alfred,

Its been a long time since I met you and or heard from you.

So this email may surprise you.

Correct me if I am wrong.

It has come to my knowledge that you attempted to get the services of Derzhowitz to represent Israel in the hearing which was postponed and now to be reconvened in November.

Obviously, I agree absolutely that Israel is entitled to the best Defence Counsel. I believe that charges were sent to Israel etc. by the Prosecution and told that they can appoint the counsel of their choice failing which a defence counsel would be assigned in their absence as was the case with the trial against Bush and Blair. This is so stated in the Charter of the Tribunal.

This is obviously a correct procedure that obtains even in the court of law of all jurisdiction.

However, I find it most troubling that you as a Judge of the tribunal took the trouble to recruit Derzhowitz as defence counsel. If it is true, it is a gross dereliction of duty and your perceived impartiality as a Judge of the tribunal. No Judge of any tribunal or court should be involved in the selection and appointment of any counsel whether for the defence or the prosecution. It is not and cannot be the duty of a Judge of any tribunal.

It is unheard of. If in happens in the Court of Law in CANADA OR ANY OTHER JURISDICTION, the judge is in contempt of his own court. Such a Judge may even be censured and or removed by the Chief Justice of the country. I am sure you are more than aware this amounts to a gross misconduct.

It is unheard of and I am truly shock that you would do this and still remain as a Judge on the tribunal. You should immediately disqualify yourself as you have by your action brought disrepute to the entire proceedings.

This is a disgrace and it is unacceptable. And you are a lawyer!

If you disagree with my views as stated above, please cite me any case authorities or legal principle that a presiding judge can involved himself / herself in the selection and appointment of a counsel whether for the prosecution or the defence.

I suggest to you as a friend and a fellow lawyer that you decline to sit as a Judge of the War Crimes Tribunal and not attend the proceedings by informing the Registrar of the Tribunal or the Chairman of the tribunal soonest possible.

Your action has caused grave embarrassment to Tun Mahathir Mohamad. He cannot obviously be involved in such matters as the Tribunal, Commission are all independent. But this independence and impartiality has now been compromised and brought into disrepute.

Please DO THE RIGHT thing and resigned as a Judge of the tribunal.

I look forward to your reply asap.

Sincerely,

Matthias Chang

MEME WARFARE: DENIAL OF DUE PROCESS

In the end I was denied any due process by the Chief Judge of the Tribunal that had now been thoroughly destabilized by "Zionist" Meme warfare undertaken against targeted Judges by Secretary-General Merican, Former Prosecutor Chang, Commissioner Chossudovsky, and Former Prosecutor Boyle.

I had in fact made no formal motion before the court and was simply replying to the email of one of the principals in the "Zionist" Meme warfare conspiracy against the Judges of the Tribunal, namely Former Prosecutor Matthias Chang.

My not appearing as a Judge at the trial of the Israel war crimes against Palestine (Nov. 20-25, 2013), however, is a convenient cover-up to those who set me up with the task of searching for "Pro-Israel" defense counsel and thus set up the trigger for "Zionist" Meme warfare designed to destabilize three Judges and the Tribunal. One wonders why the Chief Judge was pushed precipitously to rule on a legal motion that did not exist and never was made by me? Usually these matters were brought by Secretary-General Yaacob Merican to the Chief Judge. If this is the case, then it is clear the intent of this improper proceeding was yet another cover-up of the original source of the "Zionist" Meme warfare.

By the evidence, it appears that I was railroaded in an improper judicial proceeding when no motion had been made. I was politically "pushed under the bus", not afforded due process, as an attempted maneuver in "Zionist" Meme warfare to destabilize me as a Judge of the Tribunal.

Nov. 8 & 9, 2013 & Meme Warfare Aftermath – Former Prosecutors Francis Boyle and Matthias Chang continue their Meme warfare – Former Prosecutor Francis Boyle continues to circulate Meme warfare emails with attacking "Zionist" warfare against Alfred Lambremont Webre and Tun Dr. Mahathir bin Mohamad, stating "What did Mahathir know and when did he know it?"

In an expected spasm of destabilizing Meme warfare, Former Prosecutor Matthias Chang openly begins Meme warfare against Former Prosecutor Francis Boyle, calling Former Prosecutor Boyle a "Zionist".

CONTINUING REPORT ON THE FOUR PERPETRATORS OF MEME WARFARE

1. Former Prosecutor Francis Boyle - Continues to circulate Meme warfare attacks on the targeted Judges and on the Tribunal, and now has added Kuala Lumpur Foundation Secretary General Dr. Yaacob Merican and Kuala Lumpur Foundation Chairman Tun Dr. Mahathir bin Mohamad to his targets of "Zionist" Meme warfare, stating "What did Mahathir know and when did he know it?" in email broadcasts on the Internet.

2. Former Prosecutor Matthias Chang - Has begun "Zionist" Meme warfare against Former Prosecutor Francis Boyle, openly calling Former Prosecutor Francis Boyle a "Zionist" in a Nov. 9, 2013 email broadcast:

> *from:*   *matthias chang <changmatthias@hotmail.com> via bounce.secureserver.net*
>
> *to:*   *"Boyle, US" <fboyle@illinois.edu>,*
>
> *Dear All,*
>
> *I think no one should lose any sleep over the rabid rants of Francis Boyle.*

His latest email shows and exposes what he really is - an outright Zionist agent of the most vicious kind trying to scuttle the tribunal proceedings from taking place by making all kind of accusations against his former colleagues all of whom had made tremendous sacrifices for the cause of justice.

3. Commissioner Michel Chossudovsky - Is playing sly political flip flop on the Tribunal. Kuala Lumpur War Crimes Commissioner Chossudovsky (the only Jew on the Commission) first published a vicious "Zionist" Meme warfare attack on the Tribunal right after the August 21-22, 2013, and since then deleted that article from the *www.globalresearch.ca* website. Was that deletion part of Commissioner's cover-up of his part in engaging in "Zionist" Meme warfare against the Tribunal designed to destabilize the Tribunal?[7]

Then, on Nov. 1, 2013 (the same date as Former Prosecutor Chang's Meme warfare letter attacking Judge Alfred Webre), Commissioner Chossudovsky praised the Tribunal's past judgments against George W. Bush et al. as war criminals while lamenting that Lawyers Against the War were unsuccessful in blocking Dick Cheney's Oct. 31, 2013 visit to Toronto. In 2010 Cheney cancelled a trip to Toronto because of war crimes allegations by Lawyers Against the War.[8]

4. Secretary-General Dr. Yaacob Merican – After expediting an improper *in camera* decision by the Tribunal Chief Judge on a motion that Judge Webre never made, Secretary-General Dr. Yaacob Merican has gone into stealth cover-up mode, refusing to answer questions put to him by Former Prosecutor Chang as to why he started the "Zionist" Meme warfare attack to destabilize three targeted Judges of the Tribunal.

CONCLUSION

It seems a reasonable conclusion from the evidence at hand that clear from the evidence that these four individuals: Former

Prosecutor Francis Boyle, Former Prosecutor Matthias Chang, Commissioner Michel Chossudovsky, and Secretary-General Dr. Yaacob Merican all acted to create a dynamic of "Zionist" Meme warfare that was unrelated to any real facts and whose purpose and mission was to destabilize the Tribunal and three Judges thereof, Judge Eric David, Judge Michael Hourigan, and Judge Alfred Lambremont Webre.

WHO WILL INVESTIGATE THE FOUR PERPETRATORS OF "ZIONIST" MEME WARFARE?

Who will step in to investigate the roles of Former Prosecutor Francis Boyle, Former Prosecutor Matthias Chang, Commissioner Michel Chossudovsky, and Secretary-General Dr. Yaacob Merican and seek accountability for their roles in the "Zionist" Meme warfare that destabilized targeted Judges and the Tribunal?

What if one or more of these officials has acted on behalf of an intelligence agency in a Cointelpro role, as some now have come to suspect?

As a Judge on a Tribunal that, by clear *prima facie* evidence, has been destabilized by "Zionist" Meme warfare being directed against the Tribunal and its Judges, I feel it my duty to uphold my Oath of Office by letting the wider public community that supports the Kuala Lumpur War Crimes Tribunal know of the facts of this "Zionist" Meme warfare.

Thank you,

Vancouver, BC

Nov. 10, 2013

This is part II of a series of articles on the covert control methods of the Illuminati used in conjunction with other New World Order operations to target specific Truth movement organizations and workers. The article connects dots, and the reader, as always, is free to perceive

those dots as connected or not connected. Readers can access Part I in
"Jon Stewart carries out Satanic Illuminati hit on Daily Show?:
October 23, 2013" http://bit.ly/18XgqhG

[1] Kuala Lumpur War Crimes Tribunal, *http://bit.ly/17hrnaf*

[2] For a documentation of the ethnic cleansing of Palestine by Israel starting in 1948, please see Paper, Ilan (2007-09-07). The Ethnic Cleansing of Palestine (Kindle Locations 41-42). Oneworld Publications (academic). Kindle Edition.

[3] Kuala Lumpur War Crimes Tribunal hearings, *http://bit.ly/1eycJmw*

[4] Stephen DeVoy, "Meme Warfare" *http://bit.ly/1iUFNlT*

[5] Please see Organization Chart, Kuala Lumpur Foundation to Criminalize War, *http://bit.ly/17ULTkM*

[6] Judicial disqualification, *http://bit.ly/HNU6wo*

[7] See:
http://www.globalresearch.ca/search?q=kuala+lumpur+war+crimes+tribunal

[8] Prof. Michel Chossudovsky, "According to Dick Cheney "Canada is Too Dangerous". He Fears Arrest but has not Cancelled his Trip to Toronto", November 1, 2013, *http://bit.ly/1iXq1GR*

SCENE 8

UFO/ET "Disclosure" &
The Transhumanist Agenda

June 1, 2013
European Parliament
Rue Wiertz 60 1047
Brussels, Belgium

In the year 2000 when he first published the Exopolitics model online, Alfred could not have fully foreseen that, by the year 2013, Exopolitics would focus on deconstructing the implementation of the "Transhumanist Agenda" on Earth and on deconstructing the role of specific individuals within the Exopolitics community with whom only 13 years earlier he had been allied.

Alfred's awareness of the Transhumanist Agenda began in earnest in 1977 when, implementing the Carter White House Extraterrestrial Communication Study at SRI he was exposed first hand to early versions of frequency weapons using electromagnetic energies to induce confusion in targeted individuals.

A common misconception is that the Transhumanist Agenda is a future in which robots "take over" by using artificial intelligence (AI) to overrun and control humanity and the planet.

In 2013, European experts introduced Alfred to a Transhumanist Agenda built around recent technological advances in human robotization and Nano implant technologies, and acceleration of they characterized as a "global enslavement program".[163] These nano-technologies have now shifted from electromagnetic wave to scalar waves and use super quantum computers in the quantum cloud to control "pipes" a reference to the brains of humans that have been taken over via implants from chemtrails that can be breathed in and can breach the blood-brain barrier. Brain implantation can also take place via frequencies derived from an individual's DNA harvested from blood samples given as babies at birth or at medical lab tests. The human babies, children, teenagers and adults whose DNA is on file can then be brain-entrained and then controlled via scalar waves on a super-grid.

Over 1000 grids worldwide are now connected into a mind control super grid that is connected to HAARP as a master planetary mind control machine that now uses advanced scalar technologies, super quantum computers and a quantum cloud for global coordinated mind control of a growing population of robotized humans that are created via these Nano technologies for a global control and enslavement agenda known as the Transhumanist Agenda.

Alfred learned that one conservative estimate of the number of individuals whose brains had been entrained into the super grid was set in the early 2000s at 6 million persons in the European Union alone, and now is estimated to be greater. When free RF radio frequency readings were performed for citizens to ascertain if these individuals are being targeted with scalar Nano technology control weapons in a recent public RF testing in London, UK, 40% of the participating public tested positive for emitting RF frequencies, an indication that they were being subjected to non-consensual scalar mind control. In one public testing, 100% of public participants tested positive. One targeted individual testing positive for RF frequencies was a five-year old child, indicating that children are at risk of human robotization in the Transhumanist Agenda.

The European experts told Alfred that homeopathic gold may be effective protection in protecting a targeted individual against the scalar wave intrusions of the super-grid. Technologies that were thought effective against electromagnetic (EMF) mind control frequency weapons are not effective against these new scalar wave technologies.

The parties whom the European experts identified as being behind Transhumanist Agenda were familiar to Alfred. When asked for individuals and institutions operationally involved in this new mind control super grid and Transhumanist Agenda, the European legal expert indicated that his personal opinion that the Agenda is Illuminati controlled, and is implemented by military-intelligence agencies in a pyramidal organization.

The expert stated, "At the top of the Pyramid is the Mossad, which serves as the military-intelligence arm of the Rothschild bloodline banking interests. Next on the mind control implementation pyramid are U.K. agencies such as MI6 and MI6, closely connected to the British Crown and City of London Illuminati bloodline banking families. At a third tier are the Russian and U.S. military-intelligence agencies (KGB, CIA, NSA). A lower level of the pyramid includes the Swedish and German military-Intelligence agencies. The U.S. Defense Advanced Research Projects Agency (DARPA) is a leader in research on the scalar and nano-technologies for robotization and neurological torture of humans, including so-called "Smart Dust" or Morgellons, as well as the FUA, the Swedish counter-part of DARPA, and the Nobel Prize recipient Karolinska University Hospital in Sweden".

When Alfred asked if the European legal expert believed the Wallenberg Foundation may also be involved in funding mind control research, he responded that he agreed it was plausible. Alfred's ExopoliticsTV had reported that the Wallenberg Foundation may be funding the Tromso Norway HAARP facility which is responsible both for the Norway Spiral of Nov. 1, 2009 at the time of Barack Obama's Nobel Prize speech, and for the March 13, 2011 Fukushima HAARP nuclear false flag event.[164]

One European expert told Alfred he estimated that the Transhumanist Agenda can be slowed and stopped, with significant progress on protecting targeted individuals happening over the ten years from 2013. One focus of activity is alerting public awareness through media. Another focus is legislative, with activity at the European Parliament, although the group concedes that a global ban on scalar and Nano technology weapons for human harassment is necessary.

The first major inkling that a battle around the Transhumanist Agenda was taking place within the Exopolitics and UFO community that initially had received Alfred's Exopolitics model occurred in Barcelona, Spain in the summer of 2009 at the European Exopolitics Summit that initially grew out of Alfred's address book and was later appropriated by Spanish conference co-organizers.[165]

The venue for this Transhumanist confrontation was in Sitges, an historic beachside gay-friendly resort about 35 kilometers southwest of Barcelona. In hindsight, Alfred knew that a true Transhumanist confrontation between the "replicant" forces that had infiltrated and taken over the Exopolitics movement and the "Starseed" Incarnate forces that in fact had founded the Exopolitics movement early on through Alfred's efforts in the 1977 Carter White House study and even earlier.

SCENE 9

THE POPE, THE QUEEN/KING & THE OBAMA

March 13, 2013
St. Peter's Basilica,
Vatican, Rome

"*The three archetypes of the New World Order (NWO) are The Pope, The Queen/King, and The Obama*"

"*Pope Francis I = Jorge Mario Ber-GOG-lio – Gog and Magog?*"

"*Pope Francis: His Jesuitical, Extraterrestrial, "False Prophet", and Political Identities*"

"*Expert: Prince William is the Anti-Christ, the Future Zionist World King*"

"*Bush is to Obama as Pope Benedict is to Pope Francis*"

"*Obama/Soetoro is a forerunner, a sort of Satanic John the Baptist to the Anti-Christ*"

—QUOTES BY ALFRED LAMBREMONT WEBRE

The three key New World Order (NWO) Leader-Archetypes are The Pope, The Queen/King (Elizabeth/Charles/William), and The Obama. The Pope, the Queen and The Obama have all spoken in Westminster Hall, London, UK, the cathedral of the New World Order (NWO).

To Alfred, a poster circulating on the Internet in the days after Pope Francis I installation encapsulated all his own hard work and research:

> *What If The Roman Empire Rebranded Itself As The Catholic Church And Still Rules The World Via Its Proxy Corporations – The U.K. Crown And Washington, D.C.?*

On March 13, 2013, it appeared that the New World Order (NWO) archetypes reached a new stage of interim maturation with the installation of a Jesuit Pope. Alfred thought back on his own timelines of experience to comprehend this. His uncle Richard Chisholm SJ, the assistant to Pedro Arrupe SJ, the Black Pope director general of the Society of Jesus, to whom Elizabeth Windsor, the Queen, sent the Royal Yacht Britannia so Richard could join Her Majesty and become a spiritual Advisor, so Juanita told Alfred. Alfred whose journalism exposed Soetoro/Obama as the time-travel captured President who had chronovisor-teleported to Mars with Alfred's colleagues Andy and Brett in the 1980s. The NWO archetypes – The Pope, The Queen, and The Obama - so neatly within short degrees of separation from Alfred's transformational orbit.

Alfred worked to expose publicly incriminating evidence against the Pope, the Queen/King, and the Obama in his role as an investigative journalist in the public interest.

Alfred exposed the existence of Satanic networks within the Roman Catholic Church.

Satanic priests in the Catholic Church?

Fri Aug 20, 2010

Press TV interview with international war crimes lawyer Alfred Lambremont Webre.

The Catholic Church is facing pedophilia charges while seven adults have filed lawsuits accusing a California priest of child sex abuse between 1972 and up until 2001.

The plaintiffs, who include six women and one man, say they were abused by father Stephen Kiesle. They go on to say the Catholic Church has long facilitated the molestation of children by protecting the well-known child molesting priests.

This is the latest of several lawsuits where individuals say the Catholic Church is closing its eyes to sexual abuse of children by priests and church officials. The church has paid out more than 400,000 million dollars to victims of clergy sex abuse.

The following is a transcription with Alfred Lambremont Webre, who is an international lawyer specializing in war crimes. Mr. Webre shares his insights regarding these types of cases and explains how the Catholic Church has a dark history of satanic sexual abuse, which taints the hierarchal structure of the church from the father all the way up to the Pope.

Press TV: To discuss this scandal further, we are being joined by international lawyer Alfred Lambremont Webre from Vancouver, Canada. Many thanks for joining us here on Press TV. This case is not an isolated incident. There are reports alleging the current Pope being involved in a massive cover-up for the sake of the Church. Now with the Vatican's defense being that one cannot prosecute the head of a state, can there be no justice as far as the upper echelons of the church go?

Webre: I think that in this case it's not the Vatican which is being sued here. It's the diocese of Oakland so that this case can go forward. What is very interesting is the evidence in this case which is the lavation file of the accused former priest. There's a letter in there that bears the signature of the former Cardinal Joseph Ratzinger, who is now Pope Benedict XVI and there was a letter to diocese officials in which Ratzinger, the current Pope, said that the arguments for removing the accused priest were quote, "of grave significance and that the action required careful review and more time." So in this case we have the evidence with the current pope's own signature that he signed so as to protect this particular priest more and to give it more time. Now people are saying that this is a pattern of protecting the church from embarrassment. Let's turn this around. Suppose Cardinal Ratzinger, the current pope, was actually running a sexual abuse ring for "satanic worshipers" using Satanism and using sexual abuse. They were actually encouraging sexual abuse by priests on children around the world as part of a "Satanic Ritual." That's what this looks like to me as a lawyer, as a war crimes lawyer. Actually, the current Pope was covering up satanic rituals of sex abuse within the current Catholic Church, and here we have his signature of "Pope Benedict XVI" (Cardinal Ratzinger) on the letter of Stephen Keiser who's the accused priest. We have his signature and that's the evidence in this case. They can't plead sovereign immunity because it's the diocese of Oakland that is being sued.

Press TV: The church has paid millions of dollars to victims of clergy sex abuse. Now will the extent of punishment here go just as far as defaulting?

Webre: You know, there is no dollar amount you can really put on the pain and suffering of these individuals and this is really a war crime. You have a major church, a major institution, which has been committing a fraud against the children of the world, against the families of the world, and maybe a satanic organization in our midst, and has committed war crimes against humanity as that is understood under the various conventions. So, there is no price here. What exactly was the intent of Cardinal Joseph Ratzinger? We know he has Nazi ties from his childhood.

Press TV: Now with such large numbers of lawsuits being filed against members of the Catholic Church, how would you assess its standing with its thousands of worshipers around the world now?

Webre: Well, you know that's a good question. Because you have a hierarchy that is in serious trouble, and does not want to look at their actions. They are hiding behind improper defenses like sovereign immunity, that it's a state as if it goes back to a decision when they were the Holy Roman Empire. It was the Roman Emperor around 300 AD that marked into the Pope. That is what we have. We have the former Roman Emperor who's now in the Vatican in Rome. This is a historical fact. And for a religious, ethical and moral leader to hide behind the defense of sovereign immunity on a criminal prosecution of moral turpitude is beyond the pale. So, whether or not the Roman Catholic Church will survive this crisis, depends on how they are reacting. So far, they are not reacting well. Women have come forward and have wanted to be priests. They have been rebuffed completely. It appears as though Cardinal Joseph Ratzinger (the current Pope) signature is all over the crimes that have been committed here, and as an attorney, I can tell you we have a big case of "Satanism" here with the Robert Picton cases here in Canada. So, I would say that, investigators should start looking at the Catholic Church as a possible "Satanic Organization."

Press TV: I'm afraid we will have to leave it there. That was international lawyer Alfred Lambremont Webre speaking to us from Vancouver. Many thanks for your insights here on Press TV.[166]

Alfred exposed the Pope and Vatican as a morphed extension of the Roman Empire.

Lawyer likens Vatican to Roman Empire

Wed Aug 11, 2010 5:38PM

The Vatican State is "functionally" the continuation of the Roman Empire, protecting pedophile priests from prosecution, an international lawyer says.

The Vatican is the only church in the world that claims itself a "sovereign state... because 2,000 years ago, around 300 AD, the Roman

Empire chose to mold into the Catholic Church when the Roman Emperor functionally became the Pope," International Lawyer Alfred Lambremont Webre told Press TV on Wednesday.[167]

Alfred, raised in a Jesuit household under his uncle the Assistant to the Jesuit Black Pope, educated at Jesuit schools in Havana, Cuba (Belen) and Garrett Park, MD (Georgetown Preparatory School), exposes Pope Francis as the prophesized False Prophet of Revelation.

"JESUITA, JESUITA, SED JESUS NON FUIT ITA" Latin Maxim

"Oh Jesuit, Oh Jesuit! But Jesus was not like this!"

Pope Francis: His Jesuitical, Extraterrestrial, "False Prophet", and Political Identities

By Alfred Lambremont Webre, JD, MEd

VANCOUVER, BC - Already controversial within hours of his nomination to the Papacy, Argentine-born Pope Francis I has now been identified by informed hermeneutics researchers as the possible "Petrus Romanus" or "False Prophet" of the Book of Revelation.

March 13 is a significant date, both in Exopolitics and in the hermeneutical interpretation of Pope Francis I.

March 13, 2013, the date of Pope Francis I nomination, was the 16th anniversary of the Phoenix Lights, a massive spacecraft that overflew Phoenix, AZ. on March 13, 1997. March 13, 1997 is a significant event in the Exopolitical community that follows the Extraterrestrial presence on Earth.

"Ironically, a major trial opened up in Buenos Aires on March 5, 2013 a week prior to Cardinal Bergoglio's investiture as Pontiff. The ongoing trial in Buenos Aires is: 'to consider the totality of crimes carried out under Operation Condor, a coordinated campaign by various US-backed Latin American dictatorships in the 1970s and

1980s to hunt down, torture and murder tens of thousands of opponents of those regimes."

The Jesuit Oath Exposed

"Go ye, then, into all the world and take possession of all lands in the name of the Pope. He who will not accept him as the Vicar of Jesus and his Vice-Regent on earth, let him be accursed and exterminated."
Professor Arthur Noble

Are Extraterrestrials "the dragon" identified in the Book of Revelation?

One hermeneutical interpretation would have "the dragon" of the Book of Revelations identified as "Extraterrestrial civilizations that the False Prophet (putatively Pope Francis I) promotes to humanity. This role of a Jesuit Pope, promoting "Official ET Disclosure" along with other major institutions such as the United Nations and the major space-faring and extraterrestrial knowledgeable nations such as the United States, the United Kingdom, Russia, and China, would certainly fulfill one dystopian view of extraterrestrial "Disclosure", that of a false flag extraterrestrial invasion such as was predicted by Dr. Wernher von Braun on his death bed and related to Disclosure Project witness Dr. Carol Rosin.

3-13-97/3-13-13 *Extraterrestrial connection?*

March 13 is a significant date, both in Exopolitics and in the hermeneutical interpretation of Pope Francis I.

March 13, 2013, the date of Pope Francis I nomination, was the 16th anniversary of the Phoenix Light, a massive spacecraft that overflew Phoenix, AZ. on March 13, 1997. March 13, 1997 is a significant event in the Exopolitical community that follows the Extraterrestrial presence on Earth.

If there is a meaningful, synchronistic relationship between the March 13, 1997 Phoenix Lights date and the March 13, 2013 Pope Francis I nomination date, then there may be a meaningful relationship between the Extraterrestrial civilization and/or human black budget faction piloting the space ships involved in the Phoenix Lights sightings and the nomination of Jesuit Pope Francis I. As a Jesuit Pope, Francis could intentionally lead and "official disclosure" of either (1) an Extraterrestrial race behind the Phoenix Lights, which could be non-benevolent or benevolent, or (b) a False Flag "Extraterrestrial" operation by black budget human UFO craft, if in fact the Phoenix Lights were human ARVs (Alien Reproduction Vehicles).

Either way, Jesuit Pope Francis I would, under these scenarios fulfill the "False Prophet" role which leads humanity to "worship" the dragon, namely Extraterrestrial visitors or black budget false flag operation whose mission is to prop up the New World Order, including the Vatican.

Alternative hermeneutics: The Dragon as "The New World Order/Leader"

An alternative, non-exopolitical interpretation of Pope Francis I role as the False Prophet would frame him in a dominant role model supporting the imposition of a false cosmology accompanying a world police state commonly referred to as the "New World Order", supporting "anti-Christic" institutions and leaders, that is institutions and leaders that are genuinely G*D/Source-directed.[168]

In 2010 Alfred became an informal legal adviser to the International Tribunal into Crimes of Church and State (ITCCS.org), a citizen's tribunal of conscience operating under natural law, international humanitarian law, and indigenous law. Rev. Kevin Annett, whom Alfred had met while they both were fellow radio talk show hosts at Vancouver Coop Radio, was Acting Secretary of the Tribunal.[169]

The Pope & The Law

Tribunal records show that the Judgment of the International Tribunal into Crimes of Church and State against Pope Benedict XVI (Joseph Ratzinger) may have been the actual factor that forced Ratzinger's resignation from the Papacy.

International Tribunal into Crimes of Church and State (ITCCS.org) vs. The Pope (Benedict XVI)

January 30, 2013: The ITCCS International Common Law Court's Prosecution concludes its case against Thirty officials accused of Genocide in Canada, including the Pope and four top Vatican officers. The Accused do not respond to or deny the charges. The Jury of thirty-three sworn citizens then judges the evidence.

February 4: A diplomatic note is issued to the Vatican Secretariat by a European government working with our Common Law Court, concerning its impending Arrest Warrant against one of the accused, Joseph Ratzinger (aka Pope Benedict)

February 11: Joseph Ratzinger resigns as Pope

February 15: Ratzinger is given sanctuary and "legal immunity" by the Vatican

February 25: The Common Law Court Jury unanimously finds Ratzinger, Elizabeth Windsor and 28 others guilty as charged of Crimes against Humanity and Criminal Conspiracy, and sentences them to 25 years imprisonment and loss of property and authority. The guilty are given one week to comply.

March 3: The occupation and seizure of church property begins in Canada, England, the United States and Italy.

March 4: The guilty do not comply. Common Law Citizen Arrest Warrants are then issued by the Court for the detainment of Ratzinger, Windsor and others. Attempted arrests proceed.

March 7: A Public Notice declares that the legal and political authority of the governments, courts and police of the Vatican, Canada, England and other Commonwealth nations is nullified and disestablished. The Notice calls for new Constitutional Republics in these countries and for Civil Constitutions that nationalize church property and governance.[170]

International Tribunal into Crimes of Church and State (ITCCS.org) vs. The Pope (Francis I)

The International Tribunal into Crimes of Church and State (ITCCS)

ITCCS Breaking News Update - Thursday, April 11, 2013

(9 am GMT)

Pope Francis is linked to Exocet Missile Acquisition, according to British government source - Margaret Thatcher's Death and Queen's Pending Resignation are Connected

Brussels and London:

Whatever it is that dwells in Rome behind the mask of religion and empire is inexorably being revealed. And its mask slipped further yesterday with more startling revelations involving the new Pope Francis, Jorge Bergoglio.

A reliable source in the British civil service who has provided accurate internal leaks in the past to our Tribunal has revealed the following to an ITCCS officer in London:

Commencing in September of 1981, the present Pope Francis 1 acted as an agent for the Argentine military Junta to acquire Exocet missiles that were used against the Royal Navy flotilla during the Falklands War the following year.

During September and October of 1981, Pope Francis, as then-priest Jorge Mario Bergoglio, applied through his friend Roberto Calvi, a high official in the Vatican Bank, for the funds that allowed the Argentine Junta to buy "at least twenty" of the Exocet missiles at a cost of over $200 million, according to the British source.

The same source stated to an ITCCS officer in London on April 9, 2013,

"The Junta knew the British would oppose their seizure of the Malvinas so they got their man Father Bergoglio to get them the missiles, since he was friends with Roberto Calvi. Margaret Thatcher was the Prime Minister in 1982, and both she and Buckingham Palace knew that it was Bergoglio who had lined up the missile funding for (General) Videla. Thatcher in fact approved an MI-6 plan to eliminate the priest, Father Bergoglio, but that fizzled out. But now that same priest has become the Pope, and Thatcher just suddenly died, and the Queen is stepping down under rumored assassination fears, after she

had already cancelled her March 6 trip to Rome when it became clear that Bergoglio would become Pope. These are not coincidences."

After the Exocet missile deal was successfully concluded, the relatively unknown cleric, Fr. Jorge Bergoglio, was rapidly elevated in the Argentine Catholic hierarchy. He became the head of the entire Roman Catholic Church in Argentina in 1998 as part of his reward.

On June 17, 1982 - just two months after the start of the Falklands War - Bergoglio's Vatican bank associate Roberto Calvi was found dead, hanging under Blackfriar's Bridge in London.

Two books have confirmed the Vatican Bank and Roberto Calvi's link to the Argentine Exocet deal: In God's Name by David Yallop, and The Entity: Five Centuries of Secret Vatican Espionage by Eric Frattini.

Is the Jesuit Pope Francis linked to the deaths of Roberto Calvi and former Prime Minister Margaret Thatcher, and to an assassination plan against Queen Elizabeth? This evidence and recent events certainly suggest so.

On April 10, 2013, an official inquiry about these facts and questions was sent by our Tribunal to the Papal Office and to the Vatican Secretary of State. Our inquiry has gone unanswered.[171]

The Queen (Elizabeth Windsor)

Alfred helped to expose the child trafficking and genocide and murder personally engaged in by Queen Elizabeth Windsor when in Oct. 1964 in the company of her consort Prince Philip, Elizabeth Windsor took 10 aboriginal children from a residential school in Kamloops, B.C. Canada on the pretext that they were going to a picnic. The ten children were never seen again.

Assassination of key witness to murder of First Nations children personally committed by Elizabeth Windsor

In his interview with Alfred Lambremont Webre, Rev. Annett discusses the evidence the ITCCS Tribunal will be reviewing that Elizabeth

Windsor and her consort Prince Philip did in October 1964 partici-pate in the abduction and probable murder of 10 young First Nations children, taken by the Royal Couple using the power of Royal Leave from an Aboriginal residential boarding school in Kamloops, B.C.

These 10 children have never been seen since the abduction by the Royal couple during Elizabeth Windsor's then state visit to Canada as its head of state.

Key witness William Coombes assassinated

William Coombes, a Canadian Aboriginal, was to have served as a sworn witness International Tribunal into Crimes of Church and State (ITCCS) session as to crimes of torture, genocide and crimes against humanity personally committed by Elizabeth of Windsor (Queen Elizabeth II) and her consort Prince Philip in Canada in October 1964 at Kamloops, British Columbia.

In his interview, Rev. Kevin Annett sets out the prima facie evidence for Queen Elizabeth's and Prince Philip's personal involvement in the disappearance and presumed murder of these 10 Aboriginal children abducted by them from a residential school in Kamloops, BC in the period Oct. 5 - 13, 1964 and never seen again in their lives.

According to Rev. Annett's recitation of the forensic evidence, it appears that William Coombes was assassinated on February 26, 2011 in St. Paul's Hospital, Vancouver, BC, by a criminal conspiracy acting on behalf of Elizabeth Windsor and the Vatican to prevent William Coombe's testimony at the October 2011 Session of the International Tribunal into Crimes of Church and State.

On August 9, 2011 Rev. Kevin Annett was detained at Heathrow Airport as he arrived in the U.K. to deliver lectures on the work of the ITCCS Tribunal, and was unlawfully expelled from the U.K. as part of the continuing cover-up of child genocide by Elizabeth Windsor, Head of State of the United Kingdom.

Breaking News, 9/29/2011[172]

Arrest warrants for Queen Elizabeth Windsor from the International Tribunal into Crimes of Church and State were served on Buckingham Palace on the evening of Thursday, February 28, 2013. ITCCS.org Acting Secretary notes that Buckingham Palace held the ITCCS process server for three hours. The following day, Friday, March 1, 2013, Elizabeth Windsor reportedly developed a case of flu, forcing her cancellation of all public appearances and her trip to Rome. Some observers report that the Queen's public appearances may have been cancelled because of the Tribunal's arrest warrant or more likely because of a reported assassination plan against Elizabeth Windsor during her forthcoming visit to Rome.

Friday March 1, 2013: Skype message from Rev. Kevin Annett to Alfred Lambremont Webre:

Kevin Annett
3/1/13 12:04 PM

Thank you Alfred! The Court Orders have been mostly delivered - at Buckingham palace the cops arrested the man delivering it for us and held him 3 hours. All the Canadian churches are served and the PM today. Kevin Annett
3/1/13 12:04 PM

Friday March 1, 2013: Queen Elizabeth Windsor contracts stomach bug
BBC NEWS: Queen spending second day in hospital with stomach bug
Philippa Young reports on the Queen's admission to hospital in London
Queen in hospital with stomach bug
Parade goes ahead without the Queen
Sick Queen cancels Swansea visit

The Queen is spending a second day in hospital where she is being assessed for symptoms of gastroenteritis.

She was taken to London's King Edward VII's Hospital from Windsor Castle, where she had been resting, on Sunday [March 3, 2013] - her first hospital stay in 10 years.

Buckingham Palace said the Queen, 86, had been admitted as a precaution and was otherwise in "good health".

All official engagements for this week, including the Queen's trip to Rome, will be either cancelled or postponed.

News of her illness first emerged on Friday night and she cancelled a trip to Swansea on Saturday to mark St David's Day in a military ceremony.

However, earlier on Sunday she had carried out a private medal presentation at Windsor Castle.

BBC, March 4, 2013[173]

In the Tribunal proceedings against Queen Elizabeth Windsor (and her successors), Alfred noted that the Oath the UK Monarch takes upon their coronation includes the following,

> "I take this Crown provisionally until He to whom it belongs returns."

As of this writing on April 30, 2015, the sudden exposure and collapse of the ITCCS in December 2014 had still not been fully clarified. Readers can visit the following articles at News-InsideOut.com for further clarification.[174]

INVESTIGATOR: CIA, POPE JOHN PAUL II, BUSH SR. & JR., BILL/HILLARY CLINTON DO RITUAL CHILD SACRIFICE, DRINK HUMAN BLOOD. THE TRANSHUMANIST AGENDA IS THE CORE DRIVER OF GLOBAL PEDOPHILE, CHILD SACRIFICE AND CHILD-TRAFFICKING NETWORKS

By Alfred Lambremont Webre

NewsInsideOut.com

VANCOUVER, BC – *NewsInsideOut.com* correspondent and investigator Juan Lankamp, whose specialty is crimes of the Elite,[1] sets out an overview of evidence of interconnected MKULTRA, pedophile, ritual child sacrifice, human hunting parties, and abuse networks, and child trafficking networks that are interlinked with the Vatican, the DEA (Drug Enforcement Agency); the CIA, Wackenhut, and the Bilderbergers in parliaments, Churches, governments, courts, schools, child welfare institutions and the media. Juan Lankamp's revelations came in a wide-ranging nearly 2-hour interview (below) with *NewsInsideOut.com*'s Alfred Lambremont Webre.

The reality about pedophile and ritual sacrifice networks Lankamp reveals in his research and analysis is remarkable and suggests that a prime mover of global pedophile, child sacrifice and child-trafficking networks may have originated as a cooperative enterprise between Draco reptilians and US government/CIA that has the U.S. government MKULTRA entity as a major technological driver. MKULTRA and the Draco connection began during the Franklin D. Roosevelt Administration in 1933, and was further cemented through post-World War II Operation Paperclip of German intelligence and its Draco/Orion Grey networks into CIA.

THE TRANSHUMANIST AGENDA IS THE CORE DRIVER OF GLOBAL PEDOPHILE, CHILD SACRIFICE AND CHILD-TRAFFICKING NETWORKS

It would appear now from the evidence this over-all enterprise driving the global pedophile, child sacrifice and child-trafficking networks can be termed the driving force behind The Transhumanist Agenda or the New World Order. The US government (USA Corp) appears to be an important technological and infrastructure base of global pedophile, child sacrifice and child-trafficking networks as they integrate with the Transhumanist Agenda. This explains why USA agencies such as the National Security Agency (NSA) are at the forefront of the effort to torture and robotize humanity, and are intimately involved in, for example, the interface between remote neuro-mind control weapons and Hospitals that can implant victim mothers, and Family Law and Psychiatric facilities that can plot to take the victim's children for the pedophile networks.

DRACO-US GOVT.-MKULTRA-TRANSHUMANIST-RITUAL CHILD SACRIFICE/PEDOPHILE COMPLEX

Lankamp's research shows that this Draco-US Govt.-MKULTRA ritual; child sacrifice/pedophile complex in turn has infiltrated ruling and controller structures world-wide, including Churches such as the Vatican, the Anglican Church, the Monarchies, Governments (especially the USA Corp. government), Intelligence agencies, Military, Corporations, Schools, civic organizations, and multi-generational families.

Laura Eisenhower confirms the existence of such cooperative treaties and entities between the US government and manipulative Extraterrestrials such as the Draco reptilians and Orion greys in her ExopoliticsTV interview with Alfred Lambremont Webre *"Laura Magdalene Eisenhower: ET invasion has already occurred and governments do not want us to know."*[2]

During the course of his *NewsInsideOut.com* interview Juan Lankamp discusses a number of high-profile individuals from these networks for whom he has reliable eyewitness evidence of their participation in ritual child sacrifice, blood drinking and flesh eating.

These include Pope John Paul II, who according to an ex-Jesuit Jose Luciano, participated in a ritual child sacrifice in an underground bunker 40 meters from the Vatican.

USA PRESIDENTIAL CAMPAIGN 2016: The leading Republican and Democratic families involved in Presidential Campaign 2016 – Bush & Clinton – are both, by the evidence, committed participants in ritual child sacrifice, blood drinking, and pedophilia,

According to Juan Lankamp's evidence, pedophilia parties as part of the CIA-MKULTRA circuit took place in the White House under George HW Bush and George W. Bush. Both Bush Sr. and Bush Jr. participated at Area 51 in ritual human sacrifice, blood drinking and flesh eating in joint ceremonies with Draco reptilians held in underground facilities as part of a cooperative entity of Draco reptilians and the U.S. Military. Both Hillary and Bill Clinton, according to Juan Lankamp's evidence, have participated in ritual child sacrifice and are human blood drinkers. While no explicit evidence has emerged of Jeb Bush participating in ritual sacrifice, it is reasonable to expect that Jeb Bush was aware of such Bush activities and may have participated.

At the very least, as an ethical Presidential Candidate, Jeb Bush would be expected to denounce pedophilia and ritual child sacrifice by his father and brother and any other Bush family members.

All 2016 Presidential candidates should be questioned as to whether they have ever participated in pedophilia, ritual child sacrifice, or child trafficking, or in any of the networks that support such.

A NEW MODEL OF THE ACTUAL PLANETARY DRIVER OF PEDOPHILE AND RITUAL SACRIFICE NETWORKS

The Transhumanist Agenda model of pedophilia and child abuse networks is more accurate and factual than a prior model of pedophilia that focuses sole blame on Churches [such as the Vatican] or Monarchies [such as the UK, Dutch, or Belgian Throne]. This prior model of pedophile networks actually diverts attention away from Transhumanist Agenda, which is the actual current planetary driver of pedophile and ritual sacrifice networks.

THE TRANSHUMANIST AGENDA & ITS RELATIONSHIP TO PEDOPHILE AND RITUAL CHILD SACRIFICE NETWORKS WORLDWIDE

The Transhumanist Agenda can be defined as: A complex cooperative entity originating in the Draco reptilians and CIA/U.S. government using MKULTRA technology that appears now to have expanded out into a planetary infrastructure around the NSA and contracting agencies around the world, along with a dedicated grid of HAARP installations, chemtrails, Supergrids, Super computers, nano-bots, nanochips to be the prime mover entity responsible for driving pedophile and ritual child sacrifice networks world wide in power institutions such as the Vatican, Jesuits, Zionists, Churches, Monarchies, governments, intelligence, military, police, Schools, and families. Pedophile and ritual child sacrifice activities and networks world wide appear to facilitate establishing a global power base in these institutions for the ultimate robotization of humanity.

The over-all goal of the Transhumanist Agenda is the robotization of humans and the substitution of manipulatory AI for the human soul and Source connection.

Belgium: Structure of Pedophile Networks

Using Exhibits A, B, C, and D [below] prepared by ProJusticia in Belgium, Juan Lankamp in his interview reveals evidence of various components of the power structures behind the world pedophile, child ritual sacrifice and child trafficking networks. These appear to have had their origin in covert U.S. government MKULTRA programs, human ritual sacrifice and consumption programs co-run with Draco reptilians at underground bases in the US, the U.S. DEA, Vatican agencies, and CIA-DIA, Wackenhut, and Bilderberger forces, and now have extended into the world-wide NSA infrastructure known as the Transhumanist Agenda.

These pedophile and child sacrifice infrastructure networks in turn interface with the Monarchies, Vatican Popes & Cardinals, Parliaments, Governments, Courts, Police, Schools, and other networks in a nation such as Belgium. Asked whether "Belgium was the pedophile capital of the world," Juan Lankamp responded, "Belgium and the Netherlands, which used to be one country, are an important pedophile center."[175]

Draco-CIA-NSA-MKULTRA
drive ritual child sacrifice in Religions (Vatican/Jesuit/Talmudic)- Monarchies-Governments-Schools-Wars for Transhumanist Agenda

The Transhumanist Agenda
& Its relationship to pedophile and ritual child sacrifice networks worldwide

In his interview, Webre stated, "The Transhumanist Agenda can be defined as: A complex cooperative entity originating in the Draco reptilians and CIA/U.S. government using MKULTRA technology that appears now to have expanded out into a planetary infrastructure around the NSA and contracting agencies around the world, along with a dedicated grid of HAARP installations, chemtrails, Supergrids, Super computers, nano-bots, nanochips to be the prime mover entity responsible for driving pedophile and ritual child sacrifice networks world wide in power institutions such as the Vatican, Jesuits, Zionists, Churches, Monarchies, governments, intelligence, military, police, Schools, and families. Pedophile and ritual child sacrifice activities and networks world wide appear to facilitate establishing a global power base in these institutions for the ultimate robotization of humanity.

> "The over-all goal of the Transhumanist Agenda is the robotization of humans and the substitution of manipulatory AI [Artificial Intelligence] for the human soul and Source connection."

In his interview, Webre covers areas ranging from the Draco treaties with the US and Nazi governments; the central role of Dracos and the CIA-NSA-MI5-Mossad-MKULTRA apparatus in driving both the ritual child sacrifice and pedophile networks world-wide as exemplified by the recent expose in Hampstead UK; and Israeli Prime Minister Netanyahu's Talmudic attempt on 3/3/2015 in an unlawful address to the U.S. Congress to ignite WWIII as a ritual human sacrifice.

A Webre stress that the expose and public disclosure of these hidden pedophile networks is part of a planetary cleansing brought by the positive timeline.[176]

The Obama & the Law

Alfred worked to expose publicly the illegalities in the policies of U.S. President Barack Obama.

> Obama policy on assassination drone strikes amounts to war crimes: Lawyer

Yemen is not an imminent threat to the US; however, over 300 Yeme-
nis have been illegally murdered in US drone attacks this year that
includes women and children.

Press TV has interviewed Alfred Lambremont Webre, war crimes law-
yer, Vancouver about the illegality, under the United Nations Char-
ter, of US assassination drone strikes on the civilian population of
several Middle Eastern countries. What follows is an approximate
transcript of the interview.

Press TV: US assassination drone strikes are becoming quite a concern
as it is no longer just one country that's bearing the brunt of it.

The US claims they're necessary despite the civilian death toll. Can
the US continue to violate humanitarian and international law in the
name of national security?

Webre: Well, no. More and more it's becoming clear even by their own
words of US officials and by leaks now by the Arab Times that the US
laws are violations of Article 51 of the United Nations Charter, which
is the only article that permits the inherent right of self defense.

The only way that the drone attacks could be legal is if this would be
invoked in the inherent right of self-defense, that is, to protect the
country from an imminent threat of violent attack.

Now... It is very, very difficult to argue that drone attacks in Yemen or
in any other country in that region are protecting the United States
from imminent threat of violent attack even though Obama himself
argues that, oh, if the United States can target someone who is 'plan-
ning an attack' against the United States, then it is legal.

But the problem with that is that the way the US is carrying it out
violates the four principles that are contained in Article 51and that
is necessity, distinction, proportionality and humanity because
these drone attacks are carried out by secret legal standards by the
CIA.

Now... these standards have become public because of a leak through
the New York Times and they are as follows and I want to quote: all

military-aged males in a strike zone are considered targets unless ex-plicit intelligence 'posthumously' proves them innocent.

I.e. the US orders - and these are secret legal orders - assumes that any military-aged male, which I assume goes from 18 years old to 65 years old in a strike zone, which may be any zone in any of the countries in the region are considered targets unless explicit intelligence posthumously proves them innocent - meaning that they're justified unless after they're dead there's a report that comes back that says, oh, they weren't planning any imminent physical attack against the US.

This is beyond the pale, legally. Only a power that considers itself above international law...

Press TV: Speaking to CNN on drones, Obama talks about a due process, but then still says that these "targets" are eliminated because it is not possible to capture them and then try them etc etc. Isn't that a contradiction in terms?

Webre: Yeah. No, no you see that is what we call legal sophistry be-cause those aren't the true standards because the true standards and I'm quoting, "Anyone who is an area of known terrorist activity found with an al-Qaeda operative in an al-Qaeda operative zone is, quote, probably up to no good".

And they don't have precision targeting. So that by the very, very act of the drone attack say for the 300 civilians that have been killed in Yemen perhaps, perhaps they say, that one legitimate strike that would fall within that zone... But I'm not even willing to concede that - that falls within a zone that's sanctioned by Article 51 of the United Nations Charter, which is based on self-defense.

Self-defense means an imminent attack upon the United States.

That falls under crimes against humanity and genocide and aggressive war. So in that case, it is the United States, which is the aggressor.[177]

PressTV, Sept. 10, 2012

As a former constitutional law university professor, Alfred was able to bring his constitutional law expertise in exposing the Obama policies as well.

US drone strikes against constitution: American lawyer

A US war crimes lawyer says US drone attacks in countries when there is no declared war are "absolutely unconstitutional," Press TV reports.

"The drone assassination program especially when they involve US citizens in nations like Yemen where there's no declared war is absolutely unconstitutional because it violates the separation of powers between the Congress and the Executive," Alfred Lambremont Webre said in an interview with Press TV.

"The CIA will not release the legal memoranda which allegedly give the legal authority to President Barack Obama to approve these strikes, and they won't do so because it's the same patently fraudulent legal memorandum that was used by Alberto Gonzalez and [former US President George W.] Bush, [former Vice President Dick] Cheney and [former Secretary of Defense Donald] Rumsfeld in the case of torture in Iraq, Afghanistan and in Guantanamo," he added.

On Wednesday, relatives of three US citizens killed in the US assassination drone strikes in Yemen sued senior US officials.

According to the lawsuit, the killings of US-born Muslim cleric Anwar al-Awlaki, his 16-year-old son Abdulrahman al-Awlaki and naturalized US citizen Samir Khan were unconstitutional.

The victims' relatives said that the three assassinations committed by the CIA violated US legal guarantees, including the right to due process.

Webre said the families of the victims have a very strong case against the US government and its officials because they violate the Geneva Conventions.

"People should just keep on challenging these rulings in court because

403

there's nothing [to authorize them] but these fraudulent legal memoranda," he said.[178]

PressTV, July 19, 2012

Obama's National Security Council Lies about Alfred's Article

On January 3, 2012, the spokesperson for the U.S. National Security Council, Tommy Vietor, issued an official denial to Wired.com of Alfred Lambremont Webre's November 2011 article in which Alfred revealed that U.S. President Barack H. Obama, using his legal name Barry Soetoro, had participated in the 1980s U.S. Central Intelligence Agency (CIA) "jump room" teleportation program. MSNBC, Fox News and other mainstream media also published the National Security Council denial.[179]

According to the White House website, "The National Security Council (NSC) is the President's principal forum for considering national security and foreign policy matters with his senior national security advisors and cabinet officials. Since its inception under President Truman, the Council's function has been to advise and assist the President on national security and foreign policies. The Council also serves as the President's principal arm for coordinating these policies among various government agencies."[180]

In fact, Tommy Vietor was an Obama insider who in Obama's 2008 U.S. Presidential campaign was charged by Obama to take Obama's fraudulent Certificate of Live Birth to FactCheck.org and other liberal blogs so that they could distribute that meme into the campaign when issues as to the provenance of the individual known as "Barack Hussein Obama" surfaced in the campaign. [Note: For an introductory treatment of the subject of Barack Hussein Obama's provenance, please see "Alfred Lambremont Webre, "Obama/Soetoro, Time-Travel, & the US Supreme Court".[181]]

Here is Alfred's article exposing Barack Obama as participating in the CIA jump room teleportation program, as early as 1980. This is the article that earned the denial by Tommy Vietor, National Security Council spokesperson and Obama insider.

Mars visitors Basiago and Stillings confirm Barack Obama traveled to Mars

By Alfred Lambremont Webre, JD, MEd

Two former participants in the CIA's Mars visitation program of the early 1980's have confirmed that U.S. President Barack H. Obama was enrolled in their Mars training class in 1980 and was among the young Americans from the program who they later encountered on the Martian surface after reaching Mars via "jump room."

Andrew D. Basiago, 50, a lawyer in Washington State who served in DARPA's time travel program Project Pegasus in the 1970's, and fellow chrononaut William B. Stillings, 44, who was tapped by the Mars program for his technical genius, have publicly confirmed that Obama was enrolled in their Mars training class in 1980 and that each later encountered Obama during visits to rudimentary U.S. facilities on Mars that took place from 1981 to 1983.

Their astonishing revelations provide a new dimension to the controversy surrounding President Obama's background and pose the possibility that it is an elaborate ruse to conceal Obama's participation as a young man in the U.S. secret space program.

Mars training class held for future Mars visitors

According to Mr. Basiago and Mr. Stillings, in summer 1980 they attended a three-week factual seminar about Mars to prepare them for trips that were then later taken to Mars via teleportation. The course was taught by remote viewing pioneer Major Ed Dames, who was then serving as a scientific and technical intelligence officer for the U.S. Army. It was held at The College of the Siskiyous, a small college near Mt. Shasta in California.

They state that ten teenagers were enrolled in the Mars training pro-

gram. In addition to Basiago and Stillings, two of the eight other teenagers in Major Dames' class that they can identify today were Barack Obama, who was then using the name "Barry Soetoro," and Regina Dugan, who Mr. Obama appointed the 19th director and first female director of the Defense Advanced Research Projects Agency (DARPA) in 2009.

As many as seven parents of the ten students, all with ties to the CIA, audited the class. They included Raymond F. Basiago, an engineer for The Ralph M. Parsons Company who was the chief technical liaison between Parsons and the CIA on Tesla-based teleportation; Thomas Stillings, an operations analyst for the Lockheed Corporation who had served with the Office of Naval Intelligence; and Mr. Obama's mother, Stanley Ann Dunham, who carried out assignments for the CIA in Kenya and Indonesia.

From 1981 to 1983, the young attendees then went on to teleport to Mars via a "jump room" located in a building occupied by Hughes Aircraft at 999 N. Sepulveda Boulevard in El Segundo, California, adjacent to the Los Angeles International Airport (LAX).

Obama identified as having visited Mars at least twice

Mr. Basiago and Mr. Stillings have each issued public statements confirming that they both attended Mars training with Mr. Obama and later encountered him on Mars during separate visits.

On August 21, 2011, Mr. Basiago stated: "Something highly significant has happened, and that is that two individuals from the same Mars training class in 1980 (Basiago and Stillings) have met and are comparing experiences and are able to corroborate not only that they were on the surface of Mars together but that before reaching Mars via jump room they were trained with a group of teenagers that included the current President of the United States (Obama) and director of DARPA (Dugan)."

Mr. Stillings' statement, released at the same time, read: "I can confirm that Andrew D. Basiago and Barack Obama (then using the name "Barry Soetoro") were in my Mars training course in Summer

1980 and that during the time period 1981 to 1983, I encountered Andy, Courtney M. Hunt of the CIA, and other Americans on the surface of Mars after reaching Mars via the "jump room" in El Segundo, California."

In a statement made Sept 20, 2011, Mr. Basiago confirmed Mr. Obama's co-participation in the 1980 Mars training class, stating: "Barry Soetoro, a student at Occidental College, was in my Mars training class under Major Ed Dames at The College of the Siskiyous in Weed, California in 1980. That fact has been corroborated by one of my other classmates, Brett Stillings. Two years later, when he was taller, thinner, more mature, a better listener, using the name 'Barack Obama,' and attending a different college, Columbia University, we crossed paths again in Los Angeles and I didn't recognize him as the person that I had been trained with in the Mars program and encountered on the surface of Mars. In fact, doing so would have been virtually impossible in any case, because measures had been taken to block our later memories of Mars shortly after we completed our training in 1980."

Mr. Basiago states that during one of his trips to Mars via "jump room" that took place from 1981 to 1983, he was sitting on a wall beneath an arching roof that covered one of the "jump room" facilities as he watched Mr. Obama walk back to the jump room from across the Martian terrain. When Mr. Obama walked past him and Mr. Basiago acknowledged him, Mr. Obama stated, with some sense of fatalism: "Now we're here!"

Mr. Stillings states that during one of his visits to Mars, he walked out of the "jump room" facility and encountered Mr. Obama standing beside the facility by himself staring vacantly into a ravine located adjacent to the facility.

Mr. Basiago thinks that it is virtually certain that Ms. Dugan also went to Mars, because he once encountered her at the building in El Segundo where the "jump room" to Mars was located as he was entering the building to jump to Mars and she was exiting it. "I know you!" she said, greeting him as she passed him in the lobby of the building.

Strangers in a Strange Land

Basiago, Obama, Stillings, and Dugan went to Mars at a time when the U.S. presence on Mars was only just beginning but many had already gone.

Mr. Basiago states that in the early 1980's, when they went, the U.S. facilities on Mars were rudimentary and resembled the construction phase of a rural mining project. While there was some infrastructure supporting the jump rooms on Mars, there were no base-like buildings like the U.S. base on Mars first revealed publicly by Command Sgt. Major Robert Dean at the European Exopolitics Summit in Barcelona, Spain in 2009.

The primitive conditions that they encountered on Mars might explain the high level of danger involved. Mr. Basiago and Mr. Stillings agree that Major Dames stated during their training class at The College of the Siskiyous in 1980: "Of the 97,000 individuals that we have thus far sent to Mars, only 7,000 have survived there after five years."

In light of these risks, prior to going to Mars, Mr. Basiago received additional training from Mr. Hunt. Hunt, a career CIA officer, showed Mr. Basiago how to operate the respiration device that he would wear only during his first jump to Mars in July 1981, provided him with a weapon to protect himself on Mars, and took him to the Lockheed facility in Burbank, California for training in avoiding predators on the Martian surface.

When they then first teleported to Mars in Summer 1981, the young Mars visitors confronted the situation that Major Dames had covered at length during the class the previous summer – that one of their principal concerns on Mars would be to avoid being devoured by one of the predator species on the Martian surface, some of which they would be able to evade, and some of which were impossible to evade if encountered.

The Mars program was launched; Basiago and Stillings were told, to establish a defense regime protecting the Earth from threats from space and, by sending civilians, to establish a legal basis for the U.S.

to assert a claim of territorial sovereignty over Mars. In furtherance of these goals and the expectation that human beings from Earth would begin visiting Mars in greater numbers, their mission was to acclimate Martian humanoids and animals to their presence or, as Major Dames stated during their training near Mt. Shasta in 1980: "Simply put, your task is to be seen and not eaten."

It is not known whether NASA-JPL, which is located in Pasadena, California, had a hand in selecting the young people for their dangerous interplanetary mission to Mars, but it is conspicuous that all four had Pasadena, California connections.

Mr. Basiago was the son of an engineer for The Ralph M. Parsons Company, which is headquartered in Pasadena. Mr. Stillings was residing in La Canada, California, which is a suburb of Pasadena. Mr. Obama had just completed a year of undergraduate studies at Occidental College in Eagle Rock, California, near Pasadena. Ms. Dugan was attending the California Institute of Technology, which is located in Pasadena.

1980: U.S. secret Mars teleportation program and rudimentary facilities on Mars

The firsthand, eyewitness testimony of Mr. Basiago and Mr. Stillings as to the existence of a secret U.S. presence on Mars that is made possible by a revolutionary "jump room" technology that has been concealed from the public is congruent with similar accounts given by three other Mars whistle blowers:

1 *Former U.S. serviceman Michael Relfe, who spent 20 years as a member of the permanent security staff of a U.S. facility on Mars;*

2 *Former Department of Defense (DoD) scientist Arthur Neumann, who has testified publicly that he teleported to a U.S. facility on Mars for DoD project meetings; and*

3 *Laura Magdalene Eisenhower, great-granddaughter of U.S. President Dwight D. Eisenhower, who in 2007 refused a covert attempt to recruit her into what was described to her as a secret U.S. colony on Mars.*

Mars researchers, including physicist David Wilcock, estimate that as a result of the "jump room" technology that Relfe, Basiago, Neumann, and Stillings have described, the U.S. colony on Mars that Eisenhower was invited to join might number 500,000 individuals.

Secret U.S. presence on Mars and Obama's Mars connection airs on Coast-to-Coast AM on Thursday

Public revelation of Mr. Obama's secret Mars connection will continue with a special broadcast on talk radio's Coast to Coast AM this Thursday, November 10, 2011 from Midnight to 2 AM PST.

Mars visitors Andrew D. Basiago and William B. Stillings will be appearing with Mars whistle blower Laura M. Eisenhower in an historic broadcast.

This will be the first time that a mainstream media program will interview two Mars visitors on the same show and in a joint appearance with an individual invited to join the secret U.S. colony on the Red Planet.

Special Program:

http://www.coasttocoastam.com/show/2011/11/10

With multiple whistle blowers coming forward and corroborating each other's testimony, it now seems inevitable that both the cover-up of the U.S. presence on Mars and Mr. Obama's personal involvement in it will soon become matters of great public interest.[182]

Originally published at Examiner.com

The Obama White House and its CIA time travel cover-up team apparently acted stealthfully to see to it that Alfred's article exposing Obama's participation in the 1980s CIA jump room program was initially taken off of the Examiner.com website on November 22, 2011, the same date that Alfred as a Judge on the Kuala Lumpur War Crimes Tribunal found George W. Bush and Tony Blair guilty of war crimes in Iraq, just a few days before Bush traveled to Africa and subjected himself to a petition for arrest by the Kuala Lumpur Court. Alfred's contract with his newspaper Examiner.com was unlawfully cancelled, on the fraudulent grounds that Alfred was publishing "false information".

Acting swiftly, Alfred placed his article exposing The Obama (along with others of his Examiner.com articles) back online at Exopolitics.com during a 24-hour layover at the Hong Kong airport on the way from Kuala Lumpur to Johannesburg, South Africa where he was speaking at an Exopolitics conference and scheduled to visit Adam's Calendar, a site where the Anunnaki extraterrestrials first landed 280,000 years ago.[183]

During the unfoldment of the Boston Marathon false flag operation (April 15-19, 2013), Alfred called out "Barack Hussein Obama" as the Deceiver archetype.

"Identify the Perpetrator": How The Obama fulfills the "deceiver" archetype and why it is important to expose him publicly

By Alfred Lambremont Webre, JD, MEd

By the "deceiver" archetype, I refer to inter-personal, social, spiritual and exopolitical archetypes, not to any specific individual. The "deceiver" archetype refers to an archetypal social, spiritual, and exopolitical role that an individual may play in society. The "deceiver" archetype embodies duality consciousness ("I win - you lose") with an emphasis on deception, and is the obverse of Unity Consciousness ("We are all One") embodied by Christ consciousness.

The individual publicly known as "Barack Hussein Obama" is a reasonable candidate for fulfilling the "deceiver" archetype on at least the following grounds, prima facie evidence for which is set out in this article:

1 *He is practiced in institutional deception since adolescence;*

2 *As U.S. President he has covertly participated in and coordinated false flag operations causing ecocide and genocide through environmental warfare; bioweapons; and ionizing radiation.*

3   *He was elected to the highest political position of U.S. President by mass deception.*

4   *As U.S. President he has covertly participated in and served as "public Capstone" for false flag strategic deception operations intended to deceptively deprive U.S. citizens of their rights under the Bill of Rights including their right to bear arms, and ultimately to depopulate and enslave the U.S. population.*

5   *He covertly and intentionally serves as an archetypal "deceiver" asset of an international war crimes racketeering organization intent on installing a global police state known as The New World Order, and he owes primary allegiance to the New World Order crime organization.*

Each of the above five (5) aspects of the deceiver archetype of Barack Hussein Obama is documented in extenso (some might say ad nauseam) in the article below.

"Identify the Perpetrator": Why it is important to expose the deceiver "Barack Hussein Obama" publicly

"Identify the Perpetrator" is a successful strategy that individuals and groups can use when liberating themselves of abuse by a perpetrator whom they have difficulty identifying and naming not only publicly but even to themselves.

"Friendly Fascism" is a methodology that I analyzed as a Futurist at Stanford Research Institute in the mid-1970s as the system that the new world order would attempt to implement in the United States at this time. "Friendly Fascism" is the programmatic name for the integrated mind control police state that is now being rolled out in the United States, as well as in other jurisdictions around the planet. In the United States variety, "Barack Hussein Obama" serves a key role as the "friendly leader". "Barack Hussein Obama" is to "Friendly Fascism" what Adolph Hitler was to Nazism.

"Friendly fascism" includes mass mind control technologies ranging from HAARP to synthetic terror events like the Newtown and Boston

Marathon that create a "consensual trance" in the population, so the population feels it is imposing "friendly fascism" as part of its democratic process.

In this context, the consensual trance in the United States (and in the world) is still such that "Barack Hussein Obama" is to "Friendly Fascism" what Adolph Hitler was to Nazism in the 1930s. The consciousness of the typical citizen who is in a "consensual trance" assumes that the ecocidal events, the genocides like Fukushima, the false flag operations like Hurricanes Isaac and Sandy, the false flag psyops like Sandy Hook Elementary and the Boston Marathon are occur as "an act of God", natural events, or random, senseless acts of terrorists or deranged individuals in the case of false flag "terror events". In fact, all of these events are intentional acts of state terror put into operation and/or coordinated under plausible deniability around the chief executive officer of that state, in this case "Barack Hussein Obama."

Under the "consensual trance", these false flag events are, where feasible, so designed with "Barack Hussein Obama" as the Capstone who comes in after the tragedy and offers the benediction of the state that will protect the citizens, while concealing the forensic evidence establishing that it is state terror under the plausible deniability coordination of "Barack Hussein Obama" that creates the catastrophe in the first place.

Why it is reasonable to hypothesize that "Barrack Hussein Obama" fulfills the social archetype of arch-deceiver

1. "Barack Hussein Obama" is practiced in institutional deception since adolescence - The individual "Barack Hussein Obama" has since adolescence, if not childhood, become expert in hiding his origins and provenance. His legal name continues to be "Barry Soetoro". The individual assumed the name "Barack Hussein Obama" on October 14, 1982 at a court in British Columbia when he changed his name from his CIA operative pseudonym "Barak Mounir Ubayd" to Barack Hussein Obama". This change of name was concurrent with the 1982 CIA assassination by automobile crash in Kenya of a Ken-

yan civil servant by the name of Barack Hussein Obama. The fabrication of the intelligence legend of "Barack Hussein Obama", the role of
DARPA quantum access technologies in this deception, and the entire
Manchurian candidate deception in which this individual was involved can be seen in an online Powerpoint presentation:

How Intelligence Legend & Manchurian candidate Barack Hussein
Obama was created

This slideshow, originally presented at The Awakening Center, Mt.
Rainer, WA on Feb. 25, 2013, sets out the forensic and documentary
evidence showing the systematic pattern of deception and advanced
exotic technologies used in the creation and maintenance of the intelligence "Legend" of the Manchurian candidate "Barack Hussein
Obama".[184]

VIDEO: Obama/Soetoro, Time-Travel, & the US Supreme Court

A video analysis by Alfred Lambremont Webre of the creation of the
intelligence Legend and Manchurian candidate "Barack Hussein
Obama" can be seen below:[185]

2. As U.S. President, "Barack Hussein Obama" has covertly participated in and coordinated false flag operations causing ecocide and
genocide through environmental warfare; bioweapons; and ionizing
radiation.

There is sufficient documentary and forensic evidence to demonstrate
that the individual "Barack Hussein Obama" has intentionally and
knowingly participated in causing ecocide (wanton destruction of the
planet Earth) and genocide (systematic destruction of a class of human beings, or of all human beings), two prime characteristics of the
"deceiver" archetype, also known as the "Destroyer".

B.P. Gulf of Mexico Oil Spill (April - June, 2010) - As U.S. President
Barack Obama knowingly, as agent of an international war crimes
racketeering organization known as the "New World Order", directed
his Department of Energy and other agencies to participate in the
acceleration of the ecological damage to the Gulf of Mexico during

414

the B.P. Gulf of Mexico false flag oil spill to hinder the cleanup of this damage.[186]

Fukushima HAARP global radiation false flag attack (March 11, 2011) - As U.S. President, the individual "Barack Hussein Obama" intentionally ordered his Department of Energy to coordinate as part of the Fukushima HAARP global nuclear radiation attack on the northern hemisphere, taking steps to exacerbate the radiation released, discontinue radiation readings, fail to warn U.S. citizens of dangerous radiation levels over the U.S. and North America, with the purpose of causing 100,000 excess deaths in the United States alone in 2011, and causing ongoing genetic damage, depopulation and ecocide in the northern hemisphere.

Leuren Moret: 100,000 excess deaths in North America in 2011 from Fukushima

In an exclusive ExopoliticsTV interview released Oct. 22, 2011 independent scientist Leuren Moret, MA, PhD ABT has revealed that approximately 100,000 excess deaths will occur in North America 2011 that are directly attributable to the effects of deadly radiation from the March 11, 2011 tectonic-nuclear false flag earthquake and tsunami event at Fukushima, Japan.

Ms. Moret's revelation of 100,000 excess deaths in 2011 in North America from Fukushima radiation is based on official excess death data for 2011 published by the CDC (Centers for Disease Control and Prevention), set out at the end of this article.

According to Ms. Moret, the CDC mortality data show that total USA excess deaths for the period from the Fukushima event March 11, 2011 to September 3, 2011 was 34,129 excess deaths. The peak excess death rate period was April 23-May 21, 2011. May 7, 2011 was a peak excess death day with a 34% increase.

According to Ms. Moret, the governments of the USA, Canada, Japan and other governments are in knowing complicity in a cover-up of this documented radiation genocide and crimes against humanity by a now-identified international war crimes racketeering organization.[187]

Leuren Moret: Japan, U.S. and Canadian governments complicit in radiation cover-up

Evidence, documents and analysis demonstrate the intentional involvement of the individual "Barack Hussein Obama" in coordination of the ecocide and genocide of the Fukushima HAARP global nuclear false flag operation.

"*Thus, the U.S. Department of Energy (DOE), under the directorship of Dr. Steven Chu (Secretary of Energy) and Dr. Stephen Koonin, is following in the Fukushima HAARP-radiation false flag operation the same methodology that they followed in the BP Gulf Oil Spill false flag operation.*

"*Ms. Moret states, 'Dr. Steven Chu received a $500 million grant from BP Oil prior to being appointed Secretary of Energy by newly elected President Obama. Obama also received $500 million from the British Crown two years prior to his election, to begin his election campaign for US President. Upon his appointment as Secretary of Energy, Dr. Steven Chu appointed Dr. Stephen Koonin, chief scientist for BP, to run the DOE's science operations. The Queen of England personally owns BP.'*

Ms. Moret states, 'Together, DOE/BP's Secretary of Energy Steven Chu and Dr. Stephen Koonin are doing the same thing at Fukushima that they did at the BP Gulf of Mexico oil spill with full approval by President Obama. Dr. Chu and Dr. Koonin increased the exposure of the population both at Fukushima (radiation) and at the Gulf of Mexico oil spill (toxins), and they acted within the U.S. government on behalf of President Obama, so that effective action to prevent exposure could not be taken. With full Presidential oversight, the U.S. Government is increasing radiation exposure in the northern hemisphere from Fukushima, through Secretary of Energy Chu and Dr. Koonin on behalf of their benefactors the British crown and BP, with the same depopulation agenda result they had at the BP Gulf oil spill.'[188]

3. "Barack Hussein Obama" was elected to the highest political position of U.S. President by mass deception.

The individual "Barack Hussein Obama" would not have been re-elected U.S. President on Nov.6, 2012 but for the outside intervention of two major HAARP triggered environmental warfare false flag events, each of which was created by an international war crimes racketeering organization known as the New World Order, and in each of which Barack Hussein Obama participated knowingly and intentionally as an agent of the NWO organization.

These two HAARP false flag events were Hurricane false flag Isaac, (August 21-September 1, 2012,) and Hurricane false flag Sandy, (October 21-31, 2012), which are the bookends to the U.S. Presidential campaign. Hurricane Isaac was steered into the Republican convention in Tampa, Florida, cancelling its first day and depriving it of a bounce. Hurricane Sandy placed Barrack Hussein Obama back in the Commander in Chief role 10 days before the election, when his ratings had dropped precipitously to 46% and no sitting US President had ever been re-elected with ratings of less than 50% approval rating.

How 2012 HAARP Hurricanes Isaac & Sandy were created to make Barack Hussein Obama President

You can read excerpts from our Nov. 2, 2012 broadcast here:

Our headline is: Hurricane Sandy appears to be a false flag operation with multiple purposes, including, further rehearsing of the New World Order (NWO) lockdown of the USA, the United States, because that appears to be the targeted nation here.

[Hurricane Sandy's purposes include] securing the re-election of global New World Order asset Barack Obama, whose legal name is Barry Soetoro; and activating catastrophobia, fear of catastrophes, in the North American and world public in order to promote a North American Union, a world government, and other New World Order projects.

U.S. President Barack Obama's approval rating

Secondly, with regard to securing the re-election of global New Word Order asset, Barry Soetoro, (that's his actual legal name). His Man-

churian candidate name is Barack Obama and that's a manufactured name. His biological father is not the Kenyan civil servant named Barack Obama who was assassinated in a car wreck, an arranged car accident in 1982 in Kenya (arranged by the CIA). Let's see how effective that has been.

The keynote - one of the principal indicators, of whether a US president is going to be elected or not is what they call the approval rating. No sitting president with more than a 50% approval rating has failed to secure re-election. Well guess what? Barack Obama's/Barry Soetoro's approval ratings on November 1, 2012, were at 50%.

Listen to this. On October 27, 2012, (the HAARP false flag hurricane Sandy was October 22-31, 2012), just prior to the brunt of Sandy on October 27, 2012, the Obama approval had plummeted seven points from 53% to 46%. It appeared that if his republican rival, Mitt Romney, had a surge than he would win or stood a good chance of taking the presidential vote. At this stage with Obama's approval ratings above 50% as of November 1, 2012, while no one is predicting victory, no sitting president with a 50% approval rating has failed to secure re-election. It appears as though Sandy has secured that goal as well.

If we look at the bookend false flag hurricanes, the HAARP false flag Hurricane Sandy of October 22-31, 2012, and Hurricane Isaac of October 21-September 1, 2012, [they] were both environmental warfare psyops on the US and world political systems by this international war crimes, racketeering organization headed up by the British crown and the international bloodline banking syndicate, centered in the city of London that controls the HAARP-Chemtrails weapons system of mass destruction.

Hurricane Isaac, as you recall, was steered directly into the GOP, the Republican convention in Tampa, Florida, so as to cancel the initial events on the first day, and kind of deflate that convention and deflate its public profile and the bounce that Romney would have gotten. And then, hurricane Sandy came in on October 22-31, 2012, bringing up the approval rate to the required level.

Hurricane Sandy and "Friendly Fascism"

Let's switch and begin to look at what we call friendly fascism, or iron fist inside the velvet glove aspects of Sandy.

If you look at hurricane Sandy as compared to some of the other environmental war- HAARP directed false flag events, the loss of life was very low from Sandy. For example, when you compare it to the hundred and fifty thousand dead in the HAARP–Myanmar cyclone of May 2008. That's one hundred and fifty thousand dead compared to about a hundred dead. Some people say 'oh it was off-world technology that counteracted the New World Order-HAARP manipulation that kept the death toll that low'. But, I think that the more realistic perspective is that the New World Order-HAARP controllers took a friendly fascism approach. That's a term that when I was a futurist in the mid-seventies doing the proposed Carter White House extraterrestrial communications study, the term 'friendly fascism' came up. That is sort of fascism with a smile.

In a way, Barry Soetoro/Barack Obama embodies, embodies, friendly fascism. He is so user friendly from a certain point of view. And it's friendly fascism. The New World Order-HAARP controllers wanted to tilt the election to Obama but not do an environmental, genocidal, war attack like the 2008 Myanmar cyclone where one hundred fifty thousand persons were killed. They were yellow and brown, and they were in Asia, and that was a different case. Or, the 2010 Haiti earthquake that was the Vancouver winter Olympics earthquake. What occurred there is that the Canadian governor general was actually a woman of Haitian extraction. The Canadian governor general is the woman that represents the British crown, the Queen of England. The government of Haiti was resisting the Rothschild controlled companies who wanted to exploit the gold reserves and petroleum reserves that had just been discovered under Espanola, the island that Haiti sits on. So they flattened Port au Prince, the government of Haiti, and the presidential palace with an earthquake-bomb by HAARP that resulted in two hundred thousand people killed; more than Hiroshima and Nagasaki. And that certainly was not friendly fascism.

One has to look at it from that perspective. Probably it's more to re-hearse a New World Order lockdown in North America with grada-tions, while still maintaining Barry Soetoro/Barack Obama as a friendly fascism New World Order asset.

Hurricane Sandy and the New World Order

This gets us into the next subject here on THE NEWS Live, which is the whole New World Order facets or aspects of this environmental war event known as hurricane Sandy. We know that the HAARP-Chemtrails global weapons system is controlled by the city of London bloodline bankers and the British crown. The city of London bloodline bankers has been documented that they are essentially a satanic cult. It has been documented in many books. One book is called "The Il-luminati, The Cult that Hijacked the World". I urge people to google that and to read it, and to judge from themselves by the evidence.

Here we have a whole number of elements that harken back to what actually happened in WW2 during the Hiroshima bombing, where the one Christian city, (Hiroshima in Japan), was chosen for the bombing by the Manhattan Project which was, in essence, controlled from the inside by agents of the city of London-Illuminati banking consortium. One of the themes here in world genocide is anti-spirituality and anti-spiritual leaders such as the Christ. It's not a religion such as the Vatican as a political organization, but rather things of that sort. So what do we have here? Just open your minds to the fact that "Christ", "Christie", "Christ-Christ", "Christopher Chris-tie", "Christ-Christ 'e'", was a central character in this environmental war hit. And that the environmental war hit drove "Christ-Christie" into the arms of the New World Order asset, Barack Obama. The environmental war hit had the function of raising Barack Obama and "Christ-Christie" into world prominence as heroes, with the Satanic intelligence deploying this 'laughing all the way home'.

You may think that this is idle speculation but a long study of some of these elements [has been done]. For example, we've been able to iso-late that the Tromso Norway HAARP facility was used in November

9, 2009, for the Tromso Spiral that occurred the night before Barack Obama's Nobel speech in which he mentioned the war and not peace. That was one of those productions. The same Tromso Norway HAARP facility was used for the March 11, 2011, Fukushima-HAARP event.

U.S. News & World Report: HAARP Conspiracy

What was interesting was that US News and World Report is a mainstream newspaper and it actually ran a story on October 29, by Elizabeth Flock saying Conspiracy theorists [are] saying Obama engineered hurricane Sandy "as hurricane Sandy blasted the eastern seaboard, a number of conspiracy theorists have decided Barack Obama engineered the mega-storm to secure his re-election." Then they go on and talk about HAARP.

If one goes out and looks at the data just for the record, on some of the key websites like HAARPstatus.com, an independent website that has a real time sensor network from over 28 sensors placed in rural areas across the United States. During the Sandy period they recorded "the strongest HAARP readings in the projects history." They were literally "off the charts and lend credence to parallel claims that hurricane Sandy is being engineered to create mass destruction." Some of the facts, or the conclusions are that the strongest readings in the history of this project have peaked. A never before seen white shade indicates about a value higher than 10 on the scale. The scale is from 1-10 and this was above 10. HAARP status projections showed New Jersey and they showed the storm being steered. There's plenty of evidence on the Internet.

I'd like to spend the closing 2-3 minutes of this initial broadcast of THE NEWS Live just reviewing with you, the viewing audience, the false flag events that have been reaped by the HAARP-Chemtrails false flag weapons of mass destruction system. You can go to ExopoliticsTV and you can see an hour long presentation that I made to the Consciousness Beyond Chemtrails conference in Las Vegas this year that sets out all of the science behind this. Let's look at these operations and see what the script is and what the damage is.

First of all, the false flag operation of September 11, 2001. HAARP was one of the major tools used in that to bring down the World Trade Center towers. We have the 9-11 War Crimes Tribunal. You can go to its website at 911WarCrimesTribunal.org. The tribunal will be issuing its indictment, a first ever indictment, of key co-conspirators of the 9-11 conspiracy. That indictment will be issued on January 22, 2013, two days after the inauguration of the new US president.

Hurricane Katrina, another HAARP false flag, August 28, 2005.

The Haiti earthquake of 2010, two hundred thousand dead.

The BP Gulf oil spill of April 20, 2010. The Obama administration was responsible for the negligence that allowed this, with the Corexit, to ruin the Gulf of Mexico. Barack Obama with his Department of Energy and the Coast Guard actually aided and abetted BP and the British crown in doing this.

The Fukushima HAARP radiation event of March 11, 2011. Likewise, Barack Obama, the Department of Energy under David Chu, actually (no audio) radiation event. You can follow all of the documentation of this event in interviews and articles at our website, EcologyNews.com.

And now we have Hurricane false flag Isaac, (August 21-September 1, 2012,) and Sandy, (October 21-31, 2012,) around the 'Selection' of 2012 and the implementation of the New World Order lockdown.[189]

4. As U.S. President he has covertly participated in and served as "public Capstone" for false flag strategic deception operations intended to deceptively deprive U.S. citizens of their rights under the Bill of Rights including their right to bear arms, and ultimately to depopulate and enslave the U.S. population.

The individual "Barack Hussein Obama" has intentionally and consciously participated in false flag operations that are part of an established program of the Central Intelligence Agency and the U.S. national security state create internal false flag state terror events in the United States with the objectives of: (1) enacting police state stat-

ues, executive decisions and regulations which can trigger a dictatorship under the U.S. President; (2) disarming the U.S. population so that progressive elements of the population can be incarcerated and eliminated in internal concentration camps, which now number over 800 according to reliable sources.

Two recent examples of such false flag state terror events orchestrated via deceit around the persona of Barack Hussein Obama as "friendly fascist" dictator-in-waiting are:

1. The False Flag State Terror operation of Sandy Hook (December 14, 2012)

2. The False Flag State Terror operation of the Boston Marathon (April 15, 2013)

Sandy Hook as state terror against USA population

"Sandy Hook assassination on December 14, 2012 of 28 people (including 20 reported elementary students who may have been abducted into CIA/intel pedophile rings) was reportedly the 19th MKULTRA-type mass assassination in CIA/intel domestic state terror program with multiple purposes: To disarm the civilian population in preparation for a police state; to "pacify" civilian US population into mindless robots, with an international war crimes racketeering organization targeting USA as the Soviet Union was targeted for extinction in the 1990s. MKULTRA-type mass assassinations used along with GWEN and cell phone towers, HAARP mass mind control and mind control of governance (Executive, Legislative, Judicial branches of Federal, State and Municipal governments) throughout the USA. Sandy Hook correlated with Hurricane Sandy that ensured NWO asset Barack Obama/Barry Soetoro's election in 2012.

Sandy Hook as mind control false flag state terror against the U.S. population

"Sandy Hook, on December 14, 2012, included the reported assassination of 28 people, including possibly 20 reported elementary students who may have been abducted into CIA pedophile rings; that *remains to be seen. Sandy Hook was reportedly the nineteenth MKULTRA-type mass assassination in a CIA/intel domestic state terror program with multiple purposes: to disarm the civilian population in preparation for a police state; to pacify the civilian U.S. population into mindless robots, with an international war crimes racketeering organization targeting the U.S. as the Soviet Union was targeted for deconstruction in the 1990's. MKULTRA-type mass assassinations are used in this deconstruction, along with GWEN and cell towers mind control, HAARP mass mind control, and mind control targeted of governance. That is [directed mind control technologies aimed at] Executive, Legislative, and Judicial Branch bodies and officers of the Federal, State, and Municipal Governments of the United States throughout the U.S. as a nation. Moreover, the Sandy Hook false flag operation is correlated with the false flag and HAARP triggered and directed hurricane Sandy; that insured New World Order asset Barak Obama/Barry Soetoro (his real legal name) election in 2012 as THE NEWS Live reported on November 2, 2012.*

Various Layers of Sandy Hook

"Let's look at various layers of this story. First of all, Sandy Hook as [part of] a long standing (publicly funded by tax payers) CIA/intel program to disarm the civilian population in preparation for a police state known as the New World Order (NWO). It seems to be working. According to a recent pole, more Americans prioritize gun control above second amendment rights by the widest margin since President Barak Obama/Barry Soetoro took office. According to a new pole released December 24, 2012, 49% of those poled say it's more important to control gun ownership, as reported 42% believe that the constitutional rights of protecting gun ownership should be protected.

"Let's look to a second part of this and that is the structural components. How exactly is it that this program is structured of nineteen mass murders? They're slightly different in the technologies employed from assassination to assassination as say Columbine on April 20, 1999, (Hitler's birthday) to Aurora, Colorado, on July 20, 2012, around THE

DARK KNIGHT RISES. THE DARK KNIGHT RISES being a motion picture that was showing in Aurora, Colorado, where Sandy Hook appears inside THE DARK KNIGHT RISES. We're going to ask whether, in fact--symbolically as part of the mass mind control program, if Barak Obama/Barry Soetoro is 'The Dark Knight' that is 'Rising'. No racial slur intended, just matter of fact reporting.

"Here we have a statement from Admiral Gunther K. Russbacher who is a thirty-year plus veteran of the CIA and Naval intelligence, and who was held prisoner because he released a lot of this information. He was husband to a colleague of mine, Rayelan Allan. Admiral Russbacher was asked 'How are the subjects for the MK Ultra assassination programs chosen?" and he gave out a whole series of levels (one through ten or so) and this is just to show an introduction to Level One and Two. He says: "A preset group of our people (from the intelligence community) canvasses the county hospitals and immigration centers in order to find viable candidates. We locate and select people who have no close family or friends. Once they have been selected, they are put under heavy, Level One hypnosis. At this time a clear and definitive pattern of their usefulness is determined by our psychiatrists and field officers. If the candidate possesses a relatively high IQ, he will be filed in a category file, called 'call file.'"

Levels One and Two

"'If the tested applicant has more than 120 IQ, a "recall" command and an accompanying "trigger" word will be written into his personality during the Level One hypnosis session. This "trigger" will activate his recall program when we are ready for him. We then systematically do a background search and create a file for future reference. If there are no relatives, to speak of, the subject will be "recalled" and taken to a location of our choice. Further tests for vulnerability will be conducted at this location. If he passes these tests, he is then brought to Level 2 hypnosis where specific instructions are "written" (placed through hypnotic commands and suggestions) into his personality and he is given diverse small orders."

"And the Admiral concludes (He's a real whistle blower) 'If this horrendous, diabolic plan to disarm America is not exposed, we can expect to see many more killings like the ones at Columbine. Each subsequent episode will be 100 times worse than the others. In Columbine, the real people behind the killings were sending a subtle message to anyone who can decipher it: The bombs that were found were not intended to go off. They were merely there to let "key people" in Congress know what will happen the next time. In other words, instead of 15 people being killed, hundreds, maybe even thousands will be killed.'

"'In other words, instead of fifteen people being killed, hundreds-maybe thousands-will be killed and we'll see that in this latest episode, it's tied into pedophile rings which are the means by which the Federal U.S. Government and the U.S. Congress is actually controlled; through pedophile rings. So that [subtle message] is like a signal to the U.S. Congress and the Executive Branch to start action on this.'"

Hegelian Dialectic

"And we're again going from Rumor Mill News, Rayelan Allan: 'In the case of the children" (this is what occurred at Sandy Hook) "being murdered by children. This is a "CIA modified" "Hegelian Dialectic" technique. In other words, if you want society to become something different than it is, you must set up the conditions which will bring about the desired results." The Hegelian Dialectic was Thesis, Antithesis, and Synthesis. Inside the CIA, it's called Crisis Creation, Crisis Solution, and Crisis Control. A Navy Captain, Trenton Parker, describes how the CIA uses the technique in foreign countries to influence politics. You can get this at RumorMillNews.com included at the end of the article at Exopolitics.com. Crisis Creation replaces Antithesis. Horrific violence and mass murders committed by people with guns who are either programmed or in the employ of the CIA or government agencies. That's what the Crisis Creation is. The Crisis Solution replaces Synthesis. [For example,] *draconian gun laws that take the guns away from everyone including law abiding citizens. In other words, Crisis Control now becomes a new Thesis. In the case of gun violence, the new Thesis will resemble a Police State where only the government will have guns. To further illustrate the point, America is a nation full of guns and guaranteed the right to own and bear arms by the Constitution. America cannot be taken over by the New World Order and their socialist/communist agenda if American's are armed. This is the [current] Thesis--an all armed citizenry. Therefore, conditions must be created that will cause the American public to demand their Constitutional right to bear arms be rescinded. The created conditions are called the Antithesis by Hegel [Hegelian Dialectic]. It is a Crisis Creation by the CIA. In the case of an armed citizenry, the Antithesis is random, senseless and horrific murders using guns as the weapon. When these two conditions, for example, an armed citizenry and horrific violence, exist simultaneously, public hysteria can be whipped up making the public demand that there Congressional representatives outlaw all guns. This is called the Synthesis by Hegel or Crisis Solution by CIA. The Synthesis then becomes the new Thesis for triading Hegel's Dialectic. In the CIA's version of the Dialectic, the Crisis Solution brings about the new Thesis, which is Crisis Control, namely the New World Order.*

"'Now, there are variations of this as Homeland Security in the U.S. has bought up a humongous number of rounds of soft nosed bullets indicating that they plan a war against the civilian population, [or] indicating that they were planning; which may include time travel technology that indicates that the population is not going to give up the guns. And [with] that, they are going to be compelled, probably, by the International War Crimes Racketeering Organization that I believe probably includes the British Throne, The Zionist Bloodline bankers and the City of London, and others as the U.S.A. has been targeted as the Soviet Union was targeted in the 1990's. So that's what's up for the U.S. over the next several years.'"

"The plot of Sandy Hook

"Now let's look at the plot of Sandy Hook. How was the false flag accomplished? It was through the classic false flag technology using a drill. This is what they used in 9/11. They had simultaneous drills going on to mask the false flag and to set up a patsy, in this case, Adam Lanza. There are a number of solutions that have come to this. We will put the sources out on Exopolitics.com and I'll just give a summary here. If we're breaking down the day, December 14, there were actually two events: The real event that took place and Homeland Security/FEMA simulation, and those two were interlocked with various levels of police coming in; and various level of patsy; and various levels of shooters coming in.

"Emergency Drill

"'By grim coincidence, even as the terrible events were unfolding in Newtown on Friday morning, the Putnam County Emergency Response Team ("ERT") happened to be assembled for regular training in Carmel, and team members were at that very moment engaged in a mock scenario of an active-shooter in a school. The ERT is comprised of specially trained and heavily armed officers from the Sheriff's Office and the Carmel and Kent Police Departments." When news broke of the Newtown shooting, the Putnam County ERT commander called Newtown Police and offered to have the ERT respond to the Sandy Hook school, but that response was not needed because Connecticut police had already secured the scene.'" (I used to have a house in Kent, a summer home in Kent, Connecticut.)

"'When news broke of the Newtown shooting, the Putnam County ERT Commander called the Newtown Police and offered to have the ERT respond to the Sandy Hook school, but that response was not needed because Connecticut Police had already secured the scene. Therefore, they asked was Adam Lanza was conned into believing he would be participating in a drill?'"

"'So there are various layers to this. Reading it is like reading a film and you can go to SandyHookHoax.com. There are various layers.

The number one layer is the real event taking place at Sandy Hook Elementary and what that event is, is still open to question.[190]

"*Layer 1: The REAL Event - Sandy Hook Elementary Shooting*

-Layer 1A: The Operation Prep

--Layer 1B: The Actual Black-Op

---Layer 1C: Evidence Cleanup, Patsy Setup & "Official" Police Arrival

"*Layer 2: The FAKE Event – Namely the DHS/FEMA Exercise/Drill/Simulation (Simulating Sandy Hook Elementary)*

- DHS/FEMA Drills General Plot

--Ryan Lanza likely participates in DHS/FEMA Simulation

---The two operatives who were probably identified as the shooters, and if there was any abduction of the children to go into pedophile rings, as we will see, out of that area by the Jesuit run Fairfield University in Connecticut. ([Fairfield University] is an MKULTRA hub going back to 1942, and also a pedophile hub run essentially by the Jesuits and the Vatican and the CIA.)

"*Another small-scale active shooter drill also takes place nearby and then later, leads to systematic media confusion of the real versus the fake event coverage. There's just like total confusion.*

"*[Layer 3: Systematic Media Confusion - Real vs. Fake Event Coverage.]*

"*For example, what could have occurred is that Adam Lanza was with his mother and the two ops come in and say 'Adam, you are going to participate in a drill today.' And he willingly goes with him to the drill. One of the black ops in there, then shoots the mother in her own bed and then takes Adam off and sets him up as the patsy.*

"*Pedophile, Satanic, mind control*

"*What is the pedophile, Satanic, mind control, connection to Sandy Hook? This is one of the covers of the op. There's a point at which very* excellent researchers ask nine questions, and their ninth question (and the most disturbing perhaps) is where are all the bodies? That week of funerals--were all the funerals closed casket funerals? Were those phony autopsies? And were the children taken off into CIA pedophile rings?

"And we have an excellent article, and we'll put a link to that on Exo-politics.com, stating that in 1942 at the start of World War II, the Jesuits opened Fairfield University that then became a center for, eventually, MKULTRA and also pedophile rings. J.D. Salinger [an MKULTRA operative presumably stationed at Fairfield University] who had been involved in OSS in Project Artichoke which was smuggling German Jews into Palestine in support of a Zionist State; and also in Project Paperclip. And now, so that that area was the center-or is the center-of a CIA/MKULTRA pedophile presence that goes back fifty years to 1942; or more, that goes back seventy years! The question then asked is with this investigative venue, 'comes the diversionary exercise of "gun control", a national effort led by Joe Biden, a member of the Knights of Malta, a politician with an intelligence background who is sworn to protect the interests of the Vatican... Leave intact the right of armed self-defense or the gangsters will take over everything.'"

"Obama's role in Sandy Hook Psyops

"Let's ask about Obama's role. We know that we have hurricane Sandy previously (you can go to the November 2, 2012, THE NEWS Live) and we show that hurricane Sandy was HAARP directed, and Sandy Hook is a town in New Jersey that was hit by hurricane Sandy. Hurricane Sandy ensured Barak Obama's election, because right before the election, Obama's approval rating was plunging down 7 points, down to 46%, and then no U.S. President had ever been re-elected with an approval rating of less than 50%. Hurricane Sandy hit, he went into the Commander in Chief role, and the approval level went above 50% fifty percent and Obama wins.

"So we have THE DARK KNIGHT RISING that was showing at the Aurora, Colorado, shootings earlier in 2012. There's a Sandy Hook reference in the BATMAN movie, and now we have hurricane Sandy *ensuring Obama's 2012 electoral victory, [In THE NEWS Live report] we show that Obama is one of the three principals in the New World Order of upper theatre personages of the Pope, the Queen and the Obama. A section of Gotham City was renamed Sandy Hook from South Hinkley from the latest 'Dark Knight' release THE DARK KNIGHT RISES.*

"I, for one, find it difficult to believe that U.S. President Barack H. Obama aka Barry Soetoro, a lifelong CIA asset (and we have published extensively on this at Exopolitics.com) was personally uninformed about and unaware about the December 14, 2012, Connecticut shooting, the July, 2012, Boulder, Colorado, shooting and many other shootings; and prior administrations are, in fact, part of a sophisticated MKULTRA assassination Cointelpro program. If you're lifelong CIA, you sort of know that's one of there programs. Therefore, we can reasonable assume that he has constructive awareness of cultural assassinations. Therefore, the question arises is Obama himself 'The Dark Knight Rising'?

"That is, we have the coming of a police state. That's the agenda that's being pursued now around 'The Dark Knight Rising' and this dark figure. Is Barack Obama now being portrayed in this upper theatre drama in the U.S., 'The Dark Knight Rising' as one part where the guy is conducting mass assassinations and mass mind control, and the other side of the CIA personified in Obama, a lifelong CIA asset, is mind controlling the people into thinking that he's the savior? There's a lot of evidence that points that way. For example, there's an analysis of the famous video where Obama cried. Not only that those were crocodile tears, but also it is that his presentation is actually set out in hypnotic language and hypnotic techniques.

"Obama starts out very slowly with a naturally slow language (we'll put the link at Exopolitics.com) There's a common hypnotic technique in order to allow the subject time to respond to suggestions, imagine images, and feel sensations conjured by the hypnotist. And then Obama starts louder 'scripture tells us outwardly we're wasting money, inwardly we're being renewed day by day'. The process with which the *mind searches between alternative meanings is called trans-derivation. The searching through these various meanings is part of what distracts the rational part of our mind as part of hypnotic induction, even if we are not consciously aware of our search between different meanings, this trans-derivational search occurs below the level of induction.*

"Therefore, this analysis that a friend sent to me is of Obama's speech at which he cried at:

5:10 "Dutifully following instructions… the way young children some-times do"

[8:37] He says we cannot do it alone, and associates family, commu-nity to NATION.

[9:50:] Are we doing enough?… points to himself as he says the word happiness

12:40 Implies we have no choice! POWERLESS CARNAGE

13:40 - what gives our life meaning… our AXE Purpose. So now life/meaning = Axe/Purpose??

14:11 - we will fall short of what we hoped.

14:17 - With the word GOOD INTENTIONS again he points to self

14:38 - we are groping through darkness

14:47 - one thing we can be sure of - the LOVE we have - points to self/nation. 'the love we have' in other words that's the nation, that's him.

15:10 - waving hand "wonder we see through their eyes".

15:47 - AGAIN "That's what we can be sure of" - points to himself.

"So the children and Obama are the family and the nation, and the nation "can do no wrong" [15:40] protecting children. And there is the "love that binds us" [15:10].

"This is the subliminal program that Obama is laying down. And this is the Obama that this week now, has signed in the NDAA that pro-vides, essentially, that any American citizen can be declared a terrorist

and stripped of all rights, civil rights. His true self by rational analysis is coming out as the 'Dark Knight Rising'."[191]

"Boston Marathon false fag operation (April 15, 2013 Tax Day) as state terror to induce mass fear; accelerate a police state and rolling out Presidential executive orders establishing a functional martial law dictatorship

"In the 48 hours after the Boston Marathon explosions, Truth movement researchers had already deconstructed the major aspects of the Boston Marathon false flag operation.

"These included:

"1. Use of parallel drills - A bomb drill was being conducted in parallel with the Boston Marathon false flag bombing. The methodology and standard operating design of false flag operations includes parallel drills, which have multiple functions, including generating diversion of first responders and law enforcement, over-loading of psychological disinformation, masking of perpetrators, and mainstream media confusion.

"I was with Alex Jones and Gov. Jesse Ventura in New Orleans when Jesse Ventura and I did his TruTV program on Hurricane Katrina and the BP Oil Spill false flag operations. Alex Jones was very helpful and explained my points to Jesse Ventura in our conference before the program. I urge all people, especially Americans to watch this 8 min. video, explaining the evidence that the drills demonstrate the Boston Marathon event was a false flag operation. This video sets out proof of open state terror in the United States of America.[192]

"Use of Chechen mind controlled assets in Boston Marathon false flag – A Truth researcher wrote me, 'The Boston Marathon were mind-controlled Chechen terrorists', controlled through Operation Gladio, the same Gladio network that is sponsoring "Barack Hussein Obama".

"'Operation Gladio: Chechen Terrorist connections to co-founder Zbigniew Brezezinski (with David Rockefeller) of the Trilateral Com-

mission in 1973. Zbigniew Brezezinski. Well here is the tie we have been looking for. The Chechen terrorist organization associated with bombers linked to Brzezinski.

"'Again, the dirty hand of London is all over the Chechen Boston bombings, since Brzezinski/Rockefeller had ties to the Chechen terrorist orgs. This seems like a 911 replay blaming both on Moslem terrorists controlled by London assets.'

"'Subject: Chechen Terrorist connections to co-founder Zbigniew Brezezinski (with David Rockefeller) of the Trilateral Commission in 1973. Zbigniew Brezezinski

Date: Friday, April 19, 2013, 10:31 AM

"'The Boston Marathon rebels were mind-controlled Chechen terrorists. Here's the background:

"'The terrorist organization in question is the Chechen rebel group associated with the names of two of the greatest butchers of our time, Aslan Maskhadov and Shamil Basayev, both deceased even though the organization they built fights on. The foreign minister and ambassador for this terrorist group is Ilyas Khamzatovich Akhmadov (born December 19, 1960), who was granted political asylum in the United States in 2003. Akhmadov's patron is none other than Zbigniew Brzezinski...'[193]

Capstone role of "Barack Hussein Obama" in the Boston Marathon false flag operation - As in a recent state terror false flag operation at Sandy Hook Elementary School in Newtown, Conn., the role of "Barack Hussein Obama" is to serve as the "Capstone" on the pyramid of the false flag operation. The Obama stereotypically makes his entrance several days after the false flag operation at the scene of the state terror with a backdrop of the civilian victims to give a benediction.

In the case of the Sandy Hook false flag, The Obama was able to announce Gun Control legislation that was part of the mission of the false flag in the first place, and that ultimately failed in the U.S.

Senate ironically on the very day after the Boston Marathon false flag.

As you can see from the below video of The Obama speaking at the false flag Capstone ceremony (aka "Interfaith service") for the Boston Marathon false flag operation, The Obama speaks with vague platitudes and well-wishes, campaign style comparing sports franchises, etc.[194]

5. "Barack Hussein Obama" covertly and intentionally serves as an archetypal "deceiver" asset of an international war crimes racketeering organization intent on installing a global police state known as The New World Order. "Barack Hussein Obama" owes primary allegiance to the New World Order crime organization.

Upper Theatre NWO - "Barack Hussein Obama" is a major archetypal "deceiver" asset in the Upper Theatre of the New World Order (NWO). Only three archetypal NWO "deceiver" assets have been allowed to speak in the 'Temple' of the New World Order in its capital (London, UK), at Westminster Hall. Barack Hussein Obama spoke at Westminster Hall on May 25, 2011.

These three NWO "deceiver" archetypes are The Pope, The Queen/King, and The Obama. I call "Barack Hussein Obama" in his NWO "deceiver" archetypal manifestation, 'The Obama".

The Pope, The Queen/King and The Obama are the three "deceiver" archetypal figures in the New World Order panoply at this time.

The three "deceiver" archetypes are the principal Illuminati Upper Theatre ruling archetypes for maintaining the masses in the consensual trance of the Illuminati New World Order leading to a domestic police state worldwide.

The three archetypes are fulfilling the NWO "deceiver" roles. The Pope is The World Divine Intercessor. The Queen/King is The World Regent. The Obama is the third "deceiver" archetype. He is fulfilling the World President archetype.

Now there are rumors that Queen Elizabeth Windsor will either step aside or demise and that they'll skip a generation (already Prince Philip is promoting this scenario) and go to her grandson, Prince William.

435

Prince William is fully qualified to be the first Illuminati King because he and his consort, Kate, are both from City of London Illuminati banking bloodlines. The Rothschilds and the Illuminati banking bloodline will have achieved the British crown. That's their life long ambition.

The Pope - Technically, the Pope that spoke at Westminster Hall was Benedict XVI (Joseph Ratzinger) who was reportedly forced to resign because he was on the verge of being arrested for the crimes of child trafficking by prosecutors from specific European jurisdictions.

Pope Francis (I) [Julio Mario Bergoglio] -

We have already identified Pope Francis in his Jesuitical, Extraterrestrial, "False Prophet", and Political Identities.[195]

The Queen/King -

In an exclusive ExopoliticsTV interview with Alfred Lambremont Webre released June 15, 2011, author and hermeneutics expert Peter Kling has stated that Prince William, Duke of Cambridge, embodies the a "deceiver" archetype known as the "Antichrist," to be the future king of a one world government now promoted by the New World Order. Under this analysis, the present United Nations is under time schedule starting in 2013 to be morphed by the Illuminati hidden power structure into a dictatorial, police state "one world government" over which Prince William will be installed as Head of State, Illuminati king of the world. According to Mr. Kling, the "deceiver" archetype of "Antichrist" is a political and exopolitical office, not a religious one as commonly interpreted.

The one world government, and Prince William as its putative Head of State, are expected to be essentially a surrogate global state of an Anunnaki ET-Illuminati bloodline hierarchy that was installed starting approximately 280,000 according to researchers and archeological monuments such as Adam's Calendar in South Africa.

In his interview, Mr. Kling states that the occupation of Earth by the one world government and the Antichrist will be overthrown by an exopolitical liberation of Earth by ethical extraterrestrial and interdimensional forces that include a benevolent Pleiadian civilization.

Watch ExopoliticsTV interview with Peter Kling

Readers can watch the ExopoliticsTV interview with Peter Kling at the following link.[196]

Prince William has already commenced official communication releases as "deceiver" Antichrist

As Mr. Kling discussed in his ExopoliticsTV interview, Prince William and his support staff at Buckingham Palace has already commenced official communication released depicting Prince William as the "deceiver" Antichrist.

A formal photograph, officially released by Buckingham Palace and published on May 31, 2004, depicts Prince William posing in "popular" garb (blue jeans and sweater) with a lamb as he holds its rear cloven hoof is an example of an officially-sanctioned intentional communication by the U.K. Throne from Prince William as the "deceiver" Antichrist, future king of the one world government.

One source states, "On May 31st 2004, the Rothschild-controlled Associated Press, published a photograph world wide, taken by Alistair Grant. The photo shows prince William posing with a lamb like Jesus Christ, who the Bible calls the Lamb of God. What is the significance of this photograph? To the unaware observer, the photograph is perfectly innocent. But to insiders familiar with the Protocols of Zion, Freemasonry and the Book of Revelation, William is identified in the photo as the antichrist.

"The antichrist has been described in art and literature as a handsome and charming and a master of lies and deception. Freemasons call him the Bathomed, or Goat of Mendese. He is commonly illustrated with cloven hind hooves.

"Why is prince William holding up a cloven hind hoof in the photograph?"[197]

What are Solutions out of the New World Order consensual trance, deceptions, and its deceiver archetypes: The Pope, The Queen/King and The Obama?

1. *Wide and systematic public exposure of the individual "Barack Hussein Obama" as a deceiver in all of the aspects enumerated above:*

A. *He is practiced in institutional deception since adolescence;*

B. *As U.S. President he has covertly participated in and coordinated false flag operations causing ecocide and genocide through environmental warfare; bioweapons; and ionizing radiation.*

C. *He was elected to the highest political position of U.S. President by mass deception.*

D. *As U.S. President he has covertly participated in and served as "public Capstone" for false flag strategic deception operations intended to deceptively deprive U.S. citizens of their rights under the Bill of Rights including their right to bear arms, and ultimately to depopulate and enslave the U.S. population*

E. *He covertly and intentionally serves as an archetypal "deceiver" asset of an international war crimes racketeering organization intent on installing a global police state known as The New World Order, and he owes primary allegiance to the New World Order crime organization.*

2. *Citizen's Tribunal and Citizen's Grand Juries of Conscience to indict, prosecute, try and convict "Barack Hussein Obama" for ecocide, genocide, treason, and murder.*

This approach has been used successfully by the International Tribunal into Crimes of Church and State (ITCCS.org), a citizen's tribunal of conscience, in successfully prosecuting The Pope (Joseph Ratzinger)

The International Tribunal into Crimes of Church and State (ITCCS.org) has also initiated proceedings by indicting, prosecuting, trying and convicting The Queen/King (Elizabeth Windsor).[198]

3. Own your rights as citizens and engage the body politic - Become active in activities, organizations, media, and campaigns for public office that seek to expose and deconstruct the New World Order.

4. Speak out! Silence equals death! Publish or perish. Start and promote a blog. Deconstruct the New World Order widely on social media etc.

5. Expose the methodologies of the New World Order publicly by exposing false flag operations, deconstructing "deceivers" and New World Order propaganda.

6. Stay in Unity consciousness ("We are One") and commit to a Positive timeline 2013 - 2025, and the landing of Paradise on Earth.

7. Add your own steps below with your comments.

Alfred Lambremont Webre, JD, MEd

April 19, 2013.[199]

2014-2021 "TRIBULATION" & POSITIVE TIMELINE. DOES CHRIST RETURN WITH A DECLOAKING OF THE UNIVERSE FLEET?

2015 Update: Alfred Lambremont Webre, hermeneutics expert Peter Kling discuss 2015 as the 6th year in the 7 year "Tribulation" period 2014-2021, where in Sept 2015, Pope Bergoglio (the Book of Revelation's Whore of Babylon) speaks at United Nations (the "10 Horned Beast") after seeing Obama in Washington DC (the "One horn of the two-Horned beast, other being the UK Crown) where Bergoglio is speaking as the first Pope to speak in the US Congress.

In this context, the Second Coming of Christ predicted by the Book of Revelation may be a decloaking of the Universe Extraterrestrial fleet that in turn defeats the combined forces of Antichrist to liberate humanity.[200]

The publication of JOURNEY – VOLUME I on June 15, 2015 was made necessary in Alfred's view by the events scheduled around the various meetings of the Whore of Babylon (Pope

Francis Bergoglio), the Two Horned Beast (Obama/USA Corp & UK Crown) and the 10 Horned Beast (Ban Ki Moon-UN/EU Leaders) in New York at the United Nations in September 2015.

SCENE 10

MAPPING OF THE OMNIVERSE

July 2009
La Vanguardia
Avda. Diagonal 477, 3°.
E-08036 Barcelona. España

On a bright July 2009 day in Barcelona, Ima Sanchis, a veteran journalist with La Vanguardia, the leading Catalan newspaper and a top newspaper in Spain, interviews Alfred on Exopolitics for her full-page column LA CONTRA. Alfred is on a book tour of Spain as part of the launch of the Spanish edition of his book "Exopolitica: La Politica, El Gobierno y La Ley en el Universo."[201]

Toward the end of the interview in a small conference room at the La Vanguardia's Barcelona headquarters, Ima puts down her pen, turns off her tape recorder, turns to Alfred and asks pointedly,

"*¿Alfred, Como funciona el universo?*

"*¿Cuál es la relación entre los extraterrestres y la reencarnación del alma humano?*"

Translated into English, Ima Sanchis' questions mean,

"*Alfred, how does the Universe function?*

"*What is the relationship between extraterrestrials and the reincarnation of the human soul?*"

As Ima Sanchis asks her questions, Alfred recognizes her questions address key issues that most humans, philosophers, scientists, priests, and earthly religions have struggled to answer for millennia – without much objective scientific success.

It dawns on Alfred that Ima is pointing to the next pathway of research into how intelligent civilizations in the multi-verse relate to each other.

Ima's questions are the deeper questions of Exopolitics, and Alfred has not at that point yet addressed the empirical proof for any of the answers to the penetrating questions she asks.

In that moment at La Vanguardia's offices, Alfred assures Ima that indeed there was a relationship, and sketched some of the initial connections out loud.

Extraterrestrials and the Soul

Alfred returns to Madrid from speaking in Barcelona. At his hotel in Madrid, on his way back home to Vancouver, B.C., he ponders the relationships between extraterrestrials and the soul, and scribble notes to himself on hotel notepaper. His mind explores the basic similarities in communications between humans and extraterrestrials and human and souls in the 'interlife'.

Communications between human contactees and representatives of intelligent civilizations, as exemplified by the reported extraterrestrial contactee cases, are telepathic, Alfred notes.

Communications between mediums and representatives of 'soul civilizations' in the afterlife (or the 'interlife') as exemplified by the many apparently genuine reported cases of mediumistic communications with persons in the dimension of the afterlife, are also telepathic, Alfred notes.

Alfred concludes that this common factor – telepathy (non-local mind-to-mind communication) - appears to reveal a fundamental similarity in the nature of communication by humans with intelligent civilizations of 'extraterrestrials' and with intelligent civilizations of 'souls'.

Communication between humans and 'Extraterrestrials' and between humans and 'souls' appears in many cases to be inter-dimensional, non-local telepathy.

Eighteen months later in December 2010, Alfred sits at his desk in Vancouver, B.C. and begins to draft this chapter. He looks down, and one of these hotel notes is stuck under the wheels of his desk chair. Alfred has no idea how the note got under his desk chair at that moment. He had not seen the note since he arrived from Spain in July 2009.

The note on Madrid hotel paper says, in Alfred's handwriting,

"Communication with AL [afterlife] telepathic;

Communication with ET [extraterrestrials] telepathic"

Alfred concludes that telepathic communication appears to be the common denominator in this dimensional ecology. The dimensional ecology is active in parallel universes and dimensions among Earthling humans, extraterrestrials, interdimensionals, the 'interlife', the intelligent civilizations of souls and of 'spiritual' dimensional beings.

Earthling human agencies with their interdimensional artificial intelligence technology do not control all of this dimensional ecology of the multi-verse.

Alfred's own creative, scientific observations such as:

"Communication with AL [afterlife] telepathic;

Communication with ET [extraterrestrials] telepathic"

are created by Alfred's own creative subconscious or, in the dimensional ecology, by the creative prompting of his muse, guides, or other inter-dimensional helpers.

An early dialogue on the dimensional ecology

An early dialogue on the dimensional ecology appeared publicly when Ima Sanchis' interview with Alfred was published in La Vanguardia in September 2009. Alfred was hoping Ima would make an allusion to their private dialogue on how the universe functions and the relationship between extraterrestrials and the soul.

Ima starts the dialogue with key research and discoveries on another intelligent civilization in the Time-Space dimension of our solar system - the existence on an intelligent, indigenous civilization living under the surface of our nearest planetary neighbor, Mars.

Ima Sanchis does include an important question on the dimensional ecology in her published interview:

> *La Vanguardia: ¿Cómo funciona el universo? Webre: Hay muchas dimensiones y universos paralelos al nuestro. Algunas civilizaciones extraterrestres vienen de otra dimensión, otro universo paralelo, por eso los ovnis pueden aparecer y desaparecer. La Vanguardia: How does the universe function? Webre: There are many dimensions and universes parallel to ours. Some alien civilizations aliens come from another dimension, another parallel universe, that is why UFOs can appear and disappear.*

Out of this seed conversation, five years later in 2014 the mapping of the Omniverse is made public as Alfred's book *The Dimensional Ecology of the Omniverse.*

"WELCOME TO A MAP OF THE DIMENSIONAL ECOLOGY OF THE OMNIVERSE."

"Welcome to a map of the dimensional ecology of the Omniverse. Our map of the Omniverse is based on replicable, empirical prima facie evidence that is evaluated according to the law of evidence. The map establishes the existence of a dimensional ecology of intelligent civilizations in the physical universes of time, space, energy, and matter in our multiverse. The dimensional ecology includes the intelligent civilizations of souls, spiritual beings, and Source (God) in the spiritual dimensions.

"The Omniverse, this prima facie evidence establishes, is the sum of the multiverse plus the spiritual dimensions—in other words, all that is."

from *"The Dimensional Ecology of the Omniverse"* by Alfred Lambremont Webre, Introduction

Public debate on existence of afterlife, souls, reincarnation, God bolstered by new scientific evidence on roles in multiverse

VANCOUVER, BC – The scientific basis for an on-going public debate on the existence of a human afterlife, souls, reincarnation and God has been significantly bolstered by the publication of new evidence on the roles of the intelligent civilization of souls and of God in the formation of the universes of the multiverse. These findings have been released in a new book – *The Dimensional Ecology Of The Omniverse* – that proves, using replicable prima facie evidence, the existence of a dimensional ecology among the universes of the multiverse through which souls, spiritual beings and God (an Intelligent Source) are co-creating the planets, solar systems and galaxies of each of the "humungous" number of universes in our multiverse. At present, recent public opinion polls show that only 51% of humanity holds the belief in a "divine entity", and only 51 percent believe in some kind of afterlife.

Reviewing *The Dimensional Ecology Of The Omniverse*, author Barbara Hand Clow writes, "This is a must-read for anyone who wants to fully engage with many dimensions to end absolutely any fear of abandonment, death, or the future."

The Dimensional Ecology Of The Omniverse is sure to have a lasting impact on public debate and private searching about the existence of an afterlife, human souls, and God. The book's author, Canadian-American futurist Alfred Lambremont Webre, writes in the book, "Humanity now is being misinformed about the true nature of the soul, the Interlife, the mechanisms of reincarnation, and ultimately of Source (God). Religions are a large source of erroneous information about these realities. This misinformation is based on texts and ancient religious belief systems that are not scientifically correct and are yet considered sacred, as a matter of faith. Academic science prohibits teaching the reality of life after death, even though empirical evidence supports this hypothesis. Therefore, modern science is also a

445

source of erroneous information about the soul, the Interlife, and Source (God). Cultural and religious conflicts result from the ignorance imposed by religion and an antiquated scientific canon concerning any such spiritual realities. The science of spirit can demonstrate the true nature of the human soul and its spiritual and exopolitical dimensions.

The Dimensional Ecology Of The Omniverse is the result of five years work by Webre, who is a pioneer in frontier science projects. Webre directed the proposed 1977 Carter White House extraterrestrial communication study as a futurist at Stanford Research Institute. Webre's 2000 book, Exopolitics: A Decade of Contact, founded Exopolitics, the science of relations among intelligent civilizations in the multiverse. Using advanced quantum access technology, the U.S. Defense Advanced Research Projects Agency (DARPA) and the Central Intelligence Agency (CIA) time traveled his 2005 book, Exopolitics: Politics, Government, and Law in the Universe, back to 1971, when an unwitting Alfred was examined by a group of approximately 50 CIA and DARPA officials who knew Alfred would be a leading future extraterrestrial and time-travel whistleblower, and would become the developer of the Exopolitics and Dimensional Ecology models of the Omniverse.[202]

YALE LAW SCHOOL GRAD VENTURES BEYOND THE FROZEN-IN-TIME AMBIT OF CLINTON'S PRESIDENTIAL LATE-NIGHT TELEVISION DISCOURSE

Author Barbara Hand Clow writes in her review, "This is a must-read for anyone who wants to fully engage with many dimensions to end absolutely any fear of abandonment, death, or the future."

Universe Books
By Jon Kelly, Vancouver UFO Examiner
April 3, 2014

The April 2, 2014, edition of ABC's "Jimmy Kimmel Live" featured an appearance by President Bill Clinton in which the Yale Law School graduate offered what the public can only presume were seemingly unscripted executive insights concerning possible extraterrestrials, their visitations to earth and unifying influence upon human society. However, [Alfred's lecture] titled "The Dimensional Ecology of the Omniverse" promises to further enrich public understanding of these issues by offering perspective on spiritual realities perhaps novel to and unanticipated by any president in recent U.S. history.

In his new book titled *"The Dimensional Ecology of the Omniverse"* fellow Yale Law School graduate and former director of the proposed 1977 Carter White House extraterrestrial communication study at Stanford Research Institute Alfred Lambremont Webre, JD, MEd, ventures beyond the frozen-in-time ambit of presidential late-night television discourse in a way that considers "replicable prima facie evidence of the existence of a dimensional ecology among the universes of the multiverse through which souls, spiritual beings and God (an Intelligent Source) are co-creating the planets, solar systems and galaxies of each of the "humungous" number of universes in our multiverse."

COLD WAR CHILL

"We know now we live in an ever-expanding universe," President Clinton told Wednesday's "Live" audience, in a pop culture-focused appeal to mass media-informed perceptions of scientific discovery.

"We know that there are billions of stars and planets literally out there and the universe is getting bigger. We know from our fancy telescopes that just in the last two years more than 20 planets have been identified outside our solar system that seem to be far enough away from their suns and dense enough that they might be able to support some form of life," he said.

Echoing retrogressive Cold War sentiments from the 1980s,

the Rhodes Scholar proceeded to outline in brief what he described as the theory behind the American 1996 science fiction disaster film "Independence Day."

"Maybe [that's] the only way to unite this [incredibly] divided world of ours," he suggested. "They're out there. We better think of how all the differences among people on earth would seem small if we felt threatened by a space invader."

In his speech to the United Nations General Assembly, 42nd General Assembly on September 21, 1987, President Reagan then considered how "Perhaps we need some outside universal threat to make us recognize this common [bond]. I occasionally think about how quickly our differences worldwide would vanish, if we were facing an alien threat from outside this world. And yet, I ask you, is not an alien force already among us?"

REMEDY IN SPIRIT

Concerning matters of intercultural conflict Canadian-American futurist Alfred Lambremont Webre proposes in his book how these events "result from the ignorance imposed by religion and an antiquated scientific canon concerning any such spiritual realities. The science of spirit can demonstrate the true nature of the human soul and its spiritual and exopolitical dimensions."

Author Alfred Lambremont Webre, JD, MEd, appears in a forthcoming exclusive interview with journalist Jon Kelly to discuss his new book and the role offered by a science of spirit in breaking the ice between peoples of all nations, worlds and dimensions of the Omniverse.

From Exopolitics.com: "*The Dimensional Ecology of the Omniverse* is a new hypothesis integrating replicable empirical evidence from intelligent civilizations in the universes of the multiverse and from the intelligent civilizations of souls, spiritual beings, and Source (God) in the Afterlife. This new lecture demonstrates a functioning ecology of intelligence in the dimensions in the Omniverse."

448

Author Barbara Hand Clow writes in her review, "This is a must-read for anyone who wants to fully engage with many dimensions to end absolutely any fear of abandonment, death, or the future."

From Exopolitics.com: "Humanity now is being misinformed about the true nature of the soul, the Interlife, the mechanisms of reincarnation, and ultimately of Source (God). Religions are a large source of erroneous information about these realities. This misinformation is based on texts and ancient religious belief systems that are not scientifically correct and are yet considered sacred, as a matter of faith. Academic science prohibits teaching the reality of life after death, even though empirical evidence supports this hypothesis. Therefore, modern science is also a source of erroneous information about the soul, the Interlife, and Source (God). Cultural and religious conflicts result from the ignorance imposed by religion and an antiquated scientific canon concerning any such spiritual realities. The science of spirit can demonstrate the true nature of the human soul and its spiritual and exopolitical dimensions."[203]

As of this writing on May 1, 2015, Inner Traditions/Bear & Co. is scheduled to publish Alfred's book on the Omniverse in December 2015.

SCENE 11

SEPTEMBER 23, 2015 JADE HELM FALSE FLAG

May 2015
Exposing the year-long
September 23, 2015 –October 11-12, 2016
Jade Helm False Flag

NEWSINSIDEOUT REPORT: A GLOBAL EXTINCTION LEVEL FALSE FLAG EVENT IS UNDERWAY UNDER THE MEME "SEPTEMBER 23, 2015" LASTING UNTIL OCT. 11-12, 2016, CHALLENGING THE POSITIVE TIMELINE

BY ALFRED LAMBREMONT WEBRE

NEWSINSIDEOUT.COM

VANCOUVER, BC – In the course of reporting on Jade Helm 15, an apparent martial law drill exercise of the U.S. government, NewsInsideOut.com has discovered what appears to be an attempted global Extinction Level false flag event that is operating under the Meme "September 23, 2015" designed to last until Oct. 2016, and presenting a challenge to the positive timeline that has reportedly supplanted a catastrophic timeline in our Earth's timeline hologram as of December 21, 2012.

"SEPT. 23, 2015": CHALLENGE TO THE POSITIVE TIMELINE?

The "Sept. 23, 2015" year-long false flag is reportedly designed by its controllers to be a near Extinction Level event. However, the Positive Timeline Equation [Positive Future = Positive Timeline + Unity Consciousness] is thought to have supplanted and overcome an outdated Matrix Elite formula that is no longer effective, even if applied in the dimensional ecology by duality consciousness controllers like Dracos and Orion greys, renegade Anunnakis, and demonic Luciferic interdimensional entities behind the "Sept. 23, 2015" event:

Problem + Reaction = Solution [1]

"SEPT. 23, 2015" IS CODE

"Sept. 23, 2015" is code for a dimensional ecology year-long event whose memes are embedded in Illuminati cards, movies, TV, media, music, Bible Prophecy (Rapture), "Ascension", CERN demonic portals, ET invasion/false flag, killer asteroids, Jade Helm, Georgia Guidestones depopulation to 500 million humans, One World Religion, Peace & Security, Antichrist, Second Coming, with the principal upper theatre archetypes being the Pope [Whore of Babylon], USA (Obama) & UK (Crown) [Two-Headed Beast], UN/EU [Seven-Headed, Ten Horned Beast] and King of the North [Russia/Putin].

FALSE FLAG DURATION:
SEPTEMBER 23, 2015 TO OCTOBER 11-12, 2016

The initial phase of the "Sept. 23, 2015" global level false flag is scheduled for a Sept. 22-28, 2015 period around the final Tetra

Lunar Eclipse of 2014-15 [9/28/15], initiating a "Peace & Security" phase of the false flag. The final phase of the false flag is scheduled for a year later, technically on the Jewish Day of Atonement 2016 (October 11-12, 2016)

HIDDEN CONTROLLERS BEHIND "SEPT. 23, 2015" FALSE FLAG YEAR

The "September 23, 2015" [Jewish Day of At-One-Ment] False Flag was planned principally in the 4th and 3rd consciousness densities along an old catastrophic timeline and is being implemented by the following a consortium of controllers still in Duality Consciousness. NewsInsideOut.com has previously reported that the hidden controllers of humanity that have set up the Jews as a tribal ethnicity of social patsies or mind-controlled collectives for Tetrad Lunar cointelpro-like events include the Saturn-Moon mind control Matrix, under the control of the descendants of the Giants crypto-terrestrials originally from the planet Marduk (nor the asteroid belt), and now settled in the rings of Saturn, Mars, Earth's moon and Earth itself. [2]

Hidden controllers of the "September 23, 2015" false flag year can also be classified from the ranks of such documented controller classes as Dracos, Orion Greys, Anunnaki, Ancient Vampire Illuminati, Zionist Illuminati, Jesuits, Bankers, Monarchies, Coneheads, operatives of VatLonUSA, the three-city-state Empire of the Vatican-City of London-Washington, District of Columbia [founded 1871]. [3]

ILLUMINATI SKULL & BONES SHILL JOHN KERRY ON "SEPTEMBER 23, 2015"

U.S. Secretary of State John Kerry, a Yale school mate of this reporter and member of Skull & Bones [2nd Chapter of the Bavarian Illuminati, established at Yale University in 1776 to subvert to American republic to Illuminati designs] was apparently tasked by the "September 23, 2015" controllers to stage the public announcement of the end-date, or "Mass Kill Date" of the year long false flag, which is the Jewish Day of Atonement 2015 Yom Kippur (September 23, 2015), or 500 days from the public statement made in the company of the French Foreign Minister who served as Kerry's spokesperson for the Illuminati "September 23, 2015" coded announcement.

"500 Days" Until Climate Chaos
(May 14, 2014 To September 23, 2015)

Is "Climate Chaos" code for "September 23, 2015" false flag event?

French Foreign Minister & John Kerry

https://www.youtube.com/watch?feature=player_embedded&v=2QDJb6fF8pg

Design of the False Flag:
Peace & Security (Sept. 23, 2015)
to Mass Human Execution/Depopulation
(September 23, 2015)

By this analysis, an unsuspecting human population is "sucked in" by a Peace & Security Series of False Flag Global events on Sept. 22-28, 2015 as follows:

September 23, 2015: Jesuit Pope Francis Bergoglio (Whore of Babylon prophecy code] meets with President Obama in White House (One Head of Two Headed Beast prophecy code);

September 24, 2015: Pope Francis Bergoglio (Whore of Babylon prophecy code] speaks as First Pope in U.S. Congress (One Head of Two Headed Beast prophecy code);

September 25, 2015: Pope Francis Bergoglio (Whore of

Babylon prophecy code] addresses the UN General Assembly ahead of the Post 2015 Summit;

September 28, 2015: Fourth and Last Tetra Lunar eclipse 2014-15

Beginning of the 'Organization of the UN Summit for the adoption of the post-2015 development agenda [4]

According to the false flag plan, it can be deduced, a second Mass Planetary Human Execution/Depopulation occurs on Oct. 11-12, 2016, timed for Yom Kippur or the Jewish Day of Atonement in 2016.

In accordance with Jewish beliefs, acts committed against "Goyim" or non-believers on Yom Kippur are forgiven in the eyes of the Jewish God.

MASS PLANETARY DEPOPULATION WHILE ELITES GO TO MARS COLONIES?

The planned year-long false flag event, around which the U.S. government Jade Helm martial law drill is designed, may take various forms. The holographic projection, crisis actor, and managed mainstream media technologies perfected in prior false flag events such as the JFK assassination (Nov. 22, 1963); 9/11 (September 11, 2001); Hurricane Katrina (Aug. 29, 2005); Hurricane Sandy (Oct. 22, 2012); Sandy Hook Elementary (December 14, 2012) are reportedly to be applied in creating any one or more of the following "events":

1   Dimensionally-engineered/holographically created Asteroid collision or "Planet X-Nibiru" false flag event [5];

2   HAARP and directed energy weapon intentional Yellowstone seismic detonation warfare [6],

3   CERN Dimensional Hell Chaos [7]

4   False Flag ET "Invasion" or False Flag ET "Disclosure"

See also: *Project Blue Beam* - The technology of the September 23, 2015 Jade Helm year-long false flag explained?
The New World Order And Project Blue Beam
http://www.shiftfrequency.com/new-world-order-blue-beam-project/

Under cover of this "false flag" human Elites are evacuated to the secret Mars colonies operated by the Mars Colony Corporation once overseen by U.S. Vice President and David Rockefeller and Council on Foreign Relations darling Richard B. Cheney, another Yale schoolmate of this reporter who flunked out of Yale as a sophomore. [8]

Hidden controller asset Jon Stewart, who announced his retirement "unexpectedly" from Comedy Central earlier in 2015 in coordination with the September 23, 2015 year long false flag, recently announced the Elite Mars colony escape through a comedy meme sketch on the Daily Show with a Yale graduate John Hodgman comedian.

Jon Stewart & John Hodgman, The Daily Show - 2015: Mars-A Space Gated Community

https://www.youtube.com/watch?feature=player_embedded&v=m53llV2Nw3g

Misdirection & Code

As with other major false flags of the 20th & 21st Centuries (September 11, 2001 - "9/11"), for example, the hidden controllers have embedded coded public notice of this false flag in memes around Illuminati cards, movies, TV, media, music, Bible Prophecy (Rapture), "Ascension", CERN demonic portals, ET invasion/false flag, killer asteroids, Jade Helm, Georgia Guidestones depopulation to 500 million humans, One World Religion, Peace & Security, Antichrist, and Second Coming of Christ.

THE ILLUMINATI KNOW WHAT IS COMING SEPTEMBER 22-28, 2015

Besides the Illuminati cards, some of which explicitly refer to the "September 23, 2015" false flag year, the "September 23, 2015" meme is embedded in numerous popular movies ["Evan Almighty"; "Ghostbusters"; "Knowing"; "Tomorrowland"; "Deep Impact [Black President]";"Left Behind"; "Gone Girl"; "Seeking a Friend for the End of the World"; "The Number 23";], TV shows ["3rd Rock from the Sun"; "LOST'; "NCIS'], toys [LEGO Dimensions (CERN)], Music [Beyoncé'; Miley Cyrus] and news media memes ["Climate chaos"].

Renee M has created a 4-part video analysis of the "September 23, 2015" false flag that readers may want to watch at their leisure. Readers may want to view this informative series discounting Renee M's personal belief system in the "Rapture", which does not critically affect the integrity of her research as to the reality of the "September 23, 2015" false flag. [9]

Readers are recommended to watch the 14:33 video [BELOW] by Renee M summarizing some of her evidence. Renee M states that there is a second planned false flag event for October 11-12 Yom Kippur, 2016.

RENEE M. AN ASTEROID OR METEOR WILL HIT THE EARTH ON SEPTEMBER 24, 2015 - YOU HAVE BEEN WARNED!!!

https://www.youtube.com/watch?feature=player_embedded&v=1g0GaGGqzkI

HOW WILL THE POSITIVE TIMELINE & UNITY CONSCIOUSNESS EQUATION DECONSTRUCT THE "SEPTEMBER 23, 2015" FALSE FLAG?

A May 5, 2015 NewsInsideOut.com Panel addresses the issue of whether and how the Positive Timeline & Unity Consciousness

457

Equation deconstruct the "September 23, 2015" false flag.
Panel: 9/28/15 Tetra Lunar Eclipse global false flag for Jade Helm,
Pope, Congress, Obama, UN Post 2015 "Development Agenda"?
WATCH PANEL ON YOU TUBE
https://www.youtube.com/watch?feature=player_embedded&v=
8bNkW-veRCw

JADE HELM: MONETARY RESET; YELLOWSTONE SEISMIC WARFARE, NIBIRU FLYBY PSYOP, ET FALSE FLAG INVASION?

The Panel discusses what form a false flag may take as correlated to the apparent Jade Helm – 15 attempted U.S. government American people's domestic pacification program patterned on the Phoenix Program in Vietnam 1967-1974. [Please see Appendix A for a list of research resources on Jade Helm – 15].

The Panel discusses a number of alternatives, including a Monetary reset; a seismic warfare setting off of the Yellowstone Caldera (for which there is prima facie evidence of a secret program[6]); a Nibiru Flyby (for which there are meme videos now circulating on the Internet predicting a "Nibiru asteroid collision for September 24, 2015[7]); a false flag extraterrestrial invasion, such as that leaked by Operation Paperclip scientist Dr. Wernher von Braun to Dr. Carol Rosin. [Werner von Braun & Dr. Carol Rosin: False Flag Wars and Exopolitics, http://exopolitics.blogs.com/exopolitics/2006/12/eyeopening_int e.html

According to Panelist Peter Kling's book, *You can Survive Armageddon*, at this time, by adopting an alpha state of consciousness, individuals and groups access a positive timeline and exit a catastrophic timeline established by the controllers of the false Matrix in which Earth has been a captive.[11]

According to Panel member Alfred Lambremont Webre, the operation of the Positive Future Equation in the time space hologram of Earth's 3rd and 4th density itself deconstructs any such false flags that may have been constructed by false Matrix forces under conditions of Duality Consciousness ("I win/You Lose") along an obsolete catastrophic timeline no longer operational after December 21, 2012.

The Positive Future Equation is:

Positive Future = Positive Timeline + Unity Consciousness

A 27 page paper explaining it origin and operation in more detail and in four languages can be accessed at www.positivefuture.info

Some observers are contending that the positive holographic timeline did not enter into operation on [or about] December 21, 2012, and that the catastrophic timeline is still operating dominantly and will continue to do so until 2017.

That view appears by the evidence to be flawed. For an extended discussion of the evidence, please see *Creating a Positive Future: Time Science Shows Our Earth is on a Positive Timeline in our Time Space Hologram*

"It's time science, not rocket science that Earth is on a positive timeline."
Positive Future = Positive Timeline + Unity Consciousness

by Alfred Lambremont Webre
www.positivefuture.info

What can you/we do proactively to expose & deconstruct the September 23, 2015 year-long Extinction Level false flag?

We now know that the Positive Future equation suggests that in the synergy between the Positive Timeline and Unity consciousness, a critical mass of humanity is collectively and individually activated for some or more of these suggested actions and policies for a positive future, and synchronistically resources and actors are brought together in multi-dimensional universe processes to manifest a desirable result.

We can Acknowledge the September 23, 2015 event as a false flag publicly, learn about it, share about with family, friends, and networks, create chat groups, personal groups, teaching groups and support groups to share about it and all its dimensions;

We can support researchers, independent media, public groups, and others who speak out against the September 23, 2015 false flag operation and not allow assassination attempts; shilling; cointelpro; use of frequency weapons against them and their family members for attempted intimidation;

We can bear Personal Witness before, on, and after the initial days of the events that they are the September 23, 2015 false flags;

We can reach out to public officials of all levels of all nations and make them aware of the September 23, 2015 – October 16, 2015 false flag;

We can vote into office public officials who vote against and are committed to expose false flag operations and overturn laws based on false flag operations, such as the Patriot Act (USA) and Bill C-51 (Canada);

We can hold Silent Vigils (so they cannot be infiltrated by provocateurs) in public places and Common Law Tribunals presenting the evidence, prosecuting and sentencing the perpetrators of the September 23, 2015 False Flag event;

We can meditate and pray and ask for interdimensional and Divine intervention to deconstruct this planned false flag event of the Dark forces to coopt as many souls as possible and impose tyranny on Earth.

More…

RECOMMENDED READING

BBS Radio taken off-air as James Gilliland & Alfred Lambremont Webre discuss September 23, 2015 Jade Helm False Flag

http://newsinsideout.com/2015/05/bbs-radio-taken-off-air-as-james-gilliland-alfred-lambremont-webre-discuss-september-23-2015-jade-helm-false-flag/

Panel: 9/28/15 Tetra Lunar Eclipse global false flag for Jade Helm, Pope, Congress, Obama, UN Post 2015 "Development Agenda"?

By Alfred Lambremont Webre

http://newsinsideout.com/2015/05/panel-92815-tetra-lunar-eclipse-global-false-flag-for-jade-helm-pope-congress-obama-un-post-2015-development-agenda/

Peter Kling: 2014-2021 "Tribulation" & Positive Timeline. Does Christ return with a decloaking of the Universe fleet?

By Alfred Lambremont Webre

http://newsinsideout.com/2015/04/peter-kling-2014-2021-tribulation-positive-timeline-does-christ-return-with-a-decloaking-of-the-universe-fleet/

BuzzSaw's Sean Stone interviews Laura Eisenhower & News-InsideOut's Alfred Lambremont Webre on Positive Timeline & Secret Mars Colony

http://newsinsideout.com/2015/03/buzzsaws-sean-stone-interviews-laura-eisenhower-newsinsideouts-alfred-lambremont-webre-on-positive-timeline-secret-mars-colony/

Positive Timeline may result in the election in 2016 of a Positive US President, contrary to Matrix time travel pre-identification:

http://newsinsideout.com/2014/12/positive-timeline-positive-2016-us-president-contrary-matrix-time-travel-pre-identification/

VIDEO: Alfred Lambremont Webre: Positive timeline transforms planned 2015 Federal Reserve fiat US Petrodollar collapse through BRICS into Sovereignty and planetary Golden Age

This planned and unsuccessful 2015 (or so) $dollar collapse is actually one of the functional components of the Jesuit-Matrix depopulation plan that includes Fukushima radiation, GMOs, Vaccines, GeoEngineering, Wars, planned financial collapse and the Transhumanist Agenda, all orchestrated along a catastrophic timeline that is no longer operative in our time-space hologram.

461

http://newsinsideout.com/2015/01/alfred-webre-positive-timeline-transforms-planned-2015-dollar-collapse-sovereignty-brics-golden-age/

Positive Future = Positive Timeline + Unity Consciousness - An Editorial

http://newsinsideout.com/2014/12/positive-future-positive-timeline-unity-consciousness-newsinsideout-com-editorial/

ENDNOTES [204]

SCENE 12

THE POSITIVE FUTURE EQUATION

July 2014
Publication of
The Positive Future Equation
King Edward Avenue West
Vancouver, BC

Creating a Positive Future: Time Science Shows Our Earth is on a Positive Timeline in our Time Space Hologram

BY ALFRED LAMBREMONT WEBRE*

- "It's time science, not rocket science that Earth is on a positive timeline."

- Positive Future = Positive Timeline + Unity Consciousness

VANCOUVER, BC

POSITIVE FUTURE = POSITIVE TIMELINE + UNITY CONSCIOUSNESS

A key discovery promulgated in this paper is that (1) a critical mass of humanity is (2) co-creating a positive future, through conscious acknowledgement that (3) we are synergistically traveling along a positive timeline (4) in Unity consciousness.

The Positive Future equation has supplanted and overcome an outdated Matrix Elite formula that is no longer effective:

Problem + Reaction = Solution

POSITIVE FUTURE EQUATION

The Positive Future equation is:

Positive Future = Positive Timeline + Unity Consciousness

The Positive Future equation suggests that in the synergy between the Positive Timeline and Unity consciousness, a critical mass of humanity is collectively and individually activated for some or more of these suggested actions and policies for a positive future, and synchronistically resources and actors are brought together in multi-dimensional universe processes to manifest a desirable result.

POSITIVE PARADOX

The "Progress Paradox" or "Positive Paradox" of our current era is that, although our Earth dimension is on a positive time line, Earth's current bloodline Elites, Negative dimensional entities, Matrix institutions (Governmental forms, Religions; Central Banks), and War & Addiction industries are acting out operational plans that seem based on a false negative timeline, or an actual catastrophic timeline that is occurring in some other dimensional timeline than the positive timeline Earth is demonstrably on.

464

Although humanity has every objective reason to be optimistic about the future, large segments of humanity still reflect this Matric power focus on a false catastrophic timeline.

According to an April 14, 2014 Ipsos survey, In the West, 42% vs. 34% people feel pessimistic about the future, despite the objective scientific reality that humanity is on a positive timeline. China, India, Brazil, Turkey and Russia are more optimistic than pessimistic for their young – but all other countries are more likely to think things will be worse rather than better.[1]

Yet time science demonstrates that our Earth civilization is traveling on a positive timeline within our time space hologram. And time cosmology analysis demonstrates that Unity consciousness ("We are One") is the dominant universal consciousness frequency broadcast, as of December 21, 2012, through the singularity – interdimensional portal – at the core of the specific Universe in which we are based.

Catastrophic duality consciousness ("I win, You Lose") fostered by these Matrix Elites, Negative dimensional entities, and Matrix institutions can no longer can control and thrive on our current positive timeline, as a matter of density and dimensional frequency and time science. Duality consciousness is "Service to Self" and cannot survive in our new Universe consciousness density frequencies.

It is now "time" for the positive timeline to be acknowledged as a scientific reality, and for our individual and collective to transform consciously as a critical mass of ethical humans awaken to the reality of the positive timeline.

Positive timeline in synergy with Unity Consciousness

If you resonate with the positive timeline in synergy with Unity consciousness, you are encouraged to share these insights with others privately and publicly, your family, friends, networks.

Together we can build that critical mass of awakened humanity that acknowledges and collective shifts to being in a reality of a positive timeline Unity consciousness ("We are One") as the new norm.

All you have to do and all we have to do is change our minds, and the positive timeline follows, as a matter of science.

TIME SPACE HOLOGRAM & TIME LINES

One of the early key discoveries of time science is that our own universe of time, space, energy and matter contains, and is composed of time-space holograms, and may be considered itself a time-space hologram, created by a higher intelligence and composed of parallel time lines.

"Our universe includes a time-space hologram, within which our Earth human civilization exists, that is an artificial environment created by a higher intelligence. The higher intelligence that created and maintains our universe, including the time-space hologram that we inhabit, is the spiritual dimension that itself is composed of God/ Source, the intelligent civilizations of souls that incarnate in the time-space hologram, and the intelligent civilization of spiritual beings. In "Simulations back up theory that Universe is a hologram: A ten-dimensional theory of gravity makes the same predictions as standard quantum physics in fewer dimensions," Ron Cowen writes, 'At a black hole, Albert Einstein's theory of gravity apparently clashes with quantum physics, but that conflict could be solved if the Universe were a holographic projection.'

"The time-space hologram we inhabit as Earthling humans is composed of multiple timelines. Time travel and teleportation are methods by which intelligent civilizations navigate the dimensional ecology of both the Exopolitical dimensions (the multiverse) and the spiritual dimensions of the Omniverse. Teleportation consists of point-to-point movement across a single timeline. Time travel consists of movement across more than one timeline."[2]

TIMELINES = PARALLEL LANES IN A MULTI-LANE HIGHWAY

Humanity is based inside a virtual reality composed of multiple, parallel timelines.[3] In simple 3D-3rd density terms, one can visualize timelines in a time-space hologram as parallel lanes of a multi-lane highway.

As a collective consciousness, humanity can find itself on a changed timeline from a more catastrophic lane (global coastal flooding event) to a more positive lane (landing a Utopia on Earth). Catastrophic timelines (lanes in the highway) that may have been foreseen through technological time travel (chronovision), scientific remote viewing, or psychic remote viewing can fail to materialize as humanity finds itself on a positive timeline.

ORIGINS OF THE FALSE "CATASTROPHIC TIMELINE"

This paper addresses a recent Italian magazine article that misrepresented my views on the positive timeline. The magazine invited me to publish a response. The title of the Italian magazine article was: *"Alfred Webre: the global disasters that are affecting our planet, are the effects of "Kill Zone" Planet X."[4]*

Thankfully, the Italian magazine has published this, my response paper on Creating a Positive Future:

Creare un futuro positivo: la scienza sostiene che la nostra terra si trova in un momento positivo del nostro ologramma spazio-temporale

http://www.segnidalcielo.it/creare-un-futuro-positivo-la-scienza-sostiene-che-la-nostra-terra-si-trova-in-un-momento-positivo-del-nostro-ologramma-spazio-temporale/

EDGAR CAYCE REMOTE VIEWING OF 21ˢᵗ CENTURY GLOBAL COASTAL EVENT

The Italian March 8, 2014 article relies on my 1974 book *The Age of Cataclysm* that was a first book to integrate modern earth sciences with parapsychology and analyze the remote viewing predictions of psychic Edgar Cayce of a global costal flooding event occurring on Earth early in our 21ˢᵗ Century.

A global coastal event may be triggered by a variety of astronomical events causing massive tsunamis and earth changes having catastrophic effects on human civilization such as the global coastal event destroying Earth's great maritime civilization (Atlantis), caused by the solar system catastrophe of 9500 BC when a fragment of the supernova Vela entered the solar system.[5]

2010 FARSIGHT MILITARY-TRAINED REMOTE VIEWERS PREDICTED GLOBAL COASTAL EVENT OF JUNE 2013

In the course of research on potential impending transitional changes during the 2012-13 time horizon, I identified in 2010 what can be described as two parallel realities, each buttressed by independent sets of data and personal and institutional decisions – a *2012-13 catastrophic timeline* and a *2012-13 positive future timeline*.[6]

The two parallel 2012-13 timelines were quite opposite in nature.

The cataclysmic timeline envisioned 2012-13 as a time when the Earth is hit by destructive "solar flares, large meteors, tsunamis, world-wide coastal inundations, mega-catastrophe." This was congruent with the Edgar Cayce remote viewed global coastal event, as well as hermeneutic interpretation of prophecies of Earth Changes.

As evidence of a possible 2012-13 catastrophic timeline, researcher Dr. Courtney Brown pointed to the results of a recent

Farsight Institute *remote viewing study of global climate change 2008 – 2013*. Expecting to find marginal effects of global climate change on coastal areas in 2013, Dr. Brown reported instead remote viewers found a catastrophic 2013 timeline, and a global coastal event for June 2013 that devastated global coastal cities, with the U.S. Capitol in Washington, DC under water.

1971 DARPA CHRONOVISOR PROBE OF WASHINGTON, DC – 2013 GLOBAL COASTAL EVENT. US SUPREME COURT BUILDING UNDER 100 FT. OF BRACKISH WATER

In a remarkable coincidence (or synchronicity), both the Farsight Institute and a chronovisor probe in the early 1970s by DARPA's Project Pegasus chose archetypal targets in Washington, DC right across the street from each other. *Project Pegasus* chose to view the U.S. Supreme Court building in 2013 via chronovisor and Project Pegasus participant and whistleblower Andrew D. Basiago "found that the Supreme Court building was under 100 feet of stagnant water" in a chronovisor probe. U.S. chrononaut Basiago adds, "There were second, third and fourth dimensional chronovisors. I went to Washington, DC in 2013 bodily. They poured water out of my boots. That particular chronovisor was not a screen or a template. It was a cube of light in the nature of a time-space hologram that enveloped us with the result that we physically went to the time-place they had tuned in." The chronovisor was originally developed by two Vatican scientists in conjunction with Enrico Fermi and later refined by DARPA scientists.

The 2010 Farsight Institute probe targeted the U.S. Capitol building in 2013, and some remote viewer reports viewed the U.S. Capitol in ruins along side deep water.

PREDICTED 2013 GLOBAL COASTAL EVENT OCCURRED ALONG ANOTHER, CATASTROPHIC TIMELINE DIMENSION

The June 2013 global coastal event predicted by Edgar Cayce remote viewing, 1971 DARPA chronovisor probe, 2010 Farsight Institute probe in fact occurred in another timeline dimension, according to Dr. Courtney Brown, director of the Farsight Institute.

In a video update, Dr. Brown concludes that *15 February 2013 meteor event* over Russia, the largest since the Tunguska event, coupled with the close approach of the roughly 50 metre asteroid *2012 DA14* that occurred about 15 hours later may constitute the meteor or asteroid event referenced in the Farsight Institute study, which predicted a global coastal event destroying most coastal cities on the planet in June 2013. Dr. Brown states he does not expect any other meteor or coastal event between February 16, 2013 and June 1, 2013 based on the Farsight study. Dr. Brown refers to the holographic nature of reality and to the his remote viewers having possibly viewed a global coastal event happening in June 2013 on Earth in some other timeline or holographic version of Earth or parallel universe.[7]

PLANET X AND THE CATASTROPHIC TIMELINE

Some have speculated that a Planet X (Nibiru or Second Sun type flyby) would be responsible for the June 2013 global coastal event predicted by the Farsight Institute study. [8]

Dr. Brown's *interim* update appears to suggest that Dr. Brown does not expect any other meteor or coastal event between February 16, 2013 and June 1, 2013 and that the Farsight Institute report states that no global coastal event caused by Planet X can be expected through June 1, 2013.

WHY THE GLOBAL COASTAL EVENT DARPA FORESAW DID NOT MATERIALIZE

U.S. chrononaut Andrew D. Basiago writes that the 1971 DARPA probe was actually to an alternative catastrophic time line. He states, "We are now starting to discover why the global coastal flooding event that I saw when DARPA sent me to 2013 via chronovisor in 1971 didn't eventuate on this time line. NASA is now reporting that in 2012, a solar flare almost destroyed Earth. According to my source to the secret US agency the Department of Physicists, had the huge solar flare occurred six to seven days before it did, when the Earth was one degree of tilt in another position, it would have "wreaked havoc" on Earth. Apparently, the probe I was involved in at ITT Defense Communications in Nutley, NJ on November 5, 1971 for the Office of Naval Intelligence took us to an alternate time line where the devastating effects of such an event in 2012 were evident in 2013, including Washington, D.C. being 100 feet under water."

Dr. Courtney Brown's February 16, 2013 *interim* update on the Farsight Institute report and Andrew D. Basiago's conclusions regarding DARPA's 1971 chronovisor probe of 2013 appear both to conclude that the respective catastrophic timelines viewed in each study are not the actual (non-catastrophic) timelines that Earth is actually experiencing in 2013.

THE FALSE CATASTROPHIC TIMELINE & FALSE FLAG OPERATIONS

As stated, Matrix Elites, Negative dimensional entities, and Matrix institutions (Governmental forms, Banks, Religions) appear to be operating from (1) duality consciousness ("I win, You lose"), (2) to create a false catastrophic timeline and thus attempt to maintain hegemony over Earth and humanity.

Using the primary playbook of the False Flag Operation, the Matrix powers appears to be employing an End Times script, ecocide, and depopulation through Weather Warfare; Tectonic

Warfare; Biowarfare (Ebola; GMOs; Chemtrails; Famine); World War III memes; Negative dimensional warfare; Religious warfare; and other means.[9]

These efforts cannot find a stable dimensional reality along the positive timeline and have an increasingly short shelf life in the minds of a humanity that is now bathed in the universe, galactic and solar waves of Unity consciousness.

The positive timeline & Unity Consciousness

In 2012-13, *Dr. Carl Joseph Calleman*, an expert on the Mayan concepts of time and cosmology, stated in an interview with me, "the universal alternating energy wave movements end, and Earth is set on a gradual setting of a potential to reach advanced utopian planet status – a virtual 'Garden of Eden'".

Dr. Calleman writes the positive timeline *envisions* 2012-13 and the years that follow as: "2012 heralds Earth's entry into the Golden Age, and between now and then is a time of transition from life as you have known it into life totally in harmony with all of Nature."

Universe singularity now emanating energy for 'enlightened Unity Consciousness'

According to Mayan time and cosmology expert, Dr. Carl Johan Calleman, October 28, 2011 marked a portal in linear time when the singularity [interdimensional portal] at the core of our own universe began to emanate a constant "enlightened universal consciousness."[10]

Unity Consciousness is a consciousness that realizes "We are One."

Likewise, the interdimensional portal or singularity at the center of our galaxy (our galactic center 'black hole') modulates this universe consciousness energy wave as well.

This is, by any standard, exceedingly good scientific news.

Universal, alternating energy wave movements have been a feature of our universe, says *Dr. Carl Johan Calleman*, since the Big

Bang, and it is these wave movements that have shaped the nature of consciousness in our universe over the past 18 billion years.

What, you may ask, does this universal wave of unity consciousness have to do with you or your reality?

In a word, everything.

The wave of unity consciousness – like all universe energy wave emanations, creates the 'meme' or story content of our personal and our collective reality.

Dr. Calleman's discoveries are suggesting that our highest thoughts and 'memes' are/may in fact be sourced from the energy waves of the universe singularity, mediated through the galactic singularity – the black hole at the center of our galaxy the Mayans called *Hunab Ku*.

The singularity of our solar system is Sol, our sun - a dimensional portal to other galaxies, according to physicist *Nassim Haramein*.

These universe singularity energy waves serve as carrier waves of 'the universe's mind and spirit software' - the way that the intentional universe (some call it source, the 'sea of Light' or God) lets us know of its intention for consciousness in the entire universe.

As a practical matter, does it matter if you are tuned in and commit to Universal consciousness universe energy wave of unity consciousness?

Yes – the universe energy waves we humans tune in and commit to determine our planetary status and how we reach our potential as a planet.

Positive Timeline: Earth will be utopia, not a dystopia or

The good news is that our universe singularity is now emanating 'utopia' consciousness waves on its alternating energy carrier waves.

The more we humans are individually and collectively tuned into the universal energy wave of 'enlightened universal consciousness,' and committed to achieving unity, non-dualistic consciousness, then the stronger the 'positive timeline' becomes, and the more rapidly we achieve our potential as a planet – "a potential to reach advanced utopian planet status."

The Positive Paradox

The "Positive Paradox" is although that Earth is objectively and scientifically on a positive timeline in a field of Unity Consciousness, the more humanity as a critical mass fully internalize and acknowledge this reality, the more it manifests.

The term 'conscious' is used in Unity Consciousness to emphasize how important individual commitment to achieving unity consciousness is.

One psychiatrist professor I know stated, "Humans are Velcro for the negative and Teflon for the positive. Because avoiding the negative was so important in our evolution – avoiding getting eaten in the jungle – our brains tend to remember the negative and forget the positive."

Unity consciousness can be expressed in a simple realization: 'You and I are not we but one.'

Dr. Calleman *writes*, "To begin with, for all that we know it is designed to bring a shift to unity consciousness where the human mind no longer will be dominated by any dark filter. We will in other words become "transparent" and I believe this is the particular consciousness – seeing reality the way it is with no separation - that so many are waiting for. Not just any consciousness, but one that transcends the dualities of the past and aids the human beings to see the unity of all things.

"The reason that this kind of unity consciousness can be beneficial to the planet, and to mankind, is that it is one that leads to the transcendence of all separation (between man and woman, man and nature, ruler and ruled, east and west, etc). I feel that without the manifestation of such a shift in consciousness the world will sooner or later come to an end.

"People with a dualist and separating consciousness are somewhat like cancer cells in the body of the Earth with little regard to its larger whole and would eventually generate a collapse of its ecosystem. Only a shift to unity consciousness will forever stop the unchecked exploitation of the Earth and on a deeper level make us understand that we are part of creation and need to live in harmony with it. But will such a shift just happen automatically?"

CREATING A POSITIVE FUTURE

There are many modes of expression in many Earth cultures of on how to create a platform for humanity on Earth to awaken and thrive along the scientific reality of our new collective positive timeline.[11]

Here are some suggested collective actions and policies for this platform. Your suggested collective actions and policies are welcome.

You can submit your suggested collective actions and policies via any of the channels linked to below.

Truth & Disclosure – A full public disclosure of the presence of intelligent civilizations in Earth's environment and a global referendum as to whether and on what conditions humanity should enter into relations and space travel, space colonization, space governance, with organized intelligent universe, multiverse, and Omniverse society.

New Energy, Teleportation & Time Travel – A full public disclosure of secret (new energy, zero point, free, antigravity, exotic) new energy sources now available for application on Earth. Public implementation and rollout of sequestered of free energy technologies for powering dwellings, human settlements, industry, transport and propulsion, communication and many other areas.

Implementation of teleportation as a global, national, regional and local transportation system, replacing polluting fossil fuel vehicles (trains, buses, trucks, autos) and their intensive land use in highways, railways, and urban freeways, as well as of a regulated time travel public education program.

Recognition of Animals as sentient beings with rights – Worldwide grant of personhood rights to animals with concomitant rights against murder, slaughter, torture, and cruel and inhumane treatment. Special intelligent civilization status for cetaceans including whales and dolphins. Development of healthy, safe, tasty protein meat substitutes for humanity's consumption and nutrition.

Secure Online Direct Democracy at the local, regional, national, and global level – Secure virtual technology now permits the implementation of Swiss canton democracy worldwide. There is no more need for intermediaries such as City Councils, State or Provincial Legislatures, National Parliaments or Congresses, or even, ultimately in time, a gathering of nations such as the United Nations. Experience over the centuries has shown that the powers that be buy off all intermediaries. Direct virtual democracy adapts secure virtual technologies and provides virtual hack-proof citizen voting at the municipal, provincial/state, regional, national, and world level. Under direct virtual democracy, the entire city votes on municipal laws; the entire nation votes on national laws; the world population votes on global standards, all duly informed by government staff at the respective local, national and world level. Municipal Government, for example, is tasked with efficiently picking up the garbage and managing the city according to the laws passed by local virtual democracy.

Reinvention of money as a human right and public utility like air, water or electricity available for creative investment at public money utilities. A global ban on privately controlled central banks like the "U.S. Federal Reserve System" and on privately owned commercial banks. Support of complementary currencies. Licensing of consumer cooperatively owned banks. Imposition of heavy criminal penalties for violation and astronomical fines, for individuals, organizations, and nations.

Social guarantees in the form of annual income, health care, and elementary, secondary, and post-secondary educa-

tion for every person on the planet, for life. Funded by universal state pools, tax on all financial transactions and by post graduation contributions to education plan, and more. Implementation of traditional and alternative, as well as advanced extraterrestrial medical technologies.

World Debt Forgiveness – Global forgiveness of all public and private debts – a world bankruptcy for a bankrupt system and an end to the debt – fiat money prison system. Criminalization of charging interest on money and of fractional reserve lending.

Disenfranchisement of the state power of monarchies and religions worldwide – The UK monarchy and the Vatican are examples of the abuses that occur when two institutions based on non-democratic principles (Divine Right of Kings and Popes) are given established state rights in a modern democratic world.

Criminalization of the war industry – A criminalization of and global ban on war, genocide, and depopulation in all its varied forms, overt and covert. A ban on war as a dispute resolution method. A permanent ban on the design, production, or sale of weapons systems, including nuclear weapons, space-based weapons, and conventional weapons. A permanent ban on the maintenance of offensive armed forces. Imposition of heavy criminal penalties for violation and astronomical fines, for individuals, organizations, and nations.

Criminal Prosecution and Conviction of War Crimes Racketeering Organization and Restorative Justice for War Crimes Victims – Criminalization and rigorous prosecution of the international war crimes racketeering organization for a planning and implementing a genocidal depopulation program, including (and not limited to): (a) planning and triggering wars and armed conflicts through false flag operations; (b) regional and global radiation genocide and ecocide through depleted uranium (DU) and the nuclear agenda; (c) planning and implementing environmental war attacks including geo-engineering, weather warfare, HAARP, chemtrails, and scalar weapons robotization and genocide of humanity, famine, vaccines, GMO foods, DNA manipulation and more; (d) Carrying out a program of assassination and Cointelpro terror against activists, researchers and social inventors in the multiple areas of peace research; new energy; food and nutrition; radiation; democracy and electoral politics; (e) Carrying out as DOPE INC. a lethal, 300 hundred year old conspiracy to addict humanity to narcotics and to criminalize useful substances such as hemp for profit and enslavement; (f) the transhumanist agenda of population mind control through nano-weapons, emf and other weapons. There is no statute of limitations on murder. Imposition of heavy criminal penalties for violation and astronomical fines, for individuals, organizations, and nations.

HOW WILL THESE SUGGESTED COLLECTIVE ACTIONS AND POLICIES FOR A POSITIVE FUTURE MANIFEST ALONG HUMANITY'S POSITIVE TIMELINE?

The basic equation of a positive future suggests that these collective actions and policies (or variations of them to achieve essentially the same goals) will manifest out of the synergy of the positive timeline and humanity's awakening to Unity consciousness.

The Positive Future equation reflects a new level of collective manifestation by humanity and its individuals, resulting from the synergistic dynamics of the positive timeline and a humanity awakening to Unity consciousness.

JOIN & ACT

Join in our awakening communities committed to the positive timeline and Unity consciousness, including:

- **Comments Section** – Add your thoughts below

- *Email us* at Exopolitics@exopolitics.com

- **Facebook:** Discuss in Positive Future group on Facebook *https://www.facebook.com/groups/positivefuture/*

- **Positive Future News (Free):** Subscribe *http://bit.ly/1tiP0dO*

REFERENCES

* - About Alfred Lambremont Webre

http://exopolitics.blogs.com/exopolitics/2008/10/post.html

[1] People in western countries pessimistic about future for young people

Ipsos MORI Global Trends Survey

http://www.ipsos-mori.com/researchpublications/researcharchive/3369/People-in-western-countries-pessimistic-about-future-for-young-people.aspx

[2] Webre, Alfred Lambremont (2014-03-19). The Dimensional Ecology of the Omniverse (p. 17 - 18). Universe Books. Kindle Edition. *www.dimensionalecology.com*

[3] See Webre, Alfred Lambremont (2014-03-19). The Dimensional Ecology of the Omniverse. Universe Books. *www.dimensionalecology.com*

[4] "Alfred Webre: i disastri globali che stanno colpendo il nostro pianeta, sono gli effetti della "Kill Zone" di Planet X" | Segni dal Cielo - Portale web di UFO News, Cerchi nel grano, profezie maya, Convegni e seminari *http://www.segnidalcielo.it/alfred-webre-i-disastri-globali-che-stanno-colpendo-il-nostro-pianeta-sono-gli-effetti-della-kill-zone-di-planet-x/*

[5] Alfred Lambremont Webre, JD & Phillip H. Liss, PhD, The Age Of Cataclysm, (1974-New York: GP Putnam's Sons, Berkley Paperback) - *http://exopolitics.blogs.com/exopolitics/2012/07/the-age-of-cataclysm-prophetic-1974-book-now-required-reading-about-predicted-impacts-of-a-2013-brow.html*

[6] Webre, Alfred Lambremont Are you on a 2012-13 catastrophic or positive future timeline? Part 1

http://exopolitics.blogs.com/exopolitics/2011/12/are-you-on-a-2012-13-catastrophic-or-positive-future-timeline-part-i.html

[7] Webre, Alfred Lambremont, "Dr. Courtney Brown - Russia meteor & asteroid 2012 DA14 may constitute 2013 "global coastal event" remote viewed in another timeline",

http://exopolitics.blogs.com/exopolitics/2013/02/video-dr-courtney-brown-russia-meteor-asteroid-2012-da14-may-constitute-2013-global-coastal-event-re.html

[8] Webre, Alfred Lambremont, "Planet X Update: Is Earth on a positive timeline, 2013-2020?"
http://exopolitics.blogs.com/exopolitics/2013/02/is-earth-on-a-positive-timeline-2013-2020.html

[9] Please see extensive documentation at *www.Ecologynew.com*

[10] Webre, Alfred Lambremont, "GOOD NEWS! Universe singularity now emanating pre-wave energy for 'enlightened unity consciousness'"

http://exopolitics.blogs.com/exopolitics/2011/12/good-news-universe-singularity-now-emanating-pre-wave-energy-for-enlightened-unity-consciousness.html

[11] Webre, Alfred Lambremont, **10+ Policies for a Positive Future**

http://exopolitics.blogs.com/exopolitics/2013/09/10-policies-for-a-positive-future.html

10 + Políticas para un futuro positivo

http://exopolitics.blogs.com/exopolitica_mexico/2013/09/10-pol%C3%ADticas-para-un-futuro-positivo.html

UPPER THEATRE: RECOVERY

Upper Theatre: Recovery was published briefly online in 2000 as Journey I: Recovery and withdrawn awaiting its time synch

UPPER THEATRE:
RECOVERY

ALFRED LAMBREMONT WEBRE
J.D. M.ED.

INTRODUCTION BY
GERI DESTEFANO-WEBRE, PH.D.

For Gaga

Introduction to the Journey
By Geri DeStefano-Webre, Ph.D.

As a reader, you may be drawn to dismiss the information set forward in this book, out of hand. You might be entertaining thoughts like how can a man, so obviously battling mental illness be counted on as a credible witness/reporter of events so speculative and, sometimes, abstract in the extreme?

I want to quote from George Becker in his "The Mad Genius Controversy: A Study in the Sociology of Deviance."

> *"The aura of "mania" endowed the genius with a mystical and inexplicable quality that served to differentiate him from the typical man, the bourgeois, the philistine, and, quite importantly, the "mere" man of talent; it established him as the modern heir of the ancient Greek poet and seer and, like his classical counterpart, enabled him to claim some of the powers and privileges granted to the "divinely possessed" and "inspired."*

Throughout our history, as a race, there are those of us who have been described as "mad" and dangerous to the rest of the "normal" populace. The Greek Oracles of ancient times were usually so unhinged that they were sheltered very closely with every survival need attended to. They might have been mad but they were sought out by Kings and common folk alike to divine the future.

In more contemporary times, Hans Christian Andersen, of fairy-tale fame, wove some of the darkest tales plumbed from the depths of his manic-depression. I can remember, as a child, being chilled by the shadowy images his writing evoked. Such "benign" stuff these fairy tales are!

487

As a professional psychic with a PH.D. in psychology I've had the opportunity in 30 odd years to observe hundreds of clients. Some came for therapy, others to expand their psychic awareness. In my own practice I was struck most profoundly by those who were creative geniuses and tormented souls. Artists, writers, musicians, futurists, scientists, lawyers and doctors made their way to my doorstep deep in the throes of whatever mental illness possessed them. The dilemma, as a practitioner, is how to strike a balance between functioning in the "real" world and still provide an outlet for this creative genius.

It occurred to me, through the years, that certain forms of mental illness, specifically manic-depression, had a function and place within the human psyche. This mental state allowed for certain definable flashes of insight and creativity. And yet, living and surviving on the mundane level can be painful and problematic. Most people suffering with this particular challenge may be able to maintain the semblance of normal reality but only for very short periods at a time. Marriages, careers and social interactions are often at risk in the face of someone suddenly turning "visionary."

One of the catch phrases of the New Age has been "altered state of consciousness." People in all walks of life have been drawn to meditation, fire walking, drugs, enlightenment intensives, gurus, Tantra, Yoga, and psychic development to name just a few. They were drawn to the heightened sense of realities not normally accessible in our waking state. People saw these altered states as the gateway to creativity and insight. Some found IT and others still struggle. And, by some fluke of genetics, and as a result of "faulty wiring" there are those among us who just access these altered states naturally!

I see this book as a journey and as a work of courage. Alfred Webre is my husband and soul mate. Through the time we've spent together I've watched him wage a battle, sometimes fierce and unsettling, with the mental illness that has plagued and enriched his life. At the depths of one of his depressions I suggested that he update one of his books, "The

Age of Cataclysm" and perhaps write a book on his personal journey through manic-depression. My thinking at the time was he needs something to focus on and give him some purpose. That was in July shortly after "God" died and left Alfred both, devastated and exhilarated. He and I had been working together to come to grips with his attraction to cults and to move into a state of recovery. This was a task I felt well prepared for as I had done a great deal of "exit therapy" over the years with a variety of cult members.

What emerged was a book that was a combination of both of these focal points: his visionary insights into the coming times and his often, painful insights into his own state of mind. The two are inextricably connected. One could not have happened without the other.

The courage here comes from Alfred's willingness to expose his process. This is where you, as reader, will be called upon to integrate what is being presented with your own notions of mental illness. Most people will be tempted to dismiss the visionary insights because of the process that gave birth to them. Particularly if those visionary insights are uncomfortable and threatening to their "world view." It's one thing to be transported by a Rachmaninoff or Tchaikovsky Concerto (both composers apparently manic-depressive) it's another to be shown the possibility of an ETI initiative!

So I would ask you the reader to open your mind to the possibilities presented in this book. As a psychic I have been present to the more subtle ebbs and flows of reality, so called! Over the years I have watched the emerging trends of information regarding earth changes and the coming times. Scores of writers and prophets have come forward with insights and pieces to the great cosmic jigsaw puzzle. All are widely divergent in scope and vision.

Who's right? Who's wrong? Maybe that's not the real question here. The fact is that SOMETHING is afoot! There are huge shifts in the collective unconscious and there are tremendous shifts in the conscious world around us. We are being asked to wake up from our long drowsy complacency and recover! Recover our power, our unique human potential and create a new paradigm.

Part of that recovery process is to no longer perpetrate secrets. We can no longer stay in a perpetual state of denial. This is the cornerstone to recovery from any kind of substance or abuse. The AA programs of recovery have made these concepts household words all over the globe. Millions of people have tackled the challenges of recovery in their personal lives. This sets the groundwork for us all to identify and recover from an even more sinister level of abuse.

Alice Miller, the famed Swiss psychoanalyst, sets forth the theory that the child looks towards the parent for love and guidance. They trust and are loyal to that parent even when that parent abuses them. She further posits that this is why Hitler was allowed to come to power and instigate the atrocities in the German Reich. The people saw Hitler as "father" and followed blindly and through a state of denial.

Now, we are faced with a similar challenge. Our government, in the guise of the benevolent father, has been given authority to take actions, even though they are fraught with secrecy and "abuse" that are supposedly in the best interests of the populace. We can't even imagine that a democracy would be capable of depriving of us of our basic civil rights. A good father wouldn't do that! But what if our "father" and the puppet master, secret cartels are psychotic? What if they are gripped by their own delusional machinations?

It takes one to know one! Perhaps the Prophets of our coming age can see further and deeper into the vast labyrinth that envelops us. Perhaps, just consider the possibility, that because of their own struggle for recovery and their courage to fight that they present US with the roadmap to our collective recovery.

It's not a comfortable thought. Recovery never is. Recovery upsets the homeostasis, the delicate balance of nature. Some of us would just as soon be in denial and in our comfort zone.

And, we can't stay there forever. Evolution and growth are

490

difficult territories to navigate. Probably not for the faint of heart. But we DO have pilots to guide us through!

Just consider the possibility!

"Thou art Peter
and Upon this Rock
I shall found my Church"

—'HOLY SPIRIT' ENTITY,
SPEAKING TELEPATHICALLY, SEPTEMBER 1973

"Alfred is at the border between genius and madness."

—LAZARIS,
CHANNELED ENTITY, 1981

"Just because you think you are a child of destiny,
Does not mean you are a child of destiny."

—SALT SPRING ISLAND, BC
OCTOBER, 1998

"Write a book about your life. But write it as fiction.
Otherwise, no one will believe you."

—MOTHER

492

Mayan cosmology scholars now hold that during 1998-2001 the Earth is aligning with the galactic equator. The Earth's 26,000 year galactic cycle will end, according to the Mayan calendar, on December 22, 2012. This is said to inaugurate an age of earth changes.

Of UFO interest, the July 11, 1991 Mexico City UFO sighting occurred on the exact date of the Mayan Sixth Sun eclipse, predicted by the Mayan calendar in 755 AD to represent return of the "space brothers". The sighting was documented on 17 different independent video-cams. Scotland's Skywatch International has an excellent report on the July 11, 1991 sighting including computer enhancements of the video-cam images.

We're developing a "context" interpretation theory for high-synchronicity UFO events like the Sixth Sun UFO event. The theory seems to hold whether the UFO event was dimensional, extraterrestrial, geo-electromagnetic or MILAB -"Nellis AFB" (military abduction/military craft) technology.

—ALFRED WEBRE
INTERNET POST, MARCH 3, 1999

CHAPTER 1

JOURNEY

My journey is a story of three decades in the dark but illuminated worlds of cults, higher intelligence, and manic depression. The journey is still in process, and is now along the path of recovery from these dimensions. If I were asked, "What have you learned from these years of search, confusion, and truth?" I would not say they were a waste of life's precious gift. I would say that I had been given the gift of compressed living; experiencing multiple lifetimes of lessons and insights in 30 short years.

Cults, manic-depressive psychosis, and higher intelligent beings have many effects or functions in common. They each catapult the individual into a new, different level of reality that is a quantum away from the "normal" world. They each can function as microscopes; lenses through which an individual can capture and understand dimensions of reality they would never know existed. They can also create delusional, destructive worlds for the person caught in them.

When cults, manic depression and higher intelligence are brought together in one person, one result is a chaotic life lived at the intersection of spirituality, power, destiny, and delusion.

A chaotic life is some part of the story of my journey. That I am even alive to tell this tale I attribute to a higher power. The odds are that I would have perished somewhere along the way. Yet a chaotic, delusional life is not my whole story. If I look down on my life's design, I have experienced deep and lasting inner growth.

My journey into cults, manic depression and higher intelligence began in 1973 when I met the Messiah.

I call him the Messiah because that is what he called himself the second time we met, and I half believed him. The Messiah had a brilliant labyrinthine mind and was a professor of psychology at a major university in the United States of America. He told me he had been contacted some months before we met by higher intelligent beings who informed him he was the Messiah. By the time we met he had constructed an elaborate world-view of his Messiahood, integrating it into parapsychology, cognitive psychology, and prophecy. He called me his first Angel.

Soon we began meeting frequently. I had originally been referred to the Messiah because I was looking for a parapsychologist, one who could explain to me this science of the paranormal I was just beginning to learn. What I found was brilliance and psychopathology rolled into one being, the Messiah. I had not been told the Messiah had been released the month earlier from a psychiatric ward.

Some chords – of authority, knowledge, ancient knowing, latent psychosis – stirred deeply within me, and I began to seep into his reality as Messiah. I achieved an identity. If he was the Messiah, then I was the Paraclete – Greek for lawyer or advocate; symbolic of the Holy Spirit. I left my job as environmental lawyer to take up the duties of the Paraclete.

The Messiah and the Paraclete had begun a cult composed of two persons, known in psycho-pathological terms as a *folie a deux*, a folly of two.

I found myself a member and creator of a self-referent world, bending science, paranormal, prophecy, and world events to its cause. The year 1973 was a great year for the Messiah and the

Paraclete to join forces in this reality. 1973 was, according to some traditions, the year of the beginning of the fight between good and evil. It was a prophetic time of open scientific integration of the known sciences with the sciences of the paranormal and human consciousness. Extraterrestrial intelligence (ETIs for short) were having a field day, with record flaps over North America.

We found that extraterrestrial intelligence encompasses a broad reality. ETI may be extraplanetary beings; they may be beings inhabiting unknown dimensions parallel to ours. We saw that phenomena known as unidentified flying objects may or may not be our very, very human psychological perceptions of what extraterrestrial spacecraft "should" look like. We did not limit our approach to ETI solely to the study the nature of unidentified flying objects. That would be tantamount to limiting the study of human civilization to a study of its vehicles.

The Messiah and the Paraclete felt that multiple dimensions of reality seemed to be accelerating toward a global transformation, with us two beings of destiny at the center of it all.

We worked hard to prepare ourselves for this transformation. The Messiah held tutorials for me on cognitive psychology and parapsychology in all of its manifestations, from the study of precognition to cases suggestive of reincarnation. The theory of artificial incarnation held that any person could enhance their talents and abilities by imagining himself or herself the reincarnation of an important being. Within this mindset, we each became the reincarnations of prominent historical, artistic and scientific figures, appropriate to our prophetic stature.

I found my own grasp of reality shifting, taking on the Messiah's psychopathology. At times, in solitary meditation I felt a deep cosmic consciousness, expansion of being and awareness. I was able to compartmentalize the different parts of my life, and still deal credibly with a world that did not suspect my hidden prophetic world.

At the same time, I found myself becoming more and more like the Messiah, seeing world events as designed to lead me into a significant historical role. I would cry, asking "Why me?" Still, led on by the adrenaline of this delusional Mission, I continued.

One night I was visited by an alien intelligence. It came upon me as an invisible presence, expanding my being and knowing beyond what I thought capable. We conversed telepathically. It said it was the Holy Spirit and I was the Rock it would build on. The Holy Spirit entity said that as the well being of mankind fell, I would be called on. I stayed in a reverie for hours. Higher intelligence would follow me my entire journey. I kept this visitation to myself for years.

Meanwhile, the Messiah and the Paraclete needed a field theory to explain why we were the chosen, and how we would accomplish a world transformation. Our answer came from the ETIs. Together we studied and discussed the known cases of ETI encounters, and the theories of higher intelligence. We speculated that certain ETI encounters were dream-like, and perhaps subject to the laws of dream interpretation. We interpreted a number of ETI encounters as though they were dreams.

One reported ETI encounter stood out. During the encounter, one of the human contactees had fired a rifle at an alien humanoid. The contactee reported that the bullet, while in trajectory, slowed almost to a standstill, and was "turned inside out." In that very dream-like report, we thought, lay the key to the future. A single bullet turned inside out was in reality a clue which higher intelligence had embedded for us. It told us the whole story of how the transformation was to happen.

The full context of why this ETI encounter was so important came from our ongoing study and brainstorming about world conspiracies, and in particular the conspiracy behind the assassination of John F. Kennedy. The Messiah had turned me onto the Kennedy assassination conspiracy theory, and we discussed it avidly for hours. I became a conspiracy student and read widely on conspiracies in general. Together, we had mapped the terrestrial elites and the conspiratorial groups that would be threatened by an ETI landing.

498

We concluded that, as Messiah and Paraclete, we were the earthly captains of the ETIs, the humans the ETIs would rely on in bringing in a new human society.

We found that central to a conspiracy theory of the Kennedy assassination was the "single bullet theory." If the theory that a single bullet caused multiple wounds in the Kennedy assassination were discredited, then Kennedy must have been assassinated by a conspiracy. If that conspiracy were exposed, it would veritably shake the foundations of the power elite.

To complete ETI interpretation, what the ETIs were really telling us in the single-bullet, dream encounter was that the single bullet theory would be discredited, the Kennedy assassination would be seen as the product of a far-reaching conspiracy, and human society would be "turned inside out." In a word, that the current terrestrial power structure would be exposed as corrupt, and a new structure would be brought, in facilitated by the ETIs.

Of course, the Messiah and the Paraclete would be at the center of this global transformation.

Soon I started a book that would bring the Messiah and the Paraclete to public attention. I researched trends in the earth sciences, and wrote Age of Cataclysm on prophesized earth changes. While I was writing the Book, the Messiah flew to a parapsychology conference, convinced he would be declared Messiah by acclamation. On his return he was hospitalized for acute psychosis.

Rather than pulling away from him, I went to his support, arguing with his physician and family that he should be released. I felt anger at him, but it was anger that he was endangering our mission, not that our mission itself was flawed and delusional.

A major publishing house bought the manuscript and in nine months would bring out the Age of Cataclysm as one of the top of their list. We felt this was a major vindication of our mission. We readied ourselves by jointly writing another book, a field theory of reality. We called it The Messiah Game. Each day we would gather to write several more pages of analysis and manifesto. A routine set it, as well as a growing sense of listlessness.

I felt an underlying sense of separation from the Messiah, one that would increase. I just did not feel that he embodied the being and attributes of a messiah.

My sense of growing unease was a puzzle for me. Why did I ever think the Messiah was a messiah in the first place? Yet, now well into the tasks of the mission, I continued with determination to complete and succeed. I was invested in being the Paraclete, an inner archetype I had fashioned. By being the Paraclete, my life had deepest meaning; historical significance; cosmic important; and public attention.

Soon after publication, the Messiah and the Paraclete began to appear on radio and television talk shows to talk about coming earth changes. Of course, we never told anyone we were the Messiah and the Paraclete. We were just cosmic futurists with first-rate educations and track records. Some of the shows went well. I did most of the talking, as I was more in command of the research. Others of the shows were disasters.

At one major radio show, the Messiah appeared at the studio with a suitcase, and proceeded to pull a hookah water pipe out of it, and place it next to his microphone. Needless to say, the host became nervous and agitated. The Messiah was increasingly incoherent as the show progressed. After the show, I castigated him, saying, "Don't ever do that again!" I could feel my ambivalence about what had just occurred: was it a creative confrontation, or a display of psychosis?

Our breaking point was predictable, in retrospect. We were invited to be on national television in Canada. On the flight there, the Messiah was alternately withdrawn, and aggressively showing off. This time I saw his psychosis clearly.

I had fallen – after almost three years – out of the force field of the *folie a deux*, the dual madness as Messiah and Paraclete. I felt I was on the show to give out a clear message. Even the television crews applauded. The Messiah was sullen.

500

On the flight back, I broke with him. I would not see him again for almost eight years.

Soon after the break with the Messiah, I was at a party with friends. I sat in a corner, shaking my head, saying, "My head was filled with craziness." It felt like I was coming out of a dream into clarity. The Paraclete was a costume I no longer had to wear. I could feel myself as more real, my own self. Now... what to do with my life?

That was when I realized that though I had broken with the Messiah, I had not broken with the worldview and agenda that together we had forged. My own analysis and logic had put together much of our platform. My dominant thought was to continue seeking to break open the conspiracy behind the assassination of John F. Kennedy. Uncovering this conspiracy was a first lynchpin in a sequence of events that would lead to cosmic transformation of the planet.

My activist self took over, and I mailed out a proposal to re-open the Kennedy investigation to a group of notables. I soon linked up with a grass roots group of Kennedy assassination researchers, bent on reopening the investigation.

Fueled by a groundswell of public opinion, an investigation was opened in the congress. I found myself consulted by the congressional counsel, and invited to meet with the chairing congressman.

I felt I was making a difference, in the real world.

I sensed that some unseen force was leading me to complete an agenda that had been started when I was still under the delusion of being the Paraclete.

The Kennedy investigation in the U.S. Congress was now underway. To support my family and myself I sought a position as a futurist at a prominent think tank. Not any old think tank, but a think tank that was doing research on the application of psychic abilities to military spying. I introduced myself by sharing my theories of ETI strategies. That cinched the job.

True to my inner agenda, I conceived of my self as a deep cover agent for higher intelligence. Together with a prominent

ETI theorist, I developed a proposal to re-open the public ETI investigation by the government. My contacts were in the Carter White House. On trips to Washington, I would start the day at the Kennedy assassination researcher's house, to monitor the progress of the investigation, and follow that with visits to the White House on the proposed ETI investigation. Life became very racy and blurred. Later I was to find out, via the think tank security, that I might be a Soviet under cover agent! Little did anyone know I had proclaimed myself as acting for the ETIs!

Or maybe my acting for higher intelligence was really the problem.

Then illness struck: manic depression with its near fatal manic delusions; its dark, deadly depressions.

I went to New Orleans to see one of my brothers and tour the traveling King Tut exhibit. I had made an appointment to see a prominent Kennedy assassination critic the next day. It turned out I would never meet him. As I entered the Tut exhibit, a psychedelic whirling of the room about me overwhelmed me. Later I would say it felt as though someone poured LSD in my coffee.

Then began the full-blown manic episodes. There were five manic episodes over the course of several months, each followed by a forced hospitalization. When the first one struck I had not even heard of manic depression. By the time of the last one, in barely lucid moments through a painful cloud of confusion, I could guess that something was seriously wrong with my emotions and my mind. But even when drugged out and delusional in some psychiatric ward, I knew I was still on a mission with higher intelligence.

Manic depression is also known as bipolar affective disorder, a disorder of the affect or emotions and of perception as well. If not treated with medication and therapy, it can be a fatal disease. Unmedicated manic-depressives become risk-takers and may commit suicide. The flip side of manic depression is that the same risk-taking is also the source of creativity. Many of the world's great artists, poets and statesmen have been manic-depressives.

And in those first five episodes, the medication could not control my mania. My world became living symbol, and I acted out the symbols. I danced nude at the San Francisco airport, a creative modern dance photographed by crowds of giggling tourists. I drove a car in the wrong lane of traffic at top speed on a bridge several miles long.

From a hotel room, I started a campaign to become president of a neighboring university. I took my son out of school and boarded a flight to the Rio Grande Valley that had to make a forced landing because I was sobbing uncontrollably. My son was taken to social services, and I was straitjacketed and rushed by ambulance to the nearest hospital under 72-hour hold.

Inevitably came the flip side of bipolar affective disorder – depression. Mine lasted for months, the deepest most painful despair possible. I tried to commit suicide, but spat the pills out when they were in my mouth. I entered a rural psychiatric retreat for an extended stay. While there, my wife came to tell me, in the presence of the staff, that she was leaving our marriage. With my initial outbreak, I lost the first of four wives to manic depression, each marriage to be broken during a manic-depressive episode.

Manic depression is a destroyer of families and careers, and mine was no exception. Following my release, I took a leave of absence from work, and stopped my medication. I needed to feel being on the edge, and could not stand the drugged, slow thinking being I became under lithium and anti-depressants. When I returned from my leave, it was only a matter of time before I would go manic again.

That manic episode began in a hot tub. I looked at my watch and the digital numbers were racing in a symbolic sequence. In my mind, it was razor's edge whether the racing watch was signals from higher intelligence or manic delusion.

From there my mania spiraled, shattering the final threads of relationship with the think tank. In short order, it was apparent to my racing mind that I should go out onto the world and live my mission.

Thus I began my EyE period, a soaring mixture of creativity, spiritual experience, and outright psychosis. EyE was the name I gave myself as I traveled from city to city by bus and airplane, blessing each city and elevating it. I had no job and my mother became my patron and support, sending me airplane tickets or small money orders. I was in a mind-envelope, with full-blown delusion.

All characters on television would talk to me, and I saw all of post-war history as a symbolic setting for my holy coming. Music, songs, and advertisements were all covertly about me. I carried a notebook, fashioned a purse, and took notes of my experiences in the era of good feelings, as I dubbed it. In some places I was robbed; in others I was a street psychotic; still in others I would stay at decent hotels and enjoy the local opera and art museums. EyE possessed a deep, musical appreciation of a reality and world revolving about him.

EyE eventually landed at my parent's home, broke and with no permanent direction. My bizarre ceremonies and often-violent outbursts led my family to commit me to a psychiatric ward. I brought habeas corpus and won release. I still would not take the medication that would bring me out of mania; I was totally enthralled with the magic world I had discovered. I needed a private space I could call my own, where people would not get funny and move to commit me.

The solution came in a camper van, which my anxious parents financed for me, and which I dubbed the "Lordmobile." I packed it as a traveling journalist's studio, complete with typewriter, tape recorder, cameras, portable television, stereo and earphones. Within a few days journey I came upon a state park deep within the mountains, there to celebrate the first authentic Christmas, amidst the lowing Winnebagoes.

There, within the Sangre de Cristo mountains, I began my book, to document my experiences for history in humorous and pun-filled poetry. The manuscript was called *EyE G*D on Urth*, and I felt joy at the literary scope of what was becoming an epic lyric poem. Years later it would be reported to me that an eminent literary critic in England had compared the un-published manuscript to works of James Joyce. Each night after writing, I stood under the stars, listening to music on my earphones, marveling at the breadth of creation.

One night with all my heart and mind I sent out a telepathic prayer, "Calling all Angels" in creation to come to Urth and save it.

Soon I finished about a third of the manuscript, and I left the mountain lair.

The Pope, I learned, was about to make his first trip to Mexico. I secured journalist credentials as an author, and headed for a Papal enclave close on the twin volcanoes of Popocatepetl and Iztaccihuatl, and Cholula, built on the largest pyramid in the world.

Cholula was the ancient seat of the Plumed Serpent, the ancient God-Man returned. I began covering the Papal visit, but in my mind, I was EyE becoming the Plumed Serpent, and documenting it in my continuing lyric poem. My being on the scene was a cosmic signal that a new area of history was beginning.

Each day I would labor over the manuscript, incorporating the insights of EyE and the Plumed Serpent into the narrative. Then I would go to the daily Papal press conference and observe. Occasionally I would go to the Mexican capital to cover international events. I covered the presidents of a number of nations, again through the lens of my symbolic reality. I remember my solitary wave to the president of the United States as his limousine turned in front of me. I was the only person there.

The President of the United States waved back with what I took to be a wave of solidarity with EyE. I had just spent several hours in a journalist's briefing with his press secretary.

In a field up across the twin volcanoes, one day, I went into an altered state and was admitted to a conversation between the moon and the earth. The two heavenly bodies told me how it was that the moon could cause quakes in the earth to protect her against mankind.

I generally wrote while parked in this field between the vol-canoes and the pyramid. One day as I was typing the words, "I make myself an ally of the Earth," the earth trembled with an earthquake, and the Lordmobile shook. I experienced a deep oneness between the earth, my mission, and myself.

Soon the enclaves and press conferences had finished, and my manuscript felt complete. An inner voice told me my next destination – "Hollywood!"

My mind opened to the possibilities. After all, the worlds of movies and music were built on my persona. I would find a home for the manuscript there, the company of peers.

I packed the van and headed north immediately. Several days later I crossed the US border at 6AM. That night I was at the Academy Awards banquet, tape recorder in hand, ready for the next interview.

So began my three-year interlude in La-La land, the world of entertainment.

It was a respite from the rigors of EyE. I was still unmedicat-ed, but relatively grounded. I wrote a screenplay on the life of the psychic Edgar Cayce for a producer at a major studio, which like most screenplays was never produced. I re-married and spent six months in Australia seeking custody for my wife's child, kid-napped by her former husband. My marriage broke up almost immediately, a victim of a manic episode upon our return.

Australia brought me to a seminal sacred text, and with it the most rigorous and satisfying universe cosmology I had ever come upon. I spent my time during the long months waiting for the custody trial reading a chapter each day, from back to front. The book taught me that the evolution of our planet and our souls is in fact the product of profound organization by deity. Its revela-tions showed me that the theories the Messiah and the Paraclete had evolved were simplistic beyond belief.

Life back in La-La Land became luxurious and sweet. I lived in an old movie star's duplex, an ageless actress my next-door neighbor. I partied, socialized. I became a member of the Governor's earthquake preparedness committee, and returned to my old think tank in a position of honor and respect. A record company engaged me as diplomatic consultant in producing a series of records by the Pope. I flew into the Vatican on the holiest day of the year, and officials opened their offices especially for us.

Bombs also went off that morning at the Vatican, not too common an event.

Coincidence?

After a season or two, I began to find this sweet life among the lotus-eaters unsatisfying. A group of activists came to me, asking my help in producing a peace concert in San Francisco. I accepted, and immediately plunged into the war.

The peace concert was in support of the second special session on disarmament at the United Nations. My passions for the militant life were once again awakened, and I resolved to participate. The night after the final concert, I flew to the United Nations as a non-governmental delegate, and a credentialed journalist for a funky, alternative newspaper.

The UN special session was accompanied by massive public events on behalf of peace. There were large concerts, public marches in support of it. Journalists and delegates arrived from all over the world. I mingled with them, exchanging stories and leads. I attended the concerts, walked beside the marchers, and drank in the spirit of an aroused citizenry.

It soon became apparent that the designated villain was the United States.

I attended a press briefing at the US delegation, and along with other journalists, was subjected to my first experience of what must have been electromagnetic pulse, extremely low frequency (ELF) weapons.

As we sat there listening to US officials drone on, we began to feel stunned and disoriented. A fellow journalist from the Netherlands, sitting next to me, agreed that the US must have been dousing us with ELF weapons. Their purpose was to dampen our questions and forestall confrontation on the US's intransigent position on cruise missiles.

Almost as an act of fate, I ran into the Messiah, being videotaped at the United Nations about his plan for world peace. Afterward we took a quiet walk in Washington Square Park, talking over our experience. He still was convinced he was indeed the true Messiah.

The Messiah's nose was broken, and he looked the victim of assault. He told me that after we had broken, the police had taken him to a vacant lot and brutally beaten him. As we spoke, a dozen or more police cars ringed the park looking on at us and wailing their sirens in unison. How pitiful, I thought, that the state would pay men to beat up defenseless psychotics.

After the disarmament conference, I continued my reporting in Europe for a wire service and a peace journal. I covered violent attacks on women's peace camps seeking to shut down cruise missiles just miles from their homes. At a UN outer space conference, I met fate once again. A prominent woman futurist invited me to her mansion outside Washington. I accepted and moved into the stately house on Rock Creek Park. Little did I know that my coming to Washington would open the way to my entrance into the Kingdom of Heaven.

I call this Canadian wilderness cult the Kingdom of Heaven because that is what it called itself. Of course, I did not know the Kingdom was a cult when, in the company of my futurist host, I traveled to Canada visit for a short orientation.

We were met by a group of twenty or so happy souls, living in a mini-settlement in the snowy forests. During the day, I attended classes on the history of metaphysics. There were veiled allusions to something called the "cube," but I could not get anyone to talk about it.

At night I would venture out under the clear starry skies. I heard music playing somewhere in my aura. This was a magical mystery school, I concluded. I decided I wanted more, and made up my mind to take a residential course. The clincher happened when I found a copy of the Age of Cataclysm in their library.

Within a few months I was back at the Kingdom of Heaven, on a semi-permanent basis. That is where the struggle began. It was a struggle between the group, which wanted to absorb me on their terms, and myself, who wanted to participate on my own terms and not be absorbed. I was clearly a conflicting and conflicted character in the group. A nervous period of courting began.

I was courted by the Queen of Heaven and Earth, the female aspect of God, known simply as the "Queen." I knew she was the Queen by accident, when I stumbled across a royal portrait of her in queenly garb, next to a man in kingly garb. When I asked a member who the man was; "Oh one of our teachers," was the reply.

That moment of discovery would haunt me for years. As you can guess, the man turned out to be the King of Heaven and Earth. Together the King and the Queen made up the Point, a single focus of reality for the entire universe.

It was then still a matter of ambiguity as to whether the King was the Point, himself and alone.

The Queen's visits to our settlement were known as visitations, and were carried out according to a protocol that included the type of silverware at meals, and the hierarchy of seating arrangement. The Queen took a shine to me, and we would swap ETI stories. When I said we had been captains of the ETIs, she replied, "Oh, we'll get along just fine." This was the beginning of a topsy-turvy career in the Kingdom, and its aftermath.

I courted the Queen back, and sent her a framed photograph of mine, an artistic headshot. She radioed back that she had placed it in "the Alfred room." I became the human rights advocate in the group, and facilitated the adoption of the Universal Declaration of Human Rights as their standard. But all this was superficial gaming, and would soon come apart, after the Sacred Summit.

The summit was conceived by the Point to be a bridge between the Kingdom and the earthly fabric, as human society was referred to. Human people were mortals; Kingdom people were immortals. The Sacred Summit would be an entry level for chosen mortals to enter the dimension of immortality. We labored and built tables and conveniences; painted buildings; put up flagpoles for the summit. It was to be a watershed event.

The summit turned out to be three days of unfocused well-meaning conversation among a dozen people or so who came. Notable were my futurist friend and some New Age types from the Pentagon. Unbeknownst to anyone at the summit, the Queen had rigged the conference hall with hidden microphones and listened in on the proceedings with a small group of the inner chosen. I was supposed to participate as a shill for the group, but really did not understand that.

When it came my turn to speak, I spoke my mind vocally against control groups like the one hosting the conference. Well, that ended my exalted position in the Kingdom. The Alfred room was dismantled, and I was given the choice of leaving or going on the residential course as I had initially planned. I chose the residential course, in the name of persistence and spiritual adventure. Besides, I would tell myself, what other real life do I have now?

The course, held at an instructional campus, was a pleasant series of growth and spiritual exercises, based on the Atlantean method, so called because it had reputedly been last used in Atlantis. The method taught that most effective learning or communication occurred when the individuals' auras could connect a one to one, known as an "abwa".

I found the abwa experience a deepening one.

In the midst of the residential course, carloads of group members arrived wearing trucker's hats and martial swords, to tell us that the Point had declared spiritual war. We were marshaled into troop formation, read a declaration of spiritual war, and told to return to the main campus, an eight-hour drive away.

Like Candide, my fortunes in the Kingdom were to shift once again.

From Heaven's Gate, as the main campus was known, I remember being hustled into group rides that were headed to Washington, DC. What the purpose of the exercise was I could not fathom, though I shared a philosophy that the planet was in the grip of the forces of darkness, and that spiritual war was inevitable.

We arrived in Washington. Nothing happened. I saw some friends and headed back to the Kingdom of Heaven. Not the least of my reasons for returning was that the High Priestess, who was to become my third wife, was riding with us.

Back at the Kingdom, I experienced a meteoric rise. Each member took on the identity of a specific tarot card, and I became the Magician, a high member of the major arcana.

I was chosen to lead a group-wide retreat, and led them like troops in my Andean poncho and boots – the psychic guerilla. These were the troops of the Galactic Federation of Light Forces, and I was their ancient champion come to lead the troops to battle. At least, on the better days, I was. One could never know "what was what" and "who was who" on any given day in the Kingdom.

One high point came when I was commissioned to write the Throne Speech. This was the speech based on timeless reality in which the Point would proclaim itself to the world. I was admitted to the inner sanctum base, the home of the Queen and the King.

The night I arrived thunder and lightning spread across the sky as I have never seen it.

Destiny rode as I completed the Throne Speech, flirting at night with the High Priestess who lived in the same complex. A few days later I delivered the Speech before a select audience, the hierarchy of the Kingdom. There was silence, which I could not read. In my mind, at least, some prophesized event was about to happen.

The real war for the Kingdom was what happened next. Bundles of royal documents, including the Throne Speech, were given to group members who then dispersed around the world. We were to proclaim the Kingdom of Heaven on Earth, and invite humanity into it.

I was designated to Washington, and my new wife, the High Priestess, to New York. We had just recently been married at the

Point; the Queen had maintained that unless we were married the world would be blown up. So after a few desultory meetings in Washington, I headed back to New York.

Then the unthinkable happened. War broke out between the King and the Queen. There was trouble in Paradise.

Initially, as a counselor of state, I decided to take no sides.

Huge numbers of disillusioned members defected back to their normal lives. The Kingdom of Heaven as we knew it was abandoned. Lawsuits ensued over the Kingdom's properties.

The High Priestess decided to leave our marriage, concurrent with a new manic episode on my part. After a brief, but traumatic visit to the former Kingdom bases, I alighted back into the earthly social fabric.

One central fact had come out of the war in Heaven – God in his full persona had been born.

I call him God because that is what he would call himself nearly every time we met. He had been many things: King of Heaven, Lord of the Universe, King of Kings. But now he was simply God.

In the aftermath of the war in Heaven, God established himself as the sole occupant of the Point, the center of creation.

No longer did he need a cult to support him. He used to call his reality, "the cult of no cult." With the Queen safely dethroned, he was now reigning as God on earth. All reality, all evolution, art, literature, music, history had developed to this point of his landing on the planet.

My relationship to the Point now changed. God was the Point. We had a relationship of mutual admiration and mistrust at the same time. It seemed that I could not do without him, and for a while he could not do without me. In this lifetime, he was my nemesis as I was his nemesis.

I have been told ours was an ancient rivalry, born aeons ago in some former incarnations. In total there were fifteen years between my first entrance into the Kingdom, until God's untimely death of sudden heart failure. I count those fifteen years as the story of my struggle against a deep adversary, and my final vindication. Karmic contracts and obligations often determine vast passages of one's life.

After leaving the ruins of the Kingdom, I determined to keep a distance from the Point. Yet some unresolved force kept tugging me back, and I became a major financial support for God, at a distance.

Back in my earthly life once again, I rejoined society and its challenges. One of these was politics; another was law; yet another was media, particularly radio. I reestablished a life and a persona, and co-hosted the first live radio program between the United States and the then Soviet Union.

On air, I cried, "We've broken the embargo [between the US and the UUSR]!" Then came another fateful call from God.

I took the call and flew up to the Point. God gave me the honored guest treatment. When he entered my room, he looked like a creditable version of what God should look like. The matter was legal, he said. Would I help him find an attorney to represent God in a lawsuit seeking $80 million damages for invasion of privacy? It turned out that the attorney he preferred was a client of my firm. I conferred with the lawyer. He had met God and was unwilling to undertake the lawsuit.

"I met him and I was not impressed," the distinguished dean of the Canadian bar told me.

I returned to the Point to find God agitated. He believed that the forces behind this attorney would now destroy him, unless a lawsuit was filed in the next ten days. He offered me $20 million of the final judgment as my fee if I would take on the case. His tone was: do this or else. I said nothing, my inner voice conflicted. I knew the lawsuit was not worth $80 million, that perhaps there was no lawsuit at all. I also believed God to be inspired, if not actually God.

I quickly weighed everything: I could move my office from New York to Florida, the venue for the lawsuit; I could file the lawsuit, although I had never actually tried a case.

Ah - sweet adventure, as always, won out.

Thus began a single lawsuit that would stretch over the course of almost five years, and eventually become over twenty lawsuits in the courts of the United States and Canada. The cause of action was based upon a private film of God's life that a major media company had been shown on television. It was virtually unprovable without finding a copy of the broadcast film.

What the lawsuit spawned was an outright war between God and covert powers that hold sway in North America. As God's attorney, I was the infantry. God himself, with his prodigious psychic powers, was the air force. That I emerged alive was the miracle.

So great was God's magnetic hold on me that I did not perceive until after he had died that God's diagnosis, like the Messiah's was paranoid schizophrenic. It was as though life with the Messiah was training for the real battle of life with God. Curiously, the Messiah and God shared the same initials in their name. The Messiah was a featherweight to the heavyweight that God was.

To understand God's lawsuit, one has to understand God's reality. Curiously, it resembled the reality I had experienced when in full-blown psychosis from manic depression.

Music, particularly music videos, was either for good or for evil. Music videos were good as they glorified God or the vibe. Music videos that worked for the "other side" exploited negative aspects of his personal life. God ran the music industry, and cleaning up music videos was one of his special missions on earth. Nature is all its aspects worked for him. God was the birds and the animals and the forests.

The central assertion of the litigation was based on God's worldview. Hence it was deeply flawed, being sourced by a paranoid schizophrenic mind. The only hope of keeping the litigation alive lay in employing every procedural maneuver we could. This we did by endless, multiple appeals and motions. I began to slip into a God-reality. I saw everything as referent to the litigation – all the news, all politics, all media. I saw Washington as a proto-fascist center, occupied by security forces and electromagnetic population control weapons, poised to stop the litigation.

Meanwhile, came the counterattack against God himself. God was sued to set aside his adoption of the woman who would become his second wife. I rushed back to Canada and a siege mentality set in at the Point.

Government resistance to God's litigation left no doubt that there were forces determined to destroy God as an entity. ELF bombardment of the Point became a daily reality. Waves of paranoia would rise, and be beaten back. Twice I was forced to leave Canada on immigration technicalities. Once to Switzerland; once to London. In each case I was back in action within days.

Eventually God won. The case against him was dismissed and he married his adoptive daughter. Through a procedural oversight, we won a $750 million default judgment against the government, a paper victory that would never be collected.

I wrote a book about God's cases, which premiered at the London international book fair. We were poised on some new plateau.

Then darkness set in, and God destroyed my world once again.

Looking back on what transpired I could see that it was sourced in God's developing mental illness. God followed a very deliberate, twisted plan in trying to destroy me. First he moved to destroy my livelihood; then he moved to destroy my very self.

God, the person I had sacrificed so much for, whom I could not conceive would turn against me, did in fact hatch and carry out a plan sourced in raging paranoia. The crux of it was that I was a Soviet spy that had infiltrated the Point. Since the Point led NATO, I was endangering world peace simply by being where I was.

God first pressured me into bringing suit against my partners in an international legal access firm, when I really had no cause and did not want to. I was still unmedicated, and I could feel the stress bringing on a manic episode.

Then one night God came and took me into an enclave of the other cult members, accused me of being a Soviet spy, and had each member come and denounce me.

One of them was my fourth wife, whom I had married a scarce month before.

I seethed with inner rage, but maintained a martial arts balance.

God began to threaten me with physical dismemberment and death. God continued his death threats in private for several days. He told me he had taken away my soul, and damned it to the worst possible torments

A blinding blizzard had left my truck snowed in. As soon as the snow cleared, one night I saw there were no guards outside my house. I grabbed one or two belongings, started the truck and drove four days non-stop to my parental home on the border of Mexico.

The trip was a journey through hell. The Gulf war had just begun. I was in seething manic psychosis. I encountered many strange, hallucinatory phenomena. I knew I had just been saved from certain death. But at least I was alive.

Now followed a black period of depression. For two years I did not leave my home, and when I did I would experience myself as a dead being among live souls. I refused medication that would have brought me to clarity within days.

I languished, praying, watching television, reading, writing a novel. My self-esteem was low, low. I felt as though I had lost my life, and any future.

I still held on to some thread that God was good, and that he had been misinformed and misguided in what he had done to me. Once he called my house and my spirit soared. Another time I was invited to his birthday party, though later he would say he had to do it.

In the midst of my depression my mother lay dying of cancer. I knew I had to rise and go into the world again. A friend

516

offered me employment at a health center, provided I took medical treatment first. I accepted and within the month was back almost to my active self.

Quickly I rose within the center's hierarchy. I traveled widely and learned much about health, and decided to become a mental health provider. I returned to university and several years later became a counselor and therapist. I also confronted my manic depression. I attended support groups; learned about the illness; complied with medication.

Throughout these years God remained, as an unanswered question, an incomplete agenda. I screwed up my courage and I visited the Point maybe once a year, and contributed financially. In our meetings, there were undercurrents, as though both of us were dissimulating. On the surface I still treated him as God.

Underneath I felt he was a sneaky, unreliable enemy. Most of what he projected onto me was in fact about himself.

The denouement and final act came through my marriage. My wife and I met on the Internet; she is a psychotherapist and psychic. We decided to visit the Point together, so she could experience God for herself and then decide. When we arrived, we found a disheveled, incoherent negative being. God berated me for my marriage. He ranted for hours; the rest of the members watching the proceedings as though in some trance. That night we finally decided he was psychotic, and dangerous. My term for God was a psychic terrorist.

I moved my energy away from the Point. Within a few months, God was dead, of apparent massive heart failure. When I heard the news I felt a heavy negative weight had been lifted from my shoulders. I wrote his widow words to that effect.

Of all the challenges I had faced in this quarter-century, perhaps the greatest by far was that posed by God. Our relationship, nominally a spiritual one, was deeply abusive. It was terrifying to me. Though I would try to leave I felt in that double bind. If I stayed I would be destroyed; if I left I would be destroyed.

My recovery from God came only after his death. I had been working on my recovery for at least five years; becoming a therapist, treating clients, active myself in manic-depressive support groups. So great was his hold on me that until I heard the news of his death I thought he was in fact the true God, source of all creation. How could God be so horrible, I asked myself, unable to see the truth that God I had befriended was a schizophrenic, destructive being?

One common thread underlying recovery from cults, higher intelligence, and manic depression, is recovery from abuse.

My recovery from the Messiah and from the Kingdom of Heaven began once I made the decision I would no longer tolerate psychic abuse.

My recovery from my manic depression began once I decided to end my cycle of self-abuse in refusing to acknowledge that my illness might need medication and treatment.

My years with God were perhaps the greatest challenge I have faced in life. I continue to recover from my years with God. I experienced profound spiritual growth by surviving a being who was the opposite of the true God of creation. My recovery began when I decided to break the cycle of this relationship of abuse.

My years with the Messiah prepared me for surviving God. My years with God have prepared me for the next challenge, one of unparalleled spiritual magnitude.

What might be a greater challenge than trying to adapt to an abusive paranoid schizophrenic who believes he is God?

Well, it just might be entry into full interplanetary society will bring its share both of excitement and abuse.

If my guess is right, my struggle with the consciousness of the paranoid schizophrenic I knew as God might be very close to a struggle against abuse that we humans may come to wage in securing our full participation as citizens of the universe.

CHAPTER 2

ALIEN EXPERIENCER

How is my recovery from higher intelligence progressing? If there is one straight line running through my life, that line is the arc formed by higher intelligent beings.

I am an alien experiencer, as the term is now known. An alien experiencer is one who has had direct contact with some form of alien higher intelligence, other than human. This may be contact with extraterrestrial beings; it may be contact with entities from other dimensions reality. It may be both.

Contact with higher intelligence is a central experience of an alien experiencer's life. At the deepest level, that has been true in my life. Nothing has gone as deeply into my being and soul as the experience of a higher intelligence coming down and communicating upon me. That communication and its vision are what have driven me forward for twenty-five of my adult years; sometimes into peril; sometimes into promise; always into growth.

My feelings of familiarity around alien higher intelligence go back to childhood. I remember well long winter evenings as a fifth grader at my paternal grandparents' Main Line home in the early 1950s, drawing endless flying saucers on graph paper, with my grandfather's drafting tools. I drafted blueprints of flying saucers; vertical and horizontal cross-sections.

ETI encounters were even bigger in those days than now. A formation of unidentified objects had just reportedly just buzzed the White House space. No one in their right minds believed the 'temperature inversion' explanations as other than military disinformation. Of course, what did a fifth grader know about disinformation?

ETIs were also part of my pre-teen pop music life. My favorite song at my maternal grandmother's house in pre-revolution Havana was "Los Marcianos Llegaron Ya." The lyrics of the song said it all: "The Martians have already landed, dancing cha cha cha." I would dance the chachacha around the hard tile floors of the old masonry house in Vedado, and laugh, laugh, laugh.

ETIs were the icons of my 1950s grade school youth. The alleged war for the minds of the people of Earth was just beginning. Consciously, I did not know the details of any struggle between the vested interests of earth and the representatives of interplanetary society. Nor did any other average kid.

But we knew flying saucers and mother ships were real. And we knew space travel was real; and other inhabited worlds were real. We were tuned in to the essence of the human space drama, just lacking the fine details; the factual confirmations. We could quickly grasp the concept that the human race was doomed to self-destruction if our war-like ways continued.

Then a gap of unconsciousness fell upon me – sixteen years of painful, rigorous secondary, university, and graduate education in the classics, liberal arts, industrial administration, and international law. I was indoctrinated into the dominant dogma of the adult philistine world. This dogma upheld a world not too dissimilar to the world before Copernicus. Its assumptions: Earth is the center of the universe. There is no other populated planet; no other intelligent race in the universe. We humans are the highest intelligent forms in material reality.

Life is a competitive bitch, and then we die.

My formal education was infused with the dogma of organized religion. The religion of choice of my family was Catholicism, so that was my early story of dimensional higher intelligence. Catholic dogma claimed itself to be the exclusive roadmap to higher intelligence. This higher intelligence manifested in dimensions of reality known as heaven, in forms such as angels. At a quantum level of reality, the higher intelligence of the Son of God exists, who had actually incarnated as a human. At mega levels of reality, the triune entity of God exists – Father, Son, and Holy Spirit: Three divine persons and one God.

So ETI intelligence – and ETI craft and extraterrestrial travel - were the center of my childhood. And higher religious intelligence – in the dimensions of spirit and heaven - was the focus of my adolescence.

Adolescence sped into early adulthood, with its ten years of unconscious, conventional careerism. I became agnostic: religious concepts of dimensional intelligence were medieval leftovers. I became a lawyer: a high-income profession invested solely in proving three-dimensional evidence generally around the issue of who owes how much to whom. I became a cynic: the spirit; the unseen; anything outside of tangible, material reality was at best poetic, at worst living a lie.

Oh, and I was also a late child of the Sixties. Smoked dope; dropped acid and practiced Wall Street and environmental law; marched against war; sought spirituality in the country.

In early 1973, my personal volcano erupted out of its boxed reality. I went back full square center back to ETI intelligence.

By a miracle, I managed to throw off my shackles of perception, rooted most firmly at Yale. I began to perceive ETI intelligence as prime movers on the planet: the prime political, governmental, scientific, spiritual, prophetic, and even colonizing force.

Extraterrestrial intelligence (ETI) was here, dancing far more than the chachacha. ETI was here to help midwife our entry into interplanetary society, a predictable phase in the evolution of life-bearing planets. At last, our planet had reached that phase after a tortured history. Our nascent ability for space travel seemed to be the standard signal that we were ready to enter a fuller version of universe citizenship.

Extraterrestrial alien intelligence did not make up the totality of "higher intelligence" in my reality. Rather I had begun to understand that our human reality actually existed in an ecology of dimensions. As human beings, we also existed as one species in a vast, interactive ecology of intelligent species.

Other intelligent, extraterrestrial beings inhabited the vast expanse of space and planets. Other intelligent, evolved beings inhabited the dimensions of reality that co-existed with our material universe.

In short, at the age of thirty-one, I came back into an awareness I had lived as a child – that ours is a magical universe; far-reaching in its journeys; multiple in its intersecting levels; variegated in the spectra of its beings.

What I had acquired in navigating this circle was, I suppose, a heavy dose of cosmic unconsciousness, reinforced by blanket upon blanket of human-inspired, anti-ETI programming – known in the trade as disinformation.

The more I thought I knew, the more I became aware of how little I did know.

Did you ever have that experience?

There is that old saw that when the student is ready the master will appear.

So it was with me. The time was not of my choosing, but I was a seeker on some road to truth. And I the student was rushing full force down the road to cracking the inner code of reality. Who was the higher intelligence? What was their agenda? How did I fit into it? Could I decode their plans? What was their timetable? How would it unfold?

These were questions I sought day after day, night after night in an obsessive searching. If I knocked, I was sure a door would open. If I asked, I was certain, an answer would be given me. Days flew by in the spring of 1973. I could sense I was closing in on some approaching opening, some moving target which slowed as I approached it.

Then came one specific night that is now etched in my very DNA, in the nuclei of my cells. The intelligence came upon me unannounced and in the middle of the night.

Winter had turned to spring. White snow long since disappeared from the streets of lower Manhattan. At 2 am I was awake, working at the front of my loft on Greene Street, just then gentrifying from industrial to artist-gallery. Before we had converted it into an ultra modern artist space, it had been a warehouse for religious objects. We had tossed out literally barrel after barrel filled with gilt-edged holy cards of Mary, Jesus and other saints.

My son was asleep in his small back bedroom. I remember the glare of the white florescent lights on the tall frosted front windows of the loft. I was painting the shelves of my office bookcase, bright yellow and red. The silence was peaceful, calm, like a pillow spread around the white space and onto the hard maple floor.

I remember sitting for a time, as in meditation. My consciousness became single-focused. My visual field became very clear. After a while I felt encased in a translucent energy field. My consciousness deepened, thoughts resonating as powerful, resonating insights.

Gradually I became aware of a presence permeating the energy field around me. The presence then became one with the energy field, responding softly, then more loudly to my thoughts.

We spoke back and forth, each to each, just at the edges of my consciousness. With each reverberation of communication my consciousness expanded out into union with this source.

We were dialoguing, but more than that, I was integrating with the entity, in a state of profound reverence and oneness.

My feeling was of being at peace, united with the deep truth of reality – a mystic state.

We stayed in this mutuality for an indeterminate period, for what felt like a timeless embrace.

I felt in the presence of a being of the order of the gods, something far and beyond any reality I could conceive.

I felt I was being given a revelation, and I surrendered.

The dialogue – communion – at the edge of my being edged toward the center of my consciousness. I began to hear the outlines of the thoughts that grew between the entity and myself.

I became aware of the content of these thoughts. I could make out that our dialogue had to do with the agenda of spirit in our reality.

Though I could not fully hear them yet, the meanings seemed to validate what I had been deducing in my waking hours.

My mind held its focused questions as background: Who were the higher intelligence? What was their agenda? How did I fit into it? Could I decode their plans? What was their timetable? How would it unfold?

The entity now came into the center of my consciousness, holding it in invisible embrace.

Our thoughts back and forth became louder to me, more definite.

Each syllable, word of thought of the presence reverberated down the core of my being, like extended musical notes played up and down the edges of my energy field.

Then all of a sudden my thoughts spoke first, loudly in my mind.

"Who are you?" I asked.

A long deep pause. I felt safe, but forward in asking, as though I had been given permission.

Profound came back the thought from the presence.

"I am the Holy Spirit," the presence said in thought.

Silence enveloped us.

Communion embraced us.

Realization overcame my being.

Elevation caught me in its gentle hand, and I rose in frequency of thought and feeling.

I wanted to stay in this moment forever, and I stayed as long as I can remember, living in this deep embrace. I could feel my very molecules changing; altered, transforming my naïve, human state.

The Holy Spirit, holy of holies, third person of deity, my Catholic buttons said.

At any other higher level of energy gradient, I know I would have been rendered unconscious, or at least transfixed by the presence. As it was, we could communicate, and I could rest in meditation on its most recent answer.

I let my evaluative, judgmental brain processes go; and just experienced being at one with this moment.

I felt enthralled. Symbols of the "Holy Spirit" pushed me into circuits of profound reverence. My brain knew it could not the third person of all Source that was talking to me. My spirit felt like deity embraced me.

My mind did not want to leave this reverie. Its words "Holy Spirit" reverberated and reverberated.

At some moment my mind wanted to know more.

So I asked.

"And who am I?"

The Holy Spirit responded with thought waves that continued to embrace me.

"Thou art Peter and upon this rock I shall found my church."

Me? The rock on which the Holy Spirit will found its church? I was simultaneously awed and shocked.

I cannot tell you for how many years and how far this answering phrase of the Holy Spirit entity has carried me, a dominant obsession.

The literature on alien experiencers tells us that contactees are often given messianic messages, which set them off on life long missions as "appointed" messengers to humankind.

My own immediate reactions were probably not too different from other alien experiencers.

My first reaction was profound validation. "Hey... the Holy

Spirit knows what it is doing!"

My second reaction was... "Hey, this entity is playing head games with my Catholic case!"

My third reaction was... "Hey, this is happening to me now, and I really do not know what it all means."

I sank back into thought silence with the entity, baffled, embraced, feeling responsibility and awe; becoming somewhat confused.

I am not sure how long I stayed in a state of quiet reverie. It could have been an hour; it could have been less. I remember thinking that my visitation with the Holy Spirit was at an end.

Then came the second act.

I was lifted up off my chair, as if an unseen companion was helping me walk. I was turned toward the center of the loft space.

I walked slowly toward a table saw I had placed there for woodworking necessary to finishing the space.

A force ushered me up to the table saw, bent me over, and brought my head and face right up to its edge.

The saw's brand name – Rockwell - stared me in the face.

As I looked at the brand name, its letters and syllables began to morph about before my eyes.

The "ROCK" became very large and came up to my eyeballs, vibrating before me.

The "well" zoomed away from me, becoming gradually smaller, and then disappearing in an optical dissolve.

The bizarreness of the scene baffled me for a moment. I almost laughed at the cheekiness of it all. Really, now. Why do these high beings have to communicate through wavy, buzzing letters on the edge of a table saw?

Then I realized that it was all a message in symbolic code.

526

An extension of the message I had just received from the Holy Spirit entity. I did not figure this out on my own. The Holy Spirit's – or some entity's – thought voice was telling this to me in my mind.

The voice walked me through the symbols in the message, several times.

The bizarreness of the "ROCK" syllable and the "well" syllable kept dancing before my eyes. I continued in my befuddled state. I was being coaxed to understand, like a child learning elementary meanings in a language from a teaching adult.

Slowly these meanings dawned on me. The voice in my mind was firm, but gentle.

How do "well" and "Rock" relate? The question kept revolving in my mind.

The answer came in one of those "aha!" moments.

The "well" syllable had morphed small and disappeared in an optical dissolve.

I understood the meanings of symbols.

"Well" means the "wellness of the earth."

The "well" doing an optical dissolve means that the "wellness of the earth" will diminish and disappear.

I envisioned the symbols in my mind – "There will be a time when conditions on the earth will become catastrophic for human kind."

My mind turned to the "ROCK" syllable.

What did it mean that "Rock" morphed huge and magnified itself up against my eyes?

The Holy Spirit's words – "Thou are Peter and upon this Rock I will found my Church" – swirled around me. I did not want to allow that "Rock" meant me. That was too scary. On the other hand, there was an underlying thrill that the "Rock" might mean me. Sort of the ultimate life challenge.

Then, I didn't get that the "Rock" meant in fact meant me.

The "Rock" meant a reality based on the reality of the Holy Spirit entity.

The total meaning of the symbolic message came in a flash.

> *"As the wellness of the earth disappears,*
> *the Rock will come to the fore!"*

The Holy Spirit was giving me a prophecy, or vision of the future, in symbolic terms.

I took the gist of the prophecy to be that there are catastrophic times coming for the planet. And as these times come, a spiritual reality will come to the fore on earth.

It was now very late, perhaps an hour before dawn. I was sitting quietly. My mind exhausted, meditating on what had just transpired.

I felt I had entered an elite rank – humans who had been visited by higher intelligence. I felt I had been given a special message for mankind. The symbolic message was not for my benefit only, but for the benefit of the planet.

It seemed logical. Other prophecies in time had been given by higher intelligence to humans, couched in symbolic terms.

Like other experiencers of higher intelligence, I was given not only a message but also a mission. That mission felt messianic; a responsibility to tell the world of the new troubled times that were coming.

There was also a messianic ambiguity in the message. Undoubtedly, the Holy Spirit entity deliberately designed its answer to me to exploit this ambiguity.

I was told explicitly that "Thou are Peter and upon this Rock I shall found my church." In many Latinate languages, Peter and Rock are synonyms.

That message is a line from the New Testament, referring to the historical Jesus' appointing Peter his successor in spreading Christianity. Particularly in Catholicism, it is a line of profound import, signifying the ultimate authority of the Catholic Church to represent Jesus on the planet.

Why would the Holy Spirit entity deliberately blow my mind with this ambiguous designation as of me as Peter the

Rock?

Ah. Well, apparently that's the way higher intelligence is. Higher intelligent beings know how to motivate.

They know how to enroll a human being for the balance of her or his life.

They know how to couch it in symbols that will sear the soul of their human charge.

Higher intelligence knows how to implant the symbols of divinity in a way that charges the human with the sense of a unique mission on earth.

So it was with me.

My episode with the Holy Spirit entity occurred a few months into my career as a student of prophecy and the paranormal. The visitation came at a strategic moment, and propelled me forward into ever deepening alternative realities. I felt I was on a pre-destined track in my life.

I had started a mission that has lasted twenty-five years and still counting.

For over a decade, I told no one about the Holy Spirit, and kept my secret deep within my heart.

I felt I had been transformed at the molecular level. The frequencies of my being vibrating at higher rates than the humans and the reality around me. I navigated, rather then walked through the scenes of my life.

Who was the Holy Spirit? Who was I?

The answers came to me in layers. Not all at once, but in sequences of study, glimpses of insight, constant rumination over the course of two and a half decades. I still do not know, but I have a better idea of the Holy Spirit and the vast living universe surrounding that moment.

I read widely in sacred texts; revelations; psychic channeling. I read and wrote on the nature of extraterrestrial intelligence.

The world around me became vast divination – I read the ways leaves fell from a tree; the license plate numbers on cars;

the names of people I would encounter; the words of music and song.

In peak experiences, all was a living single whole, speaking to me if I would listen. Telling me more of the meaning I sought.

Some texts spoke more deeply than others did to me.

One particular sacred text seared itself into my soul. In it I had found a veritable roadmap to higher intelligence.

I learned that the universe is highly populated, highly organized, and consciously evolving.

I learned that Heaven is a place in the Universe. Were we so evolved we could in fact have dinner with God, or some more evolved concept of that communion.

I learned that the conventional knowledge we have on earth is backwards. We are not the sole, populated planet. Rather we are one of billions of life-bearing planets. The reason we may feel isolated in the universe is that the earth has been in quarantine by the universe administration. That quarantine may now be ending.

I learned that the universe itself – its local universes, galaxies, constellations, solar systems, planets – is the on-going creation of higher beings who themselves are evolving even as they create. There are regular procedures, for example, for growing a planet, and evolving life-bearing species onto that planet.

We humans on planet earth are in the outermost dimension of creation – the material plane. The higher intelligent species that create and develop our material universe are in dimensions that wrap themselves around and through ours like the multi-faced layers. Souls like ours proceed through these dimensions over the aeons, evolving themselves eventually into gods.

Our planet earth was placed in quarantine after we suffered a rebellion against the universe administration's rule and plan for us. On each life-bearing planet, there are representatives of the universe administration who come to administer and develop the planet, under a standard plan. Our planetary administrators were overthrown from within. The story of the rebellion and quarantine on our planet lives on in human scared text and myth – in the Adam and Eve story.

This may well be a true history I learned. We humans are the products of a system-wide rebellion in the millennial past. Our planet has been denied all the benefits and accouterments of organized universe society i.e. membership in universe federations, travel and cross-fertilization from other planets and dimensions, organized universe education and science, and connection with universe energy circuits, communications, and broadcasts.

I learned why the human race as a whole seemed the most violent, polluting, species-suicidal race I could conceive of. And why individual humans seemed, on the whole, beautiful individual souls striving to express themselves with goodness and truth.

We are the living remnants of the planetary rebellion. Sort of the Galapagos Islands of spiritual evolution.

Who, then, was the Holy Spirit entity that visited upon me? Well, I had a better handle on an answer. The Holy Spirit, I thought, was a dimensional being, carrying out duties in the continuing evolutionary husbandry of the planet. That higher being was probably operating under authority of the universe administration, according to approved plan.

The Holy Spirit was gaming with me. Gaming in the sense that the Being was using highly charged religious symbols – the name of the third person of deity – to cloak itself. Its mission was to enroll me in some life-long dedication under a plan.

But the distance between gaming and manipulation is very small. Wouldn't you say that the Holy Spirit being was manipulating me?

Why did the higher being not simply come clean? It could have said straight- forwardly – I am acting on behalf of an organized authority. We have chosen you and would like to enroll you in a life of challenge, with no little suffering involved.

I do not have a full answer to that. It may have to do with how higher beings teach the lower evolving orders, through very brief interventions in the perceptual framework of the human subject. The human is then left on his or her own to puzzle through the meaning of the intervention. Any direct, transparent intervention by the higher being without the veil of human symbolism would blow the human away, crippling their long-term growth.

My journey after the Holy Spirit episode took me into the deepest recesses of the study of ETI, of apparent purposeful extraterrestrial, dimensional intelligence in our reality.

I studied ETI research, and developed theories. I brought a seminal ETI proposal to the White House staff to reopen the study of ETI activity. Following my proposal to the White House, I directly experienced think tank executives officially prohibit my further work on ETI, on alleged grounds it would jeopardize their defense contracts.

In the tense atmosphere of the inner office, I heard a progressive officer tell me, "Dissimulate." Meaning, just pretend you aren't interested in ETI any more.

Then the bad guys came into the room. They were from the nuclear missile side of the think tank, grubbing after studies moneys by making sure annihilation is more accurate. Predictably, their offices were just across from the Pentagon.

I didn't dissimulate. I confronted the slimy bastards. But everyone else at the meeting caved in. And my ETI research under government auspices was abruptly at an end.

I had just experienced a mini-combat in the secret war against the ETI initiative first hand.

I tried to understand this secret war to block our re-integration with universe society. How did it relate to the Holy Spirit entity that intervened with me late one night in 1973? Over these years, I brought those few hours into mind frequently. The visitation fueled my study, my life's purpose, my sense of meaning.

What was the Holy Spirit doing with me?

I was being activated.

I was being motivated.

I was being directed.

Activation, motivation, direction is what the Holy Spirit did with me.

The Holy Spirit was enrolling me in the secret war, or more largely in the broad task of helping elevate planet earth into the society of nations.

Why me? Well my ego always thought it was because of my homespun prowess as a cross between a guerilla warrior of the mind, and a public interest mole. But that's just my ego talking, strictly within the confining binders of what I thought a cool life might look like.

In other words, I have no idea why me, except I seemed predisposed to rush in where angels feared to tread.

And I really, really want to see this planet take its place in organized universe society.

Desire. In other words I had desire.

I felt like one more delicately nurtured cog in the multi-dimensional,

interactive, dynamic plan of ETI to bring planet earth back home.

That plan is what I mean by the ETI initiative.

The true burning political, spiritual, and evolutionary question of our day is:

"Are you for or against the ETI initiative?"

And what is your particular opinion on this burning issue of the day? How do you stand, on a sliding scale from "Agree" to "Don't know" to Disagree."

Whatever your answer, it will be very instructive to you.

Look at the ETI initiative from the perspective of higher intelligence.

There is really only one organized force against the ETI initiative. Some call it the "shadow government". Others call it the "secret government." Still others call it the "Military-industrial complex."

The conventional wisdom is that the ETIs cannot land because it would cause worldwide panic.

Not! The bulk of our community of human souls would welcome an intervention by the ETIs. Just look at the polls on the subject.

We are in fact ripe for intervention by the ETIs, in mutual initiative with humans, to undertake the rights and responsibilities of interplanetary citizenship.

Our technology is at the right stage; we are ready for interplanetary travel.

Our people are at the right stage; they are by and large soulfully endowed; sufficient to belong to the universal community of human souls.

So what is blocking the integration?

As always, it's the bad guys! Our bad guys are apparently a relatively small and readily identifiable group of rotten human beings. They own the bulk of our resources, of our means of production, and have for at least fifty years controlled and manipulated our wars, our welfare, and our human potential.

Their mode of choice in the war against the ETI initiative can be summed up in these words: psychological warfare, undertaken against the human population

Their favorite war technology: covert operations, be it technological or human based.

Their arsenal of weapons in the war to keep humans from entering planetary civilization:

Secrecy laws and regulations

Secrecy regulations prohibit military personnel from even discussing ETI encounters. ETI issues are given the highest security ratings, placing them beyond the purview of even the highest elected officials.

Command and control

Command and control over military information and response in the United States – the leader of the anti-ETI pack – is limited to very specific offices of the alphabet soup. Command and control floats around so we can't get too determined a fix on it. For a while, initials like NSA, NRO ran the show. It is said ETI encounters have the highest priority response rating on all US early warning systems.

Isolation

Standard practice appears to call for all military personnel involved in an ETI encounter. For example, if a nuclear sub crew is buzzed by a giant ETI craft off Cape Kennedy, then debrief the crew, telling them it was a weather balloon, and dismantle and disperse to entirely different units, no matter what the cost.

Mind control operations

MILAB is the military's favorite elite weapon's system in the anti-ETI initiative. Using advance electromagnetic pulse mind control technology, MK-ULTRA mind control stuff, and camouflage role-playing, human abductees are taken on bogus ETI abductions. The military makes real sure they have a bad time. The whisper campaign gets out – ETI aliens are about to enslave the planet and beat you up. MILABs and other anti-ETI operations may be carried out by para-military cutouts, entities operating in the twilight of black budgets, unaccountable to public law.

Much confusion in the public mind has been created by MILAB, and its "hostile alien" stereotypes. Entire hypotheses of a secret alien plan to breed a race of ETI hybrids, and genetically take over earth have been constructed from abductee reports that have identifiable MILAB components in them.

The most objective, multi-witnessed cases of ETI encounters, such as those with a military component, on analysis confirm that the ETI's "target" if any may be the anti-ETI war itself. This war is conducted by the US military command, not by our human population.

Anti-population weapons

These are the leading edge weapons in the anti-ETI war. Mainly electromagnetic pulse weapons (EMP) like HAARP, which was sold to the US Congress and press as a research project on the aurora borealis. EMP weapons have various functions in the anti-ETI war. They are anti-population mind control weapons and can create mass hysteria, panic, depression, and disorientation in individual civilian, areas or cities they are targeted. They charge the ionosphere, and can create earthquakes, even large-scale earth changes, if the massive tectonic plates along the earth's surface are sufficiently stressed. EMP weapons apparently can also zap objects and craft in outer space. They may be perfect for zapping and destroying any ETI shuttlecraft and even mother ships that may cruise our skies, destroying them

The anti-ETI forces have been looking to make the war a hot war, and this new generation of EMP weapons and allied weapons systems has the possibility of giving them the cannon power they so obsessively believe they need.

Disinformation

Disinformation is the glue that holds the anti-ETI war together. In the early days of the war, when the US Joint Chiefs of Staff determined that it would rather fight that join interplanetary society, disinformation was their primary psywar weapon. "Swamp gas," "temperature inversion," "psychologically unstable witness," were early staple labels put out to discredit genuine ETI encounters.

The obvious question is – why did the world's first superpower make such a stupid decision?

Why did it choose to go to war with the ETI initiative, rather than co-develop a joint initiative with the representatives of interplanetary society?

There is an immediate, simplistic answer, which is my answer of choice. Then there is the more complex answer, which takes us into the swamp of details in which the entire battlefield is mired.

The simplistic answer proceeds from the following observation. Certain European countries are now de-classifying their entire ETI encounter files. The United States of America is not only not declassifying its reports of ETI encounters, but is waging a war of attrition against the ETI.

Why the difference, if the ETI phenomenon is universal?

The answer can be found at many levels, from the level of earthly power, wealth, and control of our civilization's resources, down to the very level of the human soul.

The European military is under the control of humans who are fit for interplanetary society. Their normal impulse, whether they are conscious of it or not, is to react openly, not aggressively, to the stimuli of a higher intelligent species.

In stark contrast stands the military command of the USA, beginning with the joint chiefs of staff in the early 1950s, who first militarized the ETI issue and in effect began the anti-ETI war.

Rather than opening to the ETI initiative, the military command of the USA reacted and declared war on a higher civilization, using the war technologies we have just talked about.

In allegorical terms, the lower beasts – the counter-evolutionary souls - saw the angels coming, and reacted by picking up their clubs, not running to embrace them.

The USA military command's declaration of war against the ETI may have at the core been a psychological-evolutionary thing, not a strictly military strategy thing.

Okay, now on to the next layer of the onion – who benefited from the anti-ETI war?

Many parties thought they were benefiting, all of them vested interests. Although the military by-word for the war was "avoid public panic" and "maintain public control of the

Nation," none of these parties really had the long-term public interest in mind. ETI encounters produced public amusement. Puzzlement, not panic.

Any objective analysis of the data would have confirmed this. There was no evidence the ETIs intended colonization of earth. Rather, observation and the peripheral cueing of earth's population were their apparent mission, early stages in the ETI initiative. ETI encounters were in reality peripheral cues, psychologically charged stimuli designed to make earth's population widely, but acutely, aware of a higher intelligent presence in their environment.

If anything, many ETI encounters appear to be deliberately pushing the buttons of the US military. Disabling the firing mechanisms of nuclear missile sites; buzzing the White House air space; buzzing numerous military fighter airplanes, air force bases, military submarines and ships.

Objectively analyzed, these are not hostile acts of war by the ETI. They are the playful psychological conditioning of an advanced interplanetary culture. Their goal is to teach the US military – Nuclear war is a no-no; don't even think about it, we got the White House if we want.

So, who thinks they benefit from the anti-ETI war?

Well, for one, the retrogressive elements within the US military command might think they benefit from the anti-ETI war.

"We've got another war to fight!" thinks that primitive military mind, knowing this means resources, money, research, weapons, power, self-importance, continuance of the military even unto earth's destruction.

Yeah, the US military command got another war to fight. The best kind, a secret war. No accountability. Boys and their toys. Little do they know that entry into interplanetary society means the end of war as a social problem-solving mode.

But, on their own, the US military command does not have the power and vested interests to start and sustain an ultra secret, top priority, interplanetary war own its own initiative. That is not how the culture of the US war machine functions. Going back to very early days of banana republic wars, the US military machine has always been a tool, waging war to protect the vested interests of a small circle of economic and political interests.

US military intervention is the surface shell of the true battlefield, the conflicts that ultimately are about preserving a petroleum civilization.

Energy! That is what may fuel (no pun intended) the anti-ETI war. Control of energy resources. Control of an entire planetary civilization, from its means of production, to its national governments, parliaments, legislatures, newspapers, television, and its very consumer culture.

After all, do we not have a fossil fuel and nuclear energy civilization, with devastating impacts on our planet? This fossil fuel civilization that traces back directly to predatory ruthlessness, to oligopolies that control our natural resources to this very day. Do not we see the same bloody phantom fingers again and again when we delve into the underlying struggles of war?

Come the ETI evolution, advanced ETI free energy technology will replace our fossil fuel and nuclear energy, our fossil fuel transportation. The entire resource civilization that the shadow government seeks to retain control of will be transformed.

What is the war against the ETI initiative? It is a war to preserve not only a fossil fuel civilization. It is a war to preserve the culture of war, exploitation of natural resources, degradation of the earth and of the human spirit, political and social control. The anti-ETI war is waged through psychological warfare against the human race and extraterrestrial intelligence, simultaneously.

The war against the ETI initiative is this shadow's government's last gasp. The anti-ETI war is a war of attrition against both the human community and the representatives of interplanetary society. It is a desperate attempt to hold on to the evolutionary past, by trying to fool the people one more time.

This time it is the shadow government that is the fool.

OK, what is the shadow government, how does it function and who are its leaders, captains, denizens and cannon fodder?

Oh, to answer that would be to provide a treatise of the underlying political science of earth.

The shadow government shifts and changes, and at the same time it remains oddly permanent, unchanging and stationary. It is not a single entity. It is more like a network of common values, entities and members with common goals. It has its good guys and bad guys.

There is a most important mantra in becoming aware of the shadow government. The mantra is – "I know it when I see it."

It has many, many rooms in its planetary mansion – taking new forms, growing new heads as old ones are cut off or become inoperative.

The shadow government is a font of culture. It seeks to implant and maintain a culture on earth. The closest description of this culture was what we used to call at the think tank "Friendly Fascism."

Therefore, at its core are the owners of the resources of earth, seeking to perpetuate our fossil fuel civilization through the technology of friendly fascism.

These are the monarchs, the Rockefeller bad guys, top multi-national types, world-class ideologues, evil intelligence types. Old boy ties into the covert operation agencies give the shadow government its enforcement mechanism.

They figure they own the core human civilization, its resources, and the minds within our human culture. Control is just a matter of proper programming. They start, stop, and run all wars. Networks of hyper-intelligence agencies destabilize just in the right way, creating just the right war, and the public treasury compensates them for all the costs.

What a shuck; what a scam.

Too bad when the shadow government ran into the ETI initiative and jumped the wrong way.

Can you believe the cosmic idiocy of trying to wage war on a higher civilization?

540

Other counter-evolutionary government, power, cultural, economic, religious, national, or military groups on the planet may be waging war against ETI, enrolled as "cousins" or informal fellow travelers of the shadow government.

So be it. All the better that they facilitate their self-destruct.

My theory is that the ETIs suckered the shadow government into declaring war on it. ETI, an advanced species, knew that the shadow government and its troops would take the bait, setting themselves up for virtual annihilation in a war they could not possibly hope to win.

Remember, we are only admitted into interplanetary society if we do not bring the culture and mind-set of war with us. So ETI's double bluff on the shadow government actually may be an evolutionary filter. Functionally, it is how the human wheat is separated from the chaff. At the level of the human soul, finally, after millennia, the shadow government may well be publicly surfaced on earth, dismantled, and thrown into the eternal abyss.

That is, in a few words, the simplistic over-view of the secret war on the ETI initiative being waged on planet Earth.

Some even say the shadow government is pursuing a scorched earth policy. Either we elite terrestrials stay in covert control of the ball game here on earth, or we torch it.

Fat chance. We've been there, done that, millennia ago.

Why does this group like covert operations and secrecy so much?

If the activities and persona of the shadow government were made public, they would no longer be effective. Secrecy is a prime component of their technology. Secrecy is an engineering requirement for these guys.

Bottom line: If these guys went public in their opposition to the ETI initiative, we would know how really rotten they are.

Soon, we are told, the more progressive elements in these networks want to leak out the word that an ETI initiative exists.

The war against the ETI initiative, like all wars, changes every day.

A best advice is to follow the war, at least with some degree of consciousness; say, as you would follow a high priority item in your own life.

For we are all in the war against the ETI initiative. We are what the war is ultimately all about.

Do you want to go with the terrestrial retrograde elites?

Or do you want to dance with the representatives of inter-planetary society?

I say it's a no-brainer.

So, again, how does the Holy Spirit entity fit into the ETI initiative?

Just what role does its visitation upon me play in the multi-dimensional, interactive dynamic that is my own life?

Was the Holy Spirit a hallucination, a projection of my mind? I go back in time often, trying to discern just what the Holy Spirit entity was, and what the meaning, the function of its words to me might be.

At a gut level, my hours with this higher entity feel real, tran-scendental, benign. I suppose this gut feeling is one of the main reasons I believe the ETI initiative to be benign, and part of our incorporation into universe society. I believe I had a genuine interaction with a higher being who for some specific reason related to the ETI initiative chose me to communicate with.

The term "partisan" keeps coming to my mind. Partisan war-fare has been long been a feature of human wars. Partisans are loosely organized individuals within the grass roots of a popula-tion who carry on war against an occupying military force from within the culture.

Maybe the Holy Spirit was activating me as a partisan in the larger ETI initiative. The entity's approach and its words of activation, motivation, and direction fit very much within the mold of how human partisans have been enrolled in human wars. There is a one-time activation. There is no sign of continu-ing command and control. The partisan in effect is left to carry on the mission on her or his own devices, to study the terrain and the battlefield, to live by trial and error.

That is very much the model of how I was visited upon, and then left to live my mission for a quarter century in earth's social fabric. Not an organized guerilla force of the mind, but a networked individual with a unique perspective, partisan to the cause of the ETI initiative.

At another level, perhaps my life meaning was itself another reason the Holy Spirit came to communicate with me.

In the longer-term spiritual design of my own universe career, the Holy Spirit's revelation, its intervention gave a certain elevated spin or momentum to my life. Life has been indelibly different since the night I was brought into its embrace. Very different, as I feel I migrated with it toward some other dimension, different from the mind spaces humans normally inhabit.

Mine is now a dimension with a direction. I feel as though the Holy Spirit entity enrolled me in a larger scenario unfolding not only on earth and interplanetary civilization, but in dimensions of the spirit that use planetary life as a school for souls. Over the years, I have become a more and more witting participant in this fuller universe life. My own reality has become a sort of crossover between the human life, extra-planetary life, and life in spiritual dimensions that are more real than material plane. I find myself projected into each of these dimensions, but not totally of any of them.

Who was the Holy Spirit? Well, it may be wishful thinking, but I feel the Holy Spirit's intervention with me was part of the universe administration's plan to keep earth free. Free from whom? Free from the lethal alliances and vested interests of the shadow state. Free from the counter-evolutionary forces that are waging war against our entry into full universe citizenship.

In a word, I was enrolled as a free agent on behalf of the universe administration. And that is where my loyalties have grown. My core loyalty is not solely to the ETIs and not solely to human society. But to helping build a bridge – a co-evolution between the community of human souls and interplanetary society.

It is with great joy and expectation that I carry these thoughts and insights in our secular, positivist society. My every-day world has been the world of government, environmental law, community health care and mental health therapy. Each of these worlds is sharply positivist. There has been no official finding that dimensional beings or ETI intelligence exist. Therefore to share the thoughts that there may be an ETI initiative, and a secret war instigated and maintained by a shadow human government is provocative.

I certainly hope so!

I mean, what could be more provocative than these constellations of theories, insights, and opinions?

Hey, I'm just another ETI partisan, and if I can provoke and awake and dialogue and inform and nudge human awareness, well then I am doing my interplanetary mission.

I am just a piece of a holographic puzzle called reality. But I feel very, very fortunate in being able to bring these insights to you. You may have thought of all of them. You may have thought of some. It all may be new and cognitively dissonant.

If these are provocative, well then the job is being done.

From my view, a true environmentalist, concerned about the future of Gaia, would find the promise and vision of an impending integration with extraterrestrial civilization a fundamental environmental issue.

Inter-Planetary citizenship, and the access to advanced technology that it may bring, is likely to mean the end of environmental degradation of the earth, its resources, and life forms. A new energy civilization, based on cosmic energy sources, is likely to terminate out fossil fuel civilization with prejudice.

Human health care is likely to be revolutionized as we gain access to the more advanced healing and genetic technologies.

The secrets of the human mind may likely be accessed through our integration with more advanced civilizations. We currently use but a fraction of our potential. There are dimensions of reality we only glimpse through a veil.

Our access to science, technology, social organization, economic abundance will likely advance. We are just now beginning to uncover deeper universe laws. Our notions of human reality are based, in some fundamental way, on medieval beliefs. The ETI initiative beckons us out of our own dark ages.

I would be disingenuous if I did not say that the life of an ETI partisan had its challenges. In the short quarter century of my mission to date, I have experienced self-doubt and despair. I have been seared by moments of ridicule and humiliation. I have suffered moments of defeat, been elated when I felt I communicated some insight. I have been looked up to, sought out, shunned, honored, and sometimes even accepted, all because of my allegiance to the mutual causes of humans and higher intelligence. All in the service of a higher ETI plan, whose dim outlines I can barely make out, and which seems to reside somewhere outside the conscious awareness of the vast majority of my fellow billions of human beings.

Am I in recovery from higher intelligent beings?

Well, that's hard to say.

In some sense, every day is another day of recovery from the transformational cauldron to which the Holy Spirit admitted me.

The flip side of recovery is that the Holy Spirit's transformational cauldron has become my life, which is now familiar and safe.

CHAPTER 3

THE MESSIAH

If there is one thing you could say about the Messiah, it's that he was of good heart and good will, if infirm mind. He was genuinely ethical; concerned about the fate of the universe and humanity. Kind to strangers and beggars. Brilliant in his chosen field on experimental psychology. And a good father and husband before his lost sanity.

In the distance of the years, I bear a growing fondness for the Messiah, my mad teacher. He was transparent; his heart-sourced motives were pure by and large. He was the hand dealt to me by fate. And I in turn was the moving hand dealt to the Messiah.

The Messiah and I first intersected in time-space continuum two years before he had his own run-ins with either schizophrenic voices or higher intelligent beings. When we met he was an associate professor of psychology at a prestigious university, with degrees from Harvard, MIT and McGill Universities. Seven years he was a grimy street psychotic, wandering the streets of New York in a daily search of his messiah-ship. In the intervening years came our adventure, the folly of Messiah and Paraclete.

The Messiah's enrollment as universe savior started with his delving into parapsychology. He had a sharp scientist's mind and approached the study of precognition, telepathy, psychokinesis, and reincarnation with the same vigor as he had attacked experimental and cognitive psychology. Perhaps it was the death knell of ego tolling, but he told me how no one in contemporary parapsychology had the methodological grasp that he did. His job, as he saw it, was to integrate the paranormal sciences with mainstream science, and to lead humankind from the darkness to a new dimension of universe understanding.

The Messiah's journey before we met took him through the labyrinth of the paranormal. He told me that disembodied voices spoke to him he was returning from a visit to a parapsychological institute in Eastern Europe. During this episode, he experienced more than voices alone. The Messiah's reality morphed as the voices were talking, in a way to reinforce and demonstrate their message.

His latent schizophrenia was activated, on that close thin line between mental aberration and interaction with higher beings. The voices said that he was the messiah, that he was destined to integrate all knowledge for the new era. Morphing subconscious thoughts would manifest before him, like little cartoon characters. Wristwatch hands would bounce back and forth, signaling messages from unseen dominions. He could not only read people thoughts, but see them.

Who was I to contradict that he had been visited by higher beings, enrolling him in his messianic mission? After all, they were doing the same to me. Only now do I realize that I was on one side of sanity's razor, and the Messiah, square on the other. The voices in his head were chemical artifacts, dissociated personalities. The Holy Spirit, I discerned, was a higher being, come down upon me.

So why did I follow the Messiah? He was my mentor, he was my teacher, and he was my friend. He was the personal messiah who helped liberate me from the box that was my mind. He liberated me from the arid deserts of everyday thinking, into greener pastures of the mind. He activated my own latent hallucinations, later to blossom into full-scale manic depression.

He introduced me to the secret, crazy worlds that live invisible right before our very noses, in the recesses of our minds.

At first the Messiah and I tape-recorded all our conversations. We would meet from mid-morning to early morning next day; tape and tape after tape changed into the largish black tape recorder, sentences left hanging while the tapes were changed. Day number forty-one, tape number nine. The Messiah and the Paraclete are in conversation. Recorded for the ages.

Conversation was the Messiah holding forth, peppered by the occasional phrase of prompt from me, passing the joint back to him, smoke thick in the loft.

Today's topic, well, Swedenborg's description of life after death. Emmanuel Swedenborg was a Swedish scientist and psychic of the eighteenth century. Known as one of the greatest scientists of his day, Swedenborg spent many of his later working days in trance communication with higher beings in the inner dimensions.

He developed an elaborate description of the afterlife, holding that the "dead," actually live souls, continued to live detailed lives in a series of dimensional spheres surrounding the earth. Swedenborg would visit with them, gathering data in the manner of a visiting sociologist. Some of the "dead" did not know they had passed on from earthly life.

The Messiah latched onto Swedenborg as his role model, a world-class psychic scientist. Swedenborg had paved the way for him, to be a stepping-stone for his messianic mission of integrating science and liberating mankind.

Other days we would talk about numbers, codes, and synchronicities. The Messiah told me that higher voices had given him the meaning of numbers they would use for communication. The number 2 meant "good," for example. Soon I was applying them in my own microcosm - automobile license numbers, phone numbers. I would walk down the streets of New York, spying the license plate number of passing cars, decoding their meaning. License plates became my guides. They would tell me what might happen at the meeting I was going to.

Their codes would answer my thoughts. I had found new anchors in the Alice in wonderland world of the Messiah.

Synchronicity was another fun topic for our taped conversations. The source here was Carl Jung, the psychologist. Synchronicity held that there was a dimension of meaning in the universe. The classic example is that of a scarab beetle walking into Jung's window, just as a patient was telling him a dream about a scarab beetle. Well, we were afloat in a sea of synchronicity, taken to insane extremes.

Synchronicity infused all our activities and thoughts. One of our grand synchronicities happened as we were walking in a park next to the Hudson River, visioning our roles in the coming millennium. As we spoke, a large ship came down the river, its stern emblazoned with the name, "Global Hope."

The Messiah and the Paraclete were, you see, the "global hope" for mankind.

Our synchronous antics ranged from the sublime to the ridiculous. One day, the Messiah started decoding biblical prophecy – Old Testament – to show how his coming had been foretold. He interpreted one biblical phrase to refer to his cousin masturbating and ejaculating in front of him when they were kids. Sure there was synchronicity – down to the identical names of his cousin and the biblical actor. He really believed this one. I stared and went along silently, wondering.

I soon got into the synchronicity game. My grandmother's family was from a town in Cuba called Sancti Spiritus - "Holy Spirit". I loved to find my birthday and birth-year numbers in the news. "Forty-two miners today narrowly escaped injury when..." I made detailed maps and connections between prophecy and politics, highlighting the synchronous names, sounds, dates, and patterns. The links between politics and spirituality were what most deeply mattered to me.

These were the bubbly froth on the surface of our reality. We each were deadly serious about our missions, and drifting into a hard inner core of delusion. Reality is plastic – it will mold itself into one's deepest psychological projections. Until the projections become inform or demented or delusional or hallucinatory.

Then one hits a wall.

We managed to go three years before hitting our own unique personal wall.

The Messiah really had to push me in our first attempt to announce ourselves to the world. He came to my loft one day agitated, saying it was to time make a public announcement, everyone would then see. I was skeptical, but still able to be manipulated. I didn't say no. By the time we got started I really identified with our decision to announce ourselves to earth.

We came up with a 100-page paper, numbered and bound, to be sent to all major media of earth. How typical! Another pair of crazies announcing themselves. The paper laid out what we thought was a cogent argument that we were the Messiah and the Paraclete. It proposed the beginnings of an integration of science, and a peace plan for earth. I mean we really poured our educated souls into the work. I sneaked a two-line college poem of mine at the end:

> *gentle shyness*
> *self-worried spider's mirror*

Just to give the tome that touch of sensitive consciousness.

I remember the late night we stayed up by the large loft tables addressing each paper to yet another of the world's media – news agencies, newspapers, journalists, television stations. Our wives knew we had gone off the deep end.

Then we mailed them, and waited. And waited. And waited. Nothing. Not the drop of a pin. No reaction. Now I can imagine the envelopes arriving at the mailroom and going into that circular file meant for the bizarre. In our delusional grandeur, we had sent out our announcements with the expectation of the ages.

Finally, one Sunday the phone rings at the loft. It is an editor from one of Europe's finest magazines. "Is this some kind of a joke?" he says.

"No, it is for real," I reply.

"Well, it seems like a tremendous waste of money," he says.

End of conversation. End of first announcement.

The Messiah didn't show his face around my loft for weeks. He must have been in that stage of delusional thinking where the signal back from the world is jarring and grounding.

Probably the best thing about our first announcement was that there never was a second one. The Messiah gave up trying to announce himself to the world, at least where I was involved in the announcement. There was that time he flew off to Prague to announce himself at a parapsychology conference. But for as long as we were to be together, the Messiah let go of having to tell the world that he had come.

It was after our announcement that the Messiah's latent mental illness began to surface and intensify. Within several months, he flew off to Prague to announce himself again, only to arrive back to the psychiatric ward. He called me from the hospital. "Get me out of here; they're drugging me," he agitated over the telephone. The hospital put him under a psychiatric hold order. I called my contacts in the civil liberties union to see if we could get habeas corpus. Their assessment was that the Messiah was very sick, and should not be released.

The truth is that I was living in a bubble of psychopathology myself. My head was divided. Half of it was in the world of the state legislature and foundations, on consulting contracts to pay my bills and feed my family. The other was firmly in the thought-world dreamed up by a schizophrenic, in which I was a central character.

Still, I did not break. I managed to walk bravely in both worlds, seeing them as utterly different levels of reality. In one reality I walked with the Messiah. In the next I walked with the legislature. The two never intersected. I managed to perform in both.

That we had become ganga-raj intensified the bubble. We inhaled marijuana smoke from waking until the earliest hours before dawn, constantly in the high and then the daze. Listening to the tapes of our conversations you would hear these long silences during which a joint – usually as thin as a nail – was rolled. Then gaps of silence while one or the other of us drew in the sometimes-mild, sometimes-harsh smoke.

The dope was sacred, the path of the Rasta into higher consciousness. Sometimes I would go high into the consensual sanity of the world of contracts and publishers. I like the heightened sensitivity, the blast of insight I would direct at others in the meetings. I went high to a meeting with the editor in chief of a major publishing house, and managed to quadruple my advance on a book. Hey, this is power, I thought.

Grass helped us puzzle out the plans of higher intelligence. I mean, with interactions as bizarre as theirs, it was good to be high and disassociated when trying to delve into ETI meanings. We took dope as a necessary condition of work. Without the smoke, we would not have been able to fly into the astral dimensions we needed to inhabit for our mission.

Well, psychoactive substances and psychopathology do strange things together. I think the smoke in a strange way both elevated our consciousness, and magnified the delusions of our messianic mission. He wasn't the real messiah, clearly. But the dope helped him – and me - access hyper-real thoughts and insights about ETI intentions, which we would have probably never grasped.

At the same time, the marijuana accelerated whatever pathology was in the Messiah's mind. Consequently, he became simultaneously more messianic, and more delusional.

And the bubble of delusion grew stronger and stronger around the Messiah – and me. When would this bubble burst, and how would each of us survive?

Our media appearances, spread over three years, delayed the bubble bursting. Our appearances all came after the publication of a book on earth changes, which I had engineered to be as technocratic and evidence-oriented as possible. No references to Messiah, although we present something of a messianic platform. We re-surfaced the John F. Kennedy assassination at a time when it was still somewhat dangerous to challenge the official verdict. We proposed a new political party, based on representational voting, to break the artificial monopoly of the Republican and Democratic parties in the political marketplace. Our messianic platform felt sophomoric, fixated and obsessed with the United States of America - out of all the countries on the planet.

With our media appearances limited to discussing technocratic earth changes predictions, the Messiah really felt pinned to the wall. He could not declare himself. On good days, he would chime in and participate. On bad days he would show up stoned, and rant at the media host.

My fondest memories, actually, are of our first joint appearance, at an all-night metaphysical radio talk show held one Christmas Eve. The host had his own "metaphysical expert" on the panel, to provide counter-balance. We stayed the night on the air, to the dawn. It was the first public venue where we really could unload the insights we had been developing in our bubble. Not Messiah stuff; but state of the art theorizing about higher intelligence; about the earth changes prophecies. The call-ins were hot - we really caught the audience's ear. The show was like one of our recorded marijuana-smoke sessions, only without the dope and the delusions. I thought we had begun to hit our stride.

We were finally on track in our mission – flogging information, not hallucination. After the show, the Messiah was in one of his more stable moods. I thought he got it.

But he didn't get it at other shows. The prime example was a radio talk show where he showed up in the studio with his hookah, incoherent in his Messiah head. I never knew when a schizophrenia flap would happen. There were no predictors. I think the worst always happened when I arrived at the studio first, leaving him to stoke himself up with smoke and trigger himself into hallucination.

When we would make the trip to the studio together, I usually could talk him back down into his body.

Our media exposure had paradoxical effects. One would have thought it reinforced the Messiah's bubble. In an odd way, the effect was just the opposite.

Media brought us up into the immediate glare of social reality. It magnified the creative insights we were delivering. But it also exposed the pathology of messianic delusion back directly into our eyes. It was like a plane taking off, with its bottom falling out.

One television appearance I particularly remember was a major mid-day talk show with a national host, in Washington, DC. The show itself went well, with repartee back and forth on the coming cataclysms, and the political leadership that would be required to survive. On the airplane back to New York, the Messiah and I talked, not about this fresh triumph, but about how disastrously our messianic mission was going.

We were both depressed. The depression came not because we had failed in reaching a large audience about earth changes, but because as we succeeded as mainstream thinkers, our messianic mission dimmed. As the plane was landing, he turned to me and said, "Well, maybe the best thing that can happen is that this airplane crashes now."

The plane did not crash, and we languished forward into the waning days of the Messiah and the Paraclete.

The waning days lasted a year and a half. Though the riveting force of our messianic mission had dissipated, both of us hung on stubbornly. Though I was having difficulty meeting rent and food each month, when a law school colleague called me with an offer from a Wall Street firm, I declined it. I was addicted to the messiah game, and the game was still afoot, at least in late night reveries with my smoke.

The game graduated to the slow, steady tortoise pace. Day after day we trudged back to writing our newest visionary, delusional manuscript book, aptly the Messiah Game. Perhaps, not so aptly. It was actually an academic book, a rehash of evidence for the paranormal – precognition, psychokinesis, telepathy. A restatement of major ETI cases; a review of the occult lives of Hitler, a quest for the paranormal Jesus. Hidden and nowhere in sight were the Messiah and the Paraclete. I was determined there would be a stonewall: no Messiah talk.

The Messiah, who could touch-type, was at the typewriter. I would pace and dictate the book. Some of our concepts were novel – if misguided. We developed the dream-interpretation theory of ETI encounters, and Virgin Mary sightings. Both were essentially ETIs, although one in religious archetype and the other in science fiction archetype. We brought forth a new theory of history, an under-history of the paranormal and higher beings, as the true driving force behind human events.

But underneath, I could feel a ponderous energy, off-track, glued to some fundamental delusion. The Messiah and I were on the road to nowhere.

How could I have voluntarily entered the world of the Messiah and carried out the folly of the Paraclete, both of us in fixed delusion?

I still ask myself that question.

On the face of it, the driving thread in our dual folly of Messiah and Paraclete seemed to be, not the intervention of higher intelligence, but mutual mental illness.

In psychiatric terms, the Messiah and I became prisoners of *folie a deux*, a psycho-pathological symbiosis. We took on a mutual delusion and acted it out.

Facilitated by mental illness, we could also have been termed a two-person cult, a one-on-one cultic relationship. Cultic relationships are built on the dominance, abuse, mind control of one person in the relationship over the other.

Psychopathology and cultic relationships may have been factors that led me into the world of the Messiah and the Paraclete, but were they the sole factors?

Clear away the underbrush of mental illness and cultic dynamic in the Messiah-Paraclete psychodrama. There emerges a plateau on which to trace the clever hand of higher intelligence in manipulating, leading, misleading, and guiding us.

As to mental illness, the seeds of Messiah-Paraclete *folie a deux* must lie, in some part, within myself. Years after the Messiah and I had parted, when I was in the midst of my master's degree as a counseling therapist, I did a genealogical map of mental illness in my family. The purpose of the map was to trace mental illness up through my family tree, and discover patterns that may reveal a genetic tendency.

Genetic theory now has it that some mental illnesses can be genetically transmitted. My genetic map revealed possible – some would say strong - lines of genetic tendency toward mental illness, coming down my mother's side. One generation up, two of my aunts apparently had some possible form of what could be considered mental illness. One aunt had been treated with electro-shock, a common treatment in her day for depression. Another aunt, though not diagnosed, was famous in our family for bizarre behavior. For example, she would obsessively lock and re-lock doors, even our front door at parties. Obsessive-compulsive disorder might have been the diagnosis of any reasonable mental health practitioner.

Clearly then, I was at genetic risk of having a latent mental illness or a predisposition toward it, when I went into the Messiah-Paraclete dual folly. Granted, this is a truism. Two years after breaking with the Messiah, I was myself in a florid episode of bipolar affective disorder, a lethal, lifetime mental illness known as manic depression.

However you want to parse it, I was fair game for a brainy, schizophrenic psychologist who thought he was the promised savior. We used to joke about this, at length. We were the mad scientist (Messiah) and the mad politician (Paraclete). We studied and discussed the psychiatric literature on the Messiah delusion, a fairly common one in the annals of psychosis, seeking to distinguish our folly from those found in psychiatric wards around the world.

Psychiatric researchers have even gone so far as to place three delusional Christs in a single psychiatric ward and study their delusional interactions. At least the Messiah and I did not have that problem. We each had divided our delusional turf in advance. The Messiah as Christ. I was his sidekick, the Paraclete, who could of course be the third person of deity, and thus out-rank him. Clever, eh?

Then there were the historical precedents. We went a long way with one historical *folie a deux*, which traveled the length of the medieval world proclaiming themselves God and the Prophet. They may have been considered heretics, but the people did not consider the completely insane, and at their height God and the Prophet held sway over sizable numbers of followers.

All these rationalizations cannot sweep away that early moment in my relationship with the Messiah when I perceived some aha! Realization. My mind's eye beheld this short, but lanky, blonde and balding, middle aging Jewish scholar who looked like the shadow of a Swedish film director. His mind felt like a cross between that of a Talmudic scholar and a brilliant secular intellectual.

He spoke of prophecies, inner dimensions, and paranormal reality in substantiated tones. He told me, "I am the Messiah, and you are my first angel." Whether I was merely psychologically susceptible, or actually delusional and latently psychotic, I do not know. Perhaps a mixture of both. Yet at that moment, I knew that my exploding perceptual grasp of a deep secret of my own fact had occurred. I embraced that moment of the truth of the Messiah.

Incarnational contracts? Karmic debts? Perhaps, though these things are hard to prove beyond the immediate perception of the individuals living out a re-incarnation contract. There is no way I could prove to myself, let alone to you, that the reason I fell into the Messiah's world is that I owed him from a prior life. Or that I was paying of the mechanisms of fate, that ineffable power. These are subjective forces, which probably do govern our lives, but we have not yet developed the technology to prove it to you.

Having slipped into the Messiah's world I stayed there for three years, becoming its administrator, its theorist, its articulator, its political and media arm.

I managed to maintain my balance and lived both in the Messiah's bubble and the larger bubble of our consensual world. I held jobs, earned money, reasoned, shouted, loved, and labored in society's common vineyards.

No doubt about it at all, I was sane and functioning in the real world, though considered weird by those technocrats in the foundation world to whom I had confided my earth changes work. My persona in the world of Messiah-Paraclete was another story, altogether. If for one brief encounter, the thoughts and words, and mental states of that dual merged entity know as Messiah-Paraclete had been known by, say your average psychiatric type, we would have been judged seriously delusional. The Messiah more deluded than the Paraclete, on a sliding scale of sanity.

Well, then, for a time we had our own genuine German-trained psychoanalyst. We would see him once a week. The shrink's game with me was that the Messiah was more delusional than I was. He would just listen and listen while I ranted. Once when I broke down in insight, and gape-mouthed, grasped that Messiah-Paraclete was sick, he leaned forward into my face, and with as much emotion as he could muster, said, "See; see!" Meaning, see how delusional you are.

We had our own psychiatric reality check to whom we confided everything, out of which I got only one rise in all those years. Sanity seems to be a consensual, relative definition. Did our psychiatrist make me a fit and healthy Paraclete, and a delusional human being?

So you can't write off the Messiah-Paraclete as a completely delusional, psychotic, insane, folie a deux. We were certified as – well, if not OK – then passably sane, or at least I was. And our shrink thought the dual folly was, very creative – a tolerable outlet for two aging professionals. Conclusion: The Messiah-Paraclete phenomenon cannot be written off as exclusively a product of mental illness phenomenon.

Well, then, lets explore the cultic aspect. That's certainly a more politically correct terrain. If the Messiah-Paraclete relationship was a cult; that is, a two person abusive, thought-reforming, mind-control, power-tripping personality enclosure. As a cult, it's a known psychosocial quantity, and can be evaluated and dismissed. Perhaps if we can account for our bubble as part cult and part delusional folly, then we can more easily erase the role of higher intelligent beings.

Yes. The Messiah and the Paraclete were a cult. No, the Messiah and the Paraclete were not a cult. Both are true. Both are false.

Let us repair to the psychological literature on cults. Yes, according to the accepted categories of cults, the Messiah and I enjoyed a mutual cult of personality. This is a variation on the standard cult of personality, where one dominant, charismatic leader emerges. In this case, two charismatic (to each other) personalities took on the mutual roles of respected leader to the other.

I gave over my power of veneration to the Messiah as the embodiment of Christ. The Messiah gave over his power or… well, grudging acceptance to the Paraclete as the executive wing of deity.

We were a cult, acting out mutual symbolic roles and perceptions, in special (and magical) relationship to reality.

We were not a cult, or at least not a really, really strong cult. The literature tells us that the most common aspects of the cultic relationship (where there are two members of the cult) include manipulative use of abuse, guilt, helplessness, despondency, self-blame, fear, threat, feigned kindness, isolation.

The archetypal example of this is an abusive marriage. The Messiah and Paraclete were raucous, delusional, uninhibited, obsessive, and not mutually abusive.

The issue of abuse is really tricky, though. There was no physical abuse, to be sure. We had an almost scholarly relationship in our work, our messianic debates and research. Was there psychical abuse? For example, did the Messiah abuse me by stating his messiahship, knowing I would defer by reason of my Catholic programming?

The answer is yes, at least for the first six months of our connection. The Messiah's psychical abuse would flare until I finally caught on that the Messiah was delusional and subject to psychosis. I would call him on it, using cognitive techniques, gently and abrasively leading him out of the abusive posture.

To be sure, there was objective feedback that we could be termed a cult. One leading ETI analyst wrote a book contending, in passing, that the Messiah and I were "an ETI cult." His characterization was based on a misleading newspaper clipping, the flimsiest of scholarship. I came across the book and felt somewhat hurt, as the ETI scholar and I had collaborated on a major project a few years earlier and he had not tried to contact me for comment. By serendipity, I ended up visiting his offices after I had read his book. I chose not to confront him, but chose to test his sense of ethics. He did not volunteer a query or a comment.

But he must have been on to some inner truth. We were a cult – the Messiah and the Paraclete. Flat out.

We were exactly what that ETI scholar had written in his book – a cult founded around higher intelligence.

What made us a cult? Not abuse; not manipulation. Not guilt. We were a cult of the personalities of the Messiah and the Paraclete, devoted to the workings of higher intelligence on earth.

We were guilty of the sin of appropriation – we took persona and prophecies from the sacred texts, and assumed them as our own.

Of course, higher intelligence – like the Holy Spirit - encouraged us to do so, in their own playful way. Though it is painful, the scenario reminds me of the "useful idiot" gambit. We formed a cult as useful idiots of higher intelligence, and were so encouraged in our folly.

Why did I stay with the Messiah and the Paraclete?

For many reasons, so it seems. Not the least of these is that Messiah-Paraclete was my life classroom for the duration. I was there to learn of the vastness of the universe, to be led to insights I had no clue existed. I was there to come into direct contact with an order of beings higher than our own species. These were three special years – a greenhouse for my consciousness.

And the Messiah was my mentor, my guide in this New World. Our paths were similar, when one looks at the rear view mirror. We were both intensely curious, knowledge seekers. Both of us had performed within the narrow confines of the achiever's worlds – top rate educations in disciplines that did not admit the reality of the paranormal, at universities that virtually forbade the mention of higher intelligence, ETIs, parapsychology and considered it pseudo-science.

Both of us had performed and achieved in our professional careers before higher intelligence – or mental illness – led us off into these strange dimensions. He was a scientist and professor. I was a lawyer and government official. We had already made a difference in our fields when we were chosen by our fateful interventions.

Despite my stellar private boarding school and Ivy League education, I was an ignoramus on the universe scale. I had no concept of the true powers of the human mind, and the invisible intricacy of the forces underlying our existence. I knew nothing of the orderly progression of billions of inhabited planets, of the unfoldment of the universe administration. I was totally ignorant of the determined plan of an alien ETI civilization in our midst, or even that extra-planetary or intra-dimensional species have long been in the environment of earth.

These were huge gaps in my consciousness, reflective of the gaps that our very civilization is subject to in its worldview. For it is far less offensive to say the world is flat, than to say the earth is the only inhabited planet in creation. I may have had a first-rate secular education, but I was a fool, a cosmic idiot. Hence I was fodder to be a useful idiot in some higher intelligent plan.

I may have been an international lawyer, but I new nothing of the law of galaxies and federations; of life-bearing planet development; of spiritual warfare.

That is why I had my classroom, and like the Messiah, when I came into first contact with the deeper truths of our reality, I exploded headlong from polite, progressive careerism into the raw, heady, delusional experience of the cosmos.

In this world, teachers, mentors have long played a central role in passing on the occulted knowledge, and most importantly developing the insights of their charges. When the student is ready, that master shall appear. That is the ancient formulaic dynamism of the transmission of advanced knowledge.

So too, when I the student was ready, the master appeared

Now, who shall I say the master is?

Let me take the most expansive view of Messiah-Paraclete. It was a training ground, a classroom for two souls. Our lessons were different. For the Messiah, the classroom led to the harsh world of the street psychotic, a broken family, a shattered career, and a fixed and permanent delusion. He paid dearly for the classroom, whatever the deeper lessons may be he will carry into the next dimension.

Of the two of us, the Messiah was the only one to claim that he was God. Oh, I was really fudging when I called the Paraclete the third person of deity. It was a lawyer's rhetorical trick. I was a paraclete, an advocate. But I demanded the truth, and very soon that was something the Messiah could not deliver.

My classroom had a different outcome. It was harsh, but open-ended. I managed to keep my balance, my perspective. I learned a deep lesson. If I could perceive the truth of a circumstance, then I could marshal all my forces behind that truth and it would out, eventually. I was tested, and I believe found sound.

Sound to some other drummer, higher than human, however. The classroom was one that higher intelligence had devised for me. This was a setup by higher intelligence. There is a fine line between human sanity and world of higher intelligence. Mine was a training classroom, preparing me for the tasks that lay ahead. What tasks? Well, they had yet to emerge.

One of these came powerfully to the fore during Messiah-Paraclete. I was to merge with the world of higher intelligence. I was to scour and study all that I could find. I was to live and perceive as if I was a higher intelligent being. I was to work on behalf of higher intelligence's plan – the plan of universe administration.

How was I to carry out my part?

Devilishly simply: Hold the Light. Hold our Light underneath the darkness.

My part in the Light emerged in my classroom.

I was to hold the light, as a singular young spiritual warrior, up onto the face of the darkness of war, exploitation, oppression, deceit.

So I was enrolled as a soldier of the Light. That part of darkness I had been assigned to target was both enticing and repelling. Enticing because I could get under the very skin and thoughts of spy, cop, thug, despot, torturer, murderer. Repelling because I felt that they were the scum of the earth, from the most senior conspirators against freedom, to the intelligence clerks that were now routinely monitoring my calls. I do not yield before these forces of death itself.

The Messiah brought me the fruits of his mentoring. I filled the gaps in my knowledge. Our sessions were really postgraduate seminars in cognitive psychology, dream psychology, precognition, and telepathy. We read and reviewed the evidence for reincarnation – consciousness surviving in successive lives.

I learned how to deal with psychosis. Handling the Messiah over three years developed my therapy muscles. Looking back on the exercise, that is how I really gained my skills as a psychotherapist, in the field. I now feel very comfortable in a therapeutic relationship with people coming out of psychosis.

But the classroom really belonged to the Holy Spirit. In a few hours, higher intelligent beings can turn your life inside out, and propel you in directions and dimensions beyond conception.

Thus it was that I became EyE.

EyE came alive after television interviews in Canada, when the Messiah and the Paraclete parted.

EyE set out to evaporate darkness in the world, by getting squarely in its face.

Darkness noticed, and has kept on noticing for a quarter century now.

In the aftermath of shattering Messiah-Paraclete, I came at the darkness of war like a vertical missile, holding my light, as phallic as I could be in the fearlessness of higher intelligence. I still had not grasped that light simply is, and that is how it disappears the darkness. It does not strike at darkness; it does not even envelop the darkness.

Light simply is.

I relished my singularity, change-agent for the dimensionals. I was on my own, at least without my dear, dear schizophrenic sidekick. I found I could divine corrupt war-like lines of power, and descended on Washington, DC. Within short months, the Congress opened its Kennedy-King assassination investigations, to lay bare the crawling rottenness of the hidden warfare state.

EyE refined my disciplines in spiritual warfare, what the

darkness hated and feared most. These were my expanded, trained awarenesses, honed and developed in Messiah-Paraclete. I could read my environment and see. Not the normal cues. My divinations are the movement of trees, calls of birds. The typology, embedded phrases of congressional reports are fodder for my penetrating de-coding of hidden meanings that no human ever intended.

I learned the martial arts of the spirit. Hold still within your chi, your inner energy. Turn the mass of the cruel, dim-witted Goliath of the state back upon itself. Bring the mad giant to its knees and incinerate it in its own weaponry.

But my twin platform to unearth the Kennedy assassination, and reveal the ETIs was flawed. It was born of human-thought, as though mere reforms of human institutions could effect positive change in life on earth. I was with one foot in the human rat race, and one foot in higher beings, trying to leverage these two realities back and forth upon each other.

The outcome was a sundering of EyE's mission, as I had narrowly defined it. More accurately, the outcome was the birth of EyE, my yin self, receptive to this conscious being universe we co-inhabit. I finally let go of my law school fixation with progress as changing institutional forms, and allowed the upper mind to act. Act it did, and I carried my Light across the continents for eight years, with the outer coating as prophet, writer, adviser, journalist and soldier for peace seeking my footing.

My mission was I, as light worker among other light workers. It was a vertical mission, not a horizontal one directly impacting the social fabric. The Holy Spirit and sacred texts were my silent, inner companions. Darkness bounced and evaporated in its own stench around me. I could not find it within myself to be compassionate toward darkness. I was its implacable foe, dangerous mission in itself, as one can then become the darkness.

Bipolar affective disorder struck me in mid-mission, within the year of leaving the Messiah. I was at the height of my undercover phase, descending upon Washington month after month – that capital of clandestine armored death – to place might light squarely inside the mandarins of deceit. EyE was seeking to implode Washington, that center of world military empire, now longing to be Outer-space Empire as well.

I now see my mental illness as my escape hatch from an untenable and dangerous traverse. Manic depression propelled me vertically upward into a new inner world of dazzling experience and spiraling depression. I had thought myself possessed of the power and invincibility of the Holy Spirit. In my obsessive mission, I would have come to harm had not my mind intervened and made me delusional, non-operative, hospitalized and out of work.

Manic depression brought my soul a new strength, even as my mind slipped out of orbit with the military state.

Look at the karma here. Is it not moral symmetry that the Messiah and I both exited our folly with mental illness? Mental illness can be contagious; taking on the psychosis of another can trigger one's own latent illness. In that sense, both the Paraclete and the Messiah paid for their folly of playing God. We each activated insanity in the other.

On the flip side, my manic depression was my greatest friend. Mental illness was my safety valve; my parachute to eject myself from a stratospheric flight targeted for destruction by all the missiles the forces of darkness could bring to bear on me. They whom the gods make great first they make mad, I told myself, choosing to deny that madness was a predecessor to destruction.

Through EyE I reclaimed my life. I voyaged in full descent into madness, owning it, capturing it, and turning and forging delusion into creative expression and the will to survive. Through EyE, I could see. I poured myself back into the world, blessing the cities of North America as I traveled through them, my own version of a saddhu holy man.

I was being messiah, walking in the moccasins of the Messiah. It was an exhilarating time for me. There is a fine, thin line between the consciousness of higher intelligence and human mental illness. The mentally ill are many times the closest to God among us. They can see the living flow and interconnectedness of everything.

One merges with higher beings at the peril of becoming mentally ill. Our minds, our brains, our psycho-neural circuits are not prepared for the vastness. Perhaps that is why higher intelligence forebears from direct intervention with human minds. We can end up fried in our circuitry, propelled into a dimension that our genetics cannot handle.

So it was for me, but I grasped this new level of being eagerly, and turned it creatively into my anchor. I was EyE G*d on Urth, my creation. All reality revolved around me, in a living poem. The living magic of Mexico fed me.

You will be glad to know I descended back to earth in my own body. My vehicle was Hollywood, where I settled into those blurry canyons surrounding entertainment. I became Alfred once again, with creative tentacles to the US Air Force, the Papacy, California earthquakes, the moveable parties, stuff, stuff, stuff. Falling back into the delusions of EyE. "How is Alfred?" the silver screen of Russian revolution said, and I still took it to be me.

In Hollywood, via a six-month's custody trial in Australia, I met a deeply sacred text. The frequencies of molecules within me jumped out again at seeing a detailed roadmap to the Holy Spirit, in a language poised at just the threshold that receptive humans could absorb. Try bringing your language downward into the world of animals, and you will see the skill that it demands.

Spirit picked me up out of Hollywood – I was too comfortable there and going native. It led me out once again into the world, sacred text under my arm, into the peace movement, shoulder hair and flowing beard. I was dropped first into the United Nations and brought face to face with the Messiah, both released of pain and guilt.

Spirit dropped me off to Europe, Vienna, that gateway between east and west. I played journalistic double agent. The Americans fed me stories; the Soviets fed me stories. German counter-spies kept me late at lunches. And EyE just watched, learning the labyrinth of the inner wiring of the global disinformation shuffle.

But my real agenda was earth's spiritual destiny, and I repaired back to the Netherlands, where one of the earth's reigning experts on one sacred expression of spirit worked and lived. Over dinner at his house, he parsed concepts on the return of the god of our local universe, a household spiritual name on earth. A conventional reading of this sacred text held that this Son of God would return to earth, and left the timing and form vague and indeterminate. It could be millennia from now.

The expert was then engaged in the Dutch translation this sacred text. He led me through passages, cross-references.

"There will be a great surprise," he said, beaming.

"You mean he will return now?" I asked.

"That could be, it could be someone else; but it will be a great surprise." he replied, phlegmatically.

That was enough for me.

The game was afoot, and I was once again upon a living trail.

Antennas that were honed by the Holy Spirit entity in my being burst open once again. I had graduated to a new room of spirit, not a classroom I thought, but a room of action. The expert's special clues were for me, the graduate of Messiah-Paraclete. Had I not gone through that crucible, I would not understand these new clues. For I had lived and trained in my early classroom as the living sidekick of the pseudo-Christ. Perhaps that delusional testing was in reality mock training for a true coming of divine, or cosmic, entity, surprise mystery.

My aura expanded into its blossoming antennae. I was being led, I knew, into a next task of my mission on this planet.

My mission morphed into a landing pad at the mansion of my hostess in Washington, DC. I was no longer EyE to me, but Alfred. The majesty and depth of Urantia's revelations had evaporated EyE's delusional persona, and grounded me. I was in the capital of earthly darkness, scanning every horizon for the next unfoldment of the Coming, once again ripe for the truth, or the next cosmic set-up.

Alfred New Man - fool for God. When the student is ready the master shall appear. But which master was I ready for? Had I done that deep inner work, purging my tapes, letting go of the obsession for earthly attachments, such as power? The local military clandestines had not caught up with this latest turn in my life drama, and still played their spy-like double games with me. The warrens of surveillance held vanishing power and fear over me. They were programmed mortals, vestiges of planetary rebellion, holding back the landing of the universe administration. Soon they figured all was safe and vanished back into the covert.

I was back in my territory, the crossover of political and spiritual forces. I, but not EyE. Holding a strategic vertical position in the belly of the beast. A European communist party newspaper rang me to cover legislative action on the Hill. I begged off, saying, "Human politics is not my bag any more." What a dead end, I mean. Left, right, center – these are mortal concepts leading to stagnation, ultimately to planetary death. I rang them off of me.

Earlier, before the revelations of cosmic surprises afoot, I had come across the channeled writings of my hostess, more clues given me by serendipity. The writings were stored in a loft in San Francisco, and I was given privilege to read them long before I my hostess had linked up in Vienna.

Her channelings were the reason why I had accepted her invitation to come to live and in Washington. Though a futurist – that most secular of prophets - she channeled a version of the *self-same cosmic beings as were promised in *surprise. Reading through them, I saw the blurry outlines of the history of our planet, a more evolved revealing of the truth than the fragments of the sacred testaments. My hostess had apparently tuned into some shared domain of revelation that I could also access.

Was I not being led onto the next path in my mission? One

coincidence - the secret clues of the Coming given me by the Dutch sacred text expert. Two coincidences – my hostess, channel-connected to rare levels of universe understanding and the Coming.

Aha! This is why I was in Washington. It had nothing to do with the belly of the beast. My hostess was to lead me to the next level tasks of my earthly mission. She would open my path along the upward spiral, closer to the surprise coming of the god of our local universe.

And so it was that my hostess and I journeyed together through that path up into the snows of rural Ontario, to the gates of a Canadian wilderness cult. As she said to me, "I think we've found it," I assumed we had maybe found the community we were looking for – a grounded manifestation of the universe administration. A mystery school channeling down galactic energies reclaiming the planet for deity.

I arrived in Canada, looking for God and found him. I did not know that God was the Devil and that my job was to destroy him.

How could God have been the Devil, and the Devil have been God?

It took me fifteen years at the bottom of the deepest well of my being to begin to glimpse an answer.

CHAPTER 4

GOD

Now that God is dead, I feel I can write my truth. We battled, God and I, in this dimension we call human life. I know now that it was only one of us - God or myself - that would make it out alive from our cosmic *sumo*-wrestling match. In his own eyes, he was God. To me, he became the Devil. I was his nemesis. At first, I was willing to accept him as God, and in the end he showed me that he was indeed the Devil.

My abiding memories of my early times in the Canadian base camps of the Kingdom of Heaven are of reading Urantia in the solitude of my room, as a compass against the disorientation of cultic thought-control. There were many levels to the thought control, not all with bad results. I used the insights of this particular sacred text to discern and evaluate what was sourcing the rarified energies of the Kingdom, now my mystery.

I soon fell into a push-me-pull-you. Yes, the Kingdom was a cult and I should leave; no the Kingdom was a universe admin-istration base, and I should volunteer my energies.

I soared during those days and weeks when I saw the Kingdom as a base for the universe plan on earth. The Kingdom's layout would then be a genuine base for a planetary ruler, which Urantia tells us, is a defined stage in the development of inhabited planets such as earth. In these moments, I felt I could see the unfoldment of planetary development right before my eyes.

Then my perceptual matrix would flip. I would come up against some invisible ceiling of thought and spirit in the cult. Their initiation rituals would become empty for me, vapid and garish imitations of what deity should be. The cult members, by and large, were good-willed, gentle, people who befriended me, became as robots, blindly wearing their cult-cap symbols. Foreswearing their critical faculties, pledging their allegiance to a giant, obscured lie.

But I was in a double bind. I could not fully enter into the Kingdom, and by the same token I could not fully leave.

There was, I would discover, a deeper drama holding me there. The drama was, perhaps, the residue of prior life dramas, unfolding around the history of the distant past. The Kingdom's cultic leader who called himself God and I had met before in spiritual battle on earth. Once again, we had come face to face upon this planet to close a final chapter in our struggle, the battle of the invisible titans. Delusional thoughts, perhaps in part, but nevertheless real.

The struggle between God and myself was a battle to the death.

I can see clearly now how my years with the Messiah were preparation for the battle with God, and how these years saved my life. The Messiah was a brilliant psychologist and scholar, with a breath-taking intellectual scope. His mental illness wrought his flawed his perceptions, but he brought a solid foundation of science to his messianic work.

God, by contrast, was a college dropout in psychology, who could bedazzle his cult members with pseudo-insight, but who drew blanks on even the most fundamental areas of psychology.

It was a source of constant fascination to me that the Messiah and God had the same initials in their name. I always took that to be a meaningful synchronicity, but with a changing interpretation.

Were my years with the Messiah a preparation to serve God, or to stop God?

With the Messiah I learned how to live within the world of a schizophrenic who thought himself Christ. That is a hard skill to learn, and still survive. Both the Messiah and God were hospitalized for psychotic episodes. In formal terms, God could be diagnosed as a paranoid schizophrenic with borderline personality disorder. God was devious where the Messiah was transparent. God could plan silently for months, and then turn on you with overwhelming force, lethal in its intent.

In the Kingdom, God built a cult around the projections of his schizophrenia.

Those who internalized these projections lived in some safe, delusional island of consciousness. There was some deeper level of my being which rejected these delusional projections. I was always the outsider, even after I was God's lawyer and confidante, and God himself had set aside the outer trappings of the Kingdom for a life of blue jeans and marijuana.

As a persona, God was the antithesis of the Messiah. God was tall, solidly built, fashion-conscious, a gourmet cook, elegant and dark. To those of us who fell within his sway, his power could be overwhelming. He was a master of manipulation and thought-control. God embodied the evil genius. He would suck you into his needs, and then ruthlessly cut the floor from beneath your feet.

God's projection held that all reality, every jot and tittle within the universe, revolved around his consciousness. His reality became the idiom for the cult. Sometimes his perceptions were ridiculous. "You know what it's like to be me?" he once asked me, "knowing that every time I take a shit, the world wants to shit as well?"

God felt he governed earth and all reality, he thought, through the projection of his energy – his Vibe. One weapon

God used against his enemies was to tie up their body parts by manipulating circuits of the Vibe. At times, when he perceived that one human clique or another was obstructing his wishes, he would shut down sex. "No sex for six months for them," he bragged. "I've shut down sex." Or he would contract their anuses, so that bowel movements became painful. "I've shut down their ass-holes," he would tell a dozen or so members of the cult gathered for Saturday night pool games.

If this was the ridiculous end of God maneuvers, there were also moments of the sublime. There were those subjective, quiet moments within in the womb of the cult, when one contemplated being in the conscious presence of the deity incarnated, a part of the mind of God. These flights of expansive mystical insight were the ultimate power drug of God's cult. Within the Kingdom, the peace of being next to God was known as "honey," or "cocaine," the peace beyond human understanding.

Sublime was our thrill to be in God's aura, leading the ultimate meaningful life, a missionary in service of the Source of all creation.

I still have vivid memories of that chilled Ontario winter day, trees laden down to the ground with ten-foot icicles. We the troops of the Kingdom were massing at our base, ready for the orders to descend upon New York and Washington as ambassadors for the Lord, as the cult called God. Quick excitement, electricity was in the air. We felt that rare power of embarking on a high mission as we loaded on the rag-tag fleet of Kingdom vehicles headed south.

That was the moment of thrill; then, as we hit the oblivious fabric of the United States, came the less sublime reality.

Blam! We hit the wall of a schizophrenic's delusional projections. No one we met in the U.S. knew that God had arrived, or who God was; no one knew humanity was in a spiritual war. My own sweet mother, whom I visited on a fund-raising trip to Texas, waved God's proclamations in my face, saying, "This is a cult! It's a cult!"

In his humble, hallucinating way, the Messiah's concern for the future of humanity was genuine. When he was lucid, his messianic vision was classically utopian, progressive, generous and free of grasping power hunger.

God's game, by contrast, was power in the absolute, not the human welfare. In my presence, he threatened to psychically motivate the North Koreans and Russians to rain nuclear missiles down on the United States if he were bodily threatened by the US military.

"Thy Will Be Done" was more than a figurative motto within the Kingdom. God lived inside the hallucination that his projected mind and energy could trigger nuclear conflagration on earth, or stop it at will. Whatever the cost, the highest good in all reality was his personal well being.

Within the cult and in the world at large, God carried his psychopathology to institutional extremes. He was, by his view, the "King of Kings." In his later years, God called our diminishing group of former Kingdom people around him "the cult of no-cult." Still, an informal fear-inducing protocol of acceptable behavior was informally enforced.

At our Saturday night gatherings, God, fueled with alcohol and dope, bombarded us with stream-of-consciousness diatribes. Any topic was fair game – personal attacks on members and their marriages; intimate details of his own marriage; revelations of how world nations were treating God. To avoid the searing attention of a personal attack, members of the groups retreated into personal paralysis with a particular behavior called "bob and nod". Easy, just nod at everything God says, bob up and down if he looks at you, and the paranoid-schizophrenic will not lash out at you. Inducing fear was God's primary weapon.

The King of King's obsession was ruling earth. "I run this planet," he told me in the privacy of his kitchen one afternoon as our legal battles were intensifying. "More energy runs through here on a single day than through the New York stock exchange."

All of nature supported him in his reign, the birds, the weather, the animals, the oceans, and the stars.

Television was one of God's principal tools to govern earth. His house was in the midst of a forest, by a lake on his private estate. As you drove by the winding unpaved road toward the lake, three large satellite dish antennas sprouted from the roof. Inside, God projected his thoughts and energy at a large-screen television. The screen was God's window to the world, and the world's channel back to him. God broadcast his will through the screen, out the antenna, and back into the television sets and minds of all humanity.

God took his television work seriously. He kept a regular broadcasting schedule, heavily weighted toward dead-of-the-night programming. Night was when the noise of the world fell, and he could best reach his human subjects. But night was not the only time God broadcast to the world. It happened during the day, everyday, especially on live television. Then God could talk back and forth with the television personalities, with politicians and heads of state, and get his will across.

Or so he, and we the chosen, thought and knew.

My favorites were God's public affairs broadcasts, usually through the news or public affairs live TV channels. Through public affairs broadcasts, God kept fleet alert and organized. Fleet consisted of those human souls who were more "irritable" or attuned to him, and most closely in the service of his mission to redeem the earth. Fleet members could be found in every walk of life – in military uniform, in politics, in the arts and music, and – importantly – in music videos.

Through public affairs broadcasts, God communicated directly with the leaders of the world – live and in living color. Leaders and heads of state could make or break their careers by how they came across to God. As the King of Kings, God judged his human leaders not by the plain words they uttered, but by their masonry – conscious or unconscious. Their body language, gestures, speech were judged by God for their symbolic impact. Finger wagging was a no-no. It meant that the finger-wagger wanted to shoot or destroy God. Any politician who wagged his finger at the TV camera when God was watching risked the destruction of his life and soul.

Politicians who angered God did so at their risk. He used his maximal negative psychic power to bring them down. One day, as I was visiting him, he began an attack session on TV. "You'd better leave," he told me. "This could be harmful to your health." I left his house very quickly.

No one was immune from God's wrath, not even the leader of the free world.

The last time I saw God alive, at his annual January birthday dinner, he turned to me with a face full of rage, and spurt out the words, "I've decided to send him to hell." He was referring to the current U.S. President.

About a week later, a sex scandal surrounding the President of the United States broke in the public news for the first time. Cause and effect? Well, you can be sure what God thought about the cause of the U.S. President's problems.

God's public affairs strategy was based on nation-blocks, races, religions, and social streams that he felt supported him or blocked his plans. Some embodied God more purely than others. He was NATO. He was Islam. He was the Asians. He was the Africans. Opposed to him were networks of organized crime and the secret world elite, a hidden cabal that maintains itself throughout the centuries with cultural masonry and manipulation of property, government and law.

The United States was his obsession; he had a love-hate relationship with the U.S. government, as well as the U.S. public. The public was his special flock, and had prayed to him to liberate them from organized crime. But the U.S. public was also "managed," easily manipulated by the masonry of the hidden elite – its media, politics, and culture. The anti-God media would promote themes and images that were designed to covertly undercut his sway in the United States and by extension the world public.

A vivid example of God's symbolic judgments grew out of the God's legal battles to marry his second wife, in which I served as legal adviser. In God's eye, virtually the entirety of world affairs turned into a reflection of his war against the Ontario government to free his adoptive charge and marry her. The Chinese government carried out its infamous public massacre of student dissidents at the height of God's legal proceedings.

By God's view, the massacre was a direct attack upon himself by gangs of organized crime who controlled the Chinese government. The Chinese had staged the massacre intentionally to block his marriage. The message sent to the world at large was that his bride-to-be – symbolized by the Chinese students (his bride was a high school student) – must "get down" or be crushed.

In the world of music video, God reigned supreme. Music videos were all about God, either for him or against him. Music videos were his most active broadcasting arena, amplifying the "good" videos and psychically shooting down the "bad."

God perceived "good" music videos as updates of his journey on earth, broadcast to fleet around the world. Each music video, its music, words, artists, story line, production values told the story of God on earth as it was unfolding. Tune into music videos and you would be tuned into the coming of the Lord.

An example? Well, do you remember Talking Heads in 1984? Did you know that "Burning Down the House" was all about the disintegration of the Kingdom of Heaven cult? If you didn't, then you weren't tuned in to God's Play as closely as those who were in the know.

Music videos were not all good, though. There was a war in music video land. The tuned in veejays knew this, and would talk to God live on the air while he watched the TV screen, and brought them into the workings of his mind and will. The more aware the veejay was, the more the mix of good and bad videos reflected the battle of the bands. It was hard to predict from video to video whether God would judge a particular musical artist good or bad. One band could be heroes because of a particular music video, only to be shot down by God a few months later for a video that went against him.

God's public work in the music video war formed the legal basis for the more than twenty legal cases he brought in the courts of the United States and Canada at the end of the eighties. He sued Home Box Office, Time Inc., RCA, and others for broadcasting footage of his private life that denigrated him, the central focus of the music video industry.

With God's power behind the lawsuits, he won a default judgment against the government of Ontario in the amount of $750 million. Despite the paper victory, God did not collect a penny. He was too busy trying to destroy and kill his Rival – his attorney whose quick wits had secured the default judgment in the first place.

That was God for you, the ultimate paranoid schizophrenic. Snatching defeat from the jaws of victory. God was ultimately a self-saboteur.

My battle to the death with God was the hidden cornerstone of our relationship. On the surface, I served him as sworn minion and attorney. Officially, he entrusted me with representation of the Crown, first as minister of External Affairs of the Kingdom, and then as lawyer in the courts. He lavished me with attentions, accommodations, and long evenings playing raconteur.

Down deep he believed he was playing with the Devil. "There you are, hidden, under layers and layers of masonry," he told me through the thick smoke of marijuana, as his plan to kill me was coming to a head. I was torn with grief. How could a true God want to condemn a soul who has given everything to serve him?

Our rivalry was visible almost from the first moment we came together in this life. Not that I intended consciously to confront him. It was my Light, my stand that directly challenged his God-hood. I made his Lie transparent, not by doing anything. Just by being. If God did not destroy me, he would ultimately implode himself.

Why am I now still so filled with emotion by God's memory? I search myself and I still feel the sting and danger of his betrayal. Betrayal, that's the source of my reverberation, my drive to clear the air and set the record straight about this bent, infirm man. The utter baseness of one whom would try to murder another who is risking his life for him.

God harbored dark thoughts about me from the onset of our alliance. The harder I would try and serve his interests, the darker his suspicions became. He thought I came to steal his powers, to make off with his messianic inheritance.

"I can look into the TV screen and have them talk back to me. Can you do that?" he asked me. I bobbed and nodded, and did not tell him that I too had done that, but that it was when I was psychotic in a manic episode. I was fearful he would have flown into a rage and attacked me physically on the spot.

I can still summon up the terror that I felt when he held me captive for over a week at his snow-bound base in Ontario, trying to engineer my physical assassination. When he failed at first to mobilize group opinion to kill me, he would visit me in the house where I was held under guard. "I could kill you with my bare hands," he told me while we were alone. "And I have fleet's permission to do it."

I survived an ultimate cult experience – assassination at the hands of your brother and sisters, under the direction of a charismatic but psychotic cult leader who has branded you as a traitor.

And why was I a traitor? Well, fleet told God on television that I was – they spoke back to him, and told him I was Satan, masquerading as a Soviet spy, disguised as a cult lawyer representing God. I was Evil incarnated. Now that's a notion for the ages. Or should I say, a psychological re-projection by God, who was seeing his own shadow self and was repelled by it.

I survived God's murder attempt only because I escaped in the late hours of the night, after my guards had gone to sleep. The snow had been cleared from my pickup truck. I rushed about the house, packing my blazer and my briefcase. A miracle! The truck started in the sub-freezing cold. A few hours later I had crossed the borders into the United States, then in full mobilization in the Gulf War.

I went from a war in Heaven to the war on earth, and saw that one war was just an extension of the other. God in Heaven was a tool of the war powers on earth. The forces of war on earth were a tool of God, my former client.

For God himself possessed formidable psychic powers, which he used in the most sophisticated ways to impose his will on earth. And psychic weapons were the leading edge of human warfare. God and the earthly forces of war had one very specific factor in common – misuse of psychic powers.

My judgment is that God and the war forces on earth both sought power in that narrow but diabolical arena – the use of psychic powers as instruments of destruction. I do not know if the Lord and the forces of war were actually able to coordinate in the psychic realm. I do know that God claimed that this was so. God's view was that fleet, friendly intelligence agencies and armies did his will. Those spy, police, and military agencies that did not did so at their peril.

My term at a prominent think tank in the United States brought me into direct contact with the US military's experiments in "remote viewing," the application of psychic powers to military spying. "Psying equals spying." These experiments were with human psychic spies. I knew the think tank experimenters, who in fact were my initial contacts there. I knew one of their principal psychics, a colorful character from New York. I knew of the surface design of their experiments – delving into military sites and file cabinets of military enemies, then most prominently the Soviet Union.

Understand my circumstances at the think tank once again. I was a triple undercover agent, on the surface a futurist in their elite unit of half a dozen futurists who developed policy for the organs of government in the United States.

At the next layer of the onion, I was an undercover agent, self-appointed EyE, psychic hero, vindicator sworn to bring down the forces of darkness, most especially those forces which perverted the divine powers within each of us in the cause of war.

And, in my third undercover role, I was the chosen vessel of the Holy Spirit entity, gaming in dangerous waters, to further higher intelligent being's world plan.

That was my spiritual hat, my holy man role.

In a word, I was highly motivated at the think-tank to be a triple-spy myself, gleaning the motivation and outcomes of the Central Intelligence Agency and other spy agencies' funding of the psychic spy research.

I was sure the psychic spy project was cover, mere icing on the cake to cover other, more diabolical misuses of divinely given psychic powers to the service of war.

So, I played double fake-out games with the US intelligence agencies throughout my stay at the think-tank. Being used to soft technocrats who rolled over on command, they had not idea what forces they were dealing with in EyE.

Or so I thought in the safety of my triple disguise, about to be obliterated by well-placed electromagnetic impulse rays directed by US intelligence agencies at my delicate aura.

I learned first hand that not only was psychic spying – the use of our psychic energy in an act of war – operational in the US arsenal. So too were machines that used electromagnetic energy to try and destroy the human aura, and ultimately to attempt assassination upon the human soul.

Those machines were electromagnetic pulse generators, and extremely low frequency (ELF) weapons, secretly deployed against the civilians and populations of the United States by its own covert government. Their purposes are neutralization of perceived dissidents against the state, and mind-control of the moods and thoughts of targeted mass regions of the US population.

Yes, the psychics at the think tank were just cover, stuff for newspaper headlines, and a manipulative way to surface opinion about psychic warfare without compromising the utter secrecy of these neo-Atlantean weapons.

I knew the Central Intelligence Agency ran a super-secret remote-viewing project, using batteries of psychics to induce distant targets to kill others or themselves.

God could do, in a limited way, what these batteries of psychics or ELF machines could do.

God's favorite weapon was the Boomerang. God did not have to do anything to destroy or hurt an enemy; he just had to BE: if an enemy of God harbored a hostile thought or intention, if a hostile act against God was planned or undertaken. No problem; just trust the Vibe! The boomerang would turn the negative energy against God's enemy.

Within the psychic bubble of the cult, the boomerang was all-powerful. The boomerang delivered a stunning, destructive load of negative psychic energy that literally ripped apart the lives of us erring humans. He relished telling us how a former cult member who challenged him became violently ill all afternoon, a victim of the boomerang.

And, oh how painful it was when I came under the boomerang's effect myself, for my deviant thoughts and errant motivations.

One of God's favorite boomerangs was fatal disease, like cancer. "You know," God told me when my mother died of cancer, "I've found that when a person dies of cancer, it's usually because they were opposed to me." God knew my mother forcefully opposed his cult.

Once as I was visiting God's house, I spied the name of a US Senator and presidential candidate – my one-time law school room mate – written on his lists. My guess was that God meant to give this Senator support through the TV screen, as the Senator was vocally opposed to the Central American wars.

When the Senator died of lymphatic cancer, I began to wonder. Was my friend the Senator a candidate for death by boomerang? Was he done in by covert viral warfare? Or was it just plain cancer that caused his death?

Life with God was the hall of mirrors.

The boomerang was not limited to members of the cult and their families. It also applied to the world at large; nations, police forces, armies, rock and roll bands, politicians, religious leaders, presidents and Queens all reaped the boomerang. In fact the story of contemporary history was seen as a crazy quilt careening of the boomerang through the life and times of straying human beings.

At times, it was hard to tell if the disintegration brought down on a particular human public figure was by the boomerang, or by the personal intervention of the Lord God's himself. Where the gravity of the situation merited, God would psychically swoop down on a target human, and literally blow their life away.

The Throne of England was one of God's least favorite institutions. By right of the oath a British monarch takes, the Throne was God's. God sent the Throne an annum horribilis, a meltdown of family, castles, and royal legitimacy.

*Likewise, the Pope. By rights, the Throne of Peter should have been God's. God sent the Pope a disintegrating Church, and public embarrassments. But whether it was the boomerang or God's personal intervention was hard to tell. God's destructive psychic whammies happened alike to his subjects on the planet, as well as to members of his cult.

God also ruled the earth by regularly surfing his favorite public affairs TV channel, zooming in on live hearings, speeches, and political debates. He targeted his enemies and friends, and zapped them with the psychic power of the Absolute, as the cult called him. I knew he studied his targets carefully. In his world, no political act of consequence took place but that his energy – for or against – was not involved. So far was God's political reach, that he many times regaled us with the tale of the US

Secretary of State turning to face the camera in a live hearing, and telling his Congressional panel, "Now that's Power!" Referring, of course, to the Lord of Hosts who was watching through the TV screen.

Over the years, I took my fair share of psychic whammies, both from God and from the secret - presumably US government – batteries of psychics or ELF machines. I always had a difficult time trying to trace the ELF attacks I was undergoing back to God, or to the installations of the United States government. They were so hard to tell apart, that after a while, I assumed they were intertwined.

I do not know if you have ever been at the receiving end of an ELF attack, but it is devastating. One reels with mental disorientation; there is what feels like an electrical wall that presses down all over you, driving the atoms in your body mad. If you do not know you are the victim of an ELF attack, you can end up incapacitated. If you're a veteran target of ELF government mind-control, you tend to grit you teeth and wonder, "When will this be over?" Or, as I tend to think, "How can I locate these bastards, and out them into public view?"

Several cases in point about my ELF experiences. Once, after a stint at the United Nations, I was traveling by train from New York to Toronto. The ELF wave came on as I was between cars, having a tobacco smoke. The ELF ray was so intense I lost momentary contact with where I was. I tried to move back into the railway car, but could not. I knew exactly what it was – a covert mind-control attack. So I just waited it out.

At the Point - the single Point of Consciousness on earth, as God's estate was known - ELF attacks were timed for Saturday night, when the cult would gather for dinners and pool games. They usually peaked around midnight. Their intent seemed to be to induce inter-personal conflict, disorientation, and fear. All of these are verified effects in human groups of the ELF technology. Whole cities can be whammied by ELF, and its residents put through mood changes and paralyzing fear.

In this case, the ELF attacks seemed coordinated with the

US and Canadian government's strategies to neutralize God's lawsuits against them. The more intense our legal battle became, the more intense and frequent the ELF attacks. We could not completely decipher how the ELF field was generated or targeted. Was it deployed by satellite? Was it deployed by land-based equipment? But we became expert at picking up the sub-auditory noise ELF put out just before the wave was felt, and thus enjoyed some degree of Civil Defense warning.

The attacks reached their height during the week that God's bride was in detention by the government of Ontario. After she was released by order of the court, the ELF attacks fell off, and went back to their usual Saturday night specials.

Good counter measures to ELF grew out of our experiences there. First and foremost was a strong sense of humor – laughing your way through the ELF attack rather than falling prey to the sense of panic and disorientation. A party atmosphere certainly helped – lots of loud music, good cheer, drinking and grass smoking were a good recipe for keeping your head intact.

So effective was pot in neutralizing the ELF waves, that it occurred to us that this was the real reason why the US and Canadian governments were so fiercely anti-marijuana.

Marijuana gave us an effective defense to ELF!

When a natural herb can so easily neutralize the multi-billion dollar Orwellian mind-control machine, you can see why dope would squarely collide with the government's drug enforcement policy. The drug enforcement policy is really about preventing the populace from defending itself against the ELF anti-population weapons.

During the latter days of the Point, my own experience was that I was zapped with ELF on my way to visit God, and zapped in the days directly after my semi-annual visits. My most vivid ELF memory was a trip I made to the Point, via Texas and San Francisco. At the San Francisco leg of the trip, I was bathed in ELF during the entire week of a public health conference I was attending.

Then I traveled for a weekend stay at the Point, where God's first private expletive at me was, "You crooked lawyer!" for not agreeing to move back up to the Point, his murder attempt against me notwithstanding. He apologized, but kept up the negative aggression all weekend.

When I arrived back in Texas, the psychic remote viewing or ELF attacks became so intense, that I remember seeing visible waves of energy inside the cab of my pickup truck, as I struggled to keep control of the vehicle.

They say politics make strange bedfellows. But if both God and the secret ELF machines were zapping me, were not God and the hidden government in concert at some level?

I say there is even money that the intelligence bowels of secret state, in its very depths, had God as a sort of secret psychic King, most actively during the seventies, eighties, and the beginning of the nineties. God may have been a kind of psychic icon to the rulers of the secret state.

Then again, maybe not. Maybe God was a legend in his mind only. It's hard to tell what's really what in these halls of psychic mirrors.

Or perhaps, from the way the former defense officials and other luminaries scurried their chairs to sit next to me at lunch at the US Senate, perhaps EyE was a secret occult icon?

No way: if any one was a secret King of the secret state, that King was God – or one of the other usual suspects of planetary demonology.

My career with God had two phases. One before and one after his assassination attempt against me. Both phases lasted seven years, as if in some biblical allusion.

During my second phase with God, I began a super-human struggle to regain my health, and place my Light in God's face.

After my escape from God I languished for two years at my family home, in deep clinical depression, amid various fixed hallucinations. I was convinced that I had died, and somehow left out to dry on the planet of the living. It was a very, very painful time. I spent most of my time in bed, just lolling for days on end. I became stuck in some paranoid universe, and felt that visitors to our house were sent by God to push me finally into hell. Despite family and friend's entreaties, I resisted the quickest way out of hell – anti-depressant medication.

After a year, I ventured to the edge out of the family compound, to retrieve the mail. Once or twice a friend took me out to the nature preserves and seashore close by. I cried when I saw the sunset, and its majestic colors, thinking that I was no longer an inhabitant of the land of the living. Still I resisted the anti-depressants. I spent my day in full-time monitoring of the US presidential campaign on the public affairs channels.

My mother contracted esophageal cancer, and my world began to unravel. I knew my life support would end with her coming death, and I would have to rejoin the world. A family friend threw me a life preserver and brought me into the community health movement. I now had an entire clinic looking after my health, this time a clinic full of public health doctors, whom I administered. I quickly emerged back into relatively normal mood range, seeking my reinstatement before the eyes of God.

My opportunity came, almost three years to the day from my nighttime flight from the Point to avoid certain death at the hands of the cult. Whatever my fears, I needed to stand in front of him, and silently confront him with his attempted deeds. I say silently, because God had gone to elaborate lengths to cover up his murder attempt. We were to play a pantomime for seven years. He agreed to woo me on the surface. I agreed to pretend to want to serve him. Each of us was really waiting for the opportunity to plunge the knife in the back of the other.

On my first visit, God praised my boots and my health. He pre-empted any moves I would make to delve into the dark hours when he had tried to do me in.

"Alfred probably doesn't remember anything of what was going on," God announced to the cult.

Of course, I was double-bluffing him, dissembling as if I was too confused to remember.

I watched him like a hawk, taking in every centimeter of his nervous cover up. As the evening wore on, God began to relax once he saw I did not seem to be seeking revenge.

Soon we were back in our usual routine. It was the "God and his trusted elder advisor" show. Another twist in the bob and nod shuffle on those weekends I would visit the Point.

I fell back into the cult-mind; but with a twist. I knew that God was a paranoid murderer wannabe, and I could not shake that perception. I kept my head low, and tried I to bring some measure of normal-think to other cult members.

"Thanks! We really needed that around here," one member told me after I spoke about the benefits of the Internet.

I decided money was my best way to anchor inside the cult. God loved money. I brought up fat checks during my semi-annual visits. We were both on our best behavior.

During one visit to the Point, I became "leader of the US government," A federal public health officer called me on the telephone, and God psychically picked up the call while watching live TV at his home.

"One moment I was leader of the US government; suddenly you are," He told me that evening. I did not tell him about the call, stringing him along in his delusions.

"I want to move up here," I retorted. I wanted to wrench every advantage out of my new role as leader-in-hallucination.

God ran back into the kitchen. "You hear that, dear," he told his wife. "Alfred's up to the Point!"

We shook hands on the deal. Our cat-and-mouse game had escalated. God and I were now in a Mexican standoff.

On that August day, at that very moment, my own soul mate and fifth wife-to-be was a half a continent away, unbeknownst to me. "I felt this inner activation," she later told me. "I knew everything in my life was going to change profoundly."

Spirit brought my other half and I together on the Internet, and we set out to visit the Point on our honeymoon. In the past, I had to face God's murderous intent alone, and surrounded by a malleable group of cult members.

Gaga's yin-yang power brought its own Light into God's face. The results proved fatal for God and liberating for myself.

Gaga was the nickname my soul mate and I now gave ourselves.

We decided on some psychic counter measures of our own.

In a Gaga psychic reading, we learned that many incarnations ago – Atlantean times - God had imprisoned Alfred as a tool for power, and banished Gaga. Gaga had come together in this lifetime to stop God and his psychotic power.

Soon after Gaga confronted his deteriorating sanity, God died of a massive heart attack, brought on by drugs, drink, and the psychotic blasphemy of thinking one is God.

God was dead!

I heard the news in a sobbing phone call from his widow, and later, as I was crossing the Georgia Strait from Salt Spring Island on a mega-ferry the full impact hit me.

My aging father, himself a Catholic deacon, told me, "You know, it's a horrible thing to say, but he was better off dead than alive."

Seven years before, my father had refused to believe that God had tried to murder me.

In the end, the truth was outed.

I put to rest my years with God in a letter to his widow, my own post-mortem confrontation of the evil that had possessed her husband.

> I do not know if I have ever mentioned this to you directly, but I feel a sense of moral responsibility toward you arising from my representing you in adoption proceedings several years ago. As a being, I wish to clear myself of any karma that I may have in that regard. I wish to let you know reality as I perceive it.

> Clinically: I do not believe your husband was God. Quite the contrary, I believe he probably could be diagnosed as paranoid-schizophrenic, with borderline personality disorder. His astrological

chart shows heavy delusional tendencies, and susceptibility to alcohol and drug abuse.

I believe he fits the classic mold of an authoritarian cult leader, and myself and others around him functioned as enablers or facilitators of this mold.

I believe his passing is a blessing in the end to me, and to those who were involved with him.

During my seven years in Brownsville, I undertook deep psychological work and earned a Counseling degree in part to restore my self-esteem and sense of inner self I felt I lost during the Queen-King of Heaven years of my life.

I cannot lead you or anyone else involved to these insights and conclusions. Your own process is for you to find. I enclose two pages of observations from a book on recovery from

cults and abusive relationships that I have found helpful personally.

Please know that if you would ever like to write or talk over some of these concepts, just know that you will always find an open door.

Alfred

There is one common bond in the two hidden histories of God and the Messiah. Each paid a steep price by claiming to be deity.

The Messiah's claim of deity cost him his sanity, life-long. He lost his own claim to healthy perception. But when I knew him, he was a kind soul, dressed in the smelly rags of the street psychotic.

God lost his very life, and gained banishment, possibly, to an afterlife unknown. God went over the edge in life, and arrogantly tried to abrogate the divine prerogatives of creating and nurturing human souls.

God's threat to take away our souls constant. "I take away souls," he would say. "I am the bottom line. I give souls and I take them away. No one gets off this planet without going through me"

He bragged about destroying souls of human leaders, judges, lawyers, artists and the media people who opposed him. God monitored their speeches, hearings, pronouncements, music videos, news and public affairs programs on the live TV. If these reached a threshold, God took their souls away. Of course, the whole exercise was God's delusional exercise. But what God's hallucinations did was to corrode his own soul.

God made murdering a soulless errant member easier for the cult. In his hubris, God told the cult he had taken away my soul as preparation for his attempt to destroy me. The cult believed him. I remember a bewildered cult member staring at me as though I was some vampire they were about to kill.

"He doesn't believe you have a soul," my cult wife told me, my then fourth spouse

After God's first attempt to rouse the cult to kill me failed, God raised the delusional ante.

"I took away your soul, but left it in your body," he told me during a face-off.

"That way the soul goes to Hell, as well as the body." God was really into soul torture, wishing the most horrible depravity to his imagined enemies.

At that moment, I was a captive of the cult, suggestible, in terror. After my escape, I spent two years in horror and panic, thinking that I had no soul. A psychologist would say my fixed delusion was posttraumatic stress disorder. My two years in suggestive hell are also a reflector of God's own descent into human evil.

In the safety of the rear view mirror, I now see my battle with God as the first true mission I undertook on behalf of the Holy Spirit entity. My mission was to bring my Light into the face of God's rogue soul, and watch that soul take a path of spiritual surrender or self-destruction. My test run, as it were; my pilot project; my shakedown cruise. Fifteen years of my surviving on rugged self-control, as God's troubled body and soul finally imploded in self-destruction.

If I survived my spiritual test in the battle against God, then I might be ready for other, larger missions in the future.

How has my mission since God's death developed?

I choose a very simple mission now. The KISS principle – keep it simple, stupid.

I guess my mission includes bringing spirit and the ETI initiative into the lives of those I am around. Not by evangelizing; not by preaching; not by argument or spiritual lawyering.

Just by being me and letting folks know that spirit and the ETI initiative are landing.

Divine nature and the unseen plans of the universe administration then take their own course.

That is my mission, as I see it now. That is the Light I must have been holding in the faces of the secret state for a quarter century.

I have had many guides along the way. Some guides have come and some guides have gone. None has been the absolute be all and end all. None hold the total truth for me. But each holds some measure of truth, enough to light the pathways ahead for a time.

When I first seeped into the dimensions of the Kingdom of Heaven, Urantia was my private guide. Each night, I would consult the book. Each night it told me I was steadfast on an intended path. "Hang tight," Urantia told me in divination. "You are developing a spiritual marriage with the cult." Why or how I was to pursue this marriage was not yet clear.

As the cult began to trust me, and I rose in rank to be a minister, a most unlikely ally came to aid my mission. She was the Queen of Heaven and Earth,

A mystic herself, well versed in esoteric traditions and profoundly sensitive to the workings of spiritual law.

"No wonder you have been able to stay on course all these years, Alfred, " she told me over the short-wave radio network the cult used to communicate between bases. "If it were not for Urantia, you would have lost yourself."

Soon she invited me to the Lodge by the Lake to present Urantia to a seminar of the ministers of the Kingdom.

I arrived to find God was not in present company. I felt divided. Either God had condoned our gathering because he understood what Urantia was; or he was indifferent.

Little did I know then - Urantia had evoked his profound enmity.

I sat in the circle, keeping close eye contact, bringing the words of the fifth epochal revelation to this planet.

The prior epochal revelation was a person. The human incarnation of the God that creates our local universe.

The revelation for this epoch is not a person, but a book.

Urantia is our planetary lesson plan for at least the next millennium.

Then I saw the moment had arrived. I was to proclaim the fifth epochal revelation right there, inside the Kingdom of Heaven and Earth. Layering upon layering.

I raised Urantia above my head, intoning:

"I now proclaim the fifth epochal revelation."

That will get their cultic psyches, I thought. This public act will land Urantia inside the Kingdom mind-space.

Well, it did, and two months later the Kingdom of Heaven was in civil war, disintegrating into camps of cult members caught in the destructive crossfire of a battle to the death between God and his Queen.

God's bitterness against Urantia grew after this event. He railed against it often at gatherings where I was present, knowing I had brought the seeds of his destruction into his very camp.

All this was irony, however. It was not the information of Urantia that was eating God away from the inside. God's own resistance was dragging him into the direction of early termination.

Just one fair reading of Urantia's rendering of the source and journey of the human soul would have blocked off God's destructive hallucination that he controlled human souls.

I had brought into God's reality a spiritual text. He could have stopped his self-destruction in just one opening to the majesty of how true divine creation works; how inhabited planets are developed and grown; how our own irregular planet has suffered in rebellion; what our future history and destination are.

I have one bright moment-memory of God, standing by a raging fireplace after dinner, turning to me, and calling me.

"You are Melchizidek," he said, reaching the deeper realms of my higher self. According to Urantia, Melchizidek's original mission was an emergency measure of the universe administration, at a time when consciousness of the one true God was in danger of disappearing

Years earlier in Holland over another dinner, I had listened closely to the man performing the Dutch translation of the Urantia book. His knowledge of Urantia was encyclopedic. As we finished eating, he unraveled a mystery contained within the mysteries of Urantia.

"The Urantia book says that there may be a surprise in our generation on earth," he told me.

That could be many things. It could be the Second Coming of the God of our local universe.

I did not know what this surprise might be. My mission took me on a headlong search for this surprise

Then, one Urantia friend wrote me,

"As for the Dutch comment/prediction, I would say it possibly had to do with the return of Machiventa Melchizedek."

After years with God I put away the playthings of symbol and self, and
am naked to the winds, myself alone unencumbered by my former masks.

CHAPTER 5

THE STATE

For me, that there is an ETI initiative is as apparent as knowing that the earth is round.

Weighing everything I know, the reality of an ETI initiative toward the people of earth is the most elegant and economical conclusion I can reach.

Elegance and economy of solution are the fundamental principles of the scientific method.

It may take some time and personal processing to reach your decision about reality of an ETI initiative. It truly comes down to a personal choice, a weighing in the balance. In the end, it may well become a matter of personal survival. Either you are for the ETI initiative and human evolution or you are against it, and vote that we devolve.

Ironically, if you are against our linking up with extra-planetary civilization, you may become fodder for the secret state. If you support the ETI initiative in daily life, the very mass of your moral support brings our planetary liberation closer and more real.

My own philosophy on the ETI initiative is innocent until proven guilty.

I find this philosophy useful in wading through the noise, confusion, misinformation, and mind-deadening psychological warfare surrounding the secret war against the ETI.

The ETIs are innocent – that is existing, benign and conscious agents of our own evolution – until proven otherwise.

The object is the secret war against the ETIs is to reverse this algorithm.

Guilty, evil, colonizing, non-existent, swamp gas, weather balloon, loony, dangerous hybrids, torturing, manipulative, extinction of the human race.

These embedded stereotypes of ETI are a psychological technology at work, a distortion of the scientific principle.

I say Occam's razor holds that ETIs are innocent until proven guilty. And when the totality of the relevant evidence is weighed – evidence from ETI encounters, from the shadow government's secret war, from the sacred texts and historical allusions, from the deeper history of humanity – it is apparent that ETIs are agents of our evolution.

And what is that core human entity that is charged with determining innocence or guilt in official matters?

The answer is the state. The human state is composed of our formal governmental institutions, acting under principles of international law.

That is why the shadow government wants to command and control the state in the war against the ETI initiative.

The ETI initiative is an official, programmatic approach by an extra-planetary civilization, an opening to our integration into universe society. The ETI initiative is a primal act of state both for the human state and for the intergalactic federation. There is no more fundamental and lofty official function for the human state than to mediate humanity's entry into interplanetary society.

Were the human state a healthy one, it would have responded to initiatives by the ETI long ago. It would have developed a mutual development plan with the ETI

Were the human state normal, honest, open, not infiltrated by a covert, war-like shadow government, the course of events of the ETI initiative would have been very different than has been the case for the last fifty years. We might be well along in formal integration into interplanetary society.

However, the human state can also be used as an instrument to halt our integration with the ETIs. If you control the state, you control official truth. You can carry out a program of lies, distortions, aggression, and reprisals against the human population. You can keep the good citizenry of earth unconscious, confused, and immobilized while you rape the human community of its cosmic heritage.

That is why the shadow government has deployed the state as its prime asset in the war against the ETI initiative. It is not that human states are evil per se. Rather the command and control mechanisms of the shadow government have co-opted the human state into its main instrument of anti-ETI warfare.

Human states and their inherent powers over their populations are co-opted by turning the target state into an empty shell, whose "official" actions are orchestrated not by democratic expressions of popular will, but by the covert state craft of the shadow government.

Using a nation state as a front for private gain is as old as our civilization.

What the shadow government has done is to endow covert statecraft with the most advanced technologies of population control and deception that we know on earth.

The government of the United States of America is a prime asset, a front for the shadow government in its war against the ETI initiative. There are historical and functional reasons for this predicament in which the US government finds itself.

Quite simply, the US government is the home base of the military-industrial complex, whose massive assets are the heart of the anti-ETI war machine.

The shadow government first achieved command and control of these assets as part of an anti-ETI war in the early 1950s, when the US government's Intelligence program was made hyper-secret and decidedly anti-ETI in scope. This officially occurred through an act of the US Joint Chiefs of Staff.

With the new secret command and control, the assets of the military-industrial complex were essentially freed up for an all-out war against the ETI initiative. Need to know became the prime information control technology of those controlling and carrying out the war.

In a word, the bad guys took over in an inside coup d'état.

And the United States of America as a state became an empty shell, in its most fundamental official policy area – the integration with advanced extra-planetary civilization.

Nobody was home. There was nobody there at the command center of a vast military, political, governmental, and financial state – only the bent and depraved captains of the shadow government.

If the ETIs were to say, "Take me to your leaders," which leaders would they be taken to?

Would the ETI be taken to the elected public leaders? Not likely. Our elected leaders were, in effect, window dressing, and patsies in an anti-ETI war they had no idea existed.

Would the ETI be taken to the real command and control in the shadow government? Not likely. The shadow government had already shown its only reaction to an extraterrestrial approach was aggression and hostility.

Do you see these possibilities as plausible versions of reality?

I'll be up front – in my mind, the shadow government is guilty until proven innocent. Why do I adopt this philosophy with the shadow government?

Easy – It's a survival tactic in the midst of a shooting war. I know the shadow government's intentions toward me are not benign.

Their intentions are in fact grotesque.

My working assumption: The US government had been made an empty shell, a front in the anti-ETI war, granting pseudo-legitimacy to an illicit shadow government that has hijacked the state from the inside so that it can wage war on the universe. The ETIs had no effective point of contact within the official state structure.

So ETI turned to the people, and began to cue them into ETI awareness. Long term, ETI awareness might facilitate the people's legitimate reclaiming of their very own governments so that the integration with ETI could get back on track. Ultimately this ETI awareness might include resurrecting shell-game nation states from under the very noses of the secret government. We do not know for sure, the war against the ETI initiative continues every day.

We come back to our present question – "Take me to your leader."

Who are our real, functional leaders in the secret war against the ETI?

That is a key question. Our bona fide elected leaders may not even know there is a war on to prevent our lawful integration into universe society. They may not grasp that, even with the mantle of elected political office, they do not command and control the anti-ETI war.

Well, in the ETI war, my own personal leaders are the ETIs. I'll always go for the higher thought.

And who is the enemy? Well, the enemy is the shadow government.

The enemies are those who have made the state an empty shell, and continue to use that shell against the people's linking up with extra-planetary government.

The shadow government had co-opted the state, twisting the official legitimacy and non-accountability of acts of state, into carrying out an anti-population war to deny the ETIs access to the people.

Does that mean that the state – the government of the United States is the enemy?

No. It means that the shell game that uses the resources of the US government to carry out anti-ETI warfare is blocking our heritage.

So, how to do deal with a shell game?
You expose it as an empty shell.

Much of my own research on the secret anti-population weapons of the state has come from experiencing the effects of these weapons first-hand as they were deployed and used against me for the past quarter-century.

In the state's eyes, one central condition qualified me to enjoy such a privileged as guinea pig for psychic, mind control, and electromagnetic pulse weapons.

My contact with, and espousal of, higher intelligent beings met that condition. I was an alien experiencer, and that fact alone made me an official non-entity. A citizen to be discredited under secret government mandates of the United States.

Not only was I an alien experiencer; I was an alien *activist*. I was proclaiming the reality of an ETI initiative in books, on radio and television. I was catalyzing a counter-policy against the ultra secrecy pronounced by the US government in the late 1940s and early 1950s. I was in the inner sanctum of a military-intelligence think tank, lobbying the White House for a project to re-open the alien policy.

Had I been an environmental activist, or human rights activist, I may have been targeted also. But most probably nowhere to the degree than being an alien activist has brought out, on every continent where I have traveled; in the most mundane settings; on almost every telephone and e-mail terminal I have used.

Hey, I'm not paranoid – just hyper-observant. Next time you feel tapped, just let fly with disinformation over the telephone, and watch the predictable results.

Somewhere in the bowels of the US covert world, an order went out to neutralize me. It had to be from the very center of the bowels; I cannot account for the almost total surveillance and attack that has been with me now since the 1970s. No matter where I traveled – Canada, the United States, Europe or Mexico – expertly coordinated police surveillance units shadowed me closely, isolating me from my life, and hoping I would break. There is only one unit of the US government that can marshal that kind of international police clout – the CIA, or maybe the NSA, or maybe the FBI, or maybe the RCMP, or maybe CSIS. That black box alphabet soup of population control.

Their basic tactics seemed stuck in some repetitive manual for psychological warfare (psywar for short) operations. Try and stun me with psychic attacks and ELF pulse weapons. If I go into terror, then grab me and kidnap me and disappear me. They tried this gambit at a metaphysical bookstore right beside the cathedral in Vienna.

Try to induce me to kill someone, or kill myself, with psychic remote viewing teams. Put me on total surveillance. Hear every sound in my dwellings and offices; deploy squad cars and patrolmen to follow me everywhere. Make me feel totally surrounded and hopeless. Create discord within my friends and community with ELF blasts. Make me an ultra-paranoid. Get me to talk about the surveillance so that I'll be written off as a paranoid.

And so on - all by the book, by the way. The methodology of anti-population weapons is massive and systematic

I made my countermeasures a creative ballet of all I knew. Psychic teams and ELF blasts can themselves be neutralized. In an attack, you may feel a mechanical field in your psyche, pushing terror, disorientation, or suicidal ideation.

Center your consciousness deep within yourself. Then with your mind, follow the ELF back to its source. There you will find military-intelligence types, blindly following orders. They are part of a dumb machine; tested and evaluated with public funds.

These psychetronic weapons are a profound violation of human rights. They are an historical abomination. Once the anti-population deployments of electromagnetic pulse weapons become publicly known, they become ineffective. Psychic and electromagnetic weapons work only on unsuspecting populations, which is why their existence has been discredited as the imaginary ravings of paranoids. That is part of the very engineering of the psychetronic weapon itself.

Phone tapping is now mostly automated. The computers are cued to keywords you might utter in conversation. You can express your personal zone of freedom and privacy by varying your key words creatively, and shoving them back up into the recording computers, and into the belly of the beast. It is part of citizen's resistance. Once they know you know, they're over.

Oh, and shove yourself in the face of any squad cars or walking police you think might be carrying out surveillance on you. These cops are operating as blind robots, on the basis of terse radioed instructions. They have no personal compunctions against violating your civilian rights. They are the soldiers of the secret occupation, and must either obey their orders or muster out.

Once, in a coffeehouse in downtown Vancouver, a group of us were followed by a surveillance group of about eight Royal Canadian Mounted Police. They were a typical CIA-manual psywar team, dressed with the regulation florescent vests, intended to induce cognitive dissonance. We stared them down for about an hour, with the help of German tourists who clearly were on to the game. At one point, a voice in my head told me, "Don't worry. They are just grist for the mill." I saw that they were marked for death.

Yes, the soldiers of the secret state are fodder for their own cannons in the mind-war for higher species dominance of Urth.

And who am I but a guided missile, activated by the Holy Spirit entity.

That has been my fundamental truth all these years, crashing up against the stone wall of the secret state.

I have noticed a not-too-subtle pattern, however.

Every time my guided missile has sought to penetrate or unearth the arena of the US government's role with higher intelligence, the governmental beast has clamped down shut around me, and I narrowly miss its flaying jaws.

"Where there is smoke, there is fire," I tell myself.

I am making mirth, but humor seems to be a most effective weapon in the civilian's arsenal in the war of the forces of death, against the forces of the future.

Who are the forces of death? Well the death urge appears universally in all of us in varying degrees.

I like to say you can tell the forces of death by their deeds.

I ask the following question: Is the war against the ETI initiative intended to accelerate the destruction of our planet and human species?

Or are these deeds of the shadow government life affirming?

You can answer this however you like, from whatever perspective, and I believe you will ultimately conclude that the anti-ETI war is death affirming, and our struggle to link up with interplanetary society affirms human life.

There is a large domain of the human state that is now on the whole life affirming. The best archetypes I can think of are the disaster relief worker, wildlife officer, and social statistician.

There is nothing inherently evil about the state. Our problem is that the governmental functions that would be responsible for integrating us into interplanetary society have been hijacked.

As we now know, there appears to be a command and control sector of the human state that is carrying out a terminal, twisted vision of the forces of death.

Merely trying to describe – yet alone prove - the multiple variations of the shadow government's relationship to ETI intelligence strains even my paranoid-friendly imagination.

So I will fall back on my own ego ideal, my vision of myself.

I myself long to become an underground guerilla resource in this war of the worlds, making a unique and personal contribution to help our human species survive its psychopathic force that has taken over our government. To reach out, and together with the ETI bring help our planet into universal citizenship.

That is my personal affirmation.

And in that spirit I offer you alternative healing remedies against imaginary and/or real lethal visions running the military command of one errant empty shell of a human state - the United States of America.

Do not take these lethal visions as factual; take them as possibilities. So that when you finally do perceive the shadows of death upon the wall before you, you may know what shape of beast may be casting them or not.

The first lethal vision about the secret state running the United States of America is that it is, well, lethal.

The secret command and control running the anti-ETI war through the United States of America could, if unchecked by the superior power of ETI itself, ultimately railroad the human species into extinction, planetary suicide.

Oh, I do not mean the good guys in the USA.

I mean the planetary bad guys in the USA. They are leaders in the war against the ETI initiative.

Think about it – this command and control entity has the technology to destroy humanity and severely damage the long-term ecology of the planet.

Lodged onto the body politic and body spiritual of the United States government is a giant, malignant organism, potentially lethal to us all. That malignant organism appears to have co-opted the military command and control and all of the resources and people in a shadow government in order to wage a secret war against our human species joining interplanetary society.

I do want to keep this simple, so I will merely remind you that astride this shadow government are other planetary fellow travelers – earth-oriented war nations, military-intelligence, organized corruption, armaments industries, nationalistic cabals. These fellow travelers may appear as enemies on the chessboard. In reality, they are part of a mega death-dance, and they too get enlisted in the anti-ETI war as needed.

None of these fellow travelers have the determined, hyper-secrecy around ETI intelligence that does the US shadow government. In this secrecy lies the possible causes of an extinction level event, which forever wipes our love them/hate them species from the face of earth.

Of course, I do not for a minute think that an extinction level event will happen. It could only happen if the shadow government is successful is isolating the bulk of the human population from linking up with interplanetary society, and ETI intelligence itself does not intervene to save us from ourselves.

We are still a relatively low-level intelligent species, vulnerable and developing. It is the hidden, selfish interests of a human shadow government, with its secret war against our becoming conscious of ETI, that may lead us to planetary suicide.

An objective interplanetary anthropologist sent to earth would reasonably conclude that the current policy of the anti-ETI war to deny, discredit and sabotage public knowledge of the plans of higher intelligence is the single most death-oriented policy on this planet.

Fundamentally, the secrecy policy denies the human species the ability to organize itself and constructively integrate with higher intelligence, as that becomes possible.

Let us take a walk through the some alternative futures that may await us. You will see why it may very healthy to let your mind go into scary territory.

The ultimate paranoid scenario looks like a bad sci-fi movie. The foul villain of the plot is a covert organization within the United States government, serving as point man for a global organization intent on keeping mankind ignorant and functionally enslaved.

The scenario moves through several themes. One is the obliteration of civil liberties, and the incarceration of millions of human "dissidents" In concentration camps.

ETI intelligence is the intended pretext for the installation of martial law.

One paranoid plan may be to simulate an ETI alien "invasion", parade some captured aliens on television, and proceed with the social enslavement.

Were it not so serious, the plot is almost laughable, a B movie built around standard issue covert destabilization techniques used against the populations of third world countries for fifty years.

Keep in mind that I am not advocating that these scenarios may materialize.

I am only saying that they are the ultimate sort of strategic deceptions that the
fools in the shadow government desperately consider as their war of attrition drags on and on and on. Look to the history of covert warfare in third world countries and you will see that no perversion is too great to the secret state.

Laughable, sure. Plausible? You are the judge of your own mind.

Put yourself in the shoes of the most dastardly clandestine organization within the US government that you can imagine.

Try and imagine reality as that secret organization sees it.

Now, what would that secret entity do if a higher extraterrestrial species were freely operating within its population and sovereign territory?

What does the entity do when a more advanced ETI civilization is buzzing US war craft, ships, aircraft, and military bases, with a technology that could clearly blow the human military machine away?

Is the shadow government's only response to impose a tight security blanket over these incidents, making even talking of them a violation of military regulations? No. That is but a limp military response.

As command and control, you create a secret strategy to counter the ETI initiative.

First, you want to be sure to deny the ETI initiative the human population, ETI's presumed objective.

You will want to control and capture the human population before the ETIs capture their hearts and minds.

Every instinct and sinew within your dastardly collective body will tell you to create a secret counter-enslavement for the minds of the human race!

Oh, it can be an enslavement of the mind. That is why the new generation of mind-control weapons – psychetronic and electromagnetic pulse weapons - is so functional for the anti-ETI war.

Through programs like MILAB that make the ETI aliens the bad guys; create an excuse for a social and mind control enslavement; and prepare for a war of attrition against the ETI aliens.

What is the doctrine of this war of attrition?

That's easy - Whoever holds the most human minds and hearts longest, wins.

Then there is also a more academically respectable scenario, based on the principle that human beings are stupid, and human governments ineffective. That scenario holds that since the 1950s, the official US government's response has been to stonewall on the ETI issue, because the government believes it is powerless to control it.

The government believes that to announce ETI publicly will give rise to social chaos.

Not! People do not panic because of ETI; on the contrary, they feel comfortable with ETI. There's an anti-ETI war on, and the war is not about preventing panic in mankind. The war is about preventing mankind from evolving into an interplanetary civilization, freed from the social shackles of the shadow government.

These dynamics drive the plot of the bad sci-fi movie we seem to be in.

And we everyday humans are caught in a dilemma of survival.

Do we surrender to the retrogressive counter-evolution offered by the secret US government?

Do we accept the disinformation offered by a timid, paralyzed empty shell of government policy?

Are we led into extinction by becoming more and more unconscious, apathetic until we fall into possible mass species suicide?

Or, do we actively confront our reality and survive, with a very simple switch of inner allegiance to the ETI initiative?

How can we humans jump-start out of our dilemma, caught underneath a raging information war?

That is a tall order, but a surmountable one.

One answer lies in the power of soul. Our human SOUL.

Souls are entities, and spiritual warfare is real.

Psychologically speaking, a first step in any healing is the ending of our collective denial.

Let's identify some stages in this self-healing:

- Denial

- Depression

- Anger

- Bargaining

- Acceptance

- Healing

- Action

Imagine that you, a human soul, are in profound denial about the existence of enemies who wish to capture your soul.

Who are the enemies of the human soul? Our enemies are the actions and actors behind the shadow government's war against our intended evolution.

Our souls are kept in denial by multiple deceptions.

The manipulation of human social taboos is a primary engine of our being kept in denial.

The shadow government uses psywar techniques to mask their plans, through active disinformation. The shadow government perceives it will lose control of earth through the ETI initiative, and that is an unthinkable and must be stopped. MILAB technology creates bogus craft encounters and abductions that are bizarre, unbelievable to the conventional mind. Witnesses are discredited or assassinated. Cover-ups and stonewalls are carried out. Projects are funded from covert budgets.

The result is our collective human ignorance and denial. Our channels of information and our cultural elites do not inform us of the threat. Our established information channels disinform us. Wittingly or unwittingly, they become agents in the service of the shadow government's occupation.

Our civilian knowledge of highly classified US military information is sketchy, and subject to revision. But that is the nature of research in any arena. There may be errors of detail, but one can at least form a picture of how the US war machine is treating the ETI initiative.

At its highest military level, the US government appears to be on some form of war footing against the ETI. All ETI encounters are classified as highly secret. Military personnel are forbidden by regulation to even discuss ETI encounters. Military radar tracks space intruders. There is talk of anti-ETI electromagnetic pulse weapons under development.

But who is at war with whom?

ETI intelligence, with its superior technology, has not yet chosen to "invade."

Maybe what military command and control sees as a threat is in fact an opening.

Maybe the "war" is one-sided. The US military command and control wage war against the ETIs, but the ETIs are only gaming with the shadow government's military agents.

Maybe the military mindset that began the anti-ETI war can itself be diagnosed as paranoid schizophrenic, with borderline personality disorder.

Maybe my experiences with the Messiah and with God were quite functional. Perhaps the shadow government is a psychopathological entity.

This shadow entity creates an enemy where there is none. It sees hostile acts where there is open approach.

The truth may be that the military command and control shrouds the ETI war in secrecy, precisely because if the war were open we would all see there is no basis or justification for waging war.

Initially, I became depressed when I first realized there was a shadow government waging a secret war against our joining in an interplanetary initiative, our universal heritage. Evil humans, I thought, might actually succeed in enslaving humanity, all its art, its love, its children, its experiences, and its treasures.

I thought, at first, that it was our fault. The victim syndrome, where the victim thinks it is the cause of the abuse. I wondered if perhaps the human species – *Homo sapiens* – had a fatal evolutionary flaw. That we humans might have a congenital predisposition to conflict and violence, an inbred inability to cooperate and trust.

I thought the possibility that the shadow government might succeed meant we were truly dysfunctional from an evolutionary perspective, and deserve to be enslaved, isolated from our universe brothers and sisters.

I thought that we humans had become prey to a shadow government because we were incapable of caring for our planet. For our ultimate responsibility, as universe citizens, is to husband the life-bearing planets on which we live.

Yet look at how we are destroying ours. The ozone layer is depleting; species that are the product of millions of years of genetic development are endangered and disappearing; the oceans are dying; toxic and radio-active waste are accumulating. We are turning a beautiful living entity, developed by vast universe intelligence, into a stenching garbage dump.

And our major investment as a species continues to be to war upon each other. Electromagnetic pulse weapons, nuclear weapons, weapons of mass destruction, massive military machines. Human's main institutional activity is to make war upon each other.

Are humans a suicidal race?

No, and again no. We are the victims of mass abuse. We have been imprisoned in a fossil fuel civilization, a war-based economy that serves only the interests of the shadow government.

As a species we are ready for interplanetary civilization.

Were it otherwise, our interplanetary cousins would not have offered us the ETI initiative.

At some point, my anger bargained back upon the beastly shadow government, and said, "Don't write us off the map of free existence too quickly."

We humans are unique. We have powerful spiritual souls. And that is what this earthly existence is ultimately about, anyway. Ours is primarily a spiritual reality.

By and large we humans are a spiritual population, motivated by love and the desire for divine growth. Struggling to exist and grow on a quarantined planet at the edge of a smallish galaxy, still prey to deep ignorance about our history and the darkness of predatory institutions.

It is not we who deserve to die. It is our destructive thought patterns and institutions, remnants of an ancient darker age, which deserve to be extincted so that we may survive.

Anger at those dinosaurs of war machines that keep in power a petroleum-based civilization where the greed for power and ignorance writes the rules.

They have kept us in the dark, but now we can begin to see.

Let us make the collective decision to survive and we will transform those institutions into vessels of planetary husbandry.

There are massive gargoyles guarding against our collective acceptance of the ETI initiative, and our acceptance of the destructiveness of the anti-ETI wars waged by the shadow government.

Ironically, one only needs to accept our twin reality of an ETI initiative and destructive shadow anti-ETI war to get beyond the gargoyles.

The gargoyles are fear-based, massive, and powerful, and it requires supreme human will to get beyond them and accept reality, as it seems to be.

We create the most powerful gargoyles through fears activated within our own minds. They are created by how are we programmed. By how we react to novel stimuli that take us out of familiar emotional territory.

Psychological acceptance is not blind faith; it is an inner surrender to the reality of the promise of ETI initiative, and the perils of the anti-ETI war. Psychological acceptance is all the more difficult because the war is kept secret. That means we must rely on the available, hard-won evidence, and on our intuition.

Acceptance means informing yourself and internalizing your conclusions.

Are you able to go beyond your inner programming of what ETI is all about?

Can you believe a secret government has stonewalled the ETI issue since the 1950s?

Can you believe that the ETI initiative is operating in our earthly environment?

Can you believe that the secret US government is waging an anti-ETI war, and is intentionally mislead us about it?

Can you believe that ETI has an initiative for us, to mutually bring human civilization into interplanetary society?

Can you transform your beliefs and life plan based on what you think about the ETI initiative? Can you withstand peer pressure, going against what your peers, friends and neighbors might think about ETIs? Can you challenge authoritative voices of your role models, and opinion leaders?

So how, at the eleventh hour, are we to begin to heal the human state, purge it of an anti-ETI command and control by a shadow government?

Direct appeals to the secret government, if we could access

them, seem a fruitless task. It is wedded to hyper-secrecy and has been so for some time. We would be knocking on the most durable of stone walls.

This beast will not change. It must be deconstructed.

What is that time-trodden cliché which adorns the headquarters of our information-captors, the original architects of the secret government's secret war against the liberation of peoples in developing countries, the United States Central Intelligence Agency?

"Know the Truth and the Truth Shall Set You Free"

Well, we can wave that flag as well. Break the information seal on the

ETI initiative, and we will have started the flow of life-affirming information.

ETI information is the healing.

Deep historical irony dogs each step of our awakening. In our human wars during this century, it has been government that has awakened us, mobilized us, pointed us towards a purported enemy, given us arms and orders.

This war is different. The secret government is not the solution. It is the problem.

It seeks our ultimate devolution through an amoral, destructive secrecy. What democratic participation was involved in the original decision to stonewall the ETI initiative? None. This lid of secrecy was put in place by the same gray evil souls who have led humanity to the brink of planetary destruction for the last half century.

Is there an ETI initiative or an ETI threat?

What do you think? I say that extra-planetary intelligence is here to bring us into our next level of evolution.

Remember – patriotism is indeed the last refuge of scoundrels, and it is the scoundrels of a shadow state who are trying to drive our species into the ditch. They have lost universe credibility and must go.

We are talking about saving humanity from the inside, liberating each soul in our communities from a box of apathy and programmed ignorance about an opening into an interplanetary future.

Inner awareness about the ETI initiative, personally owned by each of us, is the key to our liberation from this mind-control occupation by secret war.

There are ways that the anti-ETI war can be neutralized. The war is ultimately fought against the hearts and minds of humanity.

To win the war, we just have to resist, knowingly.

To neutralize the secret anti-ETI war, we need to come together in a community of resistance, a network of survival.

Saving humanity from the inside is the work of saving our souls, and then saving the souls of others you care about – family, friends, strangers, men, women, children. It will take knowledge, empathy, creativity, and community.

Until a critical mass of awareness is reached, this is careful, one-on-one work.

Why do we say saving our souls?

Ask the survivors of the holocausts of this century, and they will be able to tell you.

Holocaust survivors rescued their very souls, their inner divine essence, by resisting death and torture in the camps. They reclaimed their freedom to live as Divine Will intended them to.

Thus we can overcome the mind control holocaust of the anti-ETI war. Our collective human soul power can forestall this war, and blow out its lethality.

So what will the predictable responses of the shadow government be to the ETI initiative? One response is for sure, the stone wall will continue. We can expect no truth, and only suppression, from the command and control within government whose automatic response is to continue the secret war.

Martial law – invoked during 1960s anti-war demonstrations – is a possible next-level anti-ETI response. In the United States, the regulatory infrastructure of martial law has been put in place, and can be activated very quickly. Those who were the targets of martial law in the 1960's remember well the steel curtain of curfews and helicopter tear gas raids.

Alert! Martial law cancels democracy. Democratic forms are the vehicles by which the people express their will, gather power. Cancel democracy with martial law, and you've blocked the access of the people to use government for survival.

Knowledge and awareness are our first action steps. Community-based information media, like the Internet, are our tools. Community-based organizations – our families, churches, clubs, concerts and support groups – are our havens.

My mind literally jumps with action plans that can be put into effect.

Rather than lay out a hypothetical menu, let me share my own action plans with you. You know better than I do what plans you may want to activate for our survival. Perhaps what I plan to do may be of some inspiration to your own.

Hey, if we don't collaborate in waking each other up, it's may be all over, baby blue.

So, let me share a bit of stocktaking, my tools and my strengths.

Well, I'm a five-planet Gemini, and I just love to communicate, think and talk.

I've been a radio talk show host and am an Internet entrepreneur and journalist.

I am a public interest lawyer and love to activate the linkages between community groups and effective legislative action: in areas like environment, public-interest counter-intelligence, community organizing and higher intelligence to name a few.

I've devoted a quarter-century of my life to trying to lift shadow government secrecy, with negligible effect.

I've put myself out there in the world of ETI. My friends think I am sort of extraterrestrial myself.

I'm a Latino, bi-cultural all the way; so I feel certain sensibilities and social awarenesses outside the mainstream of Anglo life.

These happen to be my particular tools and sensibilities. You have your own you can self-activate.

My own objective is to help create a responsive voice, co-participating in the ETI initiative. My intent is to help activate humanity synergy in the opening to interplanetary society. My tools are awareness, consciousness-raising, persuasion, and effective social action. My vision is humanity's reclaiming of our planetary heritage.

Well, for starters, there are many possible interactive projects that could facilitate individual awareness and community organizing around the ETI initiative. With a presence in cyberspace, information can be imparted one-to-one, in discussion groups, through Website conferences, via downloaded publications.

Know the truth and it shall make you free. Use the truth and you can help free others.

Likewise, ETI consciousness-raising with family, friends, community, men, women, and children; workshops and seminars on coping and psychic survival.

The rest are venues of opportunity - Media. Articles. Interviews.

Whatever.

My goal is to spread awareness of the ETI initiative. To activate self-activation in others into useful channels. Mobilized people can in turn organize to turn the tide. They may seek to overturn lawless secrecy in their representative government. They may organize around educational and charitable vehicles. They may seek to have public resources dedicated to develop responsive plans. They may use legislative and electoral tactics to create a new governmental reality.

Me?

I plan to be a catalyst and change-agent, what I, in particular, do best.

Some would say we each have inner knowing of what we can do best, once our eyes are opened and we hear that inner drummer beating, beating, beating species survival. That drum is the beating signal of our collective souls.

The bottom line is how to mobilize fellow humans, willing to act on a species signal to push for universe linkup.

You may have noticed that we are still begging a core question here – What makes us think that we can evolve, even if the human race wakes up and becomes aware of an ETI initiative?

Merely making the human race aware and activated says nothing about the substance of the human input into an ETI initiative.

The essence of the human side of the ETI initiative is our collective awareness. Collective awareness puts the human race *en garde*.

Collective awareness creates a sea change (or "see-change") of perception among humans here on earth.

A society of humans fully aware of the ETI initiative in turn energizes the promise of the ETI initiative, and neutralizes the devolutionary attempts of the anti-ETI war.

Is this a tautological, self-fulfilling response?

Well, yes and no.

We know that secrecy is key to maintaining the war against the ETIs.

Collective human awareness of the anti-ETI war, and a determined human will to resist it neutralizes the shadow government's sway over the population and resources of earth.

The secret government's anti ETI war can work only because the government has for fifty years launched formidable resources to keep the knowledge of the ETI initiative from the human population. The anti-ETI methods have included cover-up, military secrecy regulations, discrediting of civilian witnesses, and even assassination, we are told. The anti-ETI plan has worked because, through the unethical use of power, it has succeeded in avoiding public accountability for information about ETI activity it knows to be true.

Moreover, it appears to be the policy of ETI that humanity comes to widespread knowledge about the ETI initiative on our own.

We must perform the task ourselves; set our governmental house in order.

In other words, in order to earn the right to interplanetary citizenship, we must ourselves disassemble the secret state and those structures that have kept us from even knowing about our cosmic heritage.

ETI can help us, as we become mobilized ourselves.

Anti-ETI secrecy can be evaporated by a determined public awareness of how the secret government has denied humans the opportunity to respond constructively to the ETI initiative.

There are no legitimate social or political arguments in favor of secrecy about the ETI initiative. Secrecy works against human evolution in this case.

A citizenry armed with the truth about the promise of the ETI initiative can impeach the credibility of shadow government secrecy.

And what if a secret government imposes martial law, or otherwise escalates its low intensity information warfare against its citizens?

That is an historically-based possibility, and should be treated seriously. The US government imposed martial law in other situations, such as the Vietnam War, to protect illicit policies.

Well, if martial law is imposed, then it is in our survival interest to resist this policy, as well as a violation of our fundamental human right to interplanetary citizenship.

We humans citizenry may actually have to confront those retrogressive governments who will otherwise continue our captivity-of-the-mind. We may have to evolve an information underground, in order to mobilize for the ETI initiative, and battle an increasingly oppressive secret government determined to continue its commitment to our demise.

Make no mistake – there are determined forces within the US government and its governmental cousins, who have for decades been laying a foundation for an authoritarian government of deception. During the 1970s as a futurist at that leading government think tank, the term we used to describe this form of government-by-deception was "Friendly Fascism."

It could get very rough, this business of evolutionary survival.

Our weapons are individual and public awareness, but they are not limited to that.

Our primary weapon is the human soul, that immortal, invisible being. That fragment of the God source that living humans are.

Let me illustrate what I mean, at different levels of the soul.

One meaning is the capacity of the human soul to witness its power in dispersing and evaporating deception by human institutions.

By channeling truth through your soul, you can actually disperse the manipulative energy of sophism and duplicity.

A specific instance comes to mind for me, one in which my own soul took over. Not that I won that day! My witnessing led massive surveillance down upon my head. In retrospect, I was able to neutralize the US government thought police. They had come to an illustrious think tank to stamp out my proposal to set up a re-examination of the ETI issue, carried out at the very core of the overt US government – the Presidency.

I remember the scene vividly, a slow motion tableau of confrontation. A senior official of the think tank called a fellow futurist and myself into his office one afternoon. He was an African American, friendly to my proposed ETI research, and to my views for expanding futurist research at the think tank into the more frontier, esoteric areas like ETIs and assassination research.

I was unawares of the purpose of the meeting, and he quickly filled me in.

Department of defense officials had contacted the management of the think tank, demanding that my proposal be stopped, and threatening to withdraw research contracts if the think tank did not comply.

In an instant I surmised what had happened. I had not approached any office or person of the Defense Department about the project. The only US government officials who had been approached were in the Carter White House and the National Science Foundation, who would carry out the study. The probability was that the US secret government surveillance tracking my Washington meetings had flagged my project as a risk to their lid of secrecy on ETIs.

The senior think tank official advised me to duck this one, and accept the ban on ETI research.

"Dissimulate," he said.

Two hatchet-faced thought police entered the room, sharp gleams in their reptilian eyes.

The lead nasty opened up, disparaging ETI research, saying this project would discredit the think tank and jeopardize its military contracts.

But that wasn't what the White House and the National Science Foundation said. They thought the project was meritorious and long over due.

I tersely recited some of the evidence for the existence of an ETI strategy with regard to earth.

My fellow futurist and that think tank official went into dissimulation mode, sliding quietly down in their chairs. Theirs was the body language of bureaucratic concession.

The more I tried to contain my rising indignation, the more I could not.

Battle lines were drawn. The US government agents had the power lines. I had the truth of the situation.

"Blast them," my inner voice said.

Blast them I did with a head-on channeling of the reality of an ETI presence. I veered close to the line of denouncing then as a military secrecy enforcement team. I had a wife and child at home I had to support. When I came to that line I held back.

But I blew the force, the steam, and the deception out of them. They deflated right before our eyes, falling back to shallow power moves.

When they left, it was clear my project would be stopped. I was in an inner rage, not yet knowing if I would stay at the think tank or leave.

But they had not succeeded in furthering a deception.

Everyone in that room knew that they were pushing a lie.

The secret US government lost moral force that day, in the very bowels of their power. My soul had chosen to speak. The human soul has the power to evaporate deception, and reset the moral configuration. Government deception techniques are built around creating a structure of false concepts within the minds of its targets. We had defeated that attempt at enforcing false concepts, at least for a small meeting about one project to unearth the truth about ETIs.

The human soul, in collective effort, also has the power to defeat the combining forces of evil it may encounter.

This is the spiritual power of the human soul.

In a fundamental way, our whole in this dimension we call human life is about the saving power of our souls.

We are here to save our human souls, and to push through the duality we meet here on Earth.

The duality is that of good and evil.

Duality is reflected in the darkened glass of our dual alternative futures – one as liberated human beings in interplanetary citizenship, and the other as the unconscious slaves of the shadow government, shadowed to earth.

Let us review the apparent futures facing us human souls. They are laced with good and evil intertwined. How we cope with these apparent contradictory futures is a function of how we use the power of our souls.

Our challenge as human souls is to create a positive future out of the mixture of destructive and positive forces we are facing.

We can succumb to the cover-up and terrorism of negative human forces trying to keep us in ignorance. Or we can give support to those forces within human governmental and power structures and help open up a positive transition to a trans-planetary society.

Likewise, we have the option to become enslaved at the hands of a predatory, psychopathic shadow government. Or we can blast though human self-destructive tendencies, and reach out to those parts of the universe federation that may be reaching out to us in a constructive way.

We humans apparently have been victims of a series of inter-locking cover-ups of the ETI presence. The cover-ups are like the layers of an onion.

Some of the parties participating in these levels of cover-up have been more lethal and malevolent than others. It is to our advantage to distinguish among the cover-ups, and dismantle them one by one.

At the surface level, we have a policy of stone-wall and deni-al by the

Official organs of US and other governments. Mis-information and dis-information about an ETI presence, discrediting and neutralization of witnesses have been standing orders and regulation for the US military and official US government agencies for a half-century. Theoretically, these can be turned by directives of the Congress and the executive; by mass disclosure of 50 years of disinformation.

Some have even suggested that amnesties be granted to gov-ernment officials to facilitate the process of disclosure.

Our pushing for this official government disclosure is a first step to recovering our species sanity. Disclosure will enhance our individual and species health. It will take us out of denial. It may illuminate, and throw the cleansing light of day upon other, deeper layers of determined cover-up that are more lethal to our souls.

The surface duality of good and evil may be resolved by public disclosure of ETI cover-up by the official layers of human government.

But there are deeper, more entrenched levels of ETI cover-up to be addressed by our collective souls.

At this deeper level of ETI cover-up, the duality business gets tough, the forces of darkness and light meeting in pitched and fatal battle.

The shadow human government is the first level of power and cover-up we meet, even as the official government may be opening to public disclosure.

The shadow government is not a paranoid figment of our mass imagination.

It is real. The shadow government is structured around control of resources, technology, and human masses. It networks and memberships have been documented and researched. The official government in many ways is but a tool and vehicle of the shadow government, carrying out its policies and strategic will in a dance of surface democracy.

Energy, specifically our nuclear and petroleum-based civilization is a key axis for the shadow government. The technology of higher intelligent species promises free or inexpensive energy. A rapid transition to advanced energy sources would bankrupt the shadow government. They are the individuals who own vast corporate empires that for the past century have governed human affairs, peace and war.

This is the layer of ETI cover-up that is entrenched. It has resisted cooperation with the ETI initiative for fifty years.

Who are the members of shadow government? Well, some scholars say there is a split within it now, with a progressive wing wanting to slowly leak out the reality of an alien presence. There is a conservative wing wanting to hold onto its nuclear and petroleum hegemony.

Disclosing the anti-ETI war of the shadow government is at another level, another plateau above achieving disclosure by the official human governments.

The individuals in this network of influence and power are

by and large private citizens or monarchs. They own the resources of the planet in intricate, layered corporate schemes.

We know who the ringleaders are; now how to surface them and achieve effective disclosure? Remember that these are the same individuals who have orchestrated massive covert warfare by the US Central Intelligence Agency and other covert action agencies, all in furtherance of their resources and empires.

Well, I may have brushed up against one ringleader, whose bloody fingerprints go back to the Eisenhower administration. I remember being at a family compound next to his private estate in Northeast Harbor. My hosts, enlightened capitalists, ran his development corporations in Latin America. Even with them, he had demi-god status. Sort of secret cult laughter accompanied every mention of his name.

My hosts winked and laughed "cultic" all night.

Now I have come to understand. The United States of America may be, at some real level, host to a secret planetary cult of the powerful.

There may also well be a true secret cult King of the shadow government.

I am really glad I had my fifteen years with God and the Kingdom of Heaven.

Therein, I experienced a darkened mirror of what the underlying power structure of the shadow government is really like.

The Kingdom of Heaven revolved around the consciousness and sorcery of its King, otherwise known as God.

Likewise, the shadow government can be thought of as a cult, with a secret King, and a secret King's cabinet.

The shadow government's cult may have likewise revolved around the consciousness and black sorcery of its secret cult King.

Not a pro-ETI cult; but an anti-higher intelligence cult. The shadow government has dedicated itself over the past half century to covering up a positive alien presence, and consolidating planetary wealth.

We humans have suffered wars, disease, privation, and ignorance for naught. For no good reason than the greed and destructive power of the individuals leading the shadow government.

"The enemy of my enemies is my friend," my mother used to tell me in ironic comment on geopolitics.

Well, the enemy of our collective soul development may have found its host in the anti-ETI programs of the secret state, including a rogue organization within the US military.

Ah, yes – the rogue US military. Now we get into real cowboy territory.

In the duality of good and evil, the rogue US government can be thought of as a core activator of evil on this planet.

Evil, from the bottom to the top. Read any reliable expose by CIA insiders and you will see how it secretly killed, maimed, destabilized, lied and destroyed in order to advance the property and strategic interests of the shadow cultic government.

Just how rogue the covert military anti-ETI program has been is an open question. It has always been hard to fix accountability in United States covert programs, especially in the ETI arena. Military secrecy and black budgets are so structured that lines of authority and knowledge are obfuscated, hidden from public view and democratic scrutiny.

It has always been thus, because the "rogue" US military operates under an umbrella of authority and imprimatur from the cultic shadow government. Government contracts with defense industries involved in black projects are the bottom line of the individuals who lead the shadow government. The rogue US military may be operating outside the formal legislative and executive boundaries of the official US government. But they appear to operate with the acquiescence of those super-rich individuals who are the hard-liners of the shadow government.

ETI falls under the blackest of the black budget activities of the "rogue" US government. The release of dis-information about the ETI initiative is a central part of their rogue strategy to defeat human evolution into universe citizenship. It is difficult to set out a reliable litany of their misdeeds, a catalogue of the dark projects upon which they embark.

Lines are blurry; however a symbiotic relationship is clear.

The mind-enslavement program of the shadow government is a mortal danger to our souls. So also are the activities of the rogue military.

They act together in a symbiosis of evil, whether overtly related and allied or not.

The rogue military and the shadow government are the twin evils we face in resolving the duality of good and evil on our planet.

Expose and deconstruct the rogue military and the shadow government, and evil on our planet moves backward into its own abyss. Public disclosure evaporates the power of these two evil forces, and is a key to our positive, collective futures.

One cannot underestimate the utter depravity of the rogue US military and the shadow government.

We humans cannot afford to underestimate the healing power of our community of souls.

CHAPTER 6

MANIC DEPRESSION

I have come experience my manic depression as a mirror of
my very, very human life – from heights of possibilities for
our divinely crafted souls, to the depths of depraved evil on
our planet.

Bipolar disorder mirrors the dualities of life – manic and
depressive; good and evil.

Hey, our human reality is bipolar duality in spades.

Indeed, manic-depressives may be equipped with the most
apt perceptual lens for this age. Our depressive microscope lets
us perceive the molecular depravity of dark forces on our planet.
Our manic camera opens us to the panoramic heights of global
spiritual attainment.

My name is Alfred and I am bipolar.

I have bipolar affective disorder. B.A.D.

That's the creativity disease. Some studies show that many of
the world's accomplished poets, artists, and states-persons were
manic-depressives. Risk-taking is a common impulse to both
creativity and suicide. Bipolar disorder is one of the most lethal

of brain-chemistry conditions. Untreated, the manic-depressive has few constraints on risk-taking and may channel their creative impulses into suicide or bodily harm.

I remember the strange, vaulting thoughts of my first pre-manic episode. I was walking along the street in Ipanema, just a block from the beach. Brazilian carnival was happening, and I had spent the night in samba and my crimson and gold robes. As I walked, this vision urge came upon me.

"I am going to be the first American pope!" my inner voice said.

Never mind that I was not going to be a Catholic priest – you don't need to be a priest to be a Pope.

Never mind that the Catholic Church stood for retrogressive values, oppression of the spirit.

Some awakening part of my mind was talking, then in its spiritual infancy.

Able to express it's global yen only through a constricted, institutional metaphor – American pope.

In the synapses of my brain, tiny neurotransmitters failed to re-uptake, confusing my thought-processes, and creating an inner movie to be the first American pope – itself an emotional residue from my catholic education.

My bipolar cycles during early adulthood were mild, like the Pope one. Mainly they were dysthemic – bouts of mild depression when I would take on the long face of a troubled, angry poet. Wallow deeply in emotional issues; stay in bed for long periods; withdraw from life; hold negative self-concepts for six months at a time. Perfect for the bookish graduate teaching assistant; the apprentice lawyer. Somber, inner-directed.

Now I am reflecting back in time on more than twenty years of Bipolar I, the most serious diagnosis level of manic depression.

The illness has brought me five life-crashes and the loss of four marriages and wives.

Like the inky-winky spider, I've climbed up the spout again.

Time and time again.

But my greatest weakness has turned out to be my greatest strength. My altered brain-chemistry may be evolutionarily adaptive to the interplanetary action in our earth environment.

The shadow government and rogue US military are gleamingly close to being psychotic. Daily, they create an insane world around them, through institutional deceit, misinformation, and strategic deception.

Project the worldview of the shadow forces on a giant screen, and you will see the world of a negative psychotic entity - delusional; narcissistic; destructive.

The shadow government and the US rogue military can be diagnosed as a clinically demented and dangerous entity. We are under the command and tutelage of a planetary leadership that is psychopathic.

How well my training under God and the Kingdom of Heaven now serves me to tell you that! Fifteen years under psychopathic leadership held close to a vested cover of savoir faire, psychological education, worldliness, prodigious psychic powers.

The shadow government's work may be - is - the product of a demented, depraved group mind, genocidal in potential intent, and leading to planetary suicide if not stopped.

Insanity sums up what the shadow world stands for and all it knows.

The shadow world lives within the duality of plausible denial and social camouflage. Its derangement is coupled with a surface veneer of worldly knowing. Its denizens are the amoral spy-destabilizers; the polished financier-extortionists; the genocidal assassin-soldiers.

Their psychotic world is an abomination, a cancer, a deep illness on our planetary ecology. We have lunacy for our reigning shadow government.

The rogue US military and shadow government live within a duality; appearing legitimate and sane, but in fact deadly to us all.

The point of my manic depression is that I had to become psychotic myself in order to fully perceive the shadow government for what it may be itself.

As the rogues and shadows came down heavily on me, so my bipolar disorder activated. And saved me, providing me with a haven of perception,
a new altitude they could not reach. Manic depression blew me out of my established patterns and life-tracks so that the gorgons of the secret state could no longer find me on their maps.

Their disinformation teams, psychological warfare baffles, even their electromagnetic weapons could not work on me, because I had seeped into a parallel universe. You can't bullshit a shitter. One psychotic cannot double bluff the other. We see right through.

As soon as I perceived that shadow psychological warfare technology was based on a foundation of insanity, their game was over.

Hey, I developed a *counter-psywar* based on my own creative insanity, which I ran back on them.

And guess what? It worked!

Just know that the shadow power world is insane, and its power over you evaporates. Its agents may dress in the garb and trappings of office and wealth.

But they are illegitimate, and terminally psychopathic.

The point is that the power the shadow world has on governments and populations alike is psychopathic, and based on an unstable foundation.

We, the human race, can shake loose of this power because it was never freely given over to the shadow world.

The way we begin to shake loose is to publicly expose the acts of the shadow government and the rogue US military.

Once the shadows are exposed, we human souls will be able to see and acknowledge that their acts are psychopathic, and leading to species suicide.

This process is like the healing process a patient takes to

come out of mental illness.

The first step of this healing process is to come out of denial.

Knowledge leads to acceptance and a letting go of the need to deny.

In my own little world, my allegiance to higher intelligence has been the trigger to each of my five major manic episodes. Each time I got closer to higher intelligence, the shadow world rose to stop me, and my mania was triggered.

I used to think this was a self-defeating cycle. Self-destruction activated just as I approached some level of success in pushing forward toward breakthrough to ETI.

Now I see that my manic episodes may have functioned as an unconscious survival strategy.

The causal links of my going manic are clearer to me now. My pro-ETI activities would reach a threshold, tripping some secret security cordon of the state. The shadow forces would emerge with a variety of neutralizing weapons – surveillance, electromagnetic stun weapons, and threats. I would feel vulnerable under this stress, and the neurotransmitters in my brain would create a manic episode.

Blown out of the ETI trail, I would find myself in some altered, parallel universe, manic with delusions, unable to carry out focused work or human relationships: a candidate for the psychiatric ward.

Hey, if I had not so easily escaped into my vertical manic reality, I could very well have been blown away, wasted, taken out, made nada by the gorgons of the secret state.

Interesting way to look at a mental "illness," as a survival strategy on planet earth.

For the longest time, I thought my activism against political assassination technology and Star Wars weaponry had triggered these psywar counter-measures by the secret state.

But no, it turned out to be my efforts at the Carter White House to reopen the ETI issue that brought ELF waves and secret agents down upon my head.

How do I know this? Well, by the deductive process of elimination.

I had a three-ring circus going in Washington, DC, right before the secret state unleashed its first psywar attack against me. One circus ring was the reopening of the John F. Kennedy and Martin Luther King assassinations. Our public interest counterintelligence group ran a safe house off of Dupont Circle, funneling information to friendly Congresspersons on the House Select Committee on Assassinations.

Did that activity draw out the secret counter-weapons on my head?

We lobbied Committee members and their staff, gave them information that undercut the Warren report. No, there was no visible ruffle of surveillance agents and electromagnetic beaming.

Stopping Stars Wars was a second area I was active in. Star Wars was, by some accounts, a US military cover program for getting aggressive war technology into outer space. This, we are told by universe administration sources, is prohibited. The universe administration does not want an aggressive intelligent species importing dirty weapons and war-based cultures into outer space.

So I set out to monitor the Star Wars program, in consulting visits to appropriate offices in the Pentagon.

Did my public interest mole activism bring forth surveillance agents and ELF technology? Well, perhaps somewhat. The Star Wars cover for the secret state's war against ETI intelligence may have been too close for comfort for the surveillance types. Still, the most I got on anti-Star Wars missions was mild psywar baffles thrown at me. One Pentagon secretary sat me on a chair, went across to her desk, and pretended to read a phony newspaper with the headline, SEX, printed on the side she flashed to me. I remember being unmoved, but righteously ticked off that the culture of anti-civilian psywar was so blatant within the Pentagon.

But when I started up the ETI uncover project, the surveillance agents and the ELF cranked up in full force.

I personally discovered then, in the middle years of the Carter administration, the fierce extent of a hardened ring of secrecy surrounding the US government's true attitude of hostility toward the ETI initiative.

This discovery was not academic knowledge. It was real, first hand discovery; my personal descent into a spy movie, with the bad guys coming down all around me.

As a psywar melodrama played itself out around me, I discovered that any effective attempt to penetrate this ring of secrecy brings out aggressive countermeasures, aimed at neutralizing, harming, or eliminating the individuals mobilizing the attempted project.

These psywar counter-measures are carried out with laser-like precision. If the individual is not one that can be credibly assassinated, softer techniques are brought against them.

One of the soft techniques is the use of ELF weapons and surveillance baffle teams to destabilize the individual psychologically, economically, socially. Make him or her a pariah, a nut, insane, an outcast.

So when I pressed forward into an ETI-friendly window that had opened at the presidential level, the shadow neutralizing teams went into action.

Wham ELF beams; wham surveillance teams flooding my reality.

The psywar manuals just love those psychological flooding technologies. One time my car was literally flooded with at least a dozen Secret Service vehicles surrounding it, just a few miles from the White House.

Regulation head games by the book.

What did I do? I went limp – I went into florid manic depression.

I reacted to state suppression by going into my first full blown manic episode, lasting several months, including five mandatory holds in psychiatric wards of Bay Area hospitals.

Fortunately, some very distinguished people in history have been manic-depressives who have done extremely weird things. So I had some artistic cover to hold on to as my technocratic persona as a think tank futurist was shattered to pieces.

With manic depression I self-destructed, just like the intelligence manuals said I would. No longer was I Mr. Futurist, walking the legislative and executive halls with institutional credibility behind me.

I was a mental health patient, that label-box that means non-person. Underneath it all, I felt I was being outfitted for the next phase of my Holy Spirit-inspired mission.

Manic depression typically destroys two victims – careers and families. Both of mine went down the tubes, at least temporarily. I went into leave of absence mode.

Acting out is a hallmark of a first full flush manic episode, and I did my own share of acting out my hallucinations and delusions.

It's just like having mushrooms or acid pumping through your brain, without the inner brakes.

Yes, my sixty-day initiatory manic episode was a two-month public performance. Price of admission: ability to withstand consequent humiliation.

Slow hallucinatory episodes, followed by peak flourishes; then total confusion and the mandatory 72-hour stay while filled with haldol, lithium, and antidepressants.

That painful, painful realization that all has gone wrong. Why am I in this hospital, anyway? Why is the television set talking to me? Why am I filling all these cigarette tubes with tobacco? Just who are my fellow patients?

First the manic soaring followed by hard landing in a stark psychiatric ward, my unlikely haven from the gorgons of the state.

Bipolar disorder struck me without warning even though the signs and latent symptoms had been there for three decades.

After the initial outbreaks came twenty years of struggle against this disease, it being at once my downfall and my safety net.

I developed an elaborate worldview, part fixed delusion, part psychic vision.

I saw that the whole, entire universe, every atom, jot and tittle, revolved around me, in synchrony to the thoughts of my mind.

And that vision – was it a delusion or a universal truth? – became my fixed perceptual lens for the next twenty years and beyond.

This rich, bewildering world was the gift and the burden that manic depression bestowed me.

My bewildering world also had a script.

I was the Hero, come to liberate earth from the dark forces, to help initiate the new.

Everybody, every channel was talking about my drama.

All music, all news, all conversations were really about me underneath. That is how the human species was updating itself on the progress of the liberation.

Take my interactions, for example. When others spoke to me I actually heard their subconscious minds speaking, not the surface words their minds spoke.

So when I answered their subconscious thoughts, rather than their verbal output, some would say, "You are truly wise."

Others – the majority – would hear only the non sequitur of a man in the delusional grip of bipolar affective disorder.

Who was to say I was psychotic? Subconscious speech can be the opposite of conscious conversation. I could delve and understand what my conversants were actually saying when they spoke, because I could read their inner minds. They were startled not by my ramblings, but by the truth of what they were thinking mirrored back to them.

Well, not quite.

Most of the time I did not share with others what was really

going on in my head, because if I did, they would really know my thoughts were in the realm of
the insane.

Or were they so insane, my thoughts? Maybe I was tracking on some embedded universe programming in the music, news, and human events of planetary reality.

Let us go to some specifics, in television land. I can remember sitting in the day room of some psychiatric ward after my initial manic outbreak. It was morning and the game shows were on TV. Outwardly I felt denuded. In a hospital nightgown; on mind numbing anti-psychotic drugs; a long, long distance from the futurist walking through the halls of human power in the empire's capital.

Inwardly, as I watched the TV game shows, I felt closer than ever to the hidden codes of reality's structure, its core meaning.

All of television land was talking about me and to me! All this television programming was actually keeping people up to date on the latest happenings in the Hero's drama of world liberation.

"Fred Flintstone," my son called me, as Fred Flintstone's television cartooning was programming generations of earthlings for the arduous heroic tasks of Fred, my professional nickname.

"How is Alfred?" the movie heroine asks in a film on revolution, reminding the audience to keep me in their inner thoughts.

Oh, and the numbers. There was an unwritten rule that publicly reported numbers had to be structured around my birth date or home address: 542 or 524 or 620.

But these micro-references do not do justice to the blaring, omnipresent, enveloping music that came at me through the media – it was all about me, the Hero with no faces.

Looking into the faces of the game show hosts and guests what I heard was encouragement.

"A baby is born today; it's a new birth," said one gentle lady on TV. She was, of course, talking to me and my newborn cosmic consciousness.

Hey, that was I in my oh-so-tender drugged consciousness,

awake now to the dream we all are in. It is a dream of the Hero awakening in a psychiatric ward.

What more fitting place than a psychiatric ward for my birth? The Hero with no face, born into the last quarter of the twentieth century, a century of mass insanity?

And so on, twenty four hours a day. Not even the strongest anti-psychotic medicine would erase my consciousness that I had come across some inner program of the universe, tapped into a hidden knowledge.

Flip forward to six months in the future from my first manic outbreak. I am in major depression in a psychiatric ward, a county club scene.

I had been admitted after going into chronic crying jags, trying once unsuccessfully to overdoes myself with lithium. As I popped the pills into my mouth, I realized I was acting out, and spit them back onto my open palm. Right as I spit them out, the phone rang once. I figured it was the thought police, monitoring me. Trying to let me know I was totally covered; trying to throw me into despair so I would suicide. Hey, I stopped right then. The Man is not going to get me to end my life, no way.

Depression. The neurotransmitters in my brain malfunctioning, creating confused thoughts and a feeling of despair. Depression is mostly brain chemistry illusion but its effects are very real.

I forgot all the soaring thoughts, the insights I had in the manias. They were replaced by pain.

"You're a brilliant man who just can't get it together," the ward therapist told me.

"You have no idea of the forces that lurk out there," I thought to myself.

There was no way I could tell her or my fellow patients in support group sessions that I was on a mission from the Holy Spirit which had taken me to unearth the cover-up by a secret government at war with the higher intelligence of our interplanetary society.

There was no way I could tell this psychiatric ward therapist that the television programs she was watching were actually an update on the journey of a Hero who was now a patient in her ward.

Thinking the television set is talking to me was a classic symptom of manic-depressive delusion.

Was I suffering under the spell of this classic syndrome?

Probably yes.

Was manic-depressive delusion the sole cause of my seeing some underlying thread of consciousness emanating from the television set, from all of my waking reality?

Probably not.

My brain was my antenna, and tuned into real stations of cosmic connection, but with static reception. Manic depression amped me up, so I was receiving levels of consciousness I could not see before.

I saw the interconnectedness of all things.

I gleaned the meaning, the story driving our reality.

And that story was my story, the way the Holy Spirit entity had told it to me.

"Thou art Peter and upon this rock I shall build my church."

Such were the dynamics of the delusion that fixed itself upon my mind. My reality became a vast canvas, a living painting of the adventures of EyE.

Within this living painting, the forces of evolution and the forces of regression and deception intertwined in play and counter play.

The secret state reached up its tentacles to me, trying to make me an agent of chaos, one of their street psychotics to be teleguided, used, shredded, made psiwar fodder.

One vivid memory remains, of a US presidential convention in the eighties. I was watching it on television, in my second manic episode. There were two choices for president, one a cover-up artist from the Kennedy assassination.

The other, a super spy from the secret state. My phone rang

twice as the decision was being made. Bright women CIA types asked me my opinion on the telephone (I was not hallucinating this – they were really talking to me on the phone) – the cover-up or the spy?

I double-bluffed them and answered the spy into the telephone. Like sure I'll play your game of teleguided manic robot.

Within minutes, the spy became the presidential nominee and eventually President of the US. I was later to sue the bejeezus out of him, with God as my client.

Yes, I really got to know the sewer system of the secret state, its brainwashed mind control victims. I played along with them, psychotic poet that I became, and learned their methods. How they destabilized whole nations with guinea pigs whose souls they weakened and minds they stole in the service of clandestine power.

Can you countenance that individuals can be teleguided with remote psychic viewing, and local peripheral cues like white coffee plastic cups flashed by coordinated security guards?

Can you accept that the US government actually has major psywar programs that use this mind control technology to destabilize its domestic population?

The secret US State is not a nation. It is an abomination.

And I spent a quarter century in the belly of this beast, learning its inner wiring, fighting back to bring the beast to light and ultimately dispersion and death by evaporation.

Oh, it's a family thing. My paternal grandfather wrote the book on evaporation, and I'm just following in his footsteps.

So the surveillance actually increased after I got blown out of futurist think tank technocracy. I had liberated myself into a freelance poet and warrior for the ET alliance. Infinitely more dangerous to the secret state, especially as I was hip to the psywar mind games, and turned them around against the enemy.

I called my stance police hockey.

The enhanced perception brought on by manic depression was actually my greatest strength, as well as my greatest weakness.

As the secret government continued its daily tag team head games on me, I went into a head space that the official US government was split about me. Part of it was for me; part of it against me. Nobody was indifferent, and the daily proceedings of the leaders in the legislative and executive branches were in conducted in masonic, humorous code – all about me.

All this, mind you, was before I met God personally.

When I met God and I saw he thought like me when I was delusional, I knew something was off about the guy.

After all, only one of us could have been the center of subliminal attention in all reality.

Still, God used to get pissed off when he saw that some of the governmental masonry coming out of the secret US state was really about me, not him.

That's how God came to see me as a traitor, a Judas Man. He was really jealous that my delusions were stronger than his delusions.

God thought I was the secret government's secret agent to destabilize his power over the human mind.

I thought God bought into the secret government's disinformation about me, hook, line and sinker.

Oh, that I could remember chapter and verse of those exhilarating moments when I would perceive expansive masonry about me in song and art. Or peer down into the bowels of major US governmental processes and see my masonic signatures spelled out there.

But I cannot. Perhaps then my symbol world was really all delusion, a signal system I used to escape from the snares of psywar the secret government waged against me for more than two decades.

Still, I did hear a prominent, warlike US president stumble on his UN speech in fear because he knew I was in the audience as a covering journalist.

Or was that my projection, the remnant brain chemistry of

manic episodes?

And the majesty of all those nights in the wild mountains with earphones and music and amyl nitrate.

Senor, the music said. Was that me or was that He?

One thing seems more certain. As I emerged over the years from my illness, and took on again the tasks of a public interest lawyer, the psywar of the secret state only increased.

I was psychologically stable by then, so I could test and measure my reality.

The same psywar techniques that I experienced while in manic delusions continued. I continued to be the brunt of the flooding with squad cars and sirens; the electromagnetic pulse weapons; the psywar masonry in court proceedings and papers.

All this government psywar was triggered by my activities with higher intelligence.

When I was clear and emotionally stable, I proved this state surveillance to myself and to companions. The major stressor triggering my manic episodes was without doubt the pervasive psywar of the secret state.

The secret state knew I knew too much. Its denizens knew I had penetrated to the center of their darkness, and could effectively help lift the blanket of secrecy unless neutralized, by the weapons of abomination.

Manic depression brought out my spiritual expansion. An opening of my instrument, trained in Anglo-Saxon law and Catholic dogma. Oddly enough both stultifying disciplines served as strong foundations for my expansion. Turn law and dogma inside out and you can find the seeds of universal truth.

First my blinders flew, torn off by the blinding light my neurotransmitters created during manic episodes. There is no feeling like being inside a speeding ambulance, strapped to a hospital gurney, inside a strait jacket, when you know you've been given a glimpse of the inner structure of all things.

My earth-focused perceptual bindings flew away during those years when I wandered the United States and Mexico in my Lordmobile, my mobile studio, home, and sanctuary.

The Hero awakening. But why could I not just become nothingness? Why did I not realize my ordinariness as a human being in the divine order of things?

Why not let go of Hero, let go of leadership, let go of the obsession with the secret state?

And so I did, but at every turn I would find myself back in some place that reminded me of Hero and the secret state.

As I learned more about the universal structures, the organization of reality,

I learned that we do not live here in a moral vacuum here on earth.

The themes of human history, light struggling against darkness, evolution struggling against evil, war and desolation, are not the products of a meaningless dialectic.

In historical fact, we may be a life-experiment planet gone wrong, intentionally quarantined from the rest of planetary society.

Those of us who wake up to our inner cosmic consciousness are awakening to an evolutionary drive, the will to grow out into the cosmos, as is divinely ordained.

We seek to be reunited with the rest of intelligent life in the universe, but we find ourselves blocked at every turn by a human network of greed. More valuable are the oil profits of specific individuals and royal families than the future of the community of human souls yearning for reunion with their fellow species in planetary society.

I found it hard to believe that I, with the weaknesses of my mental illness, continued to be enough on track to see what the essential plight of our human community was. To know that out in space beckoned our future. Knowing that all around us legions of dimensional and extraterrestrial beings were gradually bringing our planet into reunion. Knowing that a dark, determined force had perverted the science of statecraft for the sole reason of keeping our species ignorant, isolated, in fear.

My cosmic consciousness grew with manic depression. I saw the inner connections of all things. I realized we were all sparks of divinity growing into our own gods. I learned of the intricate administration of the visible and invisible universe, how life is grown on planets, how universe society is organized.

The more I saw and learned of reality and its working, the more determined I became to help liberate our planet from the dark, atavistic force that has become its hidden agent of doom.

It seems that we the human species cannot grow unless we are able to clear the dark resistance within us.

Expand into the cosmos with your consciousness. Understand that all is evolving outward. Watch the dark forces on earth evaporate, come apart.

Their evaporation is a dance; the dark forces are waning, increasing right before the dawn. Manic depression can bring an explosion of consciousness to envelop one in these cosmic processes. Mental illness can be a gift, depending on how one receives it into their being.

Then after this explosion of awareness we return back to the mundanities of earth. Chop wood. Carry water. Bring awareness to the furnace of you life. Awareness changes all, awareness liberates, frees one of the strictures, the pounding of the secret state, an automaton beast using techno-magic to try and stay alive.

Oh there is much more than the secret state keeping us within this prison of our planet.

There are our genetic blockers, our built in disposition to conflict, not resolution. Have we as a species reached the glass ceiling of our evolution?

If so, manic depression was my being's urge to grow, evolve, out of the limiting human mindset that this planet is all we shall ever see; that we are separate from our fellows, where as we are only expressions of one single being – the collective human soul.

There are our phobic militaristic cultures, our obsolescent religions, each claiming they have the only hold on the truth. So many versions of the one true Source, each competing against the other, committing cultural genocide in the name of truth.

There are our now blending races – brown, black, white, red and yellow – in stereotype racing for separation, pushed inflammatory by the forces of war and destruction. In reality, now seeking a multi-cultural blending. Might not each race be the product of interplanetary breeding, life experiments?

In the end, it is we humans who are creating our reality. We create the wars; we create the beauty, we create the secret state, we create the healing arts.

It is our species that itself creates our destruction and our salvation.

These are the insights manic depression brought me. A simple first-level enlightenment and traumatic method acted out through rebellious neurotransmitters in my brain.

The configurations of the planets, for sure, are helping us. Our earth moves toward the galactic center in the year 2008, and all consciousness elevates in unison, we are told. Beings caught up in the cosmic enlightening expand during this transit toward the center of the galaxy. Other beings, caught up in oppression and death, implode and self-destroy. Not to worry, then, the shards of the secret state lie in their own future, huff and puff though they might, desperate to inflict their souls' inner pain outward, onto us the living.

Our paths to this enlightenment are each different. My own path was traumatic; sudden; fraught with illness and struggle. The result was the same as if I would have come to it mens sana in corpore sano.

What emerges from my sojourn through ETI cults is the intimate connection between the cult itself and latent (and overt) mental illness. Mental illness seems to be the real glue that holds ETI cults together. Mental illness is the lens through which the ETI cult leader views the ETI phenomenon, and translates it downward to his cultic members.

God and the Kingdom of Heaven, and the Messiah and Paraclete are two examples I have personally experienced, where there is a symbiosis between mental illness, the cult leader, and the ETI cult itself.

Paranoid schizophrenia and character disorder are the most probable diagnoses for God and the Messiah. God's schizophrenia was latent, hidden, not formally diagnosed. It would have been heresy in the Kingdom of Heaven to suggest that God was schizophrenic. The Messiah's schizophrenia was diagnosed during multiple psychiatric ward stays. No matter how many times I was told that, I continued to follow him as the Paraclete.

Both God's and Messiah's peak acting out periods occurred when each of their psychoses was activated in an episode. The Messiah's acting out in European parapsychology conferences, in US media shows, with mailed proclamations to the world press all happened as the result of an active episode of this mental illness. The symptoms of the Messiah's psychosis were all there – the confused thinking, the delusion, the desperation.

Likewise, with God. He might have perceived that his bouts of acting out onto the world were divinely inspired, or signaled by higher intelligence, or brought on by fleet. In reality God's acting out in aggressive cult invasions of the capitals of the world, in bringing tedious and ill-founded law suits, in proclaiming himself through massive telexed announcements was triggered by active episodes of his latent psychosis. God's way of being in the world was defined by his character disorder, and his latent paranoid schizophrenia.

What then of we members of God's and the Messiah's cults? Were we in functional psychosis as well when we charged the halls of world media, delivering incoherent broadside missiles? Probably.

God, with his acting out, brought the entire cult of the Kingdom of Heaven into a state of mass delusion and functional psychosis. God perceived the ETI phenomenon in a delusional way, and moved to take over the world. The cultic membership followed, internalizing God's delusion and sacrificing their free will and individual sanity to the cult. The cult went from group latent psychosis to group active psychosis.

These dynamics are one of the mechanisms of the "hard landings" that we members of ETI cults experience when our leaders call for acting out in the world. In the extreme, the hard landing can turn into mass ETI cult suicide. Typically, at the Kingdom of Heaven, we would launch from our bases in Ontario onto the US capitals, Washington and New York, with God's agenda in hand. While at our home bases, all the preparations seemed logical and clear.

We were living there, at home bases, in a fully delusional reality, supported by the cult social structure and belief systems.

When we reached our destinations in the US social fabric, the landing was often hard. There was no world out there waiting to be taken over. People thought us kooky; insane for the odd and incoherent cultic message we carried. We were bewildered by a disconnect between God's mind and what we found going on in the real world. This hard landing was sourced in the mental illness of God himself. For God's delusional thought system was where we had based our own thoughts and actions.

This interpretation of the ETI cult experience cuts away the mystique, but seems to be reliable indicator of cult behavior. Study the sanity and being of the ETI cult leader, and you can plumb the depths of that cult.

Did my own latent manic depression lead to my attraction to the Messiah and to God's Kingdom of Heaven?

Yes, most probably. My latent psychosis allowed me to experience reality as God and the Messiah saw it. We were all coming at reality from a delusional perspective.

Are all my insights, discoveries, perceptions, thoughts about fringe-area research – the symbioses of extraterrestrial intelligence and the US secret government, for example – in turn psychotic, delusional, and ill founded, because I came to them in association with God or the Messiah?

Are my conclusions less reliable because my own brain chemistry has been affected by manic-depressive psychosis?

These are the continuing questions of my life, asked and answered every day.

A fellow member of a support group I attend embodied an answer to these questions, almost in serendipity. He was a former radio broadcaster, with disorders close to mine. On his gloves and pouch he had emblazoned the word "UFO." He listens to the same ETI radio programs as I do from time to time. He was sure government agents were following him because of his political beliefs. He spoke a non-stop conspiratorial blurb, connecting Y2K, survivalism and ETI cover-up. A network of toxic ideas that further activated his mental disorders.

So, how am I different from him? Why are not my experiences just the product of a disordered mind? Is he not just a reflection, a mirror of me?

Been there; done that.

Part of me may continue to be delusional. Part of me may be in enough recovery to accurately report sound and genuine perceptions.

I am doing everything I can to report accurately, healthy thoughts to you. Maybe I do have a unique perspective on the ET reality to bring to the table because of the alteration of my brain chemistry.

All this talk of the psychotic and delusional basis of cultic acting out does not invalidate the underlying validity of the ETI phenomenon itself. Just because ETI cults act out delusions based on ETIs does not mean the underlying ETI reality does not exist.

The ETI is a phenomenon unto itself. There is no consensual view among humans as to what it might in reality be. We view ETI intelligence through the lens of our human minds and apparatus. Our interpretations of the phenomenon may be biased by our human projections of what extraterrestrials should look like.

Our guesses as to ETI's plans and strategy are themselves anthropomorphic projections. As the Holy Spirit entity has shown me, the ETI phenomenon may be deeply intertwined with all of human reality, its spiritual heritage, and its mythic structures. It seems likely that the ETI game plan is not based on any simplistic genetic invasion.

But I keep coming back to the fact that my own gateway to the ETI reality was through manic-depressive illness. So strong were my societal and perceptual filters that I had blocked out the possibility that the ETI presence was here, on earth, now. These powerful social filters of mine were shattered by manic-depressive psychosis. That shattering is what allowed me to perceive that another form of higher intelligence was active in our reality, at a deep, mythic level.

The trauma and shattering I went through may be a mirror of what some significant sector of humanity may go through as the ETI initiative "lands." After all, one of the secret stated fears of the US government has been that an ETI presence may lead to mass psychosis in the human population. An ETI opening would bring a profound loss of confidence in the structures of human reality such as government and religion.

Perhaps I was allowed to be among those numerous "messengers" of the ETIs. We are ETI alien experiencers. Our task has been to experience early on what the human species may experience in the future. Pioneers, messenger molecules, pilot projects, guinea pigs. Our experience may make it easier for the human species to go through to co-existence with a higher species. We subject ourselves to ETI contact that can produce trauma, delusion, and psychosis. We take on that burden on behalf of the human race, making our landing with the ETI civilizations less traumatic, easier when that comes.

A shift is occurring in human consciousness, an opening to our planet's membership in universe society. Humans are coming to see alien experiencers as individuals who have undergone a forerunner experience on behalf of the collective human future.

A turning point in my relation to my neurochemical disorder came when I fled God in Canada to save myself from his plans to murder me. Up to that point

I had used my enhancing, occasionally delusional perceptual tools to peer deeply into reality's frontier.

The easiest way to hold the raw power of manic-depressive perception was to stay unmedicated. Against all medical advice, I took no lithium carbonate to ensure the steady flow of clear thoughts across the synapses of my brain. I took no antidepressants to smooth re-uptake of my neurotransmitters. I was fully vulnerable to the glorious heights and hellish depths of my mental chemistry.

So when I fled to the lower Rio Grande Valley of Texas, I landed in the deepest, unconditioned hell my mind had known. I was in a literal hell of my own mind's making, exacerbated by the post traumatic stress of escaping from the hell God had just tried to send me to. As I've told you, I thought I was dead, and everyone else was alive. Somehow I had managed to remain suspended in this dimensional reality to see how living people enjoy or disregard the beauty of our world.

I learned so much in two years of quiet, withdrawn observation. I had my real childhood in my parent's home. And came to know my mother and father for the first time since I left home for boarding school at the age of six.

"We've decided to save you," my mother told me.

So they made me their project in their old age, and I turned fifty, but really twelve in age relational to my father and mother.

Still I did not medicate my bipolar disorder, and chose to wallow in the seas of major depression.

My hallucinations remained fixed, particularly on live political television. When a future environmental official of the incoming US government coughed uncontrollable at a live televised conference, I perceived her cough as a signal of my continuing underground influence in US public life. Coughing, you see, was a major masonic symbol that everyone, just everyone, used to let the world know about me, good or bad.

Just three years after that episode, I delivered a live presentation to the very same environmental official at a tri-national environmental conference in Oaxaca, Mexico. I spoke from the heart and said that human health was part of the environment, silently remembering our earlier television connection. The tri-national ministers agreed and amended their official documents accordingly. Once again, I took this vaulting change in my fortunes and social impact to be yet another chapter of the mystery school I enrolled in as part of life.

Normalcy is the force that ruled my life in the 90s. I returned to the social norm of living, in all its mundane regulated aspects. Normalcy healed my illness.

I ceased rebelling against allopathic medicine, and went on medication to even out the cycles of bipolar thought. The medication reduced my libido, but increased the reliability of my perceptions. My active interest in ETI, in the secret state abated.

Of course, the secret state's interest in me did not abate. I was a federal official in the community health center movement. Every time I had to fly to the US Congress on business or for hearings, there were the multiple black station wagons, the nasty black garbed agents staring me down.

"Hey, you're a Fed, but I'm a Fed, so bug off," I sort of laughed to myself.

My family home was on an isolated country lane. So close was the electronic surveillance that when I would venture out at night to walk my dog, well, the squad car would roll right up slow against me. When I went to political meetings supporting my city council neighbor, the local police chief and about a dozen of his officers would stay outside the meeting, running police hockey games. I gamed back. The police chief's sister was my student at the university, where I taught the civil liberties course to her and about 80 future corrections officers. So I winked and joked at them, though the chief later was to become head of Texas' executions parole board.

These orders to perform active surveillance of a citizen did not come from the Rio Grande local police department. On their own they didn't give a shit what I was doing. Their orders to run psywar on me came from disembodied agents in some weird world trying to reach yet another dissident federal official right in the tranquility of the Rio Grande valley, all because of his knowledge and activities of higher intelligence on planet earth.

I stayed my goal and continued to maintain my mental health, healing two decades of full-blown bipolar madness.

"You would be a good therapist," the director of my health center told me.

So I became a therapist, after five years in graduate school while juggling my life as a Fed.

The inmate took over the healing asylum. I gave deeply to my patients. I organized manic-depressives in Texas and Mexico. I kept on my medication faithfully. My interests became the psyche, the human mind. I met my wife, also a therapist, and we started our soul mate journey.

We traveled to Canada, and met God together. God was in florid schizophrenic rave. A few months later he was dead. My karmic contract with God over. Now once again together, our bonded auras had ended a story of exploitation by God begun long ago.

And then our journey took us, guess where?

Back to the bosom of higher intelligent beings; back to the future; back to the gardens of Eden where I started as the Paraclete.

I had made the journey from mental health patient to mental health healer, and still my journey had its original destinations. Everything remains the same and yet everything is different. The Messiah and God have passed out of my aura to their own private destinies. The Holy Spirit entity remains.

So was the Holy Spirit the Joker?

"Thou art Peter and upon this rock I shall build my church," the Holy Spirit said.

What a cosmic, comic setup to throw at a terrestrial, Catholic trained, Yale lawyer!

I mean, the Holy Spirit entity must have some sharply honed sense of black humor to follow the Peter-rock line with two wild cards like the Messiah and God. Did I stand a chance at staying sane and yet attentive to my duty of obedience to divine command? To be at the service of the King of Kings, all two of them?

Now, in well-grounded mentality, stabilized by daily lithium and serotonin enhancers, I can reinterpret the Holy Spirit's forecast.

It was either:

1   a hallucination;

2   a disinformation;

3   a symbolic communication.

Of course, in the service of my ego, which still enjoys strokes, I choose to believe the Holy Spirit spoke to me in authentic symbolic communication.

Just because the visitation triggered two decades of on and off delusional activism does not mean it was inauthentic or the product of my mental chemistry.

The question I now ask myself, in stabilized reality, is not did the Holy Spirit entity speak to me, but rather, what did these words mean.

That's easy. 'Thou" means not me, but each of us humans. 'Peter" does not mean the Pope of the earth. It means a building block of the new era, the new cosmic dispensation on earth. 'Church' does not mean some new institutional order, but a dimension of consciousness.

Now we can translate what the Holy Spirit was really saying to me.

The Holy Spirit said that we humans are the base on which a new consciousness is to be built on earth.

What a positive view of the future!

You may remember, dear reader, a single characteristic which one higher intelligent species putatively active in our environment looks for in "choosing" humans for contact.

This higher intelligent species says they choose humans who are "visionary."

Is this true?

Regardless, I take this mantra as very suggestive. Visionary is an evolutionary characteristic. An intelligent species requires vision to evolve. Perhaps that is why the visionary is a very special relation to the future of the human race.

Believe me, manic depression activates every latent shred of vision an individual may have.

They whom the gods would make visionary, first they make manic-depressive or with some mood disorder.

There must be some sound evolutionary reason why manic depression and mood disorders have created such visionaries as: Baudelaire, Blake, Byron, Coleridge, Crane, Dickinson, Eliot, Hopkins, Hugo, Jarell, Johnson, Keats, Lindsay, Millay, Hans Christian Anderson, de Balzac, Boswell, Pasternak, Plath, Poe, Pound, Pushkin, Shelley, Tennyson, Thomas, Whitman, Bunyan, Clemens, Conrad, Dickens, Emerson, Faulkner, Fitzgerald, Gibbon, Gogol, Gorky,

Greene, Hemingway, Hesse, Ibsen, Inge, James, Lamb, Melville, O'Neill, Ruskin, Mary Shelley, Stevenson, Turgenev, Williams, Woolf, Zola, Berlioz, Handel, Ives, Mahler, Rachmaninoff, Tchaikovsky, Berlin, Coward, Foster, Mingus, Parker, Porter, Powell, Borromini, Eakins, Gauguin, van Gogh, Gorky, Michaelangelo, Munch, Pollock, Romney, Rosetti, Rothko and de Stael.

Now, visualize yourself as a higher intelligent species, charged with bringing the human community into the universe fold of inhabited planets.

Would you not want human visionaries like these graduates of manic depression and mood disorders leading the pack?

CHAPTER 7

RECOVERY

Recovery is a key survival process for this, our last, solely human era. I say "last", because the veil of planetary isolation may surely part within our generations, leaving behind our ordinary history, a universe quarantine we may have unconsciously endured for living memory.

Human fear and panic has been repeatedly used by all parties – from the US secret state to the more evolved ETs - as a core justification for keeping humanity in the dark about higher intelligent species in our planetary environment.

But why do we assume humans will panic at a social landing of the ETI initiative?

My guess is that the bulk of humanity would be overjoyed if the ETIs did land. They would sense that the ETIs represent liberation from the oppression of brutish human governments, a culture of war, destruction, and exploitation. Humans could feel, in fact, a freedom from the remnants of the dark ages on earth.

Some more enlightened, possible ETI observations tell us that it is bewildering that so many evil, destructive human beings live side by side with more evolved humans.

They tell us - eliminate the brutes in human power, and you greatly increase the chances of your species to evolve to inter-planetary status.

I submit it is not the ordinary human beings we have to worry about. Those who are prone to panic because of an overt ETI landing are more likely to be the retrogressive human types whose power positions are threatened by our integration with another higher species.

The historical record is, in fact, that human governments have panicked at ETI activity, and made it secret because they fear the loss of control.

The first abuse we humans have to recover from is the abusive secrecy of our governments, and its destructive discrediting, disinformation, and covert violence.

Let us even suppose that the paranoid scenario of abductee sexual violations and ETI hybrid breeding programs were in some measure true.

Government secrecy and cover-up of any ETI abduction program immeasurably compounds its harm, and makes the government in fact an agent of human abduction. In such a case, government has violated its duty of fiduciary trust toward the human population. The duty of a government is to serve and protect, not to deceive and destroy.

On second thought, an advanced ETI population may be concerned about causing fear and panic among human governments, not among the human population.

That human governments are the problem, not the human population, is what the historical record suggests. This has happened since overt ETI activity has been stepped up over the last fifty years. Public opinion polls tend to show humans as relatively receptive toward ETI activity. The US secret government has gone into a hyper-reactive, war-like stance.

So what are the ETIs waiting for?

What is underlying strategy of higher intelligence in holding back their social landing into human society?

One possible ETI logic seems to stand out very clearly.

The ETIs may be waiting until we humans clean our own house. We apparently may not be able to evolve without changing our values and our vision. ETIs intelligence may face real limitations in its planetary colonization. Perhaps the ETI initiative cannot bring the human race into full interplanetary society while it remains a war-like species.

We remain warlike because of the military-industrial interests that preserve our archaic culture of internecine violence and conflict.

ETI logic suggests that secret human government and military entities may, in fact, be the most immediate obstacles to human evolution. These destructive, retrogressive human authorities keep us on our path of war, prejudice and species suicide.

ETI intelligence may be waiting for we humans to disassemble these brutes from positions of institutional and social authority, and replace them with progressive, more visionary leaders.

Message: throw the bums out, organically, democratically, with the power of inner vision and evolutionary motivation.

We can dismantle the engines of war; the military establishments, the arms factories. Liberate secret military technology and research for our lives. It is fundamental economics that weapons systems are capital expenditures. Reroute this social capital to the human welfare, and we build the infrastructure to enter the society of planets.

Oh, you argue, war has been with us from the beginning of recorded memories and will be with us forever.

Guess what? War may have been abolished in planetary society millennia ago. We may be the evolutionary stragglers just emerging from the cave.

War may be core human aberration, kept in place on our planet only by the vested interests of our atavistic governments and military establishments – controlled by the evolutionary dregs of our species. The culture they create and maintain has one long-range outcome only – *to destroy us as a species.*

Simplistic? No, not really. The forces behind human war against the ETI initiative know full well what they are doing. They are engaging in a conscious, devious course of conduct.

One stratagem has been to cut human political leadership out of access to intelligence about ETI activity. Strategic leadership of the human war against the ETI initiative may operate under extreme secrecy, in a narrow private group, unfettered by the public scrutiny that follows political and governmental leaders.

ETI-based technology and information about ETI activity are part of our public trust. Our public trust has now been shifted to a convoluted network of clandestine, classified projects funded by black budgets paid out of our public funds, and perhaps the profits of the international drug trade. These black budgets are in turn paid into a honeycomb of private entities owned by individuals who have for decades led the anti-ETI war for their own vested interests and profit.

This anti-ETI methodology is similar to a well-documented methodology by which covert warfare has been carried out against national liberation movements in third world countries. The very same circle of vested interests that drove the clandestine wars against third world countries is driving the war against the ETI initiative.

Why are the methodologies of covert war against third world countries and those against the ETI initiative similar?

Because the same parties are behind both forms of warfare!

J'accuse!

I submit that a secret cultic King in the US shadow government may in fact have functioned as a secret world King, manipulating a deceptive war of nearly fifty years duration against an ETI race that wants us to survive and evolve.

That secret cultic King and the councils that surround this illicit throne have much to answer for – Morally, legally and spiritually. They may have attempted to appropriate from the human species what is their core right as citizens of the universe – to participate in the society of planets.

I have no doubt they will be held accountable, either through personal karma or by human law and mores.

There, I said it. Now let me amend it. Obviously a personal king may weaken, die, become senile, be no longer active as age advances and their soul becomes reluctant to embark of missions of systematic evil.

If not a personal king, there is a core of individuals and entities that function as a secret world monarchy. Their highest priority is to wage a war of deception against the ETI initiative, primarily for personal profit and power. Their strategic mindset is in service of this goal.

So how do we recover our public assets, our public trust? The ETI initiative is the most public of assets in the public trust we enjoy as custodians of our planet, Earth.

Sunshine is probably the most direct and immediate remedy. Public disclosure of what is known about ETI activity, about the ETI initiative, about the amoral blanket of secrecy under which we have labored for five decades.

Let the ETIs shine in!

Let's meet the ETIs half way. The focus of the ETIs has been to condition us upward to a sufficient consciousness to accept ETI into our reality.

Well, then. Let's move upward to a close encounter of the fifth kind. Let us intentionally create a mutual communication between our species – terrestrial and extraterrestrial.

Let's blow out the ETI cover up. It serves us no good. It is leading to our collective death. It is in the service of a narrow group of aging white men, and their rogue disciples.

Easier said than done? Oh I don't know. One way of looking at ETI activity is that of ETIs seeking an opening with empathetic humans.

"Can anybody down there hear us?" say ETI encounters.

The ETIs are gaming with us at a deep, deep level. The gaming is interactive. The more we consciously respond as a species, the more receptively the ETIs respond, and visa-versa.

Right now, because of the secrecy blackout, the only collective human voices the ETIs are hearing as a response are those of the secret state, committed to a war against them.

Let's get together and show the ETIs we are listening.

All channels active – music, politics, media, technology, finance, community, spirit.

A rising up and a renaissance of the human spirit

What does this rising up look like?

Well, paint your own picture.

- Musicians bringing us concerts to raise consciousness and resources for the ETI landing.

- An informed citizenry opening up the legislative and governmental halls, legitimizing the ETI initiative and lifting the blanket of secrecy.

- Educators and teachers leading open minds into knowledge about the extraterrestrial dimension of our planet.

- Media opening itself to broadcast the full story of the ETI cover-up and the ETI initiative.

- Spirit stirring within each human soul, each spiritual path to open our collective species to an era of Divine expansion.

- Human governments changing their hearts and minds to transform the war against ETIs into a welcome peace, opening up black projects and dismantling human military establishments.

- Legal amnesty given all government, military, contractors, others who come forward to witness their experiences, their knowledge of cover-up.

- Ending humanity's dark ages, and the beginning of an
  era of universal citizenship for humanity.

Too idealistic for you?

Well, take it a step at a time, and take a decade to do it.

With the right momentum, this vision can become a reality
in much less time.

How can this fifty-year-old cover up be unraveled?

Even more, what is going to happen once the war against the
ETI initiative is gone?

The cover up of the ETI initiative can unravel precisely because secrecy is key to the cover-up's modus operandi.

Once secrecy begins to lift, the cover-up has lost its most
powerful mechanism.

The lifting of ETI official secrecy in turns puts an inevitable
process of dismantling into play. We can identify some elements
the dynamics and structural elements of the dismantling. An
important outcome of this process is to move public opinion
from a state of apathy, to a state of determined concern. Out of
this concern a human social will to survive may be born.

As we know, some call this process a sea change.

In the European community, some governments have already begun to declassify their reports of ETI activity. Dismantling the cover-up does not jeopardize military security. The
secret state knows this. If it were to publicly argue for continued
secrecy around ETI activity on the grounds of military security,
the argument would fail for lack of any reasonable justification.
The secret state cannot allow any official admission of the
existence of ETI activity. Once there is an official admission,
then the anti-ETI war begins to unravel.

An unraveling cover-up in turn draws a crowd. Apathy is
probably the principal public attitude toward the ETI initiative.
This public apathy has in fact been the goal of the secret state's
program of anti-ETI war. Thus far, the ETI cover-up has

worked, as the secret government's main counter-strategy toward the threat of the ETI initiative. That counter-strategy may no longer be successful in maintaining public apathy once a cover-up is no longer credible.

"Where were you when you learned that the ETIs were really here?"

There may probably be no single other living memory more powerful that that of when one first became irrevocably aware of an extraterrestrial force in present contact with the earth.

Fear of the power of this primal imprint on the collective human memory continues to drive the secret government in its desperate measures to avoid those moments of publicly acknowledged contact.

Two elements are key to breaking through the cover-up into a collective, open relationship with the ETI initiative. One does not follow the other; they both are interactive.

One the one hand, we must do all we can to break the veil of secrecy – to shatter the thin veneer of social taboos hanging over the ETI initiative. This can come through legitimizing public participation in the ETI issue, ranging from joyous public benefit events and concerts, to determined public hearings in legislative and governmental forums.

We also must develop a focused, proactive outreach to the ETIs themselves. This is our own human ETI initiative, an alternative platform to the war and deception program of the secret state.

Thus far, this evolutionary human initiative has not developed. We have succumbed to the apathy that the secret state has sought to create in us.

So what are some of the possible elements of our own, human community-based ETI initiative?

Public information and consciousness-raising about ETI activity and plans seems to be a key element of our own ETI initiative. We must strive to see that our human community has access to full knowledge and educational resources about the ETIs.

A full evaluation of our existing database about ETI activity is essential to developing proactive goals. This database includes all hard data on military and civilian hard craft encounters, whether classified or not.

Importantly, evaluation of the existing ETI database includes full disclosure of governmental or para-official disinformation operations, including false or misleading information put out by military or paramilitary authorities.

ETI database evaluation also includes debriefing significant ETI witnesses, ETI enrollees, and abductees.

Evaluation also includes full disclosure of all classified technologies developed in secrecy as part of the "black" programs. Especially important is the potential application of these technologies to human welfare.

The human scientific resources devoted to the effort to develop our own human ETI initiative should be unprecedented and transnational.

Military lore tells us that the secrecy classifications assigned to the ETI initiative have been higher than that surrounding the development of nuclear weapons. Even during the height of the Cold War, a possible Soviet nuclear weapons strike upon the US military ranked as the second highest priority of the US radar detection system, after an ETI intrusion, which was the highest priority.

Our ETI data evaluation effort is meant to inform the process of developing our ET initiative. ETI data evaluation is reported publicly, its findings sifted on the Internet and on public information channels.

Oh, we must have lots and lots of "what does it all mean" committees, public, private, religious, and eleemosynary.

Let a thousand flowers bloom!

With all these elements cooking in our ETI kitchen, we can

devise the dishes of the meals we intend to serve at the ETI banquet.

One appetizer is sure to be the declaration of a Decade of Contact, a ten-year ETI initiative holiday here on earth.

What is the Decade of Contact about? It's like a half time at a sporting event.

The two teams – here the secret state and the ETIs - go off the field into the symbolic locker room.

They've played a fifty-year-long first half time, with we the spectators not even knowing there was a game going on.

During half time things are going to change in this game.

A third team is going to take the field – a team called "We the Aware People of Earth!" We'll be both fans in the stands and players on the field in the second half of the game to bring planet earth into universe reality.

So we need the Decade of Contact half time festivities to get organized as the third team on the field. To fill the stadium, to organize the half time show, complete with bands and presentations and lots of changes in the status quo.

We also need the half time to develop our own set of plays, so we can go on to the field in the second half, mediating an alliance with ETI, and bringing the secret state's idiotic anti-ETI war out into the open.

I mean, if it isn't idiotic to try and hide the fact that advanced intelligence wants to play the game on earth too, I don't know what is.

During the first half of the game, the secret state competed unethically, not letting on to us that ETI was here and trying to bring the planet into the galaxy.

Now, during our Decade of Contact half time, we can make up for that and kick their ass in the second half. If not kick their ass, then dismantle the secrecy. And ultimately the institutions of the secret state itself.

And in the second half of the game, we can dance onto the field as a determined cadre of awareness, spearheading our own human-ETI initiative, a mutual close encounter between terrestrials and the ambassadors from the rest of the universe.

So much for the appetizers! Now, let's get to the entrees of the meal. We are, after all, at a banquet celebrating our union with the society of planets. So let us create full-fledged gourmet dishes, for all tastes.

An inter-stellar travel delegation of a cross-section of aware human activists is a must! Our delegation would use ETI space vehicles to travel to ETI home and other inhabited planets of organized outer space, visit with them, and bring back a first hand report for the humans here at home.

The trip should not take too long via hyper-space. We could beam the whole journey live on earth television, so we earthlings get to see all the action.

The interviews on the trip itself, the celebrations of landing on the various planets, the greetings by the ETI folks at the other planets, tours of their cities, technology, educational and health systems. Immediate, visual, interactive experience, impact creates a liberating imprint on the collective psyche of the human race.

What a live teevee special!

And on return, we would have a round-the-world tour with the human delegation and their ETI hosts, with guests from other planets joining in the tour.

Celebration at home! Free at last, Lord. Free at last!

And now a vegan dish – the Blueprint. No more dog eat dog on this planet.

The Blueprint is a multi-media interactive matrix, mutually conceived by humans and ETI together, for this planet's development as a member of organized universe society.

The Blueprint is a constantly self-refreshing Plan for integrating earth into the society of planets. Not a one-time linear schematic, but a dynamic compass for integrating goals, accomplishments, and ever-new levels of galactic consciousness.

The Blueprint is a real-time, living readout of where our

planetary integration with ETI has been, where we presently are, and where we are going. The Blueprint allows us to measure our progress, our direction in integrating into interplanetary society. It is a self-correcting compass, and can tell us if we are off course in our progress, and where we might make necessary corrections.

Our species learning curve in joining interplanetary society is so steep that the Blueprint is a necessary tool so as not to lose our way.

This learning curve includes key evolutionary questions, such as how to integrate advanced ETI technology and contact in such a way as not to cripple or destroy human society itself.

Who will develop the Blueprint technology, or something similar?

That's easy. Its development is a joint, interactive project of humans and the ETI.

When can humans and ETI begin on developing the Blueprint?

That's more difficult to answer. It depends on the dynamics of the Decade of Contact. If the human cover-up of the ETI initiative begins to unravel and dissolve early on in the Decade of Contact, well then, the chances that working contact can be established during the Decade are increased. Working contact between humans and ETI is a precondition to our developing advanced social technologies such as the Blueprint.

If the secret government goes into a war of attrition mode, seeking to continue the cover-up by any means possible, then all bets are off. The ETI and we humans perforce must engage in planetary guerilla warfare of the mind.

Objectives of guerilla warfare of the mind are (1) breakdown of the secret government cover-up and (2) breakthrough of the human species and the ETI.

Breakdown-breakthrough is a tried and true model for transformation.

I think you can get the drift of the sort of new thinking and approach we need to break through to interplanetary society. Together, we could imagine and develop many different approaches that would involve the human will and imagination, and advance our journey into full universe citizenship.

What must be borne in mind, however, is that this effort is not a dry academic exercise, nor a business-as-usual social movement.

There is a dark force -both strengthening and weakening simultaneously - which is determined to keep the human race enslaved in ignorance. The final stages of this secret force's program are about to start to play out. The dark force is truly inhuman. The technological weapons it has assembled to keep our human population in its chains of mind are different from the weapons of mass destruction of prior eras, including the most recent nuclear era.

These secret weapons are designed for population control and ultimately destruction of the planet. Imagine the most dastardly science fiction scenario you can. A vulnerable human population held as hostage by an evil planetary force. The humans do not even know they are held captive, so tight is the secret cover-up. In their final desperation to stave off the inevitable victory of universe forces, the secret government unleashes death rays that can not only kill off human population at the mind, even soul level, but can destroy the very ecology of the planet itself.

Like the ionosphere, for example, capable of being destroyed by the HAARP electromagnetic pulse weapons systems.

It's the old dog-in-the-manger trick. If I can't win this game, no body will.

That's the secret state for you. Now don't you just love them?

If any group can probably play a dramatic role in the Decade of Contact, it will be the ETI enrollees and contactees, for many different reasons and in many different ways.

In a way, all of us humans are ETI contactees. Our planet is the subject of a highly sophisticated ETI initiative, whose goal is to bring us into interplanetary society, within our species limitations. The waves of ETI sightings and reported encounters can reasonably be interpreted as following definite strategies.

One ETI strategy appears to be peripheral cueing. ETI encounters, taken as a whole, can be seen as structured according to the psychological laws of cognition, where human awareness is created by creating subtle cues – ETI activity – in the periphery of the human environment.

Sort of things that you see at the edge of your consciousness, but not directly in front of your eyes. Like your boss's body language.

ETI encounters may function as peripheral cues, conditioning us slowly to open awareness that higher universe intelligence is in our environment.

So in that sense we humans are all ETI contactees. And we have had to pay an important psychological price for this position, due to the anti-ETI war. Most of us have not come to start paying the price of psychological recovery from the cover-up yet. But we may well pay it in the future.

That having been said, what about persons who have experienced a genuine direct ETI encounter? In many ways, they have served as guinea pigs for the human race. Some report to have been treated well, and respectfully. The perception of others having apparent ETI encounters has include the experience of trauma, including experiences that have felt like sexual, physical and psychological abuse. Many have suffered social isolation and insult, and psychological distress following their experiences.

I ask you – does my cat look at me as a human, or as a big cat? How does my cat perceive the act of my reading a book?

And remember, cats and humans are fairly close on the evolutionary scale.

In other words, it is a verified fact that humans have come into contact with phenomena that are created by higher intelligent beings. By the same token, we humans must perceive genuine ETI experiences – and bogus look-alike experiences -through the limitations of our genetic and perceptual makeup.

Human reports of ETI encounters depend on the perceptual vagaries of the experiencing human's mind. They may not be factually accurate reports of the underlying phenomena the humans believe they experienced. I recall my own experience with the Holy Spirit entity, and the multiple ways this experience could be interpreted.

Operating under extreme field conditions, a hostile government, and a fractious ETI research community have not been ideal conditions for developing a reliable methodology for interpreting ETI encounter and contactee experiences.

One of the outcomes of a proactive ETI research initiative during the Decade of Contact will hopefully be the development of these methodologies. Particularly, as the ETIs themselves can be involved in hinting at or sharing some of the strategies and techniques that they have used.

In the ETI encounter field, there are some signs of the dark presence of the secret government. Specifically, through the creation of bogus ETI abductions as disinformation techniques, using covert operations and mind control technologies, in a program describe as MILAB (Military Abductions). This psywar program – carried out as part of the over-all war of the shadow government against the ETI initiative – uses documented mind control techniques developed as part of US government's covert warfare program. MK-UTRA psychological warfare techniques; ritual torture and sexual abuse of "abductees."

The goals of this secret government psywar against the human population include creating a perimeter of fear around the ETI initiative. To intimidate and deter humans from developing a critical mass who might want to participate in the ETI initiative. To create a climate of paranoia and terror around the persona of the ETIs, denying the ETIs access to an informed human will.

This is strategic disinformation on the part of the secret state, part of their war of attrition. Its end goal is in fact devolution of the human species.

The experimenter effect, where the consciousness of the experimenter affects the outcome of the research itself, operates very powerfully in the ETI encounter field. In any single encounter, there may be as many as five different conceptual points of view of the underlying phenomena – the ETIs; the abductee or contactees; the secret government observer or perpetrator; the ETI researcher; the general public.

Right now, the perceptual gaps among the five sets of actors can be staggering. Hopefully, the dynamics of our movement to disassemble the cover-up will narrow these gaps of perception among the participants. Each participant will share and know more of the perception of the others. In this way, kind of a triangulation of perception, a determined human understanding of the full underlying facets of ETI abduction and contactee technology can be developed.

We already have a fairly advanced concept and database of the psychological characteristics of abductees, and what the functions of true abduction experiences might be.

Remember that the ETI initiative is undertaken under conditions of war. The secret military is at war with the ETIs. At the very least, ETI encounters may make sense as a "wartime" counterstrategy of ETI intelligence, created as peripheral cues to raise our collective consciousness.

The ultimate battlefield in this war by the secret government on the ETIs is the collective human mind-set, its perception of what reality really is.

That is why we humans must mobilize for survival in guerilla warfare of the mind. Standing on the sidelines is not an option for our species to survive.

The human imagination soars at what can be made possible by the dynamics of species liberation during the Decade of Contact.

Think of what we can do once we have achieved a participatory relationship with ETI intelligence. Not the least of which is an understanding of their strategies of earth-consciousness raising, their long-term strategy to bring humanity upward into the planetary federation.

Not the least of which is an understanding of just how many extraterrestrial and inter-dimensional parties are active in our earth environment, and what the origin, nature and intentions of each is.

Are there good guys and bad guys?

How can one tell?

Whom should we humans identify with more closely?

What is the inter-planetary history of ETI contact with our reality, and what can be our future?

We human can awake during this process of deep, deep recovery.

We are to recover from the effects of a long brainwashing. Our recovery is in part from those backward-looking effects of the human psyche, human culture, human mores, religions, philosophies, and sciences that might have kept us ignorant of our interplanetary heritage for millennia.

But that aspect of our recovery is not the whole of the work we must do. Nor will it be the most important in terms of the trauma that we have endured and might endure as the result of the war of attrition of the secret state.

Our most traumatic recovery may be indeed the recovery from decades of war and oppression waged on humanity by the secret government itself.

Our planet finds itself mired in violent conflict, economic and human rights oppression, poverty, environmental degradation, high tech anti-population weaponry, subversion of democracy.

Evaporation of the secret war against the ETI will not happen overnight. Our Decade of Contact is a bridge, an approach to mobilizing and coordinating human knowledge, awareness, will and momentum. Break the embargo on participation in the

ETI initiative, dismantle the secret state population war machine, and much of their oppression will begin to evaporate.

Wake up! It is neither the conflict-ridden genes of the human race, nor the contradictions of our developing planetary society that cause and maintains this violence to life.

It is the secret state – waging war upon our human species, keeping us imprisoned and separated from our interplanetary cousins, dumbed-down, hungry and poor, unhealthy, fractured and divided – that is the prime cause of the slow devolution of our planet.

We are not to blame! Our natural heritage is a cooperating partnership with our fellow civilizations on life-bearing planets.

We humans, in fact, are the victims of sustained individual and social abuse – psychological, physical, and violent abuse. A sustained and systematic pattern of abuse.

Our path out of this mire is to seek our collective, conscious recovery from the abuse of the secret state.

So what does our "recovery" from this interplanetary war of attrition mean?

A first step in any recovery from abuse – psychological, physical, social, violent or otherwise – is the acknowledgement by the victim that she or he has in fact been abused.

Consider the power of this affirmation – "I am a citizen of the universe and am entitled to reunion with my interplanetary brothers and sisters."

Call it a new section of the Universal Declaration of Human Rights.

We humans have a fundamental right – under natural law and social law alike - to full participation in the society of planets.

Governments or other entities may not interfere with the exercise of this fundamental human right of ours, whether overtly or covertly through clandestine
means.

It is that simple. The secret war of the shadow state against the ETI initiative violates the fundamental tenets of the Universal Declaration of Human Rights.

The ongoing anti-ETI war impairs the individual, human rights of every person on the planet. The war is carried out against our entire human community. It's intent, if fully carried out, may well result in the long-term devolution or genocide of the human race.

Legal implication – the secret government's war on the ETI initiative – and the world civilian population – is unlawful and contrary to established norms of international law.

The creeps of the secret state are violating fundamental international laws!

And they must be stopped from doing so in every arena we can access, with every argument we can muster, with all the force of morality and law behind us.

We have every right to appeal to the court of public opinion to stop the anti-ETI war.

We have every right to seek legal redress in every city council, county commission, state and provincial legislature, national parliament and congress in the world.

We have every right to vote out the politicians facilitating the cover up and vote in leaders who are responsive to our rights to participate in interplanetary society, and who will carry out governmental programs accordingly.

We have the right to seek that our governments bring actions in the international courts and organizations, seeking redress and positive programs to stop the anti-ETI war and vouchsafe our humans rights to ongoing communion with universe society.

We have every legal right to bring class actions and other lawsuits seeking monetary damages and injunctions against private entities, corporations, and individuals that are carrying out the cover up under public or private contract.

Why do we have these rights? Because we are citizens of the universe, and the Universal Declaration of Human Rights protects them for us. Fundamental principles of international law dictate the expansion of human rights to news areas, in which unanticipated discoveries are made.

That's the second meaning of "recovery." We must recover – take back – what is rightfully ours, our universe heritage. It has been forcefully taken from us through deception and psychological warfare, carried out with public funds.

We can take back and re-own our rights to full participation as citizens of an interplanetary world the secret government has long tried to fool us into thinking does not exist.

The entire MILAB (Military Abductions) program bears witness to the reality that the primary enemy we humans face here on earth is the secret government.

MILAB is a covert operations program, based on mind control technology developed through the CIA MK-ULTRA program during the last three decades.

The object of the program is to simulate an abduction of a target human by hostile ETI aliens.

MILAB abductions use human paramilitary personnel in masquerade as aliens, together with technologically based mind control techniques, mind screens, holographic technologies, and electromagnetic pulse technologies to simulate an alien abduction. The target human abductee's mind and perception are altered, and a practiced deception takes place. Public interest researchers have been able to develop a typical profile for MILAB abductions. MILAB abductions can be analyzed and identified as being covert paramilitary deception operations.

The purpose and goal of the MILAB program is to create a whisper campaign of negative disinformation against the ETI initiative. MILAB is part of the arsenal of weapons that the secret government uses in their war of attrition against human integration into planetary society. Invariably abductees report that MILAB abductions are traumatic experiences undertaken by cruel and manipulative ETI aliens. These reports are in turn repeated in the media, in books and reports, and in a pseudo-academic lore that the ETI initiative has as its goals the extinction of the human species in favor of a hybrid race, part human and part ETI.

So what else is new? The secret government has been using practiced deception operations against the people of earth for the last fifty years, in multiple arenas, including the ETI initiative. Assassination and social destabilization operations; anti-population mass destabilizers such as electromagnetic pulse weapons are examples that are all in the public literature.

We have a nasty, nasty rogue para-government loose on the planet, and we have had it for some time. This para-government is what we must dismantle, personnel by personnel, entity-by-entity, program-by-program, funding stream by funding stream.

Yet, how do we recover from this para-government, when its very essence is secrecy and deception? How do we uncover its labyrinth of destruction? Built into para-government programs like MILAB is an aggressive principle of secrecy. Even though individual MILAB abductions can be deconstructed, substantial components of MILAB consist of maintaining the secrecy of the program itself. MILAB is such a hot topic that at least one major television network in self-censorship has cancelled airing a segment which would have brought MILAB to public light.

Sunshine and again more sunshine.

Sunshine is a driving force of the Decade of Contact.

Secrecy abhors sunshine; public disclosure is anathema to the programs of the para-government.

The secrecy technology of para-government programs such as HAARP and MILAB become less effective as they become more publicly known; as the zone of human awareness expands during the Decade of Contact.

The Decade of Contact is a window for the human race; a window to give ourselves permission to become aware of the ETI initiative and consciously participate in this initiative. The anti-ETI war, and its components such as MILAB, will come to public scrutiny, as part of the very dynamics of the Decade.

Indeed a component part of the ETI initiative is the dismantling of military machines by we humans ourselves. An expanded human consciousness of the obligations of participating in universe citizenship will in itself be one of the main forces resulting in the dismantling of the war machine on earth.

Programs like MILAB will bite the dust as part of we humans coming into our next level of social contract. Some part of our human community may focus more on the outrages of the para-government; others may focus more on the opening to the ETI initiative itself. The over-all result will be the devastation of the para-government.

Having seen other rats desert oppressive governments in at least one social revolution I was witness to, I do not envy the denizens and soldiers of the secret state. Indeed, what to do with these reprobates, these sociopathic pseudo-soldiers? Are they indeed constitutionally and morally fit for universe citizenship?

Hmm. I would like to think about that one for a long time.

This issue has to do with the human soul; we need not be too hasty in our remedies. Perhaps transportation – that eighteenth century remedy – is enough. We have only to get the bodies and minds of the darkest of our oppressors isolated from the bulk of God-fearing humanity.

Perhaps these counter-evolutionary elements will create their own destinies as the Decade of Contact unfolds.

The ultimate recovery is that we humans recover our human souls. We recover our souls from living under the psychic tyranny of the secret state by bringing our soul power into universe citizenship.

Holding our souls free once again in an interplanetary society, which knows deeply that all intelligent sentient beings indeed possess that inner fragment of the source God.

The Soul! That may be the true battleground of the war the shadow government has waged against the human population all these decades. They have wanted to oppress our souls, and not only our bodies. In reality the true target of the secret state may have been the control of the human soul.

Otherwise, why have they waged an illicit, genocidal war against the planet's population to keep us from our destiny, which is re-union into the universal community of souls?

Sure, wars are fought at the physical level – kill the soldiers; control the bodies and minds of the conquered people.

But so they may be fought at the level of the soul. If the common soldier does not know this, then the secret generals and evil wizards of the para-government know this.

They understand they must appear good, all the while doing evil acts.

For if the human race were to know how evil they are, the very essence of their corrupt souls would be exposed and they would lose power.

All wars may ultimately be spiritual wars. The surface goal of the war may be to control the bodies of the vanquished. The underlying, truer goal may be to control the souls in those bodies by destabilizing the body and the mind of the victims of war.

So it may be with the war waged against the ETI and the human population by the secret state. The surface language of the organs of the secret state uses a language of physical warfare - weapons of mass destruction, deception operations, imprisonment and destruction of innocent human citizens. The deeper, truer goal of the secret state's war may be control of souls within the bodies of the human population, and their isolation from the community of souls in the larger universe.

A wealth of cultural and religious sources also tells us that the anti-ETI war is about the destiny of the human soul. Many sacred texts contain visions, ancient fragments of the deeper living Spirit within which we live. Some texts are virtual maps to the living structure of the universe and its divine architecture. These texts are lodestars for our souls, compasses and comforts within which we might seek direction, protection and haven from the spiritual battlefield that is earth.

Humankind's greatest spiritual enemies exist right here on earth. In our generation they can be found doing the counter-evolutionary work of the secret state. The ultimate outcome of their war – if carried to the extreme – is to reduce the human community to unconscious robots, to thwart divine will's blueprint for human souls.

If the myriad reports of how higher intelligent life unfolds in the universe are accurate, what we call matters of faith here on earth are taken as matters of scientific fact in higher planets. Higher intelligent planets live closer to the divine conscious intent in creating the soul phenomenon. Higher life was designed as a gift of the source God, a vehicle through which we could directly experience reality as God experiences it.

We find ourselves on this planet at the threshold of larger universe participation. Admission to the higher levels of the universe is not only a matter of high technology, knowledge of the organization of interplanetary society, the excitement of interplanetary travel. These aspects of universe citizenship are kind of the outer shells. The core of advanced universe citizenship is the evolutionary development of our human souls.

The soul is what lasts once our bodies fall away and wither to dust or the ashes of cremation. Your soul existed before your body and will last after your body. We create our own spiritual destiny, and life in a human body is the way we are now creating that destiny for ourselves, as individuals and as a community.

So how we lead our lives on earth – individually and collectively – does indeed matter to the long, long, long eternal future that lies ahead.

The full historical perspective is that the battle we are in now may have happened once before, in the deep millennial past. No way we can prove it, but there are sacred text sources suggesting this. The outcome of the battle was defeat of the forces seeking to hijack the planet. The long-term outcome was the imposition of universe quarantine on planet Earth.

Let's apply a soul analysis to the battlefield on earth.

The secret state appears to be a network – some would say conspiracy – of beings – using war, violence, and deception to prevent the rightful progression of human souls into a next level of universe development.

But why are they doing this? What is their underlying purpose? What do the denizens of the secret state have to gain at the soul level?

That is really the harder question. Why?

Maybe our battlefield on earth is a replay of an ancient war. Hey, that's a thought – souls driven by embedded hatreds to try and destroy the human destiny once again. This is the Bad Seed theory. The secret "staters" are cosmic hooligans, come back to wreak havoc on our planet at a strategic moment in our development.

Maybe the humans in the secret state are driven only by lower-level drives – power, control, brutality, hatred, and animosity to Spirit. Their genetic memories; the makeup of their beings is that of cosmic criminals. A specific portion of the human race appears to be criminal almost by genetics – the serial killer. They're bad shit, and we just have to deal with the secret state leaders and thugees in that way.

Maybe it is all due to ignorance and environment. The secret state is ignorant of the realm of the soul. They have been spiritually deprived. The solution is to deconstruct their dangerous worldview, and re-educate them with the insight and appreciation of the spirit. By inculcating spiritual insight in the participants of the secret state, we undercut their drive to wage spiritual warfare against the human race and the rest of inter-planetary society.

Not! Some secret staters may be redeemable as human souls. That is well beyond my powers of analysis.

I tend to believe that we are in full-fledged spiritual battle here on Earth. In some ways, that is a spiritual advantage for our evolution. The anti-ETI war of the secret state in fact provides both cover and a magnet, attracting to itself counter-evolutionary elements within the human community.

The war is a basic cosmic filter. Light is attracted to light; evil and oppression is attracted to itself – that is a cosmic filtering principle. As secret state's war enters public awareness, the secret villains of the human race and their minions will also be surfaced. This is a scientific principle in the emerging science of the soul.

When confronted with the possibility of spiritual growth, many different reactions may take place within the human soul. It is almost as though the soul has a growth or rejection trigger, which is activated when the opportunity for spiritual growth confronts it.

For some souls – probably the bulk of souls on the planet now – the opportunity for spiritual evolution seems to activate a latent yearning. These souls expand into larger participation, as universe opportunities are made available to them. In the battlefield, these souls do not panic but want to know more.

Then there are the retards of the spirit – or more accurately, against the spirit.

A spiritual approach by a higher intelligent species fills them with alarm, paranoia, defensiveness, and reaction. These beings are moved, not to explore the new reality, but to wage war against it. They attempt to keep the bulk of humanity – the souls that can feel the spirit stirring within them – in terminal captivity.

Hence the anti-ETI war arises; the lines of battle are drawn. These battle lines are not drawn by any external actor, but by the very souls of the human actors themselves responding to a common phenomenon – the opportunity for universe citizenship.

Ours is a self-defining war. Your soul will take sides depending on its basic spiritual orientation. From a soul perspective, what will determine the battle on planet earth is which way your soul will jump – into the brilliant future, or the dark, unconscious abyss.

You might say at this point, "Why me? I did not ask for this."

Well, apparently, God is the Master of surprise.

It well may be that, in the course of our long universe careers, we will never be at a stage where we will not be subject to divine surprise.

One thing we may count on, however, is that the surprise may be good as a matter of course, in the longer, divine perspective.

I mean, have we not hit the glass ceiling on this planet in our current human culture?

Do you really think that to be spoon-fed the next level of universe citizenship is in our interest as a human species?

Maybe, having to earn with by winning the war for our interplanetary citizenship is necessary, with lateral benefits.

One benefit: earning our stripes coalesces and self-identifies those human souls who really want to expand – probably most of us.

Desire to grow is a key evolutionary quality, we might surmise.

Another benefit: The really bad, irredeemable captains of the secret state become identified, and may even self-destruct. So much for these waste products of our evolution.

Yet another corollary of the anti-ETI war may well be that this is the last war we will know as a species.

War as a problem solving, conflict resolution process may finally come to an end for our species, in the aftermath of our integration into interplanetary society.

War has come to acquire the status of a religion, over time, in our relatively primitive, lower level intelligent life on our isolated planet.

As we blast our way through the oppressive and inhuman screen separating us from our interplanetary heritage, war, violence, and oppression may be their own last casualties.

War is no more.

Our childhood ends.

ABOUT AUTHOR
ALFRED LAMBREMONT WEBRE

Alfred Lambremont Webre's contributions to the development of a positive future for Earth and our living community in the dimensional ecology have included the Development of Exopolitics in his book *Exopolitics: Politics, Government and Law In the Universe* (2005 Universebooks.com); the Mapping of the Omniverse in his book 2014 book *The Dimensional Ecology of the Omniverse* (to be published as *The Omniverse* in Dec. 2015 by Bear & Co., and the Discovery of the Positive Timeline Equation, now published in *Journey – Volume I* (2015 Universebooks.com).

Alfred is a graduate of Georgetown Preparatory School in Classics, Yale University in Industrial Administration Honors and Yale Law School in international law and was a Fulbright Scholar in international economic integration in Uruguay. He has taught economics at Yale University and the Bill of Rights at the University of Texas. Alfred was general counsel to the New York City Environmental Protection Administration, a futurist at Stanford Research Institute (where he directed the proposed 1977 Carter White House extraterrestrial communication study), and was a NGO delegate to the United Nations and the UNISPACE conference. He was also an Administrator of the Brownsville Community Health Center in the Lower Rio Grande Valley of Texas as well as a Judge on the Kuala Lumpur War Crimes Tribunal and a war crimes correspondent for PressTV.

Alfred has been active in public broadcasting in the United States (WBAI-FM) and Canada (Vancouver Coop Radio); in public interest counter intelligence (Assassination Information Bureau); in deconstruction of the Transhumanist Agenda to robotize humans; in the peaceful uses of outer space (Institute for Cooperation in Space); in Life on Mars (Mars Anomaly Research Society); in multidimensional online education (Omniversity *in development*); and in news (NewsInsideOut.com; Exopolitics.com).

Alfred can be reached at *exopolitics@exopolitics.com*

INDEX

END NOTES

[1] Investigator: CIA, Pope John Paul II, Bush Sr. & Jr., Bill/Hillary Clinton do ritual child sacrifice. The Transhumanist Agenda is the core driver of global pedophile, child sacrifice and child-trafficking networks

By Alfred Lambremont Webre

http://newsinsideout.com/2014/12/investigator-cia-pope-john-paul-ii-bush-sr-jr-billhillary-clinton-ritual-child-sacrifice/

[2] Alfred Lambremont Webre, Exopolitics: Politics, Government and Law in the Universe, (Vancouver, Canada: Universebooks.com, 2005); (Granada, Spain: VesicaPiscis.eu 2009) www.universebooks.com

[3] Chicago Seven, http://en.wikipedia.org/wiki/Chicago_Seven

[4] See Alfred Lambremont Webre, "My 1970s meeting with DARPA's Project Pegasus secret time travel program", http://exopolitics.blogs.com/exopolitics/2011/08/my-1970s-meeting-with-darpas-project-pegasus-secret-time-travel-program.html; http://www.examiner.com/article/my-1970s-meeting-with-darpa-s-project-pegasus-secret-time-travel-program

[5] Phillip H. Liss & Alfred L. Webre, The Age of Cataclysm (New York: G.P. Putnam's Sons, 1974); (New York: Berkeley Medallion, 1975); (Capricorn Books, 1975); (Tokyo: Ugaku Sha, 1975); Available in PDF free at www.exopolitics.com

http://exopolitics.blogs.com/exopolitics/2012/07/the-age-of-cataclysm-prophetic-1974-book-now-required-reading-about-predicted-impacts-of-a-2013-brow.html

[6] Alfred Lambremont Webre, "Web Bot: Andrew Basiago is predicted "planetary level" whistleblower for Mars life and time travel", http://exopolitics.blogs.com/exopolitics/2011/12/web-bot-andrew-basiago-is-predicted-planetary-level-whistleblower-for-mars-life-and-time-travel.html; http://www.examiner.com/article/web-bot-andrew-basiago-is-predicted-planetary-level-whistleblower-for-mars-life-and-time-travel

[7] Alfred Lambremont Webre, "Are you on a 2012-13 catastrophic timeline? Or are you on a 2012-13 positive future timeline?", http://exopolitics.blogs.com/exopolitics/2011/12/are-you-on-a-2012-13-catastrophic-or-positive-future-timeline-part-i.html; http://www.examiner.com/article/are-you-on-a-2012-13-catastrophic-timeline-or-are-you-on-a-2012-13-positive-future-timeline-part-1

[8] Alfred Lambremont Webre, World Affairs: The Journal of International Issues, "Exopolitics And A Positive Human Future", Vol. 12 No. 2, Summer 2008; http://exopolitics.blogs.com/exopolitics/2008/11/world-affairs-the-journal-of-international-issues-exopolitics-and-a-positive-human-future-by-alfred-lambremont-webre-jd-m.html

[9] Alan J Weberman, Michael Canfield, Coup D'Etat in America: The CIA and the Assassination of John F. Kennedy, ajweberman.com

[10] Carl Oglesby, The Yankee And Cowboy War: Conspiracies from Dallas to Watergate, http://www.goodreads.com/book/show/2072443.The_Yankee_And_Cowboy_War

[11] Stuart E. Eizenstat, http://en.wikipedia.org/wiki/Stuart_E._Eizenstat

[12] Jody Powell, http://en.wikipedia.org/wiki/Jody_Powell

[13] President Jimmy Carter, http://spaceflare.com/

[14] James Earl Carter http://libertapedia.org/wiki/Jimmy_Carter; http://www.dkosopedia.com/wiki/Jimmy_Carter

[15] Alfred Lambremont Webre, JD, MEd, "Exopolitics Media Note: Is Jimmy Carter a UFO/ET Abductee?"

http://exopolitics.blogs.com/exopolitics/2008/07/exopolitics-med.html; http://www.ufodigest.com/news/0608/media-notes.html

[16] Duane Elgin, Voluntary Simplicity, http://duaneelgin.com/books/voluntary-simplicity/

[17] List of SRI International people

http://en.wikipedia.org/wiki/List_of_SRI_International_people

[18] "The Corporation", http://en.wikipedia.org/wiki/The_Corporation_%28film%29

[19] Jacques Vallée (1980). "Messengers of Deception: UFO Contacts and Cults" New York: Bantam Books.

[20] Jim Garrison, http://en.wikipedia.org/wiki/Jim_Garrison

[21] The Genographic Project, https://genographic.nationalgeographic.com

[22] Taino people, http://en.wikipedia.org/wiki/Ta%C3%ADno_people

[23] Ancient History/Americas/Ancient Cuba, "By 1550, many tribes were eradicated. Many of the Conquistadors intermarried with Native Cuban Indians. Their children were called mestizos, but the Native Cubans called them Guajiro, which translates as 'one of us'. Today, the descendants are maintaining their heritage."

http://en.wikibooks.org/wiki/Ancient_History/Americas/Ancient_Cuba

[24] Alfred L. Webre, "Evaporation", http://www.amazon.com/Evaporation-Alfred-L-Webre/dp/B000886XJQ

[25] "Occupy Adam's Calendar" Part I Extraterrestrial Genetic Manipulation: Geneticist William Brown - A film by Alfred Lambremont Webre,

http://exopolitics.blogs.com/exopolitics/2012/06/occupy-adams-calendar-part-i-genetic-manipulation-geneticist-william-brown-a-film-by-alfred-lambremo.html

[26] Alfred Lambremont Webre, "Author: ET council seeded Homo sapiens as intelligent beings with 12-strand DNA", http://exopolitics.blogs.com/exopolitics/2011/12/by-alfred-lambremont-webre-jd-med-in-an-exclusive-interview-of-author-patricia-cori-by-alfred-lambremont-webre-released.html

[27] Alfred Lambremont Webre, "Whistleblower: WWIII, a war between hostile ETs and humanity, has started", http://exopolitics.blogs.com/exopolitics/2011/06/whistleblower-wwiii-a-war-between-hostile-ets-and-humanity-has-started.html

[28] Christopher Story, "The New Underworld Order", http://exopolitics.blogs.com/exopolitics/2013/03/important-books-exposing-nwo-the-new-underworld-order-the-european-union-by-christopher-story.html (PDF download)

29 Alfred Lambremont Webre, "Archons - Exorcising hidden controllers with Robert Stanley and Laura Eisenhower", http://exopolitics.blogs.com/exopolitics/2011/12/archons-exorcising-hidden-controllers-with-robert-stanley-and-laura-eisenhower.html

30 Archons were brought into our Universe by space-faring travelers from our Universe who violated an injunction against venturing through a wormhole/stargate to a dark Universe populated by Archons.

31 Dr. Henry Makow, "The Illuminati: A Cult that Hijacked the World", http://www.amazon.ca/Illuminati-Cult-That-Hijacked-World/dp/1439211485

32 Alfred Lambremont Webre, "Good News! Universe singularity now emanating pre-wave energy for 'enlightened unity consciousness'", http://exopolitics.blogs.com/exopolitics/2011/12/good-news-universe-singularity-now-emanating-pre-wave-energy-for-enlightened-unity-consciousness.html

33 Alfred Lambremont Webre, ""Andromeda Council" - Articles & Interviews by Alfred Lambremont Webre", http://exopolitics.blogs.com/exopolitics/2011/11/andromeda-council-articles-interviews.html

34 Id. See also Dr. Henry Makow, "The Illuminati: A Cult that Hijacked the World", http://www.amazon.ca/Illuminati-Cult-That-Hijacked-World/dp/1439211485

35 Judges Of The Kuala Lumpur War Crimes Tribunal, http://criminalisewar.org/the-foundation/judges-commissioners/

36 See Dr. Michael Newton, Journey of Souls, (2008: Woodbury, Minn., Llewellyn Publications)

37 Ibid.

38 Pedro Arrupe, SJ, http://en.wikipedia.org/wiki/Pedro_Arrupe

39 Central Manati (Central Argelia Libre), http://www.ugo.cn/photo/CU/en/4098.htm

40 Czarninow is now a multinational, http://www.czarnikow.com/about-czarnikow/our-management

41   Juanita Castro, "Fidel y Raúl, Mis Hermanos: La Historia Secreta",
      http://books.google.com/books/about/Fidel_y_Ra%C3%BAl_Mis_Herm
      anos.html?id=uA1TPgAACAAJ

42   Venceremos Brigade, http://www.venceremosbrigade.net/;
      http://en.wikipedia.org/wiki/Venceremos_Brigade

43   Jean Battey Lewis, "DANCE; Awakening Cuba to 40 Years of New
      Moves", New York Times, December 10, 2000,
      http://www.nytimes.com/2000/12/10/arts/dance-awakening-cuba-to-40-
      years-of-new-moves.html?pagewanted=all&src=pm

44   Space Preservation Treaty,
      http://www.noufors.com/Space_Preservation_Treaty.htm;
      www.vcn.bc.ca/wfcvb/spct1.html, http://human-science-
      research.blogspot.ca/2005/05/how-to-proceed-with-space-
      preservation.html, vi-
      pirg.ca/archive/campaigns/past_wgs/.../space_preservation_treaty.pdf

      See also Space Preservation Act, HR 2977,
      http://www.fas.org/sgp/congress/2001/hr2977.html

45   Rebirthing-breathwork, http://en.wikipedia.org/wiki/Rebirthing-
      breathwork

46   "The Tuskegee Airmen" (TV 1995),
      http://www.imdb.com/title/tt0114745/; "Red Tails" (2012)
      http://www.imdb.com/title/tt0485985/, Asawin Suebsaeng, "'Red Tails':
      The Tuskegee Airmen Deserved a Movie That's Not Completely
      Unwatchable", Mother Jones, Sat Jan. 21, 2012 4:00 AM PST,
      http://www.motherjones.com/mixed-media/2012/01/film-review-red-
      tails-george-lucas

47   PressTV, "Satanic priests in the Catholic Church?",
      http://www.presstv.com/detail/139422.html

48   Catholic Encyclopedia, http://bit.ly/Qak6B9

49   See Henry Makow, PhD, "The Illuminati: The Cult that Hijacked the
      World", op. cit.; Christopher Story, "The New Underworld Order", op.
      cit.

50   See, for example, Alfred Lambremont Webre, "9/11 False Flag
      operation - Articles by Alfred Lambremont Webre",

http://exopolitics.blogs.com/exopolitics/2011/03/articles-on-the-911-false-flag-operation-by-alfred-lambremont-webre.html; "BP Gulf Oil Spill false flag operation: articles by Alfred Lambremont Webre", http://exopolitics.blogs.com/exopolitics/2011/04/bp-gulf-oil-spill-false-flag-operation-articles-by-alfred-lambremont-webre.html

51 Tom Flocco, "FBI memo, photo link Bush Sr to JFK Dallas murder scene", http://tomflocco.com/fs/FbiMemoPhotoLinkBushJfk.htm

52 Complete News Coverage - Kuala Lumpur War Crimes Tribunal: Bush, Cheney, Rumsfeld & 4 Lawyers Conviction As War Criminals - May 11, 2012. - Breaking News, http://exopolitics.blogs.com/breaking_news/2012/05/complete-news-coverage-kuala-lumpur-war-crimes-tribunal-bush-cheney-rumsfeld-4-lawyers-conviction-as-war-criminals-m.html

53 Alfred Lambremont Webre, JD, MEd, "My 1970s meeting with DARPA's Project Pegasus secret time travel program", http://exopolitics.blogs.com/exopolitics/2012/01/my-1970s-meeting-with-darpas-project-pegasus-secret-time-travel-program.html

54 The Genographic Project, GENO 2.0, https://genographic.nationalgeographic.com/

55 Kris Millegan, "Fleshing Out Skull and Bones: Investigations Into America's Most Powerful Secret Society", (2004: Trine Day)

56 Types of Cases, School of Medicine at the University of Virginia Medical School. http://www.medicine.virginia.edu/clinical/departments/psychiatry/sections/cspp/dops/case_types-page

57 Alfred Lambremont Webre, "Dimensions: The Ecology of the Multiverse", (2014 Universebooks.com)

58 Richard E. Sprague, "The Taking Of America, 1-2-3", Richard E. Sprague 1976. Limited First Edition 1976. Revised Second Edition 1979, http://www.ratical.org/ratville/JFK/ToA/

59 GoogleVideo: Why we need 9/11 Truth & Reconciliation by Alfred Lambremont Webre, JD, MEd

http://exopolitics.blogs.com/911/2009/12/googlevideo-why-we-need-a-911-war-crimes-tribunal-by-alfred-lambremont-webre-jd-med.html

60 Richard E. Sprague, "The Taking of America 1,2,3",
    http://scribblguy.50megs.com/takingof.htm

61 Ayocuan, La Mujer Dormida debe dar a luz,
    http://www.goodreads.com/book/show/1774306.La_Mujer_Dormida_de
    be_dar_a_luz

62 Rev Kevin Annett: 5 Judges, 58 citizen jurors try Vatican, UK Crown for
    child genocide, http://www.youtube.com/watch?v=un77lVvVRIE

63 Anthony Blunt, http://en.wikipedia.org/wiki/Anthony_Blunt

64 Queen Elizabeth II visits Melbourne City Loop, May, 1980,
    http://www.youtube.com/watch?v=lOvNsWPh_08

65 The Urantia Book, (1955: Chicago, Ill, Urantia Foundation),
    http://www.urantia.org/urantia-book/read-urantia-book-online

66 Ibid

67 California Governor's Emergency Task Force on Earthquake
    Preparedness, Western States Seismic Policy Council Policy Rec-
    ommendation 12-1 Earthquake Planning Scenarios, Appendix I, Alexa
    Traffic Rank for http://www.wsspc.org/policy/files/Adopted/Adopted_PR-
    12-1_Scenarios.pdf: unavaila-
    blewww.wsspc.org/policy/files/Adopted/Adopted_PR-12-1_Scenarios.pdf

68 Journal of proceedings, Board of Supervisors, City and County of San
    Francisco (1982), Vol 77, Part 1, Call No. 352 Sa52:7

    http://archive.org/stream/journalofjanjuneproceed77sanfrich/journalofja
    njuneproceed77sanfrich_djvu.txt

69 Gang-stalking wiki,
    http://whatreallyhappened.wikia.com/wiki/Gang_Stalking

70 De Waarheid (The Truth), the Dutch Communist Party newspaper,
    http://en.wikipedia.org/wiki/De_Waarheid

71 Thomas Banyacya, http://en.wikipedia.org/wiki/Thomas_Banyacya

72 Recommendation to Establish UN Agency for UFO Research - UN
    General Assembly decision 33/426, 1978,
    http://exopolitics.blogs.com/exopolitics/2009/02/united-nations-general-
    assembly-decision-33426-1978.html;
    http://www.ufoevidence.org/documents/doc902.htm

[73] UNISPACE2, http://www.oosa.unvienna.org/oosa/SAP/history.html

[74] ARPANET, http://en.wikipedia.org/wiki/ARPANET

[75] Jacques Vallee, Messengers of Deception, UFO Contacts and Cults (1980, Daily Grail Publishing)

[76] Alfred Lambremont Webre, "The Levesque Cases" (PSP: Ontario, 1991), http://www.amazon.com/Levesque-Cases-Alfred-Lambremont-Webre/dp/0969445903/ref=sr_1_1?ie=UTF8&qid=1369081127&sr=8-1&keywords=the+levesque+cases

[77] Ibid.

[78] WBAI-FM, http://www.wbai.org/

[79] Alfred Lambremont Webre, "The Levesque Cases" (PSP: Ontario, 1991), op. cit.

[80] Fritz Springmeier and Cisco Wheeler, "The Illuminati Formula Used to Create an Undetectable Total Mind Controlled Slave", http://www.theforbiddenknowledge.com/hardtruth/illuminati_formula_mind_control.htm

[81] A Chronology: Key Moments In The Clinton-Lewinsky Saga, http://www.cnn.com/ALLPOLITICS/1998/resources/lewinsky/timeline/

[82] Tiananmen Square protests of 1989, http://en.wikipedia.org/wiki/Tiananmen_Square_protests_of_1989

[83] Taking Heads, "Burning Down the House", http://www.youtube.com/watch?v=xNnAvTTaJjM

[84] Fritz Springmeier and Cisco Wheeler, "The Illuminati Formula Used to Create an Undetectable Total Mind Controlled Slave", http://www.theforbiddenknowledge.com/hardtruth/illuminati_formula_mind_control.htm

The Conspiracy Wiki, Monarch Mind Control, http://conspiracy.wikia.com/wiki/Monarch_Mind_Control;

Mind Control In The Field Of Art, http://www.theforbiddenknowledge.com/hardtruth/mind_control_art.htm

[85] Operation Desert Storm, http://en.wikipedia.org/wiki/Gulf_War

86   Video footage from a cooperating US station, "WRHU Instant of
      Cooperation 1986", http://youtu.be/BNbuBmH3pGw

87   Alfred Lambremont Webre, "Good News! Universe singularity now
      emanating pre-wave energy for 'enlightened unity consciousness'",
      http://exopolitics.blogs.com/exopolitics/2011/12/good-news-universe-
      singularity-now-emanating-pre-wave-energy-for-enlightened-unity-
      consciousness.html; http://www.examiner.com/article/good-news-
      universe-singularity-now-emanating-pre-wave-energy-for-enlightened-
      unity-consciousness

88   St. Leo Preparatory School, St. Leo, Florida, http://saintleoprep.com/

89   Texas Democratic Party,
      http://en.wikipedia.org/wiki/Texas_Democratic_Party

90   The Hobbit: The Battle of the Five Armies,
      http://en.wikipedia.org/wiki/The_Hobbit:_The_Battle_of_the_Five_Ar
      mies

91   List of original characters in The Hobbit film series

      http://en.wikipedia.org/wiki/List_of_original_characters_in_The_Hobbi
      t_film_series#Men

92   *Shallow Hal*, http://en.wikipedia.org/wiki/Shallow_Hal

93   *The Master* (2012 Film),
      http://en.wikipedia.org/wiki/The_Master_%282012_film%29

94   Philip Seymour Hoffman Killed in an illuminati Ritual? Many Strange
      Coincidences - 237 - Satanism Ritual Sacrifice?

      http://www.godlikeproductions.com/forum1/message2475970/pg1

95   Consent & Release Form,
      http://exopolitics.blogs.com/exopolitics/2015/04/journey-volume-i-the-
      air-war-the-day-the-earth-stood-still-twentieth-century-fox.html

96   Alfred Lambremont Webre, JD, MEd, Earth Changes: A Spiritual
      Approach

      http://exopolitics.blogs.com/earth_changes/

97   Alfred Lambremont Webre, Exopolitics: A Decade of Contact, Part I:
      http://bibliotecapleyades.lege.net/exopolitica/esp_exopolitics_0_1.htm

Part II http://www.ufoevidence.org/documents/doc1430.htm

98   N Molloy, "Exopolitics - Book Review", http://www.mail-archive.com/ctrl@listserv.aol.com/msg42363.html

99   Sally Suddock, "Book says Carter ET investigation scuttled",

      http://exopolitics.blogs.com/exopolitics/2013/05/book-says-carter-et-investigation-scuttled.html

100   June 2000 Rocky Mountain Conference on UFO Investigation

      http://business.highbeam.com/436007/article-1G1-201491179/ufo-experience-every-year-university-wyoming-conference

101   Alfred Lambremont Webre, "Exopolitics: Politics, Government and Law in the Universe", (2005: Universebooks.com), p. xii

102   This appearance does not appear on the official Coast to Coast AM program roster, http://www.coasttocoastam.com/search/?query=alfred+webre&page=1

      The notice for the Coast-to-Coast appearance on July 4, 2000 stated, "Alfred Webre is the author of Exopolitics, a remarkable assessment of the pre- and post-disclosure political implications of an extraterrestrial presence. In the same fashion as the recent Stephen King offering, Exopolitics is being sold as an eBook at http://www.universebooks.com.

      "Webre is a Fulbright Scholar and graduate of Yale University, Yale Law School and the University of Texas Counseling Program. He has been an environmental lawyer, futurist with Stanford Research Institute, community health and social activist, and has taught at Yale University and the University of Texas. Webre has also been a Non-Governmental Delegate to the United Nations, as well as a delegate to the Texas Democratic Convention."

103   See Affidavit of Alfred Lambremont Webre, sworn August 30, 2000. Op.cit.

104   Politics of UFOs/Disclosure Town Hall Meeting, Santa Clara Convention Center at Great America, Santa Clara, CA, October 13, 2000, 6:30 - 10 pm

      http://www.x-ppac.org/TownHall.html

105   Politics of UFOs/Disclosure Town Hall Meeting, Statement By Alfred Lambremont Webre, JD, MEd, Oct. 13, 2000

http://exopolitics.blogs.com/exopolitics/2013/05/politics-of-ufosdisclosure-town-hall-meeting-.html

[106] Alfred Lambremont Webre, "Towards a Decade of Contact: Preparing for re-integration into Universe society"

http://exopolitics.blogs.com/exopolitics/2012/12/towards-a-decade-of-contact-preparing-for-re-integration-into-universe-society-.html

www.exopoliticsjournal.com/vol-2/vol-2-2-Exp-Webre.pdf

[107] David Leonard, "UFO Group Demands Congressional Hearing", Space.com, May 9, 2001, http://www.space.com/searchforlife/UFO_hearings_010509.html; http://exopolitics.blogs.com/exopolitics/2006/06/do_not_publish_.html

[108] Representative Dennis Kucinich UFO, http://youtu.be/gSRWRbuMqyc

[109] "Bush, Blair found guilty of war crimes in Malaysia tribunal/ Judgment of the Court (PDF)",

http://exopolitics.blogs.com/breaking_news/2011/11/bush-blair-found-guilty-of-war-crimes-in-malaysia-tribunal-judgment-of-the-court-pdf.html

[110] India International Centre, http://www.iicdelhi.nic.in/

[111] World Affairs, The Journal of International Affairs, http://www.worldaffairsjournal.com/

[112] Alfred Lambremont Webre, JD, MEd, "Directions Towards An Exopolitics Initiative", World Affairs, http://exopolitics.blogs.com/exopolitics/2013/04/world-affairs-directions-towards-an-exopolitics-initiative-by-alfred-lambremont-webre-jd-med-.html

[113] Andrew D. Basiago, http://www.projectpegasus.net/andrew_d_basiago

[114] Kubler-Ross Model, http://en.wikipedia.org/wiki/K%C3%BCbler-Ross_model

[115] Alfred Lambremont Webre, JD, MEd, "My 1970s meeting with DARPA's Project Pegasus secret time travel program", http://exopolitics.blogs.com/exopolitics/2012/01/my-1970s-meeting-with-darpas-project-pegasus-secret-time-travel-program.html

[116] Alfred Lambremont Webre, "Exopolitics: Politics, Government and Law in the Universe", (2005 Universebooks.com) www.universebooks.com, Kindle: http://www.amazon.com/dp/B007KPF2RO

[117] Universebooks.com, www.universebooks.com

[118] Alfred Lambremont Webre, "The 1977 Carter White House Extraterrestrial Communication Study", http://exopolitics.blogs.com/exopolitics/2007/05/the_1977_carter.html

[119] Alfred Lambremont Webre, JD, MEd, "My 1970s meeting with DARPA's Project Pegasus secret time travel program", http://exopolitics.blogs.com/exopolitics/2012/01/my-1970s-meeting-with-darpas-project-pegasus-secret-time-travel-program.html

[120] Alfred Lambremont Webre, "Exopolitics Media Notes: Is Jimmy Carter a UFO/ET Abductee?"; "On The Road To Roswell & Burlington 2008: A Discussion With Jon Kelly", UFO Digest, http://www.ufodigest.com/news/0608/media-notes.html

[121] C.G. Jung, Flying saucers : a modern myth of things seen in the skies, Princeton University Press, http://archive.org/details/flyingsaucersmod00jung

[122] Free You Mind Conference 2, http://www.freeyourmindconference.com/

[123] Cathy O'Brien with Mark Phillips, "Access Denied For Reasons of National Security", (2004: Reality Marketing), p. 26 www.AccessDeniedBook.com

[124] Ingo Swann, http://www.rviewer.com/IngoSwann_encyclopedia.html

[125] List of SRI International People, http://en.wikipedia.org/wiki/List_of_SRI_International_people

[126] Alfred Lambremont Webre, J.D., M.Ed., "Exopolitics and a Positive Human Future", Exopolitics Journal, Vol 3:1 (January 2009). ISSN 1938-1719, http://exopoliticsjournal.com/vol-3/vol-3-1-Webre.htm

[127] "Carter Extraterrestrial Communication Study: UFO Studies Done and Proposed by the Carter Administration" http://exopolitics.blogs.com/exopolitics/2004/09/carter_extrater.html; http://www.presidentialufo.com/newpage11.htm

128   Ibid.

129   Ibid.

130   Disclosure Project, www.disclosureproject.org

131   Sam Nunn,
       http://bioguide.congress.gov/scripts/biodisplay.pl?index=N000171

132   Gene Laroque, http://en.wikipedia.org/wiki/Gene_La_Rocque

133   Alfred Lambremont Webre, "The 1977 Carter White House
       Extraterrestrial Communication Study",
       http://exopolitics.blogs.com/exopolitics/2007/05/the_1977_carter.html

134   "Electronically Assisted Gang-stalking"
       http://servv89pn0aj.sn.sourcedns.com/~gbpprorg/mil/mindcontrol/trans
       cript3.txt

135   The Chisholm Clan,
       http://www.rampantscotland.com/clans/blclanchisholm.htm

136   Disclosure Project Event, Simon Fraser University, Vancouver BC,
       September 9, 2001, http://www.paoweb.com/news1001.htm#Greer;
       http://www.ainfos.ca/01/aug/ainfos00349.html

137   Carol Rosin, Alfred Webre, "How to Proceed with the Space
       Preservation Treaty", Executive Summary, Institute for Cooperation in
       Space (ICIS), http://human-science-research.blogspot.ca/2005/05/how-
       to-proceed-with-space-preservation.html

138   Alfred Lambremont Webre, JD, MEd, "Four U.S. exotic black ops used
       in 9/11: Tesla time travel, antigravity UFO, directed energy weapons,
       mini-nukes", http://exopolitics.blogs.com/exopolitics/2012/02/four-us-
       exotic-black-ops-used-in-911-tesla-time-travel-antigravity-ufo-directed-
       energy-weapons-mini-.html

139   Vancouver, BC 9/11 Conference,
       http://vancouver911truth.org/index.php?option=com_content&view=ar
       ticle&id=54:announcement-911-truth-conference-in-
       vancouver&catid=22:events&Itemid=203

140   The Science and Politics of 9/11,
       http://www.prweb.com/releases/2007/07/prweb541060.htm

[141] Announcement of 9/11 War Crimes Tribunal,
http://forums.randi.org/showthread.php?t=91833

[142] GoogleVideo: Why we need 9/11 Truth & Reconciliation by Alfred
Lambremont Webre, JD, MEd

http://exopolitics.blogs.com/911/2009/12/googlevideo-why-we-need-a-
911-war-crimes-tribunal-by-alfred-lambremont-webre-jd-med.html

[143] 9/11 Treason Independent Prosecutor Act,
http://exopolitics.blogs.com/911/2009/12/the-september-11-2001-
treason-independent-prosecutor-act.html

[144] The September 11, 2001 Independent Prosecutor Act,
http://exopolitics.blogs.com/911/2009/12/the-september-11-2001-
treason-independent-prosecutor-act.html

[145] 9/11 False Flag operation - Articles by Alfred Lambremont Webre,
http://exopolitics.blogs.com/exopolitics/2011/03/articles-on-the-911-
false-flag-operation-by-alfred-lambremont-webre.html

[146] Alfred Lambremont Webre, "Secret DARPA time travel program may
hold key to understanding the deep politics of 9/11"

http://exopolitics.blogs.com/exopolitics/2012/02/secret-darpa-time-
travel-program-may-hold-key-to-understanding-the-deep-politics-of-911-
.html; http://www.examiner.com/article/secret-darpa-time-travel-
program-may-hold-key-to-understanding-the-deep-politics-of-9-11

[147] 9/11 War Crimes Tribunal, http://911warcrimestribunal.org/

[148] "9/11 Tribunal under attack for prosecuting 9/11 Accused beyond 'the
Usual Suspects'"

http://exopolitics.blogs.com/911_war_crimes_tribunal/2012/10/911-
tribunal-under-attack-for-prosecuting-911-accused-beyond-the-usual-
suspects.html

[149] Free Your Mind Conference, www.freeyourmindconference.org

[150] Alfred Lambremont Webre, "Time Travel and Political Control",
http://exopolitics.blogs.com/exopolitics/2011/12/time-travel-and-
political-control.html; http://www.examiner.com/article/time-travel-and-
political-control

151   Stephanie Relfe, B.Sc., The Mars Records, www.themarsrecords.com; www.exopolitics.com

152   Alfred Lambremont Webre, "Time Travel and Political Control", Op.cit.

153   The Affidavit of Andrew D. Basiago on 9/11, sworn September 11, 2012 - See more at: http://exopolitics.blogs.com/911_war_crimes_tribunal/2015/04/the-affidavit-of-andrew-d-basiago-on-911-sworn-september-11-2012.html

154   Kuala Lumpur Foundation to Criminalise War, http://criminalisewar.org/the-foundation/aim-of-the-tribunal/

155   Jonathan Kent, Blair, "Bush in 'war crimes trial'", BBC NEWS, Published: 2007/02/07 02:01:17 GMT, http://news.bbc.co.uk/go/pr/fr/-/1/hi/world/asia-pacific/6336333.stm

156   Mahdi Ramakrishna, Press TV, PressTV, "Bush, Blair found guilty of war crimes in Malaysia tribunal", Kuala Lumpur, Tue Nov 22, 2011 6:51PM GMT

http://presstv.com/detail/211548.html; Bush, Blair found guilty of war crimes in Malaysia tribunal/ Judgment of the Court (PDF),

http://exopolitics.blogs.com/breaking_news/2011/11/bush-blair-found-guilty-of-war-crimes-in-malaysia-tribunal-judgment-of-the-court-pdf.html

157   "Bush, Blair found guilty of war crimes in Malaysia tribunal/ Judgment of the Court", Op.cit.

158   Jim Fetzer and John Hankey, "Was George H.W. Bush Involved in Assassination of JFK?

George Herbert Walker Bush was there"

http://www.veteranstoday.com/2011/11/16/was-george-h-w-bush-involved-in-the-assassination-of-jfk/

Tom Flocco, FBI memo, photo link Bush Sr to JFK Dallas murder scene, http://tomflocco.com/fs/FbiMemoPhotoLinkBushJfk.htm

159   "George W. Bush Must be Arrested in Africa", http://www.rohama.org/en/news/6990/george-w-bush-must-be-arrested-in-africa

160   Daily Maverick – "Call to arrest Tony Blair during SA visit gains momentum", 27 Aug 2012 02:46 (South Africa) http://www.dailymaverick.co.za/article/2012-08-27-call-to-arrest-tony-blair-during-sa-visit-gains-momentum/#.UUOxCehGgWk

161   Updates-Verdict & Judgment - Complete News Coverage - Kuala Lumpur War Crimes Tribunal: Bush, Cheney, Rumsfeld & 4 Lawyers Conviction As War Criminals - MAY 11, 2012, http://exopolitics.blogs.com/breaking_news/2012/05/complete-news-coverage-kuala-lumpur-war-crimes-tribunal-bush-cheney-rumsfeld-4-lawyers-conviction-as-war-criminals-m.html

162   "Breaking: Tribunal finds Bush, seven others guilty of war crimes", http://www.globalresearch.ca/breaking-tribunal-finds-bush-seven-others-guilty-of-war-crimes/30812

163   The "Transhumanist Agenda" - EU Panel: Human robotization, Nano implant technologies, Mind control slavery, Neurological weapons torture, Gang stalking
by Alfred Lambremont Webre
Panel: Magnus Olsson, Dr. Henning Witte, and Melanie Vritschan from the European Coalition Against Covert Harassment with Alfred Lambremont Webre
WATCH PANEL ON YOU TUBE
http://youtu.be/uCEPsWF59mI
ARTICLE & LINKS:
http://exopolitics.blogs.com/exopolitics/2013/05/eu-experts-mind-control-slavery-nano-implant-technologies-human-robotization-neurological-weapons-torture-gang-stalking-t.html

164   Alfred Lambremont Webre, "Leuren Moret: Japan, U.S., Canadian governments complicit in radiation cover-up",

http://www.examiner.com/article/leuren-moret-japan-u-s-canadian-governments-complicit-radiation-cover-up

165   EUROPEAN EXOPOLITICS SUMMIT 2009

A New Paradigm for a World in Crisis

July 25-26, 2009

http://www.exopoliticsspain.es/2009/en/index.htm

166 "Satanic priests in the Catholic Church?", PressTV, Fri Aug 20, 2010
     9:39AM, http://www.presstv.com/detail/139422.html

167 "Lawyer likens Vatican to Roman Empire", PressTV, Wed Aug 11, 2010
     5:38PM, http://edition.presstv.ir/detail/138328.html

168 Alfred Lambremont Webre, "Pope Francis: His Jesuitical, Extrater-
     restrial, "False Prophet", and Political Identities"

     http://exopolitics.blogs.com/exopolitics/2011/12/2012-2025-a-positive-
     human-future.html

169 International Tribunal into Crimes of Church and State,
     http://www.ITCCS.org

170 ITCCS, How the Mighty have Fallen: The Next Steps in Reclaiming
     our World and Ourselves, March 13, 2013,

     http://itccs.org/2013/03/13/how-the-mighty-have-fallen-the-next-steps-in-
     reclaiming-our-world-and-ourselves/

171 ITCCS, "VIDEO: Pope Francis is linked to Exocet Missile Acquisition,
     according to British government source - Margaret Thatcher's Death
     and Queen's Pending Resignation are Connected",
     http://exopolitics.blogs.com/exopolitics/2013/04/video-pope-francis-is-
     linked-to-exocet-missile-acquisition-according-to-british-government-
     source-ma.html

172 Alfred Lambremont Webre, "Assassination of key witness to murder of
     First Nations children personally committed by Elizabeth Windsor",

     http://exopolitics.blogs.com/breaking_news/2011/09/tribunal-to-indict-
     vancouver-bilderberger-jim-pattison-bc-attorney-general-lawyer-rcmp-
     cfro-fm-staff-for-aiding-coverup.html

173 Philippa young, BBC, "Queen spending second day in hospital with
     stomach bug",

     http://www.bbc.co.uk/news/uk-21651425

174 The following articles on NewsInsideOut.com chronicle the sudden
     exposure and collapse of ITCCS, commencing in December 2014 for
     reasons that as of this writing are still not fully clarified:

     US Democratic Congressional candidate Hartzok attempts mediation:
     Webre accepts, Annett rejects

http://newsinsideout.com/2015/01/us-democratic-congressional-candidate-hartzok-attempts-mediation-webre-accepts-annett-rejects/

SEE ALSO:
http://exopolitics.blogs.com/exopolitics/2015/03/newsinsideoutcom-articles-by-alfred-lambremont-webre.html

175   Investigator: CIA, Pope John Paul II, Bush Sr. & Jr., Bill/Hillary Clinton do ritual child sacrifice. The Transhumanist Agenda is the core driver of global pedophile, child sacrifice and child-trafficking networks

By Alfred Lambremont Webre

http://newsinsideout.com/2014/12/investigator-cia-pope-john-paul-ii-bush-sr-jr-billhillary-clinton-ritual-child-sacrifice/

176   Draco-CIA-NSA-MKULTRA drive ritual child sacrifice in Religions (Vatican/Jesuit/Talmudic)- Monarchies-Governments-Schools-Wars for Transhumanist Agenda

http://newsinsideout.com/2015/03/draco-cia-nsa-mkultra-drive-ritual-child-sacrifice-in-religions-vaticanjesuittalmudic-monarchies-governments-schools-wars-for-transhumanist-agenda/

177   PressTV, "Obama policy on assassination drone strikes amounts to war crimes: Lawyer", Sept 10, 2012,
http://www.presstv.ir/detail/2012/09/10/260840/obamas-drone-attacks-are-war-crimes/

178   PressTV, US drone strikes against constitution: American lawyer, July 19, 2012

http://www.presstv.ir/detail/2012/07/19/251715/us-drone-strikes-unconstitutional-lawyer/

179   Spencer Ackerman, "White House Denies CIA Teleported Obama to Mars | Danger Room | Wired.com",
http://www.wired.com/dangerroom/2012/01/obama-mars/?utm_source=facebook&utm_medium=socialmedia&utm_campaign=facebookclickthru

180   National Security Council,
http://www.whitehouse.gov/administration/eop/nsc/

181   Alfred Lambremont Webre, "Obama/Soetoro, Time-Travel, & the US Supreme Court", http://exopolitics.blogs.com/exopolitics/2013/01/the-news-live-obamasoetoro-time-travel-the-us-supreme-court.html; http://youtu.be/JJB1aXgRWNw

182   Alfred Lambremont Webre, "Mars visitors Basiago and Stillings confirm Barack Obama traveled to Mars, Nov. 2011, Originally published in Examiner.com, http://exopolitics.blogs.com/exopolitics/2011/11/mars-visitors-basiago-and-stillings-confirm-barack-obama-traveled-to-mars-1.html

183   Alfred Lambremont Webre, "Occupy Adam's Calendar, Part I - Extraterrestrial Genetic Manipulation: Geneticist William Brown", http://www.youtube.com/watch?v=KLIbiOEYdKE

184   Alfred Lambremont Webre, How Intelligence Legend & Manchurian candidate Barack Hussein Obama was created,

http://www.slideshare.net/exouniversity/manchurian-candidate-barack-hussein-obama

185   Alfred Lambremont Webre, "Obama/Soetoro, Time Travel and the U.S. Supreme Court", WATCH VIDEO ONLINE, http://youtu.be/JJB1aXgRWNw,

http://exopolitics.blogs.com/exopolitics/2013/01/the-news-live-obamasoetoro-time-travel-the-us-supreme-court.html

186   Alfred Lambremont Webre, "Evidence: BP oil spill is disaster capitalism by criminal elite to depopulate and stop ET disclosure", http://www.examiner.com/exopolitics-in-seattle/evidence-bp-oil-spill-is-disaster-capitalism-by-criminal-elite-to-depopulate-and-stop-et-disclosure

COOPRADIO.ORG: The New 9/11: BP's false flag operation in the Gulf to Wreck the Environment - Leuren Moret, http://exopolitics.blogs.com/peaceinspace/2010/05/coopradioorg-the-new-911-bps-false-flag-operation-in-the-gulf-to-wreck-the-environment---leuren-moret.html

187   Alfred Lambremont Webre, "Leuren Moret: 100,000 excess deaths in North America in 2011 from Fukushima", http://exopolitics.blogs.com/peaceinspace/2011/10/leuren-moret-100000-excess-deaths-in-north-america-in-2011-from-fukushima.html

[188] Alfred Lambremont Webre, "Leuren Moret: Japan, U.S., Canadian governments complicit in radiation cover-up", http://www.examiner.com/exopolitics-in-seattle/leuren-moret-japan-u-s-canadian-governments-complicit-radiation-cover-up

For a full discussion of the Fukushima global radiation false flag, HAARP-Chemtrails depopulation agenda please see Interviews/Articles with Leuren Moret by Alfred Lambremont Webre at EcologyNews.com, http://exopolitics.blogs.com/peaceinspace/2011/09/fukushima-global-radiation-false-flag-haarp-chemtrails-depopulation-agenda-interviewsarticles-with-l.html

[189] Alfred Lambremont Webre, "Hurricane Sandy as Environmental War," http://youtu.be/u_w7n-y4oSI, http://exopolitics.blogs.com/exopolitics/2012/11/the-news-live-for-nov-2-2012-with-alfred-lambremont-webre.html

[190] The source of this scenario is: http://www.sandyhookhoax.com

[191] Alfred Lambremont Webre, "Sandy Hook as mind control false flag state terror against the U.S. population", http://youtu.be/YyrjJ88Wmvs,

http://exopolitics.blogs.com/exopolitics/2012/12/the-news-live-sandy-hook-as-state-terror-against-usa-population.html

[192] Proof! Boston Marathon Bombing is Staged Terror Attack. http://youtu.be/rEYoxwllFKc

[193] Obama, The Postmodern Coup Making Of A Manchurian Candidate

Obama Campaign Linked to Chechen Terrorism

By Webster G. Tarpley

http://www.american-buddha.com/lit.obama.webster.3.htm

[194] Obama speaks at Interfaith ceremony, http://youtu.be/or0gEXy1Jpg

[195] Alfred Lambremont Webre, "Pope Francis: His Jesuitical, Extraterrestrial, "False Prophet", and Political Identities", http://exopolitics.blogs.com/exopolitics/2013/03/informed-hermeneutics-researchers-identify-argentinian-pope-francis-1-as-possible-petrus-romanus-or-.html

722

196   Alfred Lambremont Webre, Expert: Prince William is the Antichrist, future king of one world government, http://youtu.be/4f1yUzwTQXU http://exopolitics.blogs.com/exopolitics/2012/01/expert-prince-william-is-the-antichrist-future-king-of-one-world-government.html

197   Idem

198   ITCCS, How the Mighty have Fallen: The Next Steps in Reclaiming our World and Ourselves, March 13, 2013,

http://itccs.org/2013/03/13/how-the-mighty-have-fallen-the-next-steps-in-reclaiming-our-world-and-ourselves/

ITCCS Public Notice: Great Britain Is Dissolved

http://exopolitics.blogs.com/exopolitics/2013/04/itccs-public-notice-great-britain-is-dissolved.html

199   Alfred Lambremont Webre, "'Identify the Perpetrator': How The Obama fulfills the "deceiver" archetype and why it is important to expose him publicly",

http://exopolitics.blogs.com/exopolitics/2013/04/why-it-is-reasonable-to-hypothesize-that-barrack-hussein-obama-fulfills-the-social-archetype-of-fore.html

200   Peter Kling: 2014-2021 "Tribulation" & Positive Timeline. Does Christ return with a decloaking of the Universe fleet? By Alfred Lambremont Webre
http://newsinsideout.com/2015/04/peter-kling-2014-2021-tribulation-positive-timeline-does-christ-return-with-a-decloaking-of-the-universe-fleet/

201   Alfred Lambremont Webre, Exopolitica: La Politica, El Gobierno y La Ley en el Universo, www.vesicapiscis.eu

202   See more at:
http://exopolitics.blogs.com/dimensional_ecology/2014/04/public-debate-on-existence-of-afterlife-souls-reincarnation-god-bolstered-by-new-scientific-evidence-on-roles-in-multivers.html

203   Dimensional Ecology of the Omniverse Lecture,
http://www.examiner.com/article/dimensional-ecology-of-the-omniverse-lecture-at-yaletown-roundhouse

204   END NOTES: [1] Creating a Positive Future: Time Science Shows Our Earth is on a Positive Timeline in our Time Space Hologram

"It's time science, not rocket science that Earth is on a positive timeline."

Positive Future = Positive Timeline + Unity Consciousness

by Alfred Lambremont Webre

www.positivefuture.info

[2] David Wilcock: Descendants of Giant species are the High Cabal and hidden controllers of humanity, can appear as Homo Capensis

http://newsinsideout.com/2015/02/david-wilcock-descendants-giant-species-high-cabal-hidden-controllers-humanity-can-appear-homo-capensis/

See also: Is Homo Capensis, the Big Brain Conehead, Earth's High Cabal & Covert Controller?

VIDEO: https://www.youtube.com/watch?v=4LkInRbBMDo

ARTICLE:

http://newsinsideout.com/2015/02/homo-capensis-big-brain-conehead-earths-high-cabal-covert-controller/

[3] Where does evil come from? Paul Levy: Our Wetiko (Archonic) mass epidemic of malignant egophrenia can destroy or awaken humanity

http://newsinsideout.com/2015/01/evil-come-paul-levy-wetiko-archonic-mass-epidemic-malignant-egophrenia-can-destroy-awaken-humanity/

Leuren Moret: Jesuit Depopulation Plan=Radiation + GMOs + Vaccines + GeoEngineering + Wars + $Collapse + Transhumanist Agenda

http://newsinsideout.com/2015/01/part-ii-leuren-moret-jesuit-depopulation-planradiation-gmos-vaccines-haarpchemtrails-geoengineering-wars-collapse-transhumanist-agenda-robotizationimplantsneural-controlgangstalki/

Leuren Moret: Putin Plan-HAARP the Fukushima radiation out of Russia. BRICS saves world from $collapse

http://newsinsideout.com/2015/01/part-iii-leuren-moret-putins-plan-haarp-radiation-russia-brics-saves-world-jesuit-depopulation-transhumanist-agenda/

Draco-CIA-NSA-MKULTRA drive ritual child sacrifice in Religions (Vatican/Jesuit/Talmudic)- Monarchies-Governments-Schools-Wars for Transhumanist Agenda

http://newsinsideout.com/2015/03/draco-cia-nsa-mkultra-drive-ritual-child-sacrifice-in-religions-vaticanjesuittalmudic-monarchies-governments-schools-wars-for-transhumanist-agenda/

JADE HELM ENVIRONMENTAL STATE TERROR EVENT?

YELLOWSTONE SECRET ERUPTION PROGRAM

https://www.youtube.com/watch?v=SIIThOZfC68

Nibiru Planet X Arrival Date September 24, 2015

https://www.youtube.com/watch?v=-QLVntSVMFw

Expert: Obama will bring ET false flag invasion

By Alfred Lambremont Webre

http://ufodigest.com/article/expert-obama-will-bring-et-false-flag-invasion

GEORGE: 6 billion ETs, laser safety net, assist in Earth dimensional ascension through 3rdD, 4thD to 5thDimension/Density

WATCH VIDEO/READ ARTICLE/LINKS ☺

http://newsinsideout.com/2015/03/george-6-billion-ets-laser-safety-net-assist-in-earth-dimensional-ascension-through-3rdd-4thd-to-5thdimensiondensity/

"GEORGE" Interdimensional ET: "We are helping in your frequency ascension through Contactees, Psychics, and talk show hosts"

http://newsinsideout.com/2015/02/george-interdimensional-et-helping-frequency-ascension-contactees-psychics-talk-show-hosts/

Peter Kling: 2014-2021 "Tribulation" & Positive Timeline. Does Christ return with a decloaking of the Universe fleet?

By Alfred Lambremont Webre

http://newsinsideout.com/2015/04/peter-kling-2014-2021-tribulation-positive-timeline-does-christ-return-with-a-decloaking-of-the-universe-fleet/

Letters to Earth, You Can Survive Armageddon! [Kindle Edition]

By Peter Kling

http://www.amazon.com/Letters-Earth-You-Survive-Armageddon-ebook/dp/B007TEXR3W/ref=sr_1_1?s=digital-text&ie=UTF8&qid=1430946849&sr=1-1&keywords=peter+kling

[4] Organization of the UN Summit for the adoption of the post-2015 development agenda, http://sd.iisd.org/news/unga-reaches-informal-agreement-on-post-2015-summit-organization-dates/

[5] See Renee M. An asteroid or meteor will hit the earth on September 24, 2015 – you have been warned!!! [In body of article]

[6] Jade Helm Environmental State Terror Event?

Yellowstone Secret Eruption Program

https://www.youtube.com/watch?v=SIIThOZfC68

[7] CERN - GUARD AND PROTECT YOUR SOUL & SOUL POWER - From a Friend: "Have you seen this explanation regarding what the CERN collider is all about? Could put a new slant on what Jade Helm is all about and the internment camps. This man says he experienced dark matter as a weapon. If the world is turned crazy with this plan, then They have their justification for moving in."

https://www.youtube.com/watch?v=oChedPBBdhE&index=12&list=PLQaofmgsTqjVpCVObt50iA2Mn411wSPVj

False Flag ET invasion/ET Disclosure - Predictive Programming - State Farm Insurance Ad

https://www.youtube.com/watch?v=_iSheX62EtI&feature=youtu.be

[8] VIDEO - Roundtable with USMCss Capt. Randy Cramer & UK Town Councilor Simon Parkes: Pleiadian nuke destroyed Mars ecology? Cheney ran Mars Colony Corporation

http://newsinsideout.com/2015/01/roundtable-pleiadian-nuke-destroyed-mars-ecology-cheney-ran-mars-colony-corporation/

Marine Corps: Plan to replace humanity with Mars elite DNA colony

http://newsinsideout.com/2014/12/us-marine-mars-officer-breakaway-civilization-repopulate-earth-mars-dna-pool-colonists/

[9] Renee M, The Illuminati know what is coming September 22-28, 2015 (Part 1 of 4)

https://www.youtube.com/watch?annotation_id=annotation_665413529
&feature=iv&list=PLq2qxAzE7_SRBTp5N_jayyLMuyXDkBJ6v&src_vi
d=TAamB3dqac8&v=jCoGDTi9RvI